# Personality Theories
## An Introduction

**FIFTH EDITION**

❖

# BARBARA ENGLER

UNION COUNTY COLLEGE

Houghton Mifflin Company    Boston   New York

*To my sons, Ted and Bill*

Editor-in-Chief: Kathi Prancan
Senior Associate Editor: Jane Knetzger
Editorial Assistant: Lou Gum
Senior Project Editor: Janet Young
Editorial Assistant: Nasya Laymon
Senior Production/Design Coordinator: Jill Haber
Marketing Manager: Pamela Laskey

Cover Designer: Harold Burch, Harold Burch Design, New York City

Printed in the U.S.A.

Library of Congress Catalog Card Number: 98-72020

ISBN: 0-395-90765-9

23456789-DC-02 01 00 99

# Brief Contents

**PREFACE**   XIX

**CHAPTER 1 / INTRODUCTION: EVALUATING PERSONALITY THEORIES**   1

---

PART I   *The Psychoanalytic Approach*   27

**CHAPTER 2 / PSYCHOANALYSIS: SIGMUND FREUD**   28

---

PART II   *The Neopsychoanalytic Approach*   69

**CHAPTER 3 / ANALYTICAL PSYCHOLOGY: CARL JUNG**   70

**CHAPTER 4 / INDIVIDUAL PSYCHOLOGY: ALFRED ADLER**   93

**CHAPTER 5 / PSYCHOANALYTIC SOCIAL PSYCHOLOGY: KAREN HORNEY, ERICH FROMM**   112

---

PART III   *More Recent Trends in Psychoanalytic Theory*   137

**CHAPTER 6 / EGO PSYCHOLOGY: ANNA FREUD, HEINZ HARTMANN, ERIK ERIKSON**   138

**CHAPTER 7 / HUMAN RELATIONS: MELANIE KLEIN, MARGARET MAHLER, HEINZ KOHUT, OTTO KERNBERG, NANCY CHODOROW, THE STONE CENTER GROUP**   166

---

PART IV   *Behavior and Learning Theories*   197

**CHAPTER 8 / EXPERIMENTAL ANALYSIS OF BEHAVIOR: JOHN DOLLARD AND NEAL MILLER, B. F. SKINNER**   198

**CHAPTER 9 / SOCIAL LEARNING THEORIES: ALBERT BANDURA, JULIAN ROTTER**   225

PART V    *Dispositional Theories*    255

CHAPTER 10  /  **TRAITS AND PERSONOLOGY: GORDON ALLPORT, HENRY MURRAY**    256

CHAPTER 11  /  **FACTOR ANALYTIC THEORIES: RAYMOND CATTELL, THE BIG FIVE PERSONALITY TRAITS**    282

CHAPTER 12  /  **BIOLOGICAL TRAITS: HANS EYSENCK**    305

PART VI    *Humanistic and Existential Theories*    339

CHAPTER 13  /  **HUMANISM: ABRAHAM MASLOW, CARL ROGERS**    340

CHAPTER 14  /  **EXISTENTIAL PSYCHOANALYSIS: ROLLO MAY**    372

PART VII    *Cognitive Theories*    399

CHAPTER 15  /  **PERSONAL CONSTRUCTS: GEORGE KELLY**    400

CHAPTER 16  /  **COGNITIVE-BEHAVIORAL THEORIES: ALBERT ELLIS, AARON BECK, ARNOLD LAZARUS**    419

PART VIII    *A Non-Western Approach*    449

CHAPTER 17  /  **ZEN BUDDHISM**    450

CONCLUSION  /  **PERSONALITY THEORY IN PERSPECTIVE**    475

**GLOSSARY**    489

**REFERENCES**    505

**INDEX**    527

**CREDITS**    550

# Contents

**PREFACE**   XIX

CHAPTER 1 / **INTRODUCTION: EVALUATING PERSONALITY THEORIES**   1

YOUR GOALS FOR THIS CHAPTER   1

What Is Personality?   2

What Is a Theory?   3

The Role of Personality Theory in Psychology   4

The Evaluation of Personality Theories   5

Philosophical Assumptions   7

    Recognizing Philosophical Assumptions   7

    Identifying Basic Philosophical Assumptions   8

    Evaluating Philosophical Assumptions   9

PHILOSOPHICAL ASSUMPTIONS: EXAMINING YOUR OWN PHILOSOPHICAL ASSUMPTIONS   **10**

Scientific Statements   12

    The Philosophical Basis of Science   12

    Recognizing Scientific Statements   13

    Some Basic Scientific Constructs   14

    Evaluating Scientific Statements   15

The Application of Personality Theories   16

    Assessment   16

    Research   18

    Psychotherapy   21

The Complexities of Evaluation   24

SUMMARY   24

SUGGESTIONS FOR FURTHER READING    26

---

PART I    *The Psychoanalytic Approach*    27

CHAPTER 2  /  **PSYCHOANALYSIS: SIGMUND FREUD**    28

YOUR GOALS FOR THIS CHAPTER    28

Biographical Background    29

The Origins of Psychoanalysis    31

    The Discovery of Unconscious Forces    32

    The Psychoanalytic Method of Assessment and Research    35

The Dynamics and Development of Personality    38

    The Importance of Sexuality    38

THINKING CRITICALLY: FREE ASSOCIATION    39

    The Psychosexual Stages of Development    41

    The Effects of the Psychosexual Stages    45

The Structure of Personality    46

    The Id, Ego, and Superego    47

    The Relationship of the Id, Ego, and Superego to Consciousness    49

The Ego's Defense Mechanisms    50

THINKING CRITICALLY: IDENTIFYING ĐEFENSE MECHANISMS    52

Psychoanalysis    53

    Transference    53

    The Analytic Process    54

Empirical Validation of Psychoanalytic Concepts    56

THINKING CRITICALLY: FREUD AND THE SUBJECT OF WOMEN    57

PHILOSOPHY, SCIENCE, AND ART: FREUD'S THEORY    59

PHILOSOPHICAL ASSUMPTIONS: EXAMINING FREUD    60

SUMMARY    64

SUGGESTIONS FOR FURTHER READING    66

PART II  *The Neopsychoanalytic Approach*   69

### CHAPTER 3 / **ANALYTICAL PSYCHOLOGY: CARL JUNG**   70

YOUR GOALS FOR THIS CHAPTER   70

Biographical Background   71

The Nature and Structure of Personality   73

> Psychic Energy   74
>
> The Ego   74
>
> The Personal Unconscious   74
>
> The Collective Unconscious   75

THINKING CRITICALLY: ARCHETYPES IN CULTURAL FORMS   79

> Psychological Types   81

Self-Realization   83

> Synchronicity   83
>
> Individuation and Transcendence   84

Jungian Psychotherapy   85

Assessment and Research in Jung's Theory   86

PHILOSOPHY, SCIENCE, AND ART: JUNG'S THEORY   88

PHILOSOPHICAL ASSUMPTIONS: EXAMINING JUNG   89

SUMMARY   90

SUGGESTIONS FOR FURTHER READING   91

### CHAPTER 4 / **INDIVIDUAL PSYCHOLOGY: ALFRED ADLER**   93

YOUR GOALS FOR THIS CHAPTER   93

Biographical Background   94

Social Interest   96

Finalism   96

Striving for Superiority   97

> Inferiority Feelings   98

Style of Life   99

> Birth Order   100

THINKING CRITICALLY: BIRTH ORDER AND PERSONALITY    101

Family Atmosphere    102

The Creative Self    103

Adlerian Psychotherapy    104

THINKING CRITICALLY: A LICENSE TO PARENT?    106

Assessment and Research in Adler's Theory    106

PHILOSOPHY, SCIENCE, AND ART: ADLER'S THEORY    108

PHILOSOPHICAL ASSUMPTIONS: EXAMINING ADLER    109

SUMMARY    110

SUGGESTIONS FOR FURTHER READING    111

CHAPTER 5  /  **PSYCHOANALYTIC SOCIAL PSYCHOLOGY:
KAREN HORNEY, ERICH FROMM**    112

YOUR GOALS FOR THIS CHAPTER    112

Karen Horney (1885–1952)    113

Biographical Background    113

Basic Anxiety    115

Neurotic Needs or Trends    116

The Idealized Self    117

THINKING CRITICALLY: THE TYRANNY OF THE SHOULD    119

Feminine Psychology    119

Assessment and Research in Horney's Theory    121

PHILOSOPHY, SCIENCE, AND ART: HORNEY'S THEORY    123

Erich Fromm (1900–1980)    124

Biographical Background    124

Basic Human Conditions and Needs    126

THINKING CRITICALLY: HUMAN NEEDS AND SOCIETY    129

Character Orientations    129

Assessment and Research in Fromm's Theory    132

PHILOSOPHY, SCIENCE, AND ART: FROMM'S THEORY    133

PHILOSOPHICAL ASSUMPTIONS: EXAMINING HORNEY AND FROMM    133

SUMMARY    134

SUGGESTIONS FOR FURTHER READING    135

PART III   *More Recent Trends in Psychoanalytic Theory*   137

CHAPTER 6 / **EGO PSYCHOLOGY: ANNA FREUD,
                HEINZ HARTMANN, ERIK ERIKSON**   138

YOUR GOALS FOR THIS CHAPTER   138
Anna Freud (1895–1982)   139
Heinz Hartmann (1894–1970)   142
Erik Erikson (1902–1994)   144
    Biographical Background   144
    An Enhanced Understanding of the Ego   145
    The Psychosocial Stages of Development   146

THINKING CRITICALLY: GENERATIVITY   152

    Assessment and Research in Erikson's Theory   153
    Empirical Research in Erikson's Theory   158
    Applying Erikson's Theory: The Work of Dan McAdams   159

THINKING CRITICALLY: WRITING YOUR OWN LIFE STORY   160

PHILOSOPHY, SCIENCE, AND ART: ERIKSON'S THEORY   162

PHILOSOPHICAL ASSUMPTIONS: EXAMINING ERIKSON   163

SUMMARY   164

SUGGESTIONS FOR FURTHER READING   165

CHAPTER 7 / **HUMAN RELATIONS: MELANIE KLEIN,
                MARGARET MAHLER, HEINZ KOHUT,
                OTTO KERNBERG, NANCY CHODOROW,
                THE STONE CENTER GROUP**   166

YOUR GOALS FOR THIS CHAPTER   166
Object Relations Theory   167
    Melanie Klein (1882–1960)   167
    Margaret Mahler (1897–1985)   169
    Heinz Kohut (1913–1981)   170
    Otto Kernberg (1928–  )   173
    Nancy Chodorow (1944–  )   176

THINKING CRITICALLY: SHARED PARENTING    178

THINKING CRITICALLY: CULTURALLY SANCTIONED MUTILATION    179

Relational/Cultural Theory: The Stone Center Group    180
    Shifting the Paradigm    182

THINKING CRITICALLY: DISCONNECTIONS AND CONNECTIONS    187

    Psychotherapy    188
    Other Applications    189

THINKING CRITICALLY: WORKING WITH DIVERSITY IN RELATIONSHIPS    191

PHILOSOPHY, SCIENCE, AND ART: HUMAN RELATIONS THEORIES    191

PHILOSOPHICAL ASSUMPTIONS: EXAMINING THE HUMAN
    RELATIONS THEORISTS    192

SUMMARY    194
SUGGESTIONS FOR FURTHER READING    195


PART IV    *Behavior and Learning Theories*    197


CHAPTER 8 / EXPERIMENTAL ANALYSIS OF BEHAVIOR:
              JOHN DOLLARD AND NEAL MILLER,
              B. F. SKINNER    198

YOUR GOALS FOR THIS CHAPTER    198
John Dollard and Neal Miller: Biographical Background    200
The Experimental Analysis of Behavior    200
Habits, Drives, and the Learning Process    201
Frustration and Conflict    203

THINKING CRITICALLY: THE LEARNING PROCESS    204

The Integration of Learning Theory and Psychoanalysis    205
Psychotherapy    206

PHILOSOPHY, SCIENCE, AND ART: DOLLARD AND MILLER'S THEORY    207

B. F. Skinner: Biographical Background    209
A Theory of Personality Without Personality    211
The Development of Behavior Through Learning    211
    Operant Conditioning    212
    Shaping    213

THINKING CRITICALLY: CLASSICAL AND OPERANT CONDITIONING
        IN YOUR LIFE    214

        Schedules and Types of Reinforcement    215
Psychotherapy and Behavioral Change    216
Social Utopias    218

PHILOSOPHY, SCIENCE, AND ART: SKINNER'S THEORY    219

PHILOSOPHICAL ASSUMPTIONS: EXAMINING ÐOLLARD AND MILLER
        AND SKINNER    220

Conclusions    221

SUMMARY    222

SUGGESTIONS FOR FURTHER READING    223

CHAPTER 9  /  **SOCIAL LEARNING THEORIES: ALBERT BANDURA,
                JULIAN ROTTER**    225

YOUR GOALS FOR THIS CHAPTER    225
Albert Bandura: Biographical Background    226
Reciprocal Determinism and the Self-System    227
Learning Through Observation    229
        Experimental Analysis of the Influence of Modeling    230
        Processes of Observational Learning    231
        Reinforcement in Observational Learning    233
Television and Aggression    234

THINKING CRITICALLY: FILMED VIOLENCE    235

Self-Efficacy    236
Psychotherapy and Behavior Modification    237

THINKING CRITICALLY: DEVELOPING SELF-CONTROL    239

PHILOSOPHY, SCIENCE, AND ART: BANDURA'S THEORY    240

Julian Rotter: Biographical Background    242
Internal versus External Control of Reinforcement    243

THINKING CRITICALLY: INTERNAL-EXTERNAL LOCUS OF CONTROL    245

Basic Concepts    246
Psychotherapy    247

PHILOSOPHY, SCIENCE, AND ART: ROTTER'S THEORY    249

PHILOSOPHICAL ASSUMPTIONS: EXAMINING BANDURA AND ROTTER    250

A Cognitive-Affective Personality System    250

Conclusions    252

SUMMARY    252

SUGGESTIONS FOR FURTHER READING    253

PART V    *Dispositional Theories*    255

CHAPTER 10  /  **TRAITS AND PERSONOLOGY: GORDON ALLPORT, HENRY MURRAY**    256

YOUR GOALS FOR THIS CHAPTER    256

Gordon Allport: Biographical Background    257

The Nature of Personality    258

Traits    259

Common Traits    260

Personal Dispositions    260

THINKING CRITICALLY: CENTRAL DISPOSITIONS    261

The Proprium    261

Functional Autonomy    263

A Definition of Maturity    264

Assessment and Research in Allport's Theory    266

PHILOSOPHY, SCIENCE, AND ART: ALLPORT'S THEORY    268

Henry Murray: Biographical Background    270

The Study of Personology    271

Human Needs    272

THINKING CRITICALLY: EVALUATING NEEDS    274

Assessment and Research in Murray's Theory    275

THINKING CRITICALLY: THE THEMATIC APPERCEPTION TEST    277

PHILOSOPHY, SCIENCE, AND ART: MURRAY'S THEORY    277

PHILOSOPHICAL ASSUMPTIONS: EXAMINING ALLPORT AND MURRAY    278

Conclusions    279

SUMMARY    279

SUGGESTIONS FOR FURTHER READING    281

CHAPTER 11 / **FACTOR ANALYTIC THEORIES: RAYMOND CATTELL, THE BIG FIVE PERSONALITY TRAITS** 282

YOUR GOALS FOR THIS CHAPTER    282

Raymond Cattell: Biographical Background    283

Cattell's Definition of Personality    284

Surface Traits versus Source Traits    285

Assessment and Research in Cattell's Theory    286

The Big Five Personality Traits    289

    The Study of Language    290

    The Study of Personality Questionnaires and Ratings    290

    Differences Between the Big Five and the Five Factor Model    291

    Applications of the Big Five and the Five Factor Model    292

Related Developments: Behavioral Genetics and Evolution    294

    The Genetic Influence on Traits    294

    Applications of Genetic Research    297

THINKING CRITICALLY: SHOULD WE SELECTIVELY BREED HUMANS?    298

THINKING CRITICALLY: PERSONALITY TRAITS THAT HAVE APPEARED IN FAMILIES THROUGHOUT THE GENERATIONS    299

    Evolutionary Personality Theory    299

PHILOSOPHY, SCIENCE, AND ART: FACTOR-ANALYTIC TRAIT THEORIES    300

PHILOSOPHICAL ASSUMPTIONS: EXAMINING CATTELL AND THE BIG FIVE THEORISTS    302

SUMMARY    303

SUGGESTIONS FOR FURTHER READING    304

CHAPTER 12 / **BIOLOGICAL TRAITS: HANS EYSENCK**    305

YOUR GOALS FOR THIS CHAPTER    305

Biographical Background    306

Historical Predecessors    308

Constructing a Model of Personality    310

The Identification of Superfactors    311

    The Hierarchical Model of Personality    312

    Comparisons with Cattell and the Big Five    315

    The Measurement of Traits    316

THINKING CRITICALLY: CONSTRUCTING QUESTIONNAIRE ITEMS
FOR PERSONALITY RESEARCH    318

Looking for Causal Agents of Behavior    318

THINKING CRITICALLY: THE LEMON TEST    322

The Biological Basis of Behavior and Neurosis    322
Intelligence    325
Applications of Eysenck's Theory    327
Education    327

THINKING CRITICALLY: STUDY PLACES    328

Creativity    329
Personality and Genetics    330
Psychotherapy    331

PHILOSOPHY, SCIENCE, AND ART: EYSENCK'S THEORY    333

PHILOSOPHICAL ASSUMPTIONS: EXAMINING EYSENCK'S THEORIES    334

SUMMARY    336

SUGGESTIONS FOR FURTHER READING    337

PART VI    *Humanistic and Existential Theories*    339

CHAPTER 13 / **HUMANISM: ABRAHAM MASLOW, CARL ROGERS**    340

YOUR GOALS FOR THIS CHAPTER    340
Abraham Maslow: Biographical Background    341
Human Motivation: A Hierarchical Theory    343
The Study of Self-Actualized Persons    345

PHILOSOPHY, SCIENCE, AND ART: MASLOW'S THEORY    348

Carl Rogers: Biographical Background    350
Rogers's Theory of Personality    352
Actualization    352
The Self    353
Congruence and Incongruence    354
Development of Personality    355
Psychotherapy    357
Conditions for Therapeutic Change    358
Responses to Emotional Communications    358

Supportive versus Reconstructive Psychotherapy    360

Changes in Rogers's View of Therapy    361

THINKING CRITICALLY: CULTIVATING A MORE REFLECTIVE RESPONSE    362

Assessment and Research in Rogers's Theory    362

THINKING CRITICALLY: ASSESSMENT WITH THE Q-SORT TEST    364

PHILOSOPHY, SCIENCE, AND ART: ROGERS'S THEORY    365

PHILOSOPHICAL ASSUMPTIONS: EXAMINING MASLOW AND ROGERS    367

SUMMARY    368

SUGGESTIONS FOR FURTHER READING    370

CHAPTER 14  /  EXISTENTIAL PSYCHOANALYSIS: ROLLO MAY    372

YOUR GOALS FOR THIS CHAPTER    372

Biographical Background    373

The Existential Attitude    375

Our Predicament    377

Powerlessness    377

Anxiety    378

The Loss of Values    379

THINKING CRITICALLY: THE VIABILITY OF A TRADITIONAL ETHIC    380

Rediscovering Selfhood    381

Ontological Assumptions Concerning the Person    382

Rediscovering Feelings    382

Four States of Consciousness of Self    383

The Goals of Integration    383

The Daimonic    384

Power    384

Love and Sex    385

Intentionality    386

Freedom and Destiny    386

Courage and Creativity    387

A Cry for Myth    388

THINKING CRITICALLY: THE MYTH THAT SURROUNDS OUR BIRTH    389

Psychotherapy    390

Assessment and Research in May's Theory    391

PHILOSOPHY, SCIENCE, AND ART: MAY'S THEORY    393

PHILOSOPHICAL ASSUMPTIONS: EXAMINING MAY    394

SUMMARY    395

SUGGESTIONS FOR FURTHER READING    396

---

PART VII  *Cognitive Theories*    399

CHAPTER 15  /  **PERSONAL CONSTRUCTS: GEORGE KELLY**    400

YOUR GOALS FOR THIS CHAPTER    400

Biographical Background    401

The Person as Scientist    403

Constructive Alternativism    404

THINKING CRITICALLY: HOW WE BEHAVE AS SCIENTISTS    405

Fundamental Postulate and Corollaries    405

The Reconstruction of Old Concepts    407

Assessment and Research in Kelly's Theory    409

Psychotherapy    411

THINKING CRITICALLY: ASSESSING PERSONAL CONSTRUCTS—THE REP TEST    412

THINKING CRITICALLY: ROLE-PLAYING    414

PHILOSOPHY, SCIENCE, AND ART: KELLY'S THEORY    415

PHILOSOPHICAL ASSUMPTIONS: EXAMINING KELLY    416

SUMMARY    417

SUGGESTIONS FOR FURTHER READING    418

CHAPTER 16  /  **COGNITIVE-BEHAVIORAL THEORIES: ALBERT ELLIS, AARON BECK, ARNOLD LAZARUS**    419

YOUR GOALS FOR THIS CHAPTER    419

Albert Ellis: Biographical Background    420

Philosophical Origins    422

The Theory of Rational Emotive Behavior Therapy (REBT)    422

Rational Emotive Behavior Psychotherapy    425

THINKING CRITICALLY: A SELF-HELP FORM    427

Comparisons and Contrasts with Other Theorists    428

Aaron Beck: Biographical Background    429

Philosophical Origins    430

The Theory Behind Cognitive Therapy    431

Cognitive Schemas    432

Cognitive Distortions    432

Dimensions of Sociotrophy and Autonomy    432

Cognitive Triad    433

THINKING CRITICALLY: COGNITIVE DISTORTIONS    434

Cognitive Psychotherapy    434

Cognitive Techniques    435

Behavioral Techniques    435

Assessment, Research, and Comparison with Other Theorists    435

Arnold Lazarus: Biographical Background    436

The Development of His Theory and the BASIC-ID    438

Theory of Personality    439

Multimodal Therapy    440

THINKING CRITICALLY: USING THE BASIC-ID    442

Technical Eclecticism    442

PHILOSOPHY, SCIENCE, AND ART: COGNITIVE BEHAVIORAL THERAPIES
AND THEORIES    443

PHILOSOPHICAL ASSUMPTIONS: EXAMINING COGNITIVE
BEHAVIORAL THERAPISTS    444

SUMMARY    445

SUGGESTIONS FOR FURTHER READING    447


PART VIII    *A Non-Western Approach*    449

CHAPTER 17 / **ZEN BUDDHISM**    450

YOUR GOALS FOR THIS CHAPTER    450

The Introduction of Zen to the West    451

The Origins of Zen    451

The Teachings of the Buddha    453

The Three Characteristics of Existence    455

Vasubandhu and the Eight Consciousnesses    457

Bodhidharma and the Transmission of Zen to China    458

The Practice of Zen    460

The Five Approaches to Zen Practice    464

THINKING CRITICALLY: MEDITATION   465

Enlightenment   466

Eastern Thought and Psychotherapy   468

THINKING CRITICALLY: MINDFULNESS AND THE SEARCH
FOR A HIGHER SYNTHESIS   469

PHILOSOPHY, SCIENCE, AND ART: EASTERN THEORIES   470

SUMMARY   472

SUGGESTIONS FOR FURTHER READING   473


CONCLUSION / **PERSONALITY THEORY IN PERSPECTIVE**   475

YOUR GOALS FOR THIS CHAPTER   475

PHILOSOPHY, SCIENCE, AND ART: PERSONALITY THEORIES   476

Philosophical Issues   478

The Challenge of Contemporary Personality Theorizing   479

SUMMARY   486

SUGGESTIONS FOR FURTHER READING   487


**GLOSSARY**   489

**REFERENCES**   505

**INDEX**   527

**CREDITS**   550

# Preface

*Personality Theories: An Introduction,* Fifth Edition, is designed both to explain the major personality theories and to stimulate critical thinking about them. In developing the Fifth Edition, I have continued to pursue and refine the four main objectives that have been enduring features of this text:

*To present a clear and concise picture of the major features of each important personality theory.* I have strived to present the material in an accessible style and, wherever possible, to illustrate theoretical points with concrete examples. I have presented each theory succinctly, to allow for adequate coverage of all the theories. The structure of the text itself is also clear and concise: each chapter focuses on one theory or group of related theories. Brief biographies of the theorists shed light on how they formed their theories.

*To focus on significant ideas and themes that structure the content of the personality theories.* I regularly compare the different theories to outline the distinctive characteristics and contributions of each theory and to emphasize significant ideas around which the theories are structured. Because many theories have elaborated on, modified, or refuted psychoanalysis, I have devoted substantial space to Freudian theory, providing the reader with a focal point from which comparisons and contrasts may be made.

*To provide criteria to guide the evaluation of each theory.* Many of the theories that influence contemporary thought did not develop from strict scientific methods but instead reflect philosophical assumptions. In addition, the application of a theory to a real-life situation such as psychotherapy is a creative act, demonstrating that a personality theory may function as an art. Therefore, the evaluation of a personality theory is best accomplished when the theory is broken down into its component parts—philosophy, science, and art—and judged according to the criteria appropriate to each function. Two features in each chapter—the "Philosophy, Science, and Art" sections and the "Philosophical Assumptions" boxes—refer the student back to the basic philosophical assumptions introduced in Chapter 1, relating the parts back to the whole and drawing attention to significant ideas that have generated the structure and content of personality theories. The "Conclusion" chapter at the end of the text wraps up the evaluation discussion.

*To present activities, informed by the tenets of each theory, that will provide growth in critical thinking skills.* Effective learning is not a passive process; it requires active participation. The fourth objective is accomplished through "Thinking Critically" boxes that provide activities designed to stimulate and foster critical thinking skills. Such boxes, first introduced in the Third Edition, have proven to be very popular. Many of these activities are new; others have been carefully reviewed, revised, and augmented to emphasize more clearly cultural diversity and a postmodern worldview.

# Features of the Book

Important and effective pedagogical aids continue in the Fifth Edition. To help students read with a sense of purpose and review important points quickly, each chapter begins with a list of "Your Goals for This Chapter" and ends with a "Summary," whose items are keyed to each goal. Key terms and concepts are boldfaced within the text, and a glossary at the back of the book provides definitions. Throughout, the illustration program has been revised to include more figures and tables that summarize the concepts being presented. Every chapter also includes a list of "Suggestions for Further Reading."

A number of Thinking Critically activities appear in each chapter. As discussed above, these boxes ask the student to return to material that has been presented in the chapter and reconsider it or apply it critically.

The discussion of each theorist is accompanied by a Philosophical Assumptions box (with accompanying scale on the text endsheets), in which students can compare and contrast their own philosophical views with those of the theorist.

# New to the Fifth Edition

I have revised the book in response to developments in the field of personality psychology and to feedback from instructors and students who used the previous edition. I have combined some chapters and expanded others into two on the basis of the current direction of personality exploration. Specifically, the chapters on Horney and Fromm from the previous edition have been combined into Chapter 5, *Psychoanalytic Social Psychology: Karen Horney and Erich Fromm;* and the chapters on Rogers and Maslow have been combined into Chapter 13, *Humanism: Abraham Maslow and Carl Rogers.* This is not to minimize the significance of these theorists, but rather to make room for other theories and developments that have emerged. In that connection, from the previous edition the chapter on more recent psychoanalytic theorists has been expanded into two chapters: Chapter 6, *Ego Psychology: Anna Freud, Heinz Hartmann, and Erik Erikson,* and Chapter 7, *Human Relations: Melanie Klein, Margaret Mahler, Heinz Kohut, Otto Kernberg, Nancy Chodorow, and the Stone Center Group.* The chapter on trait and temperament theories has been expanded into two chapters: Chapter 11, *Factor Analysis: Raymond Cattell and the Big Five Personality Traits,* and Chapter 12, *Biological Traits: Hans Eysenck.* In addition to these organizational changes, the text has been updated throughout and continues to emphasize multicultural, feminist, and postmodern concerns.

Further highlights of the changes in the book, by chapter, include

CHAPTER 1

❖ New graphics to illustrate the primary concepts

❖ Updated discussion of the significance of postmodern viewpoints, cultural diversity, and narrative thought as a primary form of cognition and understanding

❖ Expanded coverage of correlational studies

CHAPTER 2

- ❖ Expanded coverage of recent criticisms and rebuttals concerning Freud's theory
- ❖ Discussion of possible integration of psychoanalytic theory and cognitive science

CHAPTER 3

- ❖ Expanded discussion of Jung's archetypes
- ❖ New Thinking Critically box: "Archetypes in Cultural Forms"
- ❖ New section on synchronicity
- ❖ Applications of the MBTI in education, business, and counseling

CHAPTER 4

- ❖ New Thinking Critically box: "A License to Parent?"
- ❖ Expanded discussion on birth order in light of Sulloway (1996)
- ❖ Recognition of prevalence of Adlerian Institutes

CHAPTER 5

- ❖ Coverage of Horney and Fromm combined to form a new chapter on social psychoanalytic theories
- ❖ Updating of the bibliographic material on Horney in light of more current information
- ❖ Recognition of Horney's view forecasting object relations theory and Kohut's position
- ❖ Appreciation of the application of Horney's theory to group psychotherapy
- ❖ New Thinking Critically box: "Human Needs and Society," informed by Fromm's theory
- ❖ Appreciation of the continued interest in Fromm's theory

CHAPTER 6

- ❖ Coverage of recent psychoanalytic theorists expanded to two chapters: Chapter 6 on ego psychology and Chapter 7 on human relations
- ❖ Expansion of Anna Freud's views on adolescence
- ❖ Expanded sections on Erikson's understanding of the ego and introduction to the psychosocial stages of development
- ❖ New section on Dan McAdams's theory of identity development through life stories
- ❖ New Thinking Critically box: "Writing Your Own Life Story"

CHAPTER 7

❖ New section on Melanie Klein's contribution to object relations theory

❖ Expanded discussion of Mahler's impact on psychotherapy

❖ Consideration of the current interest in Kohut's work

❖ New discussion of Kernberg's suggested changes to Freud's drive theory

❖ Discussion of Chodorow's 1994 and 1995 writings on gender

❖ New major section on the work of the Stone Center group on human development within relationships

❖ New Thinking Critically box: "Disconnections and Connections"

❖ New Thinking Critically box: "Working with Diversity in Relationships"

CHAPTER 8

❖ Appreciation of cultural influences on reinforcement patterns

❖ Additional recognition of how reinforcement can motivate adaptive and maladaptive behavior

❖ Expansion of Dollard and Miller's influence on social and behavioral learning theory

❖ Additional information on Skinner's air crib

CHAPTER 9

❖ Updating of the bibliographical material on Bandura

❖ New section on self-efficacy

❖ New information on internal controls and moral behavior

❖ Recent trends in locus of control measures

❖ New section on Walter Mischel

CHAPTER 10

❖ Expanded discussion of Allport's influence on the study of religion

❖ Increased recognition of Allport's contribution to the dispositional approach

❖ Consideration of the resurgence of interest in idiographic approaches

❖ Expanded discussion of the Thematic Apperception Test

❖ Acknowledgments of Murray's influence on McClelland's study of the need for achievement

CHAPTER 11

❖ Coverage of trait and temperament theories expanded to two chapters: Chapter 11 on factor analytic theories, with a focus on Raymond Cattell's theory and the Big Five personality traits, and Chapter 12 on biological trait theory

❖ Expanded discussion of factor analysis

❖ Discussion of syntality

❖ Greatly expanded section on the Big Five personality traits

❖ New section on behavioral genetics

❖ New section on evolutionary personality theory

### CHAPTER 12

❖ Extended focus on the theory of Hans Eysenck

❖ Expanded discussion of historical predecessors to Eysenck's theory

❖ Detailed discussion of Eysenck's construction of a model of personality

❖ Clarification between personality dimension and psychiatric illnesses

❖ Comparisons of Eysenck, Cattell, and the Big Five

❖ Expanded section on causal agents of behavior

❖ New Thinking critically box: "The Lemon Test"

❖ Expanded section on the biological basis of behavior and neurosis

❖ New section on intelligence

❖ New sections on the applications of Eysenck's theory to education, the study of creativity, the study of personality and genetics, and psychotherapy

❖ New Thinking Critically box: "Study Places"

### CHAPTER 13

❖ Coverage of Rogers and Maslow combined to form a new chapter on humanist theories

❖ Clarification of the principle of relative potency in Maslow's thought

❖ Discussion of the organismic valuing process in Rogers's theory

❖ Discussion of Rogers's research program at the Counseling Center of the University of Chicago with reference to the case of Mrs. Oak

❖ Clarification concerning encounter groups

### CHAPTER 14

❖ New Thinking Critically box: "The Viability of a Traditional Ethic"

### CHAPTER 15

❖ Consideration of Kelly's personal construct theory as it relates to social constructionism and narrative psychology

### CHAPTER 16

❖ Rationale given for the name change in Ellis's theory

❖ New examples of Ellis's therapeutic techniques

❖ Expanded biographical information on Beck

❖ Updated biographical discussion of Lazarus

❖ Expansion of the Thinking Critically box "Using the BASIC-ID"

❖ Discussion of the influence of managed care on short-term psychotherapy

### CHAPTER 17

❖ New material on Vasubandhu and the Eight Consciousnesses

❖ Information on physiological responses that occur during the practice of Zen meditation

❖ New section on five approaches to Zen practice

❖ Influence of Morita and Naikan therapies on Reynolds's "constructive living"

## Ancillaries

The text is accompanied by an *Instructor's Resource Manual and Test Bank,* revised by Billa R. Reiss of St. John's University. The manual includes teaching suggestions for both novice and experienced instructors and multiple-choice and essay questions for each chapter of the text. A computerized version of the manual allows instructors to generate exams and integrate their own text questions with those on disk.

## Acknowledgments

I would like to thank the following theorists for reviewing and commenting on the manuscript for the Fifth Edition: Albert Bandura, Aaron Beck, Raymond Cattell, Nancy J. Chodorow, Albert Ellis, Arnold Lazarus, Dan McAdams, Jean Baker Miller and Judith Jordan (of the Stone Center), Neal Miller, and Julian Rotter.

In addition, I would like to acknowledge two special people whose help began with the Fourth Edition. Yōzan Dirk Mosig, Ph.D., a professor of psychology who has practiced Zen Buddhism for a considerable amount of time, wrote the first draft of the chapter on Zen Buddhism. The original draft that Yōzan prepared was considerably longer and had to be cut due to space limitations. Dr. Mosig has offered to answer any questions that readers may have on the material. He can be contacted c/o Psychology Department, University of Nebraska at Kearney, Kearney, NE 68849. Nancymarie Bride, Ph.D., a certified clinical mental health counselor in private practice in Westfield, New Jersey, and a close personal friend, gave me a great deal of information, some of which I was able to use verbatim, on Albert Ellis, Aaron Beck, and Arnold Lazarus for the chapter on those theorists.  I would also like to thank my colleagues and students at Union County College for their continued interest, support, and constructive comments regarding the text and its revision—in particular, Donna Lawless and Charnette Banks, reference librarians, who patiently fulfilled my every request for abstracts, articles, information, and interlibrary loans. I am also grateful to the following reviewers who thoughtfully evaluated the manuscript or provided prerevision advice:

Peter Arnett, Washington State University

C. George Boeree, Shippensburg University

Joel Frederickson, Bethel College

Rosalyn M. King, Northern Virginia Community College

Jerald J. Marshall, University of Central Florida

Suzan D. Olson, Wichita State University

Billa R. Reiss, St. John's University

Steve Slane, Cleveland State University

Susan Krauss Whitbourne, University of Massachusetts at Amherst

Finally, I would like to thank the following people at Houghton Mifflin who assisted in the development and production of the Fifth Edition: Jane Knetzger, Joanne Tinsley, Janet Young, and Karen Lindsay.

—B.E.

# Introduction: Evaluating Personality Theories

## Your Goals for This Chapter

1. Explain why the term *personality* is difficult to define.
2. Define the term *theory*.
3. Discuss the role of personality theory in psychology.
4. Describe three functions of personality theories.
5. Explain how to recognize *philosophical assumptions*.
6. Identify some of the basic philosophical issues on which personality theorists differ.
7. Explain how philosophical assumptions are evaluated.
8. Explain how science has its basis in *philosophy*.
9. Explain the characteristics of *scientific statements*.
10. Explain how scientific statements are evaluated and describe how scientists decide between rival hypotheses.
11. Describe two major techniques of assessing personality and three primary research approaches used in personality.
12. Identify three major goals of *psychotherapy* and indicate the criteria of evaluation suitable for each goal.
13. Explain why it is important to distinguish among the different functions of personality theories.

A definition for the word *personality* would be a good way to begin a book that considers various theories of personality. However, writing a definition is not that simple. A complete search for such a definition takes us back to the early history of the human race, back to the time when the first person asked, "Who am I?," thereby reflecting on his or her identity. The different answers that people have given to that question have found expression throughout history in various cultural constructs such as philosophy, religion, art, politics, and science. Each one of us begins the search anew; as children seeking identity, and later as adults reflecting upon our identity, we wonder who we are and join fellow travelers on the road in search of the self.

## What Is Personality?

Although the term **personality** is frequently used, it is not easy to define. In common speech, it usually refers to one's public image. Thus people say, "Becky has a terrific personality!" or "If only Jeff had a more dynamic personality." This common usage reflects the origin of the word *personality* in the Latin *persona,* which referred to the masks that actors wore in ancient Greek plays. In the Greek theatre, there were often more roles in a play than there were actors. Thus an actor would change *personae* to let the audience know a different role was being assumed. Such a concept of social role, however, does not include the complications that are involved in the long search to understand the self.

There is little common agreement among personality theorists on appropriate use of the term *personality* (see Figure 1.1). Gordon Allport described and classified over fifty different definitions. For Allport, personality was something *real* within an individual that leads to characteristic behavior and thought. For Carl Rogers, another personality theorist, the personality or "self" was an organized, consistent pattern of perception of the "I" or "me" that lies at the heart of an individual's experiences. For B. F. Skinner, possibly the most well known American psychologist, the word *personality* was unnecessary. Skinner did not believe that it was necessary or desirable to use a concept such as self or personality to understand human behavior. For Sigmund Freud, the father of contemporary psychoanalysis, personality was largely unconscious, hidden, and unknown.

Each theorist presents us with his or her own understanding of the term *personality.* In part, this helps to explain why there are so many different personality theories. Although such a variety of definitions and theories may be confusing and even disturbing, it does not mean that the theories are not useful. Each offers insight into the question of the self and each can be helpful to us as we develop our own answers.

## WHAT IS PERSONALITY?

It is an organized, consistent pattern of perception of the "I" or "me" that lies at the heart of an individual's experiences.

**Carl Rogers**

It is largely unconscious, hidden, and unknown.

**Sigmund Freud**

It is something real within an individual that leads to characteristic behavior and thought.

It is an unnecessary construct.

**Gordon Allport**

**B. F. Skinner**

FIGURE 1.1    The Many Views of Personality

"Personality" is not a readily defined concept. Shown here are just some of the views of personality held by different personality theorists. As you proceed through this text and examine the work of individual personality theorists, you will discover many more different views of personality.

## What Is a Theory?

Since we are referring to theories of personality, the next question is "What is a theory?" Here you may be pleased to see that there is a more definitive answer. The term *theory* comes from the Greek word *theōria*, which refers to the act of viewing, contemplating, or thinking about something. A **theory** is a set of abstract concepts developed about a group of facts or events in order to explain them. A theory of personality, therefore, is an organized system of beliefs that helps us to understand human nature.

Describing a theory as a system of beliefs underscores the fact that a theory is something that we create in the process of viewing and thinking about our world. Theories are not given or necessitated by nature; rather, they are constructed by people in their efforts to understand the world. The same data or experiences can be accounted for in many different ways, and people of varying cultures and backgrounds construct a wide variety of explanations. As we shall see, there are many theories of personality.

## The Role of Personality Theory in Psychology

Because personality addresses that important question "Who am I?," you might imagine that personality is the primary emphasis of psychology. In fact, personality is not the dominant concern in contemporary psychology; it is simply one area of specialization.

The question "What is personality?" takes us back to early human history. Awareness about the self and the world probably existed *before* deliberate reflection, philosophy, and science. In time, as people began to reflect on their ideas, philosophy developed as a mode of understanding and expression. As psychology found expression in the philosophies of Plato and Aristotle, it sought to clarify the essence of a human being and explore what it means to be a person.

By the late nineteenth century the scientific revolution had made great strides in comprehending the physical world, and people were eager to apply scientific methods to the study of human beings. Modern-day psychology emerged from a combination of various movements in philosophy and science. In 1879, Wilhelm Wundt (1832–1920) established the first psychological laboratory at the University of Leipzig in Germany to explore the experience of consciousness. By combining careful measurement with *introspection,* or self-examination, Wundt sought to reveal the basic elements and structure of the conscious mind. The psychologist could thereby emulate the natural scientist, who had been successful in identifying the basic elements of the physical world.

Wundt was successful in establishing a meticulous, systematic method of study based on the experimental method. However, his emphasis on conscious experience was criticized in the 1920s by John Watson (1878–1958), who came to be known as the father of American behaviorism. Watson recommended that in order to be a science, psychology emphasize the study of overt rather than covert behavior. *Overt* behaviors are those that we can observe directly, such as bodily movements, speaking, and crying. *Covert* behaviors are those that only the individual who experiences them can directly observe, such as thoughts, feelings, and wishes. Watson's recommendation created a curious situation for psychology. Much of what psychologists had traditionally talked about, including Wundt's research, concerned covert phenomena.

Watson pointed out that it is virtually impossible to observe mental processes directly. Therefore, he suggested that the psychologist should act as if mental processes did not exist and simply concentrate on overt behavior. While few psychologists today agree with Watson's extreme view, the behaviorist position that he generated became the dominant movement in American psychology throughout most of the twentieth century. Watson was succeeded as leader of the movement by B. F. Skinner, who took the behaviorist position to its logical extreme. Because of Skinner's influence, students of psychology rapidly discovered that, for the most part, they were not engaged in the study of the person, but in the study of behavior (usually of rats and pigeons). They were encouraged to adopt a rigorous scientific methodology that emphasized extrospective observation, or looking outward. B. F. Skinner's theory will be discussed in greater detail in Chapter 8.

Today, psychologists are very interested in the mental processes shunned by Watson and Skinner. Indeed, one current trend is toward cognitive psychology, which emphasizes how people receive, process, and react to information from their environment. On the other hand, psychology has retained from the behaviorists an emphasis on rigorous methodology emphasizing extrospective observation.

Not all of the personality theorists that we will consider agree that a rigorous scientific method is the best way to understand personality. In fact, the first theories of personality developed outside the mainstream of academic experimental psychology. While Wundt was at work in his laboratory at Leipzig, Sigmund Freud (1856–1939), who was *not* a psychologist but rather a neurologist and physician in private practice in Vienna, was employing introspection somewhat differently in his treatment of patients who were suffering from emotional problems. Instead of using introspection only to examine present phenomena, Freud also taught his patients to employ it retrospectively to examine past experiences. Thus Freud was able to examine phenomena that could not be elicited in a laboratory. Freud found introspection to be a valuable tool for discovering and exploring unconscious processes. On the basis of his clinical observations, Freud developed psychoanalysis and a theory of personality, which will be discussed in Chapter 2. Freud's method was far different from the experimental laboratory research that characterizes much of psychology today.

Some of Freud's followers became dissatisfied with orthodox psychoanalysis and founded their own schools of thought. Although these theorists were all deeply indebted to Freud, they reacted in varying ways against his theory and developed their own positions. Since the study of personality became a formal and systematic area of scientific specialization in American psychology in the mid-1930s, some psychologists have recommended that all research in personality be conducted and evaluated along strict scientific guidelines as defined by mainstream academic psychology. Nevertheless, the study of personality is the heir of two different approaches: *academic psychology* and *clinical practice* (see Figure 1.2). These traditions have never fully merged (Boneau, 1992). Examples of each, and other traditions as well, will be found in the theories discussed in this book.

## The Evaluation of Personality Theories

As we have seen, personality theory is not simply an expression of psychology as a science. Before the study of personality became a specialization of academic scientific psychology, questions of personality were generally included under the broader umbrella of philosophy. Many of the personality theories we will explore resemble philosophical investigations rather than scientific studies. The methods of science and philosophy are distinguishable but not unrelated. Science is an offspring of philosophy and its methods are the fruit of philosophy's labors. The specific mode of study and investigation characteristic of a modern

**FIGURE 1.2    Approaches to the Study of Personality**

scientist arose out of an earlier philosophical encounter with the world and retained many of its requirements. Science further demanded that theories be empirically validated, or ultimately based on sensory experience.

If scientific theories of personality have their origin in philosophy, they also lead to some form of art, or practical application. The art of personality theory is much older than the science or even the philosophy of it; from earliest times, much has been spoken and written about how to live a good life and understand people. As science has developed, however, it has provided us with new knowledge, tools, and methods of self-understanding and improvement. Theories of personality are not just armchair speculations but belief systems that find expression in ways that are designed to help us understand and improve ourselves and the world.

Philosophy, science, and art may be seen as three complementary orientations from which personality theorists work. As philosophers, personality theorists seek to explore what it means to be a person; as scientists, they hope to develop a workable set of hypotheses that will help us understand human behavior; as artists, they seek to apply what is known about people and behavior to foster a better life. Each activity is conducted according to certain rules with its own criteria for success. Just as potential athletes need to become familiar with the rules, equipment, and scoring of whatever sport they wish to engage in, students of personality need to become familiar with the different rules governing the activities of personality theorists. You will have difficulty understanding a personality theory unless you can identify the particular activity that the theorist is engaged in at a particular time and know how to evaluate it. By briefly exploring the activities of philosophy, science, and art, you can build a foundation for evaluating personality theories and understanding how they function.

# Philosophical Assumptions

No psychologist or personality theorist can avoid being a philosopher of sorts. As we have seen, the science of personality theorizing has its origins in philosophy. The very act of theorizing, or thinking about what we see, entails making certain assumptions about the world and human nature. All people—not only personality theorists—hold basic **philosophical assumptions** as they reflect on the world and their own existence. These basic philosophical assumptions profoundly influence the way in which we perceive the world and theorize about it.

The term **philosophy** comes from the Greek *philein,* "to love," and *sophia,* "wisdom"; it means the love or pursuit of wisdom. Each one of us is a philosopher insofar as we think and reflect about the world and ourselves. The search after wisdom, however, involves more than a desire for information to counter our ignorance. Wisdom denotes not merely knowing about something but knowing what ought to be done and how to do it. As philosophers, we make assumptions and judgments about the good life and how to live it.

Traditionally, philosophy has encompassed five types of language and study: logic, aesthetics, ethics, politics, and metaphysics. *Logic* is the study of correct or normative reasoning; it describes the ideal method of making inferences and drawing conclusions. *Aesthetics* is the study of ideal forms and beauty; it deals with the nature of the beautiful and with judgments about beauty. *Ethics* is the study of ideal conduct; it deals with the knowledge of good and evil. *Politics* is the study of ideal social organization; it describes those forms of social and political structures that are most appropriate for human beings. *Metaphysics* is the study of ultimate reality; it attempts to coordinate what is real in the light of what is ideal.

Very few of us have complete and articulate stances on each of these issues. Yet, insofar as our thoughts, statements, and theorizing reflect one or more of these concerns, we can be sure that they are informed by certain basic philosophical assumptions. In the same sense, very few, if any, of the personality theorists whom we will consider aim at developing complete philosophical pictures of ourselves and the world. Most consider themselves psychologists rather than philosophers. Nevertheless, in their psychologizing they raise philosophical issues and, in doing so, reflect philosophical assumptions.

## Recognizing Philosophical Assumptions

To introduce the nature and character of philosophical assumptions would take us far afield and belongs more properly in philosophy textbooks. However, it is important to recognize that personality theories do entail philosophical assumptions and to identify them when they occur.

The discourses of philosophy frequently posit a distinction between what is and what ought to be. People do not always think logically, nor do they behave in ideal ways. Philosophical statements suggest that things are not necessarily what they appear to be. *What is* is not necessarily *what should be.* For instance, the fact that many people are aggressive does not necessarily mean that aggression is right or that aggression represents what it means to be human.

Philosophical knowledge is ultimately in the form of an **epiphany** (from the Greek *epiphaneia,* which means "appearance" or "manifestation"), or a sudden perception of essential meaning. The "seeing" of philosophy is a special act of knowing, an extraordinary intuition that transcends everyday experience. Philosophical assumptions, therefore, differ from *empirical statements,* which are based on ordinary observation. The statement "All people seek what is good," for example, does not refer to something that can be seen in everyday observation. This statement refers to some kind of ultimate reality that is perceived in a different way.

Scientific statements also often refer to things that we cannot see in ordinary observation. Many important constructs in science involve imaginary concepts that cannot be seen. However, statements in science are ultimately, even if indirectly, based on empirical observation and their means of testing are different from those of philosophy.

The difference between scientific statements and philosophical assumptions lies in the nature of the observation that gives rise to the construct and the way in which it is tested. In science, all statements must be open to falsification. In fact, science is required to indicate the conditions under which its statements might be proven incorrect. If an exception is found to a scientific generalization, that generalization must be qualified. On the other hand, philosophical assumptions are not tentative hypotheses to be discarded when evidence contradicts them. There is no way to construct an empirical test that would let us falsify a philosophical assumption. If I maintain a philosophy that "All people seek what is good," I will not permit any ordinary observations to disprove the assumption. On the contrary, I can account for all exceptions and seeming contradictions in terms of my assumption itself.

Philosophical assumptions may be *explicit* or *implicit.* It is often difficult to identify a person's assumptions when they are not stated clearly. Nevertheless, almost everyone takes a stand on certain fundamental philosophical assumptions that deeply influence one's way of perceiving and understanding the world.

## Identifying Basic Philosophical Assumptions

Many of the differences among personality theories can be attributed to fundamental differences in philosophical assumptions. Some of the issues on which personality theories commonly disagree are described below. Each issue is presented here as a bipolar dimension. Some theorists may be seen as agreeing with one or the other extreme. Others are neutral toward the issue or seek a synthesis.

*Freedom versus determinism.* Theorists vary as to whether they believe that people basically have control over their behaviors and understand the motives behind them or whether they believe that the behavior of people is basically determined by internal or external forces over which they have little, if any, control.

*Hereditary versus environmental.* Theorists differ over whether inherited and inborn characteristics or factors in the environment have the more important influence on a person's behavior.

*Uniqueness versus universality.* Some theorists believe that each individual is unique and cannot be compared with others. Others contend that people are basically very similar in nature.

*Proactive versus reactive.* Proactive theories view human beings as acting on their initiative rather than simply reacting. The sources of behavior are perceived as lying within the individual, who does more than just react to stimuli from the outside world.

*Optimistic versus pessimistic.* Do significant changes in personality and behavior occur throughout the course of a lifetime? If an individual is motivated, can genuine changes be effected in personality? Can we help others to change by restructuring their environment? Some personality theories are decidedly more optimistic and hopeful than others concerning these possibilities.

## Evaluating Philosophical Assumptions

Inevitably, the personality theories described in this book represent philosophical points of view as well as scientific investigations. Some of the theories are explicitly philosophical. In others, the philosophical assumptions are not clearly stated, but they are nevertheless present. Carl Rogers openly acknowledged that his view of the self was philosophical and that his primary differences with other theorists, such as B. F. Skinner, were philosophical ones. Sigmund Freud initially conceived of his work as lacking any philosophy but finally admitted that many of his assumptions functioned philosophically. Because personality theories and our own thoughts involve philosophical assumptions, it is important that we recognize and evaluate them as such.

In empirical science, as we shall see, statements are proven false by the process of perceptual observation. Philosophical assumptions have criteria that are suitable to the epiphanic vision that underlies them. In evaluating a person's assumptions, we cannot set up a crucial test or experiment that will determine whether or not the hypothesis is justified. Philosophical assumptions have their own criteria or tests.

We are going to suggest three criteria for evaluating the philosophical assumptions that underlie personality theories. These three criteria add up to a fourth and final criterion: compellingness.

The first criterion is **coherence.** Are the philosophical assumptions of a personality theory clear, logical, and consistent or are they riddled with contradictions and inconsistencies? A philosophical system may have apparent inconsistencies, perplexing metaphors, or paradoxes and still be coherent, provided that the contradictions are ironed out within the philosophical stance itself so that the final position represents a clear, coherent whole. A person's philosophical system may also be unfinished, that is, open to further growth, but to be coherent it must have a clearly recognizable, consistent thrust.

The second criterion is **relevance.** To be meaningful, a philosophical assumption must have some bearing on our view of reality. If we do not share the same view of reality we will have considerable difficulty judging the assumption. In our postmodern world, the criterion of relevance further implies the need to be compatible with empirical reality as best we can ascertain it; thus, philosophies are invariably reshaped by scientific discoveries.

The third criterion is **comprehensiveness.** Is the philosophical assumption "deep" enough? In part, this question refers to scope. Does it cover what it intends to cover? Further, the criterion of comprehensiveness asks whether the treatment of the subject is profound or superficial. A philosophical assumption is superficial if it leaves too many questions unanswered or if it refuses to address them.

These three criteria lead to the fourth criterion, **compellingness.** The final and most important question is "Does the assumption and its underlying philosophy convince you?" A philosophical assumption convinces you if it grabs you in such a way that you find the belief inescapable. It is as if you *have* to believe in it. Actually, it is perfectly possible that a philosophical assumption may strike you as being coherent, relevant, and comprehensive, but in spite of those features it does not compel you to believe it. In such a case, the belief does not move you and you cannot "buy" it. My language here deliberately describes you as passive: "The philosophical assumption grabs you." "You are compelled." This language underscores the fact that philosophical assumptions are not merely subjective opinions that a

## PHILOSOPHICAL ASSUMPTIONS

# *Examining Your Own Philosophical Assumptions*

By looking at your own philosophical assumptions, you can better prepare yourself to recognize them in the theories of others. Each basic issue is presented here as a bipolar dimension along which a person's view can be placed according to the degree of agreement with one or the other extreme. You can rate your own views on a scale from 1 to 5. On each issue, if you completely agree with the first statement, rate the issue with a number 1. If you completely agree with the second statement, rate the issue with a number 5. If you only moderately agree with either statement, a number 2 or 4 would best reflect your view. If you are neutral toward the issue or believe that the best position is a synthesis of the two extremes, rate the issue with a number 3.

The first time you go through the items, rate each issue according to your beliefs. The second time, consider each issue in terms of your actions, the way in which you generally behave.

When you have determined where you stand on each of these major issues, a comparison of your positions can help you assess the importance of these issues to your own understanding of personality. Those assumptions that you feel very strongly about and mark with a 1 or a 5 probably play a very important role in your personal philosophy. If you are not strongly committed to any particular issue, that issue is probably not as important in your thinking about personality.

You should note that even experts differ in their responses to the statements below. The different personality theorists that we shall discuss vary markedly in their position on each of these issues. Each adopts the position that appears most commendable or compelling. Throughout the text, you will be asked to return to these assumptions to consider the stance of specific theorists and to see how your attitudes toward certain theorists are related to your own stance on these five dimensions.

| WOULD STRONGLY AGREE | WOULD AGREE | IS NEUTRAL OR BELIEVES IN SYNTHESIS OF BOTH VIEWS | WOULD AGREE | WOULD STRONGLY AGREE |
| --- | --- | --- | --- | --- |
| 1 | 2 | 3 | 4 | 5 |

**FREEDOM**                                                                                    **DETERMINISM**

People basically have control over their own behavior and understand the motives behind their behavior.

The behavior of people is basically determined by internal or external forces over which they have little, if any, control.

| 1 | 2 | 3 | 4 | 5 |
| --- | --- | --- | --- | --- |

**HEREDITARY**                                                                               **ENVIRONMENTAL**

Inherited and inborn characteristics have the most important infuence on a person's behavior.

Factors in the environment have the most important influence on a person's behavior.

| 1 | 2 | 3 | 4 | 5 |
| --- | --- | --- | --- | --- |

**UNIQUENESS**                                                                                **UNIVERSALITY**

Each individual is unique and cannot be compared with others.

People are basically very similar in nature.

| 1 | 2 | 3 | 4 | 5 |
| --- | --- | --- | --- | --- |

**PROACTIVE**                                                                                         **REACTIVE**

Human beings primarily act on their own initiative.

Human beings primarily react to stimuli from the outside world.

| 1 | 2 | 3 | 4 | 5 |
| --- | --- | --- | --- | --- |

**OPTIMISTIC**                                                                                    **PESSIMISTIC**

Significant changes in personality and behavior can occur throughout the course of a lifetime.

A person's personality and behavior are essentially stable and unchanging.

person has about the world. Rather, philosophical assumptions emerge out of a person's encounter with the world. They entail an active meeting of the person and the world that leads to a position about reality that the person finds inescapable.

The way in which philosophers create their views of the world is similar to, although more formal than, the manner in which each one of us comes up with our own view. We may not have thought as much or written about it, but each one of us, upon reflection, can probably think of a significant incident or period in our lives when we experienced something that led us to think about ourselves and our world in a different way. For example, after an illness or accident an individual often perceives life as having a new mission or purpose that was not present there before. Such experiences constitute the formative insights that shape our lives.

During the second half of the twentieth century, we have moved from a modern view of the world to a postmodern one in which no one has a monopoly on The Truth; rather, knowledge is a matter of perspective. This is not to say that there is no truth or that all perspectives are equally valuable. Our reconstructions of the past reveal an ethnocentric Western view of personhood (Hermans, Kempen, & Van Loon, 1992) that cannot be seen as innocent. Postmodernism raises a special challenge as we move to develop more globally relevant, multiculturally sensitive explanations appropriate for the twenty-first century.

## Scientific Statements

As scientists, personality theorists seek to develop a workable set of hypotheses, or tentative assumptions, that will help us understand human behavior. Scientists confirm their hypotheses by testing them according to generally agreed-upon methods. Thus, science, which comes from the Latin *scire,* "to know," is a group of methods of acquiring knowledge that are based on certain principles.

### The Philosophical Basis of Science

Science has its origins in philosophy, and, as such, it retains elements of its forebears. Thomas Kuhn (1970), a physicist who has studied the history of science, points this out when he reminds us that the observation on which scientific activity is based is not fixed once and for all by the nature of the world and our sensory apparatus but depends on a prior paradigm. A **paradigm** is a model or concept of the world that is shared by the members of a community and that governs their activities. Everyday observation and perception are shaped through education and subject to change over time. Your view of the world, for example, is very different from that of a person in ancient Greece or a member of an isolated primitive tribe. Indeed, without some sort of paradigm, we could not draw any conclusions from our observations at all.

**Scientific statements,** therefore, are statements about the world based on empirical observations arising from currently accepted paradigms. The paradigms are not derived from scientific activity but exist prior to it. The scientific viewpoint that one *should* base conclusions on perceptions that can be shared by others rather than on private, intrinsically unique, perceptions is a value statement that is not mandated by our observations but chosen by the community of scientists as more useful.

## Recognizing Scientific Statements

The keystone of science is empirical observation, and the simplest kinds of statements in science are empirical statements, such as "There is a person in the room." To know whether or not an empirical statement is valid, an individual has to be shown evidence based on sensory data regarding what has been seen, heard, felt, smelled, or tasted.

Empirical statements may be based on objective data or subjective data. If someone reports, "I see a person," we can interpret the statement in two ways. The person may be saying, "I see a *person*" or "I *see* a person." In the first case, we are referring to the object of experience or **objective data.** In the second case, we are referring to an experience of seeing or **subjective data.** Both objective and subjective knowledge refer to empirical data. The difference between them lies in the position of the observer. In objective knowledge, the position is I-it: the self is looking outward on the world as object. In subjective knowledge, the position is I-me: the self is looking inward on its own experience as the object.

Reports that are concerned with the object of experience or extrospective data are relatively simple to verify. We merely indicate the conditions under which the observation may be repeated. If a second observer does not see the reported phenomenon, we suggest that the conditions were not clearly specified; for example, the observer looked for the person in the wrong room. Or we may suspect that the original observer has a distorted sense of perception. Repeated observations of the same phenomenon under specified conditions lead to **consensual validation** or agreement among observers.

Reports that are concerned with introspective or subjective phenomena are much more difficult to validate consensually. A certain piece of art may give one person much joy but fail to move someone else. This is because subjective phenomena often occur under complex conditions and are more difficult to describe than objective information. Repeating such subjective observations may require the second observer to undergo extensive training or other experiences in order to duplicate all of the conditions. Undoubtedly, one's joy on seeing a particular piece of art depends not simply on the art itself, but also on one's culture, mood, personal history, and so forth. Considerable effort is needed to duplicate these observations but it is not impossible (Tart, 1975).

Since reports that are concerned with subjective phenomena are much more difficult to validate, some psychologists have tended to ignore them and invest their efforts in extrospective or objective findings. As we saw, John Watson recommended that inasmuch as our thoughts, feelings, and wishes cannot be directly observed by another person, the psychologist should ignore them and concentrate on overt behaviors. Few psychologists today would agree with this extreme position. Most personality theorists emphasize that we need to be concerned with both subjective and objective data in order to understand behavior.

When a number of different instances of observation coincide, the scientist may make a generalization. A **scientific** (or **empirical**) **generalization** is a conclusion that something is true about many or all of the members of a certain class. Suppose I wanted to test the statement "All aggressive people are controlling." The evidence for this statement could be a number of facts about individual members of the class. I could observe this aggressive person, that aggressive person, and other aggressive persons. If all of them were also controlling, I might conclude that all aggressive people are controlling, even though I have not examined each and every aggressive person.

Because it is impossible for me to examine each and every aggressive person who has existed in the past or might exist in the present or future, I can never know for certain that my empirical generalization is true. Indeed, misleading stereotypes are the result of premature and unwise generalizations. As a scientist, the personality theorist must leave empirical generalizations open to possible falsification.

The scientist also uses **definitions,** statements that are true because of the way in which we have agreed to use words. Some words are easy to define clearly and precisely. Other words are harder to define and subject to more disagreement. To resolve this problem, the social scientist frequently tries to develop operational definitions. An **operational definition** specifies which behaviors are included in the concept. "Stress" might be operationally defined in terms of the rate of one's heartbeat and extent of one's perspiration as measured by polygraph apparatuses, which translate such bodily changes into a printed record. It frequently is difficult to reach agreement on suitable operational definitions, and at times an operational definition distorts or even misses the concept it is trying to describe. For example, "stress" can also be defined as a subjective feeling of intense anxiety. The value of operational definitions lies in giving us a common ground of reference. Nevertheless, some critics have argued that operational definitions as developed by psychologists in the 1930s and 1940s were based on a misunderstanding of an attitude first recommended by Percy Bridgeman, a physicist, in the 1920s. In spite of repeated refutations, including one by Bridgeman himself in the 1950s, current textbooks persist in singing their worth (Green, 1992).

The most important statements in science are based on scientific constructs. A scientist uses **scientific constructs,** which are imaginary or hypothetical and cannot be seen with the naked eye or even with sophisticated optical equipment, in order to explain what we observe. The building blocks of nature, protons, neutrons, and electrons remain visibly elusive by direct observation, but are indirectly confirmed by their necessary existence in the construct. Today's atomic models require further inference to even smaller unseen particles such as quarks, leptons, and hadrons. The difficulty of not being directly observable does not imply nonexistence; rather it has provided for continual progress toward an understanding of what may be real. Another familiar hypothetical construct is that of IQ or intelligence quotient. The concept of IQ is an imaginary construct that is used to explain certain behaviors, namely, one's likelihood for academic success. Many of our concepts in science, in fact almost all of the important ones, cannot be directly seen; we can only know them through their effects.

## Some Basic Scientific Constructs

Constructs such as trait, reinforcement, and self have been created in efforts to understand personality scientifically. The concept of **trait** refers to a determining tendency or predisposition to respond in a certain way. Examples of traits are emotional stability and introversion versus extroversion. Allport, Cattell, Eysenck, and the Big Five theorists make extensive use of trait constructs in their theories. The **self** is another useful construct for understanding personality that is present in many contemporary theories. In Carl Rogers's theory the self refers to those psychological processes that govern an individual's behavior. In Albert Bandura's theory the self is conceived more narrowly in terms of cognitive structures.

Indeed, some personality theorists conceive of the term "personality" itself as a scientific construct. Thus Cattell defines personality as "that which permits a prediction of what a person will do in a given situation." For Cattell, personality is an imaginary construct that permits us to explain and predict behavior. The scientific constructs of a personality theory tie together the empirical findings of that theory and suggest new relationships that will hold true under certain conditions.

## Evaluating Scientific Statements

As we have pointed out, there is no one method of validating scientific statements. Personality theorists use a variety of techniques, some of which are very complicated, to evaluate their work. We will be looking at a number of these later in this chapter and in subsequent chapters when we discuss the specific assessment and research procedures used by different personality theorists. However, we can make some general comments about the validating techniques used by scientists.

Even though scientists may build elaborate theories referring to things that they cannot observe directly, they base their theories on perceptions of our sense organs. It is true that I cannot test the statement "John has an IQ of 110" in the same way that I can test the statement "There is a person in the room." I cannot simply look. The statement must be tested indirectly, but the test is still based on empirical observation, such as looking at John's performance on an IQ measuring device. Given the identical conditions, another person could be expected to share the same perceptions and draw the same conclusions. Scientific statements, therefore, are based on *what is* and *what occurs* in our everyday world as it appears to us through our sense organs.

Second, scientific statements must be *open to falsification.* As scientist, the personality theorist is required to indicate the conditions under which theoretical statements might be proven incorrect. If an exception is found to a scientific statement, that statement is considered to be false or in need of qualification. The generalization "All aggressive people are controlling," for example, is disproven by pointing to an aggressive person who is not controlling or qualified by indicating the conditions under which an aggressive person will not seek to control others. This helps us to understand why a scientist never claims that the information produced by scientific methods is ultimately true. Scientific hypotheses are tentative and need to be discarded when evidence contradicts them. Although scientific methods cannot be said to yield ultimate truth, they do provide a wealth of useful information to assist us in living in the everyday world. It is to our advantage, therefore, to act as if the conclusions from our scientific methods are true.

In the process of scientific investigations, the personality theorist frequently develops more than one hypothesis. Each one is examined in turn to rule out those that do not stand up under test conditions. Occasionally, the scientist is left with rival hypotheses.

Given that both are sound hypotheses, how does the scientist decide between them? In general, three criteria have been used: compatibility, predictive power, and simplicity. Each of these criteria has advantages and limitations. **Compatibility** refers to the agreement of the hypothesis with previously well-established information. This criterion is a sensible one since it is a lot easier for us to accept a new hypothesis if it is consistent with findings in other areas. However, it should not be too rigidly applied. There are times in science when a new idea completely shatters earlier theories, forcing us to revise or reconsider them.

**Predictive power** refers to the range or scope of the statement. Scientists seek not only to explain the phenomena that we observe but also to predict and anticipate them. The more predictions or consequences that we can infer from a theory, the greater its range and usefulness in generating new ideas. On the other hand, too strict a reliance on this criterion may lead to the notion that the only value of a theory lies in the amount of research and predictions it generates. Some theories express their heuristic value by integrating and encompassing ideas rather than by generating specific predictions and research projects.

The last criterion is **simplicity** or parsimony. Explanations ought to be as simple as possible. If there is too rigid an emphasis on the criterion of simplicity, the hypothesis may fail to account for all of the complexity of human behavior. However, all other things being equal, the simplest explanation is best.

We should note that in the West, theories of personality have often developed within the strict limits of a scientific paradigm. Some of the personality theorists that we will cover (such as Jung, Fromm, Horney, Rogers, Maslow, and May), however, have argued that that paradigm frequently fostered *scientism,* or the exclusive reliance on a narrow conception of science, which is inappropriate for understanding human nature. Some of these, most notably Jung and Horney, have suggested that we turn to the East for a more balanced comprehension.

## The Application of Personality Theories

If theories of personality have their origin in philosophy and seek to validate their constructs through scientific methods, they also culminate in some form of art or practical application. Personality theories have found application in many areas, such as assessment, research, and psychotherapy.

### Assessment

The assessment of personality is a major area in the application of personality theories to everyday life. *Assessment* refers to evaluation or measurement. You have probably been touched by assessment to a greater degree than you realize. In education, for example, assessment is used to measure progress and evaluate learning disabilities. Psychologists in industries and organizations use assessment to assist in job placement. Prior to deciding a course of counseling, a clinician needs to assess the individual in order to evaluate the nature of his or her problem.

The wise and judicious use of appropriate assessment techniques can be invaluable in developing individual and group potential. An accurate understanding of one's limitations and potentialities is important for self-actualization. The point to remember, however, is that there is a distinction between a person's inclination to behave in a certain way and the fact of behaving in such a way. Many personality tests are accurate predictors, but they are not guarantees of certain behaviors. Furthermore, as scientific tools, they must remain open to falsification, and our use of them needs to reflect that fact.

Good techniques of assessment seek to fulfill four evaluative criteria: standardization, objectivity, reliability, and validity.

**Standardization** involves assuring uniform conditions and procedures for administering a test. Standardization also informs us of the distribution and variability of scores for a particular test. The process of standardization makes it possible for us to know whether an individual's score is high, low, or average.

**Objectivity** refers to the avoidance of subjective bias in assessment. If a procedure is objective, qualified administrators and scorers can present it in the same way to any particular subject and obtain the same score as other qualified examiners. Objectivity is easier to obtain if responses are clearly delineated, as in a multiple-choice or true-false test where each response clearly indicates a certain factor. It is more difficult, but nevertheless possible, to develop objective criteria for scoring protracted written or verbal responses. Such criteria provide for objectivity in evaluating interviews, written essays, projective techniques, and so forth.

**Reliability** refers to the consistency of scores over time. This is similar to an oven thermometer that must register the same degree each time for the same amount of heat in order to be a consistent and useful measuring device. If you were to take an alternative form of the same test on two separate occasions, the two scores should be similar.

**Validity** asks if an assessment technique measures what it is supposed to measure. Validity is the most important, yet most difficult, criterion of all to meet. Virtually all psychologists agree that certain recognized intelligence tests are valid measures for predicting school performance. They are not all certain, however, that these tests are valid measures of that elusive quality, "intelligence."

The personality theorists discussed in this book have developed specific ways of assessing personality that are informed by and also inform their theories. These procedures range from the interpretation of dreams to statistically sophisticated and elaborately constructed tests. We will discuss each theorist's particular method, but first some general words about two major approaches to assessing personality.

### Psychometric Tests

Psychometric tests measure personality characteristics through carefully designed questionnaires developed with theoretical and statistical techniques. Psychometric testing had its origin in the psychological laboratories established at the end of the nineteenth century.

One of the most carefully researched questionnaires is the Minnesota Multiphasic Personality Inventory (MMPI), first published in 1942 and most recently revised in 1989. The MMPI is made up of over 550 self-report items or printed statements to which the participant answers "true," "false," or "cannot say." Designed to measure tendencies toward pathology or abnormal behavior, the MMPI is employed as an aid in the diagnosis of psychiatric disorders and is widely used in personality research.

Psychometric measuring devices and techniques have not been used without controversy. Many individuals view such tests as an invasion of personal privacy and are wary of the use to which the test results may be put. Often the validity of the tests is assumed rather than demonstrated. On the basis of a "carefully designed" test, we might imagine a situation in which individuals could be imprisoned for life simply because of the high probability that they might commit murder. Such a situation may seem far-fetched, yet individuals are turned down for jobs or denied educational and other opportunities on the basis of such tests.

### Projective Tests

Some psychologists, particularly in a clinical setting, also employ projective techniques. The participant is presented with a deliberately ambiguous stimulus. In responding to the stimulus, the participant will put forth personal attitudes, values, needs, and feelings.

Two of the best-known projective techniques are the Rorschach Inkblot Test and the Thematic Apperception Test (TAT), which are derived, respectively, from the theories of Carl Jung (Chapter 3) and Henry Murray (Chapter 10).

The main advantage of projective techniques is that they disguise the purpose of the test. Because the stimuli are ambiguous and the participant is free to respond in any way, it is difficult for the participant to know what would be an appropriate answer and fake a "correct" response. The difficulty with projective tests is that they are very hard to score in an objective manner that avoids subjective bias and the projection of the scorer.

## Research

Personality theorists also differ widely in the type of research methods that they use. Some follow very strict scientific guidelines in their work. Others encourage the use of a wider range of acceptable methodologies, making use of interdisciplinary and eclectic approaches. Indeed, restraints on creative and productive research may occur when the area of personality inquiry is too narrowly demarcated (Duke, 1986). Three primary research approaches used in personality are the clinical approach, the correlational approach, and the experimental approach. It is difficult to be specific about the evaluative criteria here, as they vary according to the specific activity and its canons of research.

### The Clinical Approach

Many of the personality theories that we will be considering originated in the clinical setting. The clinician conducts research through intensive interviews and observation of the participant. Clinical methods of research may also include the analysis of dreams and/or early memories. A clinician may further structure the observations by asking questions or giving one or more tests. Frequently there is considerable overlap between a theorist's methods of research and methods of assessment. A primary tool in the clinical approach to personality is the development of a *case history*, a carefully drawn biography of an individual. Sigmund Freud developed psychoanalytic theory largely on the basis of case histories (including his own).

Unlike most other research methods, the case history entails studying one individual or a small number of individuals in great depth rather than large numbers of subjects. Freud and Erik Erikson also developed case histories of prominent historical figures such as Michelangelo, Leonardo da Vinci, Martin Luther, and Gandhi.

### The Correlational Approach

In a **correlational study,** events or variables are systematically observed as they naturally occur to see the extent to which they covary, or occur together. Events that covary are said to be correlated. Correlations are expressed by a number that ranges from +1.00 to –1.00. The plus or minus sign tells us if the relationship is positive or negative. The numeric value tells us the extent of the relationship. The closer the numbers are to +1.00 or -1.00, the higher the frequency with which the two events occur or do not occur together.

Correlations can be visualized in the form of a *scattergram,* with each paired measurement of the two variables represented by a point. Figure 1.3 illustrates some possible correlations. A pattern that goes from lower left to upper right represents a positive correlation; the opposite direction, a negative correlation. A circular or undifferentiated pattern shows no relationship. The closer the pattern resembles a straight line, the more perfect the correlation.

It is important to remember that a correlation does not imply that one variable caused the other. For example, there is a high correlation between brown hair and brown eyes. This is not to say that brown hair causes brown eyes but rather that a great many people who have brown hair also have brown eyes. Nevertheless, where two variables have a high correlation it is reasonable to hypothesize that one caused the other or that a third variable caused both. However, such a hypothesis would have to be subject to further test. We are not permitted to draw that conclusion simply on the basis of a correlational study. Cattell and Eysenck make considerable use of a sophisticated correlational procedure, *factor analysis,* in developing their theories.

### The Experimental Approach

An experimental approach is favored by many psychologists because it permits them to infer a cause and effect relationship between two factors. In its simplest form, a researcher systematically varies the presence of one factor, the *independent variable,* while keeping all other variables constant. The researcher can then determine whether or not the changes in the independent variable have any effect on a particular behavior, the *dependent variable.* If so, it is assumed that the changes in the independent variable caused the changes in the dependent variable. For example, after students are provided with either positive or negative feedback following their performance on a memory test, they could be given a depression questionnaire to test for a change in mood. The two levels of feedback would serve as the independent variable and the score on the depression questionnaire as the dependent variable. Experiments can be very complex, with several independent and dependent variables.

The experimental method is considered the most precise method of psychological research. It has the advantage of permitting the experimenter to posit a clear cause and effect relationship, but it has limitations. To limit the findings of personality explorations to those that can be demonstrated only within the experimental laboratory would be to circumscribe the study of personality to merely those aspects about the person that can be

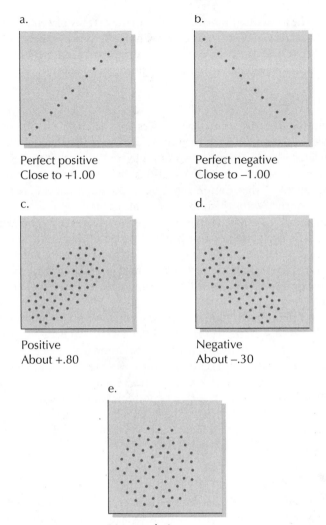

**FIGURE 1.3   Scattergrams of Possible Correlations**

A pattern that goes from lower left to upper right (a, c) represents a positive correlation between two variables. The opposite direction (b, d) indicates a negative correlation. A circular or undifferentiated pattern (e) shows no relationship. The closer the pattern resembles a straight line, the more perfect the correlation, expressed as +1.00 or –1.00.

studied by manipulation. Because of this, many questions about the ultimate meanings, purposes, and goals of human living, questions that traditionally have been and could be included in the study of personality, would be ruled out of inquiry. A wider range of acceptable methodologies is necessary (Henwood & Pidgeon, 1992).

Multiple approaches and methodologies are needed to understand the whole person. In general, the field of personality inquiry is broadening in scope (McCrae, 1996). Since Sarbin (1986) suggested that narrative might be considered a root metaphor for understanding human behavior and experience, the integrative life story has emerged as a significant vehicle for expressing and understanding personality (McAdams, 1993). Narrative thought is emerging as a primary form of cognition and self-understanding that qualitatively varies from abstract proportional or scientific thinking (Mueller & Tingley, 1990) and further enables us to understand moral development (Greenberg, 1995; Packer, 1991; Tappan, 1991). In general, the growing openness of personality theorists to more effective methods contrasts with the perpetuation by some other psychologists of a narrow view of science.

## Psychotherapy

The art of **psychotherapy** is the effort to apply the findings of personality theory in ways that will assist individuals and meet human goals. The word *therapy* comes from the Greek *therapeia,* which means "attending" and "healing"; however, psychotherapists are not interested only in healing sick people. They are also interested in understanding "normal" people, learning how they function, and helping them to function more creatively. Although in many respects psychotherapy is the flowering of personality theory, it is also the seed of it, because the desire to help people has fostered and nourished the development of personality theories. The two have gone hand in hand. Many theories of personality cannot be adequately understood without understanding the theory of psychotherapy that led to them.

### Goals of Psychotherapy

Joseph Rychlak (1968) points out that psychotherapy has three major motives or goals: the scholarly, the ethical, and the curative.

The *scholarly* motive considers therapy a means of understanding the self and human nature. Psychoanalysis, for example, was seen by Freud as a tool for discovering truths about human nature. His goal was to help the individual acquire self-understanding and to develop a comprehensive theory of human nature. He developed psychoanalysis as a method of research aimed at these ends.

The *ethical* motive considers therapy a means of helping the individual to change, improve, grow, and better the quality of life. Carl Rogers's work is an example of the ethical motive. His emphasis is on a climate created by the therapist that permits change to occur within the client rather than on cognitive understanding or the manipulation of behavior.

The *curative* motive aims directly at eliminating troublesome symptoms and substituting more suitable behavior. Most behavior therapists, for example, consider that they have been hired to do a job and seek to do it as effectively and quickly as possible. From this point of view, the therapist is responsible for creating changes, removing symptoms, and controlling behavior.

Most people enter therapy with the expectation that they will be cured or helped to improve. In this respect, the curative motive is most consistent with the popular view of psychotherapy. Because of this expectation, many people have difficulty, particularly at the beginning, in undergoing psychoanalysis or other forms of "insight" therapy. If they stay with it, however, their reasons for being in therapy change, and they begin to appreciate the value of the other motives. Obviously, the reasons for entering, continuing in, and practicing psychotherapy are many and mixed. This is why the evaluation of therapy is a difficult issue.

## Evaluating Psychotherapy

How does one go about evaluating psychotherapy? What criteria are appropriate? In 1952, Hans Eysenck stunned the therapeutic community with a report on treatment outcomes indicating that various forms of psychotherapy do not show greater effectiveness than spontaneous remission or placebo treatment. Eysenck's report created a flurry of research and comment, as **meta-analyses**\* of psychotherapy outcome studies were conducted showing that various forms of psychotherapy are consistently beneficial (Landman & Dawes, 1982; Smith & Glass, 1977). Eysenck's criterion for improvement focused on "symptom remission." Eysenck (1994) continues to reaffirm his position but acknowledges that the problem is a paradigm conflict in which different criteria are used. Garfield (1992) points out that Eysenck has been rigid in his insistence on the superiority of behavior therapy. Jones and Pulos (1993) have shown that differences in theory lead to differences in therapy. Symptom remission may be an appropriate criterion for therapies governed by the curative motive but not necessarily for those that are conducted for other purposes.

If the proportion of cures were the only criterion by which psychotherapies were to be judged, psychoanalysis and other insight therapies would have long since disappeared from the scene with the arrival of more efficient and less costly curative techniques. This, however, has not been the case. If one's criterion, on the other hand, rests on scholarly grounds, psychoanalysis emerges a clear winner. No other method of therapy has provided us with such a wealth of information about the complexity and depth of the human personality.

In brief, each method of psychotherapy must be evaluated in terms of its own goals and purposes. Behavior therapists, who aim at curing clients, are particularly interested in discovering the proportion of cures associated with various techniques. Ethical theorists, who aim at creating a suitable climate for therapeutic change and life improvement, have stimulated the study of those conditions that foster personality change and their effects. Freudian psychoanalysis asks to be evaluated in terms of its effectiveness as a method of research aimed at understanding human nature. For a summary overview of the viewpoints, their activities, and their evaluative criteria, see Figure 1.4.

---

\* A meta-analysis is a comprehensive analysis of several studies.

FIGURE 1.4   Viewpoints for Understanding and Evaluating Personality Theories

Shown here are three ways in which personality theories function. Each entails different activities that contribute to personality theory, and each activity must be evaluated according to its own criteria.

# The Complexities of Evaluation

We have suggested that science, philosophy, and application/art are three functions that personality theories encompass. Our use of this threefold approach allows us to recognize each activity as it arises and gives us a better idea of how personality theories in general, and any specific personality theory, work. It is important to identify the different aspects of a personality theory because each activity has its own rules and procedures for establishing information and each has its own criteria for judging the worth of its findings.

No theory is simply one or the other: philosophy, science, or art; each theory combines elements of all these activities. Nor are we trying to establish a model that all personality theories must follow. The fact is there is no one scientific method, philosophical approach, or psychotherapeutic strategy that would serve as an adequate model for all others.

Scientific studies of personality rely on paradigms that can only be established philosophically and generally culminate in some form of art or practical application. The desire to be scientific reflects itself in an effort to test constructs by validating evidence rather than by relying on the gut-level feeling of illumination that everyday language calls "understanding something" (Perrez, 1991).

Some psychologists have attempted to narrow the possible activity of a personality theorist to one function or interpretation of science, such as an objective experimental methodology, and ignored the philosophical assumptions on which all scientific work is based. Others have assumed that the compelling character of philosophical assumptions is sufficient to establish their credibility as scientific findings about personality. Either position is unnecessarily limiting. It is important that we distinguish among the different kinds of functions that personality theories entail so that we can recognize them when they occur and evaluate them accordingly. Part of the current problem in personality theorizing is that the theorists are not always clear about what activity they are engaged in.

As we discuss the major personality theorists in the following chapters, we will try to clarify the function of philosophy, science, and art in each theory. This should enable you to see how the theories fit into the overall framework of personality theories as philosophy, science, and art. As you will see, there is a wide variety and diversity of personality theories providing you with a rich selection from which to choose or develop your own theory of personality.

## Summary

1. The term *personality* is difficult to define because there is little common agreement on how the term should be used. In everyday speech it usually refers to one's public image. Different personality theorists present us with their own definitions of the word based on their theoretical positions.

2. A *theory* is a set of abstract concepts that we make about a group of facts or events in order to explain them.

3. Two traditions inform contemporary theories of personality. One stems from psychological laboratories and academic research. The other stems from psychoanalysis and clinical psychology. The study of personality became a formal and systematic area of specialization in American psychology in the mid-1930s, but the two traditions have never fully merged.

4. Personality theories may function as philosophy, science, and art. As scientists, personality theorists develop hypotheses that help us understand human behavior. As philosophers, they explore what it means to be a person. As artists, they seek to apply what is known about human behavior to make a better life.

5. *Philosophical assumptions* suggest that things are not necessarily what they appear to be. They are based on a special *epiphanic* vision, which goes beyond the ordinary perception of our sense organs. Philosophical statements also tend to be global and do not allow for any exceptions. Finally, they often are implicit rather than explicit.

6. Some of the basic issues on which personality theorists differ are *freedom versus determinism, heredity versus environmental* factors, *uniqueness versus universality, proactive versus reactive* theories, and *optimism versus pessimism.*

7. Philosophical assumptions are evaluated by criteria appropriate to the special act of knowing that underlies them. The criteria are *coherence, relevance,* and *comprehensiveness,* all of which add up to a final criterion, *compellingness.*

8. Science has its basis in philosophy because the ordinary observation on which science relies depends upon a prior *paradigm* that is established philosophically. The values and standards of science also function as philosophical commitments.

9. The simplest kinds of *scientific statements* are *empirical,* based directly on observation. The data on which these statements are based may be *objective* or *subjective.* When a number of different observations coincide, a scientist may make a *generalization.* Scientists also use *operational definitions,* which specify the behaviors included in a term, and *scientific constructs,* which use imaginary or hypothetical concepts to explain what we observe.

10. Scientists use a variety of techniques to evaluate their work. All of these techniques are ultimately based on observation, the ordinary perceptions of our sense organs, although some statements can be tested only indirectly. Scientific statements must be open to falsification, that is, a scientist must indicate the conditions under which a statement might be proven false. Scientists do not claim that the information produced by their methods is ultimately true. Scientific statements should be judged for their usefulness rather than their truth. When scientists end up with more than one hypothesis, the criteria they use to decide between rival hypotheses are *compatibility, predictive power,* and *simplicity.*

11. Personality theories have found application in assessment and research. Two major approaches of assessing personality are psychometric and projective

techniques. Three primary research approaches used in personality are the clinical approach, the correlational approach, and the experimental approach.

12. The three major goals of *psychotherapy* are the *scholarly, ethical,* and *curative* motives. Scholarly therapies should be evaluated on the basis of their contributions to the understanding of the self and human nature. Ethical therapies should be evaluated in terms of the suitability of the climate they create for fostering change and life improvement. Curative therapies should be evaluated on the basis of symptom remission and number of cures.

13. It is important to distinguish among the different functions of personality theories so that we can recognize each activity when it occurs and therefore evaluate each theory according to the appropriate methods.

## *Suggestions for Further Reading*

Students who are interested in pursuing Gordon Allport's effort to define the word *personality* should see his survey in Chapter 2 of *Personality: A Psychological Interpretation* (Holt, 1937). This chapter provides a compact survey of the origins of the word and the various ways in which it has been defined.

    *The Story of Philosophy* by Will Durant (Pocket Books, 1954) is a lay introduction to philosophy that tells its story by focusing on the lives and ideas of significant philosophers. The introduction, "On the Uses of Philosophy," helps to place the work of these thinkers in perspective. J. B. Conant's *On Understanding Science* (Yale University Press, 1947) gives a concise introduction to the scientific enterprise. A comprehensive history of psychology is provided in the classic work of E. G. Boring, *A History of Experimental Psychology* (Appleton-Century-Crofts, 1929), a detailed but invaluable book for the serious student of psychology.

    Books that try to place the study of psychology and personality theory within the general framework of science and philosophy are more difficult reading, but worth the effort of the interested student. The following are especially recommended: M. Turner, *Philosophy and the Science of Behavior* (Appleton-Century-Crofts, 1967); D. Bakan, *On Method: Toward a Reconstruction of Psychological Investigation* (Jossey-Bass, 1969); T. S. Kuhn, *The Structure of Scientific Revolutions,* 2nd ed. (University of Chicago Press, 1970); and I. Chein, *The Science of Behavior and the Image of Man* (Basic Books, 1972). These books stress the necessity of developing adequate conceptual structures of science and philosophy within which personality theorizing can flourish as efforts to understand the human being.

    A special issue of the *Journal of Personality* (March 1986) was devoted to methodological developments in personality research.

# PART I

# The Psychoanalytic Approach

O f all the giants of intellectual history, Sigmund Freud emerges as an unquestionable leader in helping us to understand human nature. Many of the other theories that we will study were developed as efforts to elaborate on, modify, substitute for, or refute the concepts of Freud. The systematic study of personality may be said to have begun with Freud's development of psychoanalysis at the end of the nineteenth century. Not only did Freud revolutionize psychology, his influence has been felt in all the social sciences, as well as in literature, art, and religion.

# CHAPTER 2

# *Psychoanalysis*

## SIGMUND FREUD

## *Your Goals for This Chapter*

1. Describe Freud's early use of the "talking method" and indicate the conclusions he drew about *unconscious processes.*

2. Describe Freud's concept of the role of emotions in human life. Explain why *wishes* are repressed and how they may be dealt with when brought back into consciousness.

3. Cite the instructions for *free association* and explain the premise on which the procedure is based.

4. Indicate the importance of *slips* and *dreams* and explain how they are analyzed.

5. Identify the nature of our repressed wishes and desires and explain how Freud's use of the word *libido* and his concept of *drive* lead to a new understanding of sexuality.

6. Describe the child's sexual activity and outline Freud's *psychosexual stages* of development, explaining the important events of each stage.

7. Describe how the effects of the psychosexual stages may be seen in various adult character traits and disorders.

8. Describe the characteristics and functions of the *id, ego,* and *superego.*

9. Explain how the id, ego, and superego are related in the adjusted and maladjusted personalities.

10. Explain how the id, ego, and superego are related to conscious and unconscious processes.

11. Distinguish among the three forms of anxiety that Freud described.

12. Describe the function of *defense mechanisms* and define and give examples of common defense mechanisms.

13. Describe what happens in psychoanalysis.

14. Discuss efforts to test Freudian concepts.

15. Evaluate Freud's theory in terms of its function as philosophy, science, and art.

T he stature and distinguished contributions of Sigmund Freud place him at the fore-front of contemporary personality theorists. For over forty years, Freud meticulously studied dimensions of human nature. Developing the technique of free association, he reached far into the depths of his own unconscious life and that of others. In the process, he created psychoanalysis, a unique method of research for understanding the human individual. He discovered psychological processes such as repression, resistance, transference, and infantile sexuality. He developed the first comprehensive method of studying and treating neurotic problems. His position in the history of intellectual thought clearly justifies an extended study of his ideas.

## Biographical Background

Sigmund Freud was born in 1856 in Freiburg, Moravia (a small town in what became Czechoslovakia), to a Jewish wool merchant and his young wife. Sigmund was born in a caul; that is, a small portion of the fetal sac covered his head at birth. According to folklore, this was a sign that he would be famous. Freud did not practice religion as an adult, but he remained very conscious of his Jewish origin (cf. Brunner, 1991, and Diller, 1991). His mother, twenty-one at the time of her favored first son's birth, was loving and protective, and the young boy was devoted to her (Margolis, 1989). Freud's father, Jacob, was forty-one, almost twice as old as his wife. Jacob was stern and authoritarian, but his son respected him. Only later, through his self-analysis, did Freud realize that his feelings toward his parents were mixed with fear and hate, respect and love.

When Sigmund was eleven months old, a brother, Julius, was born, but he died eight months later. A sister, Anna, arrived when Freud was two and a half. Later, four other sisters and a brother completed the family. When Freud was very young, he was very fond of his nanny and impressed by her religious teachings of Catholicism. Nevertheless, shortly after Anna was born, the nanny was suddenly fired for having stolen from the family. Sigmund was also born an uncle. His father, a widower, had two grown sons by his former marriage, and Freud's elder half-brother had a child. Freud and his nephew John, who was one year older than he, were close childhood companions. Freud was to view their early relationship as very significant to his later development. Many have thought that Freud's unusual family constellation set the stage for his later theory of the Oedipus complex.

At the age of four, Sigmund and his family moved to Vienna, where he was to live for almost eighty years. Although he was critical of Vienna, he did not leave the city until it was overwhelmed by Nazis in 1938, the year before he died. In his youth, Freud was a conscientious student. His parents encouraged his studies by giving him special privileges and expecting the other children to make sacrifices on behalf of their older brother. He was the only member of the family who had his own room; he studied by oil lamp while the others had to use candles. A natural student, Freud entered high school a year earlier than normal

*Sigmund Freud was the founder of psychoanalysis, which emphasizes the importance of unconscious forces.*

and stood at the head of the class for most of his days at the Sperl Gymnasium. He was good at languages and was an avid reader, being particularly fond of Shakespeare.

As a child, Freud had dreams of becoming a "mighty warrior" (Warner, 1991) or minister of state, but in reality professional choice was severely restricted for a Jew in Vienna. He thought of becoming a lawyer but instead began medical studies at the University of Vienna in 1873 and graduated eight years later. His studies there took longer than usual because he took his time with those areas that were of particular interest to him. He never intended to practice medicine, being more interested in physiological research; practical considerations, including occupational barriers to Jewish people and the desire to marry, led him to establish a practice as a clinical neurologist in 1881. While still a student, he made substantial and noteworthy contributions to research, publishing his findings on the nervous system of fish and the testes of the eel (Glymour, 1991; cf. Miller & Katz, 1989). He developed a method of staining cells for microscopic study and as a physician explored the anesthetic properties of cocaine. Because he initially had no reason to believe that there were dangers connected with cocaine, he was somewhat indiscriminate in using it himself and in recommending it to others. After the addictive character of the drug was discovered, Freud said he suffered "grave reproaches." However, he may have continued to use it. Cocaine claimed many physicians as casualties in the 1880s and 1890s.

Because the private practice on which Freud depended for a living brought him patients suffering from primarily neurotic disorders, his attention became focused on the problem and study of neurosis. *Neurosis* refers to an emotional disturbance, but the disturbance is usually not so severe as to prevent the individual who has it from functioning in normal society. As Freud's goal was a complete theory of humanity, he hoped that his study of neurosis would eventually provide a key to the study of psychological processes in general. He studied in Paris with the French psychiatrist Jean Charcot. On his return from Paris, Freud became influenced by a procedure developed by Joseph Breuer, a Viennese physician and friend, who encouraged his patients to talk freely about their symptoms. Breuer and Freud worked together in writing up some of their cases in *Studies in Hysteria* (1895). Freud's further investigations with Breuer's "talking cure" led to his own development of free association and later psychoanalytic techniques. Eventually they separated, as, according to Freud, Breuer could not agree with Freud's emphasis on the role of sexuality in neurosis.

In 1900 Freud published *The Interpretation of Dreams.* Initially, the book was ignored by all but a few. Nevertheless, Freud's reputation grew, and he began to attract a following. He also encountered a lot of criticism; some even said his work was pornographic. However, he may have exaggerated the degree of intellectual persecution he received. A psychoanalytic society was founded by Freud and his colleagues, and many of Freud's disciples later became noted psychoanalysts: Ernest Jones (his biographer), A. A. Brill, Sandor Ferenczi, and Karl Abraham. Originally, Carl Jung and Alfred Adler were also close associates, but later they left Freud's psychoanalytic movement to develop and stress other ideas.

In 1909, G. Stanley Hall, noted psychologist and president of Clark University in Worcester, Massachusetts, invited Freud and his associate, Carl Jung, to present a series of lectures. It was Freud's first and only visit to the United States. These lectures contained the basic elements of Freud's theory of personality, and their delivery marked the change of psychoanalysis from a small Viennese movement to one of international scope and recognition.

Freud's work, however, was by no means over. He continued to develop and revise his psychoanalytic theory until his death. At the same time he was very human, among other things superstitious and arrogant. By the end of his life, psychoanalytic concepts had been applied to and were influencing almost every cultural construct of humanity. Freud's published works fill twenty-four volumes in the *Standard English Edition.* He died in London in 1939 at age eighty-three, after many years of suffering from cancer of the jaw, in what would be called today a physician-assisted suicide (Shur, 1972). There remains a considerable quantity of archival material, which will not be released until sometime in the next century. Scholars of Freud are eager to see what additional light this material will shed on such an important figure.

## The Origins of Psychoanalysis

Sigmund Freud did not complete a perfected system. *An Outline of Psychoanalysis,* which he began in 1938, the year before he died, had as its aim "to bring together the doctrines of psychoanalysis and to state them . . . in the most concise form." But this book was never finished; in fact much of his work has an unfinished character about it. Ideas appear and are dismissed, only to reappear in a new context. His thought moves in phases, changing and synthesizing what has gone before. The only works that Freud systematically tried to keep up to date were *The Interpretation of Dreams* (first published in 1900) and *Three Essays on Sexuality* (1905). In describing Freud's theories, therefore, it is important to recognize that psychoanalysis does not represent a finished theory, but rather an ongoing process of discovery about the self.

## The Discovery of Unconscious Forces

A logical place to begin discussion of the origins of psychoanalysis is Freud's early work with Joseph Breuer. This, in fact, is how Freud began his presentation on the history of psychoanalysis to the American public in his lectures at Clark University. As we have already seen, Freud was deeply influenced by a procedure developed by Breuer, and he frequently credited Breuer with the discovery of the psychoanalytic method. Thus, psychoanalysis may be said to begin with the case history of one of Joseph Breuer's patients, who is known in the literature as Anna O. (Freud, 1910).

Anna O. was a twenty-one-year-old, highly intelligent woman. In the course of a two-year illness beginning in 1880, she had developed a number of physical and mental dis-

*Best known as the first patient treated by psychoanalysis, Anna O. (Bertha Pappenheim in real life) also became one of the first social workers.*

turbances. Among her symptoms were a paralysis of the right arm and leg, difficulty in vision, nausea, the inability to drink any liquids, and the inability to speak or understand her mother tongue. Further, she was prone to states of absence, an altered state of consciousness in which there may be considerable personality change, and later amnesia or forgetting of events that occurred during that period.

The medical profession of 1880 was quite puzzled by illnesses such as these and diagnosed them as cases of hysteria, an illness in which there were physical symptoms but no physiological basis for the problem. (Today such disorders are less common and are known as *conversion disorders*.) The cause of hysteria was a mystery. Because they could not understand or effectively treat the problem, many doctors tended to view patients suffering from hysteria with suspicion and to be punitive. Some even went so far as to accuse their patients of faking an illness.

Breuer, however, treated his patients sympathetically. He noticed that during her states of absence, Anna frequently mumbled several words. Once he was able to determine these words, Breuer put her under hypnosis, repeated the words to her, and asked her to verbalize for him any associations that she had to the words. The patient cooperated. She began to tell him stories about herself that seemed to center on one particular event of her life: her father's illness and death.

Before he died, Anna's father had been very sick. She had taken care of him until her own illness prevented her from doing so. After she had related a number of these stories, Anna's symptoms were relieved and eventually disappeared. Anna gratefully called the cure the "talking cure," or referred to it jokingly as "chimney sweeping."

For example, Anna told of a time when she was sitting by her father's bed during his illness and was very worried about him. She was trying to hide her tears so that her father would not see them, when he asked her what time it was. Since she was crying, it was only with difficulty that she could look at her watch and make out the position of the hands on the dial. Recollecting that event and the emotions she had restrained at the time restored her clarity of vision.

Later she recalled another memory. A black snake (common in the area in which she lived) appeared in the room and seemed to go toward her ill father. She tried to drive the reptile away, but it was as if she could not move her arm. She wanted to call for help, but she could not speak. Recalling these events and the emotions they included relieved her paralysis and restored her knowledge of her native tongue.

Breuer concluded that Anna's symptoms were somehow determined by traumatic or stressful events of the past and that the recollection of these events had a cathartic effect. **Catharsis** refers to emotional release. When Anna recalled the events, she did so with a great deal of emotional intensity. This evidently freed her of the symptom to which the emotion had become attached.

By mid-1882, it appeared that Anna was completely and dramatically cured. In any event, according to what may have been a myth initiated by Freud and elaborated on by Jones (1953) (Tolpin, 1993), Breuer was anxious to end the treatment, because Anna's open proclamation of love and strong demands for his services embarrassed him and created domestic problems with his wife. When Breuer announced his wish to end the case, Anna offered a phantom pregnancy as a final symptom. Breuer was very shaken by this turn of events and abruptly dropped the case. He avoided the cathartic method in treating future patients. Anna, whose real name was probably Bertha Pappenheim, eventually became well known as one of the first social workers, striving to improve the rights and status of children and women (Swenson, 1994). The entire case would probably have gone unnoticed in medical history had Breuer not mentioned it to some of his coworkers, including the young doctor Sigmund Freud, who was deeply interested.

Some time later, Freud recalled the Anna O. episode and began to use the "talking method" with his own patients. He had some measure of success and, after observing his own explorations with the technique, concluded that at the time of the original traumatic event, the patient had to hold back a strong emotion. Perhaps because of the circumstances that surrounded the event, the patient was unable to express the emotion it evoked in a normal way through thought, word, or deed. The emotion, prevented from escaping normally, had found another outlet and was expressing itself through a neurotic symptom. Until they were recalled under hypnosis, the details of the events and the emotions they involved were not a part of the patient's awareness. Thus, the patient was *unconscious* of these memories; but the unconscious memories were influencing the present behavior.

Shortly thereafter, Freud decided to give up hypnosis (cf. Aron, 1996). In part, it was a practical necessity, since not all of his patients could be hypnotized. He assured his patients that eventually they would be able to remember the traumatic events in a normal waking state. Abandoning hypnosis also proved to be an important step in Freud's discovery of resistances. He had found that assisting his patients to remember was a long process. This led him to think that although the patient consciously wanted to remember those events, some force within prevented the patient from becoming aware of them and kept the memories unconscious. Freud labeled this force *resistance*.

Recognizing resistance leads to a dynamic understanding of *unconscious processes,* or forces of which a person is unaware. You may not immediately be able to recall what you did on your last birthday, but with a little effort you probably could remember. Unconscious memories are different. You may recall having been punished as a child but be unable, no matter how hard you try, to remember why you were punished. Such a memory has been rendered unconscious or *repressed*. It can only be recalled, if at all, with considerable difficulty.

What were those ideas or thoughts that would be repressed and rendered unconscious? Freud believed that they were *wishes*. During the traumatic event, a wish had been aroused that went against the person's ego-ideal. Because it is hard for people to accept the fact that they are not what they would like to be, such incompatibility causes pain. If it causes too much pain, the wish is repressed.

Underlying Freud's theory is the concept that events and happenings in our lives evoke strong feelings. These emotions help us to evaluate our world, but in some instances the immediate expression of emotion is inappropriate or even disastrous. Ideally, one acknowledges, accepts, and guides an emotion into constructive, or at least harmless, channels of expression.

A certain amount of repression is unavoidable and necessary in order for a civilized society to exist. But the repression is not always successful or constructive. An example Freud gave during his lectures at Clark University illustrates the problems that repressed ideas can create. Suppose, he suggested, that during the course of his lecture a young man in the back of the room interrupts rudely by laughing, talking, and stamping his feet. Other members of the audience, disturbed by his behavior, forcibly eject the young man from the room and station themselves at the door to make sure that he will not reenter the hall. This unpleasant young fellow, however, bangs on the outside of the door, kicks, screams, and, in short, creates a worse ruckus than he made in the first place. A new solution is required: a compromise. Perhaps the audience will agree to permit the young man back into the lecture hall if he will agree to behave a little bit better.

Freud admitted that his spatial metaphor was somewhat misleading, but it served to illustrate his primary concepts. We eject painful wishes, not permitting them to enter consciousness, but the repressed wishes refuse to behave agreeably. Instead, they are expressed in other ways; they create all sorts of problems, produce neurotic symptoms, and so forth. The need, then, is to restore the wishes to consciousness so that we can deal with them realistically.

## The Psychoanalytic Method of Assessment and Research

Our initial discussion of the origin of psychoanalysis presented it as being simple only for the purpose of abbreviation. In fact, the process is much more complicated than the original illustrations suggest. Essentially, several opposing forces are at work. First, there is a conscious effort on the part of the patient to remember the forgotten events. Second, there is resistance, which persists in keeping the memories unconscious. Finally, there are the unexpressed emotions that continue to seek expression. If a wish cannot get out on its own identity, it will seek an outlet in a disguised form. By putting on a mask, it will manage to sneak out and find expression in the person's behavior. Although the trauma cannot be immediately remembered, it may express itself in a hidden manner through the memories and thoughts that are recalled. In order to delve behind these masks and discover the repressed ideas, Freud developed two primary procedures: free association and the interpretation of dreams and slips.

### Free Association

In **free association,** a patient is asked to verbalize whatever comes to mind, no matter how insignificant, trivial, or even unpleasant the idea, thought, or picture may seem. Free association is based on the premise that no idea is arbitrary and insignificant. Eventually, these ideas will lead back to the original problem. For example, Anna O. did not immediately remember the scene of her father's death, but her arm was paralyzed, her vision clouded, and she was unable to use her native tongue. Then, what she did talk about hinted at the hidden event. The instructions for free association are deceptively simple, but, in fact, they are very hard to follow. What happens when we try to verbalize everything that comes to mind? We may be flooded with thoughts and find it impossible to put them all into words. At other times, we may go blank and discover that nothing comes to mind. Also, the thoughts that do come may be very painful to discuss. These intruding ideas are like ore, however, for the analysis eventually reduces them from their crude state to a valuable metal. After free association, one *reflects* upon what one has said. In the process, the resistance is analyzed, understood, and weakened so that the wish is able to express itself more directly.

### The Interpretation of Dreams and Slips

In the process of free association, particular attention is paid to slips and dreams. **Slips** are bungled acts: a slip of the tongue, a slip of the pen, or a lapse of memory. Many of us dismiss such events as trivial and meaningless, but to Freud slips like these are not without meaning. The Freudian theory assumes that in our psychic life nothing is trifling or lawless; rather, there is a motive for everything.

To understand Freud's view of slips, it is important to distinguish between cause and motive. *Cause* implies the action of a material, impersonal force that brings something about. *Motive* refers to personal agency and implies an emotion or desire operating on the will of a person and leading him or her to act. For Freud, all events are *overdetermined,* that is, they have more than one meaning or explanation. To illustrate: a ball is thrown into the air; after traveling a certain distance, it falls to the ground. A causal explanation of this event would use laws of gravity to account for the ball's fall. A motivational explanation would emphasize that the ball was thrown by someone. This particular ball would not have fallen at this time if someone had not willingly thrown it. Both explanations are correct and they complement each other. Thus, it is not sufficient to argue that we make slips of the tongue because we are tired, although it is true that fatigue may provide the physiological conditions under which a slip may occur. The slip expresses a personal motive as well. Freudian theory is particularly concerned with the explanation in terms of motive.

Here is an example of a slip and its analysis, which Freud reports in *The Psychopathology of Everyday Life* (1901). He recalls how a young student was talking excitedly about the difficulties of his generation and tried to end his comment with a well-known Latin quotation from Virgil, but could not finish the line. Freud recognized the quotation and cited it correctly: *"Exoriare aliquis nostris ex ossibus ultor"* ("Let someone arise from my bones as an avenger"). The forgotten word was *aliquis* ("someone"). The student was embarrassed but, remembering the significance that Freud attached to such slips, indicated that he was curious to learn why he had forgotten the word. Freud took up the challenge and asked the student to tell him honestly and without any censorship whatever came to mind when he directed his attention to the word *aliquis.* The first thought that sprang to his mind was the notion of dividing the word as follows: *a* and *liquis.* Next came the words *relics, liquify, fluid.* These associations had little meaning for him, but he continued and thought of Simon of Trent and the accusations of ritual blood sacrifices that had often been brought against the Jewish people. Next he thought of an article that he had read recently entitled "What Saint Augustine Said Concerning Women." The next thought appeared to be totally unconnected, but following the cardinal rule he repeated it anyway. He was thinking of a fine old gentleman whose name was Benedict. At this point, Freud noted that he had referred to a group of saints and church fathers: St. Simon, St. Augustine, and St. Benedict. That comment made the student think of St. Januarius and the miracle of blood. Here, Freud observed that both St. Januarius and St. Augustine had something to do with the calendar and asked the student to refresh his memory about the miracle of blood. The blood

of St. Januarius is held in a vial in a church in Naples. On a particular holy day it miracu-
lously liquifies. The people attach a great deal of importance to this miracle and become
very upset if it is delayed. Once it was delayed and the general in command of the city took
the priest aside and made it clear to him that the miracle had better take place very soon. At
this point the student hesitated. The next thought was surely too intimate to pass on and,
besides, it had little connection. He had suddenly thought of a lady from whom he might
get an awkward piece of news. "Could it be," Freud guessed, "that she missed her period?"

The resolution of the slip was not that difficult. The associations had led the way.
The student had mentioned the calendar, the blood that starts to flow on a certain day, the
disturbance should that event fail to occur, and the feeling that the miracle must take place.
The word *aliquis* and its subsequent allusions to the miracle of St. Januarius revealed a clear
concern with a woman's menstrual period. That concern was what was unconsciously oc-
cupying the young student when he made the slip. Often a slip is not so obvious and is revealed only after a long chain of associations.

A second area explored by free association is that of dreams (1900). For Freud, the
dream is the royal road to the unconscious. It is often easy to understand the dreams of
young children, because their defenses have not yet masked their motives. They dream very
simply of the fulfillment of unsatisfied wishes from the day before. The child who has not
received candy desired during the day may dream of an abundance of it at night.

Adult dreams also express unsatisfied wishes, but, because in the adult many of
these wishes have become unacceptable to the self-concept, the dream is in disguise. Therefore, Freud distinguishes between the manifest dream and the latent dream. The **manifest
dream** is the dream as it is remembered the next morning. Such a dream frequently appears
incoherent and nonsensical, the fantasy of a mad person. Nevertheless, it presents some
kind of narrative story (Giora, 1991). The **latent dream** refers to the meaning or motive underlying the manifest dream. Analysis seeks to discover the latent meaning that is expressed
within the manifest dream. The dream wish, however, has undergone distortion, and its
mask must be removed before it will reveal its meaning.

Dreams provide a particular wealth of information because in sleep a person is
more relaxed than when awake, and resistance, so to speak, may be caught off guard. The
wishes and desires that are forbidden access in normal conscious states have a chance to slip
out. Thus, the manifest dream may be described as a disguised fulfillment of repressed
wishes.

It is possible, Freud held, to gain some insight into the process that disguises the
unconscious dream wishes and converts them into the manifest dream. This process is
called *dream work* and it has many elements. One important element is its use of symbols.
Some symbols employed in dreams are unique to the individual dreamer and can be understood only in terms of the individual's particular history and associations. Others are
shared by many dreamers. In some instances, symbols have acquired universal meanings;
such universal symbols find expression in our myths, legends, and fairy tales, as well as in
our dreams (see Bettelheim, 1977).

Freud did not believe that anxiety dreams or nightmares contradicted his concept
that dreams fulfill wishes. The meaning of a dream does not lie in its manifest context; thus,
a dream that provokes anxiety may still serve to fulfill an unconscious wish. The expression

of a forbidden wish also causes anxiety or pain to the conscious self, so an anxiety dream may indicate that the disguise was unsuccessful and permitted too clear expression of the forbidden wish.

An example of a dream that Freud analyzed in the course of his self-analysis and reported in *The Interpretation of Dreams* may help to illustrate the procedure of dream analysis. Freud had this dream when he was seven or eight years old and analyzed it some thirty years later. It was a most vivid dream in which his mother, who was sleeping with a particularly calm expression on her face, was carried into the room and laid on the bed by two or three people with birds' beaks.

Freud indicated that as a child he awoke crying from the dream, but he became calm when he saw his mother. In his subsequent analysis of the dream, the tall figures with beaks reminded Freud of illustrations in Philippson's version of the Bible. The birds appeared to be Egyptian deities such as are carved on tombs. Freud's grandfather had died shortly before the dream. Before his death, he had gone into a coma and worn a calm expression on his face identical to Freud's mother's expression in the dream. At this level of interpretation, the dream appeared to express a young boy's anxiety over the possible death of his mother. Further analysis led deeper. The name "Philippson" reminded Freud of a neighborhood boy named Philip with whom he used to play as a child. Philip introduced Freud to the slang expression *vögeln*, a rather vulgar German phrase for sexual intercourse. The term originates from the German word *Vogel*, which means "bird." Thus, on a deeper level, Freud had to conclude that the wish expressed in the dream was that of sexual (and therefore forbidden) desires toward his mother. This dream led Freud to the discovery of the Oedipus complex, which will be discussed shortly, and assisted Freud in clarifying the nature of repressed wishes and desires.

## The Dynamics and Development of Personality

According to Freud, the nature of our repressed wishes and desires is erotic. This emphasis on sexuality is an aspect of Freud's work that many people find problematic. To understand this requires one to understand how Freud redefined the term *sexuality* and how he used it in his work. Still, Freud's theoretical position on the role of sexuality and his insistence on the human being's sexual nature is threatening to some people.

### The Importance of Sexuality

In his early work, Freud viewed sexuality as a bodily process that could be totally understood under a model of tension reduction. The goal of human behavior was simply to reduce the tension created by the accumulation of too much energy and to restore a state of balance. Sexual desires could be compared to a wish to remove an itch. However, as his work developed, Freud began to emphasize the psychological character of mental processes and sexuality. His use of the word **libido** to refer to the emotional and psychic energy derived from the biological drive of sexuality testifies to this shift in his thought.

## THINKING CRITICALLY

## *Free Association*

A simple demonstration suggested by Theodore Reik (1956), one of Freud's followers, can illustrate how difficult, yet potentially valuable, the task of free association is. The exercise is hardly equivalent to the genuine psychoanalytic situation, but it shares some of its elements, has the advantage of being available to anyone, and may show that the value of free association goes beyond its use as a technique in psychoanalysis.

Using a tape recorder, choose a time and place where you can be alone and in relative quiet. Assume a relaxed position and then try to speak into the recorder whatever thoughts come to mind for a period of one half-hour or more. In general, we try to speak logically and develop points in an orderly sequence. Free association requires that we verbalize whatever occurs to us without such order and restriction. You may be surprised, ashamed, and even afraid of the thoughts that emerge. It is difficult to acknowledge hostile and aggressive tendencies, particularly toward those we love. Some of us even have difficulties expressing tender thoughts. Moreover, a petty or trivial thought is often the hardest of all to express. You will be successful if you verbalize and record all of your thoughts, regardless of their significance, importance, pleasantness, or logical order.

When you are finished, put the tape aside. After a reasonable amount of time, perhaps the next day, play the tape back and reflect upon what you have said. You will be listening to a person who reminds you of yourself in many ways, but in other respects will be unknown. You may discover that you have thoughts and impulses that you did not realize before. They may seem minor, but they will surprise you.

You can also use free association to gain greater insight into your own slips and dreams. In dream interpretation, every element of the dream is important. Therefore, you should try to remember small details that arise in dreams, particularly if they are strange or bizarre. Taking each element one by one, you simply verbalize whatever associations come to mind as you ponder it. Later you can replay the tape and reflect on your associations to see whether you can discover aspects of yourself that were expressed in the dream.

---

Freud's desire to emphasize the psychological character of mental processes is also seen in the development of his concept of **drive.** The German word he used was *Trieb,* which has been variously translated as "instinct" or "drive." Since "instinct" refers to an inborn automatic pattern of activity characteristic of animals rather than humans, translation of the word as "drive," or "impulse" (Bettelheim, 1982) seems more appropriate to Freud's intent. Freud used *Trieb* to refer to a psychological or mental representation of an inner bodily source of excitement, a form of energy that cannot be reduced to either a bodily aspect or a mental one because it combines elements of both.

In his concept of drive, Freud abandoned an earlier attempt to reduce psychological processes to physiological ones and also began to resolve a problem inherited from Cartesian philosophy. In the belief that a person is more than a machine, the French philosopher René Descartes (1596–1650) had divided all reality into two separate categories: mind and matter. Matter included all material substances, inorganic and animate, including human bodies. These things, Descartes suggested, could be understood under scientific laws. Mind, which included all conscious states (thinking, willing, feeling, and so forth), was a second kind of substance that Descartes believed could not be explained by scientific laws. For the first time in history, a sharp distinction between mind and matter was made the basis of a systematic philosophy. Descartes's philosophy led people in the West to posit the center of the person in the mind rather than in the entire organism. Freud recognized that a comprehensive view of personality must see body and mind as a unity and his holistic approach began to help repair the Cartesian split.

A drive is characterized by four features: *source,* the bodily stimulus or need; *impetus,* the amount of energy or intensity of the need; *aim,* its goal and purpose (to reduce the excitation); and *object,* the person or object in the environment through which the aim may be satisfied. If Freud had characterized drives simply by source and impetus, he could have continued to think of the sexual drive as just a bodily process. He chose to include also aim and object, which forced him to view sexuality differently and to emphasize its psychological and intentional character. Freud used the German verb *besetzen* (translated as *cathect*) to refer to investing libidinal energy in a mental representation of an object that will satisfy a desire; a person cathects an object that he or she wants. The importance of one's sexual life as a bodily process begins to diminish in favor of one's response to it. For this reason, Freud used the term *psychosexuality* to indicate the totality of elements included in the sexual drive. In Freud's view drives provide a genetic base from which later structures of personality will emerge (Cavell, 1991).

Freud suggested that there are two basic groups of impulsive drives. **Eros** refers to *life impulses* or drives, those forces that maintain life processes and ensure reproduction of the species. The key to these forces is the sexual drive, whose energy force is "libido." **Thanatos,** encompassing *death impulses* or drives, is a biological reality (Badcock, 1992) and the source of aggressiveness, and reflects the ultimate resolution of all of life's tension in death. Although Freud emphasized the importance of the death drive, his discussion of the development of personality centers around the sexual drive.

What is the purpose of sexuality? The traditional answer was reproduction. The medieval theologian Thomas Aquinas (1225–1274) argued in *Summa Theologica* that according to natural law the primary purpose of sexuality was reproduction of the species. Other purposes of sexual activity were secondary. The pleasure that attended sexual activity was permissible, and even encouraged by St. Thomas, but he recommended that it should be submissive to and never prevent the primary purpose of reproduction. If we think that the primary purpose of sexuality is reproduction, what other thoughts about sexuality will logically follow? Sexual behaviors that do not lead to reproduction, such as homosexuality and masturbation, were disapproved of or regarded as perverse.

The nineteenth-century culture in Vienna, from which Freud's theories emerged, reflected such an attitude. It is difficult for us today to appreciate the extent to which sexual impulses and desires were then forcibly repressed, especially by the middle and upper classes. The sexual act was generally viewed as beastly and undignified, but it was tolerated as an outlet for a natural shortcoming of men and for purposes of reproduction. Women were supposed to be above sexual impulses, and children were thought incapable of them.

There was considerable anxiety over what were thought to be inappropriate sexual activities and perversions. Rigid taboos were put upon masturbation and limits were set on the expression of sexuality in adult life. The body's excretory functions were taken care of with embarrassment and prudery was practiced to fanatical extremes.

At the same time Vienna was undergoing a cultural renaissance in philosophy, music, and literature. The intelligentsia was seeking the realities that lay behind the facade of the decaying Austrian empire. One such reality was sex. To a large extent, Freud shared society's puritan attitude; nevertheless, he also relentlessly searched for the reality behind the mask.

Freud suggested that the primary purpose of sexual behavior is pleasure, opening the door to a host of new ideas. Activities that do not focus on the genitals may be seen as key expressions of sexuality to the extent to which they produce pleasure. The young child, who invariably seeks pleasure in the body, may be seen as having a rich sexual life. Activities such as sucking the thumb, previously seen as separate from sexuality, may be viewed as sexual.

Freud, in effect, turned the traditional concept upside down. This reversal permitted him to account for behaviors that were previously inexplicable, such as sexual variations and infantile sexuality. Freud's redefinition of sexuality was twofold. First, he divorced sex from its previous close restriction to the genitals and reproductive activity. Second, he enlarged the concept of sexuality to include activities such as thumb sucking and sublimation that previously were not thought of as sexual.

In Freudian terms, the child, who actively seeks pleasure from many areas of the body, is **polymorphous perverse;** that is, children's activities differ in many respects from reproductive sexual activity. The sexual activity of children is essentially **autoerotic;** they seek pleasure from their own bodies rather than from the body of another person. They find pleasure in sucking their thumbs, exploring their genitals, and so forth. Only in the course of a long history of development do children progress toward reproductive activities.

## The Psychosexual Stages of Development

Freud (1905) outlined a path that children travel as they progress from autoerotic sexual activity to reproductive activity. In this journey, the libido or sexual drive invests itself in various **erogenous zones** or areas of the body that provide pleasure. Indeed, observations have shown that as children grow, they do focus on different areas of the body; this attentional sequence follows the sequence outlined by Freud. He believed that by passing through a series of **psychosexual stages** in which different erogenous zones are important, children move from autoeroticism to reproductive sexuality and develop their adult personalities.

### Oral Stage

The first stage is the **oral stage,** which lasts from birth to approximately age one. During this time, the major source of pleasure and potential conflict is the mouth. From it infants receive nourishment, have their closest contact with the mother (in breast-feeding), and discover information about the world. Infants explore new objects with their mouths. The two main types of oral activity, ingestion and biting, are the first examples of character types and traits that may develop later on. Oral activities are also a source of potential conflict because restraints may be placed on them. A mother may seek to discourage thumb sucking or stop her child from biting the breast. Thus, the focus of greatest pleasure and conflict is located for infants in the mouth.

## Anal Stage

Freud's second psychosexual stage is the **anal stage,** which is expected to occur in the second year of life. At this time, the major source of pleasure and potential conflict is activities involving the anus. Generally, toilet training occurs during this period. Toilet training involves converting an involuntary activity, the elimination of bodily wastes, into a voluntary one. It frequently represents the child's first attempt to regulate instinctual impulses. A clash of wills with the caregiver may develop. Children may obtain pain or pleasure in either retaining or expelling their waste products. These two primary modes of anal expression, retention and expulsion, are further models for possible future character traits. In their efforts to train children, parents may forget that control over the sphincter muscles and elimination is an activity that only the child can perform. As early efforts to discipline children be-

*Freud outlined psychosexual stages that children travel as they progress from autoerotic sexual activity to mature reproductive activity. During the oral stage, new objects that the infant meets are typically explored with the mouth.*

gin, the buttocks are frequently selected as a site on which to inflict pain. Since stimulation in the area causes both pleasure and pain, sadistic (pain-inflicting) and/or masochistic (pain-receiving) patterns of behavior may emerge. Subsequent forms of self-control and mastery have their origins in the anal stage.

## Phallic Stage

The **phallic stage** of development usually occurs between the ages of three and six. The characteristics of this stage are pleasurable and conflicting feelings associated with the genital organs. The child's interest in the genitals is not with their reproductive function, but with their ability to give pleasure in autoerotic activity and their significance as a means of distinguishing between the sexes. At this time, children discover that not all individuals are similarly endowed. They expend considerable energy in examining their genitalia, masturbating, and expressing interest in sexual matters. They are extremely curious, even though their curiosity outstrips their ability to understand sexual matters intellectually. They spin fantasies about the sexual act itself and the birth process, which are frequently inaccurate and misleading. They may believe that a pregnant woman has eaten her baby and that a baby is expelled through the mouth or the anus. Sexual intercourse is frequently viewed as an aggressive act by the father against the mother.

Freud pointed out that for children a fantasy can be as powerful as a literal event in shaping personality, and so in that sense it does not matter whether or not an event really occurred (cf. Juda, 1991). This point is remarkably consistent with contemporary phenomenological and cognitive points of view, which stress that what is important is not an object or event in itself but rather how it is perceived by an individual. This is not to deny that some children do endure real situations of incest or sexual abuse, or that such situations can have a pervasive negative effect on a child's personality development. Recently Freud has been criticized for abandoning his early "seduction theory," which held that adult neurosis was caused by actual incidents of sexual abuse in childhood, in favor of a theory that saw childhood sexual fantasy and immature cognitive structures as primary contributors to neurosis. Moreover, he has been criticized for suppressing the seduction theory for intellectually dishonest reasons (Masson, 1983). However, Freud's point was that the reality of seduction was important only in relation to other factors as well, such as how it is perceived by the child (May, 1991; Paul, 1985; Schimek, 1987; see also Robinson, 1993; Esterson, 1998).

The pleasures of masturbation and the fantasy life of children set the stage for the **Oedipus complex,** which Freud considered one of his greatest discoveries. Freud's concept was suggested by the Greek tragedy of Sophocles in which King Oedipus unwittingly murders his father and marries his mother. A key point is that Oedipus was unaware, or unconscious, of what he was doing. He did not realize that the man whom he met on the road and killed was his own father, nor did he know that the queen whom he later married was his mother. At the same time, he played an active role in bringing about his fate. On discovering the truth, he blinded himself. Within that Greek myth, Freud perceived a symbolic description of the unconscious psychological conflict that each one of us endures. In brief, the myth symbolizes each child's unconscious desire to possess the opposite-sexed parent and do away with the same-sexed parent.

If the Oedipus complex were to be taken literally, many people would have quickly dismissed Freud's concept as absurd and nonsensical. Incredible as it may seem, Freud suggested that children have incestuous wishes toward the opposite-sexed parent and murderous impulses toward the same-sexed parent. Do children actually desire to perform sexual intercourse and commit murder? Most preschool-age children have no clearly articulated concept of what sexual intercourse is all about. Furthermore, even if they had the will, they would lack the means to perform the act. Finally, for the preschool-age child, the permanence and reality of death are incomprehensible. As a literal depiction, Freud's concept of the Oedipus complex is clearly absurd.

Nevertheless, by this stage in development, the young boy (to tell his side of the story first) has become very fond of his mother, his primary caregiver. He loves her very much and he wants to love her as fully as possible. He senses that Mommy and Daddy have a special kind of relationship, which he wants to imitate. He becomes frustrated because he cannot imagine what the relationship is all about or perform it in a similar manner. At the same time, he wants his mother's love in return, but views love quantitatively as a fixed amount. It is as if his mother's love constitutes an apple. Each kiss or sign of attention that his father receives indicates that a big, juicy chunk has been bitten out of that apple, so that less remains for him. He cannot conceive of love as qualitative or as able to increase to fill a void. Viewing love as a quantity, the child perceives his father as a rival who prevents him from obtaining the full love that he desires from his mother. This perception creates wishes and impulses about getting rid of the father, an activity the child is powerless to carry out.

The child's feelings are very intense and conflicting, besides being too difficult for the child to cope with directly on a conscious level. Furthermore, the feelings create guilt because the child's sentiments toward his father are hostile but also affectionate. The child finds it difficult to copy with ambivalent feelings of love and hostility directed toward the same person. His rivalry culminates in **castration anxiety,** which means that he fears physical retaliation from his father, in particular that he will lose his penis.

The Oedipus complex is resolved as follows. First, the son gives up his abortive attempts to possess his mother and begins to identify with his father in terms of sexual gender. In identifying with the same-sexed parent, he adopts the moral codes and injunctions of his father. This introjection of the parent's standards of good conduct leads to the development of a social conscience, which assists him in dealing with his forbidden impulses. By identifying with his father, the boy can through his imagination vicariously retain his mother as his love object, because he has incorporated those characteristics of his father that his mother loves. Although he may not have his mother in fact, he can wait until he grows up and then look for a woman who reminds him in some ways of Mom.

The little girl undergoes a similar complex. Freud deliberately did not give it a separate name, because he wished to emphasize the universality of the Oedipal situation. Others, however, have referred to the feminine version as the **Electra complex.** The primary love object for girls is also the mother. Yet girls, on discovering the genitals of the opposite sex, abandon the mother and turn to the father instead, making possible the Oedipal situation in reverse. The disappointment and shame that they feel upon viewing the "superior" penis leads to jealousy of the male, **penis envy,** a sense of inferiority, and a feeling of resentment and hatred toward the mother, who is held responsible for the effected castration. Reluctantly, the girl identifies with her mother, incorporates her values, and optimally makes the transition from her inadequate penis, the clitoris, as her chief erogenous zone, to the vagina. Eventually, her desire for a penis expresses itself in a desire to have a baby boy. Because the female Oedipus complex is secondary, Freud suggests that it is resolved differently from that of the male; thus, the woman's ego-ideal (see page 48) is closer to its emotional origins and she appears to have less capacity for sublimation. The role that the girl adopts for herself is one that has been outlined for her by her society. Doris Bernstein, however, points out that there really is no parallel story for the girl and that Freud's wish to have *one* developmental theory blinded him to clear differences (1991).

### Latency Period

After the phallic stage, Freud believed that there is a period of comparative sexual calm from the age of about seven to puberty. During the **latency period,** psychic forces develop that inhibit the sexual drive and narrow its direction. Sexual impulses, which are unacceptable in their direct expression, are channeled and elevated into more culturally accepted levels of activity, such as sports, intellectual interests, and peer relations. Freud was relatively silent about the latency period. He did not consider it a genuine psychosexual stage because nothing dramatically new emerges. Today, the latency period as such is questioned by most critics, who suggest it is more correct to observe that children learn to hide their sexuality from disapproving adults.

### Genital Stage

With the onset of puberty, the infantile sexual life is transformed into its adult form. The **genital stage** emerges at adolescence when the genital organs mature. There is a rebirth of sexual and aggressive desires, and the sexual drive, which was formerly autoerotic, is redirected to seeking gratification from genuine interaction with others. During the latency period, children prefer the company of same-sexed peers; however, in time the object of the sexual drive shifts to members of the opposite sex. According to Freud, the genital stage is the end point of a long journey, from autoerotic sexual activity to the cultural norm of heterosexual activity. Freud believed that mature individuals seek to satisfy their sexual drives primarily through genital, reproductive activity with members of the opposite sex.

Mature people satisfy their needs in socially approved ways. They accommodate themselves to, function within, and seek to uphold the laws, taboos, and standards of their culture. These implications are clearly spelled out for both males and females. The hallmarks of maturity can be summed up in the German expression *lieben und arbeiten,* "to love and to work." The mature person is able to love in a sexually approved way and also to work productively in society.

## The Effects of the Psychosexual Stages

The lingering effects of the psychosexual stages are revealed in various adult character types or traits. Freud believed strongly that events in the past can influence the present. If the libido is prevented from obtaining optimal satisfaction during one or more of the stages because it has been unduly frustrated or overindulged, it may become fixated or arrested at that particular stage. This **fixation** creates excessive needs characteristic of an earlier stage. Various adult behaviors that have been ascribed to fixations include smoking, gossiping, overeating, collecting, and so forth. The fixated libido expresses itself in adult life according to character types or traits that reflect the earlier level of development. Hence, an orally fixated person is likely to be dependent on and easily influenced by others. At the same time, oral personalities are optimistic and trusting to the point of being gullible. Anal personalities tend to be orderly, miserly, and obstinate. Most people, of course, do not reflect a pure type, but these personality traits and their opposites have their origin in the various psychosexual stages.

All of the sexual activities that Freud considered abnormal are at one time normal sexual activities for children. Prototypes of sadistic and masochistic forms of behavior, sexual disorders in which a person obtains pleasure by inflicting pain (sadism) or receiving pain (masochism), are apparent during the toddler years. Voyeurism, obtaining pleasure from seeing sexual organs or sexual acts, is present in the curiosity of the preschool child. Homosexuality, primary attraction to the same sex, is apparent during the latency period and early adolescence when one's primary association is with same-sexed peers. Thus, Freud believed that sexual deviations may be accounted for in terms of arrested development.

Freud also viewed neurosis as the outcome of an inadequate sexual development, in particular an unsuccessfully resolved Oedipal conflict. Such people are bound to their unhappy past and respond in emotionally immature ways. These unrealistic ways are not helpful to them in the everyday world.

Freud's presentation of the stages of human psychosexual development may appear clumsy, because the gradual change from one stage to another is not as distinct as the outline implies. Therefore, the age references should be seen not as beginning and end points, but rather as focal points, where the stage is at its height. The emergence of the genital stage does not signify the end of the earlier ones; instead it transforms them. Thus, adult behavior is shaped by a complex of earlier conflicts and dynamics.

Freud's discussion of the psychosexual stages of personality was set in the framework of nineteenth-century biological determinism (Richards, 1990) and has been soundly criticized for its failure to appreciate deeply enough the influence of social and cultural factors. Nevertheless, empirical child development research argues against outright rejection of Freud's ideas on psychosexual development (Neubauer & Neubauer, 1990; Wilson, 1996). Moreover, Freud's conclusion overturned almost the entire Western tradition of thought concerning humanity. In Freud's theory, human life is subsumed under a sexual model. The way in which people invest their libido determines their future. Freud used sexuality as a model for a person's style of life: character is built up by responding to one's sexuality; the way in which a person resolves the Oedipus complex is crucial to adult personality; neurosis represents a fixation at an earlier stage of sexual development. The normal or mature individual is one who behaves conventionally, having attained the genital level of sexuality and all its implications. Furthermore, the development of culture and civilization is made possible by sublimated sexuality. Sexuality essentially becomes the model for human understanding.

## The Structure of Personality

The familiar Freudian concept of the structure of personality as an id, ego, and superego was a rather late product of his thought. Not until 1923 with the publication of *The Ego and the Id* did Freud's final theory of a threefold structure of personality emerge. In discussing the id, ego, and superego, we must keep in mind that these are not three separate entities with sharply defined boundaries, but rather represent a variety of different processes, functions, and dynamics within the person. The psychoanalytic approach to the study of the mind illuminates processes that cognitive psychologists are studying today from their perspective (Goleman, 1985). Moreover, in his writings Freud used the German personal pronouns, *das Es, das Ich,* and *das uber-Ich.* Literally translated they mean "the it," "the I," and "the above-I." The Strachey translation into Latin pronouns has made them less personal (Bettelheim, 1982), raising the issue of the desirability of attempting a new translation (Cheshire & Thoma, 1991; Likierman, 1990).

## The Id, Ego, and Superego

The **id** is the "core of our being," the oldest and original function of the personality and the basis of the other two. We know little of the id, because it does not present itself to our consciousness in naked form. Therefore, we can describe it only by analogies and by comparing it with the ego. Freud referred to it as a "chaos, a cauldron full of seething excitations." The id includes the instincts and drives that motivate us as well as our genetic inheritance and our reflexes and capacities to respond. It represents our basic drives, needs, and wishes. Further, it is the reservoir of psychic energy that provides the power for all psychological functioning.

The impersonal and uncontrollable character of the id is more readily expressed in the German language than in English. For example, the German idiom for "I am hungry" (*"Es hungert mich"*) translates literally as "It hungers me," implying that I am a recipient of actions initiated *in* me, not *by* me.

The id operates according to the pleasure principle and employs primary processes. The **pleasure principle** refers to seeking immediate tension reduction. When libido (psychic energy) builds up, it reaches an uncomfortable level of tension. The id seeks to discharge the tension and return to a more comfortable level of energy. In seeking to avoid painful tension and obtain pleasure, the id takes no precautions but acts immediately in an impulsive, nonrational way. It pays no heed to the consequences of its actions and therefore frequently behaves in a manner that may be harmful to the self or others.

The id seeks to satisfy its needs partly through reflex action. Inborn automatic responses like sneezing, yawning, and blinking are spontaneous and unlearned, and operate without any conscious thought or effort. Many of our reflexes are protective in that they help us to ward off dangers in our environment. Others are adaptive and enable us to adjust to the conditions of our environment. Newborn infants have several reflexes that help to ensure their survival. For instance, they turn their heads toward the source of tactile stimulation. This "rooting reflex" assists them in locating the nipple. Sucking is also an automatic reflex enabling infants to take in nourishment.

The id also seeks to reduce tension through **primary processes,** hallucinating or forming an image of the object that would satisfy its needs. Freud thought that visualizing a forthcoming hamburger or sirloin steak momentarily relieves our hunger pangs; such activity is also called **wish fulfillment.** It is present in newborns, in our dreams, and in the hallucinations of psychotics. Visualizing a bottle or the breast partly pacifies the infant, but it does not satisfy its hunger. Since the primary process does not distinguish between its wish-fulfilling images and real objects in the external world that would satisfy needs, it is not very effective in reducing tension. A second structure must develop if the organism is to survive.

The **ego** ("I") emerges in order to realistically meet the wishes and demands of the id in accordance with the outside world. People who are hungry have to be effective in securing food for themselves from the environment in order to meet their needs and survive. The ego evolves out of the id and acts as an intermediary between the id and the external world. It drawn on the id's energy, acquires its structures and functions from the id, and endeavors to serve the id by realistically meeting its demands. Thus, the ego is the executor of the personality, curbing the id and maintaining transactions with the external world in the interests of the fuller personality.

Whereas the id obeys the pleasure principle, the ego follows the **reality principle,** satisfying the id's impulses in an appropriate manner in the external world. The ego postpones the discharge of tension until the appropriate object that will satisfy the need has been found. Although the ego does not prevent the satisfaction of the id, it may suspend or redirect the id's wishes in accordance with the demands of reality. The id employs the fantasies and wishes of the primary process; the ego uses realistic thinking characteristic of **secondary processes,** the cognitive and perceptional skills that help an individual distinguish between fact and fantasy. They include the higher intellectual functions of problem solving, which let the ego establish suitable courses of action and test them for their effectiveness. Actually, there is no natural enmity between the ego and the id. The ego is a "faithful servant" of the id and tries to fulfill its needs realistically.

Harbored within the ego as "its innermost core" is the **superego** ("above-I"). Heir to the Oedipus complex, it represents internalized values, ideals, and moral standards. The superego is the last function of the personality to develop and may be seen as an outcome of the interactions with one's parents during the long period of childhood dependency. Rewards and punishments originally placed on us from without become self-administered as we internalize the teachings of our parents and society. As a result of the activity of the superego we experience guilt when we disobey acceptable moral standards.

The superego consists of two subsystems: the conscience and the ego-ideal. The **conscience** refers to the capacity for self-evaluation, criticism, and reproach. It scolds the ego and creates feelings of guilt when moral codes are violated. The **ego-ideal** is an ideal self-image consisting of approved and rewarded behaviors. It is the source of pride and a concept of who we think we should be.

The superego strives for perfection. It seeks moralistic rather than realistic solutions. Practically speaking, the development of the superego is a necessity. The id's demands are too strong, and young children's egos are too weak to prevent them from acting on their impulses. For a period of time, strong introjected moral injunctions—"Thou shalt nots"—are required to curb behavior. But the superego may also be relentless and cruel in its insistence on perfection. Its moralistic demands may resemble those of the id in their intensity, blindness, and irrationality. In its uncompromising manner, the superego may inhibit the needs of the id, rather than permit their ultimate necessary and appropriate satisfaction.

In the well-adjusted adult personality, the ego is the primary executor. It controls and governs both id and superego, mediating between their demands and the external world. In ideal functioning, the ego maintains a balanced, harmonious relationship among the various elements with which it has to deal. Development, though, does not always proceed optimally. The ego frequently ends up harassed by two harsh masters. One demands instant satisfaction and release. The other places rigid prescriptions on that release. Drawing on Plato's analogy, Freud described the ego as a charioteer trying to control two strong horses, each of which is trying to run in the opposite direction from the other.

Freud's final picture of personality is that of a self divided. The specific roles played by the id, ego, and superego are not always clear; they mingle at too many levels. The self is seen to consist of many diverse forces in inevitable conflict. Freud's picture of the person is not optimistic, but it is an attempt to account for the fact that as human beings we are not always able to cope with certain situations.

Although the trifold division of personality appears to be a finished structure, essentially the person is understood as a product of development. The ego and superego have evolved historically in response to specific personal situations. In the case of the superego, that situation is also interpersonal since it involves other people. It would be wrong to freeze the id, ego, and superego into systems; instead, the personality is created by a dynamic of forces that can be divided against themselves at many levels. Thus, in his mature formulation, Freud holds in tension the biological ground of the self and its historical development.

---

## The Relationship of the Id, Ego, and Superego to Consciousness

There is no easy correlation between the words "id," "ego," and "superego" and the qualities of "conscious" and "unconscious." At times, Freud tended to make the easy equation of ego with consciousness and id with unconsciousness. His discoveries, reflected in *The Ego and the Id* (1923), that aspects of the ego and the superego are unconscious, as is the id, forced him to revise his theory. "Conscious" and "unconscious" could be used only as adjectives describing qualities that psychological processes may or may not have.

If one were to diagram Freud's picture of the psyche, perhaps the best image would be Freud's own: an iceberg, nine-tenths of which is submerged under water (Figure 2.1). The surface of the water represents the boundary between conscious and unconscious. Its line intersects, or potentially intersects, all three functions of id, ego, and superego. But any spatial metaphor is ultimately misleading. "Id," "ego," and "superego" are best understood as dynamic functions of personality, while "conscious" and "unconscious" are adjectives that describe qualities that these functions may have.

The dynamic forces within the self are many. The self is not simply divided against itself by id, ego, and superego but divided against itself and the world at many levels. Conflict is the keynote of Freud's final understanding of the self. The world, Freud once wrote, is *anake* (the Greek word for "a lack"), too poor to meet all of our needs. As the id's demands increase, the ego becomes overwhelmed with excessive stimulation that it cannot control and becomes flooded with anxiety.

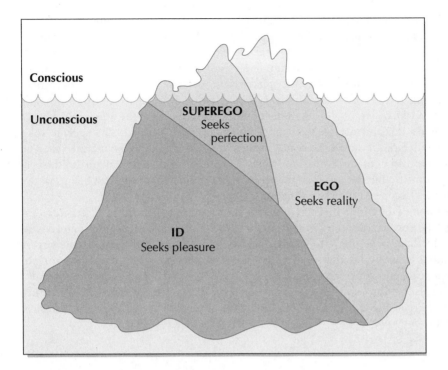

FIGURE 2.1    The Structure of Personality

Freud used the metaphor of an iceberg to depict the psyche, or personality, in order to emphasize that nine-tenths of it was submerged in the realm of unconsciousness. Whether unconscious or conscious, the three structures of the personality—the id, ego, and superego—are dynamic forces that interact at many levels as the ego tries to control and moderate the drives of the id and the superego.

## The Ego's Defense Mechanisms

Freud made a distinction among three kinds of anxiety. *Reality anxiety* refers to fear of a real danger in the external world. *Neurotic anxiety* refers to fear that one's inner impulses cannot be controlled. *Moral anxiety* is a fear of the retributions of one's own conscience. All have their basis in reality anxiety. In order for an individual to cope with anxiety, the ego develops **defense mechanisms,** procedures that ward off anxiety and prevent our conscious perception of it. Defense mechanisms share two features: they occur on an unconscious level so that we are not aware of what we are doing, and they deny or distort reality so as to make it less threatening. Defense mechanisms are not necessarily maladaptive; indeed, we cannot survive without them. They must be created to assist the developing ego in carrying out its functions. However, should their distortion of reality become too extreme or should they be used to the exclusion of other, more effective means of dealing with reality, defense mechanisms may become maladaptive and destructive, preventing further personal and social growth. Some of the more common defense mechanisms follow (see also Table 2.1).

TABLE 2.1    Defense Mechanisms

| MECHANISM | CHARACTERISTIC | EXAMPLE |
|---|---|---|
| Repression | Blocking a wish or desire from conscious expression | Being unaware of deep-seated hostilities toward one's parents |
| Denial | Refusing to believe a reality | Refusing to believe that one has AIDS or a terminal cancer |
| Projection | Attributing an unconscious impulse, attitude, or behavior to another | Blaming another for your act or thinking that someone is out to get you |
| Reaction formation | Expressing an impulse by its opposite | Treating someone whom you intensely dislike in a friendly manner |
| Regression | Returning to an earlier form of expressing an impulse | Resuming bedwetting after one has long since stopped |
| Rationalization | Dealing with an emotion intellectually to avoid emotional concern | Arguing that "Everybody else does it, so I don't have to feel guilty." |
| Identification | Modeling behavior after someone else | Imitating one's mother or father |
| Displacement | Satisfying an impulse with a substitute object | Scapegoating |
| Sublimation | Rechanneling an impulse into a more socially desirable outlet | Satisfying sexual curiosity by researching sexual behaviors |

**Repression** involves blocking a wish or desire from expression so that it cannot be experienced consciously or expressed directly in behavior. It is an involuntary act, which prevents us from being aware of many of our own anxiety-producing conflicts or remembering certain traumatic emotional events from our past. The repressed emotion seeks an alternative outlet, and resistance is required to prevent its emergence into consciousness. Nevertheless, once formed, repressions are difficult to eliminate.

**Denial** entails refusing to believe a reality or fact of life. Many people who indulge in substance abuse deny that the alcohol, nicotine, crack, or other substance could ever really hurt them. They may see it affect other people, but "that's not going to happen to me."

**Projection** refers to the unconscious attribution of an impulse, attitude, or behavior onto someone or something else in the environment. An individual who unconsciously feels hostile toward someone may project the hostility onto the other person. Such a defense reduces anxiety by placing its source in the external world, which makes it seem easier to handle. Further, it permits us to defend ourselves aggressively against our opponent and thereby indirectly express our impulses.

**Reaction formation** expresses an impulse by its opposite. Hostility, for example, may be replaced by friendship. Frequently, however, the substitution is exaggerated, thereby calling into question the genuineness of the feeling.

**THINKING CRITICALLY**

## *Identifying Defense Mechanisms*

You can familiarize yourself with the various defenses by trying to identify each of the mechanisms in Table 2.1 as you have seen them occur in someone else, and then trying to recognize instances in which you may have used them yourself. It is much easier, of course, to observe defense processes at work in someone else; however, some of the following hints may help you to spot them in yourself. Have you ever "forgotten" an important event, such as an assigned test or a dentist appointment? You may also recall momentarily forgetting the name of someone you know quite well. Such occasions indicate the tendency we all have to repress. Memory gaps about childhood events, in which you can recall only part of an event but not what preceded or followed, may indicate that the event involved certain traumatic elements that make it hard for you to remember it completely. Have your parents ever told you about an experience that you had as a child but cannot remember? Have you ever found yourself laughing at an inappropriate moment? You may have compensated for an impulse you are ashamed of by reaction formation. Have you ever provided an alibi for something you did or did not do? Could it have been an attempt to rationalize your behavior? Can you recall ever taking out your anger on someone who was helpless, such as a child or pet? Use of scapegoats is a common form of displacement. What kinds of leisure activities, sports, or creative and artistic activities do you enjoy? Through sublimation you may have been able to redirect certain antisocial impulses into socially approved and constructive behaviors. Sublimation is one of the more productive defense mechanisms available to us. In short, we all have and need defenses. Recognizing the use of a defense mechanism is not an occasion for finding fault with ourselves; rather, it is an opportunity for further exploration of our use of defense mechanisms so that they can be employed to foster instead of hinder growth.

In **regression** the person moves backward in time to a stage that was less anxious and had fewer responsibilities. Regression frequently occurs following a traumatic experience. The child who begins bedwetting again when frightened by the prospect of going to school may be showing signs of regression.

**Rationalization** involves dealing with an emotion or impulse analytically and intellectually in order to avoid feeling it. As the term implies, it involves faulty reasoning, since the problem remains unresolved on the emotional level. Aesop's fable about the fox who could not reach the grapes and concluded that they were probably sour is a classic example of rationalization.

In **identification** we reduce anxiety by modeling our behavior on that of someone else. By assuming the characteristics of a model who appears more successful in gratifying needs, we can believe that we also possess those attributes. We may also identify with an authority figure who is resented and feared. Such identification may assist us in avoiding punishment. As we have already seen, identification with the same-sexed parent plays an important role in development of the superego and subsequent personality.

If an object that would satisfy an impulse of the id is unavailable, we may shift our impulse onto another object. Such substitution is called **displacement.** A child who has been scolded may hit a younger sibling or kick the dog. The substitute object, however, is rarely as satisfying as the original object. Thus, displacement does not bring complete satisfaction but leads to a buildup of undischarged tension.

**Sublimation** rechannels an unacceptable impulse into a more socially desirable outlet. It is a form of displacement that redirects the impulse itself rather than the object. For example, sexual curiosity may be redirected into intellectual research; sexual activity into athletics. Freud suggested that sublimation was crucial to the development of culture and civilization. It is clear from biographical studies that sublimation was a defense commonly used by Freud.

Defense mechanisms, in and of themselves, are not harmful. No one is free of defenses; we need them in order to survive. Although defenses can block personal and social growth if they become predominant, they do protect us from excessive anxiety and frequently represent creative solutions to our problems. In recent years new research has begun to emerge on the development, measurement, and future potential of Freud's concepts of defense mechanisms and ego processes. Some of this work has been summarized by Cooper (1989) and Vaillant (1992a, 1992b).

## Psychoanalysis

We have seen that for Freud neurosis emerges from an unsatisfactory or arrested libidinal development, when the realistic satisfaction of erotic needs is denied. The person turns to neurosis as a surrogate satisfaction and creates a partially satisfying world of fantasy. Neurotics have no peculiar psychic content or functioning of their own that is not also found in healthy people. The neurotic is one who falls ill from the same conflicts and complexes with which normal people struggle. There are no clearly defined boundaries between illness and health. The primary question is not "Am I normal or neurotic?" but rather "To what degree is my neurosis debilitating?"

### Transference

Early in his work, Freud realized that the relationship between patient and physician was important in determining the outcome of the therapy. Nevertheless, it was with considerable embarrassment that he discovered one of his patients had fallen in love with him. We recall that a similar episode with his patient Anna O. had led Dr. Breuer to abandon the cathartic technique. Only after considerable reservations and initial attempts to discourage similar occurrences did Freud begin to appreciate the dynamics of what was happening. He discovered that the feelings that were expressed toward him as a doctor were not directed at him as a person but rather were repetitions of earlier feelings of love and affection that the patient had for significant persons in her life. Thus, Freud was forced to recognize the value of the **transference,** a process whereby the patient transfers to the analyst emotional attitudes felt as a child toward important persons. By deliberately cultivating and analyzing the transference, Freud and his patients were able to learn a great deal.

Freud distinguished between *positive transference,* friendly, affectionate feelings toward the physician, and *negative transference,* characterized by the expression of hostile, angry feelings. By studying the transference, Freud learned that his patients were relating to him in the same unsatisfactory and inefficient ways in which they had related to other important people in their lives. However, in the security of analysis, the patient could rework these earlier unsatisfactory relationships through the current relationship to a satisfactory resolution.

It is difficult to know if Freud himself ever fully recognized the implications of the transference, but its cultivation and interpretation have become crucial to the psychoanalytic technique he fathered. Transference offers the patient an opportunity to relive the emotional conflicts and cognitive structures that led to repressions and provides the analyst with a deeper understanding of the patient's characteristic ways of perceiving and reacting. The major point here is that in analysis the patient experiences conflicts under a different set of circumstances. The analyst does not respond to the patient with disapproval or rejection as earlier individuals may have done. Rather, the analyst reacts with insight and understanding, which permits the patient to gain insight into experiences and feelings and allows for change.

Freud's solution is one of *insight,* but the insight that psychoanalysis provides is a special kind of knowing that is not intellectual but existential. It touches the heart as well as the head. The solution does not lie in the realm of knowing but in the realm of doing: working through earlier conflicts. Discovering one's self is not only an intellectual act, but also an emotional experience. To use the Socratic expression: "To know is to do." Thus, therapy provides a more effective resolution of the situation that provoked the neurosis.

## The Analytic Process

In classical analysis, the patient lies on a couch and the analyst sits behind, out of view. The patient is instructed to verbalize whatever comes to mind regardless of how irrelevant, absurd, or unpleasant it may seem. During free association the patient may make a slip of the tongue or refer to a dream, both of which may be interpreted and utilized to assist the patient to acquire a deeper understanding of the problem.

In the initial phase of analysis, the patient obtains considerable relief just by being able to unburden certain thoughts and feelings to a sympathetic listener. A positive transference is developed, and the patient frequently believes that the analysis has reached a successful conclusion, even though the work of analysis has barely begun. There are as yet undisclosed and conflicting feelings. During the next phase, the analyst gently assists the patient in exploring these emotion-laden areas by pointing out and interpreting the resistance in an effort to weaken the patient's defenses and bring repressed conflicts into the open. The analyst's efforts leave the patient angry, anxious, or depressed; the analyst is now perceived as rejecting and unhelpful. Thoughts of prematurely concluding the analysis may again arise. Eventually the negative transference begins to cohere around specific areas. The patient reconstructs and reexperiences crucial episodes from childhood. The unremediated situation of the past includes not simply insufficiently resolved traumatic events but, more important, inadequately resolved interpersonal relationships and fantasies. The analyst maintains a neutral stance (Thompson, 1996), interpreting the transference and encouraging the patient to reexamine those circumstances in the light of increased maturity. The analyst's stance enables the patient to work through these situations to a more satisfactory conclusion. Last, the analyst assists the patient in converting newly won insights into everyday existence and behavior. This emotional reeducation enables the new insights to become a permanent part of the patient's personality (see Figure 2.2).

In its traditional form, analysis is a protracted and expensive procedure. The patient meets with the analyst for fifty-minute sessions an average of five times a week for a period of several years. This requires a considerable commitment in terms of time, effort, and money. Contemporary analysts have refined the process further, realizing the importance of such issues as overcoming resistance, recognizing the danger of countertransference (which proceeds from the analyst to the patient; see Goleman, 1993a; Ornstein, 1993), and working through issues on an emotional level. The goal of psychoanalysis is an ambitious one—a full understanding, reorganization, and basic change of the personality structure. Such goals cannot be accomplished quickly or easily. And, as Freud (1917) once wrote,

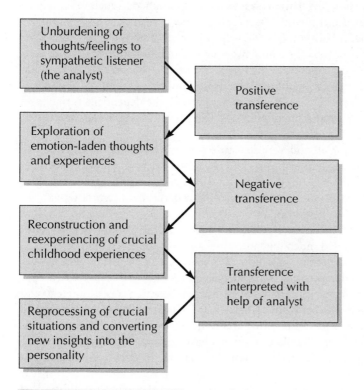

FIGURE 2.2   The Analytic Process

Shown here is a graphic illustration of what happens in psychoanalysis to help move the patient toward a full understanding, reorganization, and basic change of his or her personality structure.

"A neurotic who has been cured has really become a different person . . . he has become his best self, what he would have been under the most favorable conditions."

## Empirical Validation of Psychoanalytic Concepts

Freud's theory generated a great deal of empirical research and attempts to test his concepts. A large body of literature (for example, Fisher & Greenberg, 1977; Kline, 1972; Sears, 1943; Geisler, 1985) deals with attempts to test in a laboratory or other setting hypotheses derived from Freud's ideas to see whether they function usefully as science.

As we have seen (in Chapter 1), an experimental method is favored by many psychologists because it permits us to infer a cause-and-effect relationship between two factors. Thus, for example, Lloyd Silverman (1976) designed an experiment to test the hypothesis that depression arises from aggressive feelings that have been turned inward against the self. He tried to activate unconscious aggressive wishes to see whether or not they would result in an intensification of depressed feelings. In one session, he showed a group of participants pictures and verbal messages that were designed to elicit unconscious aggressive wishes. The images included pictures such as a fierce man with a knife and the message "Cannibal eats person." In another session, Silverman showed the same group neutral images of people reading or walking. These two sets of images constituted the independent variable. The subjects were exposed to the images for only 4/1000 of a second, so that their perception was assumed to be subliminal. Before and after the sessions, the subjects were asked to rate their feelings. Their self-ratings represented the dependent variable. As expected, the participants reported more depressive feelings after seeing the aggressive images than after seeing the neutral ones.

In yet another study, Hall and Van de Castle (1965) investigated whether or not male dreamers reported more dreams expressive of castration anxiety and fewer dreams expressive of penis envy than women. They did. Of course, Hall and Van de Castle had to carefully develop a scoring manual that spelled out specific criteria for interpreting various dream themes as indicative of castration anxiety and penis envy. They also had to show that there was agreement among different scorers. As you can see, some of these efforts to test Freud's theory have demonstrated much ingenuity and sophistication.

Not all Freudian concepts have held up well under scrutiny. For example, it has become untenable in light of modern research in embryology, biology, and female psychosexual development to view the female as a castrated male whose less-developed superego and negative view of her body is due to penis envy (Small, 1989). Wolberg (1989) suggests Freud's views on female sexuality are more illuminating about the dilemmas Freud faced when his observations did not fit his theory. Similar comments have been made about some of his case studies (Magid, 1993). Nor has it been substantiated that the male resolves the Oedipus complex by identifying with the father and accepting his superego standards out of fear (Schultz, 1990). Studies have supported Freud's idea that dreams may express in a disguised or symbolic manner an individual's emotional concerns (Breger, Hunter, & Lane, 1971) but do not confirm that they fulfill unconscious wishes (Demont & Wolper, 1958).

Other Freudian concepts, however, appear to stand up under scrutiny. These include aspects of Freud's oral and anal personality types (Kline, 1972; Masling, Rabie, &

## Freud and the Subject of Women

As you might imagine, Freud's views of the development of women have been the subject of considerable criticism and debate. In particular, many feminists have suggested that Freud's lack of understanding of female psychology reflected a male chauvinistic position.

In his famous dictum "anatomy is destiny," Freud intended to correct Napoleon's earlier motto, "history is destiny," pointing out that history is not the sole component of personality development. In his theory, Freud emphasized the importance of anatomy, in particular one's reproductive organs, as well as history. New research on sexual differences shows that much of Freud's explanation was based on incorrect information (Small, 1989). At the same time, research in ethology, behavior genetics, gender, and moral development (Sayers, 1987) indicates the importance of biology for understanding the individual (also see Neubauer & Neubauer, 1990).

Freud (1937) pointed out that the presence of two sexes is a fact of biology. Our experience of this is a matter for psychology. Biology does not cause our psychic life but our psychic life has to take it into account. The problem is not that Freud's view of women was determined by anatomy, biological determinism, and cultural restraints, but that his understanding of *all* human development was colored by the same interpretation. His discussion of the psychosexual stages of the male, no less than the female, was permeated with the notion of biological determinism and shared the same characteristics of inevitability and cultural bias. As Juliet Mitchell (1974) has pointed out, "psychoanalysis is not a recommendation *for* a patriarchal society but an analysis *of* one" (cf. Toronto, 1991). Jeffrey Okey (1991) suggests that the basic beliefs of contemporary psychoanalytic theory are very relevant to the understanding of the psychology of women. You should note, moreover, that women played a major role in the psychoanalytic movement and that Freud encouraged his daughter Anna and other women to become actively involved.

What do you think? Has Freud been unfairly maligned for his discussion of women? To what extent were his concepts a product of his social and cultural milieu? Gender is a biological division; sexuality is a social and psychological. expression (Mitchell, 1991). If the presence of two sexes is a fact of biology, how do psychology and society take it into account? Wilkinson (1989) argues that the limited impact of feminist research in psychology is due to power and politics. In order to have a greater impact, feminists will need to use social processes that establish legitimacy.

---

Blondheim, 1967; Tribich & Messer, 1974). Studies in both normal and psychiatric populations seem to confirm that psychopathology results from unconscious, conflicting aggressive or sexual wishes. Brain research has supported concepts such as unconscious processes, primary process cognition, conversion disorders, and the conflictual nature of the mind (Ducat, 1985). The concept of repression has been operationally defined as a stronger tendency to forget events identified with unpleasant or fearful associations than with neutral or pleasant events (Davis, 1987; Glucksberg & King, 1967). Defining unconscious as *unable to be verbalized* enables such processes to be subjected to experimental study (Kline, 1987). Experimental testing of these and other psychoanalytically oriented hypotheses indicates their usefulness (Hammer, 1970; Shurcliff, 1968; Silverman, 1976).

It is often difficult to translate Freud's concepts into operational procedures that allow for unequivocal testing. The operational translation of many of Freud's concepts may misinterpret and oversimplify his ideas. The Freudian theory of repression does not simply imply experiences associated with unpleasant thoughts; thus, studies on repression may deal with phenomena that are essentially different from the kind of phenomena that concerned Freud. At this time, there is no direct evidence that will substantiate concepts such as the id, ego, superego, libido, death wish, and anxiety. Moreover, if the concepts are distorted and minimized, they will not truly represent the constructs in Freud's thought. Freud's own investigations and those of other psychoanalysts hardly allow for replication because they were carried out under conditions of privacy and confidentiality.

Some critics believe that the scientific pretension of psychoanalytic theory rests on very shaky ground (Fingarette, 1963; MacIntyre, 1958). In the most vocal recent reassertions of this thesis, Grünbaum (1984, 1993) concedes that some of Freud's concepts are open to falsification, one of the criteria for evaluating scientific statements, but contends that clinical data is unacceptable as scientific support; Macmillan (1991) asserts that Freud made his theory more complex as he sought to cover over the failure of his earlier concepts to account for his observations; and Crews (1996) baldly concludes that "there is literally nothing to be said, scientifically or therapeutically, to the advantage of the entire Freudian system or any of its component dogmas." In response to these critics, Robinson (1993) wrote a sustained rebuttal suggesting that the arguments are biased and the evidence used is ambiguous. Moreover, he claims that the critics basically distort Freud and ignore his achievements in revolutionizing the way we think about ourselves.

Shevrin (1995a) has stimulated discussion on the possibility that psychoanalysis is two separate but related sciences: an applied clinical science and a basic science of the mind. And Jacobson (1996) has introduced a series of essays about the relationship between psychoanalysis and science, in which Schwartz (1996) questions why such criticisms of Freud have had such an impact, since they are based on a narrow conception of science. Other critics are very optimistic about achieving a merger of experimental operations and clinical observations in the study of psychoanalytic phenomena. Some suggest that there may be a possible convergence of psychoanalysis and recent neuroscientific information (Edelson, 1986).

The emerging cognitive psychology, which is based on generative linguistics and information science, may provide a framework with which to assimilate psychoanalysis, since psychoanalysis is essentially a cognitive psychology concerned with problems of consciousness, structure, representation, meaning, storage and retrieval, transformation, and bias in thinking. The research on awareness and cognitive processes that Freud's work has stimulated, not all of it formulated in Freudian terms, has been summarized in the June 1992 issue of *American Psychologist* and the December 1994 issue of the *Journal of Personality*. Epstein (1994) has argued for the existence of two parallel information-processing systems that seem to link up with two parallel systems of personality—one conscious and rational, the other unconscious and experiential. Kihlstrom, Barnhardt, and Tataryn (1992), however, have pointed out that the formulation of the unconscious in contemporary psychology is "kinder and gentler" than that of Freud.

Still, there are similarities in the approaches of psychoanalytic theory and cognitive science. Both draw on a multidisciplinary perspective and seek to discover and describe the mental structures that underlie conscious events. Stein (1997) has brought together efforts by researchers to create a synthesis incorporating the best of the two traditions. The work of these researchers and clinicians underscores the importance of collaboration in developing an integration between an interpretive approach that risks dismissing unconscious mechanisms as insignificant narrative devices and a narrow scientific approach that risks missing significant meaning, social context, and interaction among biological and psychological levels.

There is a wealth of information in modern psychology that was not available to Freud: the findings of anthropology regarding the cultural nature of humanity, empirical studies of mother-infant interaction and of the competence of infants, the discovery of REM (rapid eye movement) sleep, the role of emotions in individual arousal and social communication, the growth of the psychology of sex differences, and studies in cognitive style (Lewis, 1988), as well as the field of psychoanalytic infant research (Wilson, 1996). Given the information that was not available to him, the visionary nature of many of Freud's ideas and the fact that his concepts continue to engender such lively research and debate is all the more impressive. Shevrin (1995b) expresses the hope that "as psychoanalysis begins its second century it can mobilize its resources for a concerted effort toward developing a comprehensive science, by drawing on the strengths of its clinical method, psychotherapy research, and the experimental approaches now available to investigate its fundamental propositions."

## PHILOSOPHY, SCIENCE, AND ART

# Freud's Theory

Educated in the precise methods of nineteenth-century science, Freud established a reputation as a medical researcher before he developed the theory of psychoanalysis. In his writings he clearly defined and described the scientific enterprise. He asserted that knowledge is based on empirical observation and dogmatically maintained that his own theories were so based. His concepts, he claimed, were merely tentative constructs to be discarded if later observation failed to confirm them. He frequently revised his theories because new data had emerged that could not be accounted for by those theories.

Freud made careful observations of his patients in the therapeutic setting and garnered considerable information from the techniques of free association and dream analysis. He made interpretations and viewed the subsequent behavior of his patients as confirmation or disproof of his hypotheses. And he also conducted his own self-analysis, beginning in 1897 and continuing throughout his life. Data collected

## PHILOSOPHICAL ASSUMPTIONS

# Examining Freud

How would you rate Freud on each of the basic philosophical assumptions described in Chapter 1? Consult the chart on the inside front cover. Each basic issue is presented as a bipolar dimension along which a person's view can be placed according to the degree of agreement with one or the other extreme. Rate Freud's views on these issues.

When you have determined where you think Freud stands, compare your responses with those of your classmates and your instructor. You should be willing to defend your ratings, but also be prepared to change them in light of others' compelling arguments. Afterward, compare your rating of Freud with your own position on each issue and with those of other theorists. Does this comparison help you to understand why his theory does or does not appeal to you?

through self-analysis may properly be called empirical, as it is based on observation. The fact that the observer is looking in ("introspection") rather than out ("extrospection") does not make the data any less empirical, although information gathered through introspection may be more difficult to test.

Nevertheless, in determining how Freud's theory functions, we have to look not only at the data on which it was initially based, but also at the method he used to test the data. Although he claimed that he was merely extending scientific knowledge by placing the psychic life of human beings under scientific observation, Freud permitted many of his concepts to function philosophically. We have seen that an important criterion of scientific constructs is the requirement that they be open to falsification; the desire to be scientific reflects itself in an effort to test constructs by validating evidence rather than by simply relying on the compelling character of a philosophical assumption. Freud, however, defined many of his concepts as all-controlling factors in everything we do, think, and are. It is impossible to conceive of any activity in Freud's theory that does not reflect unconscious motives as well as conscious ones. The doctrine of unconscious processes is thus lifted out of an immediate empirical construct and made applicable to all possible human behavior. Even objections to the concept can be explained in terms of resistance or other unconscious processes. Sexuality is a philosophical concept insofar as Freud asserted that all human behavior can be considered in its light.

And so we see that Freud drew conclusions from careful self-observation and the observation of his patients in a clinical setting and projected those conclusions into philosophical assumptions. Although

Freud invested his theories with an aura of science, in evaluating them he made primary use of philosophical criteria, relying on their compelling power rather than validating evidence. The kind of knowing on which psychoanalysis is ultimately based is epiphanic, a form of knowing that does not rely on everyday experiences but transcends them.

It is inaccurate to portray Freud as a scientific medical doctor. To do so distorts much of the humanism present in his writings and blunts the challenge of psychoanalysis, which is to know oneself with the constant obligation to change oneself (Bettelheim, 1982).

In evaluating Freud's work, therefore, it is most appropriate to use the criteria that apply to philosophical positions and ask if it is coherent, relevant, comprehensive, and compelling.

Although Freud changed and revised his theory, in the end it presented a coherent pattern with a clearly recognizable consistent thrust. To be sure, his theory is not a finished whole. Not only did he continually modify it, but it has been revised, modified, and updated by others working within the Freudian tradition. Freud was frequently unsympathetic to efforts to modify his theory and claimed the ultimate right to declare what should and should not be called psychoanalysis, but he was not unreceptive to changes that reflected the spirit of psychoanalysis as an evolving movement of a particular form of thought and investigation.

MacIntyre (1958) suggested that Freud's theoretical work denoted a "kind of creative untidiness." His thought was characterized by illuminating insights followed by efforts at sterile systematization, yet "he never presents us with a finished structure but with the far more exciting prospect of working through a number of possible ways of talking and thinking." This may be taken as the essential character of Freud's work. He seems to be saying, "You don't have to talk that way"; that personality can be illuminated by a different picture. If you take one image and isolate it, you tend toward being either reductionistic or projectionistic. Thus Freud himself would talk several different ways at once, often flagrantly contradicting himself in order to illumine his subject. Freud depicted a person as simultaneously an economic machine, a personal history, a case, comprehended totally by sexuality, socially and historically constructed.

For Freud's ideas to be relevant in the twentieth and twenty-first centuries, they must be reworked and reformulated in contemporary terms. Many of Freud's arguments, informed by nineteenth-century culture, science, and philosophy, are clearly dated. New challenges to the ideas that have undergirded psychoanalysis require that theorists work to broaden the scope and power of psychoanalytic theory (Flax, 1994). Critiques of Freud that focus on the analysis of language and meaning (for example, Ricoeur, 1970) have been helpful in assimilating Freud's work into the greater body of philosophy. Today several of Freud's concepts are seen as foreshadowing current views on the importance of both nature and nurture by evolutionary biologistic and developmental psychologists (Carver, 1996; Koch, 1991). Freud's theory does not constitute a finished structure; it is an open one capable of continued growth.

The relevance of Freud's theory is evidenced by its impact on the Western world. Freud's faults were his virtues in that they enabled him to break through the rational optimism of the enlightenment and make possible a new view. Freud changed, perhaps irrevocably, humanity's image of itself. Since Aristotle, the essence of humanity had been located in our ability to think. This image found ultimate expression in Descartes's phrase "I think, therefore I am." In this post-Freudian world, our self-image has changed. We no longer conceive of ourselves as primarily rational animals; rather, we are pleasure-seeking, sexual, and aggressive creatures driven by our emotions. In a sense Freud begins his philosophy with "I love (or crave), therefore I am." For many, the gospel of psychoanalysis is not "good news" because it forces us to consider aspects of ourselves that we would prefer to ignore. Still, it is virtually impossible to deny Freud his influence.

The impact of Freud's accomplishments has been favorably compared with the impact of Copernicus, Darwin, and Einstein. Freud's name is a household word. Errors of the pen or tongue are commonly known as "Freudian slips," and many people cannot make one without wondering what the unconscious reason is. He grappled with ideas that were, are, and will continue to be of primary concern to us. Because of that, his theories interest, allure, and excite people.

Freud's aim was to develop a comprehensive theory of humanity. He consistently maintained that his study of neurosis would eventually provide a key to the study of psychological processes in general. Freud's quest for the truth was unrelenting; no question was too small for his consideration; no probe was too trivial; no psychological process was too insignificant for his attention. To look for meaning on the surface was, for him, to settle for appearances and superficiality. Only by risking a plunge into the depths of the unconscious could one discover the truth about oneself and others. Any contradiction or opposition to his theory was to be met by analysis of the resistance, for only through such analysis could true insight emerge.

Some (see, for example, Ellenberger, 1970; Sherman, 1995) have suggested that Freud founded a school comparable to the philosophical schools of ancient Greece and Rome. With the creation of psychoanalysis, Freud developed a movement characterized by its own rules, rituals, and doctrine of membership. As an art, Freudian psychoanalysis is an excellent example of the scholarly approach to psychotherapy (cf. Magid, 1993).

It is possible that after studying Freud, one may agree that his concepts are coherent, relevant, and comprehensive, yet remain uncom-

*Sigmund Freud stands in the front row (seventh from left) among American scientists to whom he delivered a lecture series in 1909 at Clark University. Also in the picture are William James (third from left), G. Stanley Hall (sixth), and Carl Jung (eighth).*

pelled. Freud would counter that the insight required for a full appreciation of his theory is of a particular kind, one that can be acquired only through the kind of analytic self-investigation practiced by him and his followers. Freud's theory is by no means universally accepted. Indeed, few other positions in the history of philosophical thought have been subject to as much attack, ridicule, and criticism (see, for example, Torrey, 1992). In modern science, only the theory of Charles Darwin has been met with equal scorn and resistance. Nevertheless, Freud's picture of personality is one that compels many people. His picture of the personality as beset by anxieties, governed by forces of which we are largely unaware, living in a world marked by external and internal conflicts, resolving problems by solutions informed by fantasy or reality, is a concept of personality that some people find irresistible. Nevertheless, Freud's work reflects the cultural and social values of Western Europe and North America. The concept of ego is rooted in a culture that cultivates and emphasizes the individual. Such a concept may not be as fundamental to the development of personality in collectivist societies such as Latin America, Africa, and Asia (Landrine & Klonoff, 1992; Markus & Kitayama, 1991). Still, Freud's original theory was revolutionary and formed the basis for much theoretical expansion. We can expect that psychoanalytic theory will continue to evolve in the future and will take into account a broadened cultural perspective.

# Summary

1. The case of Anna O. may be seen as the beginning of psychoanalysis. Anna O. suffered from a conversion disorder in which her right arm and leg were paralyzed, she had difficulty seeing, was nauseous, and was unable to drink any liquids or to speak and understand her mother tongue. She was also prone to states of absence. Dr. Joseph Breuer hypnotized her and asked her to verbalize associations she might have to words she mumbled during her absences. She began to tell him stories about her father's illness and death. After she had told a number of these stories, her symptoms went away.

    Freud began to use the "talking method" with his own patients and he concluded that at the time of the original trauma the patient had had to hold back a strong emotion. The patient had forgotten the event and was unconscious or unaware of it. Freud's concept of unconscious processes is a dynamic one in which certain forces repress undesirable thoughts and then actively resist their becoming conscious.

2. An emotion, prevented from expressing itself normally, may be expressed through a neurotic symptom. Wishes are repressed because they go against a person's self-concept. Underlying Freud's concept is the idea that emotions that accompany events must ultimately be expressed. If they cannot find direct expression, they will find indirect ones, such as neurotic symptoms. Ideally, the expression of emotions is nondestructive.

3. Freud developed the technique of *free association* in order to help his patients recover repressed ideas. The patient is asked to verbalize whatever comes to mind no matter how insignificant, trivial, or even unpleasant the idea might be. Later he or she *reflects* upon those associations.

4. Freud considered *slips* and dreams to be "the royal road" to the unconscious. They are analyzed by free associating to the slip itself or to the various elements of the dream. The analysis helps us to distinguish between the *manifest dream* and the *latent dream* that underlies it.

5. The nature of our repressed wishes and desires is sexual. Freud redefined the concept of sexuality as pleasure seeking. In doing so, he reversed many traditional concepts and was able to account for previously unexplained behaviors. As his work developed, he emphasized the psychological aspects of mental processes and sexuality, an emphasis apparent in his use of the terms *drive* and *libido*.

6. Freud outlined a set of *psychosexual stages* that children travel as they progress from *autoerotic* sexual activity to mature, reproductive activity. The libido invests itself in various *erogenous zones*. During the *oral stage*, the major source of pleasure and pain is the mouth. The *anal stage* follows; libidinal energy is focused on the anus and the buttocks. During the *phallic*

*stage* the genital organs become important and children experience the *Oedipus complex,* whose resolution leads to the development of a *superego* and sexual identification. The *latency period* is one of rest, and the *genital stage* begins at puberty when the sexual organs mature and the individual is able to assume the sexual role outlined by his or her culture.

7. The effects of the psychosexual stages can be seen in various adult character traits and disorders. If the libido is unduly frustrated or overindulged at an early stage, it may become *fixated.* Many adult behaviors reflect early patterns that are characteristic of the different stages.

8. The *id, ego,* and *superego* represent different functions of the personality. The id is the oldest and original function. It includes our genetic inheritance, reflexes, and instincts and drives that motivate us. It operates according to the *pleasure principle* and uses *primary processes.* The ego develops in order to realistically meet the wishes of the id. It follows the *reality principle* and operates according to *secondary processes.* The superego consists of a *conscience* and the *ego-ideal.* It strives for perfection.

9. In the mature and well-adjusted personality, the ego is the executor controlling and governing the id and superego and mediating between their demands and the external world. In the maladjusted personality, the id or the superego gains control.

10. There is no easy correlation between the id, ego, and superego and consciousness or unconsciousness. The terms conscious and unconscious are best seen as adjectives describing qualities that the id, ego, and superego may or may not have.

11. Freud distinguished reality anxiety, neurotic anxiety, and moral anxiety.

12. In order to protect us against anxiety, the ego develops *defense mechanisms* that occur on an unconscious level and deny or distort reality so as to make it less threatening. Some of the more common defense mechanisms are *repression, denial, projection, reaction formation, regression, rationalization, identification, displacement,* and *sublimation.* Freud believed that by strengthening the ego we can become more aware of our impulses and deal with them more effectively.

13. Freud's psychoanalysis emphasizes the importance of the *transference* in which the patient transfers to the analyst emotional attitudes felt as a child toward significant persons. The patient repeats with the analyst infantile and ineffective ways of relating to other people. The analysis permits the patient to reexperience and rework these relationships to a more satisfactory resolution.

14. Efforts to test Freud's concepts have been made and the results are mixed. It is difficult to translate many of his concepts into operational procedures that allow for unequivocal test.

15. Although Freud frequently suggested that his theory functioned as science, he permitted many of his concepts to function philosophically. Thus, in the final analysis, Freud's theory needs to be evaluated in terms of a philosophy according to its coherence, relevance, comprehensiveness, and compellingness.

## Suggestions for Further Reading

Freud's published works fill twenty-four volumes in *The Complete Psychological Works of Sigmund Freud: Standard Edition,* published by Hogarth Press of London, beginning in 1953. The lay reader will find the following most useful as a further introduction to the development of Freud's thought and theory. The *Five Lectures on Psychoanalysis* (1910), which were delivered at Clark University in Worcester, Massachusetts, represent a concise introduction by Freud to his own work. They are included in Vol. 11, 1957, of the complete works. More extensive presentations by Freud on his general theory are provided in *Introductory Lectures on Psychoanalysis* (1917), Vols. 15–16, 1963, and *New Introductory Lectures on Psychoanalysis* (1933), Vol. 22, 1964. Freud's classic writings on dreams, slips, and sexuality are *The Interpretation of Dreams* (1900), Vols. 4–5, 1953; *The Psychopathology of Everyday Life* (1901), Vol. 6, 1960; and *Three Essays on Sexuality* (1905), Vol. 7, 1953.

Freud's final theory of a threefold dynamic of personality was presented in *The Ego and the Id* (1923), Vol. 19, 1961. His reevaluation of the problem of anxiety and the defense mechanisms is included in *Inhibitions, Symptoms and Anxiety* (1926), Vol. 20, 1959. The various introductory lectures provide useful information on the development of psychoanalysis as a therapeutic technique. The reader may also enjoy two later essays on the subject: "Analysis Terminable and Interminable" and "Constructions in Analysis" (both written in 1937), included in Vol. 23, 1964, in which Freud tries to assess realistically the benefits and limitations of psychoanalysis. Portions of the Standard Edition are also available in paperback editions published by Norton.

Secondary sources that provide a comprehensive picture of Freudian theory are C. Brenner, *An Elementary Textbook on Psychoanalysis* (Doubleday, 1955) and C. S. Hall, *A Primer of Freudian Psychology* (World, 1954).

R. Appignanesi and O. Zarate, *Freud for Beginners* (Pantheon, 1979) uses a comic book format to introduce readers to Freud.

The serious student of Freud will also be interested in the three-volume biography, *The Life and Work of Sigmund Freud* (Basic Books, 1953–1957), written by a close friend and follower, Ernest Jones. Briefer, more popular introductions to Freud's life and work are Irving Stone, *Passions of the Mind* (Doubleday, 1971), P. Roazen, *Freud and His Followers* (Knopf, 1975), and P. Gay, *Freud: A Life for Our Time* (Norton, 1988). Bruno Bettelheim in his *Freud and Man's Soul* (Knopf, 1982) helps to clarify the essential humanism of Freud's work.

Eleanor Schuker and Nadine Levinson have edited an encyclopedic text summarizing psychoanalytic views of female psychology from Freud to the present in *Female Psychology: An Annotated Psychoanalytic Bibliography* (Analytic Press, Inc., 1991).

The June 1992 issue of *American Psychologist* and the December 1994 issue of the *Journal of Personality* summarize recent research pertinent to psychoanalysis and cognitive processes, while *Psychoanalytic Dialogues* 1996, Vol. 6, No. 4, introduces a series of essays about the relation between psychoanalysis and science. Paul Robinson, in *Freud and His Critics,* describes and rebuts major criticisms of Freud's work.

# II

# *The Neopsychoanalytic Approach*

Although he always had a group of loyal followers, it was no doubt inevitable that a dynamic figure like Freud would both attract and repel. Some of his original followers became dissatisfied with orthodox psychoanalysis, defected from the movement, and founded their own schools of thought. Carl Jung, Alfred Adler, Karen Horney, and Erich Fromm were all deeply indebted to Freud and psychoanalysis, which provided a major impetus for their work. At the same time, each reacted in varying ways against Freud's psychoanalytic theory and developed his or her own position. In many instances, certain developments in these theories have been identified as valuable elaborations or adjuncts to classical psychoanalysis. Nevertheless, each theorist presented his or her theory as one that could stand by itself, and each attracted a group of followers who continue today to champion their contributions.

# *Analytical Psychology*

## CARL JUNG

### *Your Goals for This Chapter*

1. Explain how Jung used the term *psyche.*
2. Explain how Jung's concept of the *libido* differs from Freud's.
3. Compare and contrast Freud's and Jung's concepts of the ego.
4. Identify two basic *attitudes* and four *functions.*
5. Describe the *personal unconscious* and its *complexes.*
6. Explain how Jung's concept of the *collective unconscious* enlarges upon Freud's.
7. Discuss the following *archetypes: persona, shadow, anima* and *animus, self.* Explain the use of active imagination.
8. Discuss what is involved in Jung's concepts of *self-realization* and *synchronicity.*
9. Describe some major features of Jungian psychotherapy.
10. Discuss assessment and research in Jung's theory.
11. Evaluate Jung's theory in terms of its function as philosophy, science, and art.

C arl Jung is recognized as one of the greatest and most controversial psychological thinkers of the twentieth century. It would be unfair to consider Jung only as a defector from the psychoanalytic movement. He was a mature scholar, with his own developing ideas, before he encountered Freud. Although he was closely associated with Freud for a period of time, he went on to develop an independent school of thought that contrasts markedly with orthodox psychoanalysis. He is indebted to Freud but is a personality theorist in his own right. His concept of the collective unconscious vastly enlarges an aspect of personality that was barely explored by Freud.

## Biographical Background

Carl Gustav Jung was born in 1875 in Switzerland, where he lived all his life. He was the only surviving son of a poor country pastor and scholar of the Reformed church. Jung described his father as conventional and kind, but weak. He respected his father even though he had difficulty communicating with him, especially in matters of religion, which concerned Jung throughout his life. Skeptical of the orthodox faith in which he was reared, he searched relentlessly for adequate answers. This search is reflected in his psychology, with its interest in religion, mythology, and the occult.

His mother was a powerful person. Jung felt that she was a good mother but that she suffered from emotional disturbances. He was later to describe her as possessing two personalities, one kind and loving, the other harsh and aloof.

Jung described his childhood as lonely and his personality as introverted. Two brothers had died in infancy before Jung was born and his sister was not born until he was nine. The young boy frequently played by himself, inventing games and carving a small companion out of wood to console himself. These long periods of solitude were later to find expression in his self-analysis. His psychology also reflected his predilection for being alone. Maturity for Jung is defined not in terms of interpersonal relations, as it is for Freud, but in terms of integration or balance within the self.

As a child, he not only had several close contacts and brushes with death but he was also familiar with illness. When he was a young child his mother had to be hospitalized for several months, leaving him in the care of an elderly aunt and a family maid. During his youth a series of fainting spells caused him to miss over six months of school. The boy enjoyed the freedom from formal studies that his illness afforded him and the opportunity to explore other areas that interested him but were not in the traditional academic curriculum. However, shortly after he overheard his father's anguished comment to a friend, "What will become of the boy if he cannot earn his living?" his health was restored and he returned to school. Speculation continues to this day as to whether Jung suffered from a childhood psychosis. In any event, his life is a testament to the healing power of the psyche, which can motivate a sufferer to extraordinary accomplishments (Winnicott, 1993).

*Carl Jung, initially a follower of Freud, later broke with him
and developed his own theory of personality, exploring
in depth the collective unconscious.*

Jung originally wanted to be an archaeologist, but for financial reasons he could only afford to attend the University of Basel, which did not offer courses in that area. Therefore, he chose to study medicine. He was planning to specialize in surgery when he came across a textbook by Krafft-Ebing, a German neurologist (1840–1902), that described psychiatry as invariably subjective. The description provoked Jung's interest. From early life Jung had recognized a spiritual dimension within himself that he refused to deny or minimize (Masse, 1994); here was a field that might provide the key to some of the dreams, mysteries, and obscure happenings that he had been trying to understand.

His first professional appointment was as an assistant in a mental hospital in Zurich, where he worked with Eugen Bleuler, a well-known psychiatrist who coined the term "schizophrenia." Later, he became a lecturer at the University of Zurich. He established a private practice and developed a word-association test in order to study emotional reactions.

Jung first met Sigmund Freud in 1907 after having corresponded with him about their mutual interest for a short period. The two men were highly impressed with each other and with each other's work. That meeting began an intense personal and professional relationship. For some time Freud regarded Jung as his heir apparent and he looked on him with all of the affection that a father has for his son. When the International Psychoanalytic Society was founded, Jung, with Freud's endorsement, became its first president. They traveled together to Clark University where both had been invited to lecture.

On several occasions when Jung disagreed with Freud, Freud became very upset and in a few instances actually fainted. In 1913, Jung broke away from Freud and his school. Freud described the break as "a great loss" and it was also shattering for Jung, who entered a period of extensive inner disorientation in which he could not read or write and which eventually led to his self-analysis. Many reasons underlay the break with Freud; the most pronounced point of disagreement was Jung's rejection of Freud's emphasis on sexuality. Whereas for Freud all higher intellectual processes and emotionally significant experiences are ultimately substitutes for sexuality and can be understood thereby, for Jung sexuality itself must be seen as symbolic. Sexuality and the creativity it represents have a mysterious quality and cannot be fully analyzed or completely depicted.

Thereafter, Jung developed his own school of thought, which eventually came to be known as **analytical psychology.** He wrote extensively, and his unique theories were informed by a vast array of concerns, including Eastern religions, mythology, and alchemy. Although such subjects are frequently considered scientifically suspect, Jung felt that they were essential to the psychologist and indispensable in understanding the mysterious forces of the unconscious. Some critics argue that Jung's theories foster racism and that Jung was anti-Semitic and pro-Nazi. These criticisms continue in spite of different sentiments expressed in Jung's correspondence, denials by Jungian psychologists, and assertions that analytical psychology and Nazi ideology are totally incompatible (Gaillard, 1995; Gallard, 1995). Although Jung was troubled at times, he was a sensitive individual with unique and insightful ideas. His emphasis on the importance of a psychology of cultural difference suggests his ideas can make a powerful contribution to those who are concerned about processes of political and social transformation (Samuels, 1992). Jung died in 1961 at the age of eighty-five after a long and fruitful life.

## The Nature and Structure of Personality

Whereas Freud described the structure of personality in terms of three forces that are in conflict—the id, the ego, and the superego—Carl Jung conceived of the structure of personality as a complex network of interacting systems that strive toward eventual harmony. The primary ones are the ego; the personal unconscious with its complexes; and the collective unconscious and its archetypes. Jung also described two primary attitudes toward reality and four basic functions, which together constitute separate but related aspects of the **psyche,** or total personality.

The psyche refers to all psychological processes: thoughts, feelings, sensations, wishes, and so forth. Jung used the terms "psyche" and "psychic," rather than "mind" and "mental," to avoid the implications of consciousness in the latter and to emphasize that the psyche embraces both conscious and unconscious processes.

Jung and Freud differed in their approaches to the unconscious. Freud tended to view the unconscious essentially as materials that have been repressed, whereas Jung emphasized a concept of the unconscious as the source of consciousness and the matrix of new possibilities of life.

## Psychic Energy

Different theorists often use the same words, such as *psyche, unconscious, libido,* and *ego,* to define processes and characteristics of human beings that they feel are well rendered by the term. These concepts are not interchangeable and must be understood in terms of each theory as a whole.

For Freud, the motive force of personality consists of libido, the sexual drive. Jung also used "libido" to refer to psychic energy, but his use should not be confused with Freud's definition. Jung used the term in a more generalized fashion as an undifferentiated life energy (1948). **Libido** is an appetite that may refer to sexuality and to other hungers as well. It reflects itself as striving, desiring, and willing. Psychic energy operates according to the principles of equivalence and entropy; it seeks a balance and moves the person forward in a process of self-realization.

Although Jung did not reject an instinctual basis of personality, he criticized Freud's emphasis on sexuality, suggesting that it is ultimately reductive or simplistic, as it reduces any and all activities to sexual ones. For example, the phallus represents *mana* or power as well as sexuality. Jung believed that sexuality itself must be seen as symbolic, having a mysterious quality of otherness that cannot be fully described.

## The Ego

For Freud, the ego is ideally the executor of the personality. Although Freud initially thought that the ego is primarily conscious, he later considered that a large portion of the ego is unconscious and beyond conscious control or awareness.

For Jung, the **ego** is one's conscious mind, the part of the psyche that selects perceptions, thoughts, feelings, and memories that may enter consciousness. The ego is responsible for our feelings of identity and continuity. It is through our ego that we establish a sense of stability in the way we perceive ourselves. The ego, however, is not the true center of personality for Jung. This runs counter to our everyday point of view. Most of us identify ourselves or our center as that awareness of consciousness that we have of ourselves, but for Jung, as we shall shortly see, the true center of personality is centered elsewhere.

## The Personal Unconscious

Jung compared the conscious aspect of the psyche to an island that rises from the sea. We notice only the part above water, even though a much greater land mass, the unconscious, lies below (Fordham, 1953). The **personal unconscious** is a land that is not always covered by sea and thus can be reclaimed. Here reside those perceptions, thoughts, feelings, and memories that have been put aside (for our consciousness can only hold a few items at a time), and they may be easily retrieved. The personal unconscious also includes those experiences of an individual's life history that have been repressed or forgotten. This is an aspect of the unconscious that, as we have seen, Freud also emphasized. These forgotten experiences are accessible to consciousness even though becoming aware of some of them may be an arduous process.

Experiences are grouped in the personal unconscious into clusters, which Jung calls complexes. A **complex** is an organized group of thoughts, feelings, and memories about a particular concept (1934). A complex is said to have a **constellating power,** which means that the complex has the ability to draw new ideas into it and interpret them accordingly. It can be compared to a magnet that attracts related experiences. The more constellating power a complex has, the more powerful it may become. Complexes have important implications for our interpersonal relationships, specifically influencing how we react toward others.

A complex may be organized around a particular person or object. One of Jung's examples concerns motherhood (1954). A mother complex refers to the cluster of ideas, feelings, and memories that have arisen from our own particular experience of having been mothered. It also draws into it other experiences of mothering to which we have been exposed. Each new instance of mothering that we encounter is drawn into our mother complex and understood and interpreted by it.

A complex, however, may make it difficult for us to disengage ourselves from a situation. Jung described a man who believed that he was suffering from a real cancer, even though he knew that his cancer was imaginary. The complex, Jung wrote, is "a spontaneous growth, originating in that part of the psyche which is not identical with consciousness. It appears to be an autonomous development intruding upon consciousness" (1938). A complex may act like an independent person, behaving independently of our conscious self and intentions.

A complex may be conscious, partly conscious, or unconscious. Certain elements of it may extend into the collective unconscious. Some complexes appear to dominate an entire personality. Napoleon is frequently described as being driven by inner forces to obtain power.

Jung's concept of complex may be seen as an effort to overcome the traditional categories of mind versus body and conscious versus unconscious (Brooke, 1991).

## The Collective Unconscious

Whereas the personal unconscious is unique for each individual, the **collective unconscious** is shared. Jung referred to the collective unconscious as "transpersonal"; that is to say, it extends across persons. It consists of certain potentialities that we all share because we are human (1936). Many critics believe that Jung made a unique contribution to depth psychology in his concept of the collective unconscious. Freud's concept of unconscious forces was mostly limited to personal experiences that have been repressed or forgotten. Whereas other dissenters from Freud tended to minimize the power of unconscious forces, Jung placed a greater emphasis on them and stressed the qualities that we share with other people.

All people, because they are human beings, have certain things in common. All human beings live in groups and develop some form of family life or society in which roles are assigned to various members. These roles may vary from society to society but they exist in all human groups. All human beings share certain emotions such as joy, grief, or anger. The ways of expressing these emotions may vary, but the emotions themselves are shared. All human beings develop some form of language and symbolization. The particular words may vary, but the concepts and symbols are shared. Thus, certain archetypes and symbols reappear again and again from society to society and they may be seen to have a common meaning.

Jung considered the collective unconscious an empirical concept whose existence can be demonstrated through dreams, mythology, and cross-cultural data. The workings of the collective unconscious are seen in experiences we have all had, such as falling in love with a "perfect other," feeling overwhelmed by a piece of art or music, or being drawn to the sea, and it expresses itself in shared symbols that have universal meaning.

## Archetypes

Within the collective unconscious lie the archetypes or primordial images. An **archetype** is a universal thought form or predisposition to respond to the world in certain ways (1936). The word "predisposition" is crucial to Jung's concept of the collective unconscious and its archetypes. It emphasizes potentialities, for the archetypes represent different potential ways in which we may express our humanness.

The archetypes can never be fully known or described because they never fully enter consciousness. They appear to us in personified or symbolized pictorial form and may penetrate into consciousness by means of myths, dreams, art, ritual, and symptoms. It is helpful for us to get in touch with them because they represent the latent potentiality of the psyche. In doing so, we go beyond developing our individual potentialities and become incorporated in the eternal cosmic process.

Jung wrote, "The archetype is a kind of readiness to produce over and over again the same or similar mythical ideas. Hence it seems as though what is impressed upon the unconscious were exclusively the subjective fantasy—ideas aroused by the physical process. We may therefore assume that the archetypes are recurrent impressions made by subjective reasons" (1954).

PERSONA    The **persona** refers to the social role that one assumes in society and one's understanding of it. As mentioned in Chapter 1, the Latin word *persona* refers to the masks that actors wore in ancient Greek plays. Thus, one's persona is the mask that one wears in order to adjust to the demands of society. Each one of us chooses or is assigned particular roles in our society. The persona represents a compromise between one's true identity and social identity. To neglect the development of a persona is to run the risk of becoming asocial. On the other hand, one may identify too completely with the persona at the expense of one's true identity and not permit other aspects of one's personality to develop.

SHADOW    The **shadow** encompasses those *unsocial* thoughts, feelings, and behaviors that we potentially possess and other characteristics that we do not accept. It is the opposite side of the persona, in that it refers to those desires and emotions that are incompatible with our social standards and ideal personality. It could be described as the devil within. Jung's choice of the word "shadow" is deliberate and designed to emphasize its necessity. There can be no sun that does not leave a shadow. The shadow cannot be avoided and one is incomplete without it (cf. Johnson, 1991). Jung agreed with Freud that such base and unsocial impulses may be sublimated and channeled to good ends. The shadow can also be projected onto others, with important interpersonal and social consequences such as prejudice.

To neglect or try to deny the shadow involves us in hypocrisy and deceit. Angels are not suited for existence on earth. Jung suggested a need to come to know our baser side and recognize our animalistic impulses. To do so adds dimension and credibility to personality as well as increased zest for life.

ANIMA AND ANIMUS    Each one of us is assigned a sex gender, male or female, based on our overt sexual characteristics. Yet none of us is purely male or purely female. Each of us has qualities of the opposite sex in terms of biology and also in terms of psychological attitudes and feelings. Thus, the **anima** archetype is the feminine side of the male psyche and the **animus** archetype is the masculine side of the female psyche. One's anima or animus reflects collective and individual human experiences throughout the ages pertaining to one's opposite sex. It assists us in relating to and understanding the opposite sex. For Jung, there was a distinct difference between the psychology of men and women. Jung believed that it was important that one express these opposite-sex characteristics in order to avoid an unbalanced or one-sided personality. If one exhibits only the traits of one's assigned sex, the other traits remain unconscious, undeveloped, and primitive. Those of us who have difficulty in understanding the opposite sex probably are not in tune with our anima or animus.

Jung has usually been considered friendly to women because of his assertion of the need to get in touch with one's opposite-sex archetype. However, his writings have also been criticized for including stereotypes of women as well as potentially racist comments about other groups such as blacks and primitive people. Jung stoutly maintained that the psyche of women is different from that of men and he tended to be rigid in his discussion of those behaviors that would or would not overstep the boundaries of appropriate expression of one's assigned gender role and one's opposite-sex archetype. He warned of the dangers of pushing one's capacity to behave like the opposite sex too far, so that a man loses his masculinity or a woman her femininity.

Jung believed that women's consciousness is characterized by the ability to enter into relationships, whereas men's consciousness is characterized by the ability to engage in rational and analytic thought. The persona, or social mask, differs for men and women because of the various roles that society and culture have assigned to them. The anima and the animus function in ways that compensate for the outer personality and show the qualities that are missing in outward conscious expression. Because psychological development involves integrating one's persona and one's anima or animus, Jung believed it will progress differently for the male and for the female.

A woman may react to her animus in various ways. Traditionally, women have repressed their masculine qualities and striven to fulfill their feminine role. Jung thought this might lead to an imbalance in the personality and unconscious efforts on the part of the animus to intrude upon the woman's life; he pointed out that both the anima and the animus may behave as if they are laws unto themselves and have disruptive influences. Another way to react to the animus is to identify with it, but this usually makes it more difficult for a woman to fulfill her assigned role.

However, a woman's animus need not be thought of as acting in opposition to femininity. In ideal development, the animus will lead a woman to transform her femininity into a renewed form of consciousness that overcomes the traditional dualities. The same would be true of ideal development in the male.

While Jung's theory may be interpreted as sexist, a feminist analysis of his work may be warranted (Romaniello, 1992). His comments about the anima and the animus led to the now very popular concept of an androgynous ideal. *Androgyny* refers to the presence of both masculine and feminine qualities in an individual and the ability to realize both potentialities. Considerable research has been done in the area of androgyny (see, for example, Singer, 1991).

SELF    The central archetype in Jung's understanding is that of the self. Jung's use of the term "self" differed from the usual use of the term. The **self** represents the striving for unity of all parts of the personality. It is the organizing principle of the psyche that draws unto itself and harmonizes all the archetypes and their expressions. The self directs an orderly allotment of psychic energy so that different parts of the personality are expressed appropriately. Depending upon the occasion and our personal needs, the self allows us to be socially acceptable at work (persona), outrageous at a Halloween party (shadow), emotional at a concert (shadow), and so forth. The self, rather than the ego, is the true midpoint of personality. Thus, the center of one's personality is not to be found in rational ego consciousness. For Jung, the true self lay on the boundary between conscious and unconscious, reason and unreason. The development of the self is life's goal, but the self archetype cannot begin to emerge until the other personality systems have been fully developed. Thus, it usually does not begin to emerge until one has reached middle age. Jung spoke of the realization of the self as a goal that lies in the future. It is something to be striven for but rarely achieved.

Jung (1955) believed that the **mandala,** which in Hindu and Buddhist thought is a symbol of the universe, is also a symbol of the self. The mandala is a concentrically arranged figure such as the circle, the wheel, or the cross, which Jung saw appearing again and again in his patients' dreams and in the artwork of all cultures (see Figure 3.1). It represents the self striving toward wholeness.

Jung described numerous other archetypes of the collective unconscious: birth, death, rebirth, power, magic, the child, the hero, God, the demon, the great mother, and the wise old man. Archetypes find expression in cultural forms. Rock star Madonna draws on the archetype of the great mother, as does the "grandmother" in native American folklore and Demeter, goddess of the earth, in Greek mythology. Joseph Campbell (1949) has de-

## *Archetypes in Cultural Forms*

Jung believed that there are an indeterminate number of archetypes, but some of the most common ones are:

| | |
|---|---|
| *persona* | social role or mask |
| *shadow* | the devil within |
| *anima* | feminine side of the male psyche |
| *animus* | masculine side of the female psyche |
| *self* | ultimate unity of the personality |
| *great mother* | the ultimate good and bad mother |
| *wise old man* | spiritual father |
| *hero* | conqueror of enemies and evil forces |
| *trickster* | animalistic prankster |
| *child-god* | the future |
| *hermaphrodite* | unity and wholeness |

The archetypes are ambivalent, embodying both positive and negative aspects. Frequently they appear in a mixed combination. Thus the trickster may also be a shadow figure. Yahweh, the god of the Hebrew Bible, often appears to play the role of a trickster but also culminates in the spiritual father of Judaism and Christianity.

Can you identify some of the archetypes listed above as they have appeared in cultural forms thoughout history and in our world today? It may be helpful to think of some of the myths, folklore, and fairy tales that Disney has immortalized, as well as other cultural icons you were exposed to as you grew up.

scribed the many faces of the archetypal hero figure in literature, and James Iaccino (1994) has identified archetypes in horror movies. The classic film trilogy *Star Wars* is replete with archetypal figures: Luke Skywalker plays the hero rescuing Princess Leia, the maiden, who is held hostage by evil forces. Darth Vader represents the shadow or demon, and Obi Wan Kenobi exemplifies the wise old man. "The force" itself represents *mana*. Religious symbols may also be seen as archetypes: Adam is the first man; Christ and Buddha represent the self.

Efforts to deny or destroy the archetypes place us at risk of becoming unbalanced or one-sided. For example, Myyra (1992) contends that Western culture's denial of the dreadful facets of the great mother culminated in a patriarchal society that oppressed women and destroyed nature. Therefore, we need to get in touch with the archetypes and their healing power.

At the deepest levels, Jung believed that our unconscious remains archaic, despite our scientific technology and the development of our rational powers. Freud disclaimed Jung's plea for originality in articulating the collective unconscious, stating that he (Freud)

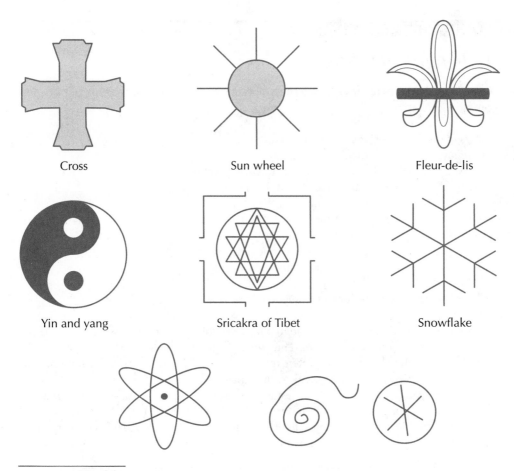

FIGURE 3.1    **Mandalas**

Jung believed that the mandala, a concentrically arranged figure, is a symbol of the self.
Mandalas appear in the symbolism of both East and West, in nature, and in our doodles.

had known all along that the unconscious is collective. And, of course, there are certain archetypal patterns in Freud's understanding of the unconscious. The psychosexual stages involve predispositions toward acting out the human drama in certain ways. The Oedipal situation that we experience is a collective archetypal myth. Symbols in dreams may be unique to the individual, but also shared. Thus, a concept of collected unconscious forces is implied in Freud's theory although certainly not clearly articulated. And whereas Freud emphasized the unique unfolding of unconscious forces in the individual's life history and personal unconscious (it is not enough to know that one has gone through the Oedipal situation—one must fully experience its particular unfolding within one's distinct family constellation), Jung emphasized the shared and collective aspects. As you might imagine, Jung's concept of the collective unconscious is an important and controversial one in personality theorizing, evoking both considerable support and opposition.

*Archetypes, universal thought forms or predispositions, appear in various cultural forms throughout history. The classic film trilogy* Star Wars *is full of archetypes: Luke Skywalker is the hero, Princess Leia is the maiden, Darth Vader is the shadow or demon, and Obi-Wan Kenobi is the wise old man.*

## Psychological Types

One of Jung's contributions to the psychology of the conscious psyche is his explanation and description of the psychological types, which arise out of the various combinations of two basic **attitudes** (1993a) and four **functions,** or ways of perceiving the environment and orienting experiences.

### The Attitudes

**Extraversion** is an attitude in which the psyche is oriented outward to the objective world. The extravert tends to be more comfortable with the outer world of people and things. **Introversion** is an attitude in which the psyche is oriented inward to the subjective world. The introvert is more comfortable with the inner world of concepts and ideas. These words have become so commonplace in today's vocabulary that many of us readily identify ourselves as introverted or extraverted. Jung labeled himself an introvert and Freud an extravert (see also Dolliver, 1994). Yet in describing people as introverted or extraverted, Jung dealt primarily with the psychology of consciousness. An individual's habitual conscious attitude is either introverted or extraverted, but the other attitude is also present, although it may be undeveloped and mostly unconscious.

## The Functions

Jung's four functions are grouped into opposite pairs. The functions of **sensation** and **intuition** refer to how we gather data and information. The sensor is more comfortable using the five senses and dealing with facts and reality. The intuitor looks for relationships and meanings or possibilities about past or future events. **Thinking** and **feeling** refer to how we come to conclusions or make judgments. The thinker prefers to use logic and impersonal analysis. The feeler is more concerned with personal values, attitudes, and beliefs. Jung suggested that one of these functions tends to be dominant in each individual and its opposite inferior. The other two functions play an auxiliary role. A professor, for example, may have so cultivated intellectual and cognitive powers that the feeling aspect of personality is submerged. Though primitive and undeveloped, feelings may nevertheless invade the professor's life in the form of strange moods, symptoms, or projections.

The two attitudes and four functions combine to form eight psychological types, which are summarized in Table 3.1.

Jung cautioned that the types as described rarely occur in a pure form. There is a wide range of variation within each type, and people of a specific type may change (though not to another type) as their personal and collective unconscious changes. No one type is better than another type. Each has its own strengths and weaknesses.

---

**TABLE 3.1    Psychological Types**

Jung's attitudes and functions combine to form eight psychological types. As you read them, note which type resembles you most closely.

| THE EXTRAVERTED TYPES | THE INTROVERTED TYPES |
|---|---|
| *Thinking:* Tend to live according to fixed rules; repress feelings; try to be objective but may be dogmatic in thinking. | *Thinking:* Have a strong need for privacy; tend to be theoretical, intellectual, and somewhat impractical; repress feelings; may have trouble getting along with other people. |
| *Feeling:* Tend to be sociable; seek harmony with the world; respect tradition and authority; tend to be emotional; repress thinking. | *Feeling:* Tend to be quiet, thoughtful, and hypersensitive; repress thinking; may appear mysterious and indifferent to others. |
| *Sensing:* Seek pleasure and enjoy new sensory experiences; are strongly oriented toward reality; repress intuition. | *Sensing:* Tend to be passive, calm, and artistic; focus on objective sensory events; repress intuition. |
| *Intuition:* Are very creative; find new ideas appealing; tend to make decisions based on hunches rather than facts; are in touch with their unconscious wisdom; repress sensing. | *Intuition:* Tend to be mystic dreamers; come up with unusual new ideas; are seldom understood by others; repress sensing. (Jung described himself as an introverted intuitor.) |

# Self-Realization

Jung did not outline stages in the development of personality nor did he consider the early childhood years to be the most important ones, as Freud did. Jung suggested, however, that the self is in the process of **self-realization.** The "psychic birth" of an individual does not really occur until adolescence, when the psyche starts to show a definite form and content. Personality development continues throughout life, and the middle years (35 to 40) mark the beginning of major changes.

Although the concept of self-realization was fully described by Jung, it cannot be said to be new with his thought. The origin of the principle takes us back to the Greek philosopher Aristotle (384–322 B.C.). Aristotle held that everything has a **telos,** a purpose or goal, that constitutes its essence and indicates its potentiality. Thus, every acorn has the essence of treeness and the potential to become a mighty oak. In the same way, each one of us has the potential to develop into a self, that is, to realize, fulfill, and enhance our maximum human potentialities. This viewpoint is essentially *teleological,* or purposeful. It explains the present in terms of the future with reference to a goal that guides and directs our destiny. Whereas Freud's view was primarily a causal one, comprehending personality in terms of antecedent conditions in the past, Jung maintained that both causality and teleology are necessary for full self-realization.

## *Synchronicity*

In addition to the principles of causality and teleology, Jung (1960) included a third component that could lead to self-realization: **synchronicity,** a phenomenon in which events are related to one another through simultaneity and meaning. In synchronicity, two events occur either at the same time or close in time (simultaneity), and, though they happen independently, they seem inextricably linked (meaning). We may dream of a friend whom we have not seen in a long time, and the next day we learn that our friend died the night before. Logic tells us that such synchronistic experiences are merely chance or coincidental, but Jung believed that at another level they are very significant; their impact on our lives is equal to that of causality. Jung suggested that such events are related through meaningful simultaneity.

Jung believed that synchronistic events arise from the simultaneous occurrence of two different psychic states. In the external world a situation occurs in the normal chain of causal events, while in the internal world an archetype emerges into consciousness. This leads one to conjecture that in some way in the example above the transpersonal collective unconscious was "in touch" with the death before the conscious mind was aware of it.

To illustrate how synchronicity can operate on self-realization, Jung (1960) cited one of his patients, who was experiencing considerable intellectual resistance to therapy. She described a dream in which she was given a golden scarab. At that very moment, Jung heard an insect tapping on the window. He let the bug in, caught it, and, noticing that it was a close insect relative to the sacred Egyptian beetle in her dream, presented it to the patient with the words, "Here is your scarab." The event broke the ice of her rationalism and permitted the therapy to move forward. Was the event merely fortuitous, or was it a moment of grace?

Jung believed that synchronicity is involved in phenomena studied by the science of parapsychology, which investigates the perceptions that come to us in ways other than through the normal five senses. He suggested that our skepticism concerning extrasensory perception is without justification and due to an ingrained belief in a constricted sense of cause and effect. Jung also linked synchronicity to *I Ching,* an intuitive traditional Chinese method of grasping a situation and choosing alternatives, in which straws are randomly divided or coins are tossed and the resultant pattern consulted to divine an answer. Jung believed that using I Ching makes it possible to overcome the limitations of conscious decision making because it grasps a situation as a whole and places its details against a cosmic background.

Jung suggested that the synchronicity factor stipulates the existence of a fourth dimension in addition to space, time, and causality, rendering the classic triad of physics a balanced set of four. Jung even collaborated with Nobel physicist Wolfgang Pauli in identifying this noncausal side to reality experienced both in physics and the psyche; their collaboration resulted in the publication of a book, *The Interpretation of Nature and the Psyche,* in 1952 (Lindorff, 1995).

## Individuation and Transcendence

Self-realization involves individuation and transcendence (1916, 1939). In **individuation,** the systems of the individual psyche achieve their fullest degree of differentiation, expression, and development. **Transcendence** refers to integration of the diverse systems of the self toward the goal of wholeness and identity with all of humanity. Jung's concepts of individuation and transcendence are difficult for the average Westerner to understand. In Western psychology, we generally think of personality in terms of an individual's uniqueness. People who do not appear to be unique are often said to "lack personality."

For Jung, individuation does not mean individualism in that narrow sense, but rather fulfilling one's own specific nature and realizing one's uniqueness in one's place within the whole. In the process of transcendence, a deeper self or essence emerges to unite a person with all of humanity and the universe at large.

Individuation and transcendence are both ongoing processes. However, the first half of life is often more concerned with the cultivation of consciousness and gender-specific behavior, while the second half of life may be more concerned with coming into closer contact with self and expressing our collective unconscious and oneness with humanity as a whole. Mary Loomis (1991) has made a comparison to a process that Native Americans refer to as the Red Road.

Thus, as the self realizes, a stormy process that may never be fully completed, it perpetually rises to a greater enhancement and realization of itself and humanity. If we view the psyche as a wheel, the hub of which is the archetype of the self, we can suggest that the true self emerges when the opposites coincide (Figure 3.2). The true person does not consist of the conscious or the unconscious, mind or body, persona or shadow, overt sexual

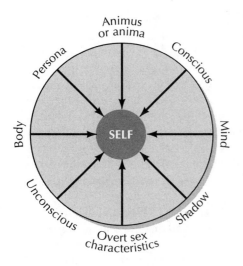

Animus
or anima

Persona

Conscious

Body

SELF

Mind

Unconscious

Shadow

Overt sex
characteristics

**FIGURE 3.2   The Coincidence of Opposites**

If we were to view the psyche as a wheel, the hub of which is the archetype of the self, the true self emerges when the opposites coincide. The resulting image is, of course, a mandala.

characteristics or complements, but of all of these. Neurosis results from a one-sided personality development. The coincidence of opposites is the ultimate goal of personality development in the Jungian view. Although both Freud and Jung emphasized the dynamic opposition of portions of the personality, they differed in the implications of this conflict. For Freud, the person is inescapably in conflict; for Jung, the person ultimately seeks harmony. Mansfield and Spiegelman (1991) have employed quantum mechanical models and symbols to deepen our understanding of the coincidence of opposites. Van Eenwyk (1991) has further suggested that chaos theory, which attempts to describe complicated systems formerly outside the range of classical mathematics and physics, illumines Jung's theory.

## Jungian Psychotherapy

Jung viewed emotional disturbance as a person's attempt to reconcile the contradictory aspects of personality. One side of the psyche, such as the conscious, adaptive, social persona, may be exaggerated at the expense of the darker, unconscious aspects. Whereas for Freud a neurosis represents the return of the repressed, for Jung it is the insistence of the undeveloped part of the personality on being heard and realized. It is difficult to describe Jung's method of psychotherapy specifically because he did not clearly outline his procedures as Freud did (see Guy-Gillet, 1996). Further, Jung maintained that no one approach is suitable for everyone. The individual who has had difficulty in accepting the sexual and aggressive urges of life may well require a Freudian interpretation. But for others, or at different stages in development, the Freudian understanding may not be sufficiently comprehensive.

In classical Freudian psychoanalysis, the analyst remains detached and reveals few personal feelings and reactions in order to facilitate the transference, whereas the Jungian analyst is more self-disclosing, foreshadowing Rogerian and other contemporary therapies. Therapy is a "dialectical procedure," a dialogue between doctor and patient, conscious and unconscious. Although the couch may be used to facilitate procedures such as active imagination, for the most part analyst and patient sit facing each other. The Jungian analyst also sees patients far less frequently than the Freudian. The frequency of visits depends on the stage that the patient has reached.

During the early stages of treatment, there is a need for *confession.* Such confession is generally accompanied by emotional release, and Jung viewed it as the aim of the cathartic method originated by Breuer and Freud. But Jung pointed out that emotional release, in itself, is not therapeutic any more than temper tantrums or other emotional outbursts are curative in and of themselves. For Freud, conscious intellectual understanding and insight renders the catharsis effective. Jung emphasized that the presence of the other, the therapist who supports the patient morally and spiritually as well as intellectually, makes the confession curative.

Projection and transference play an important role in Jungian analysis, though Jung added to Freud's concept of transference the recognition that not only significant persons from the patient's past but also archetypal images are projected onto the analyst. Jung also viewed the sexual components of the transference as symbolic efforts on the patient's part to reach a higher integration of personality. In contrast to Freud, Jung did not think that transference was a necessary precondition for therapy.

Whereas Freud treated dreams as the expression of unconscious wishes, Jung gave them a prospective function as well as a retrospective one. By prospective function Jung meant that the dream represents an effort by the person to prepare for future events. Dreams also have a **compensatory function;** they are efforts to complement the patient's conscious side and speak for the unconscious.

In interpreting dreams, Jung used the method of **amplification** (1951) rather than the method of free association. In free association, each dream element is the starting place for a chain of association that may lead far afield from the original element. In amplification, one focuses repeatedly on the element and gives multiple associations to it. The dream is taken exactly as it is with no precise effort to distinguish between manifest and latent contents. The therapist joins the patient in efforts to interpret the dream, adding personal associations and frequently referring to mythology, fairy tales, and the like in order to extend the dream's meaning. Whereas Freud tended to deal with dreams singly, Jung concentrated on series of dreams. Analysis of a series of dreams unfolds the inner life of the patient, which is taken as a guide to true-life meanings for the patient.

As a therapist, Jung also valued the use of active imagination as a means of facilitating self-understanding and the use of artistic production by the patient. He encouraged his patients to draw, sculpt, paint, or develop some other art form as a means to listening to their inner depths. In all of this, he emphasized obedience to the unfolding inner life as the appropriate, ethical fulfillment of one's humanity.

## Assessment and Research in Jung's Theory

Jung's ideas have had a significant but frequently unacknowledged impact on assessment and research in personality. Jung developed the *word-association test,* which provided the first experimental data on unconscious processes and is widely used in current laboratory research and clinical practice. The participant responds to a list of stimulus words designed to elicit emotions. An unusual response, a long pause before responding, the same response to very different words, and other factors may indicate a complex. Jung's word-association test may be termed the forerunner of later projective techniques and attempts to assess personality by techniques such as free association, sentence completion, and psychophysiological monitoring, including the polygraph, or lie detector. Indeed, Jung is credited with identifying at least two thieves through the technique of word association (Ellenberger, 1970).

A Swiss psychiatrist, Hermann Rorschach, developed the Rorschach Inkblot Test, which is heavily influenced by Jungian concepts such as introversion and extraversion. Henry Murray also was deeply influenced by Jung when he developed the Thematic Apperception Test.

Jung's typology has also led to the development of assessment and research on psychological type. The Myers-Briggs Type Indicator (MBTI) is one of the most popular tools for nonpsychiatric populations in the area of clinical, counseling, and personality assessment. The instrument, developed primarily by Katherine Briggs and her daughter Isabel Briggs Myers, is designed to implement Jung's theory of type by sorting people into groups on the basis of four separate dichotomies of indices: Extraversion-Introversion (EI), Sensing-Intuition (SN), Thinking-Feeling (TF), and Judgment-Perception (JP). You will recognize the first polarity as the two attitudes identified by Jung and the second and third polarities as the four ego functions. The last polarity indicates a preference for judgment or perception (JP): J's prefer a great deal of structure and closure in their lives and P's prefer more spontaneity and openness. The J pole refers to the two judging functions (thinking and feeling) and the P pole refers to the two perceiving functions (sensing or intuition). The preference for J or P tells which mode—J (decision making) or P (information gathering)—is shown to the outside world (see Table 3.2).

Given the four dichotomies, sixteen different four-letter types are possible. An ESFJ, for example, is an extravert who is sensing, feeling, and judging. The assessment manual provides descriptions that distinguish each type from the others. One of the distinct advantages of the MBTI is its face validity: individuals invariably recognize themselves in their types (cf. Furnham, 1990). As in Jung's original typology, no one type is preferred over other types. Each type has its own strengths and weaknesses.

The MBTI generated considerable research, some of which was summarized by Myers and McCaulley (1985). The instrument has been a very successful tool. It has enormous potential for helping people to understand learning styles and leadership types so that teachers can motivate students and employers can motivate workers by recognizing that not everyone dances to the same drummer (Keirsey & Bates, 1984). It helps relate psychological type to various topics, such as risk tolerance, problem solving, information systems design, and conflict management (Gardner & Martinko, 1996). The MBTI is widely used in organizational consulting, career counseling, and job selection, as well as in couples counseling. More research needs to be done on whether or not the findings of the MBTI apply across cultures.

Jung's techniques of research and assessment drew upon not only empirical and scientific methods, but also nonscientific and mystical approaches. Thus Jung studied a variety of cultures and periods, exploring their myths, symbols, religions, and rituals. He was interested in subjects such as alchemy and astrology. This "unorthodox blend of opposites"

---

TABLE 3.2   **The Myers-Briggs Type Indicator: Sample Questions**

In the Myers-Briggs type indicator, forced-choice questions similar to the following sort people into groups on the basis of four polar indices: extraversion-introversion (E or I), sensing-intuition (S or N), thinking-feeling (T or F), and judgment-perception (J or P).

1. Given a free evening, I would prefer to
   a. stay home by myself.
   b. go out with other people.

2. In gathering information, I am more interested in
   a. facts.
   b. possibilities.

3. In making a decision, it is more important to me to
   a. come up with a correct answer.
   b. consider the impact of the solution.

4. I prefer to do activities
   a. that have been planned in advance.
   b. on the spur of the moment.

Answers are keyed as follows: 1a: I; 1b: E. 2a: S; 2b: I. 3a: T; 3b: F. 4a: J; 4b: P.

---

(Schultz, 1990) does not always sit well with more scientifically oriented psychologists who, in spite of the widespread use of the MBTI, tend to ignore Jungian concepts.

PHILOSOPHY, SCIENCE, AND ART

# Jung's Theory

Many of Jung's discoveries, like Freud's, took place in the clinical setting. He also obtained information from sources outside the treatment room. Observations of other cultures and studies of comparative religion and mythology, symbolism, alchemy, and the occult afforded him a wealth of information. Jung considered these sources secondary but legitimate ones for psychologists seeking to uncover the mysteries of the human psyche. He believed that a comparative method of study, often used in history and anthropology, was a valuable approach in science as well.

Jung did not believe that psychologists should be bound to an experimental, scientific approach. He did believe, however, that conclusions should be based on empirical data. Jung criticized the contemporary scientific atmosphere for limiting its concepts to those of causality and emphasized the concept of teleology. After all, he pointed out, the concepts of *cause* and *goal* are not themselves found in nature but are imaginary constructs imposed by scientists. Jung urged scientists to work within a broader scope and conceptual design.

## PHILOSOPHICAL ASSUMPTIONS

### *Examining Jung*

How would you rate Jung on each of the basic philosophical assumptions described in Chapter 1? Consult the chart on the inside front cover of this book. Each basic issue is presented as a bipolar dimension along which a person's view can be placed according to the degree of agreement with one or the other extreme. Rate Jung's views on these issues.

When you have determined where you think Jung stands, compare your responses with those of your classmates and your instructor. You should be willing to defend your ratings, but also be prepared to change them in light of others' compelling arguments. Afterward, compare your rating of Jung with your own position on each issue and with those of other theorists. Does this comparison help you to understand why his theory does or does not appeal to you?

Jung's concepts are particularly difficult to study in the laboratory. As with Freud, it is virtually impossible to define many of his terms operationally or to develop a test that would disprove them. Further, Jung's interest in the occult has led many critics to dismiss him as a mystic. Consequently, scientific psychology has until recently largely ignored Jung's analytical psychology, and his position in academia is problematic (Tacey, 1997). Nevertheless, Jung has influenced developments in psychology and other disciplines.

Jung indicated that he was more interested in discovering facts than in developing a philosophy. Because his concepts were based on empirical data, in the broadest sense of the word he operated as a "scientist." However, his theory falls short of rigorous standards of compatibility, predictive power, and simplicity. Fundamentally, the Jungian quest may be viewed as a philosophical or religious one. Jung explicitly raised philosophical questions and suggested philosophical answers. For example, asserting that questions about human nature should be answered empirically is in itself a philosophical position that distinguishes science from philosophy. For Jung, the power of self-understanding stems from an appropriate philosophy of life. It should not be surprising that although Jung has been largely ignored by experimentally oriented psychologists, theologians have found his work very fruitful. His concept of God's revealing himself through the collective unconscious is particularly attractive to theologians who seek a more relevant articulation of traditional theistic concepts. Although it is complex, his theory is coherent; its relevance is attested to by the resurgence of interest in it today; and the comprehensive features of his theory are remarkable for their profundity.

As an art, Jungian therapy emphasizes a scholarly goal. With the resurgence of interest in Jung, training in Jungian analysis has become available in major American cities.

It has been argued that Jung's visionary powers and deep spirituality have helped many to find an alternative set of values to the barren materialism prevailing in Western society (Stevens, 1994). Bill W. (cofounder of Alcoholics Anonymous) credits Jung with helping him understand the importance of spirituality in recovery from addiction (W., 1988). Jung's emphasis on inborn qualities, the duality of human nature, symbolism, androgyny, and the importance of inner experiences—factors that at one time led psychologists to neglect his work—are now seen as important, if not indispensable, for understanding personality. Indeed, Jung's concept of androgyny formed the basis for the interest in androgyny that developed in the 1970s and has become well incorporated into the gender literature. Jung's interest in the developmental process with his attention to the second half of the human life span has proved valuable to social scientists who are concerned about the needs and growth of our older population (Moraglia, 1994). In particular Jung helps us deal with the reality of death (Mogenson, 1990).

In this postmodern era, Jung's concepts can further help us understand the place of the self in our talk about different cultures (Thrasher, 1991) and forge a new holistic paradigm (Clarke, 1992). Many of Jung's archetypal images tell an ecological tale of the profound dialogue between the earth and the soul (Noel, 1991).

Drawing upon Jung, Sliker (1992) explores how politics, culture, and ethnicity can be understood. She believes her model can foster discussion for resolving conflicts among various cultures.

Jung's thinking poses a significant challenge to Western thought and psychology with its emphasis on an extrospective methodology based on experimentation and causal rather than teleological or other acausal explanations. His ideas are compatible with thinking in the East, and because his goal was to regain balance, Jung believed that a dialectic between Western and non-Western cultures was essential (Bagby, 1995). It is unfortunate that many psychologists in America have been quick to dismiss the concepts of Jung. They merit more serious consideration.

## Summary

1. Jung uses the term *psyche* to refer to all psychological processes, emphasizing that it embraces both conscious and unconscious processes.

2. For Freud the *libido* consists of the sexual drive, whereas Jung used the term in a more generalized fashion as an undifferentiated energy that moves the person forward.

3. Whereas for Freud the ego is the executor of the personality, for Jung it is one's conscious perception of self.

4. Jung described two basic *attitudes* (introversion and extraversion) and four *functions* (sensation, thinking, feeling, and intuition). In each person, one of the attitudes and functions is dominant and its opposite is weaker. The other two functions play an auxiliary role.

5. The *personal unconscious* includes experiences of an individual's history that have been repressed or forgotten. These are organized into *complexes.*

6. Freud's concept of unconscious forces is mostly limited to a personal unconscious; Jung's *collective unconscious* consists of potential ways of being that all humans share.

7. *Archetypes* are universal thought forms of the collective unconscious and predispositions to perceive the world in certain ways. Some widely recognized archetypes are the *persona,* the *shadow,* the *anima,* and the *animus.* The *self* is the central archetype and true midpoint of the personality. Active imagination is a method of getting in touch with the archetypes.

8. *Self-realization* is a teleological process of development that involves *individuation* and *transcendence.* In the process, the systems of the psyche achieve their fullest degree of differentiation and are then integrated in identity with all of humanity. *Synchronicity* is a phenomenon in which events are related to one another through simultaneity and meaning.

9. In his psychotherapy, Jung sought to reconcile unbalanced aspects of the personality. It is a dialectical procedure and initially entails confession. Jung considered dreams to have a prospective function as well as a *compensatory* one; in interpreting them he used the method of *amplification.*

10. Jung's word-association test was the forerunner of projective techniques. The MBTI was developed to implement Jung's typology and is widely used in a variety of settings.

11. Although Jung's concepts were based on empirical data, he raised philosophical questions and suggested philosophical answers. His theory may therefore be seen as largely philosophical.

## Suggestions for Further Reading

Carl Jung was a voluminous writer. His *Collected Works* have been published in this country by Princeton University Press, beginning in 1953. Statements about his theory are scattered throughout these works, but Volumes 7, 8, and 9 present the major features. Because Jung is a difficult writer to follow, the lay person would be best advised to begin with books that are more directed to the general public. *Man and His Symbols* (Doubleday, 1964) is probably the best introduction to Jungian psychology. It was written by Jung and several of his disciples. Jung's autobiography, describing the spiritual journey that led to his position, is *Memories,*

*Dreams, and Reflections* (Random House, 1961). A statement of the major principles of analytic psychology as well as the theory of types and functions is included in *Psychological Types* (Harcourt, Brace, 1933a). Several of Jung's lectures were also collected in a basic introduction entitled *Modern Man in Search of a Soul* (Harcourt, Brace, 1933b).

Also recommended are the *Freud/Jung Letters* (Princeton University Press, 1974). The best secondary sources introducing Jung's ideas are F. Fordham, *An Introduction to Jung's Psychology* (Penguin, 1953); J. Jacobi, *The Psychology of C. G. Jung* (Routledge and Kegan Paul, 1942); I. Progoff, *Jung's Psychology and Its Social Meaning* (Grove, 1953); J. Singer, *Boundaries of the Soul* (Doubleday, 1973); and C. S. Hall and V. J. Nordby, *A Primer of Jungian Psychology* (Mentor, 1973). More recent reevaluations of Jung's work are J. Clarke, *In Search of Jung: Historical and Philosophical Enquiries* (Routledge, 1992) and P. Young-Eisendrath and J. A. Hall, *Jung's Self Psychology: A Constructivist Perspective* (Guilford Press, 1991). C. Downing has recently edited *Mirrors of the Self: Archetypal Images that Shape Your Life* (Jeremy P. Tarcher, Inc., 1991), in which several prominent psychologists show readers how to identify those archetypes and tap into their power.

# Individual Psychology

## ALFRED ADLER

## *Your Goals for This Chapter*

1. Explain the difference between an *intrapsychic* and an *interpsychic* emphasis in personality theorizing.
2. Define what is meant by *social interest* and explain why it must be cultivated.
3. Explain what Adler meant by *finalism* and describe some *fictional finalisms*.
4. Identify the ultimate goal of the psyche.
5. Describe how *inferiority feelings* shape one's personality.
6. Tell what is meant by an individual's *style of life*, distinguish four primary types of style, and describe how *family constellation* and *family atmosphere* may shape it.
7. Discuss Adler's concept of the *creative self* and show how it restores consciousness to the center of personality.
8. Describe some of the major features of Adlerian psychotherapy, assessment, and research.
9. Evaluate Adler's theory in terms of its function as philosophy, science, and art.

A lfred Adler chose the term **individual psychology** for his conception of personality because he was interested in investigating the uniqueness of the person. He maintained that the individual was indivisible and must be studied as a whole. His emphasis shifted from a stress on **intrapsychic** ("within the psyche") phenomena such as Freud and Jung dealt with to an appreciation of **interpsychic** ("interpersonal") relations. Adler's theory holds that understanding a particular individual entails comprehending his or her attitude in relation to the world. Thus, for Adler, the human person emerged as a social and cultural creature rather than a sexual creature. According to Adler, we are motivated by social interests and our primary life problems are social ones.

## Biographical Background

Alfred Adler, second of six children born to a successful merchant, was born in 1870 and reared in a suburb of Vienna. He described his childhood as difficult and unhappy. He suffered from rickets, a deficiency disease of childhood that affected the bones and made him clumsy and awkward. Initially, his parents pampered him, but when his younger brother was born he sensed that his mother transferred her attention to him. He felt dethroned and turned to his father, who favored him and expected great things from him.

When he was three, he saw his younger brother die in the next bed. Twice during his early childhood Adler was run over in the streets. He began to be afraid of death, and his fear was further increased by a bout of pneumonia at the age of four. Later, he traced his interest in becoming a doctor to that near-fatal illness.

At school he was an average student. At one point his teacher suggested that his father take him out of school and apprentice him to a shoemaker. Nevertheless, he rose to a superior position in school, especially in mathematics, which he originally had had the greatest difficulty in mastering. In spite of his physical handicaps, he developed courage, social interest, and a feeling of being accepted in his play with other children. His interest and joy in the company of others remained throughout his life.

His weak physique and feelings of inferiority during childhood were later to find expression in his concepts of organic inferiority and the striving for superiority. His sensitivity about being the second son was reflected in his interest in the family constellation and ordinal position of birth. His efforts to get along with others found expression in his conviction that the human being is a social and cultural animal and in the Adlerian concept of social interest.

Adler studied medicine at the University of Vienna, where Freud had received his medical training. Although he trained as an eye specialist, he became a general practitioner and later established himself as a practicing neurologist and psychiatrist. In 1902 he was invited by Freud to join a group for weekly discussions on psychoanalysis. This group eventually grew into the Vienna Psychoanalytic Society, of which Adler was the first president, and later became the International Psychoanalytic Association.

*With Alfred Adler, the emphasis shifted from intrapsychic to interpsychic phenomena. The human person emerged as a social and cultural creature rather than a sexual one.*

There are many stories concerning Adler's association with Freud and their subsequent split. Adler was never a student of Freud nor was he ever psychoanalyzed. He joined the discussions because he was interested in psychoanalysis, but from the beginning he discovered points of disagreement. By 1911 these differences appeared crucial. Adler was invited to state his position to the society, and he did, but his views were denounced, he resigned, and about one-third of the members left with him. The relationship between Adler and Freud has been further clarified by Fiebert (1997).

Adler founded his own group and attracted many followers. He served in the Austrian army during World War I. Afterward he assisted the government in establishing child guidance clinics in Vienna. Although he and Freud both practiced in Vienna during the 1920s and early 1930s, they did not associate with each other.

Adler visited the United States frequently and came here to live in 1935. He continued his private practice, accepted a position as professor of medical psychology at the Long Island College of Medicine, and lectured widely. He died suddenly in 1937 of a heart attack while on a lecture tour in Scotland; he was sixty-seven.

## Social Interest

A leading concept of Adler's individual psychology is his emphasis on the importance of human culture and society. Human society is crucial not simply for the development of an individual personality, but also for the orientation of each and every behavior and emotion in a person's life.

Human beings, like all living creatures, are driven by certain innate instincts, drives, or needs. All living organisms feel an impulse to maintain life, which causes them to seek nourishment. They have a compulsion to reproduce, which finds its expression in sex. Although much of the behavior of lower animals appears to be regulated by instincts, this is not true of human behavior. Human beings have tamed their instincts and subordinated them to their attitudes toward the environment. At times, human beings deny or disobey their natural instincts because of their social relations. A prisoner may die rather than betray her country. A young child may refuse food if he believes that such a tactic gives him an advantage in a power struggle with his parents.

This shaping of instinctual expression in terms of one's attitude toward the environment suggests that underlying all other instincts and needs is the innate characteristic of social interest (1939). **Social interest** refers to that urge in human nature to adapt oneself to the conditions of the social environment. Social interest expresses itself subjectively in one's consciousness of having something in common with other people and of being one of them. It expresses itself objectively in cooperation with others toward the betterment of human society. This innate social characteristic, while common to all, does not automatically emerge, nor does it invariably find constructive expression. It must be nurtured and cultivated if young children are to achieve adequate fulfillment of the complex demands of society and work toward its perfection (Lewis, 1991).

## Finalism

The personality and characteristics of an individual are developed by the attitudes that she or he adopts toward the social environment in early childhood. This occurs through the goal-oriented activity of the human psyche. Adler stressed the fact that the movement of all living things is governed by goals. We cannot think, feel, will, or act, except with the perception of some goal (1927). To try to understand human behavior in terms of external causes is to fail to understand psychic phenomena. If I know a person's goal, I begin to understand in a general way the individual's behavior.

When an individual behaves in a certain way we naturally ask why. Past efforts to answer that question had emphasized material and mechanical explanations. Freud maintained that it is not enough to look for physiological causes; we must also try to understand the psychological motives underlying behavioral events. However, Freud was misled by the principle of causality into regarding these motives as past and looking to the past for the explanation of all human behavior. Adler emphasized the purposefulness of human behavior by recognizing that the motivational force of every human action is the goal or future orientation of that action. This means that for Adler the human psyche is teleologically oriented. You will recall from our discussion of Jung that the term "telos" means a purpose or goal. Adler agreed with Jung that teleology is necessary for a full understanding of personality. For Adler, the goal that the individual pursues is the decisive factor and he called this concept of goal orientation the principle of **finalism** (1930).

Adler suggested that many of our guiding goals are fictions. His use of the term "fiction" may be puzzling. Adler did not equate fiction with falseness; rather he indicated that we cannot know whether or not our goals are true or false because there is no way to scientifically test them. "Fiction" comes from the Latin root *fictio,* which means "to invent," "fashion," or "construct." We are unable to have a complete understanding of things as they really are, so we structure our own idea of reality. "Fictions" are an individual's or group's interpretations of the events of the world. They are philosophical assumptions. We may assume that it is best to tell the truth, that all people are basically good, or that hard work will eventually pay off. In Adlerian vocabulary, such basic concepts are **fictional finalisms.** Adler was indebted to an earlier philosopher, Hans Vaihinger, for his concept of fictional finalisms (see Rieken, 1996). Vaihinger wrote a book, *The Philosophy of "As-if,"* in which he suggested that people create ideas that guide their behavior. Under the influence of a fiction, people behave "as if" their goals were true. If people believe that it is to their best advantage to be honest, they will strive to be so, even though there is no way in which they can ultimately test that belief as a hypothesis. It is important to note that psychologists also often pose fictional finalisms in their discussion of the good life. Concepts such as the "healthy personality" and "self-realization" function as fictional finalisms and cannot be empirically tested.

A fiction may be healthy or unhealthy. Adler maintained that it is inappropriate to judge a fiction as true or false, right or wrong; rather, the goal should be judged according to its usefulness. (Adler's concept of the **usefulness** of fictional finalisms should not be confused with the concept of usefulness in reference to scientific hypotheses, which was discussed in the introductory chapter. The scientific hypothesis is useful if it can generate predictions about experiences that we might observe.) Belief in a deity and the desire to serve it have proved to be a valuable fiction for many individuals. For others, however, belief in God and the desire to please God have had deleterious effects. Whether or not God really exists is beside the point; the point is that belief in God has a demonstrable effect, positive or negative, on the behavior and life of an individual. Healthy individuals continually examine the effectiveness of their fictions and alter their goals when they are no longer useful. They maintain their fictions in a state of flux in order to meet the demands of reality.

## Striving for Superiority

Adler suggested that the psyche has as its primary objective the **goal of superiority.** This is the ultimate fictional finalism for which all human beings strive, and it gives unity and coherence to the personality. Initially, Adler conceived of the primary motivating force as aggression. Later, he identified the primary drive as a "will to power." Then, he refined the concept of a drive toward power and suggested that the essential dynamic of human nature lies in its striving for superiority (1930). Finally, he changed from striving for individual superiority to striving for a superior society.

Adler's concept of the striving for superiority does not entail the everyday meaning of the word "superiority." He did not mean what we innately seek to surpass one another in rank or position, nor did he mean that we seek to maintain an attitude of exaggerated importance over our peers. Rather, the drive for superiority involves the desire to be competent and effective in whatever one strives to do. The concept is similar to Jung's idea of self-realization. Adler frequently used the term *perfection* as a synonym for the word "superiority." This term can also be misleading unless we recognize its origin in the Latin *perfectus,* which means "completed" or "made whole."

The striving for superiority may take the form of an exaggerated lust for power. An individual may seek to exercise control over objects and people and to play God. The goal may introduce a hostile tendency into our lives, in which we play games of "dog eat dog." But such expressions of the goal for superiority are abortive and do not reflect its constructive nature.

The striving for superiority is innate and part of the struggle for survival that human beings share with other species in the process of evolution. According to Adler, life is not motivated by the need to reduce tension or restore equilibrium, as Freud tended to think; instead, life is encouraged by the desire to move from below to above, from minus to plus, from inferior to superior. This movement entails adapting oneself to and mastering the environment. The particular ways in which individuals undertake this quest are determined by their culture, their own unique history, and style of life.

## Inferiority Feelings

The striving for superiority arises because as human beings we feel inferior. **Inferiority feelings** have their origin in our encounter as infants with the environment. As human infants, unlike other animals, we are born immature, incomplete, and incompetent to satisfy even our basic needs. There is a protracted period during which we are almost totally dependent on other people for our survival. Feelings of inferiority thus reflect a fact of existence. Such feelings are inescapable, but also invaluable, as they provide the major motivating force that leads to growth. Our efforts and success at growth and development may be seen as attempts to compensate for and overcome our imagined or real inferiorities and weaknesses. Thus, feelings of inferiority are not deviant but are the basis for all forms of human accomplishment and improvement in life (1927).

The concept of human nature as driven by feelings of inferiority first came to Adler during his practice of general medicine. He observed that many of his patients localized their complaints in specific body organs. He hypothesized that in many cases an individual is born with a potentially weak organ that may not respond adequately to external demands (1917). This "organ inferiority" can have profound effects on both the body and the psyche. It may have a harmful effect and lead to neurotic disorders, but it can also be compensated for and lead to optimal achievements. A classic historical example of compensation is found in the story of the ancient Greek, Demosthenes, who suffered as a child from a speech impediment. He learned to overcome his stuttering and became a great orator by forcing himself to shout in front of the ocean with pebbles in his mouth. Later, Adler broadened the concept of organ inferiority to include any feelings of inferiority, whether actual or imagined.

In his early writings, Adler termed the compensation for one's inferiorities the **masculine protest.** At the time, he associated inferiority with femininity. This concept finds common expression in references to "the weaker" or "the stronger" sex. Adler himself soon became dissatisfied with this shortsighted view. Women and men are different biologically, but neither sex is inferior. Later, Adler emphasized that inferiority is a condition of existence that affects males and females alike. In that sense, Adler became an early proponent of women's liberation. Basically, he recognized that the alleged inferiority of women was a cultural assignment rather than a biological one.

Adler's views were no doubt fostered by his marriage to Raissa Epstein, a member of the intelligentsia, who expected equality between them and helped him to overcome his earlier concepts of male dominance. Adler came to appreciate fully the role that culture and society has played in perpetuating male dominance and privilege. Indeed, he went so far as to suggest that psychological differences between women and men are entirely the result of cultural attitudes. Adler pointed out the devastating effect of these attitudes on the lives of children and the development of their self-confidence. He described how such biases disturb the psychological development of women and have led some of them to a pervasive dissatisfaction with their role. The "excessive pre-eminence of manliness" in our culture leads women into unhealthy forms of compensation or resignation and encourages men to unwisely depreciate and flee from women (Ansbacher & Ansbacher, 1956). Adler felt that exaggerated masculinity has a negative impact on men and women alike. He recommended the cultivation of comradeship and education for cooperation between the sexes. His ideas are confirmed today by research on sex roles and the influence of education.

## Style of Life

Each individual seeks to cope with the environment and develop superiority in a unique way. This principle is embodied in Adler's concept of the **style of life,** which was a primary theme in his later writings (1929a, 1931). Each of us shares the common goal of striving for superiority, even though there are many different ways by which we may achieve this goal. One individual may try to develop competence and superiority through intellectual skills. Another may seek self-perfection by capitalizing on physical strengths. Style of life acts in part as a perceptual filter, influencing the ways in which we view the world. These different life-styles develop early in childhood. Adler suggested that the life-style is pretty clearly established by the time a child is five years old. Thereafter it remains relatively constant. It can be changed, but only through hard work and self-examination.

The style of life results from a combination of two factors: the inner goal orientation of the individual with its particular fictional finalisms and the forces of the environment that assist, impede, or alter the direction of the individual. Each individual's style of life is unique because of the different influences of our inner self and its constructs. Adler suggested that no two individuals ever had or could have the very same style of life. Even identical twins respond to their environment in different ways.

Nevertheless, Adler (1927) felt that he could distinguish four primary types of style, three of which he termed "mistaken styles." These include *the ruling type:* aggressive, dominating people who have little social interest or cultural perception; *the getting type:* dependent people who take rather than give; and *the avoiding type:* people who try to escape life's problems and engage in little socially constructive activity. The fourth primary life-style Adler termed *the socially useful type:* people with a great deal of social interest and activity.

## Birth Order

Among the factors that lead to different life-styles are the ordinal position of birth and different experiences in childhood. Adler did not postulate any stages of development as Freud did, but he emphasized the importance of the atmosphere of the family and the family constellation. **Family constellation** refers to one's position within the family in terms of birth order among siblings and the presence or absence of parents and other caregivers. Adler hypothesized that the personalities of oldest, middle, and youngest children in a family are apt to be quite dissimilar simply by virtue of the different experiences that each child has as that particular member of the family group.

Oldest children tend to be more intelligent, achievement oriented, conforming, and affiliative. They often try to regain the glory that was theirs before they were dethroned by younger siblings. Thus, they are frequently oriented toward the past and show a high degree of concern with power, which may express itself as a desire to exercise authority, lead, or protect and help others. Adler described Freud as a "typical eldest son."

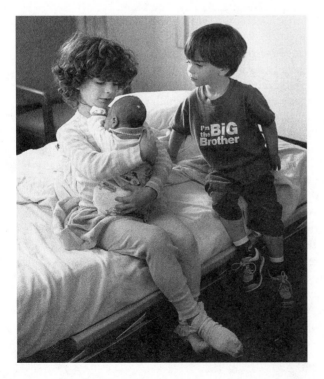

Adler suggested that the personalities of oldest, middle, and youngest child in a family often differ greatly. The first born tend to assume a nurturing and leadership role. The lastborn child risks remaining the "baby" of the family. The middle child often seems confused as to his place in the family.

# Birth Order and Personality

Read through the following lists and check those items that apply to you in comparison with your brothers and sisters. If you are an only child, check those items that apply to you in comparison with your peers.

*List A*
You tend to
  1. be more conforming
  2. be less hostile
  3. have more motivation
  4. be a better student
  5. achieve more recognition
  6. assume more leadership roles
  7. be closer to your parents
  8. like nurturing professions
  9. consult others when making a decision
  10. be less aggressive
  11. associate more with others
  12. receive high expectations from your parents
  13. have similar values to your parents
  14. seek help or nurturance from others
  15. be more anxious
  16. have more worries
  Total _____

*List B*
You tend to
  1. be more aggressive
  2. be more democratic
  3. be more independent
  4. be more popular
  5. value parents' opinions less
  6. like solitary professions
  7. fight, "get into trouble" more
  8. be a better mixer
  9. like more dangerous activities
  10. be less verbal
  11. be less likely to seek help from others
  12. be less conforming
  13. "slide by" more
  14. have been brought up less strictly by your parents
  15. be more of a "loner"
  16. have been given less attention by your parents
  Total _____

Add up your totals in each list. If you are an only or a firstborn child, the research indicates that more of the items on List A will apply to you. If you are a laterborn (but not the youngest in a large family), more of the items on List B will apply. If you are the youngest child in a large family, your pattern will be closer to that of a firstborn. If you are a middle child, you will show a combination of the characteristics of both lists. How do your findings compare with the research predictions? Can you think of other factors in your family constellation that have helped to shape your personality? Today, many students live in families other than the traditional nuclear family. They may live with a single parent or have stepparents and step- or half siblings. How might these constellations further influence personality?

The second child may feel the need to accelerate and catch up with the first child. While oldest children often dream of falling from places (dethronement), second children often dream of running to catch things. Second children are apt to be competitive and ambitious and often surpass the firstborn in achievement and motivation. However, they are not as concerned with power. Adler was a second child.

Lastborn children are more sociable and dependent, having been the "baby" of the family. At the same time they may also strive for excellence and superiority in an effort to surpass their older siblings. Adler pointed out that many fairy tales, myths, and legends (for example, the biblical story of Joseph) describe the youngest child as surpassing his or her older rivals. (It was Adler who fully developed the concept of *sibling rivalry,* in which the children within a family compete with one another.) The lastborn child who is spoiled and pampered may continue a helpless and dependent style of life into adulthood.

Only children tend to be more like older children in that they enjoy being the center of attention. Because they spend more time in the company of adults, rather than siblings, they tend to mature sooner and to adopt adultlike behaviors earlier in life. However, only children are also the most likely to be pampered, in which case, Adler wrote, "the only child has difficulties with every independent activity and sooner or later they become useless in life" (Lieberman, Shaffer, & Reynolds, 1985). Adler considered pampering the "greatest curse of childhood."

Middle children show a combination of the characteristics of oldest and youngest. If children are spaced several years apart, they have more of the characteristics of only children. The family constellation becomes further complicated when one considers all the additional possibilities such as the only brother among sisters, twins, and so forth. In recent years a considerable amount of research has been done in the area of birth order and family constellation. One of the interesting findings suggests that longer marriages may occur among partners whose birth orders are complementary. Thus, an oldest brother of sisters will probably be happier with a younger sister to a brother than with an only child, because each of them is used to that familial pattern and mode of relating.

## Family Atmosphere

The quality of emotional relationships among members of the family reflects the **family atmosphere,** which assists in determining whether or not the child will react actively or passively, constructively or destructively, in the quest toward superiority. Adler thought children who are pampered or neglected are particularly predisposed to a faulty style of life. The pampered child is one who is excessively spoiled and protected from life's inevitable frustrations. Such a child is being deprived of the right to become independent and learn the requirements of living within a social order. Parents who pamper a child make it difficult for the child to develop social feelings and become a useful member of society and culture. The child grows to dislike order and develops a hostile attitude toward it. The neglected child is one who feels unwanted and rejected. Such a child is virtually denied the right to a place in the social order. Rejection arouses resistance in the child, feelings of inferiority, and a tendency to withdraw from the implications of social life. Adler pointed out that child-rearing practices frequently consist of a continuing alternation between indulgence and rejection. The pampered child often demands undue attention and regard, which eventually leads to parental anger and punishment that are often interpreted by the child as rejection. Though few parents actually reject their children, many children feel humiliated and defeated.

Although parental "rejection" is overcome when parents learn alternative ways of handling their children that avoid pampering or neglect, Adler stressed that the individual is fully responsible for the meaning attached to parental behavior and action. Many of us harbor deep feelings of having been rejected by our parents when they actually gave us their best efforts. Thus, in the end, only the person can assume responsibility for his or her style of life.

## The Creative Self

Adler considered the concept of **creative self** the climax of his theory (1964). It is the self in its creative aspects that interprets and makes meaningful the experiences of the organism and that searches for experiences to fulfill the person's unique style of life. In other words, the creative self establishes, maintains, and pursues the goals of the individual. Adler's concept of the creative self underscored his belief that human nature is essentially active, creative, and purposeful in shaping its response to the environment.

The concept of the creative self also reinforces Adler's affirmation that individuals make their own personalities from the raw materials of their heredity and environment. In his concept of the creative self, Adler restored consciousness to the center of personality. Adler believed that we are aware of everything we do and that, through self-examination, we can understand why we behaved in a certain way. The forces of which we are unaware are simply unnoticed; they are not buried in a sea of repression.

Adler's position regarding consciousness was in such direct contrast to that of Freud that it is no wonder the two could not work together. Adler did not deny unconscious forces, but he minimized them by reducing unconsciousness to simple temporary unawareness. He opposed Freud's determinism by emphasizing the vast extent to which people can achieve conscious control over their behavior. People, Adler argued, may become largely aware of their deepest impulses and fictional finalisms, and with conscious intent create their own personalities and life-styles that will achieve their highest goals. In the end, Adler's position was almost the complete opposite of Freud's, which emphasized that our behavior is largely determined by forces of which we are unaware. Freud offered his followers the hope of being able to endure or live without crippling fear of one's unconscious conflicts, but he never offered freedom from them. By restoring consciousness to the center of personality, by again crowning the king Freud had struggled so valiantly to dethrone, Adler aroused Freud's anger. To Freud, Adler was encouraging the very illusion that Freud had sought to destroy.

For many people, Adler's optimistic view provides a welcome contrast to the pessimistic and conflict-ridden picture of human nature shown in Freudian psychoanalysis and reinstates hope to the human condition. In his optimism, Adler foreshadowed the humanistic school of personality, which will be discussed in Chapter 13; in his emphasis on the creative self as organizing behavior and emotions, he foreshadowed the cognitive-behavioral theorists to be discussed in Chapter 16.

## Adlerian Psychotherapy

Neuroses, according to Adler (1929b), entail unrealistic life goals or fictional finalisms. Goals are not realistic unless they take into account our capacities, limitations, and social environment. A person who felt extremely inferior or rejected as a child may set goals that are too high and unattainable. A person of average intelligence cannot expect to perform at a consistently outstanding level in academic work. Some individuals adopt goals that are unrealistically low. Having felt defeated and unable to cope with certain situations, such as school, people may seek to avoid situations in which they could develop and perfect those skills that would enable them to perform effectively.

Neurotics also choose inappropriate life-styles as a means of attaining their goals. In their efforts to offset feelings of weakness, neurotics tend to overcompensate. **Compensation** entails making up for or overcoming a weakness. For example, blind people learn to depend more on auditory senses. **Overcompensation** refers to an exaggerated effort to cover up a weakness that entails a denial rather than an acceptance of the real situation (1954). The bully who persists in using force may be overcompensating for a difficulty in working cooperatively with others.

Adler's terms "inferiority complex" and "superiority complex," phrases that have become commonplace in our vocabulary, also describe neurotic patterns. Individuals who feel highly inadequate may be suffering from an **inferiority complex.** In Adlerian terms, there is a gulf between the real person and excessively high life goals. Individuals who exaggerate their own importance may be suffering from a **superiority complex.** In Adlerian terms, such individuals have overcompensated for feelings of weakness. Both complexes originate in a person's responses to real or imagined feelings of inferiority.

Adler suggested that neurotics actually live a **mistaken style of life,** or *life lie.* Neurotics strive for personal aggrandizement. Their style of life belies their actual capacities and strengths. They act "as if" they were weak, "as if" they were doomed to be losers, when in fact they could create a constructive existence for themselves. They capitalize on imagined or real weaknesses and use them as an excuse rather than a challenge to deal constructively with life. They employ **safeguarding tendencies,** compensatory devices that ward off feelings of inferiority in a maladaptive rather than adaptive fashion. To be sure, we all use such protective defense mechanisms at times, but neurotics employ them in an exaggerated manner and degree.

Adlerian therapy aims at restoring the patient's sense of reality, examining and disclosing the errors in goals and life-style, and cultivating social interest. Adlerian analysis does not usually differentiate between counseling and psychotherapy (Wengler, 1995). Adler did not establish strict rules or methods for treatment; he believed that the patient's life-style should determine the procedure. On the whole, Adler's approach was somewhat more informal than Freud's. He abandoned the use of the couch, suggested that the patient sit facing the therapist, and reduced the frequency of contact between patient and doctor to once or twice a week.

The first goal of the Adlerian therapist is to establish contact with and win the confidence of the patient (1929b). Such confidence is won by approaching the patient as a peer, rather than an authority, and thereby soliciting cooperation. Whereas Freud viewed the transference, in which a patient works through earlier unsatisfactory relations by projecting them onto the doctor, as essential to the effectiveness of treatment, Adler suggested that therapy is effective because healthy features of the physician-patient relationship are transferred, or carried over, into the patient's life. Such transference need not have regressive features and is really another name for the cultivation of social interest.

Second, the therapist seeks to disclose the errors in the patient's life-style and provide insight into the present condition. The patient is led gently and gradually to recognize the errors in personal goals, life-style, and attitude toward life.

Adlerian therapy seeks to encourage the patient to face present problems and to develop constructive means of dealing with them. The therapist hopes to instill (or promote) the courage to act "as if" the old limiting fictions and mistaken life-styles weren't true. The therapist who does not make decisions or assume responsibilities for the patient may structure or suggest situations that will assist in cultivating the patient's own skills. Such deliberate attempts at encouragement enable the patient to become more courageous and to accept new tasks and responsibilities. In this sense, the therapist plays the role of an educator who reeducates the neurotic in the art of constructive living. Additionally, Adler sought to minimize latent feelings of rejection and resentment and to cultivate feelings of social interest and good will. Adler believed that only by subordinating our private gain to public welfare can we attain true superiority. The true and inevitable compensation for all the natural weaknesses of individual human beings is that of social justice for all.

Adler had a tremendous influence on psychiatrist Harry Stack Sullivan, who developed the very important concept of *participant observation,* referring to the fact that an observer of an interpersonal relationship is also a participant in it. Sullivan also coined one of today's latest buzzwords—*codependence*—which is used frequently in Al-Anon, an organization for relatives of alcoholics, to refer to individuals who, usually unwittingly, help the alcoholic remain dependent on alcohol.

Many of Adler's concepts have been used to develop more effective methods of child rearing and education (Bitter, 1991; Dreikurs & Soltz, 1964). Adler would most definitely encourage prospective parents to engage in parental training, and his work is reflected in such programs (e.g., Dinkmeyer & McKay, 1976). As creative selves, we construct the primary forces that shape our existence: our goals and life-styles. We can change these, should they become inappropriate, through insight into our errors. Through education, Adler believed, our innate and shared concept of social interest and justice could be made to flower and to provide the final and most appropriate form of compensation for our individual weaknesses. Adler was active in child guidance clinics and involved in penal reform. He was attracted to the political movement of socialism and many hours of his later years were devoted to specifying ways of educating for social justice. Adler "was radically opposed to the kind of therapy which overemphasized independence and egocentricity" (May, 1991).

## A License to Parent?

Some of Adler's concepts have been used to develop programs for more effective parenting, such as STEP: *Systematic Training for Effective Parenting* (Dinkmeyer & McKay, 1976). Such efforts raise the question of whether specific instruction and education should be required for prospective parents. Our society requires that its members obtain special training and earn credentials before they are permitted to engage in several significant activities, such as practicing medicine or law, doing electrical work or plumbing, or driving a car or a motor-cycle. Parenting is undoubtedly one of the most important jobs that any of us may be called upon to do. However, virtually anyone who is biologically capable of reproducing is permitted in our society to become a parent without any prerequisites or demonstration of adequacy to the task of parenting.

Should we require a license for engaging in the activity of parenting? After all, we now have the technology to easily prevent or terminate unwanted pregnancies. Or we could extend our programs of placing in foster care children whose parents are deemed unfit for parenting. If credentialing procedures were established, what should the prerequisites be? Should a prospective parent have the equivalent of a high school education, a certain amount of financial resources, specific courses in parenting? What other requirements would you suggest?

Questions such as these are likely to generate strong opinions. Why do they evoke such a reaction? What would be the objections and problems to implementing requirements for parenting? Where do you believe Adler would stand on these issues?

## Assessment and Research in Adler's Theory

Adler's theory, like that of many others, stemmed from clinical observations. Like Freud, Adler paid close attention to patients' nonverbal behavior as well as to what they said. He noted how they stood, walked, sat, or shook hands. He believed that nonverbal communication or behavior is indicative of a person's life-style. Adler himself conducted little systematic empirical research to validate his ideas. Instead, he viewed the importance of these data in terms of their relevance as clinical observations. Adler referred to the study of birth order, early memories, and dreams as the "three entrance gates to mental life"; these three tools constituted Adler's primary techniques of assessment.

Many early researchers attempted to test Adler's birth-order theory. Not all of the research supports Adler's findings, but his theory was valuable in stimulating further thought and research.

Zajonc and Markus (1975) believe firstborns are more intelligent and theorize that is because the intellectual climate of a family decreases as the number of children increases. This has led to a rather blustery argument with Steelman (1985, 1986), who says the educational, occupational, and income levels of the parents were not adequately controlled in the studies specified by Zajonc and Markus and could have been the primary reason (see also Zajonc, 1986).

Modern research has illustrated relationships between birth order and factors such as vocational preferences (Bryant, 1987); achievement motivation (Shell, Hargrove, & Falbo, 1986); divergent thinking (Runco & Bahleda, 1987); Machiavellianism (Gupta, 1987); introversion and extraversion (Klein, 1984); self-esteem (Kidwell, 1982); humanitarian concerns (Lieberman, Shaffer, & Reynolds, 1985); fear of success (Ishiyama, Munson, & Chabassol, 1990); health (Elliot, 1992), and perception of parental favoritism (Kiracofe & Kiracofe, 1990). Some studies discover that gender may make a difference as well on factors such as psychological health (Fullerton, Ursano, Harry, & Slusarcick, 1989; Lester, Eleftheriou, & Peterson, 1992), narcissism (Narayan, 1990), perceptions of responsibility and dominance (Harris & Morrow, 1992), and toughmindedness (Singh, 1990). Eisenman (1992) discusses causes of some of these differences in terms of parental anxieties and available time for children of different birth orders.

Noting the contradictory findings of birth order research to date, Sulloway (1996) maintains that methodological problems and an inadequate theoretical perspective have contributed to confusion rather than clarification. He draws on the work of Darwin and evolutionary science to further Adler's interest in birth order and family dynamics. Sulloway maintains that family structure in terms of sibling differences creates a set of niches that provides offspring with separate outlooks. Indeed, most individual personality differences originate from within the family, as siblings develop strategies to compete for scarce parental resources. Birth order is a crucial factor. Sulloway's most significant finding is that whereas oldest children tend to identify with their parents and authority and to sustain the status quo, younger children tend to rebel. Moreover, the repercussions of sibling rivalry extend beyond individual development to society as a whole.

Research about life-style is limited, but research in early memories, birth order, and social interest continues. Adler believed that early memories frequently summarized the essential characteristics of one's stance toward life. For example, Adler observed from a study of over one hundred physicians that their first memories often entailed the recollection of an illness or death. In the course of successful therapy, Adler also discovered that patients frequently recall previously overlooked memories that are more consistent with their new life-styles. Reichlin and Niederehe (1980) conducted research that confirms Adler's belief that early memories reflect personality traits. New research on memory, which ties it to the development of language and the ability to shape events into a story, seemingly challenges Freud's theory of infantile amnesia and may support Adler's view that our earliest memories are full of symbolic meanings (Goleman, 1993b).

In Adler's theory, dreams are goal oriented rather than reflections of the past. They reveal the mood that we want to feel and suggest how we might deal with a future problem or task. Taking note of the options we choose to follow in our dream life gives us further insight into our style of life (see Lombardi & Elcock, 1997). Research by Greisers, Greenberg, and Harrison (1972) provided evidence that dreaming may assist individuals in dealing with ego-threatening situations and their analysis may suggest alternative options.

Adler preferred the use of clinical observations rather than psychological tests in the assessment of personality (Rattner, 1983). However, a Social Interest Index (SII) and a

Social Interest Scale (SIS) have been developed by other psychologists to measure Adler's concept of social interest and test related hypotheses. A Social Interest Index has been cross-validated as a valid empirical measure of social interest (Hjelle, 1991). Measurements of inferiority need to be developed. Most available today focus on the self-concept (Dixon & Strano, 1989). Thus Adler's theory has been helpful in generating additional assessment tools.

| PHILOSOPHY, | # Adler's Theory |
| --- | --- |
| SCIENCE, | |
| AND ART | |

Adler's commitment to a philosophical viewpoint is clear in his discussion of fictional finalisms. Human beings, he asserted, are goal-oriented organisms, and all human behavior can be understood in terms of its contribution and adherence to a goal. Difficulties in living result from an inappropriate philosophy and the inappropriate style of life that accompanies it. By recognizing and cultivating the need for social justice, a person fulfills her or his ultimate potential.

Adler added *usefulness* to the criteria for judging philosophical assumptions: a philosophy is useful if it fosters productive living and enhances our lives. In doing so, he followed the pragmatic philosophy of William James (1842–1910), who argued that the meaning of a statement lies in the particular enriching consequences it has for our future experiences and the quality of our lives. Adler's emphasis on the importance of the usefulness of our goals has become very popular among psychologists and personality theorists.

Although Adler emphasized the factors in society that contribute to the shaping of personality, he did not adopt a radical environmentalist position and suggest that personality is *entirely* shaped by society. There are forces within the self, such as the drive for superiority and the creative self, that assist in shaping personality. Thus the individual plays an important, responsible role.

Adler was much more optimistic than Freud about human and societal potentialities. He saw human nature as flexible and changeable. The forward-moving tendency within the self, the drive for superiority, implies that many obstacles to growth are imposed by society rather than by human nature itself. However, through the creative self, human beings largely create their own personalities. Ultimately, Adler envisioned the possibility of creating a better society through the cultivation of our social interest. He stressed the application of personality theory through the art of psychotherapy, believing that through self-understanding and education we can construct a better world.

Critics, however, have found Adler optimistic and naive, suggesting that he may have exaggerated the potentialities of the creative self in being aware of and creating the personality that will best fulfill the individual's goals and the possibilities of change at any point in one's lifetime. Although initially Adler adhered to the notion of determinism, in

**PHILOSOPHICAL ASSUMPTIONS**

## *Examining Adler*

How would you rate Adler on each of the basic philosophical assumptions described in Chapter 1? Consult the chart on the inside front cover. Each basic issue is presented as a bipolar dimension along which a person's view can be placed according to the degree of agreement with one or the other extreme: *freedom/determinism, hereditary/environmental, uniqueness/universality, proactive/reactive, optimistic/pessimistic*. Rate Adler's views on these issues.

When you have determined where you think Adler stands, compare your responses with those of your classmates and your instructor. You should be willing to defend your ratings, but also be prepared to change them in light of others' compelling arguments. Afterward, compare your rating of Adler with your own position on each issue and with those of other theorists. Does this comparison help you to understand why his theory does or does not appeal to you?

the end he was a strong advocate of free will. At times, it appears that the creative self is exempt from or able to overcome causal laws, an idea that both Freudians and later behaviorists would have trouble with.

Adler's emphasis on the social forces that play a part in shaping personality influenced subsequent social psychoanalytic theorists like Karen Horney and Erich Fromm. Adler's optimistic constructs also influenced the humanistic school of thought in psychology (see Ansbacher, 1990). Moreover, many of Adler's concepts, particularly that of the creative self, are congruent with the contemporary cognitive emphasis in psychology. There is a whole new resurgence of Adler in the counseling and education communities (see Dinkmeyer, 1989). Institutes that offer training in Adlerian Individual Psychology have become more pervasive. They are present throughout the United States, Canada, and Western Europe, as well as in the Scandinavian peninsula, Israel, and Japan. Adlerian therapy is finding application in education, school systems, business, and counseling. Adlerian concepts have been used to explore corporate leadership (Miranda, Goodman, & Kern, 1996) and to generate new ways of working with traditional and alternative family constellations (Chandler, 1995). Acceptance of and respect for such variation contributes toward the achievement of Adler's goal of social equality (Chernin & Holdren, 1995).

Albert Ellis's system of rational-emotive therapy (1973), which holds that behaviors are a function of beliefs, draws on Adler's psychology as does the cognitive social learning theory of Julian Rotter, who studied with Adler in New York City. Thus, Adler's ideas and their application have spread even though they are sometimes not recognized as

Adlerian, possibly because Adler does not mesh with America's "intoxication with narcissism and the ego-centered self" (May, 1991).

Adler's concept of social interest is extremely significant cross-culturally. Both Christian and Buddhist concepts of religious maturity include ideas similar to Adler's social interest. Adler tried to bring understanding to a significant part of our heritage as individuals. The extreme convergence with major religions indicates he was successful (Leak, Gardner, & Pounds, 1992). Adler saw the individual as concerned not only with the self but with the entire world (Lazarsfeld, 1991). One of Adler's goals for his individual psychology was to demonstrate that it was "heir to all great movements whose aim is the welfare of mankind" (Weiss-Rosmarin, 1990). Evans and Meredith (1991) ponder whether Adlerian psychology was in advance of its time.

## Summary

1. Adler's *individual psychology* marks a shift from an emphasis on *intrapsychic* ("within the psyche") phenomena to an emphasis on *interpsychic* ("interpersonal") phenomena.

2. Adler believed that human beings have an innate urge to adapt themselves to the conditions of the environment. He named this urge *social interest* but stressed that it is not automatic and must be cultivated.

3. The principle of *finalism* means that individuals are oriented toward goals that guide their behavior. However, these individual interpretations of the world cannot be proven and are therefore called *fictional finalisms*. Adler suggested that they be judged by their *usefulness*.

4. The primary objective of the psyche is the *goal of superiority*, the desire to be competent and effective in what one does. This striving may take on the form of an exaggerated lust for power, if not properly directed.

5. As young children, we normally feel inferior, and these *inferiority feelings* lead us to seek ways in which we can compensate for our weaknesses.

6. Each individual develops a unique way of striving for superiority that is called a *style of life*. The four primary ones are *ruling, getting, avoiding,* and *socially useful*. The style of life is influenced by factors such as *family constellation* and *family atmosphere*.

7. Adler considered the concept of the *creative self* to be the climax of his theory. The creative self interprets the experiences of the organism and establishes a person's style of life. Adler's position was that the creative self is essentially conscious; he restored consciousness to the center of personality (in direct opposition to Freud's view).

8. Adlerian therapy aims at restoring the patient's sense of reality, examining and disclosing the errors in goals and style of life, and cultivating social interest. He believed the study of birth order, early memories, and dreams were the best tools for assessing personality.

9. Adler's theory emphasizes a philosophical point of view rather than an effort to study personality empirically. He also made substantial contributions to psychotherapy, education, and child rearing.

## Suggestions for Further Reading

Alfred Adler wrote a number of books and articles. Since his writings were often intended for a lay audience, they are relatively easy to understand. The classic introduction to Adlerian thought is *The Practice and Theory of Individual Psychology* (Harcourt, Brace, 1927). A shorter summary, "Individual Psychology," appears in C. Murchison (Ed.), *Psychologies of 1930* (Clark University Press, 1930). Selections of Adler's writings have also been edited and presented by H. L. and Rowena R. Ansbacher (Basic Books, 1956, 1964).

For biographical data and an assessment of Adler's contemporary influence, the reader is referred to H. Orgler, *Alfred Adler: The Man and His Work* (New American Library, 1973); H. Musak (Ed.), *Alfred Adler: His Influence on Psychology Today* (Noyes, 1973); M. Sperber, *Masks of Loneliness: Alfred Adler in Perspective* (Macmillan, 1974); H. L. Ansbacher, *Alfred Adler Revisited* (Praeger, 1984); and K. Leman, *The Birth Order Book* (Revell, 1985).

A compelling portrait of Adler has recently been provided by E. Hoffman, *The Drive for Self: Alfred Adler and the Founding of Individual Psychology* (Addison-Wesley, 1994a). F. Sulloway's *Born to Rebel: Birth Order, Family Dynamics, and Creative Lives* (Pantheon, 1996) has the potential to revolutionize our thinking concerning personality development within the context of the family.

# Psychoanalytic Social Psychology

## KAREN HORNEY ❖ ERICH FROMM

## Your Goals for This Chapter

1. Describe Horney's concept of *basic anxiety* and explain how it differs from Freud's concept of anxiety.

2. Explain how ten *neurotic needs* or *trends* can be summarized in terms of three ways of relating to others and three *basic orientations* toward life.

3. Distinguish between the *real self* and the *idealized self* and explain what is meant by the *tyranny of the should*.

4. Explain the relationship of the real self and the idealized self in normal, neurotic, and alienated individuals.

5. Compare and contrast Freud's and Horney's views of women.

6. Describe assessment and research in Horney's theory.

7. Identify what Fromm saw as our basic human condition and three common mechanisms of escape from it.

8. Explain how society shapes the fulfillment of our basic needs and leads to the development of character orientations.

9. Discuss assessment and research in Fromm's theory.

10. Evaluate Horney's and Fromm's theories in terms of their function as philosophy, science, and art.

A s we have seen, many of the theroists who followed Freud reacted against his emphasis on instincts, the view that the primary motivational forces of personality lie in instinctual drives. In particular, they criticized Freud for overemphasizing the importance of sexuality in personality formation. They acknowledged that in nineteenth- and early twentieth-century Vienna, where a strict Victorian ethos prevailed, it may well have been that many of Freud's patients expressed conflicts that clustered around guilt feelings in their sexual desires. Such conflicts appeared to be less frequent in other societies, where social and economic factors often seem to play a primary role. We have already seen a shift away from intrapsychic factors and toward interpsychic and social forces in Alfred Adler's theory.

Karen Horney and Erich Fromm emphasized the forces in society that influence personality. Horney stressed social forces that operate within the family; Fromm pointed beyond the family toward social factors within the society at large. Drawing on their own clinical experience, as well as on cultural, anthropological, and literary evidence, Horney and Fromm showed how Freud's concepts were a product of his social and cultural milieu. In turn, their own theories of personality were informed by the then emerging social sciences of sociology and anthropology, which stressed that personality is primarily a social product. They remained within the psychoanalytic framework, however, and conceived of themselves as rejuvenating psychoanalytic theory in the context of the newer sciences rather than as pioneering new theories. Their theories can be appreciated as part of the historical and social climate in which they emerged; moreover, many of the concepts they developed underlie contemporary views in psychoanalysis, and the tools they developed continue to be useful in clinical practice to this day.

# Karen Horney (1885–1952)

## Biographical Background

Karen Danielson Horney (pronounced "horn-eye") was born in 1885 near Hamburg, Germany, into an upper-middle-class family that was economically and socially secure. Her father was of Norwegian descent and her mother was Dutch. As a child, Horney sometimes traveled with her father, a sea captain. Although Horney admired her father, he was frequently stern and sullen. His intense gazes frightened her and he was often critical of her intelligence, interests, and appearance. Because of her father's long absences from home, Horney spent considerably more time with her mother, a younger, dynamic, freethinking woman who greatly influenced her daughter. Karen was devoted to her mother even though at times she felt that she favored her older brother. An experience with a kind doctor when she was twelve years old made her want to become a physician. Her adolescent diaries provide clues to her originality and independence in becoming the first to challenge Freud's ideas about women (Quinn, 1994). Mrs. Danielson encouraged her daughter to study med-

*Much of Karen Horney's work was groundbreaking for the emerging field of the psychology of women.*

icine at a time when it was unusual for women to enter that profession and in spite of rigid opposition from her husband. It was not the first time that the differences of temperament in Horney's parents led to discord. Eventually they separated and Horney's mother moved near Freiburg, where her daughter was pursuing her studies at the university. Later, Horney emphasized in her writings the role that a stressful environment plays in nurturing basic anxiety. Lack of love and encouragement, quarrelsome parents, and other stressful environmental factors lead to feelings of rejection, depression, worthlessness, and hostility. She acknowledged these feelings in herself and worked hard to overcome them.

Horney received her degree in medicine from the University of Berlin. Thereafter she was associated with the Berlin Psychoanalytic Institute. She was analyzed by Karl Abraham and Hans Sachs, loyal disciples of Freud, who were two of the foremost training analysts of the day.

In 1909 she married Oscar Horney, a Berlin lawyer. They had three daughters. As a result of their different interests and her increased involvement in the psychoanalytic movement, they were divorced in 1937. The challenges of being a career woman and a mother, and of dissolving a marriage that was no longer viable, gave her considerable insight into the problems of women. We will see that she was one of the first to oppose Freud and to speak directly to the issue of feminine psychology.

Horney spent most of her life in Berlin, but in 1932 she was invited to come to the United States and assume the position of associate director of the Chicago Psychoanalytic

Institute. Two years later, she moved to New York City, opened a private practice, and taught at the New York Psychoanalytic Institute. While in the United States, Horney met Erich Fromm; their liaison, which was both personal and professional, provoked feelings of bitterness and desire for revenge when it was over (Hoffman, 1994b).

Coming to America during the Great Depression, she began to appreciate more and more the role of environmental factors in neurosis. Her patients were not troubled primarily by sexual problems but with the struggle to keep a job and pay the bills. Economic, educational, occupational, and social pressures seemed to be foremost in inducing neurotic behavior. Although earlier she had had disagreements with the Freudian point of view, orthodox psychoanalysis with its stress on genetic and instinctual causes of behavior appeared increasingly one-sided. Eventually her dissatisfaction and the refusal of orthodox psychoanalysis to integrate or even acknowledge her ideas led her to leave the New York Psychoanalytic Society. In April 1941 she walked out singing "Go Down, Moses." Horney founded the Association for the Advancement of Psychoanalysis and the American Institute of Psychoanalysis and was dean of the Institute until her death, of cancer, in 1952.

Karen Horney concentrated on the neurotic aspects of behavior in order to help us understand why we behave as we do. She subscribed to much of Freud's work but sought to overcome what she perceived as his limitations by emphasizing social and cultural factors and minimizing biological ones. Her work provides us with a number of fascinating insights and provocative concepts that have received a lot of attention.

## Basic Anxiety

Horney suggested that anxiety is the basic human condition with which we have to deal. This idea is reminiscent of Freud's belief that anxiety is the basic condition into which we are thrust. But, unlike Freud, Horney did not see anxiety as an inevitable part of the human condition. She suggested that anxiety is created by social forces rather than by the human predicament itself.

As human beings, our essential challenge is to be able to relate effectively to other people. **Basic anxiety,** an insidiously increasing, all-pervading feeling of being lonely and helpless in a hostile world (1945), results from feelings of insecurity in these relations. According to Horney's concept of basic anxiety, the environment as a whole is dreaded because it is seen as unrealistic, dangerous, unappreciative, and unfair. Children are not simply afraid of their own inner impulses or of punishment because of their impulses, as Freud postulated in his concepts of neurotic and moral anxiety; they also feel at times that the environment itself is a threat to their development and innermost wishes. Children are dependent on their parents or caregivers for the satisfaction of many of their needs. Some parents and caregivers, however, are unable to meet children's needs satisfactorily. Horney called all of the negative factors in the environment that can provoke insecurity in a child **basic evil.** Some of these conditions might be domination, isolation, overprotection, hostility, indifference, inconsistent behavior, disparagement, parental discord, lack of respect and guidance, or the lack of encouragement and warmth. Children's fears may be objectively unrealistic, but for them they are real. In a hostile environment, children's ability to use their energies and develop self-esteem and reliance is, in fact, thwarted. Children may be rendered powerless in the face of these encroachments on their environment. Their biological dependency and the failure of parents to foster adaptive self-assertive behavior may leave them helpless. Although children may endure a certain amount of frustration and trauma, it is essential for healthy personality development that they feel safe and secure.

Some of the same concerns that occupied Horney led to the formulation of object relations theory (Ingram & Lerner, 1992). Horney's ideas on the importance of early interpersonal relationships are reflected in the writings of Heinz Kohut, whose theory is discussed in Chapter 7. Horney suggested (1939) that the emphasis on the Oedipus complex tends to detract from the significance of "early relationships *in their totality.*" This view forecasts Kohut's position that the Oedipus complex is a product of disintegration resulting from parental failure to respond with pride and empathy to the growth of their children (Quinn, 1994).

## Neurotic Needs or Trends

In the face of basic anxiety, children develop certain defense attitudes or strategies that permit them to cope with the world and afford a certain measure of gratification (1937). Many of these strategies continue into adulthood. Specifically, we use them to deal with or minimize feelings of anxiety and to assist us in effectively relating to others. Where they become exaggerated or inappropriate, these strivings may be referred to as **neurotic needs** or **trends.** Neurotic trends are the result of the formative experiences that create basic anxiety. The trends are not instinctual in nature but highly dependent on the individual's formative experiences of being either safe or insecure in the world.

Horney identified ten different neurotic needs or trends (see Table 5.1). What makes a need neurotic? For the neurotic, the need is too intense, too unrealistic, too indiscriminate, too anxiety laden. These trends lead to three types of coping strategies or primary modes of relating to other people: **moving toward** (compliance), **moving against** (hostility), and **moving away** (detachment). These types of behavior lead, in turn, to three **basic orientations** toward life: the **self-effacing solution,** an appeal to be loved; the **self-expansive solution,** an attempt at mastery; and the **resignation solution,** a desire to be free of others (1950). These orientations are interpersonal in nature, as opposed to the Freudian and Jungian character types, which are intrapsychic. Research on attachment patterns in infants suggests a distinct similarity between Horney's three basic orientations and young children's behavior.

Normal or mature individuals resolve their conflicts by integrating and balancing the three orientations, which are present in all human relations. They are able to express each mode at the appropriate time. Neurotics express one mode at the expense of other aspects of their personality. They actively, although unconsciously, repress tendencies to react according to the other orientations. This repression, however, is not successful; the repressed tendencies continue to seek expression and increase the neurotic's anxiety. As the neurotic continues to emphasize one need or mode and overlook the others, a "vicious circle" develops and the anxiety is never adequately resolved. Thus neurotics transform normal strivings into pathological ones. Table 5.1 summarizes the ten neurotic trends, three modes of relating to others, and three basic orientations toward life.

**TABLE 5.1    Horney's Ten Neurotic Trends**

| NEUROTIC TRENDS | PRIMARY MODES OF RELATING TO OTHERS | BASIC ORIENTATIONS TOWARD LIFE |
|---|---|---|
| 1. Exaggerated need for affection and approval | Moving toward (compliance): accepting one's helplessness and becoming compliant | Self-effacing solution: an appeal to be loved |
| 2. Need for a dominant partner | | |
| 3. Exaggerated need for power | Moving against (hostility): rebelling and resisting others to protect one's self from a threatening environment | Self-expansive solution: a striving for mastery |
| 4. Need to exploit others | | |
| 5. Exaggerated need for social recognition or prestige | | |
| 6. Exaggerated need for personal admiration | | |
| 7. Exaggerated ambition for personal achievement | | |
| 8. Need to restrict one's life within narrow boundaries | Moving away (detachment): isolating one's self to avoid involvement with others | Resignation solution: a desire to be free of others |
| 9. Exaggerated need for self-sufficiency and independence | | |
| 10. Need for perfection and unassailability | | |

SOURCE: Based on information in K. Horney, Self-Analysis. *New York: Norton, 1942; K. Horney,* Our Inner Conflicts, *New York: Norton, 1945; and K. Horney,* Neurosis and Human Growth, *New York: Norton, 1950. Used by permission of W. W. Norton & Co.*

## The Idealized Self

Karen Horney (1950) also distinguished between the real self and the idealized self. The **real self** represents what we are; those things that are true about us. The **idealized self** represents what we think we should be and is used as a model to assist us in developing our potential and achieving self-actualization. The dynamic of creating an idealized self in order to facilitate self-realization is universal and characteristic of each of us. An individual who seeks to be a competent doctor posits an ideal of what an effective doctor is like. In the normal individual, the idealized self and the real self largely coincide because the idealized self is based on a realistic assessment of one's abilities and potentials. But in the neurotic, the real self and the idealized self are discrepant or separated. A doctor who believes that an ideal doctor never loses a patient to death is being unrealistic. This situation can be represented diagrammatically by circles as is shown in Figure 5.1.

A person is able to recognize and develop only those aspects of the real self that coincide with the idealized self. Thus, as neurosis becomes more severe, an increasing amount of the powers and potentialities of the real self may be rendered unavailable for cultivation. In an extreme neurosis, the individual may completely abandon the real self for the sake of an idealized *glorified self.* Horney referred to this situation as one of **alienation** (or *the devil's pact*). In a state of alienation, a person identifies with the ideal self and thereby loses the true source of strength, since our only source of strength comes from who we really are.

Horney (1950) suggested that neurotics' lives are governed by the **tyranny of the should.** Instead of meeting genuine needs, those individuals create false ones. For example, some people have the idea that in order to be good they must never feel jealous, and so they posit an idealized self that does not permit feelings of jealousy. Therefore, the part of the real self that does experience feelings of jealousy is denied. The individual becomes estranged from a part of the self.

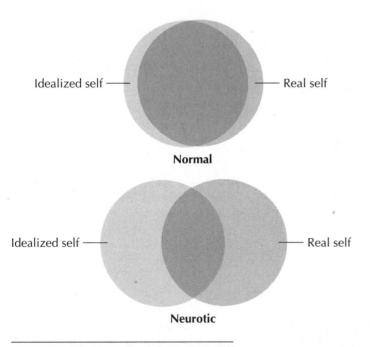

**Normal**

**Neurotic**

FIGURE 5.1   The Normal and the Neurotic Self

Circles can be used to represent the real and idealized self in Horney's theory
of personality: In the normal individual, the circles largely coincide.
In the neurotic individual, the circles are increasingly distinct.

## The Tyranny of the Should

Can you name some significant "shoulds" that you have devised to safeguard your image of self? Can you identify the origin of your "shoulds," for example, your parents, or your culture? Can you think of different types of "shoulds" that diverse cultures foster? What might happen if you were to give up one of the "shoulds" that is giving you problems?

A classic illustration clarifies Horney's point: normal individuals, by and large, are happy with and function within the everyday world. Neurotics are unhappy with the everyday world. To the extent that they are dreaming about castles in the sky, they do not function as effectively as they might. Alienated individuals try to escape to their castles. Such total identification with the idealized self renders these people virtually unable to cope.

Horney's concept of the idealized self may be seen as a constructive revision or correction of Freud's concept of the ego-ideal. Freud's concept of the superego includes two aspects: an introjected social conscience and an ego-ideal that is an idealized image consisting of approved and rewarded behaviors. The ego-ideal is the source of pride and provides a concept of who we think we should be. In her elaboration, Horney emphasized social factors that influence the development of an idealized self. Furthermore, Horney did not view the idealized self as a special agency within the ego but as a special need of the individual to keep up appearances of perfection. She also pointed out that the need to maintain an unrealistic idealized self does not involve simply repression of "bad" feelings and forces within the self. It also entails repression of valuable and legitimate feelings that are repressed because they might endanger the mask.

## Feminine Psychology

Karen Horney's interest in feminine psychology was stimulated by the fact that certain clinical observations appeared to contradict Freud's theory of the libido. In his concept of libidinal development, sexual activities and attitudes appear to be instinctual, inevitable processes unaffected by culture or society.

Freud had suggested that penis envy was largely responsible for a woman's development, that women view themselves as castrated males. Horney pointed out that both men and women develop fantasies in their efforts to cope with the Oedipal situation. She also emphasized that many men and boys express jealousy over women's ability to bear and nurse children, a phenomenon that has since been clearly seen in ethnographic accounts from many cultures (Paul, 1992), as well as in clincial settings. Horney termed this phenomenon **womb envy.** Her work suggests that womb envy and penis envy are complements (1967), reflecting the mutual attraction and envy that the sexes have for each other.

Horney believed the essence of sexual life lies in its biological creative powers; a greater role in sexual life belongs to the female because she is the one who is able to bear and nurse children. This superiority is recognized by the male and is the source of intense envy. Womb envy, rather than being openly acknowledged by most males, has often taken subtle and indirect forms, such as the rituals of taboo, isolation, and cleansing that have frequently been associated with menstruation and childbirth, the need to disparage women, accuse them of witchcraft, belittle their achievements, and deny them equal rights. Similar attempts to deal with these feelings have led men to equate the term "feminine" with passiveness and to conceive of activity as the prerogative of the male.

Both men and women have an impulse to be creative and productive. Women can satisfy this need naturally and internally, through becoming pregnant and giving birth, as well as in the external world. Men can satisfy their need only externally, through accomplishments in the external world. Thus, Horney suggested that the impressive achievements of men in work or other creative fields may be seen as compensations for their inability to bear children.

The woman's sense of inferiority is not constitutional but acquired. In a patriarchal society, the attitude of the male has predominated and succeeded in convincing women of their supposed inadequacies. But these are cultural and social factors that shape development (Eckhardt, 1991; Symonds, 1991), not biological ones.

*Horney believed that women can satisfy their creative needs internally or externally; men can satisfy their creative needs only externally, often through work.*

During her practice in the 1920s, Karen Horney believed a "flight from woman-hood" could be observed in society, in which many women inhibited their femininity and became frigid. While distrusting men and rebuffing their advances, these women wished that they were male. Such a flight from womanhood was due not to instinctual developments but to the experience of real social and cultural disadvantages that women have had to deal with. Sexual unresponsiveness, Horney pointed out, is not the normal attitude of women. It is the result of cultural factors. Our society, as has been well acknowledged, is a male society, and therefore for the most part it is not amenable to the unfolding of a woman's individuality.

Although Horney's psychology of women, which is almost a direct inversion of Freud's theory, has met with criticism because she maintained that the essence of being a woman lies in motherhood, her contributions to feminine psychology have been very valuable. In breaking away from orthodox psychoanalysis, Alfred Adler and Erich Fromm were also especially concerned about female development.

Much of Horney's work in feminist psychology and her challenge to male authority was groundbreaking for the emerging field of the psychology of women. In many ways, she was prophetic. As early as the 1920s, she observed that it was men who had written human history and men who had shaped the psychoanalytic movement. These enterprises reflected male needs and biases. She insisted that men should "let women speak, and hear *their* 'interpretations', even 'biases', if you will" (Coles, 1974). Horney as such became the first psychoanalyst who sought to define the feminine self in terms of the woman's own self and not in terms of her relationship with a man (Miccolis, 1996).

Feminine "values of closeness, love, intimacy, and sensitivity to relationships . . . as contrasted with achievement, success, power, mastery, and repression of feelings assigned to men in our culture can be readily understood in Horneyan terms." In her later writings, Horney developed a theory "that was not gender-specific, but applied to all humans. Perhaps, because Horney was a woman who saw the distortion that developed by overlooking women's identity, she was able to encompass a broader spectrum of human behavior." As such, her theory can be very helpful in "illuminating gender issues and the conflicts that women [and men] struggle with" (Symonds, 1991, pp. 301, 304).

## Assessment and Research in Horney's Theory

In her assessment of personality, Karen Horney primarily employed the techniques of free association and dream analysis. She also suggested (1942) that **self-analysis** can assist normal personality development. By analyzing one's self, significant gains may be made in self-understanding and in reaching freedom from inner bondages that hinder developing one's best potentialities.

Each one of us engages in self-analysis when we try to account for the motives behind our behaviors. A student who fails a test that she thought was unfair might ask, too, whether she had properly prepared for it. An individual who yields to another in a disagreement might ask if he gave in because he was convinced that the other's point of view was superior or because he was afraid of a possible argument. Such analyses are common in normal living.

Systematic self-analysis differs from occasional self-analysis in degree rather than kind, entailing a serious and protracted effort for self-understanding undertaken on a regular basis. Systematic self-analysis employs the tool of free association, followed by reflection on what one has thought and an analysis of the resistance that aims to maintain the status quo. When one obtains insight into one's personality, energies that were previously engaged in perpetuating neurotic trends are freed and can be used for making constructive changes. Although self-analysis can never be considered a totally adequate substitute for professional analysis of neurosis, its possible benefits for enhancing individual development merit its use.

Compared with Freudian psychoanalysis, Horney's theory recommends a more interpersonal understanding of the patient's issues. Like Freud, however, she felt that tracing the genetic sources in repetition of early patterns is critical, as is the analysis of transference.

Horney (1945) discussed four prerequisites for good decision making. First, she said, we need to be cognizant of our real feelings and wishes. Second, we need to have created our own set of values (not merely accepted those of our parents or society). Third, we have to make a deliberate choice between two opposite possibilities. Finally, we have to take responsibility for the decision that we make.

*Horney believed that children respond positively to parents who are both affectionate and firm.*

Van den Daele (1987) has suggested that Horney's theory of personality can be operationally defined and is essentially compatible with the requirements of psychological measurement. Some parallels have been noted between her concepts of "movement against others" and the idealized self and research on coronary-prone Type A behavior (Hamon, 1987). Other research that fails to support some of Freud's ideas concerning women (Fisher & Greenberg, 1977) can be seen as supportive of Horney's views (Schultz, 1990). Research on parenting styles underscores Horney's conviction that parenting patterns have a strong impact on children and that children respond positively to parents who are both affectionate and firm (Baumrind, 1972; Maccoby & Martin, 1983).

Relatively early in the twentieth century, Horney (1937) began to see a trend in America toward **hypercompetitiveness,** a sweeping desire to compete and win in order to keep or heighten beliefs that one is worthy, that has become even more pervasive as we come to the end of the century. Ryckman, Hammer, Kaczor, and Gold (1990) developed a Hypercompetitive Attitude Scale to evaluate the soundness of Horney's concept and found empirical backing for it. College men and women scoring higher in hypercompetitiveness had less self-esteem and were not as healthy psychologically as those who scored lower. Moreover, men with higher scores were more macho and thought of women as sexual objects. Kaczor, Ryckman, Thornton, and Kuelnel (1991) forecast and found that hypercompetitive men were more likely to charge rape victims as being responsible for having been raped and to view them as losers in a fierce physical fight for supremacy.

In his analysis of the contribution of Karen Horney to contemporary psychological thought, Paris (1996) suggests that her most important modification of Freud was her emphasis on an individual's current situation rather than on the past. She began by addressing current defenses and inner conflicts. Her mature theory inspired the interpersonal school of psychoanalysis and furnished a model for therapies that focus on the present.

| PHILOSOPHY, | **Horney's Theory** |
| SCIENCE, | |
| AND ART | |

Horney was an astute observer and talented clinician. She frequently tested, revised, and discarded her theories in the light of new observations. She asserted that certain therapeutic approaches bring forth desired and predictable changes in behavior, changes that can be observed during the course of therapy if not in a rigorous laboratory experiment. She was clearly engaged in scientific activity and believed that her method and therapy must be open to scientific investigation and research.

Horney was not greatly interested in abstract thinking, but her theory does reflect deep philosophical commitments, such as a belief in the process of growth and forward movement (akin to Jung's concept of self-realization) and an optimistic view of human nature. Toward the end of her life she became interested in Zen Buddhist writings and practices (see DeMartino, 1991). The underlying philosophical assumptions that support her work are both profound and compelling.

Horney's contributions to the art of psychotherapy have been particularly valuable. Her theory and therapeutic techniques have been adopted by many clinicians. Several aspects of her technique are discussed in current Freudian literature as useful additions to psychoanalysis. Clinicians are increasingly recognizing the usefulness of her concepts to the practice of group psychotherapy (Garofalo, 1996; Maiello, 1996).

Horney has been criticized for simply elaborating on concepts that were implied but not clearly expressed in Freud's writings; however, these elaborations contain valuable, original contributions. Horney clarified the ego-ideal; her concept of neurotic trends clarified Freudian defense mechanisms; and she provided significantly more insight into the psychology of women. Moreover, "her disagreements with Freud were profound" (Garrison, 1981), as she emphasized that "everything depended upon the interaction of culture and personality." Her work helped inspire the interpersonal school of psychoanalysis (Paris, 1996) and foreshadowed that of object relations theorists who emphasize interpersonal relations (Ingram & Lerner, 1992) and Heinz Kohut's ideas about grandiosity as a major developmental trend. These represent substantial and enduring contributions to psychoanalysis.

# Erich Fromm (1900–1980)

## Biographical Background

Erich Fromm was born in Frankfurt, Germany, in 1900, the only child of a deeply orthodox Jewish family. At the age of thirteen, Fromm began to study the Talmud, beginning an interest in religious literature and an admiration of the German mystic "Meister" Eckhart (1260?–1327?) that remained throughout his life. In his later years, Fromm did not formally practice religion but he referred to himself as an "atheistic mystic," and it is clear that Fromm's early religious experiences left a distinct mark on his personality and work. The moral and committed tone of his writings has a quality that has been described as reminiscent of the Old Testament prophets. He was deeply interested in religion and both his earlier and later writings reflect this concern.

Fromm wrote little about his early childhood. In his few comments, he described his early family life as tense and acknowledged that his parents were probably neurotic. His mother was "depression-prone," and his father, an independent businessman, "moody" and "overanxious." Fromm was fourteen years old when World War I broke out. He was impressed, almost to the point of being overwhelmed, by the irrationality of human behavior as it showed itself in the brutalities of war. By 1919 he had identified his political attitude as socialist and began to pursue formal studies in sociology and psychology at the University of Heidelberg. He received the Ph.D. in 1922.

Erich Fromm was trained in analysis in Munich and at the Institute of Berlin. He was one of the early *lay analysts;* that is, he had no formal medical training. The desirability

*For Erich Fromm, one's personality is a compromise between one's inner needs and the demands of society.*

of a medical background for the practice of psychoanalysis is still debated. Many psychoanalysts in America view psychoanalysis as primarily a medical method of treatment for neurotic disorders and therefore consider a medical background indispensable. Freud, however, had argued against medical training as the optimal background for an analyst and had advocated the training of lay people. He felt that analysis should be viewed as more than simply a method for the treatment of neurosis and suggested that it should also be seen as a wide cultural force offering insight into such areas as sociology, philosophy, art, and literature. Fromm's own broad understanding of the social sciences and philosophy was to enrich his understanding of psychoanalytic theory and its applications. At the same time, these interests eventually led to his severance from orthodox psychoanalysis and his criticism of Freud for his unwillingness to acknowledge the importance of social and economic forces in shaping personality.

In 1933, during the Depression, Fromm came to the United States. He helped found the William Alanson White Institute for Psychiatry, Psychoanalysis, and Psychology in New York and was a trustee and teacher there for many years. He taught at other universities, such as Yale and the New School for Social Research, and maintained an active private practice. In 1949 he was appointed professor of psychiatry at the National University in Mexico. After his retirement in 1965, he continued teaching and consulting activities. He moved in 1976 to Switzerland, where he died of a heart attack in 1980. He was almost eighty years old.

## Basic Human Conditions and Needs

The early 1920s were a time of vibrant excitement in the academic community. Nineteenth-century scholars such as Freud, Comte, Spencer, and Marx had opened the door to the analytical study of human behavior and social institutions. New disciplines of psychology, sociology, and anthropology were emerging and efforts were being made to build interdisciplinary foundations for understanding social institutions and human behavior. Erich Fromm was particularly impressed with the writings of Freud and Marx and he attempted a synthesis of their ideas.

He began with the thesis (1941) that *freedom* is a basic human condition that posits a "psychological problem." As the human race has gained more freedom by transcending nature and other animals, people have become increasingly characterized by feelings of separation and isolation. Thus, a major theme of Fromm's writings is the concept of loneliness. To be human is to be isolated and lonely, because one is distinct from nature and others. Loneliness also represents a basic human condition, and it is this characteristic that radically separates human nature from animal nature. The condition of loneliness finds its ultimate expression in the problem of death. Unlike other animals, we know we are going to die. This knowledge leads to a feeling of despair. Most of us find death incomprehensible and unjust—the ultimate expression of our loneliness.

In response to the basic condition of freedom, human beings can work with one another in a spirit of love to create a society that will optimally fulfill their needs, or they can "escape from the burden" of freedom into "new dependencies and submission" (1941). Such escape may alleviate feelings of isolation but it does not creatively meet the needs of humanity or lead to optimum personality development.

### Escape Mechanisms

Fromm (1941) identified three common mechanisms of escape from freedom: authoritarianism, destructiveness, and automaton conformity. These mechanisms do not resolve the underlying problem of loneliness but merely mask it.

In **authoritarianism,** one seeks to escape the problem of freedom by adhering to a new form of submission or domination. Individuals may permit others to dominate them or seek to dominate and control the behavior of others. In either case, the root of the tendency comes from an inability to bear the isolation of being an individual self and an effort to find a solution through *symbiosis,* the union of one's self with another or with an outside power. A common feature of authoritarianism is the belief that one's life is determined by forces outside one's self, one's interests, or one's wishes, and that the only way to be happy is to submit to those forces.

**Destructiveness** seeks to resolve the problem of freedom by the elimination of others and/or the outside world. "The destruction of the world is the last, almost desperate attempt to save myself from being crushed by it" (1941). Fromm believed that signs of destructiveness are pervasive in the world, although it is frequently rationalized or masked as love, duty, conscience, or patriotism.

The majority of individuals seek to escape the problem of freedom through **automaton conformity.** They cease to be themselves and adopt the type of personality proffered by their culture. Like the chameleon who changes its color to match its surroundings,

*In Fromm's theory automaton conformity is a common mechanism of escape from freedom. While the teen-age years are typically a time of "finding yourself," the process often entails a period of conformity. These girls are not only dressed in a similar fashion, they also have the same impassive expression on their faces.*

they become indistinguishable from the millions of other conforming automatons in their world. Such individuals may no longer feel alone and anxious, but they have paid a high price—"the loss of the self."

Fromm perceived similarities between his mechanisms of escape and Karen Horney's neurotic trends. The differences between them are that Horney's emphasis was on anxiety whereas Fromm's was on isolation. Also, Horney's neurotic trends are the force behind individual neurosis whereas the mechanisms of escape are forces in normal people. The mechanisms of escape are not satisfactory solutions. They do not lead to happiness and positive freedom. By relating spontaneously to love and work and by genuinely expressing our emotional, sensual, and intellectual abilities, we can become one again with other human beings, nature, and ourselves without forgoing the independence and integrity of our individual selves.

### Basic Needs

Our human condition of freedom gives rise to five basic needs (1955) **relatedness, transcendence, rootedness, sense of identity,** and a **frame of orientation and object of devotion.** Later, Fromm (1973) added a sixth need, **excitation and stimulation** (see Figure 5.2). These needs are part of our existence, and they must be met in order for a person to develop

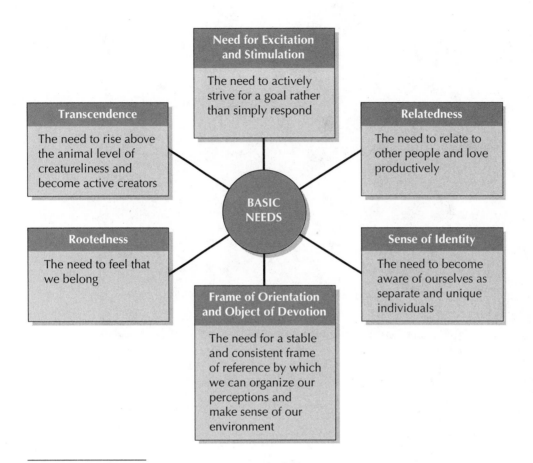

**FIGURE 5.2   Basic Needs**

Beyond the basic drive toward the affirmation of life, Fromm identified five (and later a sixth) basic needs that must be met in order for a person to develop fully (based on Fromm, 1955, 1973).

fully. Our primary drive is toward the affirmation of life, but unless we can structure our lives in such a way that our basic needs are fulfilled constructively, we either die or become insane.

Human beings create society in order to fulfill these basic needs that arise independently of the development of any particular culture. But the type of society and culture that humans create structures and limits the way in which the basic needs may be fulfilled. For example, in a capitalistic society, acquiring money is a means of establishing a sense of identity. In an authoritarian society, identifying with the leader or state provides a sense of identity. Thus one develops a final personality as a compromise between his or her inner needs and the demands of the society.

**THINKING CRITICALLY**

## Human Needs and Society

We create society in order to fulfill our needs, but the type of society that we create, in turn, structures and limits the way in which our needs may be fulfilled.

Consider the ways in which people are able to meet each of Fromm's basic human needs—relatedness, transcendence, rootedness, sense of identity, frame of orientation and object of devotion, need for excitation and stimulation—in our contemporary society.

Can you give examples of both constructive and destructive ways in which people meet each of these basic needs today? Overall, would you say that our society provides constructive opportunities for its members to fulfill their needs? Fromm suggests that if a particular society makes demands on its members that are contrary to their nature, that society warps and frustrates their human potential. Can you give specific examples of how particular cultures have or do thwart human potential? In fact, Fromm believed that no society yet developed has been able to meet all of the basic human needs constructively. But he was optimistic about the possibility of creating one. Are you optimistic? What characteristics do you think would have to be included in a society in order to permit individuals to relate to one another lovingly, transcend nature creatively, and respond productively?

---

## Character Orientations

A person's character is determined in large measure by the culture and its objectives; thus, it is possible to speak of social character types or qualities that are frequently shared by the people of a particular culture. Fromm identified five character orientations that are common in Western societies (1947): **receptive, exploitative, hoarding, marketing,** and **productive** (see Figure 5.3). The primary difference between Fromm's theory of character types and orientations and that of Freud is that Freud envisioned the fixation of libido in certain body zones as the basis for future character types, whereas Fromm set the fundamental basis of character in the different ways in which a person deals with basic human conditions.

The traits that arise from each of Fromm's character orientations have both positive and negative qualities, but on the whole Fromm saw the first four types as largely unproductive. A person may exhibit a combination of types. The first three types are reminiscent of Freud's oral and anal character types, and parallels can be drawn between Freud's and Fromm's typologies. It is in his discussion of the marketing orientation that Fromm is generally thought to have made a significant contribution and developed a new character orientation. The concept of supply and demand, which judges an article of commerce in terms of its exchange worth rather than its use, is the underlying value. Marketing personalities experience themselves as commodities on the market. They may be described as opportunistic chameleons, changing their colors and values as they perceive the forces of the market to change.

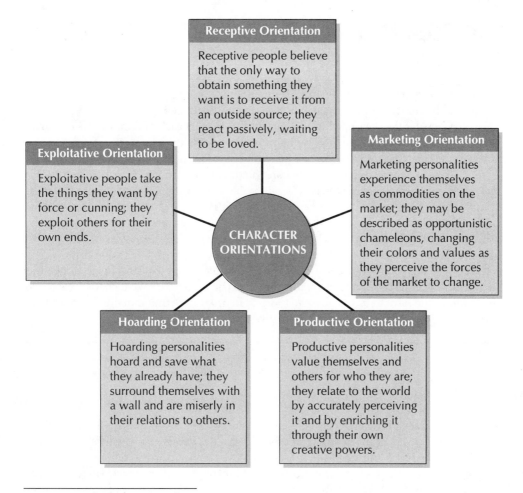

**FIGURE 5.3**   Character Orientations

Fromm identified five character orientations common in Western societies.

Fromm's description of the productive orientation tries to go beyond Freud's definition of the genital stage and describes an ideal of humanistic development and moral stance that characterizes the normal, mature, healthy personality. These individuals value themselves and others for who they are. In using their powers productively, they relate to the world by accurately perceiving it and by enriching it through their own creative powers.

Such people use humanistic, rather than authoritarian, ethics (1947). Whereas **authoritarian ethics** have their source in a conscience that is rooted outside the individual, **humanistic ethics** represent true virtue in the sense of the unfolding of a person's powers in accordance with the law of one's own human nature and the assumption of full responsibility for one's existence.

Fromm (1964, 1973) also distinguished between **biophilous character** orientations that seek to live life and a **necrophilous character,** which is attracted to what is dead and decaying and seeks to destroy life. The biophilous character is largely synonymous with the productive orientation. The desire to destroy emerges when life forces are frustrated.

Fromm believed that malignant forms of aggression can be substantially reduced when socioeconomic conditions that favor the fulfillment of human needs and potential are developed in a particular society. Productive, biophilous people comprehend the world through love, which enables them to break down the walls that separate people. Productive love, Fromm asserted, is an art. We can master its theory and practice only if we make love a matter of ultimate concern. Productive love is the true creative answer to human loneliness, whereas symbiotic relationships are immature or pseudo forms of love.

It was not until 1976 that Fromm added two basic modes or orientations of existence that compete for the spirit of humanity. The **having mode,** which relies on the possessions that a person *has,* is the source of lust for power and leads to isolation and fear. The **being mode,** which depends solely on the fact of existence, is the source of productive love and activity and leads to solidarity and joy. People whose being depends solely on the fact that they *are* respond spontaneously and productively and have the courage to let go in order to give birth to new ideas. Fromm believed that everyone is capable of both the having and being modes, but that society determines which of the modes will prevail (1976).

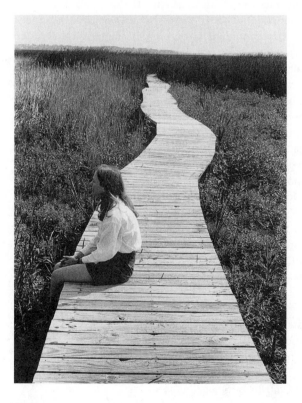

*Fromm believed that the being mode is the source of productive love and activity and leads to solidarity and joy.*

## Assessment and Research in Fromm's Theory

An example of the way in which Fromm assessed and researched culture and society was published in 1970 (Fromm & Maccoby). Psychologists, anthropologists, historians, and other experts joined together in an interdisciplinary field study of a Mexican village. With the advent of technology and industrialization, these villagers had been lured away from their traditional values and life-style. Movies and television took the place of festivals and local bands. Mass-produced utensils, furniture, and clothing took the place of hand-crafted items. Trained Mexican interviewers administered an in-depth questionnaire that was interpreted and scored for characterological and motivational factors. The Rorschach Ink Blot Test, which purports to indicate repressed feelings, attitudes, and motives, was also given. These data showed that the three main classes in the village also represented three social character types: the landowners, productive–hoarding; the poor workers, unproductive–receptive; and the business group, productive–exploitative. The findings about the village's history, economic and social structure, belief systems, and fantasies illustrated and appeared to confirm Fromm's theory that character is affected by social structure and change.

Michael Maccoby, who coauthored the Mexican village study, has done two more studies based on Fromm's character types. In the first, interviews of 250 managers in large corporations led to the identification of the "company man," a character type similar to the marketing orientation (1976). Company men seem to be marketing themselves as if they are commodities. Rather than emphasize actual job skills and knowledge, they focus on superficial packaging of themselves, which they can adapt as one might change clothes to fit various situations. A potentially new character type, **self-orientation,** which is highly narcissistic and reflects social changes that have occurred in America since the 1960s, emerged in the second study of corporate leaders (1981). This type tends to be cynical and rebellious, reflecting a breakdown in respect for authority and other traditional values. Self-indulgent and undisciplined, the self-oriented individual tends to lack loyalty and commitment to a work ethic. Maccoby's research supports Fromm's concept that historical and cultural forces shape the development of character types.

Fromm's work continues to generate interest. For example, José Brunner (1994) uses recently published material to show how Fromm was involved with the first opinion survey that employed modern psychological methods to explore electoral and political behavior. The survey was conducted by the Frankfurt Institute of Social Research between 1929 and 1931, among white- and blue-collar workers in Germany. Fromm's psychoanalytic techniques inspired the survey. Fromm's analysis of the data suggested a way of assessing the extent of democratic commitment and advanced a hypothesis regarding the interrelation of personality and politics that clarified internal discrepancies in political attitudes and behavior.

Fromm's theory emerged during a particular time in the twentieth century when psychologists were ready to appreciate the contributions of sociology and anthropology and to focus on the importance of culture and society. Even with today's emphasis on neurophysiology and renewed interest in biology, Fromm's concepts continue to enhance our understanding of the impact of social forces and to underscore the importance of our being loving, productive, and in charge of our lives (Spiegel, 1994).

| PHILOSOPHY, |
| SCIENCE, |
| AND ART |

# Fromm's Theory

Fromm rejected **scientism,** or the exclusive reliance on a narrow conception of science, deeming it inadequate for the full comprehension of human nature. He was critical of a narrow scientific approach because it tends to be reductive and it does not permit the final nuances of personality to emerge. He realized, perhaps more clearly than many, that the process of scientific activity begins with an epiphanic vision that is informed by the scientist's philosophy. Fromm's theory is a speculative and transcendental one, incorporating several vantage points that initially may appear contradictory.

We have seen how Freud's theory was a product of nineteenth-century thought, rooted and cast in the framework of a currently outdated biological determinism. Although Freud's concepts helped to shatter the nineteenth-century understanding of human nature, they require revision to meet the demands of the twentieth century. Fromm took advantage of the emerging disciplines of psychology, sociology, and anthropology, as well as new findings in other areas, to revise Freud's theory and develop his own point of view.

Although Fromm's methods of research are empirical, based on observation, they could not be described as rigorous or precise scientific techniques. In the final analysis, Fromm, like many other followers of Freud, was philosophical in his emphasis. He considered that proof grows out of the internal coherence of a theory and the theory's ability to shed light on the human condition. This "coherence theory of truth" is characteristic of the philosopher (Rychlak, 1973).

## PHILOSOPHICAL ASSUMPTIONS

 *Examining Horney and Fromm*

How would you rate Horney and Fromm on each of the basic philosophical assumptions described in Chapter 1? Consult the chart on the inside front cover. Each basic issue is presented as a bipolar dimension along which a person's view can be placed according to the degree of agreement with one or the other extreme: *freedom/determinism, hereditary/environmental, uniqueness/universality, proactive/reactive, optimistic/pessimistic.* Rate the views of Horney and Fromm on these issues.

When you have determined where you think the theorists stand, compare your responses with those of your classmates and your instructor. You should be willing to defend your ratings, but also be prepared to change them in light of others' compelling arguments. Afterward, compare your ratings of these theorists with your own position on each issue and with those of other theorists. Does this comparison help you understand why these theorists do or do not appeal to you?

Fromm wrote little about his technique of therapy. He indicated that he was a more active therapist than Freud and employed the term "activating" to describe the therapist's interventions to facilitate progress. Fromm emphasized that the therapist must *feel* what the patient is talking about and recognize the common humanity that both of them share. That element of empathy permits the patient to realize that inner feelings are shared by others.

There are clear ethical themes in the writings of Fromm. He tried to develop a norm or an ethic that presents the best answers to the problems we all face. He considered the behaviors that are most appropriate in unifying, harmonizing, and strengthening the individual to be ethical behaviors. Fromm's theory enlarges our concept of the application of personality theory to include efforts to inform and restructure society. His goals for the art of personality theory uniquely combine the scholarly and the ethical motives. In his discussions on guilt and ethics, Bacciagaluppi (1996) even suggests that Fromm anticipates some of the more recent theoretical and empirical contributions on the subject of guilt and provides an alternative framework for viewing data regarding aggression and guilt.

Although some of his writings may seem somewhat dated because they refer specifically to conditions surrounding the mid-twentieth century, his central ideas remain relevant to our contemporary situation. Many of Fromm's themes have been picked up by the humanist movement in psychology. His theory is coherent and sophisticated in its depth. A commitment to Fromm's point of view represents a commitment to the way of life espoused by his theory.

## *Summary*

1. Horney described *basic anxiety* as anxiety that results from feelings of insecurity in interpersonal relations. Unlike Freud, she did not believe that anxiety is an inevitable part of the human condition. It results from cultural forces. Research on parenting styles and attachment emphasize the importance of an affectionate and warm relationship between children and parents.

2. Basic anxiety is reflected in ten *neurotic needs* or *trends,* which lead to three ways of relating to others (*moving toward, moving against,* and *moving away*) and to three *basic orientations* toward life: the *self-effacing solution,* the *self-expansive solution,* and the *resignation solution.*

3. The *real self* represents that which a person actually is; the *idealized self* represents that which a person thinks he or she should be.

4. In a normal individual the real self and the idealized self closely coincide, but in a neurotic individual they are more separate. In extreme cases of *alienation,* a person may completely abandon the real self for the sake of the idealized self. Horney suggests that neurotics are governed by the *tyranny of the should.*

5. Horney's view of women is almost a direct inversion of Freud's. Whereas Freud suggested the phenomenon of penis envy in women, Horney pointed out the phenomenon of *womb envy* in men. She emphasized the superiority of women as reflected in their capacity for motherhood and stressed that a woman's sense of inferiority is not constitutional but acquired. In her later writings Horney developed a theory that was not gender specific but applied to all humans.

6. Horney suggested systematic *self-analysis* as an important assessment tool. Her theory has stimulated research in areas such as feminine psychology, *hypercompetitiveness,* and parenting styles.

7. Fromm identified our basic human condition as freedom; three common mechanisms of escape from it are *authoritarianism, destructiveness,* and *automaton conformity.*

8. We create society to fulfill our basic needs. In turn, it structures how these needs may be met. Society also provokes the development of certain character orientations. In his discussion of the *marketing orientation,* Fromm is thought to have developed a new type. The *productive orientation* depicts the mature individual, who is *biophilous,* that is, able to love and work in the broadest sense.

9. Assessment and research on Fromm's theory has focused on culture and society and their influence of character.

10. Horney encouraged scientific investigation of and research on her theory. Fromm pointed out the dangers of *scientism.* Both Horney and Fromm show deep philosophical commitments in their work. Horney's particular contribution to the art of personality theory has been in the area of psychotherapy; Fromm has illuminated our understanding of culture and society.

## Suggestions for Further Reading

Karen Horney's writings, clear and easy to read, have attracted a large lay audience. *New Ways in Psychoanalysis* (Norton, 1939) describes Horney's disagreement with Freudian theory: her belief that its stress on instinctual determinants is one-sided and needs to be rounded out by the consideration of cultural and social elements. *The Neurotic Personality of Our Time* (Norton, 1937), *Our Inner Conflicts* (Norton, 1945), and *Neurosis and Human Growth* (Norton, 1950) outline Horney's theory of neurosis. Identifying ten neurotic trends in the earliest book, Horney's thought developed through the concept of three modes of relating to others and, later, three basic orientations to life. In the last book, Horney introduced the concept of the idealized self. Her writings on the psychology of women have been brought together in *Feminine Psychology* (Norton, 1967). *Self-Analysis* (Norton, 1942) familiarizes the lay person with the methods and techniques of psychoanalysis. It is an invaluable work for any individual who is interested in pursuing his or her own self-understanding through analysis.

Good biographies of Karen Horney are S. Quinn, *A Mind of Her Own: The Life of Karen Horney* (Summit Books, 1987) and B. J. Paris, *Karen Horney: A Psychoanalyst's Search for Self-Understanding* (Yale University Press, 1994). A volume of papers and commentaries honoring Karen Horney's work is M. M. Berger (ed.), *Women Beyond Freud: New Concepts of Feminine Psychology* (Brunner-Mazel, 1993).

Erich Fromm's writings have had a vast appeal. He is one of the theorists most likely to be read by the lay person, for whom he wrote expressly. Fromm's first and, in the eyes of many, most important book is *Escape from Freedom* (Holt, Rinehart, 1941). In it he explored the problem of human freedom and our tendency to submit to tyranny or authority. *Man for Himself* (Holt, Rinehart, & Winston, 1947) discusses the problem of authoritarian versus humanistic ethics and outlines his five character orientations. *The Sane Society* (Holt, Rinehart, & Winston, 1955) describes the five basic human needs and considers the effects of capitalism and other social forms on character development. Fromm's most popular work is *The Art of Loving* (Harper & Row, 1956), which outlines his theory of love. The distinction between the necrophilous and biophilous orientation and Fromm's case study of Adolf Hitler are included in *The Anatomy of Human Destructiveness* (Holt, Rinehart, & Winston, 1973). Fromm's last work, *To Have or To Be* (Harper & Row, 1976), offers us a choice of two primary modes, one of which offers the potential for growth.

# PART III

# More Recent Trends in Psychoanalytic Theory

I n many respects Freud's theory was a product of nineteenth-century thought, cast in the framework of a now-outdated biological determinism. Yet it was Freud who shattered the nineteenth-century image of human nature and opened the door to a new point of view. Many of his concepts moved us forward into the twentieth century, but they require revision if they are to continue to meet the demands of our time and remain abreast of modern intellectual ideas. The thought of the analysts in Part III moves considerably beyond Freud, yet remains consistent with basic psychoanalytic doctrine. In updating and revising Freud, they have been largely responsible for the continued relevance of his theory.

For the most part, these theorists believe that the changes they have made are consistent with basic psychoanalytic doctrine. The biological grounding of human existence remains, as does the power of sexuality. Repression and transference, keynotes of psychoanalysis, remain fast in their thought. More recent analysts, however, reformed and revised psychoanalysis so that it reflects the modern world and contemporary self-understanding.

# CHAPTER 6

# Ego Psychology

## ANNA FREUD ❖ HEINZ HARTMANN ❖ ERIK ERIKSON

### Your Goals for This Chapter

1. Describe the contributions the ego psychologists, Anna Freud and Heinz Hartmann, have made to psychoanalysis.
2. Identify four ways in which Erikson extended Freud's psychoanalytic theory.
3. Explain how Erikson's theory enlarged our understanding of the ego.
4. Discuss the general characteristics of Erikson's *psychosocial stages* of development.
5. Discuss each one of Erikson's stages in terms of the Freudian psychosexual stage it reflects, the emotional duality that it involves, and the particular ego strength that emerges from it.
6. Describe how Erikson explored the role of culture and history in shaping personality.
7. Discuss Erikson's findings in the area of sex differences.
8. Discuss Erikson's methods of research and empirical research on Erikson's theory.
9. Describe how McAdams has applied Erikson's theory.
10. Evaluate Erikson's theory in terms of its function as philosophy, science, and art.

As we have seen, Freud's theory sparked a great deal of controversy and some of his original followers sought to develop separate theories. In doing so, Jung, Adler, Horney, and Fromm discarded a number of Freudian concepts that were considered crucial to psychoanalysis. Others, however, have worked within the mainstream of psychoanalysis to refine and update Freud's ideas. The thought of the analysts discussed in this chapter moves considerably beyond Freud without abandoning his key concepts and principles. The focus has changed from the study of the adult to the study of the child. The emphasis has shifted from the id to the ego. There has been an expansion of psychoanalysis as a therapeutic tool and a greater appreciation of the role of society and culture in the development of personality.

This chapter will briefly consider some contributions to psychoanalytic theory made by ego psychologists Anna Freud and Heinz Hartmann and then focus on the theory of Erik Erikson. These theorists accepted Freud's three-part division of the personality but emphasized the role of the ego, in some cases giving it a greater degree of autonomy.

Sigmund Freud believed that in optimal personality development the ego acts as an executor, effectively juggling the demands of the id and superego to meet their needs realistically. He emphasized the influence of the id, believing that the ego acts only out of borrowed energy and is at best a harassed, if not overwhelmed, commander. In his later years, Freud conjectured that the ego might have some psychological energy of its own, a position that his daughter Anna endorsed (1946). Subsequent practitioners of psychoanalysis focused on the ego and began to consider it an independent force with a larger role.

## Anna Freud (1895–1982)

Anna, Freud's youngest daughter, was her father's intellectual heir, the only member of his family to follow in his profession. After her analysis by her own father, she worked closely with him, as a highly skilled and respected colleague. After his death, she became an eminent lay psychoanalyst and international authority in her own right. Until her death in 1982, she was recognized as the guardian and elucidator of her father's revolutionary doctrine. She enlarged the application of psychoanalysis to new areas: the study of children and the exploration of the ego. She became an advocate for children and adolescents, insisting that their best interests need to be kept in the forefront. In doing so, she extended the influence of psychoanalysis into areas such as pediatrics, child care, education, and family law (see Goldstein, Freud, & Solnit, 1973, 1979).

In her efforts to clarify psychoanalytic theory, Anna Freud introduced some genuinely new and creative ideas. Her observations of children extended beyond normal or disturbed children growing up in average homes and included children who had met with extraordinary circumstances such as war, physical handicaps, and parentless homes. Her research opened the way to a new era of research in psychoanalytic child psychology under the auspices of the Hampstead clinic, with applications to a wide area of concerns associated with child rearing.

*Anna Freud, her father's intellectual heir, extended the interest*
*of psychoanalysis to the study of the child and the exploration of the ego.*

Some of Anna Freud's observations concerning children overturned previous notions of their reactions. For example, it had been widely assumed that children have an instinctive horror of combat, blood, and destruction and that war has a devastating effect on young children. However, her case studies of the effects of World War II bombings on British children, written in collaboration with Dorothy Burlingham, a long-time friend and colleague (see Burlingham, 1990, and Jackson, 1991), revealed that although wartime may lead to negative reactions, the world of the child pivots primarily on the mother.

Anna Freud's therapy stressed protective, supportive, and educational attitudes. She suggested how the classic features of adult psychoanalysis could be utilized with children four years old and upward. In working with children, she recognized that child analysis could not be conducted like the analysis of an adult. Classical techniques such as free association, the interpretation of dreams, and analysis of the transference had to be changed to correspond with the child's level of maturity. She saw the need for a long preparatory period in which the analyst is established as a trusted and indispensable figure in the child's life. She also recognized that neurotic symptoms do not necessarily have the same meaning in the life of a child that they do in the life of an adult. Her system of diagnosis, which conceives of personality as arising out of a developmental sequence, permitted her to distinguish between less serious manifestations of childhood distress, such as emotional problems of childhood that would be outgrown, and more serious disorders that threatened to fixate a child at a particular stage of development and thus jeopardize optimal personality growth. The latter, but not the former, in Anna Freud's opinion, mandated professional attention. She produced a classification system of childhood symptoms that

---

**TABLE 6.1** Anna Freud's Diagnostic Profile

Anna Freud's diagnostic profile is a careful overview of the various functionings of a patient. It provides for any stage of childhood a cross-sectional insight into the individual's overall development and mastery as well as indications for potential problems. It has nine major sections, briefly summarized as follows:

| | |
|---|---|
| I. | Reason for referral |
| II. | Description of child (personal appearance, moods, manner) |
| III. | Family background and personal history (life story and family constellation) |
| IV. | Possibly significant environmental influences |
| V. | Assessment of development in terms of:<br>development and expression of the child's drives of libido and aggression<br>development of the child's ego and superego sex developmental lines |
| VI. | Genetic assessments (signs of regression and/or fixation) |
| VII. | Dynamic and structural assessment (signs of conflicts between the ego–id, ego–superego, or ego–reality) |
| VIII. | Assessment of general characteristics in terms of:<br>frustration tolerance<br>sublimation potential<br>overall attitude to anxiety<br>progressive versus regressive tendencies |
| IX. | Diagnosis (integration and summary of above into a clinically meaningful assessment) |

*SOURCE: Based on information in A. Freud,* Normality and Pathology in Childhood, *Vol. 6 of* The Writings of Anna Freud, *New York: International Universities Press, 1965, pp. 138–147.*

---

reflects developmental issues and a formal assessment procedure known as a **diagnostic profile** (see Table 6.1). Such profiles have since been developed for infants, children, adolescents, and adults. In each profile, different aspects of psychoanalytic theory are used to organize and integrate the data acquired during a diagnostic assessment into a complete picture of the various functionings of the patient's personality and an indication of their developmental appropriateness.

Anna Freud used the term **developmental line** to refer to a series of id-ego interactions in which children decrease their dependence on external controls and increase ego mastery of themselves and their world (1965). Her six developmental lines stress the ego's ability to cope with various internal, environmental, and interpersonal situations and complement her father's discussion of psychosexual development. As children grow they progress from (1) dependency to emotional self-reliance, (2) sucking to rational eating, (3) wetting and soiling to bladder and bowel control, (4) irresponsibility to responsibility in body management, (5) play to work, and (6) egocentricity to companionship.

Anna Freud emphasized the importance of paying attention to a patient's maturation level and noted with regret that adolescence was a "stepchild in psychoanalytic theory" (1958). She developed a concept of normality for the adolescent period, acknowledging that it is a period of disharmony but suggesting that the crisis it entails is "normative" and functional. She looked at the phenomena of impulsive acting out in child and adolescent analysis and clarified the types of acting out that are normal and make a positive contribution during the prelatency and adolescence periods (see also Kaplan, 1996). It is not uncommon, for example, for an adolescent to temporarily escape the demands of society by skipping school or running away. This behavior, however, can be compounded by overreacting to it or by perjoratively labeling it.

In addition, Anna Freud learned from her work with children that there are realistic limits to analysis. Certain constitutional or environmental factors may not be open to real change through analysis, though their effects may be reduced. While recognizing the greater importance of environmental factors over internal ones in childhood disturbances, she was also impressed by the efforts of children to cope with and master extremely devastating situations.

Finally, Anna Freud systematized and elaborated on Freud's discussion of the *ego's defenses*. Whereas Freud concentrated on exploring the unconscious drives of the id, his daughter realized that in order for these to emerge in an analysis, the ego must become aware of the defenses that it is using to prevent the material from reemerging into consciousness. The ego's defenses may be inferred from observable behavior. Analysis of the defenses permits one to understand the child's life history and instinctual development. Anna Freud elaborated on the ego defenses outlined by her father and suggested some additional ones of her own (1946). She clarified the process of identification with the aggressor, in which a victim begins to react to his or her captor with gratitude and admiration. This phenomenon has since been recognized in prisoners of war and hostages. Anna Freud's graphic case descriptions illustrating these processes have become classic. Thus, a schoolboy's involuntary grimace caricatures the angry face of his teacher and testifies to his identification with the aggressor.

## Heinz Hartmann (1894–1970)

In Anna Freud's view, the ego remains inescapably bound to the id and necessarily regulated by the superego. Heinz Hartmann suggested that the ego is an important autonomous force (1958, 1964). Its energy is not necessarily derived from the id (as Freud thought), but both ego and id originate in inherited predispositions that follow independent courses of development. Thus, the ego's functions are not limited to the avoidance of pain and the service of instinctual gratification. Hartmann paid considerable attention to the synthesizing and integrative functions of the ego. He described its processes of perception, attention, memory, rational thought, and action and showed increased interest in accounting for normal behavior. Hartmann also suggested that certain spheres of ego activity may be "conflict free," that is, the ego is not perpetually in conflict with the id, external world, and superego.

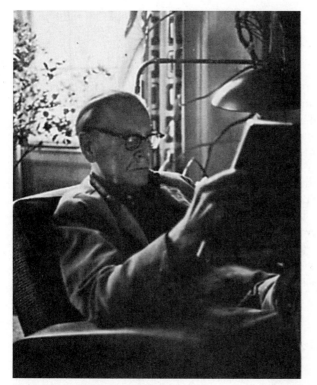

*Heinz Hartmann suggested that the ego
is an important autonomous force.*

Through experience and adaptation, many of the ego's functions may become increasingly distinct from original instinctive and defensive maneuvers.

In Hartmann's view, memory, learning, and other ego functions are *prerequisites* for the ego's interactions with the id, rather than arising out of it. They emerge independently and are then brought into service. Moreover, the ego has the capacity to neutralize sexual and aggressive energy so that they function in ways other than simple drive reduction. A defense, such as regression, may be employed in the service of the ego. Thus, a college student may be able to concentrate and study better after a weekend of play. Ego functions may be autonomous from the id and practiced for their own sake.

Hartmann's emphasis on the cognitive functions of the ego is consonant with the current interest in the role of cognition in personality formation and development (see Sampson, 1990). He conceived of adaptation as a reciprocal relationship between the organism and the environment. The organism changes the environment in order to make it more agreeable and then changes itself in order to adapt to the changes it has created. Adaptation is a continual process entailing ever more complex levels of mastery, molding, and synthesis. In its synthesizing function, the ego integrates and reconciles not only conflicts between itself, the id, the superego, and the external world, but also conflicts within itself (see also Solnit, 1994, and Schafer, 1995).

# Erik Erikson (1902–1994)

## Biographical Background

Erik H. Erikson was born on June 15, 1902, near Frankfurt, Germany, the product of an extramarital relationship. He never knew his mother's first husband or his birth father. His mother subsequently married a pediatrician, Theodore Homburger, who adopted Erik and gave him a last name. In an act that Erikson later called "loving deceit," his parents concealed the fact of his adoption from him for several years. Thus, the man who is famous for coining the term "identity crisis" did himself experience a significant identity crisis. Not only did he have to struggle with the usual quest for psychological identity, he was also unsure of his biological identity. The problem was compounded by the fact that he was raised in a Jewish home, but his genetic background was Danish. Young Erik's Nordic features made him an outcast among his Jewish peers, ironically, at the same time his German classmates rejected him as a Jew. His resolution of the identity issue may have become apparent in 1939, when, in the process of becoming an American citizen, he added the surname by which we know him, assuming the identity of Erik Homburger Erikson. He also converted to Christianity.

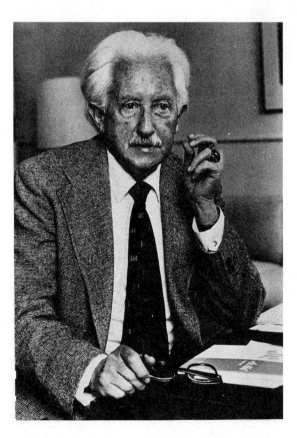

*In his discussion of psychosocial development, Erik Erikson makes explicit the social dimension implied in Freud's work.*

Erikson was able to find his professional identity in Vienna, where he and Peter Blos, a theorist and researcher on adolescence, established a progressive, nongraded school, providing children optimal freedom within an appropriate structure. After a short time, Anna Freud asked Erikson if he would be interested in beginning analysis with her and becoming a child analyst. Over the next few years, Erikson established himself as a key figure in psychoanalysis, publishing articles on education and psychoanalysis. These articles reflect the precision of the Montessori philosophy, a method of education that Erikson was studying at the time. The two complementary forms of training enabled Erikson to make a unique contribution to our understanding of child development.

Erikson left Vienna in 1933 and settled with his wife and family in Boston, where he became the city's first child psychoanalyst. In 1936 Erikson accepted a position in the Yale University Institute of Human Relations to teach at the medical school. In 1938, he learned of a unique opportunity to study child-rearing methods among the Sioux in South Dakota. Here he observed first-hand how childhood events are shaped by society and its customs, a theme he was to stress again and again in his later writings.

Between 1939 and 1960 Erikson held various positions in California and Massachusetts. In 1960 Harvard University offered him the position of professor in spite of the fact that he had never received a university or college degree. Erikson was a popular speaker at colleges and universities throughout the United States. He died on May 12, 1994, following a brief illness.

Erikson extended Freud's psychoanalytic theory in four main ways. First, he increased our understanding of the ego, showing how it is a creative problem solver that emerges out of the genetic, cultural, and historical context of each individual. Second, he elaborated on Freud's stages of development, making explicit a social dimension that was implied in Freud's theory but never clearly stated. Third, he extended our concept of development to embrace the entire life span, from infancy to old age. Fourth, he explored the impact of culture, society, and history on the developing personality and illustrated this in psychohistorical studies of famous people.

## An Enhanced Understanding of the Ego

In Erikson's theory, the ego is the part of the mind that gives coherence to experiences, conscious or unconscious. Erikson agreed with Freud that many aspects of ego functioning are unconscious, but he believed the ego has an overall unifying purpose that leads to consistent behavior and conduct. The ego has the positive role of maintaining effective performance, rather than just a negative role of avoiding anxiety. Its defenses are adaptive as well as maladaptive (1974).

Erikson did *not* believe that we can best reconstruct the ego's functions from an understanding of its dysfunctions. He elaborated on its adaptive capacities, its ability to deal with stress, to resolve vital conflict, to recuperate, and to contribute to identity formation. In the final analysis, Erikson defined the ego as a strong, vital, and positive force: an organizing capacity of the individual that leads to "that strength which can reconcile discontinuities and ambiguities" (1975).

The development of the ego was clearly outlined in Erikson's psychosocial stages of the life cycle. Ideally, at each stage the ego develops certain strengths or basic virtues that enable it to move forward. These ego strengths lay the foundation for a set of ethical rules based on ideals that we can strive for, as Erikson also conceived of the superego and human consciousness in terms of an evolutionary process.

## The Psychosocial Stages of Development

In his discussion of the psychosexual stages of development, Freud concentrated on their biological character and tended to neglect the social dimension. Nevertheless, Freud's stages reflect more than simply a psychosexual progress in which children come to terms with their sexuality. For Erikson they are definitely a psychosocial development, in which children try to understand and relate to the world and others. In effect, Erikson made explicit the social dimension implied in Freud's work.

Each of Erikson's **psychosocial stages** centers on an emotional polarity or conflict that children encounter at certain critical periods. New environmental demands introject positive and negative emotional components into the development of personality. Both emotional components are to some extent incorporated into the emerging person, but if the conflict is resolved satisfactorily, the positive component is reflected to a higher degree. If the conflict persists, or is not adequately resolved, the negative component predominates. Erikson's first four stages correspond to Freud's psychosexual stages (oral through latency). Erikson then subdivided the genital stage into four phases that represent growth and development throughout maturity.

Erikson's stages are *epigenetic* (from the Greek words *epi,* "upon," and *genesis,* "emergence"): one stage develops on top of another in a sequential and hierarchical pattern. At each successive level the human personality becomes more complex. Erikson stressed the prospective features of the life cycle and amended the logic of psychoanalysis so that early events are seen not only in terms of their contributions to later development, but as themselves directed by potentials that do not flower until later.

Erikson's psychosocial stages do not occur within a strict chronological framework. Each child has a personal timetable. However, as in fetal development, each aspect of psychosocial development has a critical period of readiness during which, if it does not flourish, it is likely to flounder. In addition, the stages progress in a cumulative rather than a linear fashion. The behaviors of one stage do not disappear with the successive stage (1969).

Erikson made psychoanalytic concepts more consistent with contemporary scientific findings. His psychosocial stages are a gradual series of decisive encounters with the environment; interactions between biological development, psychological abilities, cognitive capacities, and social influences. Erikson saw the person as a way of being in the world. Thus the first stage, rather than a cathexis of libido onto an oral zone, is a complex of experiences centered in the mouth.

Each of the eight stages entails its own **life crisis,** a crucial period in which the individual cannot avoid a decisive turn one way or the other. Each stage also provides new opportunities for particular ego strengths or basic **virtues** to develop. These psychosocial gains result from the ego's successful adaptation to its environment and must be nurtured and reaffirmed continuously.

### Trust versus Mistrust: Hope

The emotional duality of **trust versus mistrust** is the key consideration of the first stage, which corresponds to Freud's oral, sensory, and kinesthetic one (1963). The basic psychosocial attitude to be learned at this stage is whether or not you can trust the world. For a protracted period of time children are highly dependent on others for their care. Certain frustrations are inevitable and socially meaningful, but too much of either frustration or indulgence may have negative effects. Basic trust implies a perceived correlation between one's needs and one's world. If infants receive unreliable, inadequate, or rejecting care, they will perceive their world as indifferent or hostile and they will develop a high degree of mistrust. Granted, it is important that infants develop some sense of how much to trust and when to be ready for danger and discomfort. The danger lies in the extremes of trust and mistrust. This crisis is not permanently resolved during the first year or two of life, but a foundation is laid that influences the subsequent course of development.

An appropriate balance of trust and mistrust leads to the development of the ego strength *hope,* a basic human virtue without which we are unable to survive. Hope represents a persistent conviction that our wishes can be satisfied in spite of disappointment and failures (1964). Hope is the basis of faith, reflected in mature commitments.

### Autonomy versus Shame and Doubt: Will

Erikson's second psychosocial stage, **autonomy versus shame and doubt,** arises during the second and third years of life and corresponds to the anal-muscular stage in Freud's psychosexual scheme (1963). The primary emotional duality here is that of control over the body and bodily activities as opposed to a tendency for shame and doubt. "Just when a child has learned to trust his mother and to trust the world, he must become self-willed and must take chances with his trust in order to see what he, as a trustworthy individual, can will" (Erikson, as cited in Evans, 1967). The struggle for autonomy is not limited to sessions on the toilet, but extends to many other areas of life as the ego begins to establish psychosocial independence. Toddlers, who are making rapid gains in neuromuscular maturation, verbalization, and social discrimination, begin to explore independently and interact with their environment. The negativism of the two-year-old whose favorite word is "no" is evidence of the child's struggling attempt at autonomy. A temper tantrum is simply a momentary loss of self-control. Cultures have different ways of cultivating or breaking the child's will, either reinforcing or rejecting the tentative explorations of the child. Doubts about their ability for self-control may give children feelings of inadequacy or shame.

*Will,* the virtue corresponding to this stage, is a natural outgrowth of autonomy. Clearly in the toddler years only rudiments emerge, but these will build into a mature sense of will power. Will is an unbroken determination to exercise freedom of choice and self-restraint (1964) and forms the basis for our subsequent acceptance of social laws.

### Initiative versus Guilt: Purpose

The emotional duality that Erikson envisioned for the phallic or genital-locomotor stage of psychosexuality (three to five years) is **initiative versus guilt** (1963). At this period, children are active in their environment, mastering new skills and tasks. Their dominant social modality is the *intrusive* mode: their bodies vigorously intrude into space and onto other

people. Preschoolers direct their activities toward specific goals and achievements. Their in-
trusion and curiosity extends not only to sexual matters but to many other concerns of life
as well. The characteristic word of preschoolers is "why?" Parental responses to children's
self-initiated activities determine the successful or unsuccessful outcome of this stage. If
initiative is reinforced, a child's behavior will become increasingly goal oriented. Excessive
punishment or discouragement may lead to feelings of guilt, resignation, and the belief that
it is wrong to be curious about the world and ill-advised to be active in it.

Immense new faculties develop in children at this time as they begin to imagine
goals for which their locomotive and cognitive skills have prepared them. Their use of language becomes more polished. Children begin to envision themselves as growing up and
identify with people whose work and personalities they can understand and admire. Earlier
fantasies are repressed or redirected and the play of preschoolers becomes more realistic
and purposeful. They begin to engage in projects. Children are at no time more open to
learning than during these years. They are able to work cooperatively and to profit from
teachers. Their learning is vigorous, leading away from their own limitations and into later
possibilities.

Erikson believed that the Oedipus complex is both more and less than Freud made
of it. He preferred to call it an early generational complex. From the point of view of evolution, it is the child's first experience with the unrelenting sequence of generations, growth,
and death. The same-sexed parent becomes "naturally" involved in the child's early genital
fantasies at a time when the child's initiative is ready to turn away from the present situation to new goals. At the same time, the child's strong imagination and powerful locomotive skills produce gigantic, terrifying fantasies that awaken a sense of guilt and lead to the
development of conscience (Evans, 1967). Thus the Oedipal stage results in a moral sense
that establishes permissible limits and begins to attach childhood dreams realistically to the
various possible goals of one's technology and culture.

The virtue that emerges out of the duality of initiative versus guilt is *purpose,* a
view of the future giving direction and focus to our mutual efforts. Purposefulness slowly
enables one to develop a sense of reality that is defined by what is attainable (1964).

### Industry versus Inferiority: Competence

The next stage in the child's life loosely parallels Freud's latency period. Freud gave few clues
as to what was happening to personality development during this period apart from suggesting that latency involves a move from premature sexual expression to a nonactive sexual phase. Erikson agreed that during latency certain passionate and imaginative qualities
of earlier years calm down so that the child is free to concentrate on learning. However, he
pointed out that learning involves more than just a basic form of striving that takes place
throughout the life cycle and undergoes a special crisis during the school years. The focus
moves sharply from the id to the ego as the child applies to specific and approved goals the
drives that earlier motivated dreams and play. Yet the ego can remain strong only through
interaction with cultural institutions. At this time society intervenes in a more formal manner to develop the child's capacities and potentials.

During the school years (six to eleven), the primary emotional duality is **industry
versus inferiority** (1963). The term "industriousness" might be better than "industry" as it
implies being busy with something, learning to make something and to make it well. Chil-

dren in all cultures receive some form of systematic instruction at this time to teach them skills that will be needed in their society and to help them attain a sense of mastery.

New demands are placed upon children at this time. They are no longer loved simply for who they are; they are expected to master the technology of their culture in order to earn the respect of their teachers and peers. Their ability to conform and master the tasks of this level depends in large measure on how successfully they have traveled the preceding stages. If children emerge from the preceding stages with a basic sense of trust, autonomy, and initiative, they are ready for the industrious labor that "school" presupposes. But if their development has left heavy residues of mistrust, doubt, and guilt, they may have difficulty performing at an optimal level. From a psychoanalytic point of view, the child who has not adequately resolved his or her Oedipal complex may not be ready to fulfill the other demands of his or her society. If potentialities have been permitted to develop fully in the earlier stages, the child is in less danger.

The peril during this period is that feelings of inadequacy and inferiority will develop. Children begin to make comparisons between themselves and others and to perceive themselves in a more or less favorable light. The avoidance of group labels that differentiate children's performances may minimize but can in no way erase a child's consciousness of doing superior or inferior work. Children know, or think they know, where they stand.

Children at this age are ready to learn to work and need to develop a sense of *competence*, the ego strength or virtue associated with this stage. Competence entails the ability to use one's intelligence and skill to complete tasks that are of value in one's society (1964).

### Ego Identity versus Role Confusion: Fidelity

For Freud, the hallmarks of the genital stage were *lieben und arbeiten*, "to love and to work." Erikson agreed with the importance of these accomplishments, but he further divided Freud's final stage into four substages to underscore the point that "genitality is not a goal to be pursued in isolation" (Evans, 1967). In so doing, Erikson greatly enriched our understanding of adolescence and the adult years.

The primary duality during adolescence (twelve to eighteen) is **ego identity versus role confusion.** The process of forming an ego identity requires that one compare how one sees oneself with how significant others appear to expect one to be. "Ego identity, then, in its subjective aspect, is the awareness of the fact that there is a self-sameness and continuity to the ego's synthesizing methods and a continuity of one's meaning for others" (1963). Ego identity results in a sense of coherent individuality that enables one to resolve one's conflicts adaptively. Adolescents must answer the question "Who am I?" satisfactorily. If they fail to do so, they will suffer role confusion.

Erikson suggested that adolescence is a particularly crucial period. Along with rapid physical growth and changes, new psychological challenges occur. Previous continuities are called into question as young people begin to reconnect the roles and skills that they have developed into a maturer sense of identity. This integration is more than the sum total of previous accomplishments. Erikson often spoke of adolescence as a moratorium between childhood and adulthood and considered such a moratorium particularly important in a complex society.

The greatest danger at this stage is role confusion, the inability to conceive of oneself as a productive member of one's society. Erikson pointed out that "a sound ego identity

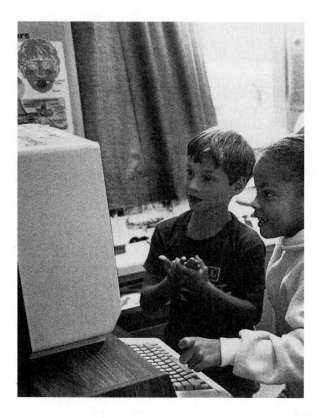

*In contemporary society, computers can be an important resource to encourage a child's sense of competence during Erikson's stage of industry versus inferiority.*

is the only safeguard against the anarchy of drives as well as the autocracy of conscience" (1958). Role confusion frequently arises out of the adolescent's difficulty in finding an occupational identity but it may also express a general inability to find a meaningful place in one's culture. The development of a positive identity depends on support from significant groups. The adolescent who cannot find a meaningful adult role runs the risk of an **identity crisis,** a transitory failure to establish a stable identity. Some young people may drop out of mainstream society for a short period, as Erikson himself did. Others may adopt a **negative identity,** one that is opposed to the dominant values of their upbringing. Where support has not been forthcoming and the climate has not been favorable to the development of inner resources, a negative identity may provide the only way of demonstrating mastery and free choice in one's culture. Negative identifications may result in unfortunate consequences—social pathology, crime, or expressions of prejudice. However, Erikson wanted us to recognize that such developments are an important testimony to the adolescent's readiness for ideological involvement. It is vitally important that a society present its young people with ideals they can share enthusiastically. The conspicuous absence of a sense of promise in any society, due to economic conditions, population trends, high unemployment, or other problems that thwart the occupational aspirations of young people, means that those adolescents will have a difficult time establishing a clear and positive ego identity. Capps (1996) suggests that Erikson's understanding of identity confusion and its ramifications has even helped inform and nurture healing efforts for Vietnam veterans and survivors of war by providing the therapeutic theory for readjustment and resocialization programs.

The virtue or ego strength developed at this time is *fidelity;* the adolescent is ready to learn to be faithful to an ideological point of view. Fidelity consists of "the ability to sustain loyalties freely pledged in spite of the inevitable contradictions of value systems" (1964). Without a constructive outlet for fidelity, the young person will either have a weak ego and suffer a "confusion of values" or search for a deviant group to be loyal to.

### Intimacy versus Isolation: Love

Young adulthood (eighteen to twenty-four) is marked by the emotional duality of **intimacy versus isolation** (1963). Intimacy refers to the ability to develop a close and meaningful relationship with another person. Erikson here applied Freud's dictum "to love and to work" as the model orientation. Isolation entails self-absorption and an inability to develop deep, committed relationships. Having grown beyond the beginnings of establishing an identity, the young adult is able to overcome the fear of ego loss and form a close affiliation with another individual. The task of young adulthood is to couple genitality with general work productiveness. Clearly, genitality is an inadequate definition of health. On the other hand, an individual's dedication to work should not be such that she or he loses the capacity to love.

Thus, it is at this point that the virtue of *love* emerges as an ego strength (1964). This is not to deny the involvement of love in previous stages, but in young adulthood the individual is able to transform the love received as a child and begin to care for others. Love further represents a mutual devotion that is able to overcome the natural antagonism involved in any relationship between the sexes. Erikson acknowledged that there are different functions of the sexes, particularly with regard to procreation; however, the capacities of the mature ego can transcend these so that male and female cooperate.

### Generativity versus Stagnation: Care

The middle years (twenty-five to sixty-four) are characterized by the conflict of **generativity versus stagnation** (1963). Generativity entails more than parenthood; it is the ability to be productive and creative in many areas of life, particularly those showing a concern for the welfare of ensuing generations. The adult actively participates in those elements of culture that will ensure its maintenance and enhancement. Failure to do so leads to feelings of stagnation, boredom, and interpersonal impoverishment. An individual who does not have children can fulfill generativity by working with other people's children or helping to create a better world for them. Thus, while the idea of generativity includes the concepts of productivity and creativity, it is much broader. A person is generative when making a contribution appropriate to her or his particular potential, be it children, products, ideas, or works of art.

Erikson suggested that because Freud stressed early inhibition of the expression of the libido or sexual drive, he underestimated the importance of the procreative desires of human beings. Erikson considered a procreative drive to be instinctual and saw generativity as a further psychosexual stage whose frustration leads to symptoms of self-absorption and indulgence.

The ego strength that emerges during the middle years is *care*. The adult needs to be needed. *Care* implies doing something for somebody. Care is also able to overcome the inevitable ambivalent feelings that are involved in the parent-child relationship. Once again, when the mature ego is able to transcend these emotions, the adult can fulfill obligations to youth.

### Ego Integrity versus Despair: Wisdom

Maturity, the final stage of life (sixty-five to death), is marked by **ego integrity versus despair** (1963). Ego integrity entails the ability to reflect on one's life with satisfaction even if all dreams are not fulfilled. Death is not feared but accepted as one among many facets of one's existence. Despair refers to regret over missed and unfulfilled opportunities at a time when it is too late to begin again. Ego integrity represents the fruit of the seven stages that have preceded. The virtue of this stage is *wisdom*. Wisdom enables an individual to bring

**THINKING CRITICALLY**

## *Generativity*

Erikson believed that the dominant task of the adult years for both men and women is generativity. Parenthood is one way of expressing generativity. Social and economic considerations, however, may make it necessary to restructure the ways in which people express this form of generativity. In America today, small rather than large families are the norm. Most households need two incomes to meet expenses.

Although Erikson's age limits have always been approximations, some teenagers today have children at much earlier ages than his theory predicts; other young adults delay marriage and child bearing. Many people in their sixties and seventies and even eighties continue to be very generative, especially as the lifespan increases. Should there be an additional stage applying to seniors? Are we out of synch with Erikson's stages? Some speak of women as having a biological clock. Do men have such a clock, biological or psychological? Although we have the technology, is it advisable for women to be having children at older and older ages? Is there a point where doing so becomes a bad idea?

Can mentoring or role modeling be a viable method of expressing generativity? Does the fact that our national debt has increased at such a fast pace indicate that the adults in power today are not as concerned about how they leave things for future generations?

Some critics suggest that Erikson's life stages, emotional polarities, and ego strengths bear the hallmarks of a white, Western, patriarchal society that would not apply well to other cultures. Does the task of generativity apply with the same force to civilizations with large populations? Try to speak with someone from a non-Western culture in order to identify what might be some more appropriate emotional challenges during the life span in that culture.

---

TABLE 6.2 The Life Cycle

| PSYCHOSEXUAL STAGE | PSYCHOSOCIAL STAGE | EGO STRENGTH OR VIRTUE |
| --- | --- | --- |
| Oral sensory and kinesthetic (Infancy) | Trust versus mistrust | Hope |
| Anal-muscular (toddler years) | Autonomy versus shame and doubt | Will |
| Phallic or genital-locomotor (preschool years) | Initiative versus guilt | Purpose |
| Latency period (school years) | Industry versus inferiority | Competence |
| Genital (Adolescence) | Ego identity versus role confusion | Fidelity |
| (Young adulthood) | Intimacy versus isolation | Love |
| (Adulthood) | Generativity versus stagnation | Care |
| (Maturity) | Ego integrity versus despair | Wisdom |

SOURCE: Based on information in Erik H. Erikson, Childhood and Society (Norton, 1950, 1963) and Erik H. Erikson, Insight and Responsibility (Norton, 1964).

life to an appropriate closure. It is the ability to stand back and reflect on one's life in the face of impending death (1964).

Table 6.2 summarizes Erikson's psychosocial stages, indicates their relationship to Freud's psychosexual stages, and lists their respective ego strengths.

## Assessment and Research in Erikson's Theory

As a researcher, Erikson has been described as "the quintessential interdisciplinarian" (Smelser, 1996). He used cultural studies, psychohistories, and inquiries into sex differences in his development of unique methods of assessment. His research is based on direct observation of a particular (configurational) kind followed by theoretical formulation (Coles, 1970).

### The Study of Two American Indian Tribes

In 1938 Erikson went to the Pine Ridge Reservation in South Dakota to observe the children of the Sioux. He had become increasingly interested in the work of anthropologists and welcomed an opportunity to observe how the events of an individual's life are shaped by societal practices. Because he traveled with an old friend of the Sioux, Erikson was able to establish a close relationship with many members of the tribe and to observe them and speak with them freely. Later, he traveled to northern California to observe a very different tribe, the Yurok.

The Sioux had originally been buffalo hunters. When the white settlers came, both the buffalo and the traditional Sioux way of life vanished amid bloody massacres. Defeated, the Sioux had become withdrawn and apathetic. In part the present behavior of the Sioux was undoubtedly due to their painful history, but Erikson found additional reasons in the Sioux child-rearing practices. Unlike most American middle-class parents who impose firm structures on their children at an early age in the belief that this will help them to become productive adults, the Sioux actively encouraged their children to be free and delayed imposing restrictions on them. The Sioux mother was at ease with her tasks of mothering and liberally breast-fed her infants. Sioux toddlers were allowed extensive liberties. Generosity was encouraged, property disregarded, and competition avoided. Boys were trained to be self-confident, boastful, spirited hunters of game and women. Girls were taught to be the wives and mothers of hunters. These child-rearing practices, probably well suited to the earlier life-style of the buffalo hunter, had continued even though the historical situation of the Sioux had changed radically. The traditional practices now could not cultivate or sustain a more adaptive system of social roles. The adult Sioux, who had been given considerable freedom as a child but whose life was now severely restricted, could cope with the dilemma only by looking back to the glorious past. The future of the Sioux tribe seemed "empty except for dreams of restoration."

The Yurok, on the other hand, showed "folkways of stinginess, suspicion, and anger" and an emphasis on acquiring and retaining possessions. Infants were weaned promptly at about six months and encouraged to be independent. Self-restraint was urged and the child was swiftly taught to subordinate all instinctual drives to economic considerations. The Yurok, who fished along a salmon river, learned to live more easily with the white settlers because their values were similar in many ways and their present work (farming, lumbering, and fishing) was both useful and familiar to them.

In describing the behavior of these two American Indian tribes, Erikson deliberately avoided talking about basic character traits even though he was aware that traditional psychoanalysts would perceive "oral" and "anal" character structures in the Sioux and the Yurok, respectively. Erikson preferred to "concentrate on the configurations with which these two tribes try to synthesize their concepts and their ideals in a coherent design for living." He pointed out that each society uses childhood in a number of ways: to give meaning to the child's early experiences of its body and other people, to channel the child's energies in socially constructive ways, and to provide an overall framework of meaning for the anxieties that social living provokes (1963).

## Psychohistories

Erikson also explored the contribution of culture and history to personality by examining the lives of significant historical figures. **Psychohistory** is "the study of individual and collective life with the combined methods of psychoanalysis and history" (1974). Freud too had examined the lives of various famous people, but Erikson refined the method of psychohistory and it is his name that is typically associated with the term.

In studying historical figures, Erikson explored how the ego strength of certain individuals is able to transform the conflicts that inhibit others so that they become leaders who make an impression on their era. Thus, in studying Martin Luther, an influential leader of the Protestant Reformation, Erikson did not focus on the pathological features of Luther's behavior as other psychiatric biographers had done. He concentrated on how Luther was able to overcome some of his limitations.

Erikson conceived of a seizure, which Luther is said to have experienced in the choir of his monastery, as a turning point in Luther's struggle for identity. Young Luther's exclamation, "It isn't me!" expressed his need to repudiate certain roles in order to break through to what he intended to be.

The focus on a key episode is apparent in Erikson's effort to understand what led Gandhi to a position of militant nonviolence. Erikson saw Gandhi's decision to put his life on the line by fasting during a local labor dispute (which culminated in a strike in Ahmedabad in 1918) as a crisis through which Gandhi was able to transform a negative Indian identity of weakness into a positive and active political technique.

Erikson's use of psychohistory has been applied by other writers to the lives of significant figures, such as Robert Hogan's analysis of Malcolm X (1976). Malcolm X was a well-adjusted, superior student, yet an English teacher criticized his choice of a law career as unrealistic and suggested that he consider carpentry instead. Malcolm knew he was smarter than most of his white classmates, but society refused him the identity he wished to choose because he was an African American. Therefore, he turned to a negative identity, becoming a "hoodlum, thief, dope peddler, pimp," before assuming the role of the militant African-American leader of the 1950s and 1960s. The interdisciplinary approach of psychohistory provides a deeper exploration of the past than what is offered by separate disciplines (Lawton, 1990; Rousselle, 1990).

## Sex Differences in Children's Play Construction

In *Childhood and Society* (1963), Erikson reported on an investigation he had undertaken with a large number of children between the ages of ten and twelve in order to explore how their inner lives might be reflected in their play. He set up a table with a random selection of toys and invited each child individually to construct "an exciting scene out of an imaginary movie" and then tell the plot. The resulting constructions accurately reflected each child's inner development when compared with other sources. However, Erikson also noticed distinct sex differences in the children's configurations (see Figure 6.1). Girls were apt to represent the interior of a room with a circle of furniture. Occasionally they included an intruder who was accommodated in the room. Boys, on the other hand, made towers and other high structures, some of which were in a state of collapse. Erikson concluded that in order to understand a child's play construction, he had to realize that girls and boys use space differently. Girls emphasized *inner space* and qualities of openness versus closedness. Boys concentrated on *outer space* and qualities of highness and lowness. These particular tendencies reminded him of the respective structures of the female and male genitals. This discovery led him to hypothesize that "one's experience is anchored in the ground plan of the body" and that there may be a "profound difference in the sense of space in the two sexes."

**Boys' play construction**

**Girls' play construction**

**FIGURE 6.1   Sex Differences in Children's Play Constructions**

In his observation of children's play constructions, Erikson noted that boys tended
to erect structures and towers whereas girls used the play area as the interior of a house.
*(SOURCE: From* Childhood and Society, *Second Edition, by Erik H. Erikson. Copyright
1950,* © *1963 by W. W. Norton & Company, Inc., renewed* © *1978, 1991 by Erik H. Erikson.
Reprinted by permission of W. W. Norton & Company, Inc.)*

  It is important to point out that Erikson's study of children's play construction,
given the age of the children (ten to twelve), does not prove that the differences are inherent. Indeed, an effort to replicate Erikson's study found no significant sex differences
(McKay, Pyke, & Goranson, 1984). The replication closely followed Erikson's original study,
and there was a high correlation among separate indicators on the presence or absence of
key characteristics that Erikson had identified as prototypical of male or female constructions. The researchers concluded that Erikson may have been incorrect in his judgment
about the data or that changes in sex-role socialization may have occurred since his original
study and thus account for the different findings.

  Erikson concluded, however, that the development of women is influenced by
their awareness of their reproductive capacity and identified a woman's maternal potential
as a key determinant of her personality. Unlike Freud, Erikson's clinical observations did
not support the idea that a girl's awareness of her sex focused on a missing penis. Rather, in
normative development, the focus is on a sense of vital inner potential. A woman's productive inner space is an inescapable factor in her development whether social, historical, and
other conditions lead her to build her life around it or not. Mayer (1996) suggests that Erikson's observations are a radical challenge to Freudian theory in that Erikson placed the experience of valuing femaleness at the center of how girls organize their sense of themselves
as "gendered."

  Erikson, like Freud, employed a male paradigm in his theory. The "eight ages of
man" are, in fact, for men. Although Erikson believed women could make significant con-

tributions in the political and work world, he did not believe they find identity in work. Subsequent research has shown that Erikson's stages of development are more satisfactory in accounting for the development of males than of females (Forisha-Kovach, 1983). Wastell (1996) has described how Erikson's stages could be broadened by taking into account both male and female development.

## Comments on Erikson's Research Methods

Erikson did not hesitate to develop techniques of study appropriate to his subject. Thus, as a child psychoanalyst he used the media of children's play and their positioning of objects in space in order to explore their inner lives. In the clinical setting, it quickly became apparent to Erikson that "basic psychological insight cannot emerge without some involvement of the observer's impulses and defenses, and that such insights cannot be communicated without the ambivalent involvement of the participants" (1975). His anthropological field work gave him further insight into how an observer necessarily participates in the lives of subjects and limits and structures the research. This finding was termed *participant observation* by Sullivan (1954); consistent with a twentieth-century understanding of science, it recognizes that we cannot speak of the observed without also speaking of the observer.

There are distinct parallels between the clinical evidence obtained and used by psychoanalysts in formulating their hypotheses and that used in the study of historical events. The discipline of psychohistory permits psychoanalysts to become aware of their own historical determinants and the historian to realize that in seeking to understand history we are also making history. The analyst asks the patient to free-associate and then reflect on those associations in order to perceive patterns and themes by which past experiences can be reconstructed. The study of a historical figure takes into account the coherence of statements, life, and time. Each event is considered in terms of its meaning for the individual at that particular stage of life and also in terms of its meaning for the life history as a whole. This means that early events need to be compatible with the developmental stage at which they occur and that there has to be a plausible continuity in the life history as a whole, just as the pieces of the developmental puzzle of an individual's life need to fall into place.

In psychoanalysis the significance of an episode, life period, or life trend is made clear by subsequent therapeutic crises that lead to decisive advances or setbacks. In biography, the validity of any relevant theme lies in its crucial recurrence in the person's development. In psychohistory we see how universal phenomena (such as the complex of emotions termed Oedipal) are reenacted in different ways by different people in different periods of history. Personal aims of an individual are framed in terms of the goals of the times and the relation of both of these to the psychohistorian's values (1974).

Some critics have suggested that the difficulty in distinguishing between historical fact and legend jeopardizes the conclusions of a psychohistorical study. Erikson was not distressed by such comments: "If some of it is legend, so be it; the making of a legend is as much of the scholarly re-writing of history as it is a part of the original facts used in the work of scholars" (1958). Such critics ask whether or not a theory corresponds to what we can observe: the empirical data. That criterion is characteristic of the scientist but it is inappropriate for the historian or psychoanalyst engaged in a retrospective activity. The reconstruction of the past in these instances can be based only on present clues, which may or may not correspond with the actual past. After all, the historical data that survive, even the most well established, survive thanks to "a previous generation's sense of the momentous" (1969).

A given world image needs to be anchored "in facts and figures cognitively perceived and logically arranged, in experiences emotionally confirmed, and in a social life cooperatively affirmed," "to provide a reality that seems self evident" (1974). Thus, Erikson considered proof to be a matter of the internal coherence or consistency of a theory and its ability to illumine the human condition.

## Empirical Research in Erikson's Theory

Adequate research on Erikson's stages of development would require extensive and costly longitudinal studies. Thus they have not been conducted. However, Marcia (1966, 1980) described four statuses implied in Erikson's concept of identity formation in adolescence by focusing on Erikson's belief that there are two components to identity formation: crisis (the struggle to reexamine old values) and commitment (making a decision and following its implications). Marcia developed an intricate interview formula to assess his statuses, which he termed *identity diffusion, foreclosure, moratorium,* and *identity achievement.* Research with his instrument by Papini, Micka, and Barnett (1989) shows correlations between different parenting styles and patterns of family communication and statuses. Additional research by Waterman (1982) suggests that if a young person undergoes an identity crisis it usually happens later than Erikson first suggested. Moreover, approximately one-third of young people do not experience a crisis but simply follow a predictable pattern. Orlofsky (1976) has described six different statuses related to the intimacy challenge facing young adults. He believes that men who achieve identity are also able to achieve a high level of intimacy. Some individuals known as *mergers* commit themselves to a relationship at the price of their own independence. Women who are mergers, for example, tend to be overly dependent on their husbands and are more likely to experience depression (Levitz-Jones & Orlofsky, 1985). Archer (1989) proposes that the identity development pattern for both sexes is comparable. However, women's identity is more likely to be based on a number of factors (occupation, marriage, mothering) whereas men focus primarily on their profession (see also Patterson, Sochting, & Marcia, 1992).

Cross-cultural efforts have been made to explore Erikson's psychosocial stages. Research has included the importance of ethnicity in the development of identity of African Americans (Aries & Moorehead, 1989), Mexican Americans (Bernal et al., 1990), and other groups (Markstrom-Adams, 1992).

Finally, Erikson's work has stimulated research on the final years of life. Whitbourne, Zuschlag, Elliot, and Waterman (1992) suggest that the last decade has seen less favorable resolution of ego integrity versus despair. Hamacheck (1990) has suggested behavioral criteria to assess the level of development during Erikson's last three psychosocial stages.

These research efforts and that of McAdams, which follows, testify to the current interest and study that Erikson's theory continues to generate.

## Applying Erikson's Theory: The Work of Dan McAdams

Dan McAdams sees three different voices emerging in Erikson's *Childhood and Society:* first, the voice of Freudian psychoanalysis describes the drives that govern psychosexual behavior; second, an anthropologically informed voice emphasizes culture and personality in the description of the Sioux and Yurok Indians; and the third voice emphasizes "human cognition, imagery, consciousness, narrative, plans, and goals." In the third voice, Erikson invokes "myths, legends, prototypes, scripts, narratives—the stories we live by" to outline the life-span development of personality and ego identity (McAdams, 1997).

Building on Erikson, McAdams (1993) suggests that each of us creates a conscious or unconscious narrative of the self, an individual myth, which develops as we proceed through the stages of psychosocial development. We develop identity and come to know who we are by constructing a "heroic story of the self," a myth that is unique to each one of us.

The first years give us a legacy of either optimism or pessimism, setting the tone for our myths. In the elementary school years, motives and themes develop, usually organized around themes of *agency,* the striving for individual independence and power, and *communion,* the striving for intimacy and union (see Bakan, 1966). Throughout our stories, *nuclear episodes* signify highs, lows, and turning points and reflect our motivation at various stages of ego development. *Thematic lines,* repeated series of similar goals, are also key components of our life stories. The adolescent period requires us to face the problem of identity, and we become self-conscious in our myth-making. We also place our stories in the context of a specific ideological setting, incorporating ethical and religious principles that provide us with a perspective from which to judge our lives and those of others.

In developing our myths, we create *imagoes,* main characters that represent our primary social roles and cravings for power and love. McAdams sees imagoes as archetypal patterns that arise out of the demands placed upon us as adults in society. McAdams's imagoes make up a taxonomy or system, observed from life but best illustrated by the gods and goddesses of mythology. Our internalized imagoes, idealized and personified concepts of the self, may take on prototypical forms such as the caregiver, the rebel, the lover, the survivor, and so forth.

In middle age we develop a "generativity script" that links our individual personal myths to the collective myths of humanity. McAdams has focused on generativity and developed a new model that draws on Erikson's theory but also makes some significant departures from it. Rather than supposing that there is a specific stage of generativity in adulthood, McAdams suggests that generativity becomes an important issue at that time because of increased cultural demand for it. As people get older, society expects that they will assume roles of responsibility for the successive generation, and it provides opportunities for them to do so. Generativity is conceived as a configuration of personal attributes that help in achieving the personal and social goals of contributing to the next generation

(McAdams & de St. Aubin, 1992). It is expressed through creating a legacy, maintaining that which is worthy, and offering these gifts to the next generation.

McAdams and de St. Aubin (1992) have explored generativity and developed a self-report scale, the Loyola Generativity Scale (LGS), to measure differences in concern with generativity (see Table 6.3).

McAdams, Diamond, de St. Aubin, and Mansfield (1997) have found that the life stories of generative and less generative adults differ in fundamental ways (see Table 6.4). Interviews with participants were analyzed in terms of five themes that had been previously identified as characteristic of commitment. Generative adults scored higher than non-generative participants on all of the themes except for early belief in having special advantage. The key difference between the two groups was that, in the stories of generative adults, negative events were frequently turned into positive ones. Generative adults were more likely to use such themes found in biblical stories, ancient folklore, and myth in making sense of their lives than are their less generative peers.

In studying narratives, McAdams seeks a middle ground between the use of a strict system of content analysis in studying stories and the view that stories are too fluid and culturally determined to be examined profitably. He calls this middle ground *prosocial constructionism.* He performs a content analysis, identifying how frequently certain predetermined themes occur, but also considers that the narratives warrant study on their own terms for the motifs that appear in them.

McAdams sees defining the self through mythmaking as an act of psychological and social responsibility. A postmodern world can no longer dictate who we are and should be. Therefore, we must construct that meaning for ourselves. Myths help us to do this. In some cases, however, if a particular myth is no longer functioning in a healthy way, it may be necessary to go back and construct a new self and new narrative materials from

---

### THINKING CRITICALLY

## *Writing Your Own Life Story*

You can deepen your self-understanding by beginning to write your own life narrative. In preparation for the larger task, begin by describing five autobiographical events: a recent high-point experience in your life, a low-point experience, an experience of commitment, an experience involving a goal, and an imagined future experience. Use as much specific detail as you can, paying attention to what happened, when and where it occurred, who was involved, and your feelings about each of the events. When you have finished, look at the narrative you have constructed to see if any of the patterns that McAdams describes emerge. Can you identify themes of agency, communion, or generativity? What imagoes appear in your story? Is there a pattern or sequence concerning negative and positive events? Do you think this is valuable data for a personality psychologist? Do you see any problems with this type of data?

In conjunction with writing your own history, you may wish to read Erik Erikson's psychohistories of Luther or Gandhi, or Robert Hogan's analysis of Malcolm X.

TABLE 6.3    **Measures of Generativity**

Engaging in several of the following activities and beliefs leads to a high measure of generativity in the Loyola Generativity Scale. How would you measure up?

❖ Volunteering to work for a charity

❖ Trying to be creative in one's activities

❖ Assuming responsibility for others who are less fortunate

❖ Having children or adopting them

❖ Teaching important skills to others

❖ Having a positive impact on others

❖ Being committed to other people, groups, and activities

❖ Providing advice to other people

❖ Believing that one's contributions will survive after death

❖ Feeling needed by other people

SOURCE: *Based on information from McAdams, D. P., & de St. Aubin, E. (1992). A theory of generativity and its assessment through self-report, behavioral acts, and narrative themes in autobiography.* Journal of Personality and Social Psychology, *62, 1003-1015.*

TABLE 6.4    **Themes Indicative of Generativity**

Generative adults are more likely to use the following themes in making sense of their lives than are their less generative peers:

❖ A worldview characterized by the need to help others

❖ Values and beliefs that indicate moral steadfastness

❖ The belief that negative experiences can be transformed into positive outcomes

❖ Anticipation of the future with prosocial goals

SOURCE: *Based on information from McAdams, D. P., Diamond, A., de St. Aubin, E., & Mansfield, E. (1997). Stories of commitment: The psychosocial construction of generative lives.* Journal of Personality and Social Psychology, *72, 678-694.*

which we can make a new story. Intense therapy, such as psychoanalysis, can enable us to do that.

# Erikson's Theory

The "coherence theory of truth" that Erikson employs is characteristic of the philosophical viewpoint in understanding personality (Rychlak, 1973). Unlike Freud, Erikson does not insist on a simply scientific pretense for his work; he openly acknowledges the presence of philosophical statements in his theory, believing that a sound personality theory requires a sound philosophical base.

Moreover, Erikson, like Erich Fromm, believes that important moral commitments lie within the psychoanalytic framework. To facilitate the understanding of these moral commitments, Erikson explored the evolution of the superego and distinguished among infant morality, adolescent ideology, and adult ethics. In doing so, he showed how epigenetic principles apply to the development of conscience.

The ego strengths that Erikson outlines may be seen as ethical values toward which the human race can strive. Ultimately, he aims for a universally applied ethical standard, a contemporary version of the Golden Rule, which he translates as "What is hateful to yourself, do not do to your fellow man" (1964). Erikson's philosophical statements are explicit, unlike Freud's, which are implicit.

Erikson's theory is highly comprehensive, accounting for many factors in personality development; he includes biological, cognitive, cultural, and historical variables in his discussion. It is also relevant, speaking to issues that concern us today. The fact that phrases like "identity crisis," "life span," and "inner space" are part of our everyday vocabulary testifies to its pertinence. His theory has had a heuristic value, stimulating thinking among historians, theologians, and philosophers, as well as psychoanalysts. Many people, professionals and nonprofessionals alike, find that his theory compels.

This is not to say that Erikson ignores empirical data or shuns verification of his concepts. He recognizes that one's philosophy must reflect a sophisticated understanding of contemporary scientific methods. However, he points out that a narrow scientific methodology is not able to account for his findings and is not appropriate for the study of personality. He urges a broader approach for the social scientist, including the adoption of research methods similar to those described in his own writings. Initially his theory did not generate much laboratory research because of its lack of specificity and operational definitions; complex concepts like *identity* do not readily lend themselves to precise measurement. Some research has been conducted on the identity crisis in adoles-

---

### PHILOSOPHICAL ASSUMPTIONS

## *Examining Erikson*

How would you rate Erikson on each of the basic philosophical assumptions described in Chapter 1? Consult the chart on the inside front cover. Each basic issue is presented as a bipolar dimension along which a person's view can be placed according to the degree of agreement with one or the other extreme: *freedom/determinism, hereditary/environmental, uniqueness/universality, proactive/reactive, optimistic/pessimistic.* Rate the views of Erikson on these issues.

     When you have determined where you think Erikson stands, compare your responses with those of your classmates and your instructor. You should be willing to defend your ratings, but also be prepared to change them in light of others' compelling arguments. Afterward, compare your ratings of Erikson's theory with your own position on each issue and with those of other theories. Does this comparison help you to understand why his theory does or does not appeal to you?

---

cence and for the most part the findings have been consistent with his theory. More recently, scholars such as McAdams have demonstrated considerable ingenuity in operationalizing such concepts as generativity in order to foster additional scholarship on them. Longitudinal studies could provide us with information on the validity of Erikson's concept of the developmental process, but such studies are expensive and lengthy. Researchers have largely focused on other personality theories that are easier to translate into operational terms.

     In recent years, however, there has been a renewed interest in Erikson's work because of the way his theory links cognitive and personality development. Erikson explicitly states that changes in a person's thinking skills will lead to changes in that person's social interactions and personality.

     Erikson's work has had an enormous impact in the clinical area. Not only have his formulations concerning ego development enriched formal psychoanalysis, they have also found wide application in child psychology, education, psychotherapy, and vocational and marriage counseling. As the median age of our population rises, gerontologists turn to Erikson's work for insight into the needs of our senior citizens.

     Erikson has been called the "closest thing to an intellectual hero" in the United States (Hall, 1983). His work is imaginative, creative, and extremely compelling. More than any other theorist, he has helped to maintain the viability and relevance of Freudian psychoanalytic theory in the contemporary world.

# Summary

1. Ego psychologists emphasize the role of the ego, giving it a greater degree of autonomy. Anna Freud also extended the interest of psychoanalysis to the study of the child. Heinz Hartmann explored the synthesizing and integrative functions of the ego.

2. Erikson extended Freudian psychoanalysis in four ways: he increased our understanding of the ego; he elaborated on Freud's stages of development; he extended the concept of development to include the entire life span; and he explored the impact of culture, society, and history on the developing personality.

3. Erikson emphasized the adaptive qualities of the ego, whereas Freud tended to emphasize defensiveness. He also described the social and historical forces that influence the ego's strengths and weaknesses, stressing its constructive rather than its repressive effects on development. He suggested that ego development reaches a climax during adolescence.

4. Erikson's *psychosocial stages* made explicit the social dimension that was implied in Freud's work. Each of Erikson's stages was established around an emotional conflict that people encounter at certain critical periods. His stages were *epigenetic,* progressing in a cumulative fashion. Each stage provided opportunities for a basic ego strength, or *virtue,* to grow.

5. *Trust versus mistrust* is the emotional duality that corresponds to Freud's oral stage. It leads to the development of *hope. Autonomy versus shame and doubt* marks the anal-muscular stage and culminates in *will.* The phallic stage is characterized by *initiative versus guilt.* The ego strength that emerges at this time is *purpose. Industry versus inferiority* is the hallmark of the latency period, whose ego strength is *competence.* Erikson subdivided the genital stage into four stages. The primary duality during adolescence is *ego identity versus role confusion.* The virtue developed at this time is *fidelity. Intimacy versus isolation* is characteristic of young adulthood and leads to the emergence of *love.* The middle years are characterized by a conflict of *generativity versus stagnation;* the ego strength that emerges is *care.* The final stage is marked by *ego integrity versus despair* and the ego strength is *wisdom.*

6. Erikson engaged in several studies that show how culture and history shape personality. He compared the child-rearing practices of two Native American groups, the Sioux and the Yurok. He undertook a number of biographical studies on important historical figures such as Luther and Gandhi.

7. In his discussion of sex differences, Erikson explored boys' and girls' concepts of *inner* and *outer space.*

8. Erikson developed techniques of study appropriate to his subject. There are parallels between the evidence used by a psychoanalyst and that used in a

*psychohistorical* study. Each event is considered in terms of its coherence with the individual's life. Empirical research on Erikson's theory stems from Marcia's theory of adolescence, research on ethnicity and identity, Orlofsky's description of young adulthood, and research on generativity and the final years of the life span.

9. McAdams has applied Erikson's theory to the study of life narratives and generativity.

10. The coherence method of truth that Erikson employs is characteristic of the philosopher. Erikson does not insist on a scientific pretense for his work. The philosophical statements entailed in his theory are explicit.

## Suggestions for Further Reading

Anna Freud's significant books and papers have been collected into a seven-volume set, *The Writings of Anna Freud* (International Universities Press, 1965–1974. Her classic work, *The Ego and the Mechanisms of Defense,* is found in Volume 2. Also significant is *Normality and Pathology in Childhood: Assessment of Development* in Volume 6. Heinz Hartmann's classic work is *Ego Psychology and the Problem of Adaption* (International Universities Press, 1958). His later papers are found in *Essays in Ego Psychology* (International Universities Press, 1964).

Erik H. Erikson's books are very readable. His first and most important book is *Childhood and Society* (Norton, 1950; 2nd ed. revised and enlarged, 1963). It describes different forms of child rearing among the Sioux and Yurok, introduces his eight psychosocial stages of development, and discusses the growth of the ego and evolution of identity. *Insight and Responsibility* (Norton, 1964) discusses Erikson's concept of the ethical implications of psychoanalysis and introduces his idea of ego strengths. The term "identity crisis" is most associated with *Identity, Youth, and Crisis* (Norton, 1968) in which he reevaluated his theory of identity in the light of historical change. Erikson's well-known psychohistorical studies are *Young Man Luther* and *Gandhi's Truth* (Norton, 1958 and 1969), a method of research that he clarified in *Life History and the Historical Moment* (Norton, 1973). Comments on sexual differences can be found in essays throughout his writings. In particular, "The Inner Space" in *Childhood and Society* and "The Inner Space Revisited" in *Life History and the Historical Moment* are recommended. To see how Erikson's view of the stages changed as he grew older, see *The Life Cycle Completed* (Norton, 1982).

Robert Coles has written a biography of Erikson, *Erik Erikson: The Growth of His Work* (Little, Brown, 1970). Following his death, the journal *Psychoanalysis and Contemporary Thought* devoted an issue, volume 19, (2), 1996, to articles based on Erikson's contributions. The best source for McAdams's life-narrative model of identity is his *The Stories We Live By: Personal Myths and the Making of the Self* (William Morrow, 1993).

CHAPTER

7

# Human Relations

MELANIE KLEIN ❖ MARGARET MAHLER ❖
HEINZ KOHUT ❖ OTTO KERNBERG ❖
NANCY CHODOROW ❖
THE STONE CENTER GROUP

## Your Goals for This Chapter

1. Describe the major ideas of the object relations theorists.
2. Identify the essential components of Melanie Klein's theory.
3. What contributions did Margaret Mahler make to psychoanalytic theory?
4. Explain how Heinz Kohut clarifies *narcissism*.
5. Describe how Otto Kernberg accounts for *borderline personality disorders* and discuss his method of treatment.
6. Describe how Nancy Chodorow's work differs from traditional psychoanalytic theory. Explain what she means by *the reproduction of mothering* and its implications.
7. Identify the Stone Center group.
8. Describe the thesis of Jean Baker Miller's *Toward a New Psychology of Women*.
9. Describe the paradigm shift made by the Stone Center group.
10. Explain the significance of *connections* and tell why *empathy* is central for growth within relationships.
11. Explain how *disconnections* are the major source of psychological problems.
12. Describe how psychotherapy can change and overcome the negative effects of disconnection.
13. Evaluate the human relations theories in terms of their function as philosophy, science, and art.

W hereas some psychoanalytic psychologists emphasize the role of the ego in personality development, others consider how people develop patterns of living out of their early relationships with significant others. Human development occurs in the context of relationships with other people on whom we are dependent initially for our very survival and with whom we interact throughout our lives. Many, if not most, individual problems reveal themselves through difficulties in getting along with other people, and most significant problems that affect the entire human race are interpersonal in origin and require cooperative solutions. The global community cannot afford to neglect the challenge of understanding how human beings get along together, why human relations go awry, and how they can be rectified.

Object relations theorists—for example, Melanie Klein, Margaret Mahler, Heinz Kohut, Otto Kernberg, and Nancy Chodorow—seek to understand the interaction between intrapsychic dynamics and interpersonal relationships. Beyond object relations, a group of women scholars working out of the Stone Center at Wellesley College have suggested a new perspective for the understanding human beings: **relational/cultural theory,** a perspective that has enormous potential to reshape our understanding as we move into the twenty-first century. Whereas the object relations theorists emphasize the intrapsychic experience of relationships with others, the relational/cultural theorists emphasize the interpsychic experience of relationships, or the connections and disconnections that occur between people in relationships.

## Object Relations Theory

In the 1950s and 1960s, American psychoanalysis was dominated by ego psychology. It emphasized conflict between internal structures and their defense in the individual psyche. Meanwhile, in Britain, Melanie Klein (1932) led child analysis in a different direction from that of Anna Freud (Brumann, 1996; Donaldson, 1996; Likierman, 1995; Viner, 1996) and initiated object relations theory. A distinction needs to be made between *object relationships,* one's external contemporary relationships with others, which were discussed by Anna Freud (Dyer, 1983), and *object relations,* the intrapsychic experience of early relationships with others. Object relations theory recognizes that from birth onward individuals relate to other people and form attachments. Object relations theorists seek to understand the interaction between intrapsychic dynamics and interpersonal relationships.

### Melanie Klein (1882–1960)

Melanie Klein initiated a shift in emphasis away from studying innate biological instincts and toward relations between people. She adhered to Freud's drive theory but proposed that drives are psychological forces that seek people as their objects. Klein believed that, in

*Melanie Klein emphasized the interaction
of unconscious fantasies and real-life experiences.*

dealing with their drives, children construct their own internal mental representations of other people and project them onto real people (externals). They then use subsequent experiences with those people to confirm or disconfirm their internal representations and to interpret their relationships with them. She also described how, primarily because of anxiety over aggressive impulses, children split objects and feelings into good and bad aspects in an effort to retain good ones as part of the self while getting rid of bad ones by projecting them onto others. This activity, however, clouds their subjective and objective perceptions and leads to distorted relations with other people. In emphasizing the interaction of unconscious fantasies and real experiences and the slow development of children's realistic relationships to the world, Klein made a major critical contribution to psychoanalytic theory.

Klein was more interested in the reality of the "inner world" than that of the "outer world." One result of her preference has been that object relations theory has been very helpful for understanding psychopathology (Dyer, 1983), and the interest in object relations has become particularly important as a framework for understanding some of the syndromes that have become a part of our popular clinical literature these days, such as borderline and narcissistic personality disorders and various forms of abuse (see also Grotstein, 1991).

## Margaret Mahler (1897–1985)

Margaret Mahler (1975) explored the processes of separation and individuation by which the child emerges from a symbiotic, or intimate, fusion with the mother and assumes individual characteristics. Her findings confirm that the biological birth of an infant and the psychological birth of an individual are not the same. The former is a distinct event, whereas the latter is a gradual unfolding process.

By studying and comparing severely disturbed and normal children, Mahler constructed a sequence of stages through which the ego passes in the process of becoming an individual. The **separation-individuation process** optimally begins about the fourth month and leads to the formation of a stable self-concept near the end of the third year. Separation implies physical differentiation and separateness from one's primary caregiver, while individuation suggests psychological growth away from one's primary caregiver and toward one's unique identity. Thus, in Mahler's view the roots of identity, ego strength, and conflict resolution precede the Oedipus complex.

Prior to separation-individuation, there are two "forerunner phases," *normal autism* and *normal symbiosis,* in which the infant's ego develops from a state of absolutely primary narcissism to a recognition of an external world. At this time there is no real separation of self from mother, but developments may occur that promote or impede the sub-

*Margaret Mahler explored the separation-individuation process.*

sequent individuation process. The separation-individuation process itself is composed of four stages: *differentiation,* the development of a body image separate from that of mother (five to nine months); *practicing,* perfecting motor abilities and developing physical independence (ten to fourteen months); *rapprochement,* increased awareness of separateness from mother, with an accompanying sensitivity to her absence that expresses a conflict between the urge to separate and the fear of loss, and a recognition that mothers have both good and bad aspects (fourteen to twenty-four months); *consolidation,* unification of the good and bad in mother with the image of her as a separate entity in the external world and the beginnings of the child's own individuality and separate personhood as seen in the development of a self-concept based on a stable sense of "me" (two to three years). Mahler's concept expresses her belief that normal, healthy infants show a "drive for and towards individuation" that is demonstrated in the separation-individuation process. Mahler's theory is receiving attention currently because her concept of a separation-individuation process is so helpful.

Jessica Benjamin (1988) observes that Mahler's research on separation-individuation was a "landmark in the theory of self" that deeply altered psychoanalytic theory and practice. It acknowledged *two* realities, both of which need to be understood: the importance of interpersonal dynamics and unconscious reality. She points out, however, that during the last twenty years, infancy research (e.g., Stern, 1985) has emphasized reciprocity and criticizes Mahler for emphasizing the separation of the child while neglecting to recognize the mother as a separate person as well.

Weingberg (1991) sees points of convergence between Mahler's theory and Stern's research into infants' development of self. However, Stern argues that infants are born with far more "hardwiring" than Mahler gives them credit for, and Stern emphasizes the role of mutuality, reciprocity, and the "holding" environment as critical to an infant's development. Other critics also believe that Mahler's idea that infants have an undifferentiated experience of self and mother is incompatible with recent findings about the sophisticated functioning of infants (Pine, 1994).

Mahler's theory has had a significant impact in the therapeutic community in facilitating analytic work with patients who have disturbed object relations (Akhtar, 1994; Skhiri, & Gaha, 1994). Historically, classical Freudian psychoanalysis has not been considered a treatment of choice for people with substance addictions or other addictive behaviors, such as obsessive gambling or shopping, overeating, or love addiction. However, Straussner and Spiegel (1996) have analyzed 12-step programs, such as Alcoholics Anonymous, in terms of Mahler's separation-individuation process and found that such programs ameliorate the ego deficiencies and difficulties in relating to other people that their members tend to have. Followers of such programs, however, would suggest that their effectiveness cannot be fully explained at a theoretical level because the programs encompass psychophysiological and spiritual dimensions as well.

## Heinz Kohut (1913–1981)

Heinz Kohut developed a new dimension in psychoanalysis that he called self-theory (1971, 1977). Extending Margaret Mahler's observations on the beginnings of individuality and the importance of the mother-child relationship, Kohut focused on narcissism and narcissistic

*Heinz Kohut developed self-theory and explored narcissism.*

character disorders that occur when an individual fails to develop an independent sense of self. He theorized that there is a narcissistic line of development that occurs distinct from and before ego and psychosexual development.

The term **narcissism** comes from the ancient Greek myth of Narcissus, who "unwittingly" fell in love with his own reflection in a pool of water. He talked to it and tried to embrace it, but all in vain as it fled at his touch. The passion with which he burned was self-consuming.

The narcissistic personality is characterized by an exaggerated sense of self-importance and self-involvement, behaviors that hide a fragile sense of self-worth. Freud believed that narcissistic and borderline disorders could not be treated by psychoanalysis because they originated before the patient was able to talk and thus were not amenable to verbal analysis. Because the libido is withdrawn from external objects, resistance is insuperable and it is difficult to cultivate a transference. However, disruptions in family relationships and in society have led to an increase in these disorders and to more efforts to deal with them psychoanalytically. Kohut and others (such as Giovacchini, Kernberg, and Spotnitz) have expanded the psychoanalytic repertoire to include techniques designed to work through transferences and resistances that stem from preoedipal phases of development.

Kohut (1971, 1977) conceived of narcissistic feelings not as qualities specific to a certain stage of development but as an aspect of personality that gradually unfolds, permeates the entire life span, and leads to a distorted sense of self. He believed that disorders of the self arise from a failure in parental empathy. Children need an adequate response to their infantile needs. To be specific, they need to be **mirrored**—to have their talk and their accomplishments acknowledged, accepted, and praised. Little children believe that they are omnipotent and they also **idealize** their parents. Such idealization enables them to develop goals. In time, most children learn that their idealized notions are incorrect and they substitute a more realistic assessment of both themselves and their parents. In part, this learning depends on parents responding positively to their children's unique, lovable, and commendable characteristics. If parents fail to respond in appropriate ways, children may be unable to develop a good sense of self-worth and may spend the rest of their lives looking without success for such acceptance. In short, narcissistic individuals are looking for an idealized parent substitute that can never be found.

With a well-developed self, one is aware of who one is and that awareness gives significance and purpose to one's behavior. In ideal development, the **nuclear self** emerges in the second year. Kohut believed that the nuclear self is bipolar. The two poles, archaic nuclear ambitions and subsequent goals, create a tension arc that fosters the development of early skills and talents. The ideal **autonomous self** has qualities of *self-esteem* and *self-confidence,* establishes both general ambition and precise goals, and develops talents and skills in order to meet them. Furthermore, the autonomous self shows a lack of dependence on other people.

Kohut believed that narcissistic disorders so prevalent today are characterized by recurrent self-absorption, low self-esteem, unimportant physical complaints, and a chronic sense of emptiness. Addiction, for example, is a "futile attempt to repair developmental deficits in the self" (1977b); cult membership provides a source of self-cohesion offsetting feelings of isolation, vulnerability, and emptiness (Feldmann & Johnson, 1995). Kohut pointed out that psychoanalysis cannot be useful unless the therapist deals first with the narcissistic disorder. Suggesting that therapists imagine themselves "into the client's skin," Kohut believed that therapists can cultivate feelings of being understood and appreciated in the patient so that the arrested growth of the patient's self can begin again. Thus, Kohut stressed empathy and introspection over the conventional psychoanalytic blend of free association and evenly suspended attention (Balter & Spencer, 1991). In the course of treatment, Kohut discovered that narcissistic patients develop idealizing or mirroring transferences to their analysts that reflect their early and troubled parent-child relationships. Therapy permits them to rework these relationships through to a better resolution.

Kohut (1977) reminded us that the "presence of a firm self is a precondition for the experience of the Oedipus complex." Kohut found that at the end of their analysis some of his patients who had primary self disorders acquired an Oedipal constellation. "This he considered to be the positive result of the consolidations of the self the patient had never achieved before" (Ornstein, 1993). Moreover, this development was associated with positive emotions, leading Kohut to believe that when children develop normally, the Oedipus complex may be a "joyful" experience. An Oedipus complex that is filled with conflict may be a sign that narcissistic parents have been unable to respond with empathy to their preschool-age child and may lead their child to turn to a fantasy life. Kohut (1977, 1984) pointed out that the necessity for children to have nurturing and affectionate parents was just currently being given genuine notice by psychoanalysts although it was well understood much earlier by neo-Freudians and humanists. Watson, Little, and Biderman (1992) found correlations between Baumrind's parenting styles and Kohut's theory, suggesting that an authoritative (rather than permissive or authoritarian) parenting style is less likely to foster narcissistic maladjustment.

Kohut (1984) pointed out that some parts of Freud's theory are "timebound" whereas other parts have a more "enduring validity." Eagle (1984) suggests that "if, as Kohut argues, forms of pathology are shifting more in the directions of narcissistic disorders; and if it is true and self psychology is uniquely appropriate to these phenomena; and if . . . the traditional theory of intrapsychic conflict is *inappropriate* to these phenomena, it follows that . . . the validity and applicability of traditional psychoanalytic theory [and I might add contemporary psychoanalytic theory] are culture—and era—bound . . . rather than . . . timeless and universal." Moreover, the increase in self disorders may be due to cultural forces such as an absence of stable beliefs and values and an attitude of cynicism that negatively affects teenagers and young adults.

Stolorow (1995) has suggested that Kohut contributed significantly to a new evolving paradigm for psychoanalysis that emphasizes intersubjectivity and relations. Kohut's self-theory has resulted in some fruitful reinterpretations of Freud's classic case studies (see Magid, 1993), and his concept of the self object continues to generate discussion and research (e.g., Basch, 1995; Lachmann & Beebe, 1995; Meares, 1996). Haitch (1995) detects a common note with the work of theologian Paul Tillich in the concept of courage in faith, essential for fighting illnesses such as cancer and alcoholism. Such current interest in Kohut's work is testimony to its revitalization of psychoanalytic theory.

## Otto Kernberg (1928–    )

Otto Kernberg (1975) agrees with Freud and Kohut that many people who suffer from narcissistic disorders have parents who were indifferent, cold, and also subtly hostile and vengeful toward them. Kernberg further underscores the atypical and high amount of self-reference in narcissistic individuals' interpersonal relationships and the dissimilarity between their seemingly exaggerated self-images and their insatiable need for approval from other people. While their craving for admiration and approval may lead others to think that narcissists are dependent, Kernberg believes that they are actually unable to trust other people and are, therefore, powerless to depend on others.

Kernberg has also focused on what are called **borderline personality disorders.** It was in the 1950s that analysts and therapists started to portray a type of patient who was unable to engage in introspection, develop insight, and work through problems. Such patients frequently had strong mood swings and were inclined to see significant others in their lives as all good or all bad. These patients displayed oral tendencies such as dependency needs or an incorporative style but also powerful aggressive tendencies, particularly with reference to their Oedipal struggles (Kernberg et al., 1989).

The psychoanalytic models of that time found such patients puzzling. The term "borderline" initially meant a person who was on the border between functioning adequately (if not neurotically) some of the time and lapsing over into psychotic episodes at other times. In time, the definition was narrowed and in the DSM-IV criteria of 1994, a person is considered to have a borderline personality disorder if he or she displays five or more specific clinical features. Kernberg would prefer, however, a diagnosis and explanation of borderline based on a causal description of early, historical relationships.

*Otto Kernberg worked with individuals with "borderline" personality disorders and developed expressive psychoanalytically oriented psychotherapy to help them.*

Kernberg introduced the notion of **splitting**—failing to consolidate positive and negative experiences between oneself and other people—to account for the intense changes that are apparent in a borderline individual's interpersonal relationships. Borderline people swing back and forth between conflicting images, seeing one and the same person as both loving and hateful rather than being able to see one loving person who at times accepts and at other times rejects. Kernberg portrays this behavior:

> In one session, the patient may experience me as the most help-ful, loving, understanding human being and feel totally relieved and happy, and all the problems solved. Three sessions later, she may berate me as the most ruthless, indifferent, and manipula-tive person she has ever met. Total unhappiness about the treat-ment, ready to drop it and never come back. (Sass, 1982)

Kernberg prefers to treat borderline patients face to face in intensive sessions three or more times a week. The therapist plays a more active role than is typical of classical psychoanalysis. Initially the stress is placed on current behavior rather than past events. Kernberg's method of treatment, which he calls **expressive psychoanalytically oriented psychotherapy,** differs from classical psychoanalysis in that a complete transference neurosis is not permitted to develop, nor is transference resolved through interpretation alone. Instead, the therapist clearly depicts and discusses the patient's seeming distortions of reality, such as a distorted view of the therapist.

Kernberg, Selzer, Koenigsberg, Carr, and Appelbaum (1989) suggest that interpretation has three stages: clarification by the patient of his or her problem, confronting the patient with unconscious internal contradictions, and interpreting the meaning of the repressions in the here-and-now and in the there-and-then.

Kernberg (1992) has suggested some changes to Freud's drive theory. He sees feelings, psychophysiological structures that evolved to assist mammals in surviving (1996a), as the building blocks of drives; and he believes that the source of libido is the emotional state of sexual excitement that embraces all physiologically activated functions and body zones engaged in the erotic arousal of a parent-child relationship. For Kernberg, the basis of personality formation lies in uniting the neuropsychological causes of primitive emotions with the first interpersonal experiences of babies and children. He proposes that personality disturbances are caused by the psychic structures that are built under the influence of early emotional events with significant others. Whereas Kohut believed that narcissistic personality disorders are the result of empathic failures, Kernberg believes that personality disorders are the result of drives that have not been neutralized.

In Kernberg's theory, aggression is a major motivating force, and rage is the necessary emotion contributing to the feeling of aggression as a drive. In this respect, he believes that Kohut failed to recognize the importance of analyzing negative transferences. Patients with narcissistic or borderline disorders frequently express hate, rage, and envy. The analyst must be able to avoid reacting with counteraggression and to maintain a posture of technical neutrality in order to clarify and interpret the transference and must be able to tolerate the ambiguity of his or her position (Kernberg, 1995a). Kernberg is careful not to let patients feel that their cure is essential to his own well-being, because such a belief tends to enhance feelings of omnipotence in a patient. The exercise of functional authority by the psychoanalyst is a necessary aspect of psychoanalytic work (1996b).

Kernberg (1994) recognizes that psychoanalysis in the United States has been hurt by declining interest, loss of prestige, and fewer prospective patients. Still, Kernberg (1996c) is optimistic about the future of psychoanalysis and encourages psychoanalytic institutes to foster more creativity in training candidates. For example, Kernberg (1992) has applied his theory to the full range of personality disorders. More recently (1995b), he has extended his treatment to encompass patients with severe eating disorders, and Lewis (1995) has suggested integrating Kernberg's expressive psychotherapy with her trauma-based approach.

Finally, Kernberg believes that self-psychology is missing a serious consideration of the cultural determinants of sexual excitement as well as the intrapsychic and biological ones.

> If you live in an Arab country where women are all covered except for the eyes, the wind lifts the veil, and it is a primal scene! If you go to beaches in Western Europe where many go topless, then you have a different attitude toward erotic stimulation than

if you were brought up in the Puritan atmosphere in the American mid-West 30 years ago. (Kernberg, 1992)

## Nancy Chodorow (1944– )

Sociologist and psychoanalyst Nancy J. Chodorow has probed the significance of psychoanalysis—in particular, object relations theory—on feminist and social theory (1996), including scholarly examinations on issues of sexual difference, gender (re)structuring, and social change.

In her initial work, Chodorow (1978) identifies a strong relationship between gender identity and the organization of work and the family in capitalist societies in the West. She points out that in the last two centuries, mothering by women has become increasingly separate from other work that had traditionally been done in the home (such as weaving). Industrialization eliminated many people who previously lived in the same household and

*Nancy Chodorow's work ranges from feminist social science to psychoanalysis.*

limited men's role in family life. At the same time, social scientists were emphasizing the significance of the mother-child relationship. Chodorow argues that "the contemporary reproduction of mothering occurs through social structurally induced psychological processes. It is neither a product of biology nor of intentional role-training." She believes that "women's mothering reproduces itself cyclically. Women as mothers, produce daughters with mothering capability and the desire to mother. These capacities and needs are built into and grow out of the mother-daughter relationship itself." On the other hand, boys' nurturing abilities are methodically limited and repressed as they are prepared to work outside the family.

Explanations of mothering rooted on biology or role socialization are not enough. There is nothing in a pregnant woman's physical or instinctual makeup that makes her especially fit to care for children past the first few months of infancy when she may choose to breast-feed. Psychoanalytic object relations theory offers a better explanation. The early relationship between mothers and infants establishes a basis for parenting in children of both sexes and "expectations that women will mother." Mothering meets a woman's psychological need for reciprocal intimacy initiated during her own infancy when she and her mother saw one another as extensions of themselves. Mothers are also close to their baby sons, but they see their sons as dissimilar and do not experience the same feeling of "oneness" they have with their daughters. Women's separation from their mothers results in their inability to recapture mother (if they establish a heterosexual relationship), whereas men may separate and still recapture mother via a relationship with an adult woman. Hence, there is pressure for women to remain "tied" or connected while there is no threat of a loss for men in separating.

Imbalances in family events stemming from women's mothering leads to a different development of the psyche in men and women. The establishment of gender identity occurs in the pre-Oedipal period and there are sex differences in the Oedipal experience due to this awareness and parental involvement. Women's personality develops in a way that emphasizes ongoing interpersonal relations but men grow to see themselves as distinct and separate. This prepares the two sexes for different roles: nonrelationship activities for men and relational activities for women. The different development of women and men further recreates women's mothering by preparing them to take "adult gender roles which situate women primarily within the sphere of reproduction in a sexually unequal society." Grown men, unused to a psychologically intimate relation, are satisfied with letting women mother.

Women and children's primary place in the home and men's involvement in the public sphere "defines society itself as masculine. It gives men power to create and enforce institutions of social and political control, important among these to control marriage as an institution that both expresses men's rights in women's sexual and reproductive capacities and reinforces these rights."

Differential feminine and masculine development leads to discrepancies in the present structure of parenting. Women's mothering assures that parenting is done. However, the process creates stresses and pressures that subvert the sex-gender system. Women who are isolated at home are more at risk for overinvesting in their children and looking for their children to meet their unmet emotional needs. Where women are permitted to do significant constructive work and have continuous good adult relationships while parenting, they are not as apt to overinvest in their children. When women are solely responsible for

---

**THINKING CRITICALLY**

## *Shared Parenting*

Recent years have seen fathers taking a greater role in parenting their children. At the beginning of the decade, economic conditions were not necessarily favorable for creative solutions to the problems posed by shared parenting (Kinkead, 1994). However, recently the economic situation has greatly improved so the time may be ripe for meeting the challenge. More companies are offering both paternity and maternity leaves, more flexible work hours, job-sharing, and daycare centers closer to the workplace, as well as more opportunities to work out of the home. Nevertheless, problems still remain. The suspicion lingers that a devoted parent cannot be as committed to work as someone less encumbered. Women still hesitate to choose between being a mother and having a career. Men may have an even more difficult time making that choice.

What do you think? Are men and women interchangeable in all parenting roles? What would an active parenting role entail for men? How do you believe your current or prospective role as a mother or father differs (or will differ) from the way in which you were parented? Research shows that fathers tend to be more playful with their children, especially with their sons. What about the positive or negative impact of rough-and-tumble play between fathers and sons and daughters?

---

parenting, it is more difficult for men to develop "a stable sense of masculine self." If we want to be free of this inequality, we will have to restructure parenting "so that primary parenting is shared between men and women."

In Chodorow's *Feminism and Psychoanalytic Theory* (1989) we can see the development of her thought during a career change from feminist social scientist to psychoanalyst. She has moved from a primarily social determinist stance toward a more psychological and internal point of view. Believing that object relations theory has not generated a sufficient description of gender or an acknowledgment of the mother's subjectivity, Chodorow extends and improves the theory via a feminist contribution. She states that object relations is in error in thinking of mothers primarily as objects for their children.

The fact that women are the fundamental caregivers is experienced very differently by boys and girls. Girls feel connected to their mothers while boys experience a feeling of threat because they have to depend on someone of another sex and later turn away from her. Girls' early development, therefore, is optimistic and positive while boys' development is pessimistic and negative, entailing repression of "affect," "relational needs" and "a sense of connection." However, when children become three or four years old, power changes to male dominance. The behaviors connected with diverse sex roles are given a new interpretation. Men have caused this new interpretation via their power and cultural supremacy, which is based on their fear and resentment of strong women due to their mother's power over them. In fact, women's maternal capacities have very positive qualities, as they generate good relationships that women, in particular, are able to participate in.

Chodorow believes that it is "crucial" for us to recognize that "the ideologies of difference, which define us as women and as men, as well as inequality itself, are produced,

**THINKING CRITICALLY**

## *Culturally Sanctioned Mutilation*

In many parts of the world, most notably in Africa and places in the Near East, clitoridectomy, or even removal of the entire vulva, is practiced with full religious and cultural sanctions. These practices are thought to ensure that the woman will be a virgin and pure when she is married. Women who have not had these procedures done are thought to be prostitutes. Therefore, mothers regularly subject their daughters to the painful and embarrassing practice even at a very young age. Such mutilation, however, effectively denies these women their sexuality and ability to fully satisfy their sexual drives (Walker and Parmar, 1993; see also Ugwu-Oju, 1993).

On the other hand, in the United States and in other parts of the world as well, many male babies are routinely circumcised. In some cases this is for religious reasons; in other cases it is done for "health purposes." While a circumcised penis is easier to keep clean, circumcision does desensitize the tip of the penis, making it less amenable to intense sexual sensation. Although such action certainly cannot compare to the destruction of women's genitals, could it be called a form of "mutilation"?

What do you think? Are these practices a sign of our continuing struggle as human beings to come to terms with our sexuality, gender fears, and power? Because these practices are culturally, and in some cases religiously, sanctioned, they could be very difficult to change.

---

socially, psychologically, and culturally, by people living in and creating their social, psychological, and cultural worlds" (1989).

Chodorow (1989) points out that Freud's theory does not simply subjugate women. "Freud tells us how nature becomes culture and how this culture comes to appear as and be experienced as 'second nature.'" Although Freud's understanding of male attitudes toward women is clear and compelling, he himself acknowledged that his understanding of feminine psychology was "shadowy and incomplete." Nevertheless, he "condemned the conditions that lead to repression and hysteria in women" (Chodorow, 1991). Freud's writings testify to and account for clinical and sociohistorical sexual diversity in both men and women. Although he gave normative status to heterosexuality, it was within a culture characterized by male-dominant gender differentiation (Chodorow, 1994). Moreover, "Freud suggests that these processes do not happen so smoothly, that this reproduction of gender and sexuality is rife with contradiction and strains" (1989).

Chodorow's speculation may be limited to families rooted in a conventional separation of labor. Some suggest that her speculation "holds only for white, middle-class nuclear families. Still it is useful in explaining how gendered personalities are recreated through the social structure of the family." Also "an important test of her theory would involve the study of boys and girls who are raised by men or in cultures where women are not devalued and parenthood is more equally shared" (Anderson, 1991).

More recently, Chodorow (1996b) expresses concern about theories positing objectivized or universal stages, drives, or unconscious fantasies that transcend cultures to explain psychological experience. She points out that in the clinical experience, psychological meaning is created in the here-and-now, with singular evidence from each person's subjective childhood and individual transferences. A person's sense of gender is a fusion of personal and cultural meaning (1995). The emphasis on objective gender, making generalizations about how men and women construct the self, often obscures subjective gender (the personal sense of one's femininity or masculinity). For one individual, invulnerable anger may be a key dimension of masculinity; for another, femininity may be encompassed in feelings of shame and guilt. Such examples illustrate the immense variation and individuality of gender definition and construction. In efforts to understand gender, placing an emphasis on the linguistic, cultural, and political construction of gender risks omitting how individual psychological processes also construct gender for the individual.

## Relational/Cultural Theory: The Stone Center Group

Beginning in the late 1970s, a group of women, friends and colleagues, have come together in an effort to improve and cultivate a better understanding of the psychology of women and eventually of all human beings. The core group consists of Jean Baker Miller, M.D., Irene P. Stiver, Ph.D., Judith V. Jordan, Ph.D., and Janet L. Surrey, Ph.D.; however, clustered around them are numerous other women, increasingly representing a more diverse community. Much of the work has been facilitated by the Stone Center for Developmental Services and Studies at Wellesley College in Massachusetts (now part of the Wellesley Centers for Women) under the leadership of Jean Baker Miller.

The Stone Center core group are trained and practicing clinicians who started by looking at the experiences of the women they worked with and began to suspect that traditional theories of human nature and development misunderstood, disregarded, or devalued several aspects of women's experiences. Moreover, the conventional models were having an insidious effect on women. The theory that has emerged from the work of these women is unique in that it is primarily a collaborative effort. Although individuals may organize and express ideas a little differently, the generation and growth of their concepts has essentially come from the group. Their contribution has significant implications for personality theory and psychotherapy as well.

A significant precursor to the theory that has emerged from the Stone Center was Miller's 1976 work *Toward a New Psychology of Women*. In that book, Miller argued that the psychological development of both sexes has been constrained and contorted by a "framework of inequity" in which one sex was thought to be of more worth than the other. The strict stereotypes portraying dominant males and subordinate females were hindering both men and women from reaching their full potential. Miller suggested a new foundation in which concepts traditionally associated with the two sexes (strength versus weakness, dependency versus autonomy) could take on new significance and purpose. Key to her message was the concept of affiliation and relationship. She asserted that women have critical and essential strengths, as yet unrecognized by our society, that can provide a creative balance to the human problems with which we are grappling. Her work undermined the male-focused paradigm of classical psychoanalysis and showed how concepts previously devalued because they have generally been associated with women (e.g., cooperation, giv-

*Shown here are some contributors to the Stone Center group, which has been the catalyst of a new view of human development that focuses on connectedness. From left to right: back row—Yvonne Jenkins, Natalie Eldridge, Judy Jordan, Janet Surrey; front row—Maureen Walker, Jean Baker Miller, Irene Stiver.*

ing, and nurturing) are in reality dormant strengths. Miller pointed toward a new truth—the initial development of all human beings begins in affiliation and relation (rather than self-enhancement)—and suggested the need to place our faith in others rather than in our own individual power, achievement, and self-sufficiency.

Research at the Stone Center has been influenced by the work of Nancy Chodorow, who made it clear that object relation theory does not reflect the ways in which the early bond between mother and daughter creates different boundaries between them than between mother and son—boundaries that are further entrenched by the child-rearing patterns of Western culture. The Stone Center also draws from the work of Carol Gilligan (1977, 1982, 1990), whose studies of girls' and women's psychological and moral development emphasizes the importance of connection with, responsibility for, and care of others.

Research by the Stone Center group suggests that the basic organizing feature of women's growth is the feeling of *connectedness* to others (Miller & Stiver, 1997). The ability to make and keep relationships is the source of a woman's sense of self and of worth. Women actively participate in the development of others, and they use their power to facilitate the growth and unfolding of both children and adults. Such participation in other people's psychological growth is an integral aspect of human life, providing a new psychological model of human development *"within relationships"* (Miller & Stiver, 1997).

The knowledge of how to develop relationships that facilitate growth is not confined to either gender, nor is it tied to an innate or biological source. As a general rule, however, society has assigned to women the role of participating in the psychological development of others, and thus it is primarily from the lives and experience of women that we can best learn about the possible impact of a relational approach to human development.

## Shifting the Paradigm

In asserting that women's life experiences are an appropriate starting point from which to understand human nature, the women of the Stone Center are challenging long-standing assumptions of psychological development. Throughout Western history and culture, the paradigm of human nature has been a male one, emphasizing autonomy and independence. Becoming a self-sufficient individual is commonly seen as the goal of psychological development. This aim is reflected in psychoanalysis, where independence and separation are the model for health. Although Erikson's stages begin with relatedness, the model quickly moves into subsequent stages that stress autonomy and self-development. Women's strength in being able to relate to others has regularly been devalued and debased as a sign of weakness (Miller, 1991). According to the Stone Center group, basic beliefs about who we are develop within the mutual connection of interpersonal relationships, not in the process of separating from each other.

Initially, the Stone Center group described their theory variously as "self-in-relation" or "the relational self." However, the virtue of setting up a new theory of "self" has itself been questioned, as they have shifted into an emphasis on relational development and the movement of relationships. "Connection" has replaced "self" as the key ingredient or focus of development (Surrey, 1990). It is **connections** that are the basic origins of growth and development and **disconnections** that derail us and block our growth. Reconceiving and recognizing the important role of relationships and connections changes the whole base of current psychological theory and thinking and requires major alternations in our concepts about what fosters growth and healing and what leads to problems and pain.

Thus the Stone Center group (Miller & Stiver, 1997) is proposing a paradigm shift in our thinking about human nature that moves away from individualistic values to relational ones and that places connection at the center of our thought (see Table 7.1). Whereas earlier theorists described a process of separation-individuation, Surrey (1991) proposes the concept of *relationship-differentiation,* a process that entails increasing levels of complexity within the framework of human relationships. The two-directional process of the mother-daughter relationship is an early model of relational development, providing us with a pattern for studying and learning about emotional connectedness and reciprocal empathy. The self unfolds in the matrix of significant relationships. Rather than entailing a task of separation, the path is one of developing capacity for entering into relationships and relational competence. Other aspects of the self, such as autonomy, develop within the prior situation of being in relation and do not negate the importance of relationship. In relationship, separate selves interact and coexist. Relationship does not always entail continuous physical connection, but there is continuous psychological connection, and the awareness of the

TABLE 7.1    **Stone Center Group**

The Stone Center group is proposing a new paradigm for understanding human nature that emphasizes human interconnectedness rather than separation and individuation.

|  | TRADITIONAL PARADIGM | STONE CENTER PARADIGM |
| --- | --- | --- |
| Process of development | separation-individuation | relationship-differentiation |
| Goal of development | self | connections |
| Model | male | female |
| Health | self-sufficiency | relational competence |
| Ill health | dependency | disconnections |
| Values | individualistic | connecting |

*According to the Stone Center paradigm, basic beliefs about who we are develop within the mutual connection of interpersonal relationships.*

presence of the other is the basis of one's self-experiences. Within this new paradigm, the adolescent experience is not necessarily one of separation but rather of altering the relationship so as to facilitate and affirm one's own growth (Surrey, 1991).

## Connections

Human beings seek **connections.** Earlier drive theories of psychoanalysis suggested that human beings seek primarily pleasure or gratification. The very name *object relations* reflects a perception of other people as objects that fulfill or frustrate our drives. Traditionally, the view of our basic formative relationships has not been based on **mutuality,** a way of relating and sharing in which all are fully participating. Freud's model of human development stressed the competitive and aggressive qualities of the male relationship. Rather than focus on the Oedipus complex or a feminine version of it, Stiver (1991a) suggests that we look at the ongoing intense, often conflictual, relationships of mothers and daughters and fathers and daughters and study the different roles that mutual empathy and empowerment play in order to clarify the connections that we seek.

Central to the new emphasis is a reconception of **empathy,** which entails experiencing the feelings and thoughts of another while simultaneously knowing one's own different feelings and thoughts. Empathy has often been thought of as a setback to mature functioning, characterized by regression and symbiosis, in which there is a break of ego boundaries and a merging with another individual. Earlier, Kohut (1978) had observed that "empathy is a fundamental model of human relatedness"; he even stressed the importance of empathy. However, he did not describe its origins or clearly envision it as a reciprocal interactional process. Jordan (1991) suggests that a more adequate definition of empathy envisions it as a process involving both cognitive and affective aspects that evolves to become increasingly complex, sophisticated, and mature. Developing the capacity to be empathetic requires modeling, practice, and mutual response.

Miller (1986) describes the type of empathic dialogue and interchange that fosters connection. Ann is telling Beth that a mutual friend, Emily, may have a serious disease.

> Tears are in Ann's eyes and her voice sounds sad and fearful. Beth says, "Oh, how sad." Beth's voice and expression are sad and there is also some fear in them.
>
> Ann then says, "Yes, but I have this other awful feeling—like fear. Like I'm scared—as if it could happen to me." Beth replies, "Me, too. It is frightening to hear this. Maybe we all feel as if it's happening to us."

An empathetic response adds to what was initially expressed and leads to a fuller acknowledgment and expression of thoughts and feelings. At first, Ann and Beth are hesitant about expressing the depth of their feelings; but as they each acknowledge and share their emotions, they are able to express them more profoundly, to imagine how Emily must be feeling, and to move from that to discussing how they would like to be with Emily during this difficult period. In the conversation that follows, Ann and Beth are able to explore their feelings and thoughts more fully. As the interaction proceeds, both become increasingly motivated and able to act. Because of the greater lucidity and accuracy that results from their conversation, they decide together to call Emily, visit her, and take other appropriate action.

In contrast, when Ann tries to share the news with her husband, Tom, a very different scenario occurs.

> Tom replies, "Well, it's a terrible thing. In the end, she'll have to do the best she can. She should get a second opinion. I hear the Sloan Clinic is very good on these kinds of cases. Have you called her back yet? Did you call my sister Helen about the birthday party she's trying to arrange for my mother next week? We should really do something about that if it's going to come off."

Tom does not respond to Ann's feelings. Instead he tells her what to do, what Emily should do, and then changes the subject, giving directions to Ann about an impending party. Whereas Ann felt empowered after her conversation with Beth, she feels uncertain after the interchange with Tom. In addition to the feelings of fear and sadness that she was unable to express, she also feels that she has lost connection.

Mutual empathy fosters mutual empowerment (Miller & Stiver, 1997), which is characterized by *zest*, the feeling of authentic connection. In addition, mutual empathy leads to the ability to take *action* in the situation, to increased *knowledge* of ourselves and others, to a *sense of worth* and of the legitimacy of our feelings, and to the *desire to make more connections.*

Mutuality is thus a crucial element of growth that fosters relationships. It does not mean sameness or equality but rather a way of relating, a shared activity in which all are fully participating. In the creative process of mutuality, something new arises based on the contributions of each person. Individuality is not being sacrificed to the group; rather, we are being ourselves as much as possible while also responsibly responding to others. The self and other become "mutually forming processes" (Miller & Stiver, 1997).

## Disconnections

The major source of psychological problems is **disconnection,** the break that is experienced when a person cannot engage in mutually empathetic and empowering relationships (Miller & Stiver, 1997). Disconnections can be either major or minor. Minor disconnections occur frequently and need not be problematic. They can even lead to growth and to improved connections, particularly if people feel safe enough to discuss the disconnection with someone who can hear and respond to the experience. The ability to reconnect after a disconnection is itself empowering. If disconnections continue over long periods of time, however, they are more difficult to resolve. They begin to appear to be natural, and a person may feel unjustified in being distressed over the disconnection. Disconnections pose the greatest problem in relationships of unequal power, because they hold the greatest potential for danger and harm to the less powerful individual. Attack or abuse in such relationships would be sources of major disconnections.

When another person does not share their feelings with us, we may feel alone in our emotions and angry because of their unresponsiveness. The situation will be compounded if we make an effort to reconnect and are further rebuffed. Because the feelings are

*In relationships of unequal power, disconnections*
*can be quite threatening to the less powerful individual.*

ours, we may feel it is our problem, not the other person's. We move from feelings that are already difficult to handle, such as sadness or fear, to a much more complicated and confused combination of emotions.

Difficult feelings are best handled in connection with others. When children are not able to talk about their feelings—for example, their sadness at a death in the family—they feel frightened and confused. They also begin to believe that there is something wrong with them and their feelings. The ultimate outcome is psychological isolation, which is the most terrifying and damaging emotion that we can experience. More than just being alone, we are being actively prevented from connection and are powerless to change that situation. After experiencing repeated disconnections, individuals will try to connect in whatever ways they possibly can. If they are powerless to change the relationship, they will try to change themselves. In order to be what others seem to want, they will deny their own feelings. On the surface, the person may seem to be compliant, but internally he or she experiences increasing disconnection and fear of trying to establish new connections. Anger is inevitable. It becomes difficult to form accurate relationship images of oneself or others.

## THINKING CRITICALLY

# *Disconnections and Connections*

Consider a situation recently in which you felt a deep sense of disconnection and the feeling that you were misunderstood. Carefully go over the dialogue, both verbal and nonverbal, that occurred in that event. Can you identify the specific phrases, behaviors, or actions that led you to feel misunderstood? How did you react? Did you try to press further and reestablish connection (and what happened then), or did you give up the pursuit and accommodate yourself to the other person? How did you feel in the aftermath of the episode?

Also consider a situation in which you felt a deep sense of connection. Carefully go over the dialogue, both verbal and nonverbal, that occurred in that event. Can you identify the specific phrases, behaviors, or actions that communicated empathy and helped you believe that you were being understood and that you were understanding the other person? Can you identify the transition point at which the movement from mutual empathy moved into mutual empowerment? If you have trouble recalling a situation of mutual empathy and empowerment, create such a situation in your imagination and identify the elements that it would include.

---

This leads to the *central relational paradox:* people who have experienced trouble in relationships continue to try to make new connections, but they are hindered from doing so because they cannot permit themselves to acknowledge the full range of their experience and feelings as they need to do in order to establish relationships.

Disconnections and violations happen to people at all ages; however, our most basic relational images are created early in life, when we are the most vulnerable to disconnection and least able to form new connections that might change the images. Thus abused or raped women who suffered from disconnections in childhood often believe they are unworthy and to blame for what happened to them. Much of the psychological suffering caused by depression, addictions, and eating disorders comes from trauma created by disconnected, distressed families. Dysfunctional relationships are at the core of many of our current social problems: incest, sexual abuse, and violence. In the past, clinicians commonly blamed the early mother-child relationship for problems primarily perpetuated by men. Too often, mothers were given full responsibility for child rearing without having necessary social support.

Disconnected families are characterized by three outstanding patterns (Miller & Stiver, 1997): *secrecy,* which denies "unacceptable" reality; *parental inaccessibility,* which precludes mutually empathetic relationships; and *"parentification,"* which requires the child to act prematurely as the grown-up. A conspiracy of silence often arises in a family in which incest occurs. In milder forms, children may be admonished not to discuss something "outside of the family." Adult children of alcoholics testify to inaccessibility in their childhood homes, as alcohol renders a parent either barely present or eruptive and angry. Depression may also leave a parent unable to connect with children. In such households, children may be required to assume parental responsibility while they themselves are still in need of active parenting. The three patterns both arise from and perpetuate chronic disconnections.

Some people learn to survive disconnections. They develop strategies for staying out of relationships, such as emotionally disengaging through inattention, preoccupation, withdrawal, or the use of alcohol or drugs. They may develop a strategy of role-playing in order to win approval and give the illusion of connection. Role-playing may appear to be adaptive, but it does not permit authentic engagement. People may replicate earlier traumatic family interactions, preventing the development of current authentic relationships. These survival tactics leave people suffering, disempowered, and out of touch.

## Psychotherapy

Fortunately, people can establish new relationships that will enable them to overcome the negative effects of disconnection. Studies of resilience in children show that resilience is enhanced by a temperament that facilitates relationships and by having a close relationship with at least one person. Some people can make far-reaching changes. Women in battered-women's shelters, for example, may, through mutual empathy, join together to take appropriate legal and political action.

Psychotherapy can provide a path to increased authentic connections (Miller & Stiver, 1997). The Stone Center group believes that most psychological problems are a result of the basic relational paradox: they are consequences of the effort to avoid engaging in relationships. The Stone Center group emphasizes identifying the origins of disconnection; the goal of therapy is to help the patient make mutual empathetic connections. Essentially, their therapy creates a new relationship between therapist and patient that is crucial to the process of healing.

Traditional clinicians are trained to distance themselves from their feelings in order to be objective and neutral. Stone Center therapists remain open to their own experiences and permit themselves to be moved by their patients' feelings. When a clinician is able to feel along with a patient, the therapist herself changes. The patient is aware of this and knows that she has had an effect on the therapist by expressing her feelings and thoughts; she is now making a connection that contradicts her earlier experiences. It is a process of "moving in relationship"; the therapist and patient are moving toward mutual empathy.

The therapist's responsibility is to facilitate the process of moving in relationship. The clinician must let the patient know when and how the patient is affecting her. This helps people believe that they can experience and sort out feelings with another person. Negative feelings or wishes can be recognized and accepted for what they are without need for interpretation. One can acknowledge how difficult it is to feel critical or angry feelings, particularly in a therapy situation. The ability to do so enhances the therapeutic relationship, which is not simply the means to the end but "both the means and the end" (Miller & Stiver, 1997).

The therapy technique used by the Stone Center group transforms traditional psychotherapy concepts such as transference. In classical analysis, the therapist maintains an attitude of neutrality and objectivity to facilitate the patient's process of projecting feelings toward people in his or her past onto the therapist. Conversely, the Stone Center group believes that neutrality can hinder the process of therapy because it prevents the patient from seeing the differences between the current relationship and past ones. The safety that an empathetic relationship provides actually facilitates transference, letting the patient explore previous relational images and begin to change them. Rather than trying to interpret the transference, which could be perceived as criticism, the group believes that being empathetic to the power of the patient's earlier relational image and conveying respect for how she dealt with the earlier circumstances communicates the difference between the therapeutic relationship and earlier ones.

Freud viewed countertransference, the clinician's conscious and unconscious feelings about the patient, as an impediment. The Stone Center group believes that countertransference may either facilitate or impede the therapist's ability to connect with a patient. The clinician must pay attention to any feelings of disconnection she might be experiencing and must focus on moving back toward connection. It is important to take seriously the paradox that patients want to make connections but are afraid to establish them.

The Stone Center clinicians disclose more of their own feelings than do classical psychoanalysts. They recognize that silence and nondisclosure may have a negative effect on therapy and lead to disconnection. If a situation in the therapist's life makes it difficult for her to be fully attentive (e.g., a death in the family), it may help for her to admit this to the patient. Too much disclosure, however, can be burdensome and overwhelming to a patient.

The process of therapy is difficult and demanding. Painful feelings emerge that would be impossible for a patient to explore except in an empathetic relationship with another person. The clinician's role, however, is not simply to be nice and caring. In order to move in relationship, the therapist must try to share the other person's experience in all its facets, including the cultural matrix in which it arises. The relationship of the therapist and patient is structured by the demands of therapy and its goal is the growth of the patient. The limits of the therapeutic relationship must be recognized—it should not be seen as a friendship or a replacement for family.

Furthermore, although the relationship is mutual, a power differential obviously exists. The therapist needs to be aware of this and be willing to discuss it. The therapist and patient are equal partners in the therapeutic endeavor; the sole difference is that it is the therapist's job to promote the movement toward more connection in the relationship.

## Other Applications

Effective therapy leads to the ability to forge deeper connections with others and with the larger community. Following therapy, people are often motivated to begin to rectify deeper disconnections in the larger world. Because our surroundings affect us, both patients and therapists need to be among colleagues and peers with whom they can share their experiences. Specifically, 12-step groups patterned after Alcoholics Anonymous are effective and vital because of the mutual empathy and empowerment they foster.

The relational model reconceives many traditional concepts such as anger, dependence, courage, shame, and sexual desire and orientation. *Anger* is a necessary signal that something is wrong in a relationship and needs to be changed (Miller & Surrey, 1997). Women have a tendency to confuse anger with violence or oppression (Bernadez, 1988), and they have not been trained to assert themselves in appropriate and effective ways. *Dependence* is redefined as a process of letting other people help us to cope physically and emotionally with experiences and tasks when we do not have sufficient skill, confidence, or energy to do so by ourselves. This definition permits us to see ourselves as "enhanced and

*In relational/cultural theory, courage is no longer a solitary accomplishment but an action taken in spite of fear and supported by the encouragement of others. These women are training for a wilderness hike to benefit Elizabeth Stone House, a shelter for women who have been abused.*

empowered through the very process of counting on others for help" (Stiver, 1991b). *Courage* can be redefined in a contextual relational manner so that it no longer refers to a solitary accomplishment but to an action taken in spite of fear and supported by the encouragement of others (Jordan, 1990). *Self-esteem* emerges from relational confidence rather than mastery or self-efficacy (Jordan, 1994). *Shame* is a deep yearning for connection while perceiving oneself as unworthy of it (Jordan, 1997b). The expression of *sexual desire* can be seen in a framework of empathic communication rather than one of achievement and performance (Jordan, 1997a). Rather than quickly dismissing the *fusion,* or intense intimacy, of lesbian relationships as pathological, one might view it as a pattern that allows women to express their relational strength (Mencher, 1997).

The initial Stone Center group was largely white, middle class, and well educated. They acknowledged that their perspective was limited by their own experiences, and they did not try to suggest that their work was representative of all women. In recent years, they have expanded their work by seeking the perspectives of minority and lesbian women (Jordan, 1997a). Turner (1997) has shown how a relational approach validates significant aspects of African American women's experience. Study groups have also been formed in which women with chronic illnesses or disabilities are the participants. More work needs to be

### THINKING CRITICALLY

## *Working with Diversity in Relationships*

Stephen Bergman and Janet Surrey (1997) use the following questions to foster dialogue between men and women.

1. Name three strengths the other gender group brings to relationships.
2. What do you most want to understand about the other gender group?
3. What do you most want the other gender group to understand about you?

First answer the questions individually and then in groups of the same gender before attempting to share the answers with an entire group of members of both genders. In the discussion, pay particular attention to the impasses that arise and may lead to disconnection and the ways in which the different groups seek to resolve them. The impasses in the groups are easier to recognize as different relational styles meet one another. Two common impasses that emerge in gender groups are the *Dread/Anger Impasse,* in which men retreat and women begin to get angry, and the *Product/Process Impasse,* in which women try to open up the process of communication and men try to fix a problem. It is important to experience the conflict without negatively expressing it and to work on staying in connection in order to foster understanding, curiosity, and empathy for the other group. This activity can also be adapted to working with members of diverse groups of different ethnicities, religions, and orientations.

*Source:* Bergman, S. J., & Surrey, J. L. (1997). The woman-man relationship: Impasses and possibilities. In J. V. Jordan (Ed.), *Women's Growth in Diversity,* 260–287. New York: Guilford Press.

done on the experiences of Native and Asian American women and on the impact of class on all women. Although the Stone Center group believes that their general statements are meaningful, they realize that their relational approach must be integrated with the experience of marginalized groups.

Tatum (1997) suggests that the practice of racism is like continually breathing in smog. It destroys both the oppressed and the oppressor. It is not an individual problem but a social one. A concerted effort must be made to develop understanding across different groups, emphasizing that empathy involves appreciating the differences of others as well as acknowledging similarities.

| PHILOSOPHY, | **Human Relations Theories** |
| --- | --- |
| SCIENCE, | |
| AND ART | The human relations theorists do not insist on a simply scientific basis |

for their work. As clinicians, their work is based on empirical observation. At the same time, they emphasize the need for an interdisciplinary perspective, as is clearly seen in Chodorow's work.

Many variables, such as biological, cognitive, cultural, sociological, and historical factors are addressed. The theories also speak to issues that concern us today, such as personality disorders that have become more pervasive and the need to rethink the issues of gender and parenting. The theories have a heuristic value, stimulating thinking among historians, sociologists, literary people, and philosophers as well as psychoanalysts. Psychoanalysis is a good example of a science that has resisted the tenets of natural science and maintained aspects of the literary and descriptive language of everyday life (Jager, 1989).

This is not to say that these theorists ignore empirical data or shun verification of their concepts. However, they believe that a narrow scientific methodology is not appropriate for the study of personality, and they urge a broader approach for the social scientist.

Their theories have not generated much laboratory research because of their lack of specificity and operational definitions. Complex concepts such as Kernberg's *splitting* do not readily lend themselves to precise measurement. Longitudinal studies could provide us with information on the validity of some of their ideas, such as Chodorow's notion of the reproduction of mothering, but such studies are expensive and lengthy. Researchers have largely focused on other personality constructs that are easier to translate into operational terms.

The *Mutual Psychological Development Questionnaire* (MPDQ), a standardized self-report inventory, has been developed by the Stone

---

**PHILOSOPHICAL ASSUMPTIONS**

 *Examining the Human Relations Theorists*

How would you rate the object relations and relational/cultural theorists on each of the basic philosophical assumptions described in Chapter 1? Consult the chart on the inside front cover. Each basic issue is presented as a bipolar dimension along which a person's view can be placed according to the degree of agreement with one or the other extreme: *freedom/determinism, hereditary/environmental, uniqueness/universality, proactive/reactive, optimistic/pessimistic.* Rate the views of the object relations and relational/cultural theorists on these issues.

When you have determined where you think the theorists stand, compare your responses with those of your classmates and your instructor. You should be willing to defend your ratings, but also be prepared to change them in light of others' compelling arguments. Afterward, compare your ratings of these theorists with your own position on each issue and with those of other theorists. Does this comparison help you to understand why these theorists do or do not appeal to you?

Center group to measure perceived mutuality in close relationships. The MPDQ permits empirical research that may help answer questions about how people perceive their intimate relationships and may also be useful in the clinical setting, although it was initially developed using nonclinical populations. As the MPDQ is applied to relationships in other populations, it may help us understand gender, racial, and ethnic contextual factors that inform the relational aspects of psychological growth.

The work of the object relations and relational/cultural theorists has had an enormous impact in the clinical area. Much of their work is being integrated into a variety of therapeutic approaches and has been particularly helpful in clarifying syndromes such as those presented by victims of trauma and abuse. Dysfunctional family systems—those having problems related to incest, addiction, or such traumatic experiences as Holocaust survival, for instance—can be more clearly understood in relational terms, as can the processes of recovery.

Further progress in understanding human relationships may be made by forging theoretical links with neurology, cognitive and developmental psychology, evolutionary theory, literature, linguistics, information and systems theory, and philosophy (Krystal, 1990; Paul, 1989). In addition, links could be forged with the theories of the Russian psychologist Vygotsky, who focused on issues such as the social origins of the intrapsychological level of functioning, the interfunctional nature of consciousness, and the need to take into account mediational needs. These ideas are very different from the individualistic underpinning of Western psychology, especially in the United States. Vygotsky believes the boundaries between individuals are much more permeable and the boundaries between individuals and the sociocultural tools they use are more difficult to preserve (Wertsch, 1990).

The current work in psychoanalysis is imaginative and creative. These theorists have helped to maintain the viability and relevance of Freudian psychoanalytic theory in the contemporary world. For all the criticism of psychoanalytically oriented theories that declares the lack of "'scientifically demonstrated' hypotheses—it is also a commonly overlooked fact that none of the modern competitive theories (cognitive, behavioral, or humanistic) have withstood similar rigid scientific tests to validate their claims to legitimacy as acceptable theories underlying the conceptualization and application of psychotherapy" (W. L. Kelly, 1991). These theorists clearly demonstrate that psychoanalysis is far from dead.

The paradigm shift suggested by the Stone Center group is a major alteration in basic philosophical assumptions and underpinnings that has enormous potential to reshape the way in which human beings in Western cultures have conceived of themselves. By putting the primary emphasis on the relationship as the origin and matrix of human development, the group challenges the "I"-centeredness that has pervaded Western conceptualizations of and thoughts about the person and personality. This refocus not only has tremendous implications for understanding ourselves, but it also has vast potential to be a very curative and healing force in human nature at a time in which such a power is sorely needed.

## Summary

1. Object relations theorists look at how people develop patterns of living out of their early relationships with significant others, particularly their mothers.

2. Melanie Klein emphasized the interaction of unconscious fantasies and real experiences in the development of children's object relations.

3. Margaret Mahler explored the processes of *separation* and *individuation* by which the child emerges from a symbiotic fusion with the mother and develops individual characteristics. She constructed a sequence of stages through which the ego passes in the process of becoming an individual.

4. Heinz Kohut accounted for *narcissism* and narcissistic character disorders that occur when an individual fails to develop an independent sense of self. He has developed psychoanalytic techniques designed to work through transferences and resistances stemming from pre-Oedipal phases of development.

5. Otto Kernberg introduced the notion of *splitting* to describe the interpersonal relationships of individuals with *borderline personality disorder,* and he developed a method of treatment called *expressive psychoanalytically oriented psychotherapy.* More recently, he has focused on aggression and has suggested changes to Freud's drive theory.

6. Nancy Chodorow places gender identity explicitly in the framework of the division of labor by sex in the workplace and the family. She believes that mothering by women reproduces cyclically, producing daughters with the desire and capacity to mother but sons whose nurturing abilities are limited and repressed. Family structure needs to be transformed so that primary parenting is shared between men and women.

7. The Stone Center group is a group of women who have developed a new collaborative theory of human development within relationships.

8. Jean Baker Miller's thesis is that both sexes have been constrained by a framework of inequity and that the concepts of affiliation and relationship are central to the development of human beings.

9. The Stone Center group makes a paradigm shift away from a concept of separation-individuation and individualistic values to a concept of *relationship-differentiation* and relational values.

10. According to the Stone Center group, *connections* are the basic origins of growth. *Empathy,* experiencing the feelings and thoughts of another while being aware of one's own different feelings and thoughts, fosters connections and leads to growth within relationships.

11. The Stone Center group sees the major source of psychological problems as *disconnection,* which prevents people from engaging in mutually empathic relationships.

12. Psychotherapy can change and overcome the negative effects of disconnection by establishing new relationships that empower individuals. The emphasis is on creating a new relational experience that fosters healing.

13. The relational/cultural theorists do not insist on a simply scientific bases for their work, but make explicit philosophical assumptions. They include many variables in their discussion, believing that a narrow scientific methodology is not appropriate for the study of personality. Their work has had an enormous impact in clinical psychology.

## Suggestions for Further Reading

Many of the writings of object relations theorists, especially Otto Kernberg, are difficult reading, but they are well worth study by the serious student. The best introduction to Margaret Mahler's work is *The Psychological Birth of the Human Infant* (Basic Books, 1975). Heinz Kohut's position is stated in *The Restoration of the Self* (International Universities Press, 1977). Kohut also wrote *How Does Analysis Cure?* (University of Chicago Press, 1984).

Otto Kernberg's titles are quite forthright descriptions of the contents. He has written *Borderline Conditions and Pathological Narcissism* (Jason Aronson, 1975), *Internal World and External Reality* (Jason Aronson, 1980), *Psychodynamic Psychotherapy of Borderline Patients* (Basic Books, 1989), and *Aggression in Personality Disorders and Perversions* (Yale University Press, 1992). Perhaps most readable is his article "'Mythological Encounters' in the Psychoanalytic Situation," published in Hartocollis and Graham, eds., *The Personal Myth in Psychoanalytic Theory.*

Nancy Chodorow's doctoral dissertation became *The Reproduction of Mothering* (University of California Press, 1978). She has also written *Feminism and Psychoanalytic Theory* (Yale University Press, 1989).

The writings from the Stone Center are very readable, in spite of the fact that they require a shift in focus from the usual presumptions of Western culture. Our language, traditionally, has not been well suited to capturing the flavor of relational thinking because it is rooted in individualistic ideation. However, the group works very well within the confines of language, and the limitations of the words do not hinder understanding of the new concepts and meanings.

Jean Baker Miller's revolutionary work *Toward a New Psychology of Women* (Beacon Press, 1976) argues that both sexes have been constrained by a framework of inequity and that the concepts of affiliation and relationship are central to the development of human beings; it provides the foundation for the subsequent work of the Stone Center group. *Women's Growth in Connection,* by J. V. Jordan, A. G. Kaplan, J. B. Miller, I. P. Stiver, & J. L.

Surrey (Guilford, 1991), is a collection of the initial papers that came out of the Stone Center. The core concepts of the relational model—empathy, mutuality, and empowerment—are presented. Miller and Stiver coauthored *The Healing Connection: How Women Form Relationships in Therapy and in Life* (Beacon, 1997), which concisely summarizes the types of interactions in relationships that lead to empowerment, growth, and development, as well as the negative consequences of disconnection. Jordan has edited *Women's Growth in Diversity* (Guilford, 1997a), a work that illustrates how relational theory embraces and enhances the understanding of women and men from many diverse backgrounds and groups. Additional working papers are included in the Stone Center Working Paper Series (1982–present), covering other pertinent topics and including the latest research and thinking in this new far-reaching approach. These papers are available from the Stone Center, Wellesley College, Wellesley, MA 02181-8268.

**PART**

# IV

# *Behavior and Learning Theories*

One of the most puzzling questions in personality theorizing has been the dichotomy between internal and external determinants of behavior. Is behavior caused by inner predispositions or tendencies that lead a person to act in a certain way or is it caused by the situation in which one finds oneself? A dominant trend in American psychology during the past century has been the behaviorist movement with its emphasis on learning and experience as the primary forces that shape behavior. Rather than postulate complex personality structures and dynamics within the individual, behavior and learning theories focus on those factors in the environment that determine an individual's conduct. However the either/or nature of this debate has been mitigated in light of more recent dispositional theories in which a combination of both biology and society, as well as other factors, is involved.

Most behavior and learning theories begin in the psychological laboratory where infrahuman (lower-than-human) species, such as rats or pigeons, are studied. Theoretical speculation is avoided in favor of careful observation and experimentation. Behavior theorists have been increasingly committed to a rigorous methodology, trying to perfect the techniques of psychology and raise them to the sophistication of the natural sciences. This has permitted precision and economy in theory construction as well as clear empirical foundations for the major concepts of their theories. Part IV presents major contributions to the behavior and learning approach to personality theory and shows their outstanding influence.

# *Experimental Analysis of Behavior*

## JOHN DOLLARD AND NEAL MILLER
## B. F. SKINNER

### *Your Goals for This Chapter*

1. Describe how behavior and learning theorists study personality experimentally.
2. Identify the early contributions of Pavlov, Watson, Thorndike, and Hull.
3. Define and give examples of *habits, drives,* and *reinforcers.*
4. Describe the four main conceptual parts of the learning process.
5. Discuss findings from research into the learning process.
6. Explain how Dollard and Miller have integrated learning theory and psychoanalysis.
7. Describe Dollard and Miller's practice of psychotherapy.
8. Evaluate Dollard and Miller's theory in terms of its function as philosophy, science, and art.
9. Explain why Skinner emphasizes overt behavior and avoids developing a theory of personality.
10. Describe the process of operant conditioning, and compare it with classical conditioning.
11. Distinguish among different schedules and types of *reinforcement* and indicate their effectiveness.
12. Discuss Skinner's concept of *behavior modification* and explain how it has been successfully employed.
13. Describe Skinner's concept of a utopian society.
14. Show how Skinner's position includes philosophical assumptions as well as scientific statements.
15. Evaluate Skinner's theory in terms of its function as philosophy, science, and art.

J ohn Dollard, Neal Miller, and Burrhus Frederick Skinner are behavior and learning theorists who emphasize experience and learning as the primary forces that shape human behavior. Dollard and Miller's orientation has been called *psychoanalytic learning theory* because it is a creative attempt to bring together the basic concepts of Freudian psychoanalytic theory with the ideas, language, methods, and results of experimental laboratory research on learning and behavior. Skinner espoused a point of view now known as **radical behaviorism.** Believing that a stimulus-response theory of psychology can account for all of the overt behaviors that psychologists seek to explain, Skinner omitted the psychoanalytic underpinnings and simply relied on behaviorist principles. In doing so, he suggested that the term "personality" and personality theories are superfluous. However, his work includes points of interest to students of personality and has had an impact on subsequent developments in the field. Thus, Skinner is typically included in books on personality theories.

*John Dollard (left) and Neal Miller transformed Freud's concepts into the terms of learning theory and experimental psychology.*

Dollard and Miller's and Skinner's views on personality stem from experimental and laboratory procedures rather than clinical investigations. However, the principles that they developed have been widely applied in areas such as education, psychotherapy, industry, and corrections.

## John Dollard and Neal Miller: Biographical Background

John Dollard and Neal Miller were both born in Wisconsin. They taught and worked together at the Institute of Human Relations at Yale University, which was founded in 1933 in an effort to explore the interdisciplinary relationships among psychology, psychiatry, sociology, and anthropology. Dollard and Miller's joint efforts resulted in a personality theory based on Clark Hull's reinforcement theory of learning and Freud's pschyoanalytic theory. This integration resulted in a behaviorist theory that became representative of the mainstream of American psychology throughout most of the twentieth century.

John Dollard, born in 1900, was granted the A.B. from the University of Wisconsin and the M.A. and Ph.D. from the University of Chicago. His primary interests were in sociology and anthropology, and he was a strong advocate of interdisciplinary studies, which is evident in his 1937 field study, *Caste and Class in a Southern Town,* that depicts the position of black Americans in that period. Neal Miller, born in 1909, was granted the B.S. from the University of Washington, the M.A. from Stanford, and the Ph.D. from Yale. His primary interests lay in experimental psychology. Both men underwent psychoanalytic training, each held a number of significant positions, and each authored several books or articles, in addition to their affiliation and collaboration at the Institute of Human Relations.

John Dollard died in New Haven, Connecticut, in 1980. Neal Miller spent more than twenty years at Rockefeller University, and, since 1985, has been a research affiliate in the psychology department at Yale University.

## The Experimental Analysis of Behavior

Before discussing the work of Dollard and Miller, it will be useful to take a brief look at some of the origins of the experimental analysis of behavior.

Behavior and learning theories have their roots in a philosophical point of view known as **empiricism,** which suggests that all knowledge originates in experience. John Locke (1632–1704), one of the first empiricist philosophers, suggested that at birth the mind is a blank slate on which sensory experience writes in a number of different ways. Locke's phrase "blank slate" (or tabula rasa) expressed the philosophical view of empiricism in its classic form just as Descartes's "I think, therefore I am" expressed the essence of rationalism.

Behavior and learning theories hold that valid knowledge arises out of experience and needs to be continually checked against it. Thus, behavior and learning theories are largely based on the experimental analysis of behavior. The behavior of individual organisms is carefully studied in controlled laboratory settings and the relationship between the behavior and factors in that environment is articulated.

Although behavioral theory is singularly American, the historical background of the approach begins in Russia where Ivan Pavlov (1849–1936) demonstrated and articulated a form of learning known as **classical conditioning.** In a classic laboratory situation, Pavlov took a hungry dog and presented it with food, an **unconditioned stimulus** that normally elicits salivation, an **unconditioned,** or **automatic, response.** Then he simultaneously paired the food with the sound of a bell, a *neutral stimulus* that does not normally elicit salivation. The dog salivated to the paired food and sound of the bell. After several presentations of both food and bell, Pavlov was able simply to present the sound of the bell, and the dog salivated. The sound of the bell had become a **conditioned stimulus** that elicited a **conditioned response.** In other words, Pavlov showed that by pairing an unconditioned stimulus with a neutral stimulus, he could elicit a response that previously would have been elicited only by the original stimulus.

John Watson (1878–1958), the father of American behaviorism, expanded classical conditioning into a theory of **behaviorism** in which he recommended that psychology emphasize the study of overt rather than covert behavior. Watson's point of view was quickly adopted by many American psychologists. The behaviorist movement became the dominant movement in psychology in America. Even today, the distinctive methodology of American psychology reflects Watson's emphasis on objectivity and extrospection.

Another figure in the history of learning theory is Edwin Thorndike (1874–1949). Thorndike conducted several experiments with animals in order to gain further understanding of the learning process. He formulated many important laws of learning. The law that is particularly important for our purposes is the **law of effect,** which states that when a behavior or performance is accompanied by satisfaction, it tends to happen again. If the performance is accompanied by frustration, it tends to decrease. We now recognize that the law of effect is not necessarily universal. Sometimes frustration leads to increased efforts to perform. Still, most psychologists believe that the law of effect is generally true.

A final figure to consider is Clark Hull (1884–1952), whose systematic theory of learning based on the concept of drive reduction will be discussed shortly, as it directly influenced the development of Dollard and Miller's theory of personality.

## Habits, Drives, and the Learning Process

Dollard and Miller emphasize the role of learning in personality and place less stress on personality structure. They suggest (1950) that the structure of personality can be defined very simply as habits.

**Habits** refer to some kind of learned association between a stimulus and response that makes them occur together frequently. Habits represent a temporary structure because they can appear and disappear; because they are learned, they can also be unlearned. This is a much simpler concept of the structure of personality than we have encountered before. The primary concern of Dollard and Miller's theory is to specify those conditions in the environment that encourage the acquisition of habits.

The primary dynamic underlying personality development and the acquisition of habits is **drive reduction** (1950). Dollard and Miller drew heavily on Clark Hull's systematic theory of learning based on the concept of drive reduction. A **drive** is a strong stimulation that produces discomfort, such as hunger. Hull believed that learning occurs only if a response of an organism is followed by the reduction of some need or drive. The infant learns to such the breast or a bottle of milk in order to relieve hunger. If sucking the breast or bottle did not result in some drive or need reduction, the infant would not continue to perform that activity. Dollard and Miller point out that reducing a drive is reinforcing to an individual, and thus an individual will behave in ways that relieve the tension created by strong drives.

**Primary drives** are those associated with physiological processes that are necessary for an organism's survival, such as the drives of hunger, thirst, and the need for sleep. We rarely observe primary drives in a direct form because society has developed some means of reducing the drive before it becomes overwhelming. Thus, primary drives, by and large, are satisfied through secondary drives. **Secondary drives** are learned on the basis of primary ones. Dollard and Miller consider them to be elaborations of the primary drives. An example of a secondary drive is being motivated to eat at 6:30 P.M., or one's usual dinner hour. Other secondary drives are wanting to earn money in order to buy food, and satisfying other drives of physical comfort in the normal mode of one's culture.

Dollard and Miller also distinguish between primary and secondary reinforcers. A **reinforcer** is any event that increases the likelihood of a particular response. **Primary reinforcers** are those that reduce primary drives, such as food, water, or need for sleep. **Secondary reinforcers** are originally neutral but they acquire reward value on the basis of having been associated with primary reinforcers. Money is a secondary reinforcer because you can use it to buy food. A mother's smile or a word of praise is also a secondary reinforcer, associated with a state of physical well-being.

We acquire habits and develop specific behavioral responses through the process of learning. As infants each of us begins life with the basic equipment needed to reduce our primary drives: reflex responses and an innate hierarchy of response. **Reflex** responses are automatic responses to specific stimuli. All of us blink automatically to avoid an irritant to the eye or sneeze to eliminate an irritant to the nose. Such reflexes are important for our survival. **Hierarchy of response** refers to a tendency for certain responses to occur before others. For example, an animal runs to avoid a shock rather than cringe and bear it in pain. If a response is unsuccessful, however, an organism will try the next response in the hierarchy. Learning, in part, involves reinforcing and/or rearranging the response hierarchy.

Dollard and Miller (1950) suggest that the learning process can be broken down into four main conceptual parts (see Figure 8.1):

A **drive,** as we have already seen, is a stimulus impelling a person to act, but in no way does the drive direct or specify behavior. It simply impels.

**FIGURE 8.1    A Simple Diagram of the Learning Process**

In the process of learning, one *wants* something (DRIVE), *notices* something (CUE), *does* something (RESPONSE), and *gets* something (REINFORCEMENT).

A **cue** refers to a specific stimulus that tells the organism when, where, and how to respond. The yellow arches of McDonald's may act as a cue directing us to stop and get something to eat. The ringing of a bell or the time on a clock is a cue to students to enter or leave the classroom.

A **response** is one's reaction to the cue. Because these responses occur in a hierarchy, we can rank a response according to its probability of occurring. But this innate hierarchy can be changed through learning.

**Reinforcement** refers to the effect of the response. Effective reinforcement consists of drive reduction. If a response is not reinforced by satisfying a drive, it will undergo **extinction.** Extinction does not eliminate a response but merely inhibits it, enabling another response to grow stronger and supersede it in the response hierarchy. If present responses are not reinforcing, the individual is placed in a **learning dilemma** and will try different responses until one is developed that satisfies the drive.

Dollard and Miller suggest that all human behavior can be comprehended in terms of the learning process. It is through the learning process that one acquires secondary drives. These drives may form a very complex system, but the underlying process by which they are developed is essentially the same: drive, cue, response, reinforcement. Even our higher mental processes can be understood in terms of the learning process. Thoughts are cue-producing responses in the brain. Reasoning consists of internal chains of drive, cue, response, and reinforcement, in which one thought serves as a cue for the next thought, and so forth. What is reinforced is determined by cultural patterns. Thus normal behaviors differ from society to society, as is apparent in the various behaviors of different social classes and immigrant groups in the United States, where different behavior patterns have been rewarded.

## Frustration and Conflict

Dollard and Miller have conducted extensive studies on different aspects of the learning process. A number of these studies have been in the area of responses to frustration and conflict (Miller, 1944, 1951, 1959). **Frustration** occurs when one is unable to reduce a drive because the response that would satisfy it has been blocked. For example, the child who is not permitted to take a cookie from the cookie jar is frustrated. If the frustration arises from a situation in which incompatible responses are occurring at the same time, the situation is described as one of **conflict.** Dollard and Miller used Kurt Lewin's (1890–1947) concept of approach and avoidance tendencies to distinguish among several different types of conflict in which an individual seeks to approach or avoid one or more goals. They developed ways of graphically presenting different types of conflict and of plotting the strengths of various forces involved in them. Thus, the child who is required to choose between two attractive objects, a toy and a bar of candy, can be diagrammed as follows:

## THINKING CRITICALLY

### *The Learning Process*

The four steps in the learning process as outlined by Dollard and Miller can be fruitfully used to help us understand some of our own habits and frequent responses. Choose a habit that you engage in frequently. Remember that "habit" simply means a learned association between a stimulus and a response. The habit may be positive, such as locking your car when it is parked in a questionable neighborhood, or negative, such as overeating. What are the basic underlying primary and subsequent secondary drives that your behavior seeks to fulfill? What are the specific secondary cues that trigger your response? What are the consequences of your behavior that reinforce the habit? Such an analysis may assist you in discriminating between cues that trigger specific behaviors and reinforcements that strengthen them.

You might also wish to discuss the four steps in the learning process with someone from another culture or background to see if it applies equally as well.

with a circle representing the child and plus signs representing each desired goal. (An undesired goal would be represented by a minus sign.) The arrows indicate that there are forces moving the child in the direction of the goals (or away from them). The intensity of the force varies as the child moves closer to or further from each goal.

The value of these graphic presentations lies in the fact that if we could measure the complex forces that impel human behavior and if we could develop formulas that encompass all of the variables involved, we could also predict a person's actions in reference to a particular goal. Human situations are so complex that such prediction is not possible at present. But Dollard and Miller's experiments with **infrahuman species** have shown that we can be quite successful in predicting the behavior of simple laboratory animals under controlled conditions.

Conflicts, in brief, result from some sort of opposition between our tendencies to approach or avoid certain objects and goals. Dollard and Miller distinguish among several different types of conflict. In an *approach-approach conflict,* the individual is simultaneously attracted to two goals that have positive value but are incompatible. (You are in love with two people at once and are forced to make a choice.) In an *avoidance-avoidance conflict,* a person faces two undesirable alternatives. (The hot plate is burning your hands but if you drop it you will spill the food.) In an *approach-avoidance conflict,* one goal both attracts and repels the individual. (Your date is both attractive and obnoxious.) These conflicts may be diagrammed simply, as is shown in Figure 8.2. In everyday life, of course, the situation is seldom so simple. Therefore, it is often necessary to consider compounded situations of conflict, such as a *double approach-avoidance conflict,* in which an individual must deal simultaneously with multiple goals that both attract and repel.

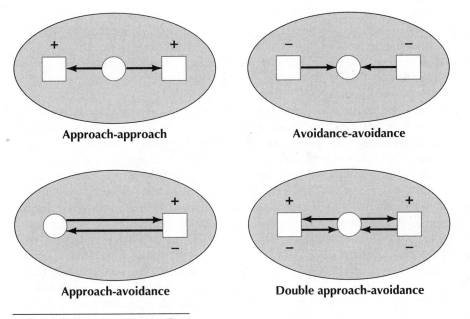

**Approach-approach**

**Avoidance-avoidance**

**Approach-avoidance**

**Double approach-avoidance**

FIGURE 8.2   **Diagramming Conflicts**

The conflicts that Dollard and Miller describe may be diagrammed simply as shown here.

## The Integration of Learning Theory and Psychoanalysis

In their attempt to integrate learning theory and psychoanalysis, Dollard and Miller adapted many Freudian concepts and reconceived them in learning theory terms. They appreciate the importance of unconscious forces underlying human behavior but they redefine the concept of **unconscious processes** in terms of their own theory.

There are two main determinants of unconscious processes. First, we are unaware of certain drives or cues because they are *unlabeled*. These drives and cues may have occurred before we learned to speak and therefore we were unable to label them. Other cues may be unconscious, because a society has not given them adequate labels. In our society, we have essentially one word for snow, although we might further describe it as dry or slushy. In certain Eskimo cultures, there are thirty or more different words for the various textures of snow. Such a society is certainly much more aware of the different variations in snow than we are. Distortions in labeling may also affect one's conscious perception. Through distorted labeling, an emotion such as fear may become confused with another emotion, such as guilt. Thus, an individual may react in frightening situations as if guilty because of a distortion in labeling.

Second, unconscious processes refer to cues or responses that once were conscious but have been repressed because they were ineffective. Dollard and Miller point out that repression is learned like all other behaviors. When we repress, we do not think about certain thoughts or label them because they are unpleasant. Avoiding these thoughts reduces the drive by reducing the unpleasant experience.

Dollard and Miller also articulate many of the other defense mechanisms that Freud outlined: projection, identification, reaction formation, rationalization, and displacement. In each case, however, they are seen as learned responses or behaviors and they are articulated in terms of learning. For example, identification entails imitating the behavior that one has learned from another. Displacement is explained in terms of generalization and the inability to make proper discriminations.

Dollard and Miller posit four critical training stages in child development: the feeding situation in infancy, cleanliness training, early sex training, and the training for control of anger and aggression. These are critical training stages in the child's development in which social conditions of learning imposed by the parents may have enormous consequences for future development. The parallel to Freud's stages is obvious. The conflict situation of feeding in infancy is reminiscent of Freud's oral stage, cleanliness training is reminiscent of Freud's anal stage, and early sex training as well as the effort to control anger and aggression are elements of Freud's phallic stage. Dollard and Miller agree with Freud that events in early childhood are vitally important in shaping later behavior. Further, they suggest that the logic of these events may be comprehended within the learning process as they have outlined it. Whereas Freud's stages unfold biologically, the outcomes of Dollard and Miller's stages are controlled by learning. Thus, the infant whose cry when hungry brings immediate relief in the sense of being fed learns that self-generated activity is effective in reducing drives. The infant left to "cry it out," may learn that there is nothing self-generated that can be done to reduce the drive and begin to develop a passive attitude toward drive reduction. Thus, in their incorporation of Freud's theories, Dollard and Miller reconsidered and elaborated his ideas in the light of learning theory principles.

It was easy to merge Freud's and Hull's theories because both of them are based on drive reduction and share the common feature of determinism. Dollard and Miller's work helps us appreciate the role of learning in the development of defenses and other psychoanalytic structures. However, there are significant differences between Freud's concepts and Dollard and Miller's articulation of them, so that the translation is not exact. For example, whereas for Freud anxiety, conflict, and repression are inevitable aspects of the human condition, for Dollard and Miller they are simply learned responses. Nevertheless, by transforming Freud's concept into the terms of learning theory and experimental psychology, Dollard and Miller rendered Freud more palatable to a large number of people. It is less threatening to believe that unconscious processes and defense mechanisms are learned and may therefore be unlearned than to conceive of them as largely universal and inescapable. In Freud's view, one could merely try to recognize them in order to cope with them more effectively. In addition, Dollard and Miller's work stimulated a great deal of scientific research and experimental testing of Freud's concepts.

## Psychotherapy

We have seen that for Dollard and Miller behavior is learned in the process of seeking to reduce drives. Deviant behavior is also learned, but in the neurotic the behaviors that have been learned are frequently self-defeating and unproductive. Dollard and Miller (1950) refer to neurosis as a **stupidity-misery syndrome.** The patient has strong, unconscious, and unlabeled emotional conflicts. The neurotic has not labeled the problem and therefore does not discriminate effectively, generalizing and applying old, ineffective solutions to current problems and situations. A young man whose father was a tyrant may have learned in early childhood that he had to react meekly in order to avoid his father's wrath. Unable to discriminate between his father's attitude and the attitude of other authority figures in his life, the young man may generalize his response to his father to later authority figures who in fact are not tyrants. In such situations, his meek response may not be the most appropriate one. Dollard and Miller (1950) suggest that "neurotic conflicts are taught by parents and learned by children."

Therapy involves unlearning old, ineffective, unproductive habits and substituting new, more adaptive, and productive responses. For example, fear, a learnable drive that reinforces responses that reduce it, can motivate either adaptive or maladaptive behavior. If thoughts on a certain topic provoke fear, and if the individual has learned to reduce the fear through responses that block the fear-eliciting thoughts, then this repression prevents the reasoning that could lead to adaptive behavior. Psychotherapy aims to reduce such fears so that reasoning and planning can occur. Dollard and Miller (1950) refer to two phases in therapy. In the **talking phase,** neurotic habits are studied, examined, and identified so the patient may unlearn them. Essentially, this procedure entails providing appropriate labels for the patient's responses. When we label a repression appropriately, the repression is lifted because we have erased the distortion. You may recall the fairy tale of Rumpelstiltskin, who loses his demonic powers once he is confronted with his name. When the repressions are correctly identified and labeled for what they are, their power to harm the individual disappears.

The second phase of therapy is the **performance phase.** During this phase, the patient acquires new, more adaptive and productive responses and habits and is encouraged to apply them. Training in *suppression* (the conscious, deliberate stopping of a thought or an action) can be helpful. The patient can be trained to suppress, rather than repress, thoughts or actions that reinforce old habits and at the same time, be deliberately exposed to new cues that will evoke different responses.

Dollard and Miller's theory of therapy represents a bridge to the more directive and active therapies of other learning theories such as Skinner's. It is pragmatic and action oriented. Whereas Freud thought it necessary to work through past problems for an analysis to be successful, Dollard and Miller believe that historical recollection is effective only if it is instrumental in creating change. If historical recollection is unnecessary for change to occur, it is only a short step to exclude that emphasis on the past and concentrate on the behaviors of the present as Skinner and other subsequent learning and behavioral cognitive theorists do.

---

| PHILOSOPHY, | # Dollard and Miller's Theory |
| SCIENCE, | |
| AND ART | |

Dollard and Miller developed their theory of personality through laboratory studies and experimentation. They try to base their statements on empirical evidence and submit theoretical differences to observational tests. They recognize, perhaps more than many other theorists, that a theory is useful according to its effectiveness in leading to predictions that can be tested. As a scientific theory, therefore, Dollard and Miller's work has been very attractive to many psychologists because of its use in validating evidence.

Empirical evidence, however, has not always given as much support to Dollard and Miller's theory as the theorists imply. What an organism can learn is limited by **species-specific behavior**—complex, rather than reflex, behaviors that occur in all members of a species. Some stimuli are more relevant to a particular species than others; responses also differ. Pigeons peck, chickens scratch, and pigs root. It is difficult, if not impossible, to alter these behaviors. One cannot easily generalize from a rat to a human being.

As we have seen, Dollard and Miller have rendered many psychoanalytic concepts into the constructs of a scientific theory. Many consider this a substantial contribution to the viability of Freud's ideas. Whether psychoanalysis has gained or lost in the process, however, is a matter of considerable debate (Rapaport, 1953). Some would point out that in the process of translation Freudian concepts have lost considerable dynamism and have been emptied of their original intent. Others suggest that Freud's in-depth clinical study of humans illuminates the dynamics of human personality far more than Dollard and Miller's research with rats does.

Ideally, if we could measure forces that impel human behavior and develop sophisticated formulas that encompass all of the variables involved, we could predict complex human behavior; the applications of such a science would be mind-boggling indeed. Dollard and Miller's theory has been quite successful in predicting the behavior of simple laboratory animals under controlled conditions. However, the mazes that individual humans run, even within the same society, are very different (1941). Dollard and Miller's views have been central to the field of personality since they first published their major work, *Personality and Psychotherapy,* in 1950. They were among the first to seek to emulate a purely scientific model in understanding personality.

Dollard and Miller combined the insights of Freud's psychoanalysis with the principles of learning theory, a combination that structured both the field of psychology and introductory psychology texts during the bulk of the twentieth century. They collaborated on an exploration of the relationship between frustration and aggression (Dollard, Doob, Miller, Mowrer, & Sears, 1939) and introduced the concept of imitation (1941) that was later expanded upon by Albert Bandura. In recent years, the behaviorist position has been revamped to include an emphasis on cognition. These contributions, considered in Chapter 9 (the social learning theories of Albert Bandura and Julian Rotter) and Chapter 16 (the cognitive-behavioral theories of Albert Ellis, Aaron Beck, and Arnold Lazarus), attest to the enduring significance of the learning approach that Dollard and Miller popularized.

## B. F. Skinner: Biographical Background

B. F. Skinner was born in 1904 in Susquehanna, Pennsylvania. His father was an ambitious lawyer; his mother was bright and of high moral standards. A younger brother, of whom he was fond, died suddenly at the age of sixteen. Skinner was reared in a warm, comfortable, and stable home, permeated with the virtues and ethics of small-town, middle-class America at the turn of the century. His parents did not employ physical punishments but their admonitions succeeded in teaching their son "to fear God, the police, and what people would think." His parents and grandparents, to whom he was close, taught him to be faithful to the puritan work imperative, to try to please God, and to look for evidence of God's favor through "success." Later, Skinner (1983b) suggested that childhood reinforcements shaped his own adult behavior.

As a child, Skinner was fascinated with machines and interested in knowing how things work. He developed a mechanical device to remind himself to hang up his pajamas, a gadget that enabled him to blow smoke rings without violating his parents' prohibition against smoking, and a flotation system to separate ripe from green elderberries. For many

*B. F. Skinner believed that the term "personality" was ultimately superfluous.*

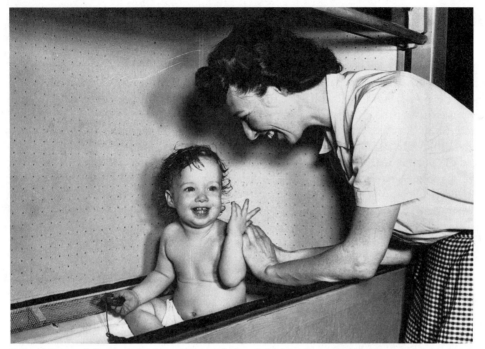

*When his second daughter was born, Skinner designed this aircrib to simplify her care and give her unrestrained movement in a temperature-controlled space.*

years he tried to design a perpetual motion machine, but it did not work. When his second daughter was born, he invented an aircrib to simplify her care and give her unrestrained movement in a temperature-controlled space (1985).

Skinner was also interested in animal behavior. He caught and brought home the small wildlife of the woodlands in central Pennsylvania, such as snakes, lizards, and chipmunks. His interest in biology was later reflected in his training of animals.

Skinner was an excellent student. Majoring in English at Hamilton College, a small liberal arts school in upstate New York, he thought seriously of becoming a writer. He sent a few short stories to the poet Robert Frost, who encouraged him to write. He decided to take a year or two off to write, but he quickly became discouraged and decided he could not write as he "had nothing important to say." During this interlude, he read books by Ivan Pavlov and John Watson, whose work impressed him, and he decided to begin graduate studies in psychology at Harvard. He received the Ph.D. in 1931.

He taught at the University of Minnesota for nine years and was chairman of the department of psychology at Indiana University before he returned to Harvard in 1948, having established a reputation as a major experimental psychologist and having written an influential book, *Walden II*, which describes a utopian society based on psychological principles.

Skinner died in 1990 after a battle with leukemia. He was 86.

# A Theory of Personality Without Personality

Skinner, the leading heir of the behaviorist position, took the beliefs and concepts of Watson's behaviorist theory to their logical extreme. He concurred with Watson that it is unproductive and foolish to refer to structures of the personality that cannot be directly observed. Thus, Skinner developed a psychology that concentrates not on the person but solely on those variables and forces in the environment that influence a person and that may be directly observed, presenting behaviorism and learning theory in its purest and most extreme form.

For Skinner the term "personality" was ultimately superfluous, as overt behavior can be completely comprehended in terms of responses to factors in the environment. The effort to understand or explain behavior in terms of internal structures such as a personality or an ego is to speak in terms of "fictions," because the terms are not very helpful. First, they are presented in such a way that they cannot be directly observed; second, it is very difficult to deduce operational definitions from them; and, last, it is virtually impossible to develop systematic and empirical means of testing them (1953; see also Moore, 1992). Instead, Skinner suggested that we concentrate on the environmental consequences that determine and maintain an individual's behavior. One can consider the person as if empty and observe how changes in the environment affect the individual's behavior.

It is also unnecessary to posit internal forces or motivational states within a person as causal factors of behavior. Skinner did not deny that such states occur: they are important by-products of behavior. He simply saw no point in using them as causal variables because they cannot be operationally defined and their intensity cannot be measured.

Rather than try to determine how hungry someone was, Skinner tried to determine what variables or forces in the environment affect an individual's eating behavior. What is the effect of the time period that has elapsed since the last meal was eaten? What are the consequences of the amount of food consumed? Such factors in the environment can be specifically defined, measured, and dealt with empirically.

Skinner also differed from other researchers in that he emphasized individual subjects. Typically, he studied each animal separately and reported his results in the form of individual records. Whereas other experimenters draw their conclusions on the basis of the performance of comparison groups as a whole, Skinner believed that the laws of behavior must apply to each and every individual subject when it is observed under the appropriate conditions. He encouraged psychology to remain within the dimensional system of natural science, suggesting that to move away from that model makes it difficult to continue to call psychology a science (1983a).

# The Development of Behavior Through Learning

At birth, the human infant is simply a bundle of innate capacities but consequent behaviors can be comprehended in terms of learning. Thorndike's law of effect stated that when a behavior or performance is accompanied by satisfaction it tends to be stamped in or increased. If the performance is accompanied by frustration, it tends to decrease. Omitting

*Animals have been taught to perform interesting feats through techniques that Skinner has articulated as shaping and operant conditioning.*

Thorndike's reference to internal states, Skinner derived a very simple definition of reinforcement. A **reinforcement** is anything that increases the likelihood of a response. It is the effect of one's behavior that determines the likelihood of its occurring again. If a young child cries or whines, perhaps parental attention will follow. If the behavior results in reinforcement, chances are the child will repeat that behavior pattern. If the behavior does not result in reinforcement, that is, if the child is ignored and does not receive attention, then it is likely that the behavioral response will cease and the child will behave in alternative ways to find patterns of behavior that are reinforced.

## Operant Conditioning

Skinner (1938) distinguished between two types of behavior: respondent and operant. **Respondent behavior** refers to reflexes or automatic responses that are elicited by stimuli. A beam of light causes the pupil of one's eye to contract. Tapping the knee on the right spot makes the leg jerk forward. When our fingers touch hot metal, we reflexively pull our hand away. Such behaviors are unlearned: they occur involuntarily and automatically.

Respondent behaviors may, however, be conditioned or changed through learning. Respondent behaviors were involved in Pavlov's demonstration of classical conditioning. Pavlov's dog learned to salivate to the tone of a bell. An infant learns to suck at a nipple.

These are reflexes or automatic responses that have come to be performed in the presence of the previously neutral stimulus through the process of association.

**Operant behaviors** are responses emitted without a stimulus necessarily being present. They occur spontaneously. Not all of a newborn's movements are reflex responses. Some of them are operant behaviors in which the infant acts on the environment. An infant swings an arm or moves a leg and certain consequences follow. These consequences determine whether or not the response will be repeated. Skinner believed that the process of **operant conditioning** is of far greater significance than simple classical conditioning. Many of our behaviors cannot be accounted for in terms of classical conditioning. Rather, they are originally spontaneous behaviors whose consequences determine their subsequent frequency.

There is a clear distinction between the nature of a respondent behavior and an operant behavior. A respondent behavior is evoked or elicited by a stimulus. Operant behavior is emitted or freely made by the organism. The nature of reinforcement also differs. In classical conditioning, the stimulus is the reinforcement and it precedes the behavior. In operant conditioning, the effect of the behavior is the reinforcement. Thus, in operant conditioning the reinforcement follows the behavior.

Operant conditioning can be systematically described by depicting the behavior of a rat in an operant conditioning apparatus, a piece of laboratory equipment that Skinner designed in order to train animals and conduct research. Commonly known as a "Skinner box," the apparatus makes possible controlled and precise study of animal behavior.

When a food-deprived rat is first placed within the box, it may behave in a variety of random ways. The rat may first walk around the box and explore it. Later, it may scratch itself or urinate. In the course of its activity the rat may at some point press a bar on the wall of the box. The bar pressing causes a food pellet to drop into a trough under the bar. The rat's behavior has had an effect on the environment. The food acts as a reinforcement, increasing the likelihood of that behavior occurring again. When it occurs again it is reinforced. Eventually, the rat begins to press the bar in rapid succession, pausing only long enough to eat the food.

When a food-deprived rat is conditioned in a Skinner box to press a bar and is reinforced for that behavior with food, we can predict pretty accurately what the rat is going to do in subsequent sessions in the Skinner box. Furthermore, we can control the rat's behavior by changing the reinforcement. When the desired behavior occurs, it is reinforced. Appropriate reinforcement increases the likelihood of that behavior occurring again.

## Shaping

Frequently the behavior that one wishes to train an organism to perform is a complex, sophisticated one that the organism would not naturally be expected to do shortly after entering the box. Suppose you wished to train a pigeon to peck at a small black dot inside a white circle. If you were to wait until that behavior spontaneously occurred, you might wait a very long time. Therefore, Skinner employed a procedure termed **shaping,** in which he deliberately shaped or molded the organism's behavior in order to achieve the desired behavior.

Initially, the pigeon moves randomly about the box. When it moves in the direction of the circle, it is reinforced by a pellet of food in the trough below the circle. The next time it approaches the circle, it is again reinforced. Later, it is required to approach the circle more closely before it is reinforced. Later still, it is not reinforced until it pecks the white circle. Finally, the pigeon is reinforced only for pecking at the small black dot within the circle.

Through shaping, Skinner was able to induce animals to perform unique and remarkable feats; he taught pigeons how to play Ping-Pong and to guide missiles to their target. His pigeons never actually were put to work guiding missiles, but Skinner showed that it was possible for them to do so. Using behavioral-shaping methods, other animal trainers have been able to produce unusual tricks and feats.

Skinner believed that most animal and human behavior is learned through operant conditioning. The process of learning to speak one's native tongue involves reinforcing and shaping of operant behavior. The young infant emits certain spontaneous sounds. These are not limited to the sounds of its native tongue but represent all possible languages. Initially, the infant is reinforced for simply babbling. Later, the child is reinforced for making sounds that approximate meaningful words. Eventually the child is reinforced only for meaningful speech. Skinner (1986) suggested that verbal behavior evolved from signaling, imitating, and other nonverbal behaviors, following the rules of contingencies of reinforce-

## THINKING CRITICALLY

# *Classical and Operant Conditioning in Your Life*

You have learned many things through classical and operant conditioning. Through the process of association you have probably learned to pair a wide variety of objects with events that give meaning to your life and influence your behavior. Can you identify some incidents of classical conditioning in your life? For example, one of my students is claustrophobic, afraid of being in small, enclosed places. As a young child she made the mistake of playing in a discarded refrigerator. Fortunately, she was rescued in time, but the incident had a lasting impact on her life. Similarly, many of us have distinct preferences for or aversions to certain things. As a young child, I enjoyed sitting next to my father as he played the piano and we sang together. To this day, I find particular enjoyment in a song fest around a piano.

Operant conditioning is even more important in our lives than simple classical conditioning. Many of our behaviors involve complex shaped responses such as tying our shoes, rolling up a back pack, or playing a musical instrument. Think of the relationship between a parent and a child. Describe some ways in which a parent might reward a child for appropriate behaviors. What are some of the ways in which parents encourage children to learn to walk, talk, and perform well in school? Consider some of the behaviors that you perform because you find them reinforcing and identify those that you have learned through operant conditioning. Can you also identify ways in which people from other cultures and societies shape their children? These deliberations should help you to recognize the pervasive importance of classical and operant conditioning in our lives.

ment. Thus, the process of shaping is involved in learning to speak, as well as many other human behaviors.

## Schedules and Types of Reinforcement

A practical necessity led Skinner to explore the effect of different **schedules of reinforcement.** In the 1930s, commercially made food pellets were not available. Skinner and his students found that it was a laborious, time-consuming process to make the eight hundred or more food pellets a day that were necessary to sustain his research. Skinner wondered what the effect would be if the animal was not reinforced every time it performed the desired behavior. This question led to the investigation of various schedules of reinforcement.

Skinner (1969) described three schedules of reinforcement and their effectiveness. In **continuous reinforcement,** the desired behavior is reinforced each time that it occurs. A continuous schedule of reinforcement is extremely effective in initially developing and strengthening a behavior. However, if the reinforcement is stopped, the response quickly disappears or undergoes extinction.

In **interval reinforcement,** the organism is reinforced after a certain time period has elapsed, regardless of the response rate. Interval reinforcement may be given on a fixed or a variable basis. If it is **fixed,** the same time period elapses each time (such as five minutes). If it is **variable,** the time periods may differ in length. This type of reinforcement schedule occurs frequently in the everyday world. Employees are paid at the end of each week. Students are given grades at certain intervals within the year. Interval reinforcement produces a level of response that is more difficult to extinguish than responses that have been continuously reinforced. However, the level of response tends to be lower than the level produced by other kinds of schedules.

In **ratio reinforcement,** reinforcement is determined by the number of appropriate responses that the organism emits. A factory worker may be paid according to the number of pieces that he or she completes. Ratio schedules of reinforcement may also be fixed or variable. If they are **fixed,** the number of responses required prior to reinforcement is stable and the same each time. If they are **variable,** the number of appropriate operant behaviors that must occur prior to reinforcement changes from time to time. Whereas a continuous schedule of reinforcement is most effective for initially developing and strengthening a behavior, a variable ratio schedule is most effective thereafter in maintaining it. Responses maintained under the conditions of variable ratio reinforcement are highly resistant to extinction and less likely to disappear. Gambling casinos have learned this lesson well. Their use of the principle of variable ratio schedules keeps many a gambler at the table long after the money allotted for gambling has disappeared.

Where reinforcement is haphazard or accidental, the behavior that immediately preceded the reinforcement may be increased even if it is not the desired behavior. Athletes often engage in personal rituals before positioning themselves for play because of an earlier fortuitous connection between that behavior and success. Such behaviors are *superstitious,* yet many ineffective habits and common superstitions have their origin in chance reinforcement. Some of these behaviors are culturally transmitted and reinforced. Now that research has confirmed the effects of various types of reinforcement, we can systematically apply effective schedules of reinforcement to shape desired behavior.

In addition to primary and secondary reinforcers, Skinner (1953) described the effects of **generalized conditioned reinforcers** such as praise and affection, which are learned and have the power to reinforce a great number of different behaviors. Moreover, they can be self-given. As we grow older, we move from primary reinforcers to more generalized types. Initially, young children will respond to food or something that meets their basic needs. Later, they respond to an allowance. At the same time, they associate these reinforcers with the praise and affection that accompany them. Eventually, children will work primarily for the reinforcement of praise, which can be self-given.

Skinner (1972) distinguished positive reinforcement, punishment, and negative reinforcement. **Positive reinforcement** occurs when a behavior is followed by a situation that increases the likelihood of that behavior occurring in the future. **Negative reinforcement** comes about when a behavior is followed by the *termination of an unpleasant situation,* increasing the likelihood of that behavior in similar situations. Taking an aspirin is negatively reinforcing because it relieves a headache. **Punishment** occurs when a behavior is followed by an unpleasant situation designed to *eliminate* it.

Skinner (1953) observed that punishment is the most common technique of behavioral control in our society. Children are spanked if they misbehave and lawbreakers are fined or imprisoned. Punishment may stop or block a behavior but it does not necessarily eliminate it. The organism may seek other means of acquiring the same ends. Punishment creates fear but, if the fear is diminished, the behavior will recur. It can also lead to undesired side effects: anger, hatred, or helplessness.

Skinner (1953, 1971) suggested the use of methods other than those based on aversive stimuli to eliminate behaviors that are not desired. One may ignore the behavior until it undergoes extinction or one may permit satiation to occur. **Satiation** entails permitting the behavior to occur until the individual tires of it. A child may be allowed to turn a light switch on and off until she becomes bored. One may also change the environment that provokes the behavior. Fragile objects may be placed out of a young child's reach. Finally, one can promote behaviors that counteract and inhibit the undesirable behaviors through positive reinforcement.

Skinner emphasized that positive reinforcement is most effective in initiating and maintaining desired behaviors. All too often we do not recognize how we inadvertently give positive reinforcement to a behavior that is not desirable. The child who is seeking attention may be *positively* reinforced by a parental scolding because the scolding affords the child attention. By identifying our reinforcement patterns, we can strengthen those that are most effective and develop more efficient means of controlling behavior.

## Psychotherapy and Behavioral Change

Skinner explained maladaptive or neurotic behavior in terms of environmental contingencies that sustain and maintain it. The neurotic or psychotic has been conditioned by the environment to behave in inappropriate ways. If we wish to change an individual's behavior, we can restructure the environment in such a way that it will no longer sustain maladaptive behavior and it will reinforce desirable behavior. Thus, in describing neurosis, Skinner did not find it necessary to refer to explanatory fictions, such as repression or conflict because maladaptive behavior can simply be reduced to the variables in the environment that reinforce and sustain it.

The role of therapy is to identify the behaviors that are maladaptive, remove them, and substitute more adaptive and appropriate behaviors through the process of operant conditioning. Skinner concurred with Dollard and Miller that there is no need to review the individual's past or encourage reliving it. Therapy is not dependent on self-understanding or insight. Some insight may occur, but such self-understanding is not necessary for behavioral change.

The contrast between Freud and Skinner emerges clearly in their attitudes toward therapy. As we have seen, Freud's intent was primarily scholarly. He sought to increase an individual's self-understanding, and psychoanalysis is relatively uninterested in specific behavioral change. Skinner's interest, on the other hand, was totally pragmatic and curative. **Behavior modification** seeks to eliminate undesired behaviors by changing the environment within which they occur.

Skinner's approach to behavior modification has been notably successful in areas where traditional insight therapy has failed or is inappropriate. One of its more spectacular successes has been with mute individuals, who for obvious reasons are not amenable to traditional therapies, which are largely based on talking. Dr. O. I. Lovaas (1966) has used a systematic program of shaping to teach autistic and mute children to speak. First, he identifies something that is reinforcing to the child. Since food is generally reinforcing for children, it is commonly employed. Initially, Lovaas reinforces the child with a small piece of food every time he or she makes a sound. Gradually he shapes these sounds until they approximate words. Eventually, he reinforces the child only for communicating in full sentences, and so forth. The reinforcement of food is coupled with praise and affection so that the type of reinforcement grows from primary and secondary reinforcers to generalized conditioned reinforcers that can be self-applied. These methods are also generalized to include training in other desired behaviors.

Since sustaining the newly learned behavior depends on maintaining a supportive environment, Lovaas includes parents and other significant figures in his program of behavior modification. Parents and other influential figures such as teachers are taught to systematically apply the same reinforcers to similar situations in the home or school. In this way the circle of the environment is widened to permit greater control.

Skinner's influence has also extended into many areas. With Sidney Presley, Skinner developed the *teaching machine,* a device whereby students may be taught without the need for an ever-present human instructor. Skinnerian principles also underlie numerous systems of individualized and programmed instruction. In such programs, the work is broken down into small units, each of which must be mastered before a student is permitted to proceed to the following unit. The student is virtually being shaped while mastering the material. There is immediate reinforcement in the sense of feedback to the student on correct and incorrect answers. Some computer-assisted instruction programs are based on Skinnerian principles and many suggest the need for a more systematic application of his ideas in our schools.

His methods have been employed in schools for the mentally retarded, mental institutions, and rehabilitation centers. In many of these institutions, a **token economy** has been established. The person is reinforced for appropriate behaviors by being given tokens of some kind that may subsequently be exchanged for special privileges or things. Making

one's bed, getting dressed, talking to other patients, and other desirable behaviors are reinforced by tokens that can be exchanged for candy, watching TV, and other amenities that
would not normally be provided. Last, Skinner's concepts and principles have been applied
systematically in industrial and business settings to encourage greater productivity through
a performance-improvement system based on accurate feedback and positive reinforcement. However, in the last couple of decades in America, perhaps due to the feeling that we
need to be harder on crime, there has been less use of methods relying on the insights of
psychological findings in all of these areas and a return to more punitive measures. That is
unfortunate.

## Social Utopias

Skinner's interest in the environment that shapes the individual and his bent toward a technological and reformist orientation (Smith, 1992) led quite naturally to his interest in the
design of an ideal environment or a utopian society. In 1948 Skinner wrote *Walden II,* a
book that described his concept of a utopia. **Walden II** was a behaviorally engineered society designed by a benevolent psychologist who employed a program of positive reinforcements. Because positive rather than aversive means were used to shape behavior, residents
sought those reinforcers and willingly behaved in socially responsible and productive ways.

In 1971 Skinner wrote *Beyond Freedom and Dignity* and again argued for the creation of a behaviorally engineered society, pointing out that most major problems today—
war, overpopulation, unemployment, inflation, and so forth—are caused by human
behavior. What we need, he said, is a behavior technology that will enable us to cope with
them. Such a technology cannot be established, however, unless we give up several cher-
ished "fictions," such as the notions that people are responsible for their own behavior and
that human beings are autonomous. For Skinner, human behavior is controlled by forces in
the environment and the concept of free will is a superstition. We feel free when we are
abundantly reinforced and have learned effective behaviors. The clue to our behaviors and
emotional states lies within the environment rather than the individual.

In Skinner's view (1984), operant conditioning is to the origin of behavior what
natural selection is to the origin of the species in Darwin's theory. Skinner's emphasis on the
environment did not negate the impact of heredity, but it did stand in sharp contrast with
the position taken by cognitive psychologists who suggest that certain learned behaviors are
due to cognition rather than environmental variables. Behaviorism may have lost its dominance in psychology because it could not assimilate the construct of **intentionality,** which
is, according to many current psychologists, crucial to understanding human behavior and
adaption (Hibbard, 1993).

In his utopian speculation, Skinner shifted from scientist to social philosopher.
Presenting us with a form of social Darwinism, he suggested that "survival is the only value
according to which a culture is eventually to be judged" (1971). Further, his concepts were
informed by the philosophical assumption that a human being is nothing more than an organism, a bundle of behavior, shaped by his or her environment. During evolution, the environment shaped the behavior that survives in our genes. After birth, environmental
conditioning shapes each one of us in this life. We need more, not less, control, Skinner argued. To his critics, he pointed out that human beings are already controlling and being

controlled. The process of controlling should not be denied but rather studied and understood so that we can implement it effectively in developing the society that we want. We have the power to develop a behavioral technology. To ignore this is to run the risk not of no control but rather of continued ineffective or deleterious control.

Skinner mellowed with age and conceded that psychologists and other people do not possess the means or the motivation to implement his utopian schemes (1981). In the end, the very reasoning of behaviorism explains its lack of success. If, as behaviorism maintains, people do not initiate actions on their own but simply act in ways in which they have been conditioned, they cannot change on the basis of predictions. Problems such as pollution, energy depletion, nuclear contamination, and other environmental issues have not been dealt with effectively because they have not yet happened in sufficient extremes to reinforce behavioral change. Survival of the species may depend on our ability to use scientific forecasts to change cultural practices (1990). By then, however, it may be too late.

| PHILOSOPHY, |
| :--- |
| SCIENCE, |
| AND ART |

# Skinner's Theory

Skinner provided a great deal of experimental data and research to support his ideas. More than any other contemporary theorist, he stimulated research, undertaken to validate the concepts of behaviorism. His own work was characterized by the intensive study of individual subjects, primarily drawn from infrahuman species, the careful control of laboratory conditions through automated apparatus, and an emphasis on variables easily modified by manipulating the environment.

Skinner's concepts clearly evolved from experimental laboratory investigations and he showed tremendous respect for well-controlled data. His constructs have been empirically tested and have held up well under the scrutiny of the scientific method. His theory is elegant in its simplicity. It is also admirable in its ability to predict and control behavior, particularly in infrahuman species. Although he set out to avoid theorizing, he presented a theory of human behavior, if not a theory of personality, and even played the role of a social philosopher.

But Skinner did not always recognize the kinds of evidence on which his various statements are based. He frequently presented his social philosophy as if it were an empirical science with all the appropriate validating evidence. For example, Skinner observed that an individual may be controlled by the manipulation of the environment. This is an empirical statement that holds up under test. However, one cannot jump from that empirical observation to the conclusion that human beings are *nothing but* organisms controlled by their environment and claim that the conclusion is simply based on validating evidence. The conclusion entails a philosophical commitment that Skinner acknowledged (1972).

Skinner himself went beyond the development of a scientific theory. In designing his utopia he invoked ethical commitments. He sug-

## Examining Dollard and Miller and Skinner

How would you rate Dollard and Miller and Skinner on each of the basic philosophical assumptions described in Chapter 1? Consult the chart on the inside front cover. Each basic issue is presented as a bipolar dimension along which a person's view can be placed according to the degree of agreement with one or the other extreme: *freedom/determinism, hereditary/environmental, uniqueness/universality, proactive/reactive, optimistic/pessimistic.* Rate Dollard and Miller's views and then Skinner's views on these issues.

When you have determined where you think the theorists stand, compare your responses with those of your classmates and your instructor. You should be willing to defend your ratings, but also be prepared to change them in light of others' compelling arguments. Afterward, compare your ratings with your own position on each issue and with those of other theorists. Does this comparison help you understand why their theories do or do not appeal to you?

gested, for instance, that the value of a society lies in its ability to survive, that human beings should give up the conceits of freedom and dignity. These are ethical considerations, not empirical ones. As such, they need to be evaluated in terms of their adequacy as philosophy.

Skinner regretted that psychology persisted in its search for internal determinants of behaviors, suggesting that humanist psychology, the helping professions, and the recent emphasis on cognitive psychology represent three obstacles in the continued development of psychology as a science of behavior (1987, 1988). He continued to argue for psychology as an experimental science and analysis of behavior in spite of controversy over the possible decline in the popularity of behaviorism (see Lambert, 1988; Place, 1988; Power, 1988).

Skinner's theory, as we have noted, works well in predicting and controlling behavior, particularly the behavior of infrahuman species. It also deals effectively with human behavior when that behavior occurs under situations of positive or negative reinforcement; in everyday terms we would say that it is effective in dealing with human situations that are surrounded by reward or punishment.

Skinner provided behaviorist explanations for complex human behaviors such as language acquisition, decision making, memory, and problem solving; however, his theory is less successful in these areas. For example, although there can be no question that operant conditioning, reinforcement, and shaping play a large role in the child's acquisition of language, these concepts alone do not fully explain how the child learns to speak (Chomsky, 1959; Hayes & Hayes, 1988). Skinner's theory does not account for the child's creative use of language. He did not tell us how it is possible for the child to come up with a new sentence never heard before. Nor do Skinner's concepts account for the meaningful errors that the child makes in learning to speak. The child who says, "I branged it home," may have never heard the verb *branged*. The error shows us that the child understands the use of the suffix -*ed* in expressing the past tense without the assistance of formal lessons in grammar.

Of all the theorists discussed in this book, Skinner and Freud have generated the most controversy and criticism. Both theories offend us because they attack our illusion that we are in full control of our behaviors. Yet their responses to the concept of our lack of self-control differ widely because of the very different philosophical assumptions that undergird their work. Freud, a pessimist, offered us hope of gaining a small margin of control over the unconscious forces of which we have been unaware through the painful process of self-understanding. Skinner, an optimist, believed that the answer lies in recognizing our lack of control, renouncing our ambitions for inner control, and committing ourselves to being more effectively controlled by a behaviorally designed technology.

## Conclusions

We have seen that Dollard and Miller developed a psychoanalytically oriented behavioral theory in which they combined the insights of Freud's psychoanalytic position with the principles of learning theory. Skinner took what he saw as the logical step that follows from Dollard and Miller's approach. If a stimulus-response theory of psychology can account for all of the overt behaviors that psychologists seek to explain, why not omit the psychoanalytic underpinnings and simply rely on behaviorist principles (Rychlak, 1973)?

The learning and behavior theories of Dollard and Miller and Skinner have strongly influenced American psychology. Throughout much of the twentieth century, the behaviorist movement was a dominant trend. Their emphasis on a rigorous scientific approach set the model for subsequent psychological investigations. However, while their theories seem to be able to account for the learned behavior of animal species and for the learned habits and simple behaviors of human beings, they are less able to explain complex human behaviors. Blackman (1991) sees contacts between Skinner's emphasis on behavior as a biological phenomenon and Mead's social behaviorism and Vgotsky's general genetic law of cultural development. It is not surprising that the radical nature of Skinner's theory, which took the learning and behavior theory of Dollard and Miller to a logical extreme, led to the development of an alternative approach to learning and behavior (discussed in Chapter 9), which, while emphasizing situational factors, also reintroduces covert factors such as cognition.

# *Summary*

1. Behavior and learning theories explore personality experimentally by studying behavior in laboratory settings. Their precise methods reflect an *empirical* point of view and the careful manipulation of variables under specified controlled conditions.

2. Early behaviorists include Pavlov, who explained the process of classical conditioning, Watson, whose theory recommended an emphasis on overt behavior, Thorndike, who formulated the *law of effect,* and Hull, who clarified the concept of *drive reduction.*

3. Dollard and Miller describe the structure of personality in terms of *habits* that may be learned and unlearned. They distinguish between *primary* and *secondary drives* and *reinforcers* as the primary motivating forces of personality.

4. Human behavior can be understood in terms of the learning process, which is broken down into four main conceptual parts: *drive, cue, response,* and *reinforcement.*

5. A number of experiments have been conducted on the learning process, especially in the area of *frustration* and *conflict.* Experiments with infrahuman species have been quite successful in predicting the behavior of simple laboratory animals under controlled conditions.

6. Dollard and Miller have adapted many Freudian concepts and integrated them into learning theory terms. Unconscious processes are reconceived as unlabeled drives and cues. The defense mechanisms and critical stages of development are also reconceived in terms of the learning process. The translation, though inexact, has helped to popularize Freud and stimulate experimental study of his ideas.

7. Dollard and Miller's therapy represents a bridge to the more directive and active therapies of other learning theories. Behavior therapy involves unlearning ineffective habits and substituting more adaptive responses. During a *talking phase,* the patient learns to label responses accurately. In the *performance phase,* deliberate training in suppression is carried out.

8. Dollard and Miller's theory of personality seeks to emulate a scientific model and places a great deal of emphasis on empirical research.

9. Skinner chose to describe variables and forces in the environment that shape overt behavior rather than to develop a theory of personality because he believed that the term "personality" and concepts of internal structure are ultimately superfluous. Behavior is best understood in terms of responses to the environment.

10. *Operant conditioning* involves reinforcing and *shaping* the spontaneous responses. It differs from *classical conditioning* in terms of the nature of the

behavior (which is freely made rather than elicited by a *stimulus*) and the nature of the *reinforcement* (which follows rather than precedes the behavior).

11. Skinner distinguished three different *schedules of reinforcement—continuous, interval,* and *ratio reinforcement*—and described their effectiveness. A continuous schedule is more effective for initially developing a behavior but a variable ratio schedule is more effective for maintaining it. Skinner also described the effects of *generalized conditioned reinforcers* and distinguished among *positive reinforcement, negative reinforcement,* and *punishment.*

12. *Behavior modification* therapy consists of restructuring the environment so that undesired behaviors are eliminated and more desired ones substituted. Skinner's approach has been successful in situations where traditional insight methods are inapplicable. His methods have also been used in therapeutic communities, education, and industry.

13. Skinner advocated the development of a social utopia, a behaviorally engineered society that employs a program of positive reinforcers to shape behavior.

14. In his utopian speculations, Skinner's statements reflected philosophical assumptions as well as scientific generalizations by not allowing for any exceptions and by invoking values and ethical commitments.

15. Skinner's theory clearly evolved from experimental laboratory investigations and emulates a strict scientific approach. However, Skinner acknowledged the philosophical assumptions that underlie his theory.

---

## Suggestions for Further Reading

For students who are interested in a historical introduction to the experimental movement in psychology, E. G. Boring, *A History of Experimental Psychology* (Appleton-Century-Crofts, 1929) is an encyclopedic survey. A classic statement of John Watson's behaviorism may be found in his book *Behaviorism* (Norton, 1925).

Dollard and Miller have jointly written two books that describe their effort to develop a theory of personality. Of primary interest is *Personality and Psychotherapy: An Analysis in Terms of Learning, Thinking, and Culture* (McGraw-Hill, 1950). In this work, the authors outline how they have applied the concepts of learning theory to reconsider many of the insights and observations of Freudian psychoanalysis. They translate Freud's theory of personality, therapeutic concepts, and procedures into learning theory terms. The book is an outstanding introduction to the learning and behavior approach to personality.

*Social Learning and Imitation* (Yale University Press, 1941) represents an early attempt to apply Hull's principles of learning to the study of personality. It is a good introduction to an effort to use learning theory to understand personality. Dollard and Miller have also written several articles. Some of these are cited in the References.

B. F. Skinner's most influential work is *The Behavior of Organisms* (Appleton-Century-Crofts, 1938), in which he formulates a theory of behavior in terms of the principles of conditioning. However, the lay person will probably be more interested in *About Behaviorism* (Random House, 1974), in which Skinner clarifies his position in a highly readable way. Also of interest are his utopian speculations in *Walden II* (Macmillan, 1948) and *Beyond Freedom and Dignity* (Knopf, 1971). Skinner was in the habit of writing down ideas as they occurred. In twenty-five years he filled over one hundred spiral-bound notebooks. A selection of these have been published in *Notebooks* (Prentice-Hall, 1982).

Students may also be interested in part two of Skinner's autobiography, *The Shaping of a Behaviorist* (New York University Press, 1985). Daniel Bjork, *B. F. Skinner: A Life* (Basic Books, 1993), provides a compelling portrait of the man whose ideas had such a transforming impact on American psychology, education, and society. An even-handed evaluation of Skinner's work is provided by Robert Nye's *The Legacy of B. F. Skinner: Concepts and Perspectives, Controversies and Misunderstandings* (Brooks/Cole, 1992). Also recommended is Marc Richelle, *B. F. Skinner: A Reappraisal* (Lawrence Erlbaum Associates, 1993).

# Social Learning Theories

## ALBERT BANDURA ❖ JULIAN ROTTER

## Your Goals for This Chapter

1. Explain what Bandura means by *reciprocal determinism* and identify the three factors that enter into it.
2. Explain what is meant by *observational learning*.
3. Identify three factors that influence modeling.
4. Describe the four processes that enter into observational learning.
5. Discuss the role of reinforcement in observational learning and compare Bandura's concept of reinforcement with that of Skinner.
6. Discuss the controversies surrounding television and film aggression.
7. Explain the concept of *self-efficacy*.
8. Describe Bandura's contributions to behavioral modification.
9. Evaluate Bandura's theory in terms of its function as philosophy, science, and art.
10. Identify the two major trends in personality research that Rotter's theory integrates.
11. Describe the *I-E Scale* and discuss the construct it measures and the findings to which it has led.
12. Describe the four variables that Rotter includes in his formula for predicting behavior.
13. Discuss applications of cognitive social learning theory in the area of psychotherapy.
14. Evaluate Rotter's theory in terms of its function as philosophy, science, and art.
15. Discuss Mischel's contributions to personality theory.

Interest in a cognitive and social behavior and learning approach has grown rapidly. The theories of Albert Bandura and Julian Rotter emerged out of the behavior and learning tradition but they seek to correct some of the shortcomings of radical behaviorism. Cognitive and social behavior and learning theories reflect the careful scientific procedures and methodology that characterize the behaviorist approach. At the same time, they have broadened many original learning theory concepts and integrated them with other current movements in psychology.

These theories have also moved from very simple laboratory situations to more complex ones and have increasingly used human rather than animal subjects. Laboratory conditions have been made more similar to the everyday life of people. Some of the contingencies under investigation are very complex, but laboratory procedures have become increasingly sophisticated in order to deal with them.

Albert Bandura believes that human behavior can be explained by a reciprocal determinism that involves behavioral, cognitive, and environmental factors. His theory reflects the behavior and learning tradition's emphasis on extrospection. Nevertheless, Bandura believes that it is desirable to reintroduce internal cognitive variables, such as **self-efficacy,** a person's perception of his or her effectiveness. Julian Rotter stresses that it is the subjective meaning and interpretation of the environment that actually regulates our lives. The effectiveness of reinforcement and the decision as to what we will learn depend on internal cognitive factors. The result is two theories that seek to correct some of the flaws of earlier behavior and learning theory and combine its insights with newer findings in the area of cognition and social psychology.

## Albert Bandura: Biographical Background

A small town in Alberta, Canada, where most of the cold fronts originate, was the childhood home of Albert Bandura. He was an only son, born on December 4, 1925, to wheat farmers of Polish descent who already had five daughters. Bandura has written little of his early years. We know that he attended a high school where there were only twenty students and two teachers. The students had largely to educate themselves, yet almost all of them went on to professional careers.

In college, Bandura initially enrolled in a psychology course because it met at a congenial time: his carpool companions, engineering and premed students, wished to arrive very early in the morning. He was captivated by the course and decided to major in the subject. He received his B.A. from the University of British Columbia in Vancouver in 1949 and his M.A. and Ph.D. from the University of Iowa in 1951 and 1952. There was a strong Hullian emphasis at Iowa, yet Bandura felt that the psychology department was very forward looking. He spent a year as a clinical intern at the Wichita (Kansas) Guidance Center and then accepted a position at Stanford University, where he rose through the ranks and has been ever since. He became a full professor in 1964 and in 1974 was awarded an endowed chair.

*Albert Bandura believes human behavior is due to a reciprocal determination that involves behavioral, cognitive, and environmental factors.*

At Stanford, Bandura began field studies on social learning of aggression, particularly considering the role of modeling; this research led him to explore the components underlying observational learning. His current research continues his interest in the power of modeling; investigates how people influence their own motivation and behavior, especially through their perception of self-efficacy; and studies the causes of stress reactions and depression.

An active scholar and writer, Bandura has published several important books and a great many articles. He has received many awards for his contributions to psychology and has been a consultant to several organizations. He was elected president of the American Psychological Association in 1973. At the present time, he teaches two undergraduate seminars at Stanford on the psychology of aggression and personal and social change. He enjoys hiking in the Sierra, dining in Bay Area restaurants, and the San Francisco Opera.

## Reciprocal Determinism and the Self-System

Earlier learning theories primarily depended on principles of reinforcement to account for how behavior is developed or changed. Contemporary social learning theories emphasize that causal influences on behavior do not simply go in one direction (Bandura, 1996). Both producers and products of their environment, people have cognitive, vicarious, self-regulative, and self-reflective capacities that influence their behavior and provide some measure of control over it.

According to Bandura (1978), human behavior is due to a **reciprocal determinism** that involves behavioral, cognitive, and environmental factors. All three factors operate as "interlocking determinants" of one another. If we were to diagram the process, each factor would have arrows pointing toward it and toward the other two (Figure 9.1) to show their reciprocal interaction.

In Bandura's concept of reciprocal determinism, although environmental stimuli influence our behavior, individual personal factors such as beliefs and expectations also influence how we behave. The selection of a tuna fish sandwich for lunch is not simply determined by the menu and other environmental stimuli but also by one's attitude toward tuna fish and an expectation as to how it will taste. Further, the outcomes of our behavior serve to change the environment. A rush on any particular item will cause a restaurant or household to run out of it and perhaps subsequently to order an extra supply.

Many psychologists have agreed with Bandura that behavior arises from the interactions of a person and the environment rather than from either factor alone. However, earlier conceptualizations have either seen the person and situation as separate agents that combine to produce behavior or considered the behavior that they produce a by-product that does not enter into the causal process. Bandura believes that his concept is significant because it emphasizes the reciprocal nature of the interaction among all three factors (1989, 1991a).

Although actions are regulated by their consequences, external stimuli affect behavior through intervening cognitive processes. While they are behaving, people are also thinking about what they are doing. Their thoughts influence how their behavior is affected by the environment. Cognitive processes determine which stimuli we will recognize, how we will perceive them, and how we will act upon them. Cognitive processes also permit us to use symbols and to engage in the type of thinking that enables us to anticipate different courses of action and their consequences. Because we act reflectively rather than automatically, we are able to change our immediate environment. In so doing, we arrange reinforcements for ourselves and influence our own behavior.

Processes relating to the self play a major role in Bandura's theory, but he does not conceive of the self as a psychic agent controlling behavior. Instead he uses the term **self-system** to refer to "cognitive structures that provide reference mechanisms," a "set of subfunctions for the perception, evaluation, and regulation of behavior" (1978). Thus the *self* in social learning theory is a group of cognitive processes and structures by which people relate to their environment and that help to shape their behavior.

Television viewing is a good example of the way in which behavioral, cognitive, and environmental factors may be interlocked. Bandura points out that

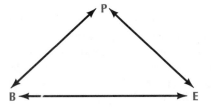

**FIGURE 9.1   A Diagram of Reciprocal Determinism**

Bandura suggests that human behavior is due to a reciprocal determinism that involves three interacting factors. In this diagram, *B* signifies behavior, *P* the person, and *E* the environment.

personal preferences influence when and which programs, from among the available alternatives, individuals choose to watch on television. Although the potential televised environment is identical for all viewers, the actual televised environment that impinges on given individuals depends on what they select to watch. Through their viewing behavior, they partly shape the nature of the future televised environment. Because production costs and commercial requirements also determine what people are shown, the options provided in the televised environment partly shape the viewers' preferences. Here all three factors—viewer preferences, viewing behavior, and televised offerings—reciprocally affect each other (1978).

The relative influence of the three interlocking factors varies in different individuals and in different situations. In a reciprocal interaction process, one and the same event can be a stimulus, a response, or an environmental reinforcer, depending on where in the sequence we begin our analysis. Thus, it is useless to search for an ultimate environmental cause of behavior. Moreover, chance encounters frequently play a role in shaping the course of a human life. In a chance encounter, each separate chain of events has its own causal determinants but their occurrence together arises fortuitously (1986). The science of psychology cannot predict the likelihood of chance encounters but it can clarify the factors that influence their impact (1986).

# Learning Through Observation

Bandura is best known for his emphasis on the process of learning through observation or by example. Bandura points out that most human behavior is learned by following a model rather than through the processes of classical and operant conditioning.

Bandura suggests that behavior is learned through observation either intentionally or accidentally. This is how children learn to play with their toys, to perform household chores, and to develop other skills such as riding a bicycle. The young child learns to speak by hearing the speech of others and imitating it. If learning a language were totally dependent on classical or operant conditioning, it could not be accomplished so readily, since the child would not be reinforced until after spontaneously uttering a sound that approximated a real word. In practice, parents repeat meaningful words over and over again to their children, who mimic those words as they learn to speak.

In many cases the behavior that is being learned must follow the same form as the modeled activity. Driving an automobile, for example, requires us to follow a prescribed method of action. However, learning through observation can also encompass new behaviors. Observers have been able to solve problems correctly even after the model has failed to solve the same problem. Thus observational learning exceeds mere imitation: the observer learns from the model's mistakes and successes. Learning through observation can account for innovative and creative behaviors. Bandura suggests that observers draw similar features from different responses and create rules of behavior that permit them to go beyond what

A key aspect of Bandura's theory is observational learning. Here a young American Indian watches the feet of an elder to learn how to dance during a Pow-Wow.

they have seen or heard. Through this type of synthesis, they are able to develop new patterns of conduct that may be quite different from those they have actually observed (1974).

## Experimental Analysis of the Influence of Modeling

Bandura's theory of **observational learning** is largely based on experimental analysis of the influence of modeling on behavior. In a typical modeling experiment, the subject observes another person performing a behavior or sequence of behaviors. Afterward the subject is observed to see whether or not the model's behavior is imitated. The subject's behavior is compared with that of a control group who did not observe the model to see if there are any significant differences.

Bandura's most famous study involved the use of a Bobo doll, a large inflated plastic figure about four feet tall (Bandura and Walters, 1963). Young preschool-aged children observed an adult playing with the doll in an aggressive fashion. The adult vigorously attacked the doll, hitting and kicking it while shouting things like "Sock him in the nose!" "Throw him in the air!" Other children did not see the adult playing with the doll aggressively. Later, when the experimental group was given the opportunity to play with the Bobo doll themselves, their behavior was similar to that of the model. It was twice as aggressive as that of the control group.

Through manipulating various independent variables in this kind of experiment, Bandura and his colleagues (1977) have demonstrated three factors that influence modeling.

First, the *characteristics of the model* affect imitation. We are more likely to be influenced by someone who we believe is similar to ourselves than by someone who is different. Simpler behaviors are more readily imitated than complex ones and certain kinds of behavior seem more prone to imitation than others. Hostile and aggressive behaviors are readily copied, especially by young children.

The *attributes of the observer* also influence modeling. People who are lacking in self-esteem or who are incompetent are especially prone to imitate a model. So too are highly dependent individuals and those who have been rewarded previously for conforming behavior. A highly motivated individual will also emulate a model in order to master a desired behavior.

Last, the *reward consequences associated with a behavior* influence the effectiveness of the modeling. Participants are more likely to imitate a behavior if they believe that such actions will lead to positive short- or long-term results. Bandura believes that this variable is stronger than the other ones.

## Processes of Observational Learning

Bandura believes that models influence learning primarily through their informative function. Learning through observation is not a simple matter of imitation. It is an active judgmental and constructive process. Through exposure, observers acquire symbolic representations of different ways of doing things and these ideas serve as guides for their own behavior. Observational learning is governed by four interrelated processes: attentional processes, retention processes, motor reproduction processes, and motivational processes (1977).

A number of variables influence *attentional processes.* Some of these have to do with the characteristics of the model, others with the nature of the activity, and still others with the subject. Some models are more noticeable than others and thus more readily copied. Charismatic models command considerable attention, whereas persons low in interpersonal attractiveness tend to be ignored.

Bandura points out that certain associations determine the types of activities we will be exposed to. The people with whom one regularly associates limit and structure the kinds of behaviors that one will observe. For example, those who live in an inner city where hostile gangs stalk the streets are more likely to learn aggressive modes of response than those who are reared in a pacifist commune.

Television has greatly enlarged the range of models that are available to people today, whereas our great-grandparents were pretty much limited to modeling sources within their own family and community. Personal qualities, such as our own interests, needs, wants, and wishes, also determine what we attend to.

A second system involved in observational learning is the *retention process.* When you observe someone's behavior without immediately performing the response, you have to represent it in some way in order to use it as a guide for action on later occasions.

There are two basic forms of symbols or representational systems that facilitate observational learning: *verbal* and *imaginal*. If you are trying to remember "Big Mac" you can do it either by remembering the words *BIG MAC* or by developing a visual image of two all-beef patties, special sauce, lettuce, cheese, pickles, onion, on a sesame-seed bun. These symbols may then be present to us when the actual stimulus is not.

The third mechanism of modeling involves *motor production processes*. In order to imitate a model, an individual has to convert the symbolic representation of the behavior into the appropriate actions. The response has to be carried out in space and time in the same way that the original behavior was. Motor production processes involve four sub-stages: cognitive organization of the response, initiation of the response, monitoring of the response, and refinement of the response.

The skills that we learn through observational learning are perfected slowly through a process of trial and error. We follow the behavior of a model and then seek to improve our approximations through adjustment and feedback.

The final system involved in observational learning is made up of *motivational processes*. Social learning theory distinguishes between *acquisition,* what a person has learned and can do, and *performance,* what a person actually does. People do not enact everything that they learn. Most of us have the theoretical know-how to rob a store. We have seen robberies in real life or on television and we are acquainted with the behaviors that are entailed in committing that crime. However, this does not mean that we will go out and do it.

We are more likely to engage in a modeled behavior if it leads to consequences that we value and less likely to engage in it if the results are punitive. We also learn from observing the consequences of others' behavior. Finally, we can engage in self-reinforcement. We generate evaluative responses toward our own behavior and this leads us to continue to engage in behaviors that we find self-satisfying and to reject those of which we disapprove or that feel uncomfortable.

No behavior occurs without sufficient incentive. Proper motivation not only brings about the actual performance of the behavior but it also influences the other processes involved in observational learning. When we are not motivated to learn something, we do not pay attention and so there is little we select to retain. Moreover, we are not willing to practice hard or to engage in the kind of trial-and-error activities necessary for the successful reproduction of a task. Thus, motivation emerges as a primary component in learning through observation.

Bandura notes that many imitative behaviors occur so rapidly that it is easy to overlook the processes underlying observational learning. However, it is important to postulate them in order to understand the phenomenon and to predict the circumstances under which learning will occur. In early development, children's modeling consists largely of instantaneous imitation. With age, children develop symbol and motor skills that enable them to follow more complex behaviors. Positing these processes helps us to specify the different variables that are involved in observational learning, develop hypotheses concerning them, and find ways of testing these hypotheses experimentally. In short, they enable us to make more accurate predictions. These constructs also help us to understand those instances in which an individual does not appear to learn from observation. Failure to reproduce a modeled behavior arises from insufficient attention, inadequate symbolization or retention, lack of physical capacities, skill, or practice, inadequate motivation, or any combination of these.

## Reinforcement in Observational Learning

Bandura suggests that almost any behavior can be learned by an individual without the direct experience of reinforcement. We do not have to be reinforced to pay attention to vivid images or loud sounds: the impact of the stimulus itself commands our attention. Nor do we have to be directly rewarded in order to learn something. Driving home from work each day, I pass a gas station along the route. One day, when I am out of gas, I drive directly to the station, demonstrating that I had learned where it was even though I was not directly reinforced for doing so. Observational learning is often seen to occur where neither the model nor the observer is directly reinforced and there is a delay between the original behavior being modeled and the later response.

Bandura believes that observational learning occurs through symbolic processes *while* one is being exposed to the modeled activity and *before* any response has been made. Therefore, it does not depend on external reinforcement. Where such reinforcement plays a role in observational learning, it acts as a facilitator rather than a necessary condition. Its role precedes rather than follows a response. It serves an informative and incentive function. The individual's anticipation of a reward or punishment influences how he or she behaves.

Social learning theory considers a broad range of reinforcements including extrinsic, intrinsic, vicarious, and self-generated consequences.

*Extrinsic reinforcement* is external. Its relationship to the behavior is arbitrary or socially arranged rather than the natural outcome of the behavior. Receiving a medal for a good athletic performance or an *A* on a term paper is an extrinsic reinforcement. Extrinsic reinforcement is clearly effective in creating behavioral change and has an important role to play in early development. Many of the activities we need to learn are difficult and tedious to perform initially. They do not become rewarding until we have become proficient in them. If we did not receive positive encouragements in the early stages of learning such behaviors, we would quickly become discouraged and stop learning them.

Depending on the activities involved and the way in which rewards are used, extrinsic incentives can increase interest in activities, reduce interest, or have no effect. It is what people make of incentives rather than the incentives themselves that determines how extrinsic rewards affect motivation.

*Intrinsic reinforcement* is naturally related to the behavior. Some behaviors produce a natural physiological effect; for example, relaxation exercises relieve muscle fatigue. In other instances it is not the behavior itself or the feedback that is rewarding, but how we feel about it. Playing a difficult piece of music well leads to a feeling of accomplishment. The self-satisfaction sustains the practice of the behavior.

*Vicarious reinforcement* occurs when we learn appropriate behavior from the successes and mistakes of others. Vicarious learning can take the form of either a reward or a punishment. A child who sees a sibling being spanked for a misdemeanor quickly learns not to do the same thing.

*Self-reinforcement* refers to the fact that people have self-reactive capacities that permit them to control their own thoughts, feelings, and actions. People do not behave like weathervanes that shift in different directions according to the external pressures that are placed upon them. Instead, they regulate their own behavior by setting standards of conduct for themselves and responding to their own actions in self-rewarding or self-punishing ways.

Self-reinforcement increases performance primarily through its motivational function. One runner might be satisfied by completing a mile in five minutes; another would want to finish it in less time. The standards that govern self-reinforcing responses are established by teaching or by example. High standards are frequently emulated because they are actively cultivated through social rewards.

After individuals learn to set standards for themselves, they can influence their behaviors through self-produced consequences. Bandura believes that most of our behavior as adults is regulated by the continuing process of self-reinforcement (1992).

## Television and Aggression

Some of Bandura's experiments were specifically designed to investigate the influence of television viewing on the development of aggressive responses. In many different variations on his classic Bobo doll studies, Bandura studied the impact of a live model as opposed to a filmed model and a cartoon model. The aggressive film model was just as effective in teaching aggressive forms of behavior as the live model. The cartoon character was somewhat less influential but nevertheless successful. In each study, children who observed an aggressive model (live, film, or cartoon) performed more aggressive responses than did children who observed a nonaggressive model or no model at all (1973).

Bandura has concluded that frequent exposure to aggression and violence on television encourages children to behave aggressively and he has been very concerned about the aggressive models that our culture provides.

Bandura's demonstrations led to considerable attention to the possible relationship between violence in society and violence on television. It was suggested that several real-life instances of aggression and risk taking had actually been triggered by similar episodes on television or in the movies. For example, death was the result when teenagers copied a stunt from the movie *The Program* in which the "tough" hero lies down at night in the middle of a busy highway (Hinds, 1993). Concern over behaviors such as this led to a number of studies throughout the 1960s and 1970s. With the increased popularity of video games, attention turned to the effects of these on aggression as well (Cooper & Mackie, 1986; Silvern & Williamson, 1987).

The results have been mixed. Much of the early research suggested a causal relationship between observing violence on television and aggressive behavior (Berkowitz & Powers, 1979). On the other hand the initial research may have been based on simplified concepts of cause and effect. The cumulative effects of watching television over a long period have not yet been evaluated (Comstock & Strasburger, 1990). Moreover, other factors such as personality characteristics of the viewer may make a difference (Russell, 1992). Duhs and Gunton (1988) discuss methodological and definitional problems in the research and conclude that on the basis of it, no particular policy advice is sustainable. They also express

## THINKING CRITICALLY

## *Filmed Violence*

What are your thoughts concerning the violence we are seeing in American society and in the television and film industry that reflects it? Do you believe that government intervention would be a good thing?

In order to think carefully about this question, it would be helpful if you formulate the strongest possible argument that you can muster both for and against the position. Once you have synthesized the main pros and cons of the issue, state your own opinion and support it with reasons and examples.

It may be of interest for you to know that one reason behind the violence in American films "is that violence, which needs no translation, sells well abroad." In 1980 about 30 percent of film income came from abroad. By 1993 it had increased to nearly 50 percent. Another factor to consider is that Hollywood's rating system is far more disturbed by sex than by violence (Weinraub, 1993).

What are some other factors that play a role in fostering aggressive behavior, such as influences in the home and culture and society at large, individual dispositions, and situational factors?

---

the concern that policymakers may be misled by present empirical findings to propose meaningless and even counterproductive restrictions.

In the past decade, the major television networks' new programs have been less violent (although still replete with sex and strong language), but violence, often seemingly pointless, on cable and in films has not decreased (Shea, 1997). However, legislation controlling violent content may just be an easy way of avoiding the more difficult root issues of crime, poverty, and gun control. As the debate escalates, "the movie and television industries say they face a difficult, if not unsolvable, problem: how [as art forms] to reflect the violence in the United States without exploiting it" (Weinraub, 1993). Comstock and Strasburger (1990) believe that the negative effects of television viewing can be alleviated by increasing the undesirability of aggressive behavior and increasing knowledge and skepticism about the medium, leading children and parents to be more critical watchers.

Our society is most definitely a violent one. Many children no longer feel safe either at school or in their own homes. However, one of the factors that we frequently overlook is that most parents employ corporal punishment as a means of disciplining their children. Corporal punishment has deeply embedded roots in many religious and cultural traditions. But parents who hit are sending their children clear messages of anger and rejection. They are also modeling aggressive behavior as a viable solution to problems, thus influencing their children to act out aggression. Bandura (1973) reminds us that children whose parents employ a lot of corporal punishment are often very aggressive. They are also less obedient (Power & Chapleski, 1986). We need to raise the question: Is the violence of society and culture also fostered by physical abuse of children in the name of discipline? And we must recognize that the answer is, Yes! And we also need to recognize that children born in poverty are more likely to have parents who are authoritarian or neglecting and who employ corporal punishment (Dornbusch, Gross, Duncan, & Ritter, 1987; Farran, Haskins, & Galligher, 1980).

# Self-Efficacy

Bandura (1977, 1997b) has developed and elaborated on the concept of **self-efficacy,** people's belief that they can successfully perform behaviors that will produce desired effects. Efficacy beliefs work together with other social and cognitive determinants in enabling people to cope with everyday life. Self-efficacy is not to be confused with self-esteem. Self-esteem entails judgments of self-worth, whereas self-efficacy entails judgments of personal capacity. Efficacy beliefs develop independently of performance and give us a basis for predicting whether one will engage in a behavior. Usually people do not try to do things they do not believe they can do. Self-efficacy is also not to be confused with *locus of control*. Rotter's locus of control, which will be discussed later in the chapter, anticipates whether actions will influence outcomes. Self-efficacy anticipates whether a person can perform certain actions and is a better predictor of behavior.

Self-efficacy is one component of social cognitive theory. It plays a central role in governing our thoughts, motivations, and actions. It influences factors such as acquisition of knowledge, choice of activities, and levels of motivation. Perceived self-efficacy also has a generative capacity that activates and coordinates other cognitive, social, and emotional subskills.

In order to do something well, we need both skill and efficacy beliefs. Many people know how to drive; not all of them are able to successfully operate a car under extremely challenging or dangerous conditions. The belief in one's ability to drive does not necessarily coincide with one's actual proficiency.

Self-efficacy arises from past accomplishments that serve as indicators of ability, from vicarious experiences that alter our beliefs through comparison with others, and from social influences (e.g., verbal persuasion), as well as from physical and emotional states. These sources are selected, interpreted, and integrated into a total estimate of self-efficacy that in turn influences subsequent cognitive, motivational, emotional, and selective processes.

Over the course of our lives, our self-efficacy beliefs may change. Different periods of life create different challenges that can alter our development of agency and self-efficacy beliefs. Social conditions and life events, which may or may not be under our control, influence us. Nevertheless, we still have some choice over the environments we are exposed to and over our reactions to situations.

Efficacy beliefs are collective as well as individual. *Collective efficacy* refers to a group's shared belief in its ability to organize and carry out actions that will lead to fulfillment of certain group goals. The sources and functions of collective efficacy are similar to those of individual self-efficacy. Efficacy beliefs may vary cross-culturally; some cultures may emphasize individuality and individual self-efficacy, whereas others place the interest of the group above the individual and foster collective efficacy.

Efficacy beliefs influence our lives in several ways. They contribute to the development of academic confidence and success. Both students' beliefs in their ability to learn academic subjects and teachers' beliefs in their ability to motivate and encourage learning affect academic performance, as does the collective institutional conviction that the school is an important influence on students. If the student body of a particular school comes from largely socioeconomically disadvantaged conditions, a strong sense of institutional efficacy will be more difficult to maintain.

Those of us who are active in sports can readily acknowledge how efficacy beliefs affect almost all areas of athletic functioning. Our ability to work hard at a sport, to persevere, concentrate, compete, avoid distractions, and cope with discouraging slumps are all mediated by self-efficacy.

Self-efficacy structures vocational choices, educational preparation, and level of accomplishment. Research on self-efficacy in business decision making shows its powerful impact. Wood and Bandura (1989) had managers participate in a computer-simulated organization. The participants had to match employees' talents to particular subfunctions. They also had to learn and use new procedures to achieve challenging levels of organizational performance. Managers who were led to believe that they could not be as effective as other managers and who received negative feedback deteriorated in their performance, whereas those who were led to believe that they could acquire the skill and were given positive feedback improved their organizational functioning.

Self-efficacy even modifies the biological systems of the body involved in health and disease. We can influence our health by controlling our behavior and environment. Although efficacy cannot entirely account for the course of an illness or disease, it can have a major impact. Prognostic judgments and medical information may change our beliefs concerning personal efficacy and thus alter health outcomes. Capitalizing on the information we have in this area could help us develop effective programs for preventing disease and promoting health (see also 1997a).

It is important to foster the development of efficacy. In the future, women and ethnic minorities will increasingly make up more of the workforce. Many of these people avoid entering the fields of science, technology, and economics because they lack efficacy beliefs in their quantitative skills. The challenge is to improve their sense of efficacy, as society will be increasingly depending on them for accomplishments in these areas.

Growing global interdependence and rapid social and technological change require us to learn to exercise some control over our lives (Bandura, 1995). Efficacy beliefs structure the ways we select, construct, and manage our environment and adapt to changing social conditions. If we believe in "empowering" people, we must recognize that empowerment can only arise through a sense of efficacy that permits people to believe that they can effect changes personally and collectively. In a time when many people are crippled by beliefs of powerlessness, Bandura (1997b) believes that we need social initiatives that will foster collective efficacy and influence the conditions that shape our lives and those of our children.

## Psychotherapy and Behavior Modification

Since observation is central in the learning of behaviors, it also has a useful place in modifying undesirable behaviors. Bandura has added to the techniques of behavior modification the systematic use of *modeling* as an aid in changing behaviors. Modeling has been used to reduce fears in children and adults, to teach domineering and hyperaggressive children to be more cooperative, to teach language skills to autistic children, to increase communication facility in asocial psychiatric patients, to lessen anxiety and improve performance in college students, and to facilitate many other behavior changes. In each case, a model or models illustrate or explain an appropriate way of handling a situation and the patient is encouraged to emulate the model. Thus, in order to eliminate a strong animal phobia, a subject might watch filmed and live models progressively interact with the animal in question and then be encouraged to engage in increasingly intimate interactions with the animal along with the model. Results have shown that modeling procedures are clearly instrumental in reducing and sustaining a reduction in fears and in making other behavioral changes.

Bandura (1977) points out that people who behave in abnormal ways generally have a poor sense of self-efficacy. They do not believe that they can successfully perform the behaviors that will enable them to cope with everyday life. Their lowered expectations lead them to avoid situations that are threatening and in which they do not believe they could perform well. Where situations cannot be avoided, they try only a little and give up quickly. As a result, they do not engage in activities that might demonstrate their abilities and serve to change their sense of self-efficacy.

Bandura's therapeutic strategies are designed to help patients improve their perception of their own effectiveness. He recommends that therapists use a variety of techniques in order to enhance their patients' self-confidence. Thus, in treating a group of *agoraphobics* (people who are afraid of public places), Bandura used a number of different procedures. Initially, Bandura met with the agoraphobics in small groups where he or cotherapists helped them to identify and rank those situations that aroused fear in them. He also taught them how to use relaxation techniques and how to substitute positive thoughts for self-debilitating ones. Then, through graduated field experiences, he encouraged them to engage in successful interactions with their feared objects and settings. Appropriate responses and behaviors were modeled by therapists and ex-agoraphobics. Exposure to feared situations was taken gradually, one step at a time, in order not to overwhelm or discourage the client. Through successful experiences, the subjects were able to improve their sense of self-efficacy and to increase the length of time they spent in intimidating situations. Gradually, the field therapists lessened their guided participation and support. Thus, through a variety of techniques, Bandura and his associates were able to increase self-efficacy and modify behaviors (1980).

Corcoran (1991) suggests that in his concept of self-efficacy Bandura may be shifting "from a cognitive-behavioral model to a largely cognitively based approach to motivation and behavior."

In those cases where behavior modification has stressed a change in the environment, Bandura points out that it usually has had only a short-term effect. As long as the person is under the control of the therapist or in a carefully monitored environment, the behavior is controlled; once that external control and support is gone, the behavior regresses. Reciprocal determinism assumes that behavior is controlled by both the person and the environment. It is possible, therefore, to indicate the conditions under which behavior will generalize and hold up over time and the conditions under which it will not. The conditions under which change is maintained are

**THINKING CRITICALLY**

## Developing Self-Control

Techniques informed by social learning theory can be used to develop ways of changing your behavior. By carefully observing your behavior and the factors that lead to it, you can begin to see how to influence an undesired activity and change it. The environment can often be varied so that either the stimuli that precede the activity or the consequences that follow it are changed. Through a strategy of behavioral programming, a person can gradually eliminate inappropriate behaviors and substitute more desirable ones.

In developing a program of self-control, the first step is to decide on a particular behavior pattern that you would like to modify. Carefully monitor and observe that behavior so that you can determine the conditions under which it is likely to occur. Your observation should be very specific. You need to count, chart, and evaluate each instance. It is helpful to keep a behavioral diary or chart. This is one way in which social learning theorists assess behavior. Next, make a list of graduated objectives that would shape you in developing a more appropriate behavior. Do not be overambitious. Select only one problem area and break it down into small, manageable steps. Consider the techniques that would help you achieve your objectives. Are there any factors in your environment that you could change in order to facilitate the development of more appropriate behaviors? A student who has difficulty studying might consider the time and place where studying normally occurs. Is it an area and time that is free from distractions and interruptions? Perhaps you would study more effectively in the library. Leaving the phone off the hook during study hours can eliminate intruding phone calls. Are there any models whose behavior you could emulate? Finally, you should develop a systematic schedule of reinforcements for appropriate behaviors that lead toward your objectives. Make sure that the reward is something that you value and are willing to work for. And then be sure that you employ it as a means of reinforcement.

---

—when the new behavior has functional value for the individual

—when there are strong social and environmental supports for the behavior

—when an individual's own self-evaluation becomes an important reinforcer

Many inappropriate behavior patterns are immediately rewarding but have long-range negative effects. Examples are overeating, smoking, and alcohol and substance abuse. In such cases, the task of the therapist is to help the individual acquire some capacity to control her or his own behavior. There are several different elements involved in *self-control*, but one that Bandura has explored carefully is delay of gratification. *Delay of gratification* involves the self-imposed postponement of an immediate reward in favor of a more significant reward in the future. The student who decides not to cut class may forgo the fun in the coffee shop over the next hour but stands a greater chance of getting a good grade in the course. Bandura's studies have shown that modeling can influence the ability to delay gratification (Bandura & Mischel, 1965). In our achievement-oriented society, the ability to delay gratification is a desired, if not necessary, skill. Bandura believes that most individuals who are able to delay gratification were reared in homes where parents modeled the delay of reward and emphasized its importance. However, adults can also be taught to delay gratification. Bandura believes that research on self-control is our most promising approach to the management of detrimental behavior (Evans, 1976).

Recently Bandura (Bandura, Barbaranelli, Caprara, & Pastorelli, 1996) has been working on a conceptual model exploring the levels of internal control that permit people to disengage from moral behavior. Social cognitive theory bases moral agency in a self-regulatory system composed of self-monitoring, judgmental, and self-reactive subfunctions that permit people to exercise control over their behavior and evaluate their conduct in terms of internal standards and situational circumstances. Destructive conduct may be made acceptable if it is linked to what the person considers a worthy purpose, if responsibility is diffused, and if victims are vilified. Moral disengagement supports destructive behavior by reducing prosocial feeling and prior self-censure and by encouraging cognitive and emotional reactions that favor aggression. Similar mechanisms are present in interpersonal aggression and delinquent conduct.

Bandura has responded sharply to charges that behavior modification entails manipulation of human beings and denial of their freedom. He points out that procedures used to create a behavior pattern that is convenient to the reinforcer but of little value to the subject usually do not produce lasting results. Bandura does not see this as a regrettable state of affairs because otherwise it would be too easy to develop procedures that would enslave people (Evans, 1976). A client comes to a therapist with a request for help in changing behavior. The relationship is not that of a controller (however benevolent) and an unwitting subject: it is a contractual relationship between two consenting individuals. Behavior modification increases rather than limits an individual's freedoms. For example, the individual with a strong fear is not really free but crippled by limiting behavioral responses.

| PHILOSOPHY, | |
|---|---|
| SCIENCE, | |
| AND ART | |

## Bandura's Theory

Heir to the behavior and learning tradition in American psychology, Bandura's theory is rapidly becoming one of the most popular approaches to the study of personality. It is particularly appealing to academic psychologists because it lies within the mainstream of American psychology. It strongly emphasizes experimental research and clearly emulates a scientific model.

Bandura's reintroduction of internal variables, his emphasis on reciprocal determinism, and his investigation of human subjects allow his theory to deal with complex social responses more adequately than radical behavior and learning theories. B. F. Skinner's learning theory can account for the learned behavior of animals and very simple learned habits and behaviors of human beings; it does not explain complex human behaviors like decision making and creativity well. Bandura's account clearly includes those kinds of complex activities, permitting scientific analysis of a wide range of human behaviors. Bandura's work has helped to overcome the earlier behaviorist view of human nature as a machine whose output depends upon the input provided. Indeed, Bandura's theory underscores the vast differences between a human being and a computer.

Bandura's theory is clearly grounded in empirical research and amenable to precise laboratory methods of investigation. It has stimulated research in other areas. It economically states major constructs in relatively simple terms. And it is compatible with our existing concept of the world.

Bandura's work has been criticized, however, for its emphasis on overt behaviors, in spite of his reintroduction of covert factors, and for its excessive bias against psychoanalysis, which leads him to ignore distinctly human problems such as conflict and unconscious motivation.

We have also seen that learning and behavior theorists have sometimes failed to appreciate that scientific work is based on philosophical assumptions. Skinner, for example, for many years did not acknowledge the philosophical commitments that inform his work. Although Bandura does not explicitly discuss his philosophical assumptions, with the exception of reciprocal determinism, he is more sophisticated than Skinner in his recognition that scientific efforts rest on philosophical assumptions. He also avoids elevating his empirical conclusions into philosophical ones.

In spite of their desire to limit their activities to empirical science, learning and behavior theorists invariably raise philosophical issues and ethical questions (Rottschaefer, 1991). This is particularly evident in their efforts to apply their theories toward the improvement of human behavior and society. Bandura has developed significant new forms of psychotherapy, like modeling. He has spoken candidly about the dangers of aggressive models. Other findings from observational learning theory have been taken from the laboratory and applied to problems in the everyday world, clearly demonstrating the practicality of Bandura's approach but implying an underlying philosophy as well.

Bandura has helped revitalize the learning and behavior approach by infusing it with a cognitive dimension and by acknowledging some of its philosophical underpinnings. The scientific emphasis makes his approach an extremely popular one. His influence will undoubtedly continue to be substantial.

Like Bandura's, Julian Rotter's theory also seeks to correct some of the shortcomings of earlier behavior and learning theory and to incorporate new findings in or from cognitive psychology.

## Julian Rotter: Biographical Background

Julian Rotter was born in Brooklyn, New York, in 1916. He has not yet written about his early life or indicated how it might have influenced his theory other than to say that throughout his school years he was an avid reader. In his junior year in high school, unable to find any new fiction to read in one of his frequent visits to the Avenue J Library in Brooklyn, he browsed in the philosophy and psychology section and came across some books by Alfred Adler and Sigmund Freud. By his senior year he was seriously interested in psychology and was interpreting his friends' dreams. He also wrote a paper on "Why we make mistakes" (1982).

Rotter would have liked to major in psychology but because he was unaware of any professional opportunities in psychology and because of the financial pressures of the Great Depression, he selected chemistry. However, he took electives in psychology, and when he graduated he actually had more credits in that discipline than in chemistry. He also met and studied with Alfred Adler, from whose theory he came to appreciate the unity of personality and the goal-directedness of behavior.

Rotter graduated from Brooklyn College in 1937. Adler's sudden death that very summer and the encouragement of professors led him to go to the University of Iowa to

*Julian Rotter explored locus of control, an individual's perception that reinforcements are controlled by internal or external forces.*

study with Kurt Lewin. He arrived in Iowa with enough money to survive only a few weeks, but was able to find a job as a part-time research assistant. From Kurt Lewin's field theory, he came to appreciate the interrelatedness of behavior and the fact that many factors are responsible for any single behavior. His writings show the influence of Adler and Lewin as well as of learning theorists such as E. L. Thorndike and Clark Hull. Rotter received his M.A. in 1938 and the Ph.D. in psychology from Indiana University in 1941.

During World War II, Rotter served as a psychologist and personnel consultant in the U.S. Army. Following the war, he took a position at Ohio State University, where George Kelly was the director of the clinical psychology program. At Ohio State, he developed his social learning theory of personality and first described it in a book entitled *Social Learning and Clinical Psychology* (1954). He also conducted a great deal of research based on his theory.

Rotter went to the University of Connecticut in 1963, where he was a professor in the department of psychology, director of the Clinical Psychology Training Program, and a diplomate in clinical psychology of the American Board of Examiners in Professional Psychology. In 1976–1977, he was president of the Eastern Psychological Association. Currently an emeritus professor at the University of Connecticut, he continues to teach courses in psychodynamics and the construction and validation of personality measures. Rotter's view has come to significantly influence thinking about personality in contemporary psychology.

## Internal versus External Control of Reinforcement

In his early years, Rotter conducted a series of experimental studies designed to tell whether or not people learn tasks and perform differently when they see reinforcements as related or unrelated to their own behaviors. The results of these experiments led him to develop the **I-E Scale,** a significant assessment tool that measures an individual's perception of *locus of control* (1966). An individual may come to believe on the basis of past experiences that the reinforcements received depend on certain behaviors or, conversely, may come to believe that reinforcements are controlled by outside forces (1966). Internally controlled individuals assume that their own behaviors and actions are responsible for the consequences that happen to them. Externally controlled people believe that the locus of control is out of their hands and that they are subject to the whims of fate, luck, or other people. Internal versus external control of reinforcement refers to a continuum of belief of which we have cited the two extremes. Competence, mastery, helplessness, powerlessness, or alienation are but a few of the terms used to describe whether or not people believe they can control their own lives. Rotter's concept of locus of control is not the same as Bandura's concept of self-efficacy. Self-efficacy refers to the belief that one is able to perform certain actions. Locus of control anticipates whether one's actions will influence outcomes. Rotter believes that his construct has an advantage over others because it is an integral part of a formal theory from which predictions can be made.

Although various measuring devices have been developed to assess locus of control as a stable personality characteristic, Rotter's scale remains one of the most widely used. The I-E Scale consists of twenty-three forced-choice items and six filler items. The participant indicates which of each pair of items applies best. The final score can range from zero to twenty-three, with higher scores indicating greater externality. Rotter does not indicate any cutoff score that separates internals from externals, but norms have been published for various groups to facilitate comparisons. On a national sample of high school students, the mean score was 8.50. The lowest mean score reported by Rotter was 5.94 among a group of Peace Corps trainees (1966).

The I-E Scale has been widely used in research and has led to a number of significant findings: internality increases with age; as children grow older, their locus of control tends to become more internal; internality becomes stable in middle age and does not diminish in old age, contrary to popular views of the elderly as dependent. Certain parental practices help to foster a belief in internal control: warm, responsible, supportive conditions and the encouragement of independence (de Mann, Leduc, & Labrèche-Gauthier, 1992; Lefcourt, 1976).

Several studies have shown that internals are more perceptive and ready to learn about their surroundings. They ask more questions and process information more efficiently than externals. They have greater mastery tendencies, better problem-solving abilities, and more likelihood of achievement (Agarwal & Misra, 1986). Thus, internal prison inmates know more about the institution and conditions affecting their parole and are more likely to be paroled (Rotter, 1966). Internals are better versed about critical political events that may influence their lives (Ryckman & Malikiosi, 1975).

Internal locus of control appears to protect one against unquestioning submission to authority. Internals are more resistant to influences from other people. They make more independent judgments and try harder to control the behavior of others (Lefcourt, 1976). They tend to assume more responsibility for their own behavior and attribute responsibility to others. As a result, they are more likely to be punitive and less sympathetic than externals.

Internals are more likely to know about the conditions that lead to good physical and emotional health and to take positive steps to improve their health such as quitting smoking, avoiding substance abuse, and engaging in regular exercise (Bezjak & Lee, 1990; Powell, 1992; Rosolack & Hampson, 1991). They suffer less from hypertension and are less likely to have heart attacks. When they do become ill, they cope with the illness more adequately than externals (Strickland, 1978, 1979). Internals also derive more benefit from social support (Lefcourt, Martin, & Saleh, 1984) and are more likely to use contraception (Visher, 1986).

Externals are more likely to conform (Singh, 1984) and prefer not to have to make a choice (Harrison, Lewis, & Straka, 1984). Externals tend to be more anxious and depressed, as well as more vulnerable to stress. They develop defensive strategies that invite failure in coping with a task and use defensive strategies afterward to explain their failures. They attribute their lack of success to bad luck or to the difficulties of the task (Drwal & Wiechnik, 1984; Lester, 1992).

Some research has shown sex differences in locus of control, with females tending to be external (de Brabander & Boone, 1990). The increase in external scores for women in the 1970s may reflect greater awareness of external constraints on their ability to meet their goals at work and in other settings (Doherty & Baldwin, 1985). However, family socioeconomic status is an even stronger correlate of locus of control (Young & Schorr, 1986), as well

# Internal-External Locus of Control

You can assess your own belief in locus of control by selecting the one statement from each pair that best describes your belief. The following are sample items taken from an earlier version of the I-E Scale but not used in the final version. You can discover whether you are inclined toward internal control or external control by adding up the choices you make on each side. Items on the left indicate internality and items on the right indicate externality.

| *I more strongly believe that:* | *Or:* |
| --- | --- |
| Promotions are earned through hard work and persistence. | Making a lot of money is largely a matter of getting the right breaks. |
| In my experience I have noticed that there is usually a direct connection between how hard I study and the grades I get. | Many times the reactions of teachers seem haphazard to me. |
| The number of divorces indicates that more and more people are not trying to make their marriages work. | Marriage is largely a gamble. |
| When I am right I can convince others. | It is silly to think that one can really change another person's basic attitudes. |
| In our society a person's future earning power is dependent upon his or her ability. | Getting promoted is really a matter of being a little luckier than the next guy. |
| If one knows how to deal with people they are really quite easily led. | I have little influence over the way other people behave. |
| In my case the grades I make are the results of my own efforts; luck has little or nothing to do with it. | Sometimes I feel that I have little to do with the grades I get. |
| People like me can change the course of world affairs if we make ourselves heard. | It is only wishful thinking to believe that one can really influence what happens in society at large. |
| I am the master of my fate. | A great deal that happens to me is probably a matter of chance. |
| Getting along with people is a skill that must be practiced. | It is almost impossible to figure out how to please some people. |

Do you concur with Rotter that an internal locus of control is more conducive to positive social adjustment and functioning?

*SOURCE: Reprinted from Julian B. Rotter, "External Control and Internal Control,"* Psychology Today Magazine, *June 1971, 5, 42. Copyright © 1971.*

as not being a member of a vulnerable population, "such as children, medical patients, lower level employees, and the elderly" (Thompson & Spacapan, 1991).

Rotter believes that extreme belief in either internal or external locus of control is unrealistic and unhealthy. He has hypothesized a curvilinear relationship between locus of control measures and assessments of maladjustment (Rotter & Hochreich, 1975). However, it is clear that many favorable characteristics have been associated with internal locus of control and it has been proposed that an internal orientation is more conducive to positive social adjustment and functioning. The locus of control construct is durable and has had a major impact (Lefcourt, 1992). Some of the more recent research is cross-cultural (e.g., Banks, Ward, McQuater, & De Britto, 1991; Murk & Addleman, 1992; Saeeduzzafar & Sharma, 1991). One trend in more recent research is to develop locus of control measures for specific domains such as health. This specificity may facilitate prediction but it detracts from Rotter's initial concept of locus of control as a generalized expectation.

## Basic Concepts

Rotter's empirical observations about individual differences led to a more general motivational theory in which behavior potential, expectancy, reinforcement value, and the psychological situation are seen as four variables that can be measured and related in a specific formula that enables us to predict a person's behavior in any given situation (Rotter & Hochreich, 1975).

The **behavior potential** refers to the likelihood that a particular behavior will occur in a given situation. Rotter uses the term "behavior" broadly to refer to a wide class of responses that includes overt movements, verbal expressions, and cognitive and emotional reactions. In any given situation, an individual could react in a number of different ways. The behavior potential is specific both for the particular behavior and for the related reinforcement. Thus, we must know what goal the behavior is related to before we can tell how likely it is to occur.

**Expectancy** refers to individuals' subjective expectations about the outcome of their behavior. It is an estimation of the probability that a particular reinforcement will occur if one behaves in a certain way in a given situation. What does Johnny expect will be the outcome of his temper tantrum? The answer to that question will influence the likelihood of a tantrum occurring.

**Reinforcement value** refers to the importance or preference of a particular reinforcement for an individual. In a given situation, Mary may refuse to wash Dad's car if she thinks that the only reward for the task is a verbal thank-you. On the other hand, she might be anxious to wash the car is she believes that she will receive ten dollars for the chore. The reinforcement value of a particular reward differs from individual to individual. Some children are more eager to please their parents than others. People also engage in activities for different reasons.

The **psychological situation** refers to the psychological context in which the individual responds. It is the situation as defined from the perspective of the person. Any given situation has different meanings for different individuals and these meanings affect the response. Rotter's concept of the psychological situation takes into account the importance of both dispositional and situational influences. It recognizes that an individual may have a strong need for aggression but may or may not behave aggressively in a particular situation depending on reinforcement expectancies. Rotter believes that the complex cues of each situation arouse in individuals expectations for behavior reinforcement outcomes and for reinforcement sequences.

Rotter has used a number of different techniques in his efforts to measure the variables that enter into his formula. Some of these rely on self-reports of the individual. Ranking methods in which individuals are asked to rank verbal descriptions of reinforcements from the most to the least reinforcing have been used to measure reinforcement value. Verbal questionnaires in which participants are asked to predict the likelihood of success in various tasks have been used to measure expectancy. Behavior potential can be measured by asking people what they think they will do in certain situations. Behavioral observations have also been used to indicate the strength of these constructs. Individuals may be observed actually behaving in ways so as to receive one reinforcement over another. A subject choosing one alternative over another is thought to be indicating a higher level of expectancy for the chosen alternative. Observations of an individual's behavior over a long period of time give us an indication of how frequently certain behaviors tend to occur. The development of precise measuring techniques for these constructs, however, is only at a very early stage.

## Psychotherapy

Rotter's concepts have found application in the field of clinical psychology. In general, Rotter (Rotter & Hochreich, 1975) suggests that maladjusted individuals are characterized by low freedom of movement and high need value. **Freedom of movement** refers to a person's expectation that a particular set of responses will lead to a desired reinforcement. **Need value** refers to the importance attached to goals. Individuals who are adjusted have a high freedom of movement and realistic goal levels. Maladjusted individuals believe that they are unable to get the gratifications they desire through their own efforts. Instead of working toward their goals realistically, they seek to obtain them through fantasy or they behave in ways that avoid or defend against failure. Problem behaviors, such as substance abuse and delinquency, have been shown to be associated with a discrepancy between an individual's need values for recognition and his or her freedom of movement for getting it.

Low freedom of movement may result from a lack of knowledge or ability to develop the behaviors that are necessary to reach one's goals. An individual who is mentally retarded may have low expectancies because of an inability to learn basic skills. Low freedom of movement may arise from the nature of the goal itself. If a goal is antisocial, behaving in ways that fulfill the goal invites punishment. An expectancy for failure can also arise from the mistaken generalization of experiences of frustration from one area to another. A child whose paralyzed leg prevents participation in sports may erroneously generalize to assume being disliked by others. Individuals who were severely punished as children may generalize from those experiences to the present. Maladjusted individuals often apply expectations and behaviors from one situation to another inappropriately. They tend to seek immediate rewards and deny the long-term consequences of their behaviors and they emphasize the gratification of one need to the exclusion of others.

A social learning therapist would seek to help a maladjusted person by reducing the discrepancy between need value and freedom of movement. Rotter points out that it is

*In Rotter's theory, adjusted individuals usually have a high sense of freedom of movement and realistic goal levels.*

essential that the therapist be flexible. In time, he hopes that patients can be systematically matched to therapists, since therapists vary in their effectiveness with different methods and patients. In general, cognitive learning theory emphasizes a problem-solving orientation to therapy and the development of problem-solving skills such as looking for alternative means of reaching a goal, analyzing the consequences of one's behavior, and discriminating among situations. The therapist assumes a highly active and directive role.

Rotter frequently advocates use of environmental change in order to effect personality change. He may try to alter the attitude of those who live with the patient or recommend a change in school or job. His work on the importance of an appropriate environment for change has led to a new conception of the mental hospital as a therapeutic community in itself. In other instances, Rotter employs various behavior strategies such as systematic desensitization, aversive conditioning or covert sensitization (the association of undesired behaviors with aversive stimuli in one's imagination), assertiveness training, and behavioral training in specific skills.

With its cognitive emphasis, Rotter's social learning theory also emphasizes the need to cultivate insight into one's own motives as they have developed from past experiences, insight into the motives of others, and insight into the long-term consequences of one's behavior. Rotter points out, however, that it is not enough for clients to understand the origins of their problems; they must also be taught new behaviors that will overcome them. Social learning theory conceives of psychotherapy broadly in the context of social interaction. The therapist's role is to help the patient develop a more satisfactory relationship with his or her social environment.

The cognitive approach to personality promises to be a very fruitful one. Cognitive factors may provide the link that will help us transcend the traditional dichotomy between dispositional and situational factors in behavior. Distinctive cognitive and behavior patterns determine the unique meaning that stimuli and reinforcers have for different individuals. An individual's cognitive style influences adaption to the world and interpersonal competence. Recently, there have been efforts to construct complex information-processing models that might eventually simulate a wide variety of human mental activity. In addition, there has been increased contact between cognitive psychology and neurophysiology based upon the belief that cognitive systems might be tied to underlying neural systems. Most of the research in personality today involves cognitive elements at some point. There is little doubt that the emphasis on cognition has grown and will continue as an important factor in the discussion of personality.

|  |  |
|---|---|
| PHILOSOPHY, | |
| SCIENCE, | |
| AND ART | |

# Rotter's Theory

Rotter's cognitive social learning theory creatively combines traditional learning theory with an interest in cognition. Rotter's position represents a significant departure from B. F. Skinner's radical behaviorism but retains the important emphasis on a strict methodology and the classical features of the learning tradition. Thus, his theory is very appealing to experimentally oriented researchers. It also appeals to those who are attuned to advances being made in cognitive studies. His emphasis on cognitive factors is greater than Albert Bandura's. In brief, his theory is very much in line with current trends in academic psychology.

Rotter's research is rigorous and well controlled even though he permits introspective methods in addition to the objective observation of behavior. Indeed, he has fostered a new appreciation of introspection as a methodological technique and in doing so has made a valid correction of the rigid narrowness that characterizes radical behavior and learning theory.

As a science, Rotter's theory excels. His terms are operationally defined and measurable, and lend themselves to empirical test. His theory readily meets the criterion of verifiability. Empirical support for his theory has been strong, particularly regarding his concept of locus of control. His work has considerable heuristic value and may eventually enable us to predict behavior. Rotter's theory has stimulated research and has found wide application in the clinical setting, where the I-E Scale has proved very useful. Because his concepts are stated as simply as possible, his theory compares well with more complex rival theories.

Rotter's theory has been criticized, however, for its lack of depth

**PHILOSOPHICAL ASSUMPTIONS**

## Examining Bandura and Rotter

How would you rate Bandura and Rotter on each of the basic philosophical assumptions described in Chapter 1? Consult the chart on the inside front cover. Each basic issue is presented as a bipolar dimension along which a person's view can be placed according to the degree of agreement with one or the other extreme: *freedom/determinism, hereditary/environmental, uniqueness/universality, proactive/reactive, optimistic/pessimistic.* Rate Bandura's and Rotter's views on these issues.

When you have determined where you think the theorists stand, compare your responses to those of your classmates and your instructor. You should be willing to defend your ratings but also be prepared to change them in light of others' compelling arguments. Afterward, compare your ratings of Bandura and Rotter with your own position on each issue and with those of other theorists. Does this comparison help you understand why their theories do or do not appeal to you?

and for the fact that it takes few risks in hypothesizing and does little more than summarize existing, generally well-known knowledge (Cartwright, 1979).

# A Cognitive-Affective Personality System

Walter Mischel has studied with George Kelly and Julian Rotter and worked with Henry Murray. His work exemplifies some of the current thinking related to Bandura's and Rotter's contemporary scientific approaches to personality. This research also reflects psychologists' renewed interest in cognition.

Mischel initially emphasized behavioral specificity in his discussion of human behavior. *Behavioral specificity* (1968) means that an individual's behavior is determined by the specific situation. Mischel initially thought that we behave consistently in the same manner in different situations only to the extent that these situations lead to similar consequences. When the consequences are different, we learn to discriminate among different situations and behave accordingly. Which reaction we show at any particular moment depends on discriminative stimuli: where we are, whom we are with, and so forth. As did other social learning theorists, Mischel emphasized behavioral specificity rather than trait consistency (trait theories are discussed in Part V).

Mischel's work stimulated a person-situation debate that commanded the attention of personality theorists for the next two decades. In the process, Mischel has tempered his position and conceded that it is overgeneralizing the concept of traits rather than the concept itself that is dangerous. In some instances, postulating dispositions could be helpful (1983). The debate has underscored the need to study how personality and situations both contribute to behavior rather than simply attributing behavior to one or the other.

Mischel (1973) attempted to reconstruct the idea of individual trait variations in light of concepts derived from the study of cognition and social learning. These have been further refined in his latest model (Mischel & Shoda, 1995).

Most recently, in collaboration with Yuichi Shoda, Mischel suggests a cognitive-affective personality system, called CAPS for short (Mischel & Shoda, 1995). The system considers both the stability of personality and the variability of behaviors across situations. In Mischal and Shoda's view, personality is seen as a stable system that mediates the selection, construction, and processing of social information that generates social behavior. Individuals differ in their selection of situations to attend to, in their encoding of the situations, and in their emotional responses to them. These differences interact with other individual mediating processes, such as expectancies and behavioral scripts and plans, in determining behavior. Patterns of variability in behavior are not unwanted errors but reflections of the same stable underlying personality. This system makes it possible to account for both the unchanging qualities of the underlying personality and the expected variability of behavior across situations.

In order to accurately predict weather, meteorologists need to be aware of specific atmospheric processes that are responsible for changing weather patterns, not just overall climatic trends that tell us that Florida is usually warmer than New York. Similarly, personality theories must conceive of personality in terms of individual mediating processes, as well as predisposing behaviors. If we want to know why two people differ in the extent to which they display honesty across situations, it is not sufficient to simply look at differences in the levels of the trait of honesty that they possess. We need to also consider the unique pattern of where and when they differ in displaying the trait.

In Mischel and Shoda's theory, individuals are described in terms of both the distinctive organization of their cognitions and feelings and the psychological features of situations. There is a stable pattern of variability within the individual that marks his or her distinctive behavior organization and profile. This conception of personality focuses on both the relationships between psychological features of situations and the individual's pattern of behavior variation across situations. Focusing on the interaction between personal and situational variables allows researchers to make precise predictions concerning stability and change in behaviors. For example, Wright and Mischel (1988) were able to accurately predict that children with strong aggressive tendencies would act more aggressively in certain high-stress situations than children with low aggressive tendencies but that there would be little aggressive behavior from either group in specified low-stress situations. They focus on a conditional approach to dispositions, seeing them as clusters of behavior contingencies that link situations and behavior.

Mischel and Shoda believe that their approach accounts for both individual differences in behavior in general and stable profiles of behavior variability across situations by seeing them as expressions of the same personality system. Their theory can also resolve the problem of consistency that has long been debated by personality theorists. People who are similar in their overall level of a trait such as honesty may show different, yet predictable, patterns in specific situations. The variation across situations is neither random nor representative of common differences in normative levels of behavior. Rather, it is a predictable indication of the organization of the personality system itself. Mischel and Shoda believe that this organization within a person remains fairly stable unless new development, learning, or biochemical changes occur.

The stable situation-behavior profiles generated by the personality system allow both the individual study of persons in their life contexts and also the general characterization of a group or type of individuals. They permit psychologists to describe individuals in terms of stable qualities that do not change across situations, as well as in terms of individual psychological processes that lead to different reactions in different situations.

## Conclusions

Bandura's, Rotter's, and Mischel's theories are good examples of contemporary scientific approaches to personality. Cognitive and social learning theorists appreciate that we cannot understand an individual's behavior or personality without also asking what is going on in his or her mind. Moreover, they realize that the mind and its processes can be investigated scientifically. Bandura and Rotter have combined the insights of earlier behavior and learning theories with contemporary findings in the area of cognition and social psychology.

As we have seen, learning and behavior theories tend to limit the kinds of phenomena psychologists can study and the ways in which they can investigate the phenomena. Their preoccupation with objective methodology and overt behaviors may constrain psychological investigation and prevent a more holistic understanding of human nature.

The validating evidence of the scientist is seldom as insightful or compelling as the epiphanic vision of the philosopher. This may be the price that Bandura and Rotter pay for the precision, power, and predictability of their work. Nevertheless, it has been their deliberate choice to restrict their assumptions and mechanisms to those that can be embraced by an exact scientific methodology. Thus, although they do not evoke deep insight or new philosophical understanding, they do provide precise, accurate, and measurable constructs.

## *Summary*

1. According to Albert Bandura, human behavior is due to a *reciprocal determinism* that involves behavioral, cognitive, and environmental factors. Their relative influence varies in different individuals and in different situations.

2. Bandura believes that most human behavior is learned through the process of *observational learning,* by following a model.

3. Three factors influence modeling: *characteristics of the model, attributes of the observer,* and *reward consequences associated with the behavior.*

4. Bandura has described four processes that enter into observational learning: *attentional processes, retention processes, motor reproduction processes,* and *motivational processes.*

5. *Extrinsic, intrinsic,* and *vicarious reinforcement* and *self-reinforcement* all play

a role in observational learning. Unlike Skinner, Bandura does not believe that direct reinforcement is necessary for learning to occur.

6. Bandura believes that frequent exposure to aggression and violence on television encourages children to behave aggressively. Research on the question has been mixed.

7. *Self-efficacy* refers to people's beliefs that they can successfully perform behaviors that will produce desired effects.

8. Bandura has added the systematic use of *modeling* as a therapeutic technique of behavior modification and developed strategies designed to help people improve their sense of self-efficacy. He has also conducted research in the area of self-control.

9. Bandura's theory clearly emulates a scientific model.

10. Julian Rotter's theory integrates two major trends in personality research: learning theory and cognitive theory.

11. Rotter developed the *I-E Scale* to measure internal versus external control of reinforcement. The scale has been widely used in research and has led to a number of significant findings.

12. There are four main concepts in Rotter's cognitive social learning approach: *behavior potential, expectancy, reinforcement value,* and the *psychological situation.* These four variables can be measured and related in a specific formula that enables us to predict a person's behavior in any given situation.

13. Rotter's concepts have been applied in the field of clinical psychology and therapy to account for maladjustment and develop strategies of change.

14. Rotter's theory excels as a scientific theory, but he and Bandura have been criticized for a lack of depth.

15. Mischel emphasizes *behavioral specificity* in his discussion of human behavior. Recently, he has collaborated with Shoda in suggesting a cognitive-affective system of personality.

## Suggestions for Further Reading

Albert Bandura's writings are quite difficult and highly technical. The most comprehensive statement of his position is *Social Learning Theory* (Prentice-Hall, 1977). His concept of personality also emerged in two articles written for the *American Psychologist:* "Behavior Theory and the Models of Man" (1974, *29,* 859–869) and "The Self System in Reciprocal Determinism" (1978, *33,* 344–358). Also significant is *Aggression: A Social Learning Analysis* (Prentice-Hall, 1973).

The best introduction to Julian Rotter's theory is *Personality,* co-authored with D. J. Hochreich (Scott Foresman, 1975). Students who are interested in his point of view will also want to consult J. B. Rotter, J. E. Chance, and E. J. Phares, *Applications of a Social Learn-*

*ing Theory of Personality* (Holt, Rinehart, & Winston, 1972) and H. M. Lefcourt, *Locus of Control: Current Trends in Theory and Research* (Erlbaum, 1976).

The classic statement of Mischel's theory is "Toward a cognitive social learning reconception of personality" in *Psychological Review,* 80, 1973, 252–283. Mischel's newest work with Shoda is summarized in (1995) "A Cognitive-Affective System Theory of Personality: Reconceptualizing Situations, Dispositions, Dynamics, and Invariance in Personality Structure." *Psychological Review,* 102, 246–268.

# V Dispositional Theories

The oldest and most persistent approach to personality is the dispositional. People have always described one another by talking about their differences and putting them into general categories. People have been described as hot-tempered or placid, shy or aggressive, masculine or feminine, intelligent or dull, and so forth. Even though our specific actions may vary according to the situation we are in, we conceive of ourselves as the same person and recognize a certain regularity or pattern in our behavior. These qualities appear to be long-term dispositions or traits that can be used to characterize our personality.

Part V concentrates on the contributions of dispositional theorists who emphasize the importance of long-term characteristics in personality. At the same time, any classification system, by its very nature, tends to be arbitrary. Many of the theorists included in this part could also be given other "labels." For example, Allport could well be called a humanist. Increasingly we are becoming impressed with the fact that emerging theories influence other developing neighboring theories so that it is rather difficult to expressly pinpoint many theories as belonging to just one category.

### CHAPTER 10

# Traits and Personology

## GORDON ALLPORT ❖ HENRY MURRAY

### *Your Goals for This Chapter*

1. Discuss Allport's definition of personality.
2. Distinguish between continuity and discontinuity theories of personality.
3. Explain how *common traits* differ from *personal dispositions*.
4. Distinguish among three levels of personal dispositions.
5. Explain why Allport coined the term *proprium* and identify his seven *propriate functions*.
6. Discuss the concept of *functional autonomy*.
7. Discuss Allport's concept of maturity.
8. Distinguish between *nomothetic* and *idiographic* approaches to the study of personality and give examples of each.
9. Evaluate Allport's theory in terms of its function as philosophy, science, and art.
10. Describe the study of personology.
11. Identify the units by which Murray suggests behavior can be studied.
12. Explain how Murray studied human *needs*, and identify Murray's twenty basic human needs.
13. Explain what Murray means by *press* and give examples.
14. Discuss assessment and research in Murray's theory and describe the *Thematic Apperception Test*.
15. Evaluate Murray's theory in terms of its function as philosophy, science, and art.

Gordon Allport and Henry Murray were dispositional theorists who emphasized the complexity of personality and the need for an interdisciplinary approach to its study. Critical of narrow conceptions of personality and research, they believed that new methods of study were required to capture the richness and fullness of an individual's personality. Gordon Allport's theory emphasized the uniqueness of the individual, the contemporaneity of motives, and a holistic view of the person. Allport paved the way for the humanistic approach, which we will consider in Part VI. Indeed, he was the first to coin the term "humanistic psychology" in 1930 (DeCarvalho, 1991). Henry Murray's theory was distinguished by its explicit discussion of motivation and the careful construction of a list of needs that characterize and direct human behavior.

## Gordon Allport: Biographical Background

Allport was born in 1897 in Indiana and grew up near Cleveland, Ohio. He described his practical but humanitarian home life as the son of a country doctor as one characterized by "plain Protestant piety and hard work." Allport wrote little about his childhood; he indicated that he spent much of it alone. He was adept at language, but poor at sports and games.

After he graduated from high school, his brother Floyd, who also became a distinguished psychologist, encouraged him to apply to Harvard, where Floyd had gone. As an undergraduate, Allport concentrated on both psychology and social ethics and in his spare time engaged in social service activities. He ran a boys' club in Boston's West End, served as a volunteer probation officer for the Family Society, and assisted other groups.

Upon graduation, he accepted an opportunity to teach English and sociology at Robert College in Istanbul, Turkey, in a venture that was an early forerunner of the Peace Corps. He enjoyed teaching and accepted a fellowship from Harvard for graduate study in psychology. He received his Ph.D. only two years later, in 1922. His dissertation, "An Experimental Study of the Traits of Personality," was also the first American study on personality traits.

Another fellowship for travel abroad gave an opportunity for Allport to meet Freud. Allport described their meeting as follows. When he arrived, Freud sat silent, apparently waiting for Allport to state the reason for his visit. Allport was simply curious. Then, an incident came to mind that he thought might interest Freud, because it concerned a small boy who had a phobia that appeared to be set very early in life. He told him about an event that had happened on the streetcar on the way to Freud's office. A small boy who was obviously afraid of dirt kept saying to his mother that he didn't want to sit on a dirty seat or next to a dirty man. When Allport finished, Freud looked at him and said, "And was that little boy you?" Allport was surprised, but he regained his composure and changed the subject. Still, he was shaken and he never forgot the incident. He began to feel that Freud's ascription of most behaviors to unconscious motives was incorrect and that an alternative theory of motivation was necessary. In his own theory, Allport did not probe into the dark

*Gordon Allport emphasized that traits are bona fide structures within a person that influence behavior.*

side of personality; he did not concur with Freud's emphasis on sexuality and unconscious motivations.

On his return from Europe, Allport became in instructor in social ethics at Harvard, where he developed and taught what was probably the first course offered in personality in this country. In 1926 he left to take up an assistant professorship in psychology at Dartmouth, but in 1930 he returned to Harvard, this time to stay. His contributions to Harvard were many. Most notably, he was an early advocate of interdisciplinary studies and a leader in the creation of the department of social relations, which combined degree programs in psychology, sociology, and anthropology. His professional honors were manifold and he was a popular and respected teacher. He died in 1967, one month before his seventieth birthday.

## The Nature of Personality

As we mentioned in Chapter 1, Allport described and classified over fifty definitions of personality before he developed his own in 1937. After working with this definition for many years, he revised it in 1961. His final definition is: "Personality is the dynamic organization within the individual of those psychophysical systems that determine his characteristic behavior and thought." Each word in this definition is carefully chosen. Personality is *dynamic* (moving and changing), *organized* (structured), *psychophysical* (involving both the mind and the body), *determined* (structured by the past and predisposing of the future), and *characteristic* (unique for each individual).

For Allport, personality is not a mere fiction or imaginary concept but a real entity. He wanted to suggest that one's personality is really *there*. He referred to the concept of personality as a hypothetical construct, which is currently unobservable because it cannot be measured empirically. However, Allport suggested that personality is an inference that may someday be demonstrated directly as a real existence within the person, involving neural or physiological components. At one time the planet Pluto was a hypothetical construct, postulated long before any telescope could observe it. In time, science was able to point directly to it. Allport also hoped that neurophysiological and psychological research will in time show us the way to directly locate our present hypothetical construct of personality. In this connection, Allport was rather prophetic in recognizing that in the future much of psychology's research would focus on the brain.

Allport (1960) distinguished among continuity and discontinuity theories of personality and argued for a discontinuity theory. A **continuity theory** suggests that the development of personality is essentially the accumulation of skill, habits, and discriminations, without anything really new appearing in the person's makeup. Changes are merely quantitative relative to the amount of inputs. Such continuity theories are **closed systems.**

A **discontinuity theory** suggests that in the course of development, an organism experiences genuine transformations or changes so that it reaches successively higher levels of organization. Here growth is conceived as qualitatively different. Walking is considered very different from crawling, talking is viewed as discontinuous with babbling, and so forth, even though these behaviors emerge out of the earlier ones. If we picture personality as an organism into which inputs are introduced, a continuity theory merely sees the inputs accumulating, whereas a discontinuity theory suggests that at times during its development, the organism reorganizes, regroups, and reshapes these inputs so that the structure of personality changes radically. Such theories view the person as open and active in consolidating and integrating experience. Change is qualitative rather than merely quantitative. Theories that posit stages of development of personality have the potential to imply discontinuity, because each stage entails a different organization of personality from the stage before it. Allport believed that Freud's psychoanalytic theory, though outlining stages of development, did not fully realize this potential because of its primary emphasis on the individual and intrapsychic factors. Elements within Freud's theory pointed toward discontinuity, but it remained semiclosed.

## Traits

With the possible exception of Raymond Cattell, Allport has explored the concept of **trait** more fully than any other personality theorist. Allport proposed a biophysical conception of traits as neuropsychic structures (1937). He emphasized that traits are bona fide structures within a person that influence behavior; they are not simply labels we use to describe or classify behaviors.

Allport defined a trait as a determining tendency or predisposition to respond to the world in certain ways. Traits are consistent and enduring; they account for consistency in human behavior. Allport suggested that traits may be considered the ultimate reality of psychological organization. The trait, like personality, is not in principle unobservable. In time, trait theorists may be able to measure traits empirically.

Allport distinguished between individual traits and common traits (1937). In his later writings, to clarify his position, he used the terms "common traits" and "personal dispositions."

## Common Traits

A **common trait** is a hypothetical construct that permits us to compare individuals within a given culture. Although no two people can be said to possess identical traits, we can discover roughly comparable traits that allow us to compare the predispositions that are held in common with other persons. Normal people in any given culture tend to develop along similar modes or lines of adjustment. In a competitive society, most individuals develop a level of assertiveness or ascendance that can be compared with the level of assertiveness in others. There are several aspects of personality in respect of which all people in a given culture may be compared.

## Personal Dispositions

Comparisons may be made among individuals but in the last analysis no two individuals are exactly alike. A **personal disposition** is, like a trait, a general determining characteristic, but it is unique to the individual who has it. Although comparisons cannot be made among personal dispositions, personal dispositions are necessary if one is to reflect accurately the personality structure of a particular individual. Whereas common traits place individuals into comparable categories, personal dispositions, if correctly diagnosed, more accurately describe the individual's uniqueness.

Each one of us has personal dispositions that are of greater or lesser importance. If a personal disposition is so pervasive that almost every behavior of the individual appears to be influenced by it, it is called a **cardinal disposition.** An example would be an extreme lust for power, so intense that virtually every act of the individual can be seen to be governed by that desire. Allport believed that cardinal dispositions are quite rare. Nevertheless, some figures have been described as possessed of a cardinal disposition—for instance, Mother Teresa's and her lifelong dedication to aiding the poor.

**Central dispositions** refer to highly characteristic tendencies of an individual. They provide the adjectives or phrases a person might use in describing the essential characteristics of another individual in a letter of recommendation (e.g., intelligent, responsible, independent, sensitive, caring). Allport suggests that the number of central dispositions necessary to describe the essential characteristics of an individual normally varies between five and ten. **Secondary dispositions** are more specific, focused tendencies that are often situational in character and less crucial to the personality structure. A person may have a large number of these. A man might be domineering and aggressive at home in his role as

---

## *Central Dispositions*

Think of a close friend or someone whom you know well. On a blank sheet of paper, try to describe your friend's personality by jotting down those words or phrases that express his or her essential characteristics. Include those qualities that you consider of major importance in an accurate description. Then do the same thing for yourself. Count the number of words or phrases necessary to describe your friend or yourself. Chances are the number falls between five and ten. Allport suggests that the number of highly characteristic central dispositions along which a personality is organized generally falls within that range. In his own research the average was seven. Does your evidence support his hypothesis?

---

father but behave submissively when confronted by a police officer who is giving him a ticket.

Cantor (1990) points out that the concept of personal dispositions can be complemented by a cognitive view providing what Allport (1937) called a "doing" aspect of personality, by centering on how dispositions are cognitively symbolized and kept in social interaction. This view shows how people understand life tasks in terms of their most available schemas (or primary patterns of understanding the world), by imagining different future selves and developing cognitive methods to shape their behavior. This view asks the question, How do people change their schemas and tasks because of their experience? An accent on the doing side can also help us understand the changeability of personality.

An important distinction between common traits and personal dispositions is the way in which each is established and assessed. The concept of common traits lends itself to traditional psychometric research (rating scales, testing instruments, and so on). The concept of personal dispositions requires new methodologies that permit the unique individuality of the person to emerge. We will explore this further in the section on assessment and research.

---

## The Proprium

Allport's humanistic orientation can be seen most clearly in his concept of the *proprium*. Allport coined the term in order to avoid the terms "ego" or "self," which he believed are often used as catchall phrases for those elements of personality that cannot be accounted for in any other way. Allport's **proprium** refers to the central experiences of self-awareness that people have as they grow and move forward. Allport purposely chose a term with the prefix "pro" to connote forward movement.

The proprium is defined in terms of its functions or the things that it does. Allport described seven **propriate functions** (1961). None of them is innate; rather, they develop gradually over time as an individual grows from infancy to adulthood. Together, the activities of the proprium constitute an evolving sense of self as known and felt.

The first propriate function to emerge is the sense of **bodily self.** It consists of sensations in the body and entails coming to know one's body limits. Certain parts of the body are emphasized as more important than others. Thus, young children, when instructed to wash their faces and hands, wash the palms and the front of the face but invariably overlook the back of their hands and behind their ears. Most of us, even as adults, tend to locate the self in the head region. This bodily sense, which is learned, remains the foundation of our self-awareness.

The second propriate function, the sense of **self-identity,** refers to the awareness of inner sameness and continuity. Infants are not aware of themselves as individuals and cannot distinguish themselves from other objects. Gradually, out of an undifferentiated whole, the infant comes to distinguish between inner and outer. The external world is developed first; later, the child discovers a sense of "I." These first two propriate functions begin to emerge from eighteen months onward. The development of self-awareness also depends on maturation of the central nervous system. However it cannot be reduced to simple maturation (Kagan, 1991).

Between the ages of two and three the third propriate function, **self-esteem,** develops. Self-esteem refers to the feelings of pride as the child develops the ability to do things. It is comparable to Erikson's stage of autonomy, which reflects the child's need to feel control over the self and other objects. Two-year-olds are eager to do things for themselves and usually do not want others to help them. One mark of the child's emerging sense of self-esteem is negativism. The child employs the word "no" to assert freedom from adult control. A certain amount of negativism is necessary for the development of self-esteem.

Between the ages of four and six, two other propriate functions emerge: self-extension and self-image. **Self-extension** refers to a sense of possession. Children recognize that certain toys and certain people belong to them and identify them as "my ball," "my daddy." Self-extension leads into a valuing of others because of their relationship to oneself. In the adult years one's children are perceived as extensions of one's self. **Self-image** refers to a sense of the expectation of others and its comparison with one's own behavior. Children come to understand parental expectations and to see themselves as fulfilling or not fulfilling those desired roles. This early self-image lays the foundation for development of conscience and, later, intentions and goals.

Between the ages of six and twelve, the propriate function of **self-as-rational coper** develops. Children discover that they can use their own rational capacities to solve problems. They begin to perceive of themselves as active, problem-solving agents, who can develop a sense of competence in what they do. Allport compared the self as coper with Freud's concept of the ego as the executor of the personality.

Last, during adolescence, the function of propriate striving emerges. **Propriate striving** refers to the projection of long-term purposes and goals and the development of a plan to attain them. Such efforts are essential for the development of self-identity, which Erikson had pinpointed as the primary feature of adolescence.

Allport believed that there is a marked difference between the infant and the adult. The infant is a dependent, impatient, pleasure-seeking, "unsocialized horror," largely governed by unlearned biological drives, who can tolerate little delay in the fulfillment of those drives and reflexes. The infant has the potentialities for personality, but "can scarcely be said to have personality" (1961). Given the appropriate security and affection, the child will grow in the direction of developing a proprium. The child will be transformed from a biologi-

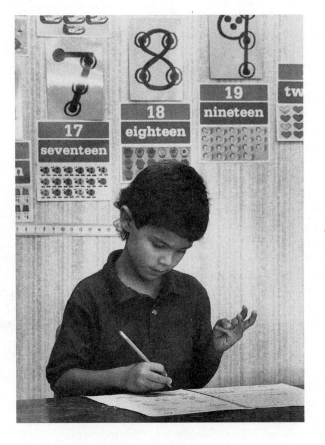

*Between the ages of six and twelve, the propriate function of self-as-rational coper develops as children discover that they can use their intellectual capacities to solve problems.*

cally dominated organism to a psychologically mature adult. The adult person is discontinuous from the child. The adult emerges from the child but is no longer governed by the child's needs.

Not only is there a radical discontinuity between the child and the mature adult; Allport also suggests that there is a radical discontinuity between healthy adults and neurotics. The life of neurotics is marked by cognitive crippling. In their efforts to find security, neurotics react in rigid, inflexible ways. Such individuals continue to behave as children, dominated by infantile drives and conflicts. Their propriums are undeveloped and their motives remain tied to original needs.

## Functional Autonomy

Closely related to Allport's concepts of the proprium and discontinuity is his concept of **functional autonomy,** which implies that adult motivation is not necessarily tied to the past. A given behavior may become a goal in itself regardless of its original intention. Thus, adult motives are not necessarily related to the earlier experiences in which the motive or activity initially appeared; they are contemporaneous with the behaviors themselves.

For example, let us imagine that young Johnny's father was a baseball fan. During his spare time and on Saturdays he played baseball with his son. Originally, Johnny played baseball with his Dad to gain his attention and to please him. During his school years, Johnny also played baseball with the other children in his neighborhood and was an active member of Little League. He discovered that he was competent in the game and, what is more, he enjoyed it. In high school and college, he played in the intramural sports program. Later, he was recruited to play with a major league. Today, as he is standing at bat for the Yankees or Dodgers, does it make sense to insist that his motive for playing baseball continues to be that of pleasing his father? Does it not seem more reasonable to suggest that he plays because he enjoys the game and the financial rewards that it brings? His present motives are entirely different and free from his original motives. There may be a historical tie, but there is no functional tie. His motive is functionally autonomous.

Allport refers to two levels of functional autonomy: perseverative functional autonomy and propriate functional autonomy.

*Perseverative functional autonomy* refers to acts or behaviors that are repeated even though they may have lost their original function; they are not controlled by the proprium and have no genuine connection with it. A teenage girl may, in a spirit of rebellion against her parents, begin to smoke cigarettes, which she knows will annoy them. As an adult, she may continue to smoke cigarettes, long after her period of teenage rebellion. Perseverative functional autonomy refers to repetitive activities such as compulsions, addictions to drugs or alcohol, ritualistic or routine behaviors.

*Propriate functional autonomy* refers to those acquired interests, values, attitudes, intentions, and life-style that are directed from the proprium. Abilities frequently convert into interests. The person selects those motives that are important and organizes them in a fashion that is consistent with his or her self-image and life-style.

Allport acknowledged that not all behaviors are functionally autonomous. Among the processes that are not are: drives, reflexes, constitutionally determined capacities such as physique and intellect, habits, primary reinforcements, infantilisms and fixations, some neuroses, and sublimations. At times it is difficult to determine whether or not a motive is functionally autonomous. Further, certain motives may be autonomous only to a certain degree. Nevertheless, Allport believed that many of the motives of the healthy, mature adult may be considered to be governed by propriate functional autonomy. Allport's rationale for developing the concept of propriate functional autonomy is the desire to underscore the concept that we live in the present, not in the past.

## A Definition of Maturity

As we have seen, Allport believed that there is a radical discontinuity between the neurotic and healthy personality. Allport concurred with Carl Jung that too many personality theorists center their discussion of personality on the characteristics of the neurotic and view health simply as the absence of neurotic symptoms. In his discussion (1961), Allport posited six criteria of maturity.

**1. EXTENSION OF THE SENSE OF SELF**    Mature adults genuinely participate in important realms of human achievement. They are interested in others and consider the welfare of others as important as their own. Their sense of self is not limited to their own selves but embraces many interests.

**2. WARM RELATING OF SELF TO OTHERS**    Mature adults are able to relate intimately to other persons in appropriate situations. They are compassionate and able to tolerate many differences in human beings. In their relationships, they neither impose themselves on others nor hinder their own freedom of self-identity.

**3. EMOTIONAL SECURITY (SELF-ACCEPTANCE)**    Mature people are able to accept themselves and their emotional states. Their emotions, even though they are not always pleasant, do not lead them into impulsive acts or actions that hurt others. They are sufficiently secure in who they are to accept themselves and not wish to be somebody else.

**4. REALISTIC PERCEPTION, SKILLS, AND ASSIGNMENTS**    Mature adults do not need to create a fantasy world but live in "the real world." They are problem solvers and have developed the appropriate skills to complete their assigned tasks and work. Moreover, their work is not a burden to them, it is a responsibility whose challenge can be accepted without self-pity.

**5. SELF-OBJECTIFICATION (INSIGHT AND HUMOR)**    Self-insight is difficult to acquire. Mature people know what they can do, what they cannot do, and what they ought to do. They have no need to deceive either themselves or other people. An important corollary of insight is a sense of humor. Mature individuals are able to laugh at themselves rather than feel threatened by their human weaknesses. Such humor is to be distinguished from the ordinary sense of the comic. The sense of humor to which Allport referred entails recognizing the ludicrous behaviors we share with others because of our common humanity.

**6. UNIFYING PHILOSOPHY OF LIFE**    Maturity entails a clear understanding of life's goals and purposes. In the mature person, this philosophy is clearly marked and outwardly focused. It is strongly informed by a set of values that may but does not necessarily include religious sentiments. Further, a unifying philosophy of life is governed by a generic conscience. The *must* conscience of childhood is replaced by the *ought* conscience of the adult. Whereas the child's values are introjected from others, the adult's values arise from a chosen style of being and are based on propriate judgments.

Essentially, maturity for Allport is summed up by expression of the propriate functions to a high degree and freedom from one's past. Allport indicated that human beings are always in the process of *becoming* (1955). The urge to grow and fulfill oneself is present from birth. We have the ability to develop and follow a creative life-style. Further, with maturity we can consciously design and effect our plans without being hindered by unconscious forces of the past. His theory holds echoes of Jung's concept of self-realization and Adler's construct of the creative self and points toward the concepts of Rogers and Maslow.

Maslow explicitly acknowledged Allport's influence on his interest in the study of self-actualized persons.

## Assessment and Research in Allport's Theory

Allport wrote extensively on methods of inquiry and investigation that are useful for the study of personality, and some of his own research in the area is considered classic. Allport pointed out that personality is so complex that every legitimate method of study should be included in its pursuit. He was critical of those who limit their research and do not encourage or permit the study of personality concepts that are not easily submitted to empirical test. At the same time, he was also critical of applying methods appropriate to the study of neurotic individuals to the normal individual.

Allport's view of personality as open and discontinuous does not lend itself very well to study by the traditional methods in academic psychology, which seek to discover general laws that apply to all individual cases. The emphasis, particularly in American psychology, has been on a **nomothetic** (from the Greek *nomos,* law, and *thetēs,* one who establishes) approach, studying large groups of individuals to determine the frequency with which certain events occur and from this to infer common traits, general variables, or universal principles. Normalcy is often conceived as that behavior that occurs most regularly. Thus, the behavior that is considered normal for a two-year-old is the behavior that is shared in common by most two-year-olds. Allport encouraged an **idiographic** (from the Greek *idios,* one's own, and *graphein,* to write) approach that centers on the individual, employing techniques and variables that are appropriate to understanding the uniqueness of each person and uncovering personal dispositions. Although such methods are difficult, time consuming, and often expensive to evolve, their aim is to account for the unique event that is theoretically just as open to lawful explanation as the frequent event.

In the 1940s, over three hundred letters written to a young married couple by a woman (Jenny Masterson) between her fifty-ninth and seventieth years came to Allport's attention. Although Allport denied it, he and his wife were probably the young couple to whom the letters were written (Winter, 1993). He and his students analyzed these letters to determine Jenny's central dispositions. In studying these documents, Allport tried to note the frequency with which certain themes or ideas appeared. He asked other people to read the letters and assess Jenny in terms of her traits. He also discussed Jenny's personality in terms of different personality theories. Allport believed that the study of personal documents, such as diaries, autobiographies, and letters, could be a potentially valuable idiographic approach.

In his analysis of Jenny's correspondence (1965), Allport looked for recurring patterns and was able to identify eight unmistakable central dispositions that he believed were significant for understanding her personality: quarrelsome-suspicious, self-centered, independent, dramatic, aesthetic-artistic, aggressive, cynical-morbid, and sentimental. Allport then conducted a formal *content analysis* of the letters. The research technique of content analysis provides a systematic, objective, and quantitative way of describing written or spoken communications. Jenny's comments in the letters were classified into different categories (e.g., independence, hostility, affective, love of art, cynicism) and a frequency count was taken. The data were then subjected to a study by factor analysis (a complex statistical analysis). The findings of factor analysis were quite similar to Allport's own.

In his preface to *Letters from Jenny*, Allport wrote: "To me the principle fascination of the letters lies in their challenge to the reader (whether psychologist or layman) to 'explain' Jenny if he can. Why does an intelligent lady behave so persistently in a self-defeating manner?"

With Philip Vernon and Gardner Lindzey, Allport developed a Study of Values Scale, a dimensional measurement designed to examine individuality. The scale measures six common traits originally delineated by Spranger (1928): the theoretical, aesthetic, social, political, religious, and economic. Because the test reflects the relative strengths of these six values within one's own personality, one individual's score cannot be compared with any-one else's. The test has been widely used in counseling and vocational guidance and has proved to be a significant research tool in studies of selective perception.

Allport and Philip Vernon also initiated research into expressive behavior during the early 1930s. **Expressive behavior** refers to an individual's manner of performing. Every behavior has a coping and an expressive aspect. The *coping aspect* refers to what the act does to deal with or adapt to the task at hand. The *expressive aspect* refers to how the act is done.

Ordinarily we pay more attention to coping behavior than to expressive behavior. But expressive behavior, because it is more spontaneous, can be highly revelatory of basic personality aspects. Allport and others conducted considerable research on several expressive features of personality: the face, voice, posture, gesture, gait, and handwriting. They discovered that there is a marked consistency in a person's expressive behavior. In some instances, Allport was able to deduce certain traits and make accurate judgments about an individual's personality. Allport suggested that further research in this area is highly desirable because a person's expressive manner and style may be the most important factor in understanding the personality.

Another outgrowth of Allport's personality theory has been his interest in religion as a healthy, productive aspect of human life. He initiated a major study of how religion was treated in college textbooks on psychology (Vande Kempe, 1995). In order to introduce religion into the comprehensive study of personality, Allport wrote *The Individual and His Religion* (1950), in which he presented religion as normal during a time when many psychologists viewed it as a primarily dysfunctional human phenomenon. Allport's distinction between intrinsic and extrinsic orientations in religion, a distinction between people who are motivated from within and those who are motivated by external forces, has contributed to research on understanding the relation between religion and prejudice. Churchgoers on the average are more prejudiced than nonchurchgoers, even though most advocates of treating all people equally are religiously motivated. Allport discovered a curvilinear relationship between religion and prejudice. The extrinsic attitude is correlated with prejudice, but the intrinsic is correlated with very low prejudice (1968). Allport fathered a line of theory and research on the social psychology of prejudice, focusing on the destructive effects of prejudice and discrimination against African Americans and other ethnic minorities.

In his authoritative study on prejudice (1954), Allport centered on racial and religious prejudice. However, identical forces occur with reference to women or any other minority. Allport suggests that first a group is compelled to respond in a specific way; then they learn specific traits in order to adapt and those same traits are employed as confirmation that the group is inferior. Thus, for example, women are often seen as weak when they communicate their need for relationships. The same need, however, could be seen as healthy and constructive for improving human relations among people of diverse cultures (Symonds, 1991).

# Allport's Theory

Allport's personality theory is a highly creative one. Although many of his ideas are reminiscent of other theories, he combined others' insights with his own to develop a truly unique approach. His original concepts, like personal dispositions, the proprium, and functional autonomy, are highly controversial and extremely stimulating. In his emphasis on the uniqueness of the individual and the contemporaneity of motives Allport foreshadowed the humanist theories of Rogers and Maslow. Indeed, the emphasis in his theory is not on the past but on forward movement.

Allport maintained that because personality is so complex, every legitimate method of study should be included in our efforts to comprehend it. He used rigorous scientific methods to establish common traits. At the same time, he pointed out that we need to develop alternative methods that help us understand the uniqueness of each individual. In his own research, Allport recognized the value of other methodologies and used information drawn from literature, philosophy, art, and religion, as well as from science. Allport believed that an open system of personality encourages the invention of new methods of research; these methods aim at rigor but do not forfeit the study of certain aspects of personality because present scientific methodologies cannot embrace such study.

Allport realized that to understand the whole human being, it is necessary to comprehend the individual philosophically as well as scientifically. "The philosophy of the person is inseparable from the psychology of the person" (1961). Indeed, any psychological stance, Allport pointed out, is implicitly linked to basic philosophical assumptions.

Allport's discussion of traits influenced a line of dispositional approaches to personality that culminated in the work of Raymond Cattell, the Big Five theorists, and Hans Eysenck, whose work is covered in Chapters 11 and 12. It also provoked debate concerning the importance of long-term dispositions as opposed to the influence of the particular situation, a debate that was initiated by Mischel and discussed in Chapter 9.

Allport's concept of functional autonomy has been the subject of a great deal of controversy and criticism. In presenting his theories to the public, Allport's concern was to teach and provoke interest rather than to make statements that are above reproach. Thus, it is often very difficult to differentiate between what he assumed and what he established through empirical procedures. The concept of functional autonomy is not a construct that lends itself to operational definition, predictions, or empirical tests. The phenomena that Allport explained as functionally autonomous can also be explained by rival constructs. Further, Allport did not clearly describe the developmental processes that underlie functional autonomy.

Still, Allport's concepts are highly congruent with recent developments in personality theory. His emphasis on discontinuity is picked up by humanist and cognitive theorists. His concepts of functional autonomy and propriate functions harmonize with recent expansions in psychoanalysis. The goal of psychoanalysis is to strengthen the functioning of the ego. The intent of the reconstruction of the past in psychoanalysis is to permit the patient to work through the past so that it loses its grip. By becoming aware of one's unconscious motivations, one is free to behave differently in the future if one so wishes. Thus, the intent of psychoanalysis is congruent, if not synonymous, with the development of propriate functional autonomy.

Allport was not a practicing psychotherapist and did not develop a specific therapeutic technique. Nevertheless, many of his ideas, like functional autonomy, propriate functions, and the radical discontinuity between normal and neurotic adults, have been useful to clinicians.

Allport did not develop a school of followers, but his theory has had considerable impact. His work offers a bridge between traditional academic psychology, which emphasizes psychometrics and nomothetic studies, and clinical psychology, which concentrates on a more idiographic approach to the understanding of personality. Allport's emphasis on personal documents has been a guiding light for their use in analyzing and understanding personality (Wrightsman, 1993). Furthermore, his early analysis of the language used to describe personality has been seen as laying the empirical and conceptual groundwork for the eventual development of the Five-Factor Model of personality (John & Robins, 1993).

There has been a resurgence of interest in idiographic approaches to the study of personality. Because of the emphasis on personal and unique determinants of behavior, an idiographic approach should provide greater accuracy in explanation and prediction. Lamielle (1981) argues "against continued adherence to the long dominant 'nomothetic' paradigm for personality research" because from it we cannot make any legitimate interpretations at the level of the individual. Lamielle suggests a strategy, which he terms *idiothetic,* that combines features of idiographic and nomothetic research in a way that does justice to individuals but that also invokes the use of norms. Pelham (1993) affirms that idiographic, or within-subjects, techniques grasp the truth of phenomenological reality where nomothetic, or between-subjects, techniques are unable to. Thus nomothetic research is not very helpful to a theory of personality that seeks to comprehend the uniqueness of individuals (Lamielle & Trierweiler, 1986). DeCarvalho (1990) has argued that Allport's complex and unifying suggestion in the late 1960s for a humanistic psychology was an exceptional happening in Western psychology that illuminates the conflict between an experimental as compared to an experiential approach to psychological exploration.

# Henry Murray: Biographical Background

Henry A. Murray was born in New York City on May 13, 1893. His parents were well-to-do and Murray grew up as a privileged American boy in a time before automobiles, motor-boats, or movies. Winters were spent in the city in a brownstone on what is now the site of Rockefeller Center. Summers were spent on Long Island, where he enjoyed outdoor physical activity, animals, and the woods in back of his home.

Murray did not believe that he qualified as a typical Freudian child. It was difficult for him to recognize the presence of an Oedipal complex in his life. His training analysis did not uncover any indications of hidden resentment toward his father. On the other hand, his childhood evokes several Adlerian themes. Murray recalled an incident at about four years of age when his mother suggested that the queen and her son pictured in a fairy-tale book were sad because of the prospect of death. Later he suggested that memory embodied feelings of having been abandoned (left to die) by his mother in favor of his siblings because he was difficult to care for. This led to an early development of self-reliance as well as tender feelings of pity toward his mother and others with emotional problems.

Unlike Allport, Murray received little formal training in psychology. After six years in two private schools in New York City, he went to Groton, a private preparatory school in Massachusetts. He obtained his B.A. from Harvard, where he majored in history but re-

*Henry Murray's term for the study of individuals was* personology.

ceived only below-average grades. It appears he was more interested in going out for the crew team. Yet he went on to medical school at Columbia University and graduated at the top of his class. Later he received an M.A. in biology from Columbia and a Ph.D. in biochemistry from Cambridge University.

In contrast to Allport, whose meeting with Freud left him somewhat skeptical about unconscious processes, Murray spent three weeks with Carl Jung in Zurich during an Easter vacation from Cambridge and emerged a "reborn man." He had "experienced the unconscious" and thereafter devoted himself exclusively to psychology and to probing the deepest recesses of personality.

A new biography (Robinson, 1992) suggests Murray had a number of troubling intellectual and emotional shortcomings and, while he kept a traditional marriage, he was also involved in a torrid affair with Christiana Morgan, a talented married woman who was also interested in the work of Carl Jung. Morgan made important contributions to the early development of psychoanalysis, especially in the area of feminism and also to Murray's theory of personality, for which she was never given proper recognition (Douglas, 1993); she also coauthored the Thematic Apperception Test (TAT), a significant projective technique widely used in personality assessment. Nevertheless, Murray was a highly regarded professor of psychology at Harvard University from the 1920s to the 1960s, where he set up the Harvard Psychological Clinic expressly to study personality.

Murray gathered around him a group of capable young and mature scholars, many of whom are notable psychologists in their own right. He was awarded the Distinguished Scientific Contribution Award of the American Psychological Association and the Gold Medal Award of the American Psychological Foundation for his contributions to psychology. Murray died in 1988.

## The Study of Personology

Murray, like Gordon Allport, emphasized the complexity of personality and the need for interdisciplinary research in personality. He suggested that the concept of personality is a hypothesis, a construct that helps us account for an individual's behavior. As opposed to Allport, who saw personality as a real entity, Murray did not believe that the concept of personality refers to any real physical substance. An individual's personality is dependent upon brain processes, and hence the anatomical center of personality is the brain. There is an intimate relationship between cerebral physiology and personality. Neurophysiological processes are the source of human behavior.

In his study of **personology,** which is Murray's term for the study of individual "human lives and the factors that influence their course" (1938), Murray emphasized the understanding of normal individuals in natural settings. He believed that psychologists should primarily concern themselves with the detailed and careful study of individual lives.

In studying the individual, Murray believed that it is useful to separate the total behavior of a person into identifiable and manageable units. His basic unit is a **proceeding,** a short, significant behavior pattern that has a clear beginning and ending. Proceedings are interactions between the subject and another person or object in the environment, for example, picking up a book, writing a letter, or holding a conversation. Proceedings may be internal (imagined) or external (real). A succession of proceedings constitutes a *serial.*

Thus, a friendship or a marriage consists of a serial of proceedings that needs to be studied as a whole. A planned series of proceedings is a *serial program*, which leads toward a goal such as becoming a lawyer. Serial programs may stretch into the future for months or even years. Each proceeding in the series may be seen as having a subgoal that brings the individual closer to the final goal. Serial programs are governed by a mental process known as *ordination*. This enables us, once we understand our world, to develop a strategy for coping with it. Ordination also permits us to develop *schedules* or plans for resolving conflicting proceedings. A schedule, like a family budget, tries to accommodate all of the competing needs and goals by permitting them to be expressed at different times.

Some aspects of Murray's theory of personology were drawn from Freud's theory. However, Murray did not hesitate to redefine terms or to elaborate and enrich Freud's concepts. Thus, he used the terms id, ego, and superego in describing the basic divisions of personality but added his own meaning.

Murray agreed with Freud that the id is the source of basic drives and needs, but he emphasized that the id contains positive impulses as well as negative ones. The superego is an internalized representation of the social environment, indicating when, where, how, and what needs can be expressed. The ego is the "organized, discriminating, time-binding, reasoning, resolving, and more self-conscious part of the personality" (1938). Its role is to facilitate the id in meeting its impulses; its effectiveness in doing so affects an individual's adjustment. Murray assumed a more active role for the ego, in line with the ego psychoanalysts discussed in Chapter 6.

## Human Needs

Murray's most significant contribution to the study of personality was probably his extensive research on human needs. He constructed what is undoubtedly the most careful and thorough list of human needs found in psychology.

Murray (1938) defined a **need** as a construct representing a force in the brain that organizes our perception, understanding, and behavior in such a way as to change an unsatisfying situation and increase our satisfaction. A need may be aroused by an internal state, such as hunger, or by an external stimulus, such as food.

An observer can infer a need from the following signs: a typical behavior effect or pattern, the search for and avoidance of certain kinds of press (discussed on pages 273–275), the expression of a specific emotion, and signs of satisfaction or dissatisfaction with the effects of one's behavior. In addition, a subject can usually confirm the presence of a need through subjective reports.

From his intensive study of individuals at Harvard (1938), Murray constructed a list of twenty basic needs, which are listed and briefly defined in Table 10.1. Although this list has been revised and modified since that time, it remains highly representative of a comprehensive overview of human needs.

Not all of the needs are present in everyone and the needs vary in their strength and intensity. Murray believed that there is a hierarchy of needs, a concept later elaborated on by Maslow (Chapter 13). Where two or more needs conflict, the most important need will be met first. Some needs are *prepotent*, which means they become very urgent if they are

TABLE 10.1  Murray's List of Needs

| | |
|---|---|
| Dominance | To control one's human environment |
| Deference | To admire and support a superior other |
| Autonomy | To resist influence or coercion |
| Aggression | To overcome opposition forcefully |
| Abasement | To submit passively to external force |
| Achievement | To accomplish something difficult |
| Sex | To form and further an erotic relationship |
| Sentience | To seek and enjoy sensuous impressions |
| Exhibition | To make an impression |
| Play | To relax, amuse oneself, seek diversion and entertainment |
| Affiliation | To form friendships and associations |
| Rejection | To snub, ignore, or exclude another |
| Succorance | To seek aid, protection, or sympathy |
| Nurturance | To nourish, aid, or protect a helpless other |
| Infavoidance | To avoid humiliation |
| Defendance | To defend the self against assault, criticism, and blame |
| Counteraction | To master or make up for a failure by restriving |
| Harmavoidance | To avoid pain, physical injury, illness, and death |
| Order | To put things in order |
| Understand | The tendency to ask or to answer general questions |

SOURCE: From Explorations in Personality *by Henry A. Murray. Copyright 1938, renewed 1966 by Henry A. Murray. Used by permission of Oxford University Press, Inc.*

not satisfied, such as the need for food or to eliminate waste. Other needs may be met together. An actor may be able to meet achievement and exhibition needs in one and the same performance.

To characterize an individual's behavior simply on the basis of needs is to give a one-sided portrait. This is why Murray introduced the concept of **press,** forces from objects or persons within the environment that help or hinder an individual in reaching goals. Stimuli that arouse needs motivate us to look for or avoid certain kinds of press. Examples of press are cultural discord, family discord, poverty, accident, loss of possessions, presence of siblings, maltreatment by contemporaries, religious training, encouragement, friendship, sexual abuse, and illness. It is important to distinguish between *alpha press,* actual

*Murray is best known for his contribution of a comprehensive list of human needs. Sometimes multiple needs—play, sentience, and nurturance, for example—can be satisfied by a single activity.*

## THINKING CRITICALLY

### Evaluating Needs

Look over Murray's list of twenty needs and study their definitions. Think of instances in which the needs have applied to your life and make a list of the needs that seem to be important to you. When you have finished your list, select the five most important needs and rank them, with 1 indicating the strongest need and 5 indicating the weakest. In evaluating your own hierarchy of needs, it will be helpful if you consider specific events in your life when the needs were apparent.

It will also be helpful for you to consider the way in which diverse cultures and eras foster and encourage the development of different needs. Can you think of needs that you have in the 1990s that may not be characteristic of people in another place and culture? Do you think that Murray's list of needs is itself culture bound? Are you aware of other human needs that are not on Murray's list?

properties or attributes of the environment, and *beta press,* the individual's subjective perception of the environment. The beta presses are the determinants of behavior.

## Assessment and Research in Murray's Theory

Henry Murray was a pioneer in the area of assessment, as aspect of personality theory that is increasingly the focus of attention and concern. Like Allport, Murray emphasized an idiographic approach to personality, which focuses on the individual, rather than the usual nomothetic approach, which deals with groups. The basic principle of Murray's concept of assessment was that multiple indicators are required to adequately assess an individual's performance. In other words, one single test could not adequately describe an individual. It is preferable to use multiple instruments administered by multiple assessors from different areas of specialization. Murray also believed that if feedback were provided to the individual, improved performance could be achieved.

In a unique interdisciplinary effort at Harvard, Murray led a staff of twenty-eight different specialists in studying fifty-two male undergraduates for a period of six months. Together they amassed a great deal of data through interviews, tests, questionnaires, and observations, using an array of clinical, psychoanalytic, experimental, physiological, and life history methods. By having several trained researchers observe the same individual, Murray believed he could cancel out personal errors in assessment. A diagnostic council permitted several observers to study the same subject and then integrate their findings into a final diagnosis. This type of interdisciplinary approach was unprecedented at the time.

Murray's concept of assessment has been generalized to programs and institutions; for example, multiple indicators of assessment have been used to accurately reflect their performance. Douglas Bray pioneered the use of assessment for personnel selection and the evaluation of performance at AT&T. The assessment center approach is widely used today for the selection of executives and leaders in industry and government.

Murray himself developed several techniques for assessing personality. The best known is the **Thematic Apperception Test (TAT)**, developed by Murray and Christiana Morgan, which is widely used as a projective device. The TAT consists of a series of thirty ambiguous pictures (for example, see Figure 10.1). The subject is asked to make up stories for the pictures, telling what led up to the event, what is happening, what the characters in the picture are thinking and feeling, and how the event will turn out. The responses to the TAT suggest how the subject thinks in relation to the physical and social environment. Responses are noted in terms of predominant themes and special attention is paid to those forces that emanate from the "hero" in the picture or from the environment. Through the data, the examiner can infer how the subject relates to other people and molds the environment to meet personal needs. There are special scoring guides, but many clinicians also develop their own system of analysis.

Because the stimuli are ambiguous and the subject is free to respond in any way, it is believed that any meaning the subject gives to the story must come from within. It is said that the subject projects meaning into the story, and thus the TAT is called a projective test. In the TAT we are dealing with imaginative projection rather than a Freudian defense

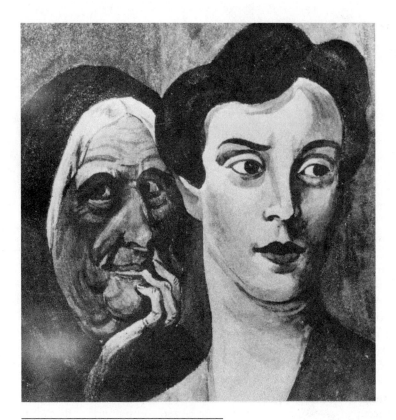

FIGURE 10.1   Thematic Apperception Test

mechanism of projection. Subjects unwittingly project their own attitudes and feelings onto the pictures and thereby reveal themselves.

TAT stories are interpreted in terms of *needs* and *press.* The interaction of need and press together with the outcome of a story make up a *simple thema.* Simple themas that run through several stories become *complex themas,* which help to characterize an individual's mode of functioning. Themas are merely symbolic; they are not considered literal translations of actual subject behavior. Their inference is a hypothetical construct that guides the clinician in evaluating an individual's personality dynamics.

The TAT has proven to be a valuable personality assessment device. It and the Rorschach Ink Blot Test are the most widely used projective techniques. A Children's Apperception Test (CAT) has also been developed by Percival Symonds. The TAT, along with Murray's system of needs, has influenced the development of other assessment techniques, such as the Edwards Personal Preference Schedule and the Jackson Personality Research Form. Moreover, the TAT is frequently used as a research tool for further study of Murray's needs, especially achievement and affiliation.

Murray's theory stimulated David McClelland to research extensively the need for achievement (NAch) (McClelland, Atkinson, Clark, & Lowell, 1953). Informed by Freud's concept of unconscious motivation, McClelland developed a modified version of the TAT

**THINKING CRITICALLY**

## The Thematic Apperception Test

Look at the picture in Figure 10.1 and describe what the picture means to you by making up a narrative for it. What story does the picture tell? What led up to the events in the picture? What is happening? What are the characters in the picture thinking and feeling? How are things going to work out? When you have finished, review the material in the text on Murray's theory and the TAT and see if you can identify some of the items that Murray would look for in your response. Review Murray's list of human needs. Which of these needs are reflected in your story? Are there examples of press that are helping or hindering the fulfillment of goals? Do any themes emerge in which need and press interact together with the outcome of the story?

For example, a picture of a woman and child might bring forth a story of a child who failed at an important task, was comforted, and able to try again. This story could indicate a belief that although failure to meet the need to achieve leads to dejection, the press of nurturance facilitates counteraction. However, an individual with a strong need for abasement might tell the story of a parent telling a child exactly what to do.

---

to assess achievement motivation. High-need-achievement subjects might respond to a picture of a young man with an open book sitting at a desk with stories of wanting to achieve and striving to do well. Low-need-achievement subjects might talk about reading for pleasure or daydreaming. McClelland identified several behavioral differences between people with high and with low need achievement. He also found out that, just as individuals differ in terms of their need to achieve, entire societies do so as well. His work eventually led to exploring conditions and developing techniques that cultivate the need for achievement in both children and adults (1961).

PHILOSOPHY,
SCIENCE,
AND ART

## Murray's Theory

Murray's pioneering studies helped to shape the growth of personality theory in this country. He was largely responsible for bringing Freud to the attention of academic psychologists and stimulating a great deal of scientific research on Freudian concepts. Although Murray tried to provide operational definitions and specific data, he recognized that he did not have sufficient data to justify calling his theory a scientific construct. The proceedings of his diagnostic council also fall short of today's typical standards in scientific research. Nevertheless, Murray was a forerunner in fostering scientific research in personality theorizing and a pioneer in the area of assessment.

Murray advocated an interdisciplinary approach to the study of personality, which was unprecedented. He was equally at home studying the literature of Herman Melville, the writings of Freud, and the latest empirical data as possible sources of knowledge about human nature. At the Harvard Psychological Clinic, he generated an atmosphere in which lively and creative minds could work together, exchanging ideas and developing syntheses. He spoke of the virtues of bringing different approaches and specialties together to shed light on human nature, and of the need to expand our scope beyond that of a narrow, limited model.

Recent essays on personology, such as McAdams (1992), stress that the "person can be said to be a history—a subjectively composed and construed life story that integrates one's past, present, and future." In addition, people develop their own scripts, most of which are both innate and learned (Tompkins, 1992).

Murray was uniquely successful in avoiding a one-sided picture of personality. He tried to strike a careful balance between constitutional elements and environmental factors. He recognized the importance of both past and future events. His theory embraces both behavioral and experiential aspects. Although he is not explicit about his philosophical position, his efforts are clearly rooted in a humanistic philosophy that encourages a comprehensive and holistic view of human nature. His concepts were "organismic when the rest of psychology was atomistic" (White, 1992).

Murray's classification of needs is considered more useful than any other classification of its type. Most subsequent and current research

## PHILOSOPHICAL ASSUMPTIONS

### Examining Allport and Murray

How would you rate Allport and Murray on each of the basic philosophical assumptions described in Chapter 1? Consult the chart on the inside front cover. Each basic issue is presented as a bipolar dimension along which a person's view can be placed according to the degree of agreement with one or the other extreme: *freedom/determinism, hereditary/environmental, uniqueness/universality, proactive/reactive, optimistic/pessimistic.* Rate Allport's and Murray's views on these issues.

When you have determined where you think the theorists stand, compare your responses with those of your classmates and your instructor. You should be willing to defend your ratings, but also be prepared to change them in light of others' compelling arguments. Afterward, compare your ratings of Allport and Murray with your own position on each issue and with those of other theorists. Does this comparison help you understand why their theories do or do not appeal to you?

on needs for power and achievement can be traced to his work. His emphasis on the brain's physiological processes foreshadows contemporary appreciation of the importance of biological and chemical forces in the human organism. Finally, Murray's Thematic Apperception Test, widely used as a diagnostic tool, represents his major contribution to the art of personality theory. Indeed, several personality tests are based on his work.

## Conclusions

Together, Gordon Allport and Henry Murray stimulated a great deal of interest and research in personality in American psychology. Each emphasized the uniqueness of the individual. Allport's theory emphasized the contemporaneity of motives and a holistic view of the person. His concept of the proprium emphasized the difference between the child and the healthy adult. Murray explicitly discussed motivation; his careful construction of the list of twenty needs and his work in the area of assessment has contributed significantly to ongoing personality research. Both Allport and Murray emphasized that personality is very complex and urged that its study be both interdisciplinary and idiographic. With the contemporary resurgence of interest in idiographic techniques, their pioneering efforts are even more appreciated.

## *Summary*

1. Allport described and classified over fifty definitions of personality before finalizing his own definition: "Personality is the dynamic organization within the individual of those psychophysical systems that determine his characteristic behavior and thought."

2. Allport distinguished between *continuity* theories of personality that are closed and admit little change and *discontinuity* theories that are open and provide for extensive growth.

3. Allport distinguished between *common traits,* hypothetical constructs that permit us to make comparisons between individuals, and *personal dispositions,* which are unique to each person. Common traits and personal dispositions are studied by different research methods.

4. There are three levels of personal dispositions: *cardinal, central,* and *secondary.*

5. Allport coined the term *proprium* to refer to the central experience of self-awareness that a person has in growing and moving forward. Allport

described seven *propriate functions:* sense of *bodily self, self-identity, self-esteem, self-extension, self-image, self-as-rational coper,* and *propriate striving.*

6. The concept of *functional autonomy* implies that adult motivation is not necessarily tied to the past. There are two levels of functional autonomy: *perseverative* and *propriate.*

7. Allport was one of the first theorists to discuss the healthy personality. He posited six criteria of maturity.

8. The *nomothetic* approach to the study of personality studies large groups of individuals in order to infer general variables or universal principles. The *idiographic* approach centers on the individual, using techniques that are appropriate to understanding the uniqueness of each person.

9. Allport respected and used the methods of rigorous science in establishing common traits, but he also recognized the value of other methods and the need to understand the individual philosophically as well as scientifically.

10. Murray's term *personology* refers to his unique interdisciplinary study of the individual, which employs a wide array of clinical, psychoanalytic, and experimental methods.

11. Murray separated a person's behavior into identifiable units. The basic unit is a *proceeding,* a succession of proceedings is a *serial,* a planned series is a *serial program,* and a plan for resolving conflicting proceedings is a *schedule.*

12. A *need* is a construct representing a force in the brain that organizes our perception, understanding, and behavior in such a way as to lead us to change an unsatisfying situation. Needs can be inferred from behavioral signs and confirmed through subjective reports. The twenty basic needs that Murray identified are: dominance, deference, autonomy, aggression, abasement, achievement, sex, sentience, exhibition, play, affiliation, rejection, succorance, nurturance, infavoidance, defendance, counteraction, harmavoidance, order, and understanding.

13. A *press* is a force from the environment that helps or hinders an individual in reaching goals. Murray distinguishes between *alpha press* and *beta press.* Examples of press are poverty, illness, and encouragement.

14. Murray urged an interdisciplinary and idiographic approach to the study of personology. He set up a diagnostic council in which several different specialists would study an individual and integrate their findings. The *Thematic Apperception Test (TAT)* is a projective device in which a subject makes up a story for ambiguous pictures. These stories may be interpreted in terms of needs, press, and thema.

15. Murray's interdisciplinary approach was unprecedented. It helps to underscore the values of an interdisciplinary approach to understanding personality and the limitations of a narrow model.

## Suggestions for Further Reading

Allport was a prolific author whose many writings have a clear teaching intent. He sought to describe and illustrate his concepts vividly. His writings are enjoyable to read and of great interest to the student of personality.

Allport's pioneer effort in personality theory was *Personality: A Psychological Interpretation* (Holt, 1937). This work constitutes the initial presentation of his theory, distinguishing between common and individual traits and introducing the concept of functional autonomy. A revised and updated statement of his position is given in *Pattern and Growth in Personality* (Holt, Rinehart, and Winston, 1961). In this work, Allport introduced the concept of personal disposition and emphasized the uniqueness of each individual. The book is highly readable and strongly recommended as an introduction to Allport's thought. *Becoming: Basic Considerations for a Psychology of Personality* (Yale University Press, 1955) underscores Allport's humanistic and futuristic approach. In it he discussed the criteria for maturity. Also recommended are *The Person in Psychology: Selected Essays* (Beacon Press, 1968), which contains a group of Allport's important articles; and *The Nature of Prejudice* (Beacon Press, 1954), Allport's classic study. Special tribute was extended to Gordon Allport in the work edited by K. H. Craik, R. Hogan, and R. N. Wolfe. *Fifty years of personality psychology. Perspectives on individual differences* (Plenum Press, 1993).

Considering the extensive amount of research that Murray did, he wrote very little. He studied Melville intensively for twenty-five years and is widely respected as a Melville scholar through his valuable articles on that author. Unfortunately, his writing tends to be stiff and formal and he had a penchant for coining new words that makes him difficult to read. The student who is interested in his work is encouraged to read *Explorations in Personality* (Oxford University Press, 1938), his major work, written in collaboration with colleagues at the Harvard Psychological Clinic, which describes the findings of his monumental study undertaken there. Also useful is "Outline of a Conception of Personality," written with C. Kluckhohn and included in C. Kluckhohn, H. A. Murray, and D. M. Schneider (Eds.), *Personality in Nature, Society, and Culture* (Knopf, 1953). A most delightful read is his autobiography, in E. G. Boring and G. Lindzey, *A History of Psychology in Autobiography,* Vol. 5 (Appleton-Century-Crofts, 1967). Robinson's biography is *Love's Story Told* (Harvard University Press, 1992).

# Factor Analytic Theories

## RAYMOND CATTELL
## THE BIG FIVE PERSONALITY TRAITS

### Your Goals for This Chapter

1. Cite Cattell's definition of *personality* and compare his interest in personality theorizing with those of other theorists.
2. Distinguish between *source* and *surface* traits and give examples of each.
3. Explain how Cattell identified traits through *factor analysis*.
4. Describe how Cattell hopes to facilitate the prediction of behavior.
5. Identify the terms most commonly used to describe the *Big Five*.
6. Discuss how the Big Five originated from the study of language and the study of personality questionnaires and ratings.
7. Describe the differences between the Big Five and the Five Factor Model.
8. Discuss applications of the Big Five.
9. Define *behavioral genetics* and distinguish between the *genotype* and the *phenotype*.
10. Explain how twin studies contribute to behavioral genetics.
11. Explain the concept of *heritability* and discuss heritability estimates of the Big Five.
12. Discuss applications of genetic research.
13. Describe how *evolutionary psychology* influences personality theory.
14. Evaluate factor analytic trait theories in terms of their function as philosophy, science, and art.

A central issue in personality theorizing has been the importance of genetic and environmental factors in shaping personality. In the lay person's mind, differences in behavior have often been thought to result in part from general physical characteristics that are inherited. Thus we have common stereotypes such as "Fat people are jolly" or "Redheads are hot-tempered." Similarly, it has been thought that an individual's potential is clearly limited by inherited factors. Thus, although a better diet may help us grow taller or act more intelligently, limitations may have been imposed by our genetic makeup.

For many years, personality theorists debated over whether personality is influenced by inner biological patterns or by the experiences an individual has had. This dispute, variously known as the issue of *heredity versus environment* or the *nurture versus nature* controversy, was frequently conducted in a way that suggested that one or the other had to be the primary factor. Today, most theorists recognize that the answer is both. The term *interaction* means that *each affects the other*. Trait and temperament views recognize that the contributions of heredity and the environment are not merely additive but rather complex combinations.

Raymond Cattell uses factor analysis, a sophisticated psychometric technique, to explore personality. The whole of Cattell's theory is complex and very difficult for the lay person to comprehend; here we will provide an overview of important points that will be helpful in understanding contemporary trends in trait and temperament theories. A major current trend in personality theory is the emergence and development of what has come to be known as the Big Five personality traits. Cattell's theory and research on the Big Five personality traits wrestle with the issue of nature versus nurture. They do not deny the influence of environmental forces on personality; they take an interactionist view. However, they often seek to clarify the role that genetic factors play.

## Raymond Cattell: Biographical Background

Raymond Cattell was born in Staffordshire, England, in 1905. His childhood was happy. England became involved in World War I when Cattell was nine. He later acknowledged that the war had a significant impact on him.

Cattell received his B.S.C. from the University of London in 1924 at the age of nineteen. He majored in chemistry and physics, but his interest in social concerns led him to pursue psychology, in which he earned a Ph.D. in 1929. His graduate work was also undertaken at the University of London, where he studied under Charles Spearman, a distinguished psychologist who developed the procedure of factor analysis that Cattell would later employ.

The following years were difficult. Employment was hard to come by for a psychologist, so Cattell worked at several part-time jobs. Meanwhile, he continued his own research. The depressed economy and his own poor health led to several lean years, during which he was haunted by poverty and his marriage broke up. Nevertheless, he remained steadfast in his dedication to his work.

*Raymond Cattell has extensively used factor analysis to identify traits and study personality.*

In 1937, the University of London awarded Cattell an honorary doctorate of science for his contributions to research in personality. That same year he served as a research associate to E. L. Thorndike at Columbia University in New York. Subsequently, he became a professor of psychology at Clark University and later at Harvard, the University of Illinois, the University of Hawaii at Manoa, and Forrest Institute of Professional Psychology in Honolulu, Hawaii. As of this edition, Cattell has retired from teaching duties, but he is still writing.

Cattell has received several honors and made significant contributions to the study of personality. Although his primary emphasis has been on the study of personality through the techniques of factor analysis, he does not lack interest in or concern with other areas of psychology.

## Cattell's Definition of Personality

Cattell begins with a tentative definition of **personality**. "Personality is that which permits a prediction of what a person will do in a given situation" (1950). He believes that a full definition of personality must await further investigation into the types of concepts that are included in the study of behavior. His general statement may be expressed in the formula $R = f(P, S)$, which reads: A response ($R$) is a function ($f$) of the person ($P$) and the stimuli ($S$).

Cattell observes that the response and the stimuli can be precisely determined in an experiment in which the experimenter carefully structures the situation. However, the person is a less well known factor that needs further exploration.

Cattell's definition of personality provides a striking and important contrast between his approach to personality research and that of other theorists, such as the Freudians. Freud developed psychoanalysis as a means of understanding one's self and developing a comprehensive theory of human nature. He was particularly concerned not with the efficacy of psychoanalysis as a predictive tool but with the compelling character of the vision of one's self or humanity that it provided. Cattell, on the other hand, is concerned with the power of a construct to predict future events. His stance is that of the empirical scientist who derives from his or her theory propositions that are subject to empirical test. In a sense, prediction is more difficult than explanation, as it is easier to account for events that have happened than to predict them. Prediction is also useful in that it enables us to anticipate what will happen in certain situations. On the other hand, a theory may have considerable predictive power and garner an impressive array of validating evidence, but still fail to provide a comprehensive or compelling explanation. In his theorizing, Cattell provides an exemplary instance of a scientist who is concerned with validating evidence.

Cattell believes that the exploration of traits will assist us in understanding the structure and function of personality. Knowledge of underlying traits will allow us to make predictions about our own behavior and that of others. Although Cattell, unlike Allport, is interested in the physical and neurological components that influence behavior, he does not maintain that the traits he is exploring necessarily have any real physical or neural status.

## Surface Traits versus Source Traits

Cattell reminds us that if a trait theory is to be useful, the traits postulated need to go beyond the overt behaviors that an individual shows. Just as any successful hypothesis in science refers to future experiences that might occur if the hypothesis turns out to be useful, a successful trait construct goes beyond simply asserting that a particular behavior pattern exists. To argue that Dale is lazy because of a lazy disposition is to argue in a circle and not provide genuinely useful information. To argue that Pat is honest, thoughtful, and disciplined because of an underlying source variable or trait of ego strength is a much more useful way to proceed. The underlying trait of ego strength accounts for the surface manifestation and also permits us to speculate about other related characteristics, such as assertiveness or confidence, that Dale or Pat will display.

Thus, Cattell distinguishes between surface traits and source traits (1950). **Surface traits** are clusters of overt behavior responses that appear to go together, such as integrity, honesty, self-discipline, and thoughtfulness. **Source traits** refer to the underlying variables that seem to determine the surface manifestation, in this case, ego strength.

The study of source traits is valuable for several reasons. Because they are probably few in number, source traits permit economy in describing an individual. Second, source traits presumably have a genuine structural influence on personality and thus determine the way we behave. Thus, knowledge of a particular source trait may permit us to go beyond mere description and make predictions about additional behaviors that we might observe further.

Source traits may have their origin in heredity or environment. From extensive research, utilizing factor analysis techniques. Cattell has identified sixteen basic **temperament** and **ability** source **traits** that he suggests represent the "building blocks" of personality (1966). The traits are presented in Table 11.1 as bipolar dimensions. These traits also form the basis of Cattell's best-known and widely used assessment test, the Sixteen Personality Factor Questionnaire (16PF).

## Assessment and Research in Cattell's Theory

Cattell's personality theory made its major impact through his methods and techniques of researching and identifying traits. Cattell's primary tool has been factor analysis.

Cattell begins by gathering large masses of data from a great many individuals in a variety of ways, such as life records, self-report questionnaires, or projective tests. All of the

---

**TABLE 11.1   Cattell's Sixteen Basic Source Traits**

Raymond Cattell identified sixteen basic source traits that represent the building blocks of personality. Certain traits are indicative of an outgoing temperament, while others indicate a more reserved disposition.

| | | |
|---|---|---|
| outgoing | — | reserved |
| more intelligent | — | less intelligent |
| high ego strength | — | low ego strength |
| assertive | — | humble |
| happy-go-lucky | — | sober |
| strong conscience | — | lack of internal standards |
| adventuresome | — | shy |
| tough-minded | — | tender-minded |
| trusting | — | suspicious |
| imaginative | — | practical |
| shrewd | — | forthright |
| apprehensive | — | self-assured |
| experimental | — | conservative |
| group-dependent | — | self-sufficient |
| casual | — | controlled |
| relaxed | — | tense |

data garnered from these sources are subjected to the complex, sophisticated statistical technique of **factor analysis.** Factor analysis is essentially a correlational procedure that describes large amounts of data in smaller, more manageable units by interrelating many correlations at one time. Hundreds, or even thousands, of variables can be considered in a single study. Factor analysis is based on the assumption that if several variables correlate highly with one another, it is possible that a common dimension underlies them.

The first step in factor analysis is to make up a correlational matrix by computing a correlational coefficient for each variable to show how it relates to every other one. This tells us the degree to which each variable or measure covaries with the others. The second step is to scan the correlational matrix and look for any patterns that emerge. Computers are used in the process. The computer looks for a set of scores that seem to go together, that is, that are similarly high or low. When it finds such a cluster, it indicates that an underlying factor could account for the many relationships in the original matrix. A *factor* is a subset of highly intercorrelated measures (see Table 11.2).

The next step is to compute a correlation between each of the identified factors and each of the original variables. These correlations reflect what Cattell refers to as the "loading" of the variables on the factors and tell us to what degree each measure is related to each factor. A high positive correlation indicates that the measure is strongly related to the factor. A high negative correlation suggests that the measure is related but in an inverse way. The final step is to name the factors. Whereas the procedures for extracting factors are established mathematically, subjective judgment enters into the process of labeling and interpreting them.

Factor analysis enables researchers to draw conclusions such as: similar scores in reading, vocabulary, and spelling tests are due to a common underlying factor of verbal ability, whereas performance in addition, subtraction, and multiplication depends on mathematical ability. Many of the studies undertaken involve a great deal of mathematical computation. The advent of the computer made factor analysis a feasible technique for personality research.

Thus, beginning with hundreds of surface personality traits, Cattell has discovered through factor analysis which of the traits cluster and occur together with the greatest frequency. These traits are then placed together under a common source trait, thereby reducing the number of traits to be dealt with and making them easier to handle.

In the end Cattell hopes that he can use the information garnered to facilitate the prediction of behavior. Given the ability to describe an individual in terms of various traits and the understanding of how these traits enter into certain behavior response patterns, we would be able to apply this information to a particular instance. Eventually, we may be able to predict how a particular individual might respond in a given situation. In order to predict behavior, Cattell (1965) suggests that we need to develop a "dynamic calculus," consisting of a set of **specification equations** that include the various traits and environmental situations that influence behavior. An example of a simple specification equation is

$$R = s_1 T_1 + s_2 T_2 + s_3 T_3 + \ldots + s_n T_n$$

This equation simply means the following: The response ($R$) equals the sum of the characteristics of the person ($T_1, T_2, T_3 \ldots T_n$). Each trait is weighted according to its relevance to the particular situation; that rating constitutes the situational index ($s_1, s_2, s_3 \ldots$). If a partic-

**TABLE 11.2   Factor Analysis**

HYPOTHETICAL CORRELATIONAL MATRIX

| VARIABLE (MEASURE) | A | B | C | D | E | F |
|---|---|---|---|---|---|---|
| a (reading) | +1.00 | +.60 | +.50 | +.15 | +.20 | +.10 |
| b (vocabulary) | | +1.00 | +.50 | +.15 | +.10 | +.10 |
| c (spelling) | | | +1.00 | +.10 | +.20 | +.15 |
| d (addition) | | | | +1.00 | +.60 | +.60 |
| e (subtraction) | | | | | +1.00 | +.60 |
| f (multiplication) | | | | | | +1.00 |

A visual scan of this matrix tells us that there are clusters of variables (measures) that may belong together.

FACTOR MATRIX

| VARIABLE (MEASURE) | FACTOR 1 | FACTOR 2 |
|---|---|---|
| a (reading) | +.70 | +.15 |
| b (vocabulary) | +.60 | +.15 |
| c (spelling) | +.60 | +.10 |
| d (addition) | +.10 | +.70 |
| e (subtraction) | +.10 | +.65 |
| f (multiplication) | +.05 | +.60 |

The factor matrix tells us that reading, vocabulary, and spelling all have high loadings on Factor 1, whereas addition, subtraction, and multiplication have high loadings on Factor 2.

ular trait is highly relevant to the response, its corresponding situational index would be high. If a particular trait is irrelevant to a response, the situational index would be zero. If the trait inhibits or detracts from the response, the situational index would be negative. The model is basically a very simple one.

For example, suppose $R$ were to stand for the classroom performance of a professor. The factor of intelligence would be very important because an instructor needs to understand the subject and know how to communicate it to others. Thus, the characteristic of intelligence would be assigned a high situational index. The characteristic of assertiveness might also be important, but less so than intelligence. Therefore, it would be assigned a lower number. Each trait that is relevant to classroom performance would be included until all the elements in the equation were filled in. We would then be able to predict how an instructor might behave in the classroom. Cattell has applied some of his methods to the area of personnel selection, where he has had considerable success in predicting job satis-faction and worker effectiveness.

Cattell's formula is based on addition, and thus it has been criticized for not pro-viding for possible interrelations or interactions among traits. A more complete formula would also need to include factors other than traits, such as **state**, an individual's temporary mood and emotion, and **role**, one's presentation of self in a particular social situation. Cat-tell acknowledges that we may eventually need more sophisticated formulas but suggests that his specification equation is a useful starting point.

Just as the study of individuals may be facilitated by the exploration of underlying traits, the study of groups and institutions that shape personality may be facilitated by the objective measurement of **syntality**, Cattell's term for the dimensions that permit us to de-scribe and differentiate among groups and institutions (1948). Again, factor analysis is an important tool in identifying the syntality of social institutions, ranging from the family to larger cultural groups such as nations. Cattell's work in syntality has led to the development of sets of factors and matrixes that can enable us to begin to measure and examine the dif-ferences and relationships among people in various groups. Cattell believes that variations among cultural groups (for example, whether Americans are more extroverted than the British but less so than Canadians) can be specified and quantified so as to aid in anticipat-ing behavior and developing appropriate responses, an important task in today's global world.

## The Big Five Personality Traits

Cattell provided the theoretical groundwork for much of the current research in the mea-surement of personality. That work has culminated in the emergence of five primary factors that form a potential basic model for delineating the structure of personality. Some have even suggested that a consensus on the factors now exists, popularly known as the **"Big Five"** (Goldberg, 1990, 1993; John, 1990; McCrae & Costa, 1987).

Although somewhat different labels have been used for the Big Five factors, the most commonly used terms are *Neuroticism, Extraversion, Openness, Agreeableness,* and *Conscientiousness* (Loehlin, 1992). An acronym for remembering these factors can be formed by rearranging the first letters of each factor to form the word *OCEAN* (John, 1990, p. 96).

Still, it is premature to say that there is a clear consensus. Although there is a high level of agreement that there are five dimensions, there is some disagreement (or dispute) concerning the exact nature of each of the five factors. Scholars do not even always use the same five terms. Historically, the Big Five arise out of two different attempts to identify ba-sic factors in personality. One major source of the Big Five was the study of language, which led to a descriptive model of personality traits that has been replicated across different lan-guages. A second source was the factor analysis of personality questionnaires, which led to an explanatory hypothesis, the *Five Factor Model (FFM),* of dispositional biological traits that are substantially inherited. Both sources are similar in many ways, but they are not identical (John & Robins, 1993). However, attempts have been made to merge the two (Mc-Crae & Costa, 1997).

## The Study of Language

Initial support for the Big Five comes from the analysis of language—specifically, of terms in the vernacular that have been used to describe personality. Sir Francis Galton (1822–1911), an English scientist, was one of the first to propose a "lexical hypothesis" suggesting that significant differences among people that affect how they interact with one another are encoded in words. Over time, people recognize and label those characteristics that are crucial for interpersonal relationships. These words are used frequently and reflect our understanding of the world and of other people (Goldberg, 1993).

Allport found 17,953 words in the English language that could be referred to as personality attributes (Hall & Lindzey, 1957). The words that people use to describe one another are observable attributes rather than underlying causal traits. However, within the vocabulary of synonymous terms, clusters develop that reflect the most important attributes. The fact that there are clusters leads one to ask how many terms we actually need to cover all of the characteristics. Lewis Thurstone, an early developer of factor analysis, was the first to suggest that as few as five common factors might be sufficient to account for all of the adjectives that people use to describe one another. He concluded that the "scientific description of personality" might be simpler than previously thought (1934).

Cattell (1943) used Allport's list as a basis for his factor analysis of the structure of personality and reduced the list to his sixteen personality factors. To hone the number to sixteen was in itself an enormous task, considering the primitive calculators of the mid-1940s. To this day, although Cattell has been given credit for launching the scientific research that led to the Big Five factors, he has yet to adopt the model, believing that five factors are too few a number. Whereas Cattell identified over a dozen factors from his analysis, later researchers, using the same data, were only able to consistently replicate five. Norman (1963) was the first to identify factors similar to the current Big Five, and it was Goldberg (1981) who reviewed research on them and argued for their power and consistency. Digman (1990) and John (1990) reviewed studies in diverse languages (such as Japanese, Chinese, and German) from different cultures and found cross-cultural support for the Big Five model.

## The Study of Personality Questionnaires and Ratings

The second major source of support for five basic factors comes from the study of personality questionnaires and ratings. This activity led to the **Five Factor Model** (**FFM**). Although questionnaires developed by Cattell and Eysenck have been used, the most research in this area has been done by Paul Costa and Robert McCrae, whose prodigious work and publication in the last two decades has bolstered the acceptance of a five-factor model for understanding personality structure. Costa and McCrae (1985; McCrae & Costa, 1989, 1990) originally developed an objective assessment device, the Neuroticism Extraversion Openness Personality Inventory (**NEO-PI**), to measure the broad personality dimensions of Neuroticism, Extraversion, and Openness. When they realized that their dimensions were very similar to three of the Big Five factors, they revised it to form the Neuroticism Extraversion Openness Personality Inventory, Revised (**NEO-PI-R**), adding scales to measure

Agreeableness and Conscientiousness and demonstrating that their inventory scales converged with the Big Five factors that had emerged from the study of language. Thus the revised test was developed precisely to assess the Big Five (Costa and McCrae, 1992).

The NEO Personality Inventory consists of thirty scales with ten items each. Subjects are asked to indicate on a 5-point scale (*strongly agree* to *strongly disagree*) whether or not certain descriptions apply to them. No major revisions of the basic model are anticipated in the near future, but a customized software version is a possibility within the next five years (Costa & McCrae, 1997).

In scoring and analyzing the inventory, six particular facets are considered within each of the Big Five factors. These are summarized in Table 11.3. Each of these Big Five factors captures the essential nature of a larger group of specific characteristics that are related to one another. Each of the five categories includes more specific traits, many of which may be further broken down. Thus a hierarchy of traits is created. For example, the factor of Extraversion encompasses the more specific trait of gregariousness, which could include the even more precise characteristic of friendliness. The more specific the attribute (and its measurement), the better able we are to predict specific behavior in a given situation. Thus a specific measure of friendliness lets us predict how much one will smile and talk in a social situation more accurately than does the more global measure of Extraversion. The NEO-PI-R inventory permits the assessment of personality both at the level of the specific characteristics and also at the more general level.

## Differences Between the Big Five and the Five Factor Model

The Big Five, stemming from studies of language, simply provides a summary description of attributes. No assumption is made as to whether or not the traits actually exist or as to their possible causes. It is purely a description, not an explanation.

The Five Factor Model is an interpretation of the Big Five factors. It seeks to advance some additional claims that do not necessarily follow from the discovery of five basic

---

**TABLE 11.3  Facets Encompassed Within the Big Five Factors**

In scoring and analyzing the NEO Personality Inventory (NEO-PI), six particular facets are considered within each of the Big Five factors (Costa & McCrae, 1992).

| NEUROTICISM | EXTRAVERSION | OPENNESS | AGREEABLENESS | CONSCIENTIOUSNESS |
|---|---|---|---|---|
| anxiety | warmth | fantasy | trust | competence |
| angry hostility | gregariousness | aesthetics | straightforwardness | order |
| depression | assertiveness | feelings | altruism | dutifulness |
| self-consciousness | activity | actions | compliance | achievement striving |
| impulsiveness | excitement seeking | ideas | modesty | self-discipline |
| vulnerability | positive emotions | values | tender-mindedness | deliberation |

dimensions in language. First, it asserts that we can describe personality structure in terms of five broad categories, each of which includes more specific attributes, and that individuals can be described by their scores on the measure of the broad concepts or the subsets. Second, it suggests that differences among people in these dimensions are stable over time, have a genetic basis, and are due at least in part to some still-to-be-specified internal mechanism. Thus the Five Factor Model sets forth additional, farther reaching theoretical claims than does the Big Five.

Theorists differ on the extent to which the Five Factor Model refers to causal mechanisms that exist within the person. Although Cattell is interested in the physical and genetic components that influence behavior, he does not assert claims of such status for the traits he uncovers. Eysenck is very clear that his goal is ultimately to identify the causes of components of personality (see Chapter 12), but he clearly recognizes the limits of factor analysis. McCrae and Costa remind us that we need to be wary of too quick a movement from language-based descriptions of personality to conclusions concerning its basic structure. "No one would argue that an analysis of common English terms for parts of the body would provide an adequate basis for the science of anatomy, why should personality be different?" (McCrae and Costa, 1985).

Most researchers in the Five Factor Model do not take a clearly causal stance and are very careful about specifying particular mechanisms. They "acknowledge that there must be some neurophysiological or hormonal basis for personality, but it is unlikely that we will ever find a single region of the brain that controls Neuroticism, or a neurotransmitter that accounts for Extraversion, or a gene for Openness" (McCrae & Costa, 1990). Others remain satisfied with a view that limits the five dimensions to a helpful descriptive summary of observed regularities of behavior without claiming to be a classification system based on causal and dynamic grounds.

## Applications of the Big Five and the Five Factor Model

Because the Five Factor Model is based on the findings of the Big Five, hereafter we will simply refer to the Big Five with the understanding that, in some cases, research is specifically based on the Five Factor Model.

Research on the Big Five has resulted in several applications. Most notably, it has been successfully used to predict job performance. Many of the traits reflected in the Big Five structure are related to those needed for positive achievement in work. For example, measures associated with the dimension of Conscientiousness are often helpful in predicting job success (Barrick & Mount, 1991), as are measures related to Agreeableness (Tett, Jackson, & Rothstein, 1991). Looking at some of the Big Five measures in terms of requirements for successful performance in specific occupations may permit employers to make intelligent decisions concerning job candidates. Successfully driving a truck, for example, requires an individual who is conscientious and emotionally stable; an impulsive, sociable individual is more likely to cause problems on the road (Hogan & Hogan, 1995).

Earlier use of personality measures by organizations led to considerable reservations about the practice because of problems of faking, low validity, and the potential for ethical abuse. However, newer data suggests that well-developed personality measures can successfully predict job performance and increase fairness in the employment process. Well-constructed personality questionnaires do not systematically discriminate against people with disabilities (Hayes, 1996), women, or the elderly or people of minority-group status (Hogan & Hogan, 1995). Instead, they can be used as a force for "equal employment opportunity, social justice, and increased productivity" (Hogan, Hogan, & Roberts, 1996).

Personality measures can also contribute to the prediction of job satisfaction. Tokar and Subich (1997) used several different measures to survey the job satisfaction of adults employed in various occupations and concluded that the Big Five personality dimensions contribute significantly to the prediction of job satisfaction. In particular, Extraversion and low Neuroticism were unique predictors. Holland (1996) has linked the Big Five with his typology of persons and work environments to underscore that people work well when there is a good fit between their personality type and the characteristics of the work environment. Thus optimal use of human resources can certainly be facilitated by the framework of the Big Five (Goldberg, 1993).

The Five Factor Model has become so compelling that a variety of instruments has been developed and many existing instruments have been modified to assess it (Widiger & Trull, 1997). Because it originated in the study of ordinary language, the Big Five structure is ideally suited for use in analyzing and understanding descriptions developed by individuals in working on their life histories, the constructs that emerge from Kelly's Role Construct Repertory Test (to be discussed in Chapter 15), and other idiographic or person-centered research (John & Robins, 1993). The NEO-PI-R has been useful in diagnosing personality disorders (McCrae & Costa, 1989; Widiger, 1993), as well as in determining types of treatment. For example, an extravert might do better in group therapy, whereas an introvert might be more comfortable in a one-on-one situation. This wider approach to assessment appears to be a growing trend (Funder & Sneed, 1993).

The Big Five construct can also be useful in showing us how concepts in personality theorizing are related. Thus Adler's *social interest*, Horney's *moving toward*, and Erikson's *basic trust* may all be seen as aspects of Agreeableness.

The Big Five have been replicated in both Western and non-Western languages. However, the factors that emerge across cultures do not completely coincide (Yang & Bond, 1990), suggesting that there are also important cultural differences in personality structure. When Shweder and Bourne (1984) permitted people in India and the United States to freely choose any terms to describe an acquaintance, trait terms were more frequently used by the Americans and situational action responses by the Indians; thus people in the United States would be more likely to describe someone as helpful, whereas people from India would describe the actual instance of helping, such as, "My friend reaches out to help people when they fall down." These findings suggest that the Indian view of personality is less individualistic and more socially embedded than the American view. McCrae and Costa (1997) compared data from studies that used six translations of the NEO-PI-R from different language families with the American factor structure. After the factors were rotated in an appropriate manner, the various samples (German, Portuguese, Hebrew, Chinese, Korean, and Japanese) revealed structures similar to the American factors. Because diverse cultures and languages were represented, McCrae and Costa believe that the result indicates that personality trait structure transcends cultural differences and may be universal. This is not to say that the five factors play the same role in every culture, but it is now possible to look at the specific cultural manifestations of common personality dimensions. Such cross-cultural replicability further points out the need for an evolutionary understanding of how differences among people have been encoded into everyday language.

# Related Developments: Behavioral Genetics and Evolution

## The Genetic Influence on Traits

Cattell was particularly interested in assessing the relative importance of heredity and environment on personality. The same interest has led other researchers to study genetic influences on traits. This research lends additional support to the Big Five theory. **Behavioral genetics** is the field of study that explores the cause of individual differences in human behavior in terms of heredity. The discipline makes an important distinction between the **genotype,** the genetic makeup of an individual, and the **phenotype**, the individual's observable appearance and behavior that arise out of the interaction of his or her genotype with the environment. Techniques of study have been developed that seek to separate the phenotypic variation of a population into genetic and environmental aspects.

By focusing on a specific characteristic and comparing various subjects in different environments, behavioral geneticists can help us understand the relative contributions of heredity and environment. If children who are unrelated are adopted, raised in the same family, and grow up to be similar in regard to a trait such as extraversion, we may conclude that the shared family environment had a more important role in the development of that trait than did heredity; if they tend to be dissimilar (as they in fact do), we might conclude that the genetic contribution was the more significant one.

Twin studies are the most popular design for behavioral genetic studies. Twins naturally arouse our curiosity and also provide a convenient population with which to explore the comparative contributions of nature and nurture. Twins are two separate individuals, yet they are very much alike. Myth and literature are replete with stories in which similar events happen to both twins. There are documented instances in which a pair of twins who were raised separately since birth are reunited and discover that they share a great deal in common, such as using the same brand of toothpaste, having spouses with the same first name, owning the same make of car, or having similar jobs, hobbies, health problems, and so forth. How can we account for such occurrences?

The logic behind the method of studying twins can be easily understood. Identical, or *monozygotic* (MZ), twins develop from a single fertilized ovum or egg; they have the same genes and the same parents and, from a genetic point of view, they are clones of each other. Any differences between two MZ twins must be due to dissimilar experiences. Fraternal, or *dizygotic* (DZ), twins develop from two fertilized ova; they share the same parents but have different genes and are no more alike than regular siblings. Differences among those twins must be due to both genetic effects and separate experiences.

Cattell (1960) advocated the technique of *multiple abstract variance analysis* (MAVA), which studies twins and siblings who have been reared either together or apart.

*While monozygotic (identical) twins are very similar, they are not exactly the same—as is illustrated by this picture of the text author (on the right) and her sister.*

However, before the early 1980s, twin and adoption studies were done outside of the mainstream of psychology and had little impact on the field. The study of genetics emphasized animal studies. Selective breeding gave clear evidence for a genetic contribution to temperament. In a recent confirmation of this finding, many people who purchased dalmatians as pets because of the movie *101 Dalmatians* returned the dogs when they realized the shortcomings of the breed (e.g., they are prone to deafness; urinary stone and skin problems; their temperament can make them hard to train; and they can become aggressive as adults). In the 1960s, two studies began to focus attention on human behavioral genetics and twin studies. Erlenmeyer-Kimling and Jarvik (1963) summarized the twin and adoption studies done up to that time and suggested that heredity is an important factor in **IQ** scores. Heston (1966) conducted an adoption study that revealed the importance of heredity in the development of schizophrenia. However, interest was quickly squelched when Jensen (1969) provoked tremendous controversy by suggesting that differences in IQ scores between blacks and whites may be due to genetics.

In the last several decades, the design of genetic studies has become highly sophisticated and varied, going far beyond the simple comparison of MZ and DZ twins. A wider range and greater number of studies have incorporated samples of adult twins and their offspring, as well as other combinations of siblings and families, both biologically related and adopted. New methods of testing hypotheses have increased the usefulness of available data. Earlier concerns regarding environmental effects and differences in the development of twins and singletons have been allayed. These are no longer seen as jeopardizing the effectiveness of the research for the purpose of genetic determination of traits. The analysis of blood tests for DNA markers has eliminated any questions regarding the zygosity of particular sets of twins because identical twins have the same markers.

Behavioral genetics uses the statistic of heritability to express the proportion of phenotypic variation that may be due to genetic variation. **Heritability** is an estimate of the degree to which a trait or characteristic is caused by the genotype rather than the environment. Geneticists look at a particular trait and compare the correlation between monozygotic (identical) twins on the trait with the correlation among singly born individuals. This comparison provides a ratio. For the characteristic of height, the ratio is .9; this means that 90 percent of the differences in height among people is genetic, and the remainder is due to the environment. It is important to note that this does not mean that 90 percent of your height is due to your genes and the remaining 10 percent of your height is due to your environment; the ratio applies to an entire biological population growing up in a particular environment, not to individuals within the population. The fact that the heritability estimate of height is 90 percent means that almost all of the height differences are due to genetic factors.

Heritability estimates can be somewhat misleading by themselves because there are different ways to define and calculate heritability. These differences can produce varying numbers. Moreover, genes affect traits in a probabilistic rather than a predetermined manner. Nevertheless, heritability statistics help us know to what extent heredity can influence a trait. A significant degree of heritability does not mean that the environment has no role in the shaping of a trait, but it does place some boundaries on the extent of its potential contribution. Heritability studies can also clarify the degree to which a trait may be due to shared environmental experiences (i.e., a common family environment or the same diet) as opposed to experiences unique to the individual.

Thomas Bouchard has been fascinated by twins ever since he read an article about a pair of separated twins who had been reunited and found that they shared an uncanny number of past and present traits and behaviors. Bouchard founded the Minnesota Center for Twin and Adoption Research in 1979; ever since, it has been at the forefront of investigative work in the area of genetic influences on behavior. Hundreds of sets of twins have been tested and studied extensively at the center. Its study of monozygotic twins raised separately is the largest continuous study in the field. As a result of these studies, many concordant traits and behaviors have been confirmed.

Summaries of the behavioral genetic twin study literature for the Five Factor Model have been provided by Loehlin (1992) and Bouchard (1994). Earlier studies may have overestimated the genetic influence on personality, but heritability estimates exceed 40 percent for all of the factors. In Lang and Livesley's (1996) assessment of genetic influence on the Big Five, the specific estimates are: Neuroticism, 41 percent; Extraversion, 53 percent; Openness, 61 percent; Agreeableness, 41 percent; and Conscientiousness, 44 percent (see Figure 11.1). Openness shows the greatest effect and Extraversion, the second greatest. The estimates of the influence of shared family environment are small. Most of the environmental variance was due to nonshared influences. These findings have also been replicated in cross-cultural studies.

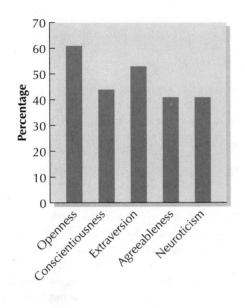

**FIGURE 11.1**   Genetic Influence on the Big Five

In a twin study assessing influences on the Big Five, Lang and Livesley (1996) found heredity estimates exceeding 40 percent for all of the factors. *(SOURCE: Adapted from Lang, K. L., & Livesley, W. J. [1996]. Heritability of the big five personality dimensions and their facets: A twin study.* Journal of Personality, 64, 577-597.*)*

## *Applications of Genetic Research*

Twin and adoption studies permit us to estimate genetic influences indirectly by noting how relatives resemble one another. However, new and sophisticated techniques are revolutionizing genetic research on personality by identifying specific DNA markers and genetic mechanisms that are believed to result in differences in behavior. These DNA markers may be assessed inexpensively, using a drop of blood or saliva. With DNA markers, researchers have been able to distinguish chromosomal regions and to isolate genes and gene products for single-gene disorders. However, most behaviors are not the result of the action of a single gene. Rather, many genes having varying effects contribute to behavior variation and vulnerability to certain problems. The genes in these multiple-gene systems are labeled *quantitative trait loci* (QTL), and DNA markers are helping us identify and locate them. The challenge is to identify genes involved in complex behaviors that entail multiple-gene effects, as well as nongenetic contributors (Saudino & Plomin, 1996). We already have a fairly complete map of the genes of the mouse, and the Human Genome Project, designed to map the genes of the human, is moving forward with due speed. In the coming years, we will see new QTL mapping techniques that will permit us to use genetic markers as direct indicators of genotypes.

None of the data on the heritability of personality traits suggests that inheritance is either the primary factor or a more significant one than the environment. At best, research suggests that the heritability of many behaviors is in the range of 30 to 50 percent. This means that only about ⅓ to ½ of behavior variation is due to genetics; the majority of the variance is due to environment. Evidence of heritability varies from trait to trait, with those associated with temperament having the highest degree of heritability and those relating to attitudes and beliefs having the least (Buss & Plomin, 1984). However, the more we

**THINKING CRITICALLY**

## *Should We Selectively Breed Humans?*

Cattell (1972) suggests that we consider selective breeding as a means of cultivating desired traits in human beings. Twin studies show that heredity plays a large part in determining personality. Selective breeding has long been accepted as a way of developing superior animals, fruits, and vegetables. Ancient people used plants, such as queen anne's lace and rue, to deliberately limit their populations (Kolata, 1994). Actually, many people selectively breed by choosing their mate on the basis of appearance, intellect, and so forth. The couple who decide to limit family size or abort a "defective" fetus are also engaging in their own form of selective breeding. These informal efforts at selective breeding have led to significant, but not necessarily optimal, changes in the distribution of the human population. Arguing that the goal is not to create an ideal type of person or master race, but rather a diversity that would maximize evolutionary progress and the survival of humanity, Cattell suggests that governments extend their concern to the genetic quality of their populations.

In time, psychology and medicine will permit us to directly determine those mental and physical traits that are most desirable. In the meantime, Cattell suggests that a reasonably efficient criterion can be developed based on economics: birth rate proportional to income. That is, parents who have demonstrated their ability to contribute to society would be encouraged to have more children, whereas others who have not demonstrated that ability and cannot afford to raise children would be discouraged through government taxation and other forms of manipulation. Because earnings are not always fairly related to social worth and contribution, some adjustments would be needed for important social occupations (such as teaching, religion, and research) where supply and demand in the market does not provide an adequate evaluation. But, on the whole, Cattell believes that relating family size to earnings would result in a positive eugenic trend. What do you think?

❖ Should we consider selectively breeding humans on a more deliberate basis?

❖ Is Cattell's assumption, that an individual's worth to society can in most cases be measured by his or her income, appropriate?

❖ What other considerations do you think need to be taken into account besides economic ones?

❖ What impact might selective breeding have on cultural and racial balances?

❖ Should decisions continue to be made individually or socially, at a national or even international level?

❖ The Clinton administration has made population control a key in its foreign policy of "sustainable development" in the Third World. It has halted additional funds for exploring human cloning. Do you concur?

These are issues that deserve serious thought by anyone who is interested in the future of the human race. What difficulties do you envision might arise in trying to be fair to all people?

**THINKING CRITICALLY**

## Personality Traits That Have Appeared in Families Throughout the Generations

Interview your parents, grandparents, and, if possible, even great-grandparents to determine possible inherited traits.

❖   What personality traits appear in the family throughout the generations?

❖   What are the similarities and differences in traits over the generations?

❖   What seem to be the most common traits?

Many times, older family members can remember traits such as shyness, creativity, depressive disorder, alcoholism, or high intelligence that seem to run in families.

You might also try to interview identical twins (or even just one of the twins) to see what traits they share with each other. As an identical twin, I can affirm that although my twin sister and I are not completely alike, we are still very similar to one another.

Such activities might help you to appreciate that genes do have an impact on our personalities.

know about a trait genetically as well as environmentally, the better equipped we will be to develop prevention and intervention strategies.

Bouchard and others (1990) hypothesize that genetic differences primarily affect psychological differences in an indirect way, by influencing the effective environment of the developing child. In other words, inborn abilities and predispositions guide individuals in their selection of the environmental experiences that will have an influence on them. In general, we seek out environments that are compatible with our inherited tendencies. Such gene/environment interaction does not detract from the significance of parenting, education, and other interventions.

The fact that a trait is genetically influenced does not mean that it cannot be changed. Genetic expressions can be extensively altered by modifications in the environment. Because many problems that may have genetic roots cannot be treated as effectively once they are fully formed (for example, psychopathology and alcoholism), early detection of people at risk provides our best means of prevention. Early identification of infants who inherit an inability to metabolize a certain protein (phenylketonuria [PKU]) has led to treatment through dietary restrictions that prevents the mental retardation that formerly resulted. However, the ability to detect potential problems early raises significant ethical questions about what should be done with that information.

### Evolutionary Personality Theory

Studies in heritability remind us of our close connections to the biological world and our evolutionary history. They lead us to ask how we have adapted to life and what role evolution plays in the development of personality. David Buss (1995) has suggested that **evolutionary psychology** may provide the conceptual tools for bringing together diverse threads in psychology and the study of personality.

From an evolutionary perspective, the Big Five traits represent strategic differences summarizing the "most important features of the social landscape that humans have had to adapt to" (D. Buss, 1995). Information from the social environment was incorporated into psychological mechanisms. Many of the significant features of our evolved psychological mechanisms are social in character because many of our significant problems are social. In the course of evolution, people who were able to correctly discern and act on individual differences had a selective advantage over those who were oblivious to them. Awareness of relative tendencies to be dominant or submissive assisted the development of a social hierarchy. Perception of the willingness of others to be cooperative or aggressive helped in forming alliances. Appreciation of another's expertise permitted one to solicit help. Recognition of the reliability of another enabled trust. Over time, people developed psychological mechanisms that were sensitive to these and other important differences. The Big Five persisted and became robust because of their usefulness in human adaption. Bringing an evolutionary perspective to them clarifies why they have been so pervasive.

Evolutionary psychology can help us overcome the false dichotomies that have often clouded discussions of the nature of psychological mechanisms by placing them in one or the other of two separate classes, such as genetic *or* environmental, cultural *or* biological, etc. (D. Buss, 1995). Heritable individual differences may lead to different utilization of psychological mechanisms. Those who are muscular and strong learn different strategies for dealing with people than those who are lean and frail do. They will probably have a greater success using an aggressive strategy than their frailer peers would. These differences can point individuals toward different ways of adapting; over time, these strategies become stabilized. What were previously considered to be separate dichotomies are more appropriately seen as aspects of one unified process of evolution.

David Buss (1995) distinguishes between evolutionary psychology and sociobiology. Adherents of sociobiology frequently advocate a view of human beings as "fitness maximizers," suggesting that psychological mechanisms aim to maximize inclusive fitness. Buss believes that this is a fallacy that confuses the origins of psychological mechanisms with their nature. Psychological mechanisms that evolved in the process of adapting to problems do not necessarily continue to ensure fitness. For example, the human preference for fatty foods at one time probably helped us adapt by increasing our caloric intake. Today, however, that preference is not necessarily in our best interest. According to Buss, it is more helpful to see human evolution in terms of adaptive problem solving than of fitness maximizing. Employing an evolutionary approach to personality may help bring some of the current diverse threads in psychology into a coherent whole.

| PHILOSOPHY, |
| SCIENCE, |
| AND ART |

# Factor Analytic Trait Theories

Cattell's theory of personality is based on highly objective and precise scientific techniques. At its height Cattell generated more empirical research than any other personality theorist (Wiggins, 1984), although his findings were not always replicated. A perusal of the material on personality published in the *Annual Review of Psychology* over the decades of the 70s and 80s attests to the significant research that Cattell's theory generated.

Cattell's theory reflects the current emphasis on quantitative methods and empirical data. Few other theorists have been as precise or as operational in their definitions. Furthermore, few theorists have been as rigorous in subjecting their concepts of underlying personality variables to empirical test. In its adherence to a strict methodology and its generation of a vast quantity of research, Cattell's theory is a meritorious example of a scientific approach to personality.

To identify Cattell as a scientist is not to ignore the fact that his theory arises out of his philosophical commitment to an empirical approach. His theory suggests that he views the world as lawful, consistent, and controllable. Moreover, Cattell suggests that a system of ethical values, which he calls *beyondism,* may be developed on the foundation of science. Beyondism is based on the view that humanity is in the process of a physical and biological advance. Moral laws that will foster and ensure this evolutionary process need to be developed. Such ethics will enable us to adapt to a wider range of circumstances and will give us a better chance of survival. Strictly speaking, Cattell's new morality cannot be said to arise from science. Scientists may have discovered the process of evolution, but the judgment that such evolution is good and should be fostered is a value judgment that takes us outside the realm of validating evidence and into the realm of philosophy. The moral issues that Cattell raises, such as the advisability of selective breeding as a means of cultivating certain traits, deserve serious debate. Herein lies the value of science for Cattell and others who cherish the importance of validating evidence: our intuition is subsequently checked by explicit logic and experimentation.

Cattell's theory is not as popular as other theories among psychologists, and it is almost totally unknown among the general public. In part this lack of popularity is due to its complexity, but it is also due to a feeling that factor analysis creates an artifact or a para-person that has no relationship to a real person. As we have seen, it is difficult for the conclusions of a scientific method to command the same degree of compellingness as a philosophical vision.

The Big Five, which is also based on factor analysis, has received a great deal of attention as a significant contribution to personality theory. In spite of its current popularity, however, there is no unanimous agreement concerning the Big Five. Cattell believes that five factors are too few, whereas Eysenck, who is discussed in Chapter 12, believes that three will suffice. Pervin (1994) expresses concern that there has been a premature consensus equating personality with the Five Factor Model that does not do justice to the dynamic nature of personality. McAdams (1994) suggests that a personality psychology that is limited to traits provides us with only a psychology of the stranger, merely giving information about people that we need to know when we know nothing else about them. Nevertheless, the Five Factor Model is an important one in personality theory, especially so because it has provoked a great deal of research even though it may not be the final integrative model.

The present interest in behavioral genetics is a helpful shift after the predominance that was placed on the environment by the behaviorist movement. However, we need to be careful not to move from a simplistic emphasis on the environment to an equally simplistic emphasis on biology (Plomin, Chipner, & Loehlin, 1990). Moreover, an emphasis on genetics easily gives rise to controversial issues, such as that of selective breeding. Cattell was scheduled to receive a lifetime achievement award from the American Psychological Association in August of 1997. However, the award was postponed because of charges that some of his writings are racist, an accusation that Cattell denies, stating that his remarks have been taken out of context.

As research in behavioral genetics continues, some questions will be answered and others asked about the genetic components of traits and temperaments, their stability, and their cultural components (Woodall & Matthews, 1993). Evolutionary psychology will provide a helpful framework within which to examine the adaptive nature of temperament and traits (Buss, 1991b) and may help us reconceive of the duality of nature and nurture as two aspects of one evolving process (D. Buss, 1995).

Cattell's theory and the Big Five that resulted from it are carefully constructed theories that are well rooted in empirical data. They

## PHILOSOPHICAL ASSUMPTIONS

### *Examining Cattell and the Big Five Theorists*

How would you rate the factor analytic theories on each of the basic philosophical assumptions described in Chapter 1? Consult the chart on the inside front cover. Each basic issue is presented as a bipolar dimension along which a person's view can be placed according to the degree of agreement with one or the other extreme: *freedom/determinism, hereditary/environmental, uniqueness/universality, proactive/reactive, optimistic/pessimistic.* Rate the views of Cattell and the Big Five theorists on these issues.

When you have determined where you think the theorists stand, compare your responses with those of your classmates and your instructor. You should be willing to defend your ratings, but also be prepared to change them in light of others' compelling arguments. Afterward, compare your ratings of these theorists with your own position on each issue and with those of other theorists. Does this comparison help you understand why these theories do or do not appeal to you?

have enormous potential for teaching us about human personality and for predicting behavior. Indeed, Cattell believes that, in time, by applying appropriate rules of reference, psychologists will be able to predict human behavior as accurately as astronomers predict the stars and planets. The rigorous methodology and approach of these theories, as well as of Eysenck's theory (Chapter 12) are characteristic of the scientific enterprise at work.

# Summary

1. Cattell defines *personality* as that which will permit prediction of what a person will do in a given situation. His interest in personality theorizing is clearly oriented toward prediction.

2. *Surface traits* are clusters of overt behavior responses that appear to go together. *Source traits* are the underlying variables, which may have their origin in heredity or in influences of the environment. Cattell has identified sixteen basic *temperament* and *ability traits.*

3. Cattell uses *factor analysis* to identify traits. Factor analysis is a correlational procedure that interrelates many correlations at one time and identifies common dimensions that underlie them.

4. Cattell hopes to develop a "dynamic calculus" consisting of a set of *specification equations* to facilitate the prediction of behavior.

5. The most commonly used terms to describe the *Big Five* are *Neuroticism, Extraversion, Openness, Agreeableness,* and *Conscientiousness.*

6. The study of language led to a *descriptive model* of personality traits that has been replicated across languages. The study of personality questionnaires led to an *explanatory hypothesis* of traits.

7. There are differences concerning the exact nature of each of the five factors because of various ways of conducting a factor analysis. Researchers also differ on whether the five factors go beyond description to provide a causal analysis.

8. Research on the Big Five has been successfully used to predict job performance and job satisfaction, to diagnose personality disorders, and to determine therapy.

9. *Behavioral genetics* explores the cause of individual differences in terms of heredity. It distinguishes between the *genotype,* genetic makeup, and *phenotype,* observable appearance and behavior.

10. Twin studies are useful in behavioral genetics because they permit us to make comparisons that suggest the genetic determination of traits.

11. *Heritability* is an estimate of the degree to which variance in a trait is due to genetics. Heritability estimates exceed 40 percent for all of the Big Five factors.

12. Genetic research helps us learn about the genetic basis of traits so that we can develop prevention and intervention strategies for problematic conditions.

13. *Evolutionary psychology* helps us understand that psychological mechanisms such as the Big Five evolve because they solve specific adaptive problems in human ancestral environments.

14. Factor analytic trait theories are excellent samples of scientific theories of personality.

---

## Suggestions for Further Reading

Cattell has been prolific, writing over thirty books and three hundred articles. His work is technical and difficult to digest. However, an introductory primer to his theory is provided in *The Scientific Analysis of Personality* (Aldine, 1965), which is not too technical and is aimed at a lay public. He also provided an update of his theory, which was published in L. A. Pervin's *Handbook of Personality* (Guilford, 1990).

Also readable and exciting because of the ethical issues that it raises is Cattell's *A New Morality from Science: Beyondism* (Pergamon, 1972). Beyond that the interested reader has a vast array of primary sources to choose from. Critical reviews of Cattell's work are found in S. B. Sells, "Structured measurement of personality and motivation: A review of contributions of Raymond B. Cattell," *Journal of Clinical Psychology,* 1959, *15,* 3–21, and L. R. Goldberg, "Explorer on the run," *Contemporary Psychology,* 1968, *13,* 617–619.

A good overview of the development of the Big Five is provided in L. R. Goldberg (1993), "The structure of phenotypic personality traits," *American Psychologist, 1,* 26–34. McCrae and Costa's work is most easily accessible in *Personality in Adulthood* (Guilford, 1990). For twin studies, the best sources are J. C. Loehlin, *Genes and Environment in Personality Development.* (Sage, 1992) and T. J. Bouchard, Jr. and P. Propping, *Twins as a Tool of Behavioral Genetics* (Wiley, 1993). For a statement of Buss's position, see "Evolutionary personality psychology" in *Annual Review of Psychology,* 1991, vol. 42, 459–491. The journal articles are difficult to read, but research in these areas is growing at such an incredible speed that it is necessary to read them to keep current with the field.

# Biological Traits

## HANS EYSENCK

### Your Goals for This Chapter

1. Describe some of the historical predecessors to Eysenck's theory.
2. Explain how Eysenck seeks to construct a model of personality.
3. Describe the superfactors that Eysenck has identified through factor analysis and compare them with those of Cattell and with the Big Five.
4. Describe how Eysenck measures traits.
5. Identify the hypothesized causal agents of *extraversion-introversion, emotional stability-neuroticism,* and *psychoticism* in Eysenck's theory.
6. Describe the biological basis of behavior and neurosis.
7. Discuss Eysenck's contribution to understanding intelligence.
8. Describe some of the applications of Eysenck's theory.
9. Evaluate Eysenck's theory in terms of its function as philosophy, science, and art.

I n his personality theory, Hans Eysenck seeks to go beyond the descriptive factor analytic concepts of Cattell and the Big Five to provide a model of personality that can be tested. He has done this by connecting *superfactors,* which he has identified through factor analysis, with psychophysical entities such as arousal and excitation. This model makes possible a great many testable hypotheses that may be verified through experimental procedures. Adamant about the need for psychology to follow the rigors of scientific procedure and to clearly specify how its concepts may be disproved through falsification, Eysenck is highly critical of dynamic, humanistic, existential, or phenomenal approaches to personality that do not affirm the primacy of experiment and falsifiable theory.

Highly outspoken and unafraid of controversy, Eysenck advocates a **biosocial** approach to personality, emphasizing biological and genetic factors as well as social and environmental ones. His superfactors are biological in nature and determined largely by genetic influences. They are the product of evolutionary forces. Thus Eysenck's work continues to focus on many of the interests that were introduced in Chapter 11.

## Biographical Background

Berlin, Germany, was the birthplace of Hans Eysenck, who was born on March 4, 1916. Germany was losing World War I, and many suffered from the mass unemployment, high inflation, and political turmoil that followed that loss. Thus the war had a significant impact on Eysenck as it had on Cattell; fewer than half of his school classmates reached middle age. His parents, well-known actors, divorced when he was two. He was raised by his maternal grandmother. Eysenck's father encouraged him to become an actor, but his mother dissuaded him and he followed her "more sensible" advice.

In school, Eysenck, a Lutheran, had been taunted with the label "white Jew" because he sympathized with the plight of the Jews. Eysenck left Germany at the age of eighteen. His hatred of the Nazi regime led him to study politics and become a socialist. Later he developed serious reservations about socialism and left the party, but continued to be interested in political issues.

After traveling around Europe, Eysenck settled in England and prepared to attend the University of London. Someone suggested he study the newly emerging science of psychology, to which Eysenck replied, "What on earth is psychology?" (1982). When assured, "You'll like it," he embarked on his distinguished career as a psychologist. Psychometrically oriented, the University of London was an exciting place to study psychology, and in 1940 Eysenck received the Ph.D.

Eysenck was hired as a research psychologist at Mill Hill Emergency Hospital. There, he independently conducted a study on the reliability of psychiatric diagnoses and prescribed treatments at the hospital. Eysenck's undercover research demonstrated that there was very little agreement among psychiatrists concerning diagnoses and treatment. Later, using factor analysis, Eysenck concluded that disorders could be embraced under two

*Hans Eysenck seeks to go beyond a descriptive
analysis to a causal analysis of personality.*

major personality factors: neuroticism and extraversion/introversion. His findings led him
to publish *Dimensions of Personality* (1947).

When World War II ended, Eysenck became director of the psychology department at Maudsley Hospital, the most prestigious teaching psychiatric hospital in England.
There he established a program of behavior therapy as well as a program of study that was
scientifically oriented and relied on the interdependence of clinical and experimental research. He also organized a behavior genetics division. In 1955, he was awarded a chair of
psychology at the University of London. In 1988, he was awarded the Distinguished Scientist Award of the American Psychological Association. At present he is a member of the
Board of Scientific Affairs of the American Psychological Association.

A prolific writer whose output exceeds even that of Cattell, Eysenck has written for
both technical and lay audiences. Most of his work has been in the area of individual differences. However, his diverse interests have led him to explore fields far different from simply the biological basis of traits and the experimental study of learning, memory, and
conditioning. He has written about psychopharmacology, sexual behavior, and the causes
and effects of smoking and heart attacks and other related problems, as well as the psychological study of ideology, media influences, extrasensory perception, and astrology. He has
not hesitated to criticize psychoanalysis, psychotherapy, and nonempirical theories of behavior. In turn, his theory has been both praised and denounced. In 1985 Eysenck retired,

but he continues to lecture, conduct research, and write on coronary heart disease and cancer, IQ, and the psychophysiology of the brain.

## Historical Predecessors

In describing his theory of personality, Eysenck readily acknowledges that the model that culminates in his own work is a structure that has been built by several bricklayers who have contributed to the slow, steady process of research into temperament and personality (1981).

One of the earliest efforts to describe personality in terms of dispositions was made by the Greek physician Hippocrates (460?–377? B.C.), who suggested that personalities could be classified according to a predominance of certain body fluids, or **humors,** which reflected the four elements of the cosmos. His position was elaborated upon by another Greek physician and writer, Galen (130?–200?). A predominance of blood led to a **sanguine** character, marked by sturdiness, high color, and cheerfulness. A predominance of mucus led to the slow, solid, and apathetic **phlegmatic** personality. A predominance of black bile led to the **melancholic** or depressed personality, whereas yellow bile infused the irascible and violent **choleric** personality.

Immanuel Kant, a German philosopher (1724–1804), updated and popularized Hippocrates' doctrine of the four temperaments in his *Anthropologie.* He organized them according to two basic comparisons: feelings and activity. Melancholic represented weak feelings; sanguine, strong feelings. Phlegmatic represented weak activity; choleric, strong activity. The primary difference between the views of Hippocrates, Galen, and Kant and those of contemporary theorists is that the earlier ones depicted *types* rather than *traits.* Types or **typologies** imply distinct, discrete, and separate categories into which an individual can be placed. **Traits** refer to continuous dimensions that individuals possess to varying degrees. Modern **trait theories** recognize that individuals vary considerably with regard to the same characteristic. For instance, we can speak of two types of statures, tall or short. Within any given population, however, we find a continuous gradation of statures between tall and short. Most of the population tends to fall in the middle area between extremes of height.

It was Wilhelm Wundt, the founder of the first psychological laboratory, who took the important step of changing categorical types into continuous dimensions. He suggested that the four temperaments exhibit high or low positions on two measures: changeability and emotionality. If we picture Wundt's two dimensions as two intersecting axes, with the four temperaments each situated in one of four quadrants, Wundt's two-dimensional depiction of personality anticipated Eysenck's model (see Figure 12.1).

Subsequently, Jung's depiction of two basic attitudes helped popularize the terms *extraversion* and *introversion* and link them with normal personality types. Jung also suggested a link between each of the attitudes and certain neurotic disorders. However, Eysenck believes that from the point of view of science, Jung's contribution to the study of personality types has been primarily negative, as he permitted mystical notions to override empirical data.

Ernest Kretschmer, a German psychiatrist (1888–1964), was also interested in normal personality types and their abnormal complements. However, he is best known for his

FIGURE 12.1    The Four Temperaments Along a Two-Dimensional Continuum

If we picture Wundt's dimensions of changeability and emotionality as two intersecting axes, the four temperaments are situated with one in each of the resulting four quadrants.

suggestion that people could be classified on the basis of their body measurements. Although Kretschmer's work was very influential, it was criticized because it was difficult to fit every individual into his framework.

William Sheldon (1899–1977), an American disciple of Kretschmer, described individuals in terms of traits based on physiques and temperaments (see Table 12.1). Sheldon's theory became very popular and continues to have some influence; it is also important because it marked the transition from earlier typologies and trait theories to a much more sophisticated approach to understanding personality. Sheldon laid the groundwork for and helped to create a significant movement in contemporary personality theory—*psychometric trait theory*—that found fruition in the work of Cattell and in the Big Five factor theory of personality (discussed in Chapter 11) and in Eysenck's approach, which is the focus of this chapter.

In surveying earlier efforts at characterizing temperaments that preceded his approach, Eysenck was impressed with a strong sense of historical continuity. Current work

TABLE 12.1    Sheldon's Relationships Among Components of Physique and Temperament

| PHYSIQUE | | TEMPERAMENT | |
|---|---|---|---|
| COMPONENT | DESCRIPTION | COMPONENT | DESCRIPTION |
| Endomorphy | Predominance of soft roundness | Visceratonia | General love of comfort, relaxation, sociability, people, and food |
| Mesomorphy | Predominance of muscle, bone, and connective tissue | Somatotonia | Tendency to seek action and power through bodily assertiveness |
| Ectomorphy | Predominance of linearity and fragility | Cerebrotonia | Predominance of restraint, inhibition, and concealment |

may be more comprehensive and developed with more sophisticated statistical methods under better controlled conditions, but it clearly continues an approach begun many centuries earlier. Earlier theories may strike us as quaint and outdated, and in many respects they are; however, they presaged many concepts in modern psychology and continue to influence personality theorizing.

# Constructing a Model of Personality

In Eysenck's view (1982), people are biosocial animals. He sees psychology as standing at the crossroads of the biological sciences (such as genetics, physiology, neurology, anatomy, biochemistry, and pharmacology) and the social sciences (history, sociology, anthropology, economics, sociometry, etc.). At the same time, he believes that psychology must become more of a true science. The academic study of human behavior must follow scientific methods of research and investigation to arrive at valid conclusions. Eysenck is committed to the classical hypothetical-deductive method of physics in which one begins with a hypothesis or tentative explanation from which can be deduced predictions with which to test the hypothesis. He points out that science constantly searches for proof—confirmation or disconfirmation through the consistent use of the experiment method or another appropriate method of testing. Many psychologists, however, simply engage in literature, writing about human nature but not in a manner that permits us to arrive at agreed-upon truths. Psychology must disengage itself from dynamic, humanistic, existential, phenomenal, or other approaches that deny the primacy of experiment and falsifiable theory. Such methods are pseudoscientific and do not follow the rigors of scientific procedure, which Eysenck seeks to apply to the study of personality.

Thus Eysenck insists on a strict, carefully delineated, scientific model of personality that focuses on two distinct aspects. The first is a description of personality derived from factor analytic studies. The second is a causal analysis based on experimental tests of deductions. This twofold approach reflects Eysenck's conviction that a model of personality must reflect the interaction of individual differences with the general normalities of human behavior (1981). Although it is possible to make general laws on the basis of observed regularities of human behavior, individuals behave differently in various situations. The laws of psychology need to reflect this interaction of individuality and generality.

In the past, experimental psychologists interested in establishing general laws and psychometricians interested in individual differences tended to go their own separate ways and to have little to do with each other. Eysenck believes that scientists in both areas need to work together cooperatively in order to develop a scientific psychology. Experimental psychology must understand individual differences in order to recognize and distinguish which responses in an experiment are due to the manipulation of an independent variable and which are due to individual differences in reaction to the same situation. Unless they can make this distinction, experimenters may mistakenly believe that varying responses invalidate the effects of the independent variable when they are actually due to individual differences. Psychologists who wish to explore individual differences need to use the concepts and methods of experimental psychology as tools to enable them to build a theoretical structure that links both approaches. By themselves, factor analytic studies cannot discover the cause of the factors they identify. They can simply give birth to further correlational studies. The only way out of this circle is to introduce outside criteria based on other theories that seek to identify the cause of the factors. Most such theories of causation will come from the area of experimental research. Using the tools of experimental psychology will permit personality theorists to make predictions that can be tested and thus make possible the development of a causal theory of personality. Thus psychometrics and experimental studies can complement and support each other; they can actively cooperate to develop a scientific model of personality.

Theories must consider the results of both correlational and experimental studies in making predictions and must carefully spell out the precise conditions under which a predicted event will occur. For example, what specific intensity and duration of stimuli is needed in order for the expected results to occur? Will the results vary with people of different personality temperaments? Under conditions of low stimulation, introverts may be more highly aroused than extraverts, but under high stimulation, the opposite may be true. Without specifying the exact measurements and conditions, we may not be able to interpret the results of an experiment. We may be misled into thinking that a theory has been falsified, when, in fact, the problem was with one of the conditions. The failure of a single prediction should not lead to a hasty abandonment of an entire theory but rather to a rethinking of the process and the conditions under which the predicted result was expected to occur. Scientific theories should not be abandoned simply because anomalies exist; they should only be abandoned when a better theory is available (1981).

Thus Eysenck is not troubled by the fact that his theory frequently encounters deviations from the expected predictions. The existence of such anomalies shows that the theory is scientific because it is subject to error and open to correction. "[W]hatever my model may be lacking, it certainly does not lack the quality of falsifiability" (1981). As part of the normal process of scientific development, a theory must take into account irregularities as they occur and account for them within the theory. When his model has failed to hold up under experimental testing, Eysenck has revised it. Thus when his preliminary attempt to develop a causal theory based primarily on a neural model of inhibition and excitation was experimentally disconfirmed he changed it to a biological model of arousal.

The steps that Eysenck has taken in constructing and revising a model of personality may be summarized as follows: (1) He hypothesizes the relationship between various personality traits. (2) He conducts factor analytic studies to identify clusters of traits that indicate underlying superfactors. (3) He constructs a biological theory to account for the behaviors associated with the underlying superfactors. (4) He generates hypotheses from the theory concerning specific testable psychophysical, neurological, or hormonal components. (5) He then conducts experimental studies to validate the theoretical prediction. (6) He revises the theory where needed in light of the results of the experimental studies. The following discussion will clarify these procedures.

## The Identification of Superfactors

Eysenck draws from biology, historical typologies, learning theory, factor analysis, and experimental studies in order to understand personality. He uses factor analysis in his work, but his use of it is more deductive than that of Cattell. In Cattell's research, conclusions were drawn from the clusters that appeared in the process of factoring. Eysenck begins with a clear hypothesis about possible underlying variables and then uses statistical analysis to test his hypothesis. Moreover, Eysenck considers factor analysis at best a preliminary tool that paves the way for subsequent laboratory and experimental research to gain a causal understanding of the factors that have been posited. As he stated to Richard Evans,

> I think probably of all of the factor analysts you may know, I'm the one who thinks the least of it. I regard it as a valuable adjunct, a technique that was invaluable under certain circumstances, but one which we must leave behind as soon as possible in order to get a proper causal type of understanding of the factors and to know just what they mean. (Evans, 1976)

As we have seen, Eysenck is extraordinarily rigorous in his adherence to a scientific method and outspokenly critical of nonscientific or prescientific theories of personality.

## The Hierarchical Model of Personality

Eysenck defines personality as "a more or less stable and enduring organization of a person's character, temperament, intellect, and physique which determines his unique adjustment to the environment" (1970). Eysenck views personality as a hierarchy (see Figure 12.2). At the bottom of the hierarchy are *specific responses,* behaviors that we can actually observe, such as someone answering a phone. The next level is that of *habitual responses,* clusters of specific behaviors that characteristically recur in similar circumstances, such as buying groceries or giving parties. Above this are more generalized traits, clusters of related habitual

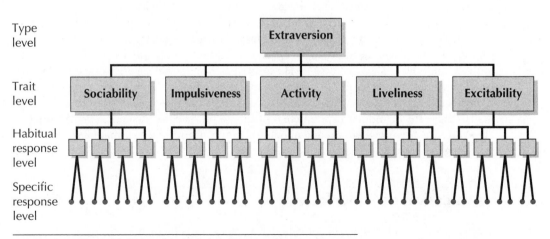

FIGURE 12.2    Eysenck's Hierarchical Model of Personality Development

*(From H. J. Eysenck,* The Biological Basis of Personality, *1967, Courtesy of Charles C. Thomas, Publisher, Springfield, Illinois.)*

responses such as the source traits that Cattell identified. At the top of the hierarchy, related clusters of traits make up broad general dimensions or basic types, such as extraversion or introversion. Eysenck's research has focused on the identification of these superfactors. Moreover, he has sought not only to describe behavior in terms of basic typologies but also to understand the causal factors behind the behavior.

When Eysenck conducted a review of temperament theories, he observed that there were distinct patterns in the various typologies that had been used throughout history to describe personality. He sought to test the hypothesis that the behavior included in Hippocrates' ancient typology could be accounted for by two fundamental personality dimensions or superfactors: introversion versus extraversion and emotionality versus stability.

The **extraversion versus introversion** dimension reflects the degree to which a person is outgoing and participative in relating to other people. Extraversion-introversion is a continuous dimension that varies among individuals. Some people tend to be friendly, impulsive, and talkative whereas others tend to be reserved, quiet, and shy. These dimensions are similar to Jung's two basic attitudes.

The **emotionality versus stability** dimension refers to an individual's adjustment to the environment and the stability of his or her behavior over time. Some people tend to be well integrated and emotionally stable, while others tend to be poorly integrated, emotionally unpredictable, and neurotic. In Eysenck and Rachman's (1965) words: "At the one end we have people whose emotions are labile, strong and easily aroused; they are moody, touchy, anxious, restless, and so forth. At the other extreme we have the people whose emotions are stable, less easily aroused, people who are calm, even-tempered, carefree, and reliable." In both dimensions, most people fall somewhere in the middle of the two extremes. Eysenck suggests that these basic dimensions of personality may be summarized as shown in Figure 12.3. The inner circle shows Hippocrates' four temperaments. The outer ring shows the results of factor analysis studies of the intercorrelations among traits. The traits, which are on a continuum, clearly reflect the two fundamental dimensions of emotional security versus neuroticism and introversion versus extraversion.

Following his research in the first two superfactors, Eysenck investigated a third one: **psychoticism** (see Figure 12.4). Psychoticism is usually characterized by the loss or distortion of reality and the inability to distinguish between reality and fantasy. The person may have disturbances in thought, emotion, and motor behavior, as well as hallucinations or delusions. The psychoticism factor also includes some degree of psychopathy: disorders characterized by asocial and impulsive behavior, egocentricity, and an absence of guilt (Eysenck & Eysenck, 1976) Unlike the dimensions of extraversion/introversion and emotionality/stability, psychoticism is not a dimension with an opposite pole; rather, it is an ingredient present in varying degrees in individuals.

It is important to clarify that the personality dimensions of emotional stability-neuroticism and psychoticism merely indicate that one has a leaning in certain directions, a *constitutional predisposition;* they do not imply the psychiatric illnesses will actually come about. Other prerequisite conditions, such as possible additional genetic factors (Eysenck, 1976) and sufficient environmental stressors (Eysenck, 1994b), would have to be present for a disorder to develop. Moreover, psychotic disorders are very different from neurotic disorders. Eysenck does not believe that neuroticism and psychoticism exist on a continuum. There are different routes to each of these conditions. A person may become more and more neurotic without becoming psychotic.

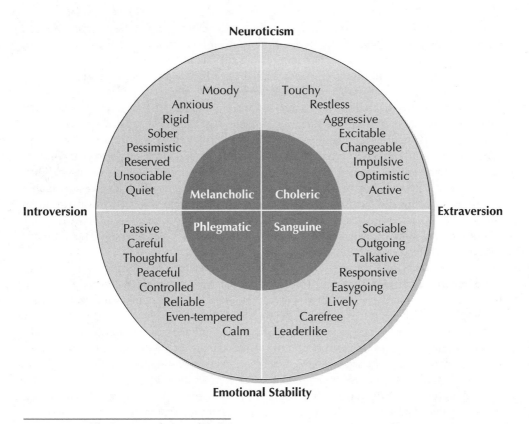

**Neuroticism**

Introversion

Extraversion

Moody
Anxious
Rigid
Sober
Pessimistic
Reserved
Unsociable
Quiet

Touchy
Restless
Aggressive
Excitable
Changeable
Impulsive
Optimistic
Active

Melancholic    Choleric

Phlegmatic    Sanguine

Passive
Careful
Thoughtful
Peaceful
Controlled
Reliable
Even-tempered
Calm

Sociable
Outgoing
Talkative
Responsive
Easygoing
Lively
Carefree
Leaderlike

**Emotional Stability**

FIGURE 12.3    The Intercorrelation of Traits

The inner circle shows Hippocrates' four temperaments. The outer ring shows the results
of factor analysis studies of the intercorrelations between traits done by Eysenck and
others.

Eysenck originally conceived of extraversion as a blend of sociability and impul-
sivity. When he developed the idea of psychoticism, however, he transferred several impul-
sivity items from extraversion to psychoticism.

Although environmental factors have a significant role to play, Eysenck believes
that individual differences in the three major superfactors are primarily due to genetic determinants. Recognizing a genetic basis for personality dimensions implies that they are
universal. Thus we can expect that they may be found in the animal kingdom, as well as in
the human domain. We can also predict that the temperaments tend to be stable throughout an individual's life. We can further anticipate that they appear throughout history and
in cross-cultural studies and that they surface in all types of various personality inventories
and measures. Empirical studies give support to all of these hypotheses (Eysenck, 1985).
"Identical factors have been found cross culturally in over 35 different countries covering
most of the globe, from Uganda and Nigeria to Japan and mainland China, from the Capi-

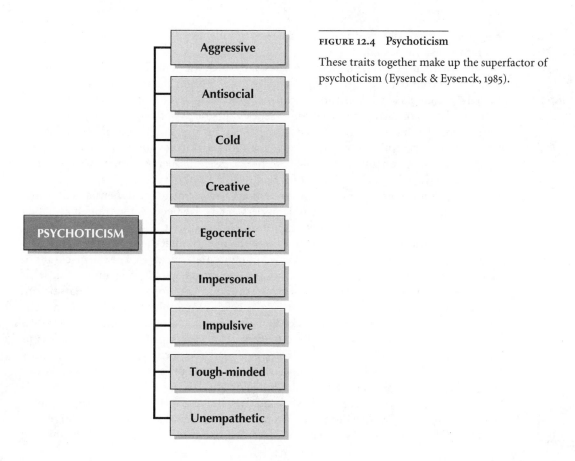

**FIGURE 12.4   Psychoticism**

These traits together make up the superfactor of psychoticism (Eysenck & Eysenck, 1985).

talist countries of the West and the American continent to Eastern-bloc countries such as the Soviet Union, Hungary, Czechoslovakia, Bulgaria, and Yugoslavia" (Barrett & Eysenck, 1994). "Such cross cultural unanimity would be unlikely if biological factors did not play a predominant part" (Eysenck, 1990).

## Comparisons with Cattell and the Big Five

There are some significant differences between the theories of Eysenck and Cattell. Cattell's theory is primarily concerned with traits, Eysenck prefers to emphasize supertraits. Eysenck also believes that Cattell gives too much importance and value to factor analysis. Whereas factor analysis is a useful tool for suggesting clusters, there is a great deal of subjectivity involved in the use of the technique. Factor analysis basically tells us how many dimensions we need to accommodate items that are related to one another. However, just as the lines of longitude and latitude drawn on a map to help us identify specific cities and places are arbitrary, the exact position of axes on which items are identified in factor analysis is also chosen rather than mandated.

In many respects, the factor theories of Eysenck and Cattell are quite similar. However, Cattell considers the scope of personality to be broader than does Eysenck. Further, Cattell's sixteen personality factors are *oblique,* which is to say that the various factors may also correlate with each other, whereas Eysenck's superfactors are *orthogonal,* or without further correlations. Indeed, Eysenck's supertraits, introversion-extraversion and emotional stability-neuroticism are essentially the same as further intercorrelations among Cattell's sixteen personality traits, which produce a lesser number of orthogonal or second-order factors. Cattell criticizes Eysenck for limiting the scope of personality in his questionnaire items, but Eysenck notes that those questions are specific to the dimensions they seek to assess and do not represent the whole of personality. He believes the traits that Cattell stresses are more limited than his own superfactors (1972a).

Eysenck agrees with the champions of the Big Five that the most important traits are supertraits that can be further subdivided into more specific ones. The Big Five traits of extraversion versus introversion and emotionality versus stability are quite similar to Eysenck's dimensions of introversion-extraversion and emotional stability-neuroticism. Goldberg (1993) suggests that Big Five measures of low Agreeableness and high Conscientiousness or will to achieve are aspects of Eysenck's dimension of psychoticism-normality.

Eysenck would have us believe that the relative merit of these positions has to come from a realm other than that of factor analysis. When experimental research shows that a relationship can be found between a trait and a psychophysical measure, "then we can begin to think that this factor has a claim to reality and is more than just a statistical artifact" (1982). Thus Eysenck seeks to go beyond Cattell's descriptive theory by developing a testable theory of individual differences. In this sense, he would applaud those who seek to establish links between the Five Factor Model and causal mechanisms that exist within the person.

## The Measurement of Traits

Before taking a look at Eysenck's efforts to develop a causal theory, we need to consider how traits are measured. Accurate measurement is an important component of both the descriptive and the causal aspects of Eysenck's work. Without reliable and accurate ways of quantifying concepts, we are not able to translate them into adequate operational procedures. Eysenck has been very active in developing appropriate measures for quantifying his concepts.

Traits can be measured in several ways. People can be asked to rate themselves, providing answers to a paper-and-pencil questionnaire or in a structured interview. Psychologists can rate others through the use of controlled observation in a naturalistic setting or in an arranged specific one. A researcher can set up an experiment in real life or in the laboratory. The specific technique chosen must fit the requirements of the theory, the situation, and the participant. Thus one would not give a questionnaire to a two-year-old but would rely on parental ratings or controlled observation. In general, a combination of methods is used to ensure greater reliability and validity.

Personality inventory questionnaires became very popular during the first part of this century. A number of them were developed to measure characteristics such as intelligence, emotional instability, and extraversion/introversion. Eysenck (1957) was critical of early ratings and inventories used in personality assessment. He observed that inventory constructors have mistakenly assumed that individuals answer questions truthfully. In some cases, people deliberately answer a question falsely to avoid being judged in a negative way. Moreover, people do not always know the truth about themselves. In one experiment, 98 percent of the subjects "claimed to have a better than average sense of humor" (1957). The fact is that in a normal bell-shaped curve, about 50 percent of the population score in the average range.

The problem with personality inventories stems from the fact that there is no objective outside criterion against which to make measurements. Eysenck (1957) notes that psychologists were able to overcome some of the difficulties involved in questionnaires when they gave up the notion of *interpreting* the answers and simply dealt "with the objective fact that a person puts a mark on one part of the paper rather than in another."

Eysenck constructed improved personality inventory questionnaires using a method that he calls **criterion analysis.** He begins with a hypothesis concerning a possible underlying variable, for instance, emotional stability versus neuroticism. He then identifies two criterion groups: a group of people who have been clearly identified as emotionally stable and another group who have been identified as neurotic. He gives each group of questionnaire and observes how many yes and no answers there are in each group to each question. If it is clear that there is a greater tendency for one group to answer a particular question in the affirmative or negative, then that question may be a good item for distinguishing between the two groups.

Eysenck makes it clear that he is not concerned with the *reasons* for the answers, but simply the fact that there are significant differences in the two groups' answers. By studying the differences in answers to multiple questions, it is possible to determine probabilities and develop a questionnaire that will distinguish between the two groups and rank each individual along a continuum. The use of criterion groups helps to show how sensitive a question is to a particular variable, such as emotional stability versus neuroticism. The approach is strictly empirical and makes use of complex statistical analysis.

Contemporary questionnaires and rating procedures are much more sophisticated and more carefully constructed than earlier ones. Tested by complex statistical studies and experimentation, and with careful procedures for establishing reliability and validity, the resulting instruments can be useful tools for the psychologist who wishes to measure personality. Eysenck has constructed a number of paper and pencil self-report inventories to measure the dimension of introversion/extraversion. Among them are the Maudsley Personality Inventory, the Eysenck Personality Inventory, and the Eysenck Personality Questionnaire. These inventories have been used in an extraordinarily large number of research projects.

## Constructing Questionnaire Items for Personality Research

It is not an easy task to develop questions that will distinguish among people in different groups. Here are some sample questions for Extraversion, Neuroticism, and Psychoticism from the Eysenck Personality Questionnaire-Revised.

1. Do you usually take the initiative in making new friends?
2. Does your mood often go up and down?
3. Do you prefer to go your own way rather than act by the rules?
4. Are you mostly quiet when you are with other people?
5. Are your feelings easily hurt?
6. Do you take much notice of what people think?
7. Can you easily get some life into a rather dull party?
8. Are you a worrier?
9. Would you like other people to be afraid of you?

The following personality dimensions are indicated if specific questions are answered in the ways shown: Extraversion: 1-Yes, 4-No, 7-Yes; Neuroticism: 2-Yes, 5-Yes, 8-Yes; Psychoticism: 3-Yes, 6-No, 9-Yes.

Try your hand at developing discriminating questions. Come up with your own questions for each of the three variables. Use as your criterion group for each variable people whose answers for all of the sample items of the EPQ-R are indicative of that variable. How do your items measure up? Do they provide a useful indicator of that variable? Obviously, this exercise will only provide you with a very general notion of how difficult it is to construct adequate personality inventories. *The questions are taken from Personality and Individual Differences, 6, Eysenck, S. B. G., Eysenck, H. J., & Barrett, P. A revised version of the psychoticism scale, 21–29. Copyright 1985, with permission from Elsevier Science.*

## Looking for Causal Agents of Behavior

In his discussion of personality, Eysenck has gone beyond a descriptive analysis to a *causal* analysis that hypothesizes the agents that may cause certain behavior patterns.

In his early descriptive research, Eysenck pointed out that individuals differ in the reactivity of their brains and central nervous systems and in the speed with which they develop conditioned responses. His first causal explanation (1957) traced the difference between extraversion and introversion to variations in central nervous system levels of inhibition and excitation. He suggested that individuals with weak excitatory and strong inhibitory potentials are likely to become extraverted, whereas individuals with strong excitatory and weak inhibitory potentials are likely to become introverted. In extraverts, their less sensitive, less aroused, and more inhibitory brain processes require them to look for continual outside stimuli in order to overcome their own passivity. These individuals are insensitive to low-intensity stimulation because their strong inhibitory processes suppress it. They need to seek more stimulation and can tolerate much higher levels of it before their cortical processes act protectively to inhibit further increases. On the other hand, the more sensitive, more aroused, and less inhibitory introvert needs to withdraw from the outside world in order to avoid being overwhelmed. These individuals are quickly satiated at rather low levels of stimulation.

Clark Hull's drive theory (briefly described in Chapter 8) helped to clarify the relationship between excitation and inhibition. As drives intensify, reinforced learned habits are strengthened. However, responses that are continuously repeated lead to a type of neural fatigue and to inhibition that lowers the effect of the original drive. Eysenck (1964) describes how you can experience this inhibition by tapping your index fingers as rapidly as possible. In a little while, one of your fingers will take an "involuntary rest pause," interrupting the rhythm for just a brief fraction of a second.

Relating the relationship between excitation and inhibition to extraversion and introversion, Eysenck predicted that introverts can be more readily conditioned than extraverts because they have a higher drive (excitatory processes) and weaker inhibitory processes. This prediction was tested by Frank (1956), who found that introverts could be more easily conditioned to blink an eye in response to a tone. However, subsequent efforts to replicate Frank's findings were unsuccessful, leading Eysenck (1967) to specify additional parameters that must be met in order for the predicted result to occur. This is just one example of anomalies that have arisen in the course of trying to test his theory. Such anomalies led Eysenck to develop further conditional explanations that complicate his original position. However, they also led to his second causal model.

In 1967, Eysenck revised his theory and hypothesized that specific biological functions were responsible for excitation and inhibition. This second explanation traced the difference between extraversion and introversion to levels of cortical arousal and the difference between emotional stability and neuroticism to levels of visceral brain activity.

Eysenck (1967) suggests that introversion-extraversion is related to arousal thresholds in the ascending reticular activating system (RAS) of the brain and that emotional stability-neuroticism is related to differences in visceral brain (VB) activation (see Figure 12.5). The primary function of the RAS is to regulate levels of arousal ranging from sleep to states of high alertness. Destruction of these tissues causes an animal to sleep almost continuously, whereas stimulation will cause it to become more aroused. Thus the RAS controls the brain's level of excitability and its responsiveness to stimuli.

Eysenck believes that intraverts may have higher levels of RAS reactivity than extraverts. Thus, given identical stimulating conditions, the state of arousal would be higher in introverts than in extraverts. The high level of arousal may create a constraint on their behavior and contribute to the specific traits, such as reserved and careful, that generally characterize introverts. In the same way, the low levels of arousal experienced by extraverts may lead to an absence of constraints and a predominance of impulsive and outgoing behavior normally associated with extraversion.

Eysenck hypothesizes that emotional stability versus neuroticism is due to differences in visceral brain activity. The visceral brain includes the limbic system and the hypothalamus, which are both involved in motivation and emotional behavior. They exert their influence through the autonomic or involuntary nervous system. Eysenck theorizes that individuals who have a low threshold of visceral brain activation—and thus are readily vis-

FIGURE 12.5   The Reticular Activating System and the Visceral Brain

The anatomical structures that Eysenck hypothesizes may be responsible for inherited differences in introversion-extraversion and emotional stability-neuroticism.

cerally aroused—may be very emotional in their behavior and more susceptible to neurotic disorders. In short, Eysenck suggests that there is a causal connection between biological functions of the brain and the basic personality dimensions of emotional stability-neuroticism and introversion-extraversion.

The 1967 theory of the biological basis for introversion-extraversion placed the emphasis on excitation rather than inhibition. This emphasis led to a shift in efforts to test the model away from the hypothesized effects of inhibition and toward the effects of RAS arousal. McLaughlin and Eysenck (1967) offered a test of the new model by combining it with the Yerkes-Dodson law of motivation and performance. The Yerkes-Dodson law maintains that the relationship between motivation and performance is curvilinear. As motivation increases, performance increases until an optimal point is reached, after which increasing motivation decreases performance. Optimal performance generally occurs at moderate levels of arousal. You can confirm this from your own experience. Without sufficient motivation, we will simply not put forth the effort to accomplish a task; however, too much pressure may lead to such a high level of motivation that it actually interferes with our performance. The relationship between motivation and performance also varies with the difficulty of the task. A higher level of motivation may be required to complete a very simple task in order to sustain concentration and avoid boredom. A lower level of motivation leads to better performance on a very difficult, complicated task.

McLaughlin and Eysenck (1967) predicted that, given a very difficult task, stable extraverts would have the strongest performance and neurotic introverts would have the weakest; the high level of arousal and motivation of the introvert would interfere with successful task performance, whereas the low arousal and motivation of the extravert would facilitate it. The researchers made predictions for the other types as well and for varying levels of task difficulty. They sorted participants by the four types and gave them either an easy or a difficult learning task that involved paired nonsense syllables. On the whole, the results were as predicted, sustaining Eysenck's theory of arousal, especially in reference to the stable extraverts. However, another irregularity arose. Normal introverts did not do as well as neurotic ones. Even though the difference was not statistically significant, it raised further questions provoking additional clarification of the theory.

As noted early in this chapter, one of the strengths of Eysenck's model of personality is his willingness to adjust his theory so that it specifies the exact conditions under which certain generalizations are true. Eysenck's theory allows for specific prediction and test. For example, if introverts have strong excitatory brain processes and relatively weak inhibitory effects, they should and do react more quickly in certain structured laboratory situations such as eye-blink conditioning (Eysenck & Rachman, 1965). Electrocardiogram studies and other electrophysiological studies also lend some support to Eysenck's theory (1970). It has even been possible to indicate introversion or extraversion by comparing the amount of salivation produced when lemon juice is applied to someone's tongue with the amount created without lemon juice. Introverts produce considerably more salivation than extraverts (Corcoran, 1964). This suggests that the same physiological functions control both salivation characteristics and introversion-extraversion characteristics. Research has also shown that introverts are more sensitive to stimulant drugs while extraverts are more sensitive to depressant drugs (1970).

Eysenck's theory that reticular activating system arousal can account for the differences in the reactions of extraverts and introverts continues to garner support from other scholars (e.g., Bullock & Gilliland, 1993). Some researchers, however, attribute the differences in reactions to brain mechanisms other than the reticular activating system (Stelmack, 1990).

It has been more difficult to develop a causal theory for psychoticism than for introversion-extraversion and emotional stability-neuroticism. Efforts to identify the biological factors that underlie the superfactor of psychoticism are still very preliminary. However, Eysenck (1982) believes that psychoticism may be related to a person's sex-hormone balance. Androgens are present to a considerably lesser degree in women than in men. Men in general receive higher scores on measures for psychoticism. As a group, criminals and psychopaths also score high on measures for psychoticism, and this group for the most part is male. Prior to menopause (at which point their androgen levels increase), women are less likely to become schizophrenic than are men. Schizophrenics and people who score high on psychoticism have lower levels of serotonin, a chemical neurotransmitter in the brain. These factors led Eysenck to suspect that psychoticism may be traced to hormonal differences and variations in neurotransmitter levels. Nevertheless, research in these areas, asso-

## The Lemon Test

You can get some rough measures of introversion-extraversion and develop a greater appreciation for the underlying physiological functions of Eysenck's superfactors by trying this simplified version of the lemon test developed by Corcoran (1964). Tie a length of thread to the center of a double-tipped cotton swab so that when you hold it by the string the swab hangs perfectly horizontally.

Swallow three times and immediately put one end of the cotton swab onto your tongue. Hold it in your mouth for thirty seconds. Remove the swab and put four drops of lemon juice on your tongue. Swallow and immediately place the other end of the swab on the same spot in your mouth. Hold it there for thirty seconds and then let the swab hang.

If you are an extravert, the swab will remain close to horizontal. If you are an introvert, one end will hang down noticeably, indicating that you produced a large amount of saliva in response to the lemon juice.

Try this with several participants whom you have previously identified as introverts or extraverts and compare your results. The lemon test is predicated on the assumption that the same physiological functions control both salivation characteristics and introversion/extraversion characteristics. What other physiological characteristics can you come up with that may also be controlled by the same functions that control introversion-extraversion, and what kind of predictions can you make that could be tested?

---

ciating the superfactor of psychoticism with hormones and neurotransmitters, is very preliminary.

It is important to remember that Eysenck's theory is speculative. He does not describe the actual workings of the brain. He acknowledged that his hypothesis "must stand and fall by empirical confirmation" (1965). In the past twenty-five years there has been enormous growth in research on the biochemistry of the brain and its functions. It is possible that some major personality dimensions have biochemical roots and may someday be explained in those terms.

### The Biological Basis of Behavior and Neurosis

Tying both dimensions of introversion-extraversion and emotional stability-neuroticism to biological bases permitted Eysenck to distinguish among four extreme types of personality based on the particular combination of the processes of reticular activating system arousal and visceral brain activation. These four types are summarized in Figure 12.6.

Because introverts have sensitive nervous systems, Eysenck believes that they are more easily civilized. The ease with which they become conditioned also makes them more vulnerable to anxiety-based neuroses, which are conditioned emotional responses. Extraverts, on the other hand, have less sensitive and more inhibitive cortical processes; they

**Visceral Brain Activation**

FIGURE 12.6    **The Biological Basis of Personality**

Tying his dimensions to biological bases permitted Eysenck to distinguish among four types of personality. *(SOURCE: Based on information in H. J. Eysenck,* The Biological Basis of Personality. *Springfield, Ill.: Charles C. Thomas, 1967.)*

seek additional stimulation and are slow to develop conditioned responses. Because socialized behavior depends largely on a well-conditioned conscience developed in childhood, extraverts are more likely to develop psychopathic disorders. Thus Eysenck suggested that neurotics become so because their cortical and emotional states interfere with the learning of appropriate responses or facilitate the learning of maladaptive ones. Neuroticism could be viewed as excessive stimulation discharged by the visceral brain, leading to a high degree of emotionality that may combine with an extremely high or low cortical arousal of the reticular activating system to form a particular neurosis.

Behavior itself is not inherited; certain structures of the nervous system are. The phenotype, the individual's observable appearance and behavior, arises out of the genotype's interaction with the environment. Figure 12.7 diagrams the hypothesized chain of events that leads from the genotype to the phenotype. The genotype evolves into inherited anatomical structures, which include the cortex, the autonomic nervous system, the ascending reticular activating system, and the visceral brain. Individuals differ widely in the particulars of these structures. These differences lead to the development of different habitual levels of arousal and thresholds for emotional response, which can be seen in laboratory experiments. Through interactions with a particular environment, these tendencies lead to the various emotionally stable or unstable, introverted or extraverted phenotypic patterns of behavior and primary traits that have been identified through factor analysis (1970). Expressed in a formula, $P_B = P_C \times E$, "Behavioral personality equals the constitutional personality times environment."

The distinction between the genotype and the phenotype is an important one. Eysenck is not suggesting that genes determine the outcome for any given individual. Genes are not certain predictors for specific patterns of behavior or development. Many genes express themselves only under certain conditions. Our genetic predispositions are affected by the specific experiences we have from conception onward.

FIGURE 12.7    The Personality Phenotype

A diagram of the interplay between genotype and environment, which leads to the phenotype of extraverted-introverted personality. *(SOURCE: H. J. Eysenck,* The Structure of Human Personality, *London: Methuen & Co. Ltd., 1970, p. 456. Copyright H. J. Eysenck, 1970.)*

Thus, even though people differ in the extent to which they are genetically predisposed to neurosis, Eysenck believes that neurotic behaviors themselves are learned. In this respect he shares similar views with the behavior and learning theorists on the origin and treatment of neurotic disorders and is a staunch advocate of behavior therapy. However, his recognition of the biological basis of personality is also consistent with biological therapies: physical or chemical interventions, such as drugs, may affect the brain or other body functions and thus provoke or inhibit certain behaviors.

## Intelligence

A final superfactor that Eysenck believes plays a major role in personality is *intelligence*. Intelligence is not always considered a personality trait or discussed in the context of temperament. However, it is a dimension of personality that is generally considered to be very significant. Indeed, Eysenck has written, "If we were reduced to describing a person in just three figures, then I have no doubt that we would get the closest approximation to his real nature by using these figures for an assessment of his intelligence, his extroversion, and his neuroticism" (1965).

From Francis Galton's early unsuccessful efforts to develop tests of intelligence based on head size, muscular strength, and visual acuity, the efforts to define and measure intelligence accurately and fairly have been fraught with difficulties. Eysenck (1994a) distinguishes between *biological intelligence,* the physiological, neurological, and anatomical bases of intelligence, and *psychometric intelligence,* the numerical measure designed to reflect intelligence. Psychometric intelligence is generally defined in terms of **IQ.** It is made up of Spearman's *g* factor, the general factor with which other measures of intelligence tend to correlate highly, and various primary factors that have been identified subsequently by Thurstone (1948), Guilford (1967), and others. Psychometric intelligence is largely due to biological intelligence, but it is also influenced by environmental and social factors. It is clear that there are biological bases to intelligence because of the clear genetic origins of individual differences in this area. Eysenck mentions that we sometimes also refer to *practical* or *social intelligence,* the successful application of one's intelligence to life experiences. Practical intelligence depends on many other factors beyond IQ. In general, practical intelligence is too broad a concept to be scientifically helpful. Thus Eysenck primarily emphasizes the biological and psychometric definitions of intelligence and tries to relate them to personality using a theoretical-experimental model. He believes that his efforts to connect these concepts of intelligence experimentally will be more fruitful than limiting the discussion to a theoretical psychometric approach, as was done previously.

It is generally believed that the psychometric measure of intelligence is not correlated with personality. Earlier studies that tried to develop a correlation were unsuccessful. Eysenck (1994a) believes they were doomed to failure from the start because they were based on a "simple blunderbuss approach" in which correlations were made at random without any preliminary a priori hypothesis.

Factor analysis studies of personality and of intelligence test scales generally result in a number of factors that appear to be independent because the analysis is limited to single dimensions. But if we look for personality factors in groups varying in intelligence or for intelligence factors in groups varying in specific personality dimensions, we are able to discover some interesting relations.

There are a number of different variables that, if carefully sorted and specified in advance, begin to indicate a relationship between intelligence and personality. One such variable is work speed. When tests are timed, extraverts have an advantage, whereas in extended tasks, introverts, characterized with higher cortical arousal, can be more careful and less constrained. When a test is administered over a long period of time, the performance of extraverts declines toward the end of the testing period. This is not to say that introverts and extraverts differ in their total IQ scores but that different test administration conditions affect them differently, especially those relating to time pressures.

A second variable is cognitive style. The cognitive style of extraverts tends to be faster, less accurate, and less reflective than that of introverts. This difference in cognitive style becomes more apparent as the task to be performed becomes more ambiguous. Howard and McKillen (1990) successfully tested this hypothesis by administering a perceptual maze test under ambiguous and unambiguous conditions. Their study was characterized by the careful construction of a specific hypothesis, the development of appropriate measures relating to well-delineated aspects of both personality and intelligence, and a focus on how the problem was solved rather than simply on the solution itself.

We can conclude from such studies that intelligence is not related to personality per se but that performance on IQ tests may be related to personality variables. However, simple attempts to correlate a personality test with an IQ measure will not be successful. It is necessary to deduce hypotheses from well-established theories of performance and develop experimental conditions to test them. Global IQ scores must be separated into distinct factors such as mental speed, persistence, and error checking. Each of these can be correlated with separate aspects of personality, such as extraversion-introversion and emotional stability-neuroticism. Conditions must be arranged to test for the differentiated parameters. Eysenck believes that this approach—combining psychometrics with experimental psychology—will prove more promising for the study of intelligence (1994a).

Because intelligence has a clear genetic basis, it must also have a biological basis, which would account for differences between individuals. Eysenck believes that the physiological mechanism for intelligence is related to *evoked potential*. Sensory (such as auditory or visual) stimulation activates neurons that send messages to the nervous system, causing electrical activity in the brain. This electrical activity, or evoked potential, can be measured by an electroencephalogram, a simple noninvasive procedure in which electrodes are placed on the skull, a stimulus is presented, and the evoked potential is recorded in terms of waves or cycles per second. These waves vary in complexity. More complex evoked potential patterns are present in people of high intelligence; those with lower intelligence show simpler evoked potential patterns. These variations are evidently due to the frequency of errors made within the brain in transmitting the incoming messages provoked by the stimulus. Low rates of error are associated with more complex evoked potential patterns. Simpler evoked potential patterns are associated with higher error rates. Eysenck believes that as information is relayed through the cortex, errors may occur at the synapses. The tendency to make errors contributes to a low IQ, whereas a low tendency to make errors contributes to a high IQ. Eysenck also anticipates that high-IQ individuals have shorter reaction and inspection times (Eysenck & Eysenck, 1985). It is important to note that all of these expectations can be formulated into hypotheses, which can then be subjected to experimental test.

Eysenck believes that his work with evoked potential has revolutionized the field of intelligence research, although much remains to be done (1982). In time, Eysenck hopes we can develop a simple physiological reaction test that can measure intelligence with the same accuracy and validity as more complex IQ tests. Such a direct physiological measure of intelligence would help us to avoid the cultural bias that has haunted the history of test development and to ensure fairness in selection processes that currently employ measures of intelligence.

# Applications of Eysenck's Theory

Eysenck's research has the potential for considerable social applications. Eysenck believes that a scientific model of personality can help us to accurately predict social behaviors in light of various personality constructs. Figure 12.8 outlines the causal steps entailed in making such predictions.

## Education

One area in which Eysenck's research, especially that on intelligence and performance, has significant implications is education. Teachers have long recognized that children's personalities influence their responses to the classroom situation and to the particular method of teaching that is used.

Most innovations in education and other areas, such as criminal justice, are initially welcomed with enthusiasm but quickly discarded once it appears that they are no more successful than those that preceded them. The problem, Eysenck (1996) points out, is that they are not tested in a manner that clearly establishes the conditions under which they will succeed. All individuals are exposed to the new method under the assumption that it will have the same effect on everyone. This assumption, however, is unfounded. The laws of psychology must pertain to individuals, not simply to a general model of a person, as though people were clones of one another.

For example, in education there has been considerable debate over the merits of *discovery* learning, in which students are encouraged to explore for themselves and to construct facts and theories rather than having concepts formally presented to them as in *re-*

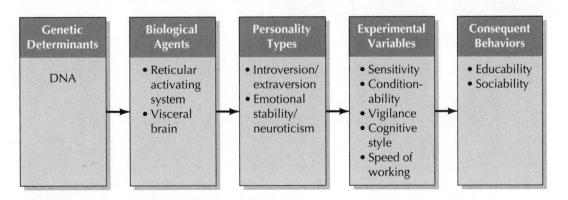

**FIGURE 12.8    From Genetic Determinants to Behavior**

This diagram illustrates causal factors and relationships that contribute to personality types and to consequent behaviors.

*ception* learning. Empirical studies did not show a significant difference in the results of the two methods because the research did not clearly articulate the conditions under which the difference would become apparent. When assessment of the approaches took into account the personalities of the students (Leith, 1974), it became apparent that children who are extraverted learn best in a situation that emphasizes discovery, whereas children who are introverted profit more from the traditional approach.

These findings have tremendous significance for education. In the lower grades, there tends to be a more relaxed atmosphere and an emphasis on discovery methods; in the higher grades, the classroom is more formal, and reception modes of presentation more prevalent. By the time a student enters college, the lecture method has become pervasive. Is it any wonder that the "good students" at that level are generally introverts (Leith, 1974)?

Honey and Mumford (1992) have developed a Learning Style Questionnaire (LSQ) based on a model developed by David Kolb (1984). Correlations of the LSQ and personality factors have been investigated by Jackson and Lawty-Jones (1996). The results support a hypothesis that personality is causally related to learning styles, but further refinement is needed to make the LSQ a more precise tool.

The potential for education is highly significant. In addition to the implications of introversion and extraversion, research must be done on the impact of other factors, such as emotional stability, psychoticism, age, and stages of development. As Eysenck (1996) points out, in both the United States and the United Kingdom, there is concern that the educational process is not serving our children very well. Teachers at every level could be helped to become aware of the differing impact that individual personality variables have on learning style and performance; appropriate measures could be generated to assess those variables; and educational methods could be developed and utilized to take advantage of the findings.

### THINKING CRITICALLY

## *Study Places*

You can get a better idea of the implications of personality variables for learning and academic performance by considering the atmosphere in which you prefer to study. When you go into a library or another place with the intent to study, what do you look for? If you are an introvert, you will probably look for a solitary, quiet place where there are few distractions. If you are an extravert, you may prefer an open area where others are present and there is some noise. Those were the predictions and findings of Campbell and Hawley's (1982) research based on Eysenck's theory. Earlier recommendations for study areas usually favored the preferences of the introvert without recognizing that individual differences matter. What other implications do you imagine the dimensions of introversion and extraversion might have for study preferences, such as number of study breaks, deadline pressures, and so forth?

## Creativity

Eysenck (1993) has developed a theory designed to relate creativity to personality in a more explicit manner than has been done before. He uses his dimensions of personality to explain many of the behaviors identified with creative achievement. He suggests that there is a causal chain connecting individual DNA configurations to creative behaviors. His theory is very speculative, but as is the case with the rest of his work, it is formulated in such a manner as to be testable.

Eysenck distinguishes between creativity as a dispositional personality trait, which he calls *originality,* and creativity as it refers to exceptional *creative achievement.* The trait of originality is normally distributed among the population. Creative achievement such as Einstein's theory of relativity, on the other hand, is very rare, occurring in a J-shaped distribution. Many people are creative, but only a small number of people are responsible for most major creative works in science and the arts. Originality is a necessary but not a sufficient condition for creative achievement. Other factors include cognitive abilities (pertinent forms of intelligence), environmental variables (such as a socio-cultural-economic climate favorable to the particular creative act), and personality factors (such as motivation and persistence). These work together synergistically to generate creative achievement.

High scores on the dimension of psychoticism are positively correlated with creativity as a trait and as an achievement. Eysenck's hypothesis that psychoticism is causally related to creativity is further confirmed, he believes, by evidence that psychotics, high P (Psychoticism) scorers, and creative achievers employ an identical cognitive style (1993). The cognitive style shared by psychotics, high P scorers, and creative achievers is to be *overinclusive* in their thinking. The process of finding answers to problems is directed by notions of what is and what is not relevant. Some people demonstrate a wide concept of relevance, or overinclusive thinking; other people have a narrower concept. These differences can be assessed by the use of a word association test that takes note of unusual and unexpected responses. The overinclusive cognitive style generates a greater number of ideas, increasing the likelihood of new, divergent, and creative responses.

The difference between an overinclusive cognitive style and the style most people use has to do with selectivity in human information processing in which past memories influence present perceptions. Reliance on past experience is helpful in that it creates patterns and structures how we perceive new information. However, it also limits novel ideas. It leads us to automatically associate "cup" with "saucer." The normal inhibitory processes that limit associative connections appear to be weakened in creative persons, as well as in psychotics and high P scorers. This may be due to a relative lack of cortical inhibition that can be further traced to varying levels of dopamine and serotonin in synaptic transmission. The final link in the chain from creativity to genetic inheritance would appear to be the hippocampus, a structure in the brain related to learning, recognizing novelty, and remembering.

Eysenck acknowledges that although there is some factual support for his theory, it is extremely speculative. The details may be in error, and some of it may have to change. However, the theory has the advantage of suggesting paths of research and generating testable hypotheses that are subject to experimental test and falsification. It is a theoretical model that can be adjusted in light of subsequent experimental research.

## *Personality and Genetics*

Eysenck has long been convinced that personality has a strong genetic component. An early paper now primarily of historical interest, "The Inheritance of Extraversion-Introversion" (1956), supported his position with facts and figures from a study of twins in South London. Today, methods of biometric genetic analysis are much more advanced and sophisticated.

Earlier in this century, many people advocated crude eugenics programs and crusaded for and succeeded in passing laws based on genetic notions—for instance, laws that restricted the entry of "inferior" immigrants into the United States and permitted the sterilization of persons considered to be feebleminded. In Nazi Germany, the same pattern of thinking culminated in the mass extermination of "inferior groups." The horror and shock that accompanied news of the events of the Holocaust was partly responsible for the subsequent strong emphasis that psychology placed on behaviorism, which emphasized the environment and minimized heredity.

In describing the biosocial nature of human behavior, Eysenck wrote:

> Human behavior [has] both biological and social causes; it's time the pendulum started swinging back from an exclusive preoccupation with social causes to an appropriate appreciation and understanding of biological causes. . . . Biological causes act in such a way as to predispose an individual in certain ways to stimulation; this stimulation may or may not occur, depending on circumstances which are entirely under environmental control. (1967)

Modern methods of analyzing the various factors that determine phenotypic behavior have a wide variety and scope. Some of these methods have been discussed in Chapter 11. Today, analysis goes beyond the simple determination of heritability to look at interaction with the environment.

Eysenck contributed a recommendation on measurement to the study of heritability. Eysenck suggested that, rather than using one score from one measure of a general factor, a full battery of tests measuring the same factor be given. A factor analysis of the intercorrelations of all the scores from those tests could then be computed and the resulting score used. Eysenck believes that this procedure would prevent results from being confounded by scores that actually measure other intervening factors. Using just one measure increases the chance that other, irrelevant variables will affect the results. By using such measures, Eysenck can suggest, for example, that the broad heritability of intelligence is 80 percent (1982).

Drawing on his own research and that of others, Eysenck maintains that there is evidence for strong genetic determinants of differences in intelligence, personality, social and sexual behavior, criminality, mental disorder, and many other aspects of human social interaction. "Clearly we cannot inherit behavior, whether it is the kind of behavior that gives rise to the trait theories of personality or the problem solving type of behavior that gives rise to the concept of intelligence and primary aptitudes. All that we can inherit is some form of anatomical structure or physiological-biochemical-hormonal functioning of the intact organism" (1982). Therefore, we need to look for anatomical, physiological, and neurological structures and functions that underlie the diversity that we observe. Further research should lead us to the underlying biological structures that are the product of genetic influences and evolutionary forces.

Even though Eysenck believes that the differences in personality are essentially due to genetic factors and that environmental factors are not as important as popularly believed, he finds, too, that the relationship between heredity and behavior is not a simple one. Eysenck's superfactors are polygenetic—that is to say, several genes interact together to make up the trait. The individual effect of each separate gene may be small, but together they create the greater impact. This is why it is unrealistic to think that we are going to be able to easily identify single genes that underlie specific behaviors, behavioral problems, or disorders. It also helps us to understand the importance of making clear distinctions, such as recognizing that although the personality dimension of psychoticism and the psychiatric disorder of psychosis may share some common genetic elements, other genes may also contribute to the fully developed illness (1976).

Some of the biological structures that Eysenck believes underlie personality, mental disorders, and intelligence have been described. In addition, Eysenck (1982) suggests three main lines of evidence that support a genetic factor in criminal behavior. First, cross-cultural studies show that criminal, antisocial, and psychopathic behavior is related to psychoticism, a dimension of personality that has already been shown to have a large genetic component. Second, studies of twins indicate that monozygotic twins are likely to have a higher concordance of criminal behavior than are dizygotic twins. (As a twin, I must remind you that this does not mean that twins are more likely than other people to be criminals, simply that if one monozygotic twin displays antisocial tendencies, the other is likely to as well.) Third, studies show that adopted children tend to resemble their biological parents more than they do their adoptive ones. This does not rule out environmental influences, but it clearly indicates that an important role is played by genetic factors.

Genetic factors also influence sexual behaviors. In spite of efforts by some researchers to establish that culture and learning are primary in determining sex differences in submission, dominance, assertiveness, aggression, and nurturance, the evidence suggests that biological factors play a strong role. This is not to deny that social forces shape the expression of those factors; Eysenck, for example, ventures that cultural forces may be more important for women, who are more likely to be influenced by them, than for men (1982).

## Psychotherapy

It would be a mistake to conclude that because genetic factors play a large part in the initiation and maintenance of negative behaviors, such as neurotic disorders and criminal activities, we can do little about them. Even though people differ in the extent to which they are genetically predisposed to certain types of behavioral tendencies, the behaviors themselves are learned. In this respect, Eysenck shares with the behavior and learning theorists similar views on the origin and treatment of neurotic disorders and is a staunch advocate of behavioral therapy and modification.

Eysenck's interest in psychotherapy began with his survey of "The Effects of Psychotherapy" (1952a), described in Chapter 1, which created an enormous impact that continues to haunt some quarters. Although Eysenck was not saying that psychotherapy was useless, he was saying that there was no acceptable evidence for its efficacy. In many cases, simply waiting for spontaneous remission to occur was just as effective. Eysenck suggested that psychologists rely on experimental studies of learning and emotion and develop methods of treatment from them rather than emulate classical Freudian psychoanalysis. His paper gave a tremendous impetus to behavior therapy. There are many problems with studies of psychotherapy (such as methodological questions, adequacy of control, criteria of improvement, etc.); therefore, Eysenck believes that subsequent refutations of his position need not be taken seriously because of their suspect data and flawed methodology (1982).

Behavior therapy began as a way of taking academic knowledge stemming from experimental laboratory studies and the theories behind them and applying that knowledge to psychiatric problems. Eysenck (1982) holds that treatment methods should be based on experimental laboratory data. Although most of that work originated with animals, theories of learning and conditioning can be applied to human clinical problems.

Learned-helplessness experiments with animals provide a good example. In learned-helplessness experiments, dogs who have been conditioned to jump across a small hurdle to avoid an electric shock when a light blinks continue to jump long after the potential of shock has been taken away. They continue to associate the blinking light with the shock. The animals can be taught to stop jumping by preventing the response and by *flooding*. The hurdle is raised so high that the dog cannot jump over it; the light blinks; and the dog experiences fear, panic, and anxiety in the shock-free environment. Eventually, the dog calms down. After the treatment is repeated a few times, the dog no longer jumps even when the conditioned stimulus (the light) is presented.

Similarly, individuals with obsessive-compulsive disorder continue their behavior long after it has become self-defeating and purposeless. An effective treatment has been used with patients who needed to wash their hands immediately after any suspicion that they have been soiled. After describing the procedure and getting permission, the therapist directed the patients to dirty their hands. The patients were not permitted to satisfy their strong need and desire to wash their hands. After realizing that they could tolerate the resultant fear, panic, and anxiety, the patients' obsessive-compulsive responses subsided (1982).

In a similar fashion, Eysenck has been able to help depressed patients. Animal studies have linked depression with insufficient positive reinforcement. To counteract their depression, patients are trained to increase the rate of positive reinforcement they receive by interacting with the environment in a positive way (constructive communication, problem solving, self-assertion, etc.) in spite of their depressed mood.

Eysenck views his theory and approach to behavior therapy as less rigid and more inclusive than that of Skinner. Skinner avoided the use of terms such as "anxiety" in his strategy, describing them as mentalistic. Eysenck does not see any problem with introducing anxiety as an intervening variable. He believes that such meditational concepts are helpful and even desirable in understanding and analyzing human behavior (1982).

Eysenck (1982) distinguishes between the terms *behavior therapy* and *behavior modification*. Behavior therapy is basically informed by classical conditioning and primarily used to treat neurotic disorders on an individual basis. Behavior modification is based on operant conditioning, deals with undesired behaviors, and is generally applied to groups in a closed environment, such as schools, prisons, hospitals, and so forth. Eysenck's efforts have been directed toward behavior therapy, but he believes that behavior modification can be a useful tool. Referring to concerns that have been raised about the ethics of using behavior therapy and modification, Eysenck points out that, in a misguided effort to apply findings and change behavior, some "treatments" (that should more accurately be termed "torture") have been developed and used in prisons and other settings. Appropriate training is needed to prevent uninformed practitioners from putting together collections of methods and labeling them as behavior therapy. On the other hand, Eysenck questions the ethics of psychodynamic therapists who treat patients with time-consuming and costly methods that create stress and other potential negative effects and that have never been proven to be effective.

Eysenck's emphasis on the biological basis of personality is also consistent with biological therapies: physical or chemical interventions, such as drugs, affect the brain or other body functions and thus provoke or inhibit certain behaviors. Medication can influence the underlying biological system and thus change an individual's subjective experience and behavior. Again we see Eysenck's concern with individual differences. Effects of drugs are patient-specific; so are different types of therapies. Certain types of therapies may work better with certain types of patients. Extroverts, for example, may do well in a group situation, whereas introverts may be more comfortable in a one-on-one setting.

Eysenck's interests have extended to other health areas as well (1995b). He has associated the probability of developing certain health problems such as heart disease or cancer with various personality traits (1989). He has also described appropriate behavioral therapy to increase one's chances for longevity (1995b). These writings are not as clearly tied to his theory as are some of his other writings. Once again, the importance of genetic factors does not mean that individuals have no control. Biological and emotional factors may predispose us to, for example, cardiovascular disease; however, in the light of this information, we can avoid potentially dangerous situations such as an unhealthy diet and learn appropriate new responses.

Eysenck reminds us that most human problems are psychological and due to human actions. Problems such as war, famine, pollution, and so forth are caused in large measure by human behaviors and can only be controlled by a better understanding of human nature. Part of that understanding entails acknowledging that individuals differ in their traits and intellectual abilities. A commitment to equal rights need not entail the naive belief that biologically we all are similarly endowed. The fact is that we are not genetically equal; our social and political commitments to equality must rest on other grounds. However, while recognizing the tragic consequences of earlier eugenic efforts, Eysenck unabashedly supports a meritocracy in which the most competent people are chosen for important social positions and occupations. To do otherwise, he says, is to run the risk of a "mediocracy" and to fail to protect ourselves (1975).

| PHILOSOPHY, | **Eysenck's Theory** |
|---|---|
| SCIENCE, | |
| AND ART | In evaluating his own theory, Eysenck wrote, "I have usually been against the establishment and in favor of the rebels. Readers who wish to inter- |

pret this in terms of some inherited oppositional tendency, some acquired Freudian hatred of father substitutes, or in any other way are of course welcome. I prefer to think that on these issues the majority were wrong and I was right. But then of course I would think that; only the future will tell" (1982).

Eysenck believes that his greatest contribution to personality theory has been to connect ideas that had been vaguely anticipated by earlier philosophers with causal theories of behavior. In his theory, concepts such as extraversion-introversion and emotional instability-neuroticism are clearly tied to a biosocial model. Eysenck's theory of personality seeks to avoid the circular arguments often involved in studies of personality that are limited to factor analysis and to root itself as well in experimental research. "Ultimately," Eysenck writes, "all theories will suffer disproof and replacement by a better theory. Until that day comes, and I don't expect it to be all that far distant, my theory may serve as an example of what personality theories ought to be like" (1982).

Essentially, Eysenck's approach, like that of Cattell and the Big Five theorists, is a nomothetic rather than an idiographic one. However, as Eysenck reminds us, this does not jeopardize the concept that each individual is unique. The uniqueness is found in the particular combination of traits within an individual, even though the traits themselves are common to everyone. Eysenck reminds us, "to the scientist, the unique individual is simply the point of intersection of a number of quantitative variables" (1952). Thus his typology may well be complemented by stud-

## PHILOSOPHICAL ASSUMPTIONS

### Examining Eysenck's Theories

How would you rate Eysenck on each of the basic philosophical assumptions described in Chapter 1? Consult the chart on the inside front cover. Each basic issue is presented as a bipolar dimension along which a person's view can be placed according to the degree of agreement with one or the other extreme: *freedom/determinism, hereditary/environmental, uniqueness/universality, proactive/reactive, optimistic/pessimistic.* Rate the views of Eysenck on these issues.

When you have determined where you think Eysenck stands, compare your responses with those of your classmates and your instructor. You should be willing to defend your ratings, but also be prepared to change them in light of others' compelling arguments. Afterward, compare your ratings of Eysenck with your own position on each issue and with those of other theorists. Does this comparison help you understand why his theories do or do not appeal to you?

ies of the unique individual, but Eysenck would want such studies to be governed by a strict rubric of scientific methodology.

Studies have used cardiovascular reactivity, brain wave amplitude, and other sophisticated indices to measure arousal and to try to confirm or disconfirm Eysenck's theory. The results of the studies are mixed. Some support it; some do not. Newer research suggests that the reticular activating system is not as general a system as Eysenck indicates; that is, the RAS does not affect the entire brain. Usually, levels of stimulation vary throughout the brain so that some parts of the brain are stimulated while others are not (Zuckerman, 1991). This makes it hard to make general statements about levels of arousal in connection with extraversion and introversion.

Because research in biology and on the nervous system is growing at such a rapid pace, it is understandable that Eysenck's theory is based on a view of the nervous system and the brain that may be quickly dated. Eysenck's theory also undoubtedly oversimplifies a very complicated system. The efforts to test his theory are frequently plagued by anomalies. Eysenck is extremely willing to adjust his theory and model of personality to accommodate irregularities and to specify the exact conditions under which certain generalizations are true. The problem is that as more adjustments are made, the basic model becomes less powerful as a theory and risks becoming just a collection of explanatory concepts. Nevertheless, Eysenck has ambitiously tried to encompass fields as divergent as psychometrics, experimental psychology, neurophysiology, and genetics into his theory, and it would be naive and unrealistic to imagine that a simple theory composed of only a few dimensions and laws could encompass such a wide range.

Eysenck's theory is a superb model of a scientific approach to personality. There is considerable support for his "type" approach. It is in his recent ideas regarding brain function that there is disagreement. It is important to reiterate that Eysenck's speculation is a hypothesis, not a factual description of how the brain works. Research has not yet provided direct empirical data to fully support it. Eysenck's concept of scientific activity is, however, somewhat narrow. There are alternative ways of gathering empirical data and operationally defining terms, which Eysenck disallows even though other scientists would permit them. Moreover, Eysenck's own procedures are not as objective or purely scientific as he contends. For example, the data of factor analysis may be interpreted in various ways. Also, the conclusions of factor analysis studies are only as good as the original data. The average individual has undoubtedly been more directly influenced by the trait approach to personality than by any other approach. Most people have been assessed by some device based on the trait approach, for instance, an intelligence test, an achievement test, or an aptitude test. Such psychometric measuring devices and techniques have not been used without criticism. Most of the constructs supposedly indicated by these tests cannot be measured directly. Often the validity of the tests is assumed rather than demonstrated.

On the other hand, the judicious use of appropriate assessment techniques can be invaluable in developing individual and group potential. Accurate understanding of one's limitations and abilities is important for developing one's potential.

Trait and temperament theories are controversial because, among other things, they imply that some personality differences are genetically based. Eysenck has said that people "are created equal in the sight of God and as regards the judicial system, but they are not created equal as far as beauty is concerned, or strength, or intelligence or a great many other things" (as quoted in Evans, 1976). This is not to say, however, that heredity is the sole determinant of personality. All of the theorists discussed in this chapter emphasize the interaction of biology and society. Heredity may place limits on an individual's potential, but environment probably determines where within that range his or her actual behavior will fall.

The recognition of similarities and differences among all people enables the effective development and application of a social philosophy that intends to provide equal opportunity for all people in our global community to achieve their potential. Such a recognition underscores the desirability of a reciprocal relationship between the philosophy, science, and art of a personality theory. Scientists should be aware of the ways in which philosophical assumptions inform their work and, in turn, of the ways in which their findings influence ethical and social decisions.

## Summary

1. Some of the historical predecessors to Eysenck's theory are Hippocrates, Galen, Kant, Wundt, Jung, Kretschmer, and Sheldon.

2. Eysenck seeks to construct a model of personality by giving a description of personality based on factor analysis and then identifying the biological causes of personality through experimental studies.

3. Eysenck has identified the superfactors of *extraversion-introversion, emotional stability-neuroticism,* and *psychoticism*. There are similarities but significant differences between Eysenck, Cattell, and the Big Five theorists.

4. Eysenck rigorously employs scientific methods in assessment. He has criticized the shortcomings of early versions of ratings and inventories, constructed more accurate questionnaires, and developed a number of self-report inventories to measure the dimensions he has identified.

5. Eysenck suggests that extraversion-introversion is related to arousal thresholds in the *ascending reticular activating system* of the brain and emotional stability-neuroticism to differences in *visceral brain* activity and that psychoticism may be due to *hormonal* levels.

6. Eysenck connects personality and neurosis to biological bases and to the interplay between the genotype and the environment.

7. Eysenck believes that intelligence is related to *evoked potential*.

8. Eysenck's theory has found applications in many fields, such as education, the study of creativity, criminal justice, and psychotherapy.

9. Eysenck's theory is an excellent model of a scientific approach.

## Suggestions for Further Reading

A highly prolific writer, Eysenck has authored about seventy-five books and one thousand articles. The level of readability varies widely. A work that is relatively easy for the lay person to understand is *Psychology Is about People* (Open Court, 1972). Other popular books include *Crime and Personality* (Routledge & Kegan Paul, 1964) and *Uses and Abuses of Psychology* (Penguin, 1953).

Eysenck's psychometric work has been summarized in *The Description and Measurement of Personality* (Eysenck & Eysenck, 1969, Routledge & Kegan Paul) and his experimental work in *The Dynamics of Anxiety and Hysteria* (Eysenck, 1957, Routledge & Kegan Paul), as well as in later papers and writings. The definitive statement of his cortical hypothesis of arousal is found in *The Biological Basis of Personality* (Charles C. Thomas, 1967). A three-volume collection of research essays related to his theory has been published under the title *Readings in Extroversion–Introversion* (Staples, 1970–1971). The latest full account of his position is in *Personality and Individual Differences: A Natural Science Approach* (Plenum, 1985), written with his son Michael. His autobiography, *Rebel with a Cause,* was published in London by W. H. Allen in 1990.

# Humanistic and Existential Theories

The humanistic theories of Abraham Maslow and Carl Rogers emerged in the 1950s in an effort to correct the limited concepts of human nature of both classical psychoanalysis and radical behaviorism. Maslow and Rogers disagreed with the dark, pessimistic, and largely negative picture of personality presented by Freudian psychoanalysis. They also disagreed with the picture of the person as a machine or robot that characterized the early behavior and learning approach.

Maslow and Rogers emphasized a view of the person as an active, creative, experiencing human being who lives in the present and subjectively responds to current perceptions, relationships, and encounters. The humanistic view of personality is a positive, optimistic one that stresses the tendency of the human personality toward growth and self-actualization.

Rollo May's existential theory also began to appear in the 1950s. It represents a singular effort to bring together the psychoanalytic tradition in psychology and the existential movement in philosophy. May is deeply aware that the technology that we have developed has yet to provide satisfactory answers to the most fundamental questions of human existence. In today's postmodern society our social security numbers have become more important than our names. In the midst of our abundant technological advance, the person appears to have been lost. In combining the insights of psychoanalysis and existentialism, May has developed a theory that is clearly expressive of our concerns in the final decade of the twentieth century.

# Humanism

## ABRAHAM MASLOW ❖ CARL ROGERS

## Your Goals for This Chapter

1. Explain why Maslow has been called the father of humanistic psychology.
2. Distinguish among *motivation, metamotivation, D-needs,* and *B-needs* and indicate the importance of these distinctions.
3. Describe Maslow's *hierarchy of human needs.* Cite studies that show that the needs are essential for optimal human life and development.
4. Describe how Maslow defined and studied *self-actualized persons,* as well as the key dimensions of self-actualized persons.
5. Explain what is meant by a *peak experience* and give examples of experiences that might be recognized as peaks.
6. Describe some of the criticisms of Maslow's portrait of the self-actualized person.
7. Evaluate Maslow's theory in terms of its function as philosophy, science, and art.
8. Explain the following concepts in Rogers's theory: *phenomenal field,* self-actualization, organism, *self.* Explain how emotions affect the process of self-actualization.
9. Explain what Rogers means by *congruence* and *incongruence* and identify denial and distortion as two processes that may lead to incongruence.
10. Discuss what is meant by *unconditional* and *conditional positive regard* and recognize their roles in influencing personality development.
11. Describe three therapist attitudes that lead to change.
12. Distinguish among five different responses to emotional communications.
13. Discuss *person-centered psychotherapy,* describing its supportive character, changes in Rogers's conception of it, and efforts at empirical validation.
14. Evaluate Rogers's theory in terms of its function as philosophy, science, and art.

Even though historical analysis reveals that humanistic psychology had no single founder (De Carvalho, 1991), Abraham Maslow has been described as its spiritual father. An articulate, persuasive writer, he described humanistic psychology as a "third force" in American psychology. He criticized both psychoanalysis and radical behaviorism for their limited conceptions of human nature. "The study of crippled, stunted, immature, and unhealthy specimens," he wrote, "can only lead to a crippled psychology" (1970). The study of human nature as a machine, typical of radical behaviorism, cannot comprehend the whole person. Maslow offered his view as a complement rather than an alternative to these two other forces. He did not reject the contributions that psychoanalysis and behaviorism have made, but he believed that the picture of human nature needs to be rounded out. In particular, Maslow sought to emphasize the positive rather than the negative side of human nature. The brighter side of humanity is emphasized in his concept of the self-actualized person.

For Carl Rogers, a person's behavior is completely dependent on how he or she perceives the world and its events. Rogers's theory of personality describes the **self** as an important element of experience; it is largely due to Rogers's efforts that the self has re-emerged as a useful construct for understanding personality. In much of behaviorist thought the concept of the self had been ignored as a remnant of earlier religious or philosophical views. Rogers presented the self as a scientific construct that helps to account for what we observe. The self is Rogers's term for those psychological processes that govern our behavior. At the same time, his theory emphasizes the organism or the total person.

## Abraham Maslow: Biographical Background

Abraham Maslow was born in 1908 in Brooklyn, New York, the first of seven children. His parents were Russian immigrants. As his father's business improved, Maslow's family moved out of the slums and into lower-middle-class neighborhoods. The young Maslow found himself the only Jewish boy in the neighborhood and a target of anti-Semitism. Embarrassed by his physical appearance and taunted, isolated, friendless, and lonely, he spent a great deal of his early years cloistered in the library in the companionship of books.

Maslow was not close to either of his parents. He was fond of his father but afraid of him. He described his mother as schizophrenic and later wondered how he had turned out so well in spite of his unhappy childhood. His mother clearly favored his younger brothers and sister and mercilessly punished her eldest son at the least provocation. Recalling a painful memory, Maslow told how his mother once killed two stray cats he had brought home by smashing their heads against the wall. Later, Maslow admitted that he hated his mother and all that she stood for (Hoffman, 1988). They were never reconciled and he did not attend her funeral. His mother's brother, however, was a kind and devoted uncle who spent a great deal of time with him and may have been responsible for Maslow's mental stability.

*Abraham Maslow has been called the spiritual father of humanistic psychology.*

Later, Maslow suggested that life didn't begin for him until he married and began studying at the University of Wisconsin. He discovered John Watson and was totally absorbed in behaviorism, which he saw as a very practical way of improving society. Maslow received a solid grounding in empirical laboratory research. His doctoral research concerned the sexual and dominance characteristics of monkeys.

After receiving the Ph.D. from Wisconsin in 1934, Maslow returned to New York and began to teach at Brooklyn College. New York was a vibrant place for a young psychologist during the 1930s. Many European psychologists, psychiatrists, and others of the intelligentsia who had come to America to escape the Nazis were in New York. Maslow eagerly met and learned from them. He was influenced by Erich Fromm, Karen Horney, and Alfred Adler. He was also impressed by the anthropologist Ruth Benedict, who inspired him with her optimism about the potentialities of society.

Within such an eclectic climate, it was probably inevitable that Maslow's interest in behaviorism would diminish. The birth of his first daughter was the "thunderclap that settled things" once and for all. All of his experimentation with rats and primates did not prepare him for the mystery of the child. Behaviorist theory might explain what was observed in the laboratory, but it could not account for human experiences. The advent of World War II also profoundly affected Maslow. His attention turned more fully to research on the human personality in an effort to improve it, "to show that human beings are capable of something grander than war and prejudice and hatred" (Hall, 1968).

Maslow remained at Brooklyn for fourteen years. In 1951, he moved to Brandeis University where he stayed until one year before his premature death in 1970. Maslow had become a very popular figure in the field of psychology. Shortly before his death he had embarked on a fellowship that would have enabled him to undertake a large-scale study developing a philosophy of economics, politics, and ethics informed by humanistic psychology.

## Human Motivation: A Hierarchical Theory

Maslow believed that human beings are interested in growing rather than simply restoring balance or avoiding frustration. He described the human being as a "wanting animal" who is almost always desiring something. Indeed, as one human desire is satisfied, another arises to take its place. In the drive to self-actualize, the individual moves forward toward growth, happiness, and satisfaction.

Maslow (1970) distinguished between motivation and metamotivation. **Motivation** refers to reducing tension by satisfying deficit states or lacks. It entails **D-needs** or deficiency needs, which arise out of the organism's requirements for physiological survival or safety, such as the need for food or rest, and motivate the individual to engage in activities that will reduce these drives. Motivation and the D-needs are powerful determinants of behavior. **Metamotivation** refers to growth tendencies. It entails **B-needs** or being needs, which arise out of the organism's drive to self-actualize and fulfill its inherent potential. B-needs do not stem from a lack or deficiency; rather, they push forward to self-fulfillment. Their goal is to enhance life by enriching it. Rather than reduce tension, they frequently heighten it in their quest for ever-increasing stimuli that will bring a life lived to the fullest.

Motivation and the D-needs take precedence over metamotivation and the B-needs, because they dominate the organism when both needs are thwarted. Unsatisfied deficiency needs hinder movement toward the B-needs (see Sumerlin & Bundrick, 1996). An individual who is desperate for food is unlikely to be concerned with spiritual goals like truth or beauty. Within the D-needs, physiological needs are stronger than safety needs. Thus, in *Les Miserables,* Jean Valjean risks his safety and future for a loaf of bread.

Maslow (1970) proposed a **hierarchy of needs** based on the principle of relative potency. In order of their strength, the five basic needs are: physiological needs, safety needs, belonging and love needs, self-esteem needs, and self-actualization needs (see Figure 13.1). As each need is satisfied, the next higher order need attains importance. Some individuals, because of their circumstances, find it very difficult to satisfy even the lowest needs. The higher one is able to go, however, the greater physiological health and self-actualization one will demonstrate.

1. *Physiological needs.* The strongest needs of all are the physiological ones that pertain to the physical survival and biological maintenance of the organism. They include the need for food, drink, sleep, oxygen, shelter, and sex. If these biological needs are not met for a protracted period of time, an individual will not be motivated to fulfill other needs.

2. *Safety needs.* Safety needs refer to the organism's requirements for an orderly, stable, and predictable world. The young child, who is helpless and dependent, prefers a certain amount of structured routine and discipline. The absence of these elements makes the child anxious and insecure. Individuals who live in unsafe environments or suffer from job insecurity

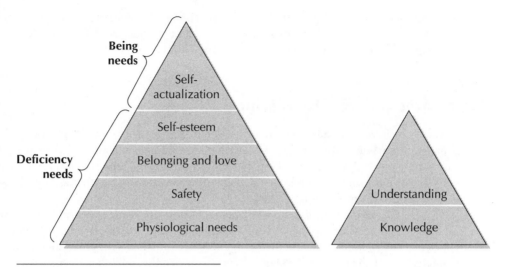

FIGURE 13.1    Maslow's Hierarchy of Needs

may need to spend a great deal of time and energy trying to protect themselves and their possessions.

3. *Belonging and love needs.* Once the physiological and safety needs are met, needs for love and belonging arise. The individual seeks affectionate and intimate relationships with other people, needing to feel part of various reference groups, such as the family, neighborhood, gang, or a professional association. Maslow noted that such needs are increasingly more difficult to meet in our technological, fluid, and mobile society.

4. *Self-esteem needs.* Maslow described two kinds of esteem needs—the need for respect from others and the need for self-respect. Self-esteem entails competence, confidence, mastery, achievement, independence, and freedom. Respect from others entails recognition, acceptance, status, and appreciation. When these needs are not met an individual feels discouraged, weak, and inferior. For most people, the need for regard from others diminishes with age because it has been fulfilled and the need for self-regard becomes more important.

5. *Self-actualization needs.* If the foregoing needs have been met, the needs for **self-actualization** may emerge *if* the individual has the courage to choose them. These needs are difficult to describe because they are unique and vary from person to person. In general, self-actualization refers to the desire to fulfill one's highest potential.

Self-actualization is possible only if the lower needs have been sufficiently met so that they do not detract from or engross a person's basic energies. Rather than organize their behavior toward tension reduction, individuals whose deficiency needs are satisfied may, in fact, seek states of increased optimal tension in order to enhance their opportunities for self-actualization. Higher needs may become as compelling as food to the hungry. In short, those who are living on a B-level have a radically different motivation from those who are still striving to satisfy deficit states.

In addition to the hierarchy just outlined, Maslow posited the important human needs to *know* and *understand* (1970). These form a small but powerful hierarchy of their own, in which the need to know is more potent than and prior to the need to understand. Children, by nature, are curious; when their cognitive impulses are satisfied, they seek further comprehension and understanding. Clinical studies also convinced Maslow that in some individuals aesthetic needs are very important: "They get sick [in special ways] from ugliness, and are cured by beautiful surroundings; they *crave* actively, and their cravings can be satisfied *only* by beauty" (1970). These needs are not sharply delineated from the needs of the earlier hierarchy; they overlap with them and are interrelated.

Maslow (1970) encouraged a more careful study of all situations that foster and fulfill the satisfaction of our basic needs: among them, constructive marriages, close friendships, healthy parent-child relationships, positive educational settings, and satisfying employment. For Maslow, every human relationship is potentially a therapeutic one. Indeed, studies show that good relations may protect us from stress by making our immune systems more resilient (Goleman, 1992). One task of psychology is to try to identify those qualities that promote good human situations rather than poor ones. We can then better foster relationships that enable us to grow.

## The Study of Self-Actualized Persons

Maslow has been described as preoccupied with healthy persons rather than with neurotics. He conducted an extensive, although informal, study of a group of persons whom he considered to be self-actualized. The study generated such interest among other psychologists that Maslow published his findings as an initial, tentative attempt to study optimum health and a focal point for further empirical research (1970).

Maslow defined *self-actualizing persons* as those who are "fulfilling themselves and doing the best that they are capable of doing" (1970). His subjects consisted of friends and personal acquaintances, public figures living and dead, and selected college students. Not all of his subjects were deemed fully actualized. Studying these individuals, their personalities, characteristics, habits, and abilities enabled Maslow to develop his definition of optimal mental health.

By ordinary standards of laboratory research, what Maslow did in his study was not true research. He was quick to acknowledge that his investigation was not conducted along strict scientific lines. His descriptions were not based on standardized tests nor were his conclusions obtained from controlled experimental situations. Moreover, his definition of a self-actualized person tended to be a subjective one: the self-actualized person was one whom Maslow deemed to be self-actualized. Nevertheless, Maslow pointed out that the canons of rigorous scientific procedures would not have encompassed or permitted research into the areas that he was studying. Further, he presented his data as only an initial observation and effort to study health as opposed to neurosis. Maslow hoped that future studies would yield more information as to the nature of self-actualization and confirm or disprove his own expectations.

---

**TABLE 13.1   Characteristics of Self-Actualizers**

---

Maslow identified fifteen characteristics of self-actualized persons that emerged from his study (1970). For simplicity, these have been grouped under four key dimensions.

*Awareness*

Efficient and accurate perception of reality

Continued freshness of appreciation without preconceptions

Tendency to have peak experiences

Clear ethical awareness and standards but not necessarily conventional ones

*Honesty*

Philosophical sense of humor that pokes fun at our shared human pretensions

Deep feeling of kinship with all humanity

Selective and deep interpersonal relations with small circle of intimates

Democratic character structure accepting of all people

*Freedom*

Detachment and a need for privacy

Autonomous and independent of culture and environment

Creativeness characterizing whatever they do

Spontaneity, simplicity, and naturalness

*Trust*

Problem- rather than self-centered

Acceptance of self, others, and nature for what they are

Resistance to cultural conformity

---

Following his investigation, Maslow described several characteristics of self-actualized persons (1970). These have been listed in Table 13.1. The self-actualized person frequently experiences what Maslow called a peak experience. A **peak experience** is an intensification of any experience to the degree that there is a loss or transcendence of self. These kinds of experiences are often termed mystical or religious, but Maslow emphasized that they do not necessarily entail traditional religious labels or interpretations. A peak experience may be provoked by a secular event as well. Events that may be mundane and ordinary to others, such as viewing a work of art or reaching a sexual climax, may be the sparks that trigger a peak experience for you.

During a peak experience, the individual experiences not only an expansion of self but also a sense of unity and meaningfulness in life. For that moment, the world appears to be complete and the person is at one with it. The experience lingers on and transforms one's

*Intense concentration on an activity may provoke a peak experience, in which there is a loss or transcendence of self.*

understanding so that things do not seem to be quite the same afterward. Research using a questionnaire about peak experiences has confirmed the characteristics Maslow described (Privette, 1986). Maslow believed that *all* human beings, not only self-actualizers, are potential peakers. People at any stage can have peak experiences, though they are what Maslow considered a moment of self-actualization. Maslow distinguished between "transcenders" and the "merely healthy": Transcenders are inclined to have peaks; the merely healthy tend not to. Some people have peak experiences but they suppress them and therefore do not recognize them when they occur. In other cases, one may inhibit a peak experience, thereby preventing its occurrence.

Self-actualizers are able to distinguish between the goal that they are striving for and the means by which they are accomplishing it. For the most part, they are focused on ends rather than means. At the same time, they often consider as ends activities that are simply means for other people. They can enjoy and appreciate the journey as well as the destination.

The picture Maslow drew of the self-actualized person is a composite. No one person that he studied possessed all the qualities of the self-actualized. Each of them demonstrated the characteristics to varying degrees. Maslow's definition of self-actualization did not imply perfection but a higher level of functioning. As such, self-actualizers may show many lesser human failings. They frequently have silly, wasteful, or thoughtless habits. At times they are vain and take too much pride in their achievements. They may sometimes lose their tempers. Because of their concentration on their work, they may appear absentminded, humorless, or impolite. At times their kindness toward others leads them to permit others to take undue advantage of them. At other times they may appear to be ruthless and inconsiderate in their relations with other people. Sometimes they are boring, even irritating. In short, they are not perfect.

The number of people who achieve self-actualization is relatively small, less than 1 percent of the entire population. Concepts such as "the self-actualized person" may apply to only a select few. Obviously, the possibility of self-actualization is limited or even closed to large numbers of the human population, whose environment and life-style have yet to meet the lesser needs depicted in Maslow's hierarchy, let alone the higher needs. This is not to say, however, that some groups of people are by nature unable to self-actualize. Maslow did point out that some people can be healthier than their environment. He concluded that they have some kind of inner freedom but did not specify how or why.

| PHILOSOPHY, |
| SCIENCE, |
| AND ART |

## Maslow's Theory

Maslow's theory clearly points away from pure science toward the broader outlines of philosophy. He reminded us that human beings create science, establish its goals, and use its technology for their own purposes. Maslow believed that it is misleading to think science is value-free, since its procedures are employed for human purposes. We may use science to create mechanistic robots out of human nature or we may use it to increase human freedom and potential. Maslow suggested that we conceive of science as a problem-solving activity rather than a specific technology. Only the goals of science can dignify or validate its methods.

Maslow's study of self-actualized persons lacks the rigor and distinct methodology characteristic of strict empirical science. His work underscores the fact that the canons of rigorous scientific procedures do not necessarily encompass or permit research into important human questions. The tension between the demands of the subject matter of psychology and the requirements of good science continues to concern psychologists.

Maslow suggested the need for a broader definition of science and the development of methodologies appropriate for the human subject. His "third force" became a very powerful force in psychology and its impact was reflected in the creation of a new division of the American Psychological Association, called Humanistic Psychology.

Maslow's portrayal of the self-actualized person is optimistic, generating much confidence in human potential. Yet some critics suggest that his picture may be simplistic, neglecting the hard work and pain that is involved in growth and development and ignoring the phenomenon of tragedy. Maslow's research originated in an era of growth and prosperity accompanied by a seemingly limitless view of human potential. But is this picture realistic? In fact, the likelihood of self-actualization may be more remote than Maslow indicated. Perhaps it is naive to hope to reduce all conflict and more justified to assume that we can merely strengthen the ego, enabling it to be more effective in its executive functions. Freud, we recall, was pessimistic about reducing human conflict.

Some critics further suggest that Maslow's view of the self-actualized individual is based on American values of individual achievement. Because of cultural training, many people in Western societies tend to believe that personality is best rooted on a high sense of positive self-esteem. Thus parents in middle-class America are encouraged to take steps to develop positive self-esteem in their children, especially their sons (Josephs, Markus, & Tafarodi, 1992; Markus & Kitayama, 1991), and psychological disorders such as anxiety and depression are often seen as a failure to develop such autonomy, achievement, and feeling of self-worth. However, people in many non-Western cultures cultivate very dissimilar personalities. In Japan and China, an autonomous self is not stressed and children are taught to cooperate and not to demonstrate their superiority so as to avoid diminishing other people (see Kitayama & Markus, 1992). As a result, people perceive themselves to be part of a whole and define themselves in terms of the group.

When Kitayama and his coworkers compared the responses of Japanese and American university students asked to indicate the frequency and origin of certain emotions, Japanese students associated positive feelings with good interpersonal relations rather than personal achievements, whereas the opposite was true of the Americans (Kitayama & Markus, 1992).

Likewise, even within the same culture gender differences may apply. Thus in North America a woman's self-esteem tends to be based on interpersonal relations whereas a man's tends to be based on personal accomplishments (Josephs et al., 1992). Lerman (1992) reminds us that Maslow did not demonstrate how the environment frequently fails to permit the gratification of basic needs of women and other subjugated groups. She believes, however, that there is a place in his and other humanist theories for contributions from a feminist examination of the environment and its potential impact on the well-being of humanity. Such an inquiry would require the elimination of sexism and careful examination of blind spots.

However, others (such as Chang & Page, 1991) believe that cross-cultural comparisons among Maslow, Rogers, Lao Tzu, and Zen Buddhism point more toward a universality of human experience in that they all share the assumption that people have an actualizing tendency that fosters positive growth. Miller (1991) suggests that placing self-actualization in the context of transpersonal psychology removes its elitism and fosters cross-cultural comparisons with Eastern concepts. Rather than emphasize one concept of an ideal, Coan (1991) suggests we look at the diverse ways in which people can realize their potential.

Clearly, more attention needs to be given to the processes within the individual and various cultures and societies that permit self-actualization and creativity to flower. In Maslow's words, "How good a human being does society permit?" (1970). In what instances can an individual overcome and compensate for needs that have not been met in life? As it stands, Maslow's discussion of self-actualization is descriptive rather than functional. He describes the characteristics of the self-actualizer but does not tell how these characteristics may be concretely acquired.

Near the end of his life, Maslow urged the promotion of a "fourth force" to deal with spiritual and religious issues. By articulating the concept of peak experiences, Maslow believed that he had brought all major religions under the rubric of the natural science of psychology. He felt that a study of positive forces that foster self-actualization and an improved culture should be a primary focus of psychology.

## Carl Rogers: Biographical Background

Carl Rogers was born in 1902 in Oak Park, Illinois, a suburb of Chicago. He was the fourth of six children. Rogers's parents, educated and conservative middle-class Protestants, instilled in their children high ethical standards of behavior and emphasized the importance of hard work.

Rogers had little social life outside of his large family, but this did not bother him. He was an avid reader and developed a certain level of independence early in life. When he was twelve, the family moved to a farm. Farm life spurred his interest in science and increased his ability to work independently. He was fascinated with the literature on scientific agriculture that his father brought home. Rogers worked hard at his chores on the farm; he raised lambs, pigs, and calves. He also collected, studied, and bred moths. A superior student, Rogers entered the University of Wisconsin, a family alma mater, with the full intent of studying agriculture. However, in his second year, he decided to prepare for the ministry. After his graduation in 1924, he married Helen Elliot and moved to New York City to begin preparation for the ministry at Union Theological Seminary.

Rogers's fate, however, was not to become a minister. During his final years at college, Rogers found himself departing from his parents' fundamentalist ways of thinking (see Thorne, 1990). The liberal philosophical approach toward religion fostered at Union Theological Seminary and the insights Rogers gained from participation in several YMCA conferences led him to feel that he could not work in a field that would require him to profess a specific set of beliefs. This was a difficult period for both Rogers and his parents but it nurtured Rogers's growing conviction that one must ultimately rely on personal experiences for developing a philosophy of life (see also Dolliver, 1995). His interests were turning toward psychology; therefore, he transferred to Columbia University Teachers College, where he was introduced to the philosophy of John Dewey and began his training in clinical psychology.

In 1931, Rogers received the Ph.D. and joined the staff of the Rochester Guidance Center, where he helped develop a highly successful child study department. Here, Rogers first met what was to be many years of opposition from members of the psychiatric profession who felt that psychologists and counselors should not be permitted to practice or have

*Carl Rogers is perhaps best known for the method of psychotherapy he developed.*

any administrative responsibility over psychotherapy. In 1939, when Rogers was made the director of the center, a vigorous campaign was waged to unseat him. No one criticized his work, but the general opinion was that a psychologist simply could not do this kind of work. Fortunately, the board of trustees decided in Rogers's favor.

In 1940, Rogers accepted an appointment as professor of psychology at Ohio State University. He worked with intellectually adept graduate students and began to clearly articulate his views on psychotherapy using college students as his primary data base. In 1945, he moved to the University of Chicago where, as professor of psychology and executive secretary of the counseling center, he again championed his view that psychologists and counselors could effectively conduct therapy. Rogers's efforts, along with others, led to the reconciliation of psychiatry and psychology as two professions in search of a common goal. This reconciliation and challenge were reflected in Rogers's appointment as professor of psychology and psychiatry at the University of Wisconsin in 1957. In 1963, Rogers became a fellow at the Center for Studies of the Person in La Jolla, California. Throughout his life, Rogers referred to himself as a counselor.

In his final years, Rogers sought to bring together in encounter groups people from conflicting political factions, such as Protestants and Roman Catholics in Belfast, Ireland. As his son David observed, "Over his career, he moved from one-on-one psychotherapy, to small groups, to nations" (Goleman, 1987). He was planning to return to South Africa to lead a second encounter session with blacks and whites when he died in 1987 of a heart attack following surgery for a broken hip.

## Rogers's Theory of Personality

Rogers (1959) maintained that each individual exists in the center of a phenomenal field. Rogers was influenced by a philosophical movement called **phenomenology.** The word *phenomenon* comes from the Greek *phainomenon,* which means "that which appears or shows itself." In philosophy, phenomenology seeks to describe the data, or the "given," of immediate experience. In psychology, phenomenology has come to mean the study of human awareness and perception. Phenomenologists stress that what is important is not the object or the event in itself but how it is perceived and understood by the individual. The **phenomenal field** refers to the total sum of experiences. It consists of everything that is potentially available to consciousness at any given moment. As you read you may not be aware of the pressure of the chair on your buttocks, but when attention is drawn to this fact you become conscious of it.

The organism, or person as a whole, responds to the phenomenal field. Rogers's emphasis here is on the individual's perception of reality. In this respect he was consistent with the recent emphasis on cognition in psychology. For social purposes, we agree that the perceptions commonly shared by others in our culture are the correct perceptions. However, reality is essentially a very personal matter. Two individuals walking along at night may see an object by the road and respond very differently. "One . . . sees a large boulder and reacts with fright. The other, a native of the country sees a tumbleweed and reacts with nonchalance" (1951, p. 484). The individual's perception rather than the reality itself is most important. Suppose a young boy were to complain that his father was dogmatic, authoritarian, and dictatorial. In fact, an impartial observer might conclude that the father was open and democratic. Rogers would point out that what the father is really like is meaningless; what is important is how the boy perceives his father.

It follows that the best vantage point for understanding an individual is that of the individual. Rogers pointed out that the individual is the only one who can fully know her or his field of experience. Rogers acknowledged that it is not always easy to understand behavior from the internal frame of reference of another person. We are limited to the individual's conscious perception and communication of experiences. Nevertheless, such an empathic understanding of the experiences of another is useful in understanding a person and therefore useful in understanding personality processes.

## *Actualization*

The primary tendency of the organism is to maintain, actualize, and enhance itself. This actualizing tendency is part of a universal life force (van Kalmthout, 1995); it follows lines laid down by genetics and may also be influenced by temperament (Ford, 1991). The particular type of seed that is planted determines whether or not the flower will be a chrysanthemum or snapdragon, but the environment can greatly influence the resulting bloom. The process of actualization is neither automatic nor effortless; it involves struggle and even pain. The young child may struggle with the first step but it is a natural struggle. Thus, each organism, or living being, moves in the direction of maturation as it is defined for each species.

Behavior is the "goal-directed attempt" of the organism to meet its needs as it perceives them (1951). This goal-directed behavior is accompanied by emotions that, unless they are excessive or inappropriate, facilitate the behavior. Rogers's view of emotions is a very positive one. Fully experiencing one's emotions facilitates growth, whereas the denial or distortion of emotions may permit them to raise havoc in our lives. Rogers suggested that actualization occurs most freely when the person is open and aware of all experiences, be they sensory, visceral, or emotional. Our inner experiences are intrinsically growth-producing. An **organismic valuing process** subconsciously guides us toward productive growth experiences provided that it has not been overlaid with external rules and societal values that preclude healthy self-actualization (1964).

## The Self

Out of the interaction of the organism and the environment, and in particular the interaction with significant others, there gradually emerges a structure of self, or a concept of "who I am" (1951). As young children interact with their environment in the process of actualization, they acquire ideas about themselves, their world, and their relationship to that world. They experience things that they like or dislike and things that they can or cannot control. Those experiences that appear to enhance one's self are valued and incorporated into one's self-image; those experiences that appear to threaten the self are denied and rendered foreign to the self.

The **self-concept** is a portion of the phenomenal field that has gradually become differentiated. It is composed of those conscious perceptions and values of "me" or "I," some of which are a result of the organism's own valuing of its experiences and some of which have been introjected or taken over from important others. Because the self-concept comes in part through others the potential for dissociation or estrangement exists (and usually occurs to some degree). As a result, the actualizing tendency may be perverted into behaviors that do not lead to actualization. The self-concept, then, is an object of perception. It is the person as she or he perceives herself or himself. Thus we have a distinction between the organism or real self in the process of actualization, and the self as perceived, or object. The "self" that one forms may be at variance with the real experience of one's organism because it includes values that are taken over from other people rather than the actual experiences of the organism.

For example, a young boy quickly learns that his parents withdraw their affection when he hits his baby brother. Even though hitting his brother is a satisfying act, the boy forfeits his satisfaction in order to conceive of himself as lovable to his parents. He denies that he wants to hit his brother. When children deny or distort their experiences, they are no longer aware of them. They begin to experience the attitudes of others, such as their parents, as if these were the direct experiences of their own. Through such distortion, an individual may come to experience any expression of anger as bad and therefore may no longer accurately perceive that at times its expression is satisfying. In such cases the experiences of the self and that of the organism do not coincide.

Rogers did not believe that the self-structure must be formed on the basis of denial and distortion. The child values experiences as positive or negative. If a parent is able to accept the child's feeling of satisfaction and also accept her or his *own* feelings that certain actions are inappropriate, the parent can help the child curb actions without threatening the integrity of the child's self-concept. The parent can make it clear that the action of hitting the baby is wrong. Nevertheless, the feelings of satisfaction from the aggression and the child's desire are recognized and accepted.

The experiences that occur in our lives are either symbolized, ignored, denied, or distorted. If an experience is *symbolized*, it is accepted into consciousness, perceived, and organized into a relationship with the self. Experiences are denied or distorted if they appear to be inconsistent with the self-structure. Young women who are brought up to believe that aggression is unfeminine may deny or distort their natural feelings of anger and find it difficult to be assertive because they seek to behave in ways that are feminine. Likewise, men frequently deny or distort natural feelings of being nurturing because they find them inconsistent with being masculine. In short, the individual's awareness is highly dependent on the self-concept.

## Congruence and Incongruence

There is a need for the self as perceived and the real self, the organism, to be congruent. A state of **congruence** exists when a person's symbolized experiences reflect all of the actual experiences of the organism. When one's symbolized experiences do not represent all of the actual experiences, or if they deny or distort them, there is a lack of correspondence between the self as perceived and the real self. In such a situation, there is **incongruence** and possible maladjustment. Diagrammatically, we can show this with overlapping circles, much as we depicted Horney's distinction between the real self and the ideal self (Figure 13.2).

When an individual denies or distorts significant sensory and visceral experiences, certain basic tensions arise. The self as perceived, which primarily governs behavior, is not an adequate representative of the true experiences of the organism. It becomes increasingly difficult for the self to satisfy the organism's needs. Tension develops and is felt as anxiety or uncertainty.

Rogers (1951) offered the following example. A young mother conceives of herself as a "good and loving mother." She cannot recognize her negative, rejecting attitudes toward her child because they do not coincide with her self-image. Nevertheless, these negative attitudes exist, and her organism seeks aggressive acts that would express these attitudes. She is limited in expressing herself only through channels that are consistent with her self-image of being a good mother. Since it is appropriate for a good mother to behave aggressively toward her child when the child's behavior is bad, she perceives a great deal of the child's behavior as bad and punishes the child accordingly. In this manner, she can express her negative attitudes but retain her self-image of being a good mother.

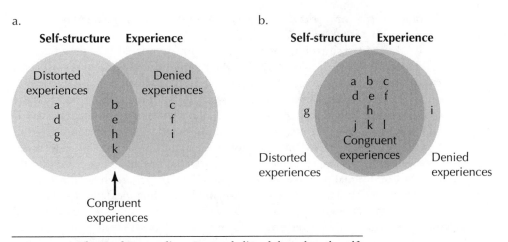

**FIGURE 13.2   The Total Personality**   Rogers believed that when the self-concept is congruent with the experiences of the organism, the person is free from inner tension and psychologically adjusted. Diagram *a* depicts a personality in a state of psychic tension. Diagram *b* shows a personality in a state of relative congruence, wherein more elements of experience have been integrated into the self.

When the self-concept is congruent with the experiences of the organism, the person is free from inner tension and psychologically adjusted. Rogers made it clear that he did not advocate the free and unrestrained expression of all our impulses and emotions. Part of the reality of the organism's experience is that certain social and cultural values require suppression of certain activities. Nevertheless, one's self-concept can include both the desire to behave one way and the desire to behave in other, more socially accepted ways. If parents can accept their feelings of rejection for their children as well as their feelings of affection, they can relate to their children more honestly.

When people become aware of and accept their impulses and perceptions, they increase the possibility of conscious control over their expression. The driver who is adept on icy roads knows the importance of steering "with the skid" in order to gain control over the car. In the same manner, by accepting all experiences, a person acquires better self-control.

## Development of Personality

Rogers did not posit any specific stages of personality development from infancy to adulthood. He concentrated on the way in which the evaluations of others impede or facilitate self-actualization. Although the tendency to actualize follows genetic determinants, Rogers noted that it is subject to strong environmental influences.

The young child has two basic needs: the need for positive regard by others and the need for positive self-regard. **Positive regard** refers to being loved and accepted for who one is. Young children behave in such a way as to show their strong need for the acceptance and love of those who care for them. They will undergo significant changes in their behavior in order to attain positive regard.

In an ideal situation, positive regard is unconditional. It is given freely to children for who they are regardless of what they do. **Unconditional positive regard** is not contingent on any specific behaviors. A parent can limit or curb certain undesirable behaviors by objecting only to the behaviors and not disapproving of the child or the child's feelings. A parent who sees a child scribble on the wall may say, "Writing on the wall destroys it. Use this blackboard instead." Here, the parent limits remarks to the behavior itself. But the parent who says, "You are a bad boy (girl) for writing on the wall," has shifted from disapproval of the behavior to disapproval of the child. Such regard is no longer unconditional.

**Conditional positive regard** is given only under certain circumstances. Children are led to understand that their parents will not love them unless they think, feel, and act as their parents want them to. In such cases, the child perceives the parent as imposing **conditions of worth,** specifying the provisions under which the child will be accepted, such as being pretty or earning top grades. Such conditions of worth may lead the child to introject values of others rather than of the self and lead to a discrepancy between the self-concept and the experiences of the organism.

**Positive self-regard** follows automatically if one has received unconditional positive regard. Children who are accepted for who they are come to view themselves favorably and with acceptance. It is very difficult, however, to view oneself positively if one is contin-

*According to Carl Rogers, the young child has two basic needs: the need for positive regard by others and the need for positive self-regard.*

ually the target of criticism and belittlement. Inadequate self-concepts such as feelings of inferiority or stupidity frequently arise because a person has not received adequate positive regard from others.

In the course of development, any experience that is at variance with the emerging self-concept is denied entrance into the self because it is threatening and evokes anxiety. If children are taught that it is wrong to feel angry, they may begin to perceive the emotion of anger itself rather than certain *expressions* of anger as dangerous or incorrect.

Research on social cognition concurs with Rogers's belief that self-perception is important in personality development and that congruence is needed for psychological health. Moreover, research has shown that people try to verify their self-concept even if the self-concept is negative. Thus people who have a negative self-concept often choose partners who think unfavorably about them. Perhaps disapproving judgments increase their perception that their world is predictable. In this view, people "may go to great lengths to maintain the perception that they are in touch with social reality, however harsh that reality may be" (Swann, Stein-Seroussi, & Giesler, 1992).

Rogers believed that supportive parents and a creative environment can facilitate psychological adjustment (1951). Longitudinal studies have suggested a positive correlation between Rogers's prescribed child-rearing practices and a composite index of creative potential in early adolescence (Harrington, Block, & Block, 1987). Individuals who have experienced a positive development are more likely to become fully functioning people. Rogers did not provide as extensive a description of the self-actualized individual as Maslow did. However, he suggested five characteristics of the **fully functioning person.** These have been summarized in Table 13.2.

## Psychotherapy

Carl Rogers is best known for the method of psychotherapy that he developed, known originally as **client-centered** or **nondirective therapy** and more recently as **person-centered.** Rogers not only originated this type of therapy but also carefully studied it to determine what makes it work. As a scientist, he tried to define operationally the conditions that underlie successful therapy to generate hypotheses that can be empirically tested. He led a large-scale research program at the Counseling Center of the University of Chicago on the outcomes of psychotherapy (Rogers & Dymond, 1954), specifying the conditions that lead

---

TABLE 13.2    **The Fully Functioning Person**

1. *Openness to Experience:* Aware of all experiences without a need to deny or distort them.

2. *Existential Living:* Able to live in the moment without preconceived structures.

3. *Organismic Trust:* Trust in their own experience; not bound by other people's opinions.

4. *Experiential Freedom:* Free-choice agents; assume responsibility for decisions and behaviors.

5. *Creativity:* Able to adjust creatively to changes and seek new experiences and challenges.

to change and describing cases in which change did and did not occur. Rogers's leadership in demanding empirical validation of psychotherapy was a significant contribution, particularly considering his phenomenological and idiographic orientation.

## Conditions for Therapeutic Change

Rogers's studies suggested that there are three necessary and sufficient therapeutic attitudes for change. By *necessary,* Rogers meant that these three therapist attitudes are essential and must be present. By *sufficient,* he meant that if the client is uncomfortable with his or her present self and perceives these attitudes, change will occur. No other conditions are required. Not only did Rogers maintain that these three attitudes underlie his method of therapy, he also suggested that they underlie any good relationship and successful therapeutic technique, and lead to the development of the same attitudes in the client (1961).

The first attitude is **empathy,** the ability to experience another person's feelings as if they were one's own, but never lose sight of the "as if." Through empathy, the therapist is able to put him- or herself in the client's shoes without trying to wear those shoes or lose his or her own shoes. The therapist understands the client's internal frame of reference and communicates this understanding, largely through statements that reflect the client's feelings.

The second attitude is one of **acceptance,** in which the therapist does not posit any conditions of worth. Acceptance essentially means a nonjudgmental recognition of oneself and the other person. Through acceptance the therapist lets the other person be. In a climate of acceptance or unconditional positive regard, the client will be able to explore those feelings and experiences that were previously denied or distorted and can drop earlier conditions of worth and defenses to be open to organismic experiencing. In doing so, the client's self-concept will gradually become more congruent with the actual experiences of the organism.

The final attitude is **genuineness.** The effective therapist is genuine, integrated, free, and deeply aware of experiences within the relationship. The therapist need not be a model of perfect mental health in all aspects of his or her own life and may have shortcomings and difficulties in other situations. But within the relationship of therapy, the therapist needs to be congruent.

Given these conditions, Rogers believed that positive, constructive personality changes will occur. We are assuming, of course, that the individual's environment will permit change, and that the individual is accessible to counseling (i.e., is not suffering from a psychosis that would prevent the expression of feelings and problems).

## Responses to Emotional Communications

Rogers did not use any special techniques, such as free association or dream analysis, in his therapy. The direction of the therapy is determined by the client. In Rogerian therapy, if there were any instructions, they would be, "Talk about whatever you would like to talk about." The client determines what will be discussed, when, and to what extent. This is why Rogers's form of therapy has been labeled "client-centered." The client who does not want to talk about a particular subject is not pressed to do so. The client does not even have to talk at all. Rogers felt strongly that his clients had the ability to understand and to explore their problems and that given the appropriate therapeutic relationship, that is, an attitude of acceptance, they would move toward further self-actualization.

In Rogerian therapy, the therapist communicates the attitude of acceptance largely through statements that reflect the client's feelings. We can understand this better by distinguishing among different kinds of responses to emotional communications. Rogers developed a number of studies in which he explored how people communicate in face-to-face situations in everyday life as well as in therapy (Rogers & Roethlisberger, 1952). Consider the following hypothetical communication: "The doctor keeps telling me not to worry, but I'm frightened of this operation." There are many different ways in which one could respond to such a statement. Rogers discovered that most responses fall into one of five categories used in the following order of frequency in everyday life: (1) evaluative, (2) interpretative, (3) reassuring, (4) probing, and (5) reflective. Each of these responses tends to lead toward a different consequence.

An **evaluative response** places a value judgment on the person's thoughts, feelings, wishes, or behavior. One might say, "You shouldn't be afraid of the operation." Evaluative responses may have their place when the listener is specifically asked to give an opinion or to disclose values or attitudes. However, because evaluative responses are judgmental, they tend to detract from an attitude of basic acceptance of the other individual. Our natural tendency to approve, disapprove, judge, or evaluate another person's comments is a primary barrier to understanding in communication, often leading to a defensive reaction in the speaker and to a situation in which each party simply looks at the problem from her or his own point of view. A person who is defensive is no longer open to further exploration of anxiety.

An **interpretative response** is an effort on the listener's part to tell the original speaker what the problem really is or how the speaker really feels about the situation. One might say, "That's because you're afraid of being unconscious during the operation." Interpretation is a technique that is frequently employed in intensive therapy. When properly used and given with skill, empathy, and integrity, interpretations can be potent catalysts for growth. But in the hands of an amateur, interpretation can be a dangerous tool. In the first place, the interpretation may be wrong. Second, if it is correct, it must be properly timed. If an interpretation is ill timed, it may be rejected because the speaker was not ready for it and may further make the speaker feel misunderstood and reluctant to discuss the issue further.

A **reassuring response** attempts to soothe the original speaker's feelings. It implies that the speaker need not feel that way. One might reply, "Many others have come through the same operation well." Reassuring responses may be helpful in conveying acceptance to the speaker or in encouraging a person to try out new behaviors that might help to resolve a problem. However, an individual frequently perceives reassurance as an attempt to minimize the problem. Introducing other people's problems or one's own in an effort to pacify may suggest that the listener is not taking the speaker's problem seriously or wants to dismiss it.

A **probing response** seeks further information. One might ask, "What is it about the operation that frightens you?" Additional information can be very helpful in assisting the listener to understand the problem. All too frequently, however, a probing response is taken to be an infringement of privacy. The individual may inwardly react, "That's none of your business." Rogers would recommend that a probing response be avoided or presented in such a way that the speaker is free to drop the subject. One might simply ask, "Would you like to talk about it?" in which case the speaker is free to say, "No, I'd rather not," if the subject is too painful.

The **reflective response** seeks to capture the underlying feelings that are expressed in the original communication. One might say, "You're very scared." An effective reflective statement does not simply echo the original words or thoughts of the speaker, it tries to zero in on the underlying emotion that was expressed. It is most effective if the listener uses her or his own words and responds in a manner that matches the depth of the original communication.

A distinction should be made between a reflective response and mere restatement. A *restatement* repeats the *thought* of the original comment, whereas a reflective comment seeks to express the underlying *emotion*. Reflective responses are useful because they tell the speaker that the listener is interested and understands what he or she is trying to say. A reflective response is most likely to encourage the speaker to elaborate and explore the problem further. In addition, it assists the listener to understand the other person's internal frame of reference. For these reasons, it is probably the most fruitful response to employ, particularly for a lay person and even for a skilled therapist in the initial phases of a relationship.

Rogers believed that meaningful therapy is not confined to the professional therapist's or counselor's office. Any relation can be therapeutic when it has the necessary and sufficient conditions. Most people could use practice in cultivating the reflective response inasmuch as it is the most fruitful but least used response. Rogers's theory strongly pertains to the development of effective interpersonal and communication skills (see Table 13.3).

## Supportive versus Reconstructive Psychotherapy

Different methods of psychotherapy vary in their ambitions. Some therapies aim at strengthening adaptive behaviors and others seek to reorganize the basic personality structure. At one end of the spectrum, psychoanalysis stands as an example of **reconstructive psychotherapy.** Through analysis of the resistances and transference the analyst seeks to remove defenses so that the analysand can communicate true feelings and integrate his or her personality. On the other hand, many psychotherapeutic techniques are best characterized as **supportive psychotherapy,** since they seek to strengthen adaptive instincts and defenses without necessarily tampering with the underlying personality structure. Clearly, reconstructive psychotherapy is a much more intensive undertaking, which accounts for the long duration of psychoanalysis. Although he was not averse to providing insight when the occasion merits it, Rogers's approach tends to be supportive rather than reconstructive.

One technique is not better than the other; rather, we need to recognize that for different people, in different circumstances, and perhaps even at different times in their lives, one approach may be more suitable than another. Rogers pointed out that we all can benefit from counseling. Although we may not be suffering from overt problems that seriously affect our lives, we may not be functioning as well as we would like.

TABLE 13.3  **Response to Emotional Communications**

Roger's research showed that most responses to emotional communications fall into one of five categories (listed in left column in the order of frequency with which they are used, which is not necessarily the order of the most helpful responses). In the right column is an example of each type of response to the emotional communication: "I'm really worried about Stephen. His grades have fallen, and I think he may be into drugs."

| TYPE OF RESPONSE | EXAMPLE |
| --- | --- |
| *Evaluative:* Places a value judgment on the person's thoughts, feelings, wishes, or behavior | "You mustn't feel that way. Worrying never helped any situation." |
| *Interpretive:* Identifies the real problem or underlying feelings | "That's because you feel guilty because you smoked some pot when you were young." |
| *Reassuring:* Attempts to soothe the person's feelings | "Most kids go through periods like that; it's probably nothing to worry about." |
| *Probing:* Seeks further information | "What is he doing that makes you think he's into drugs?" |
| *Reflective:* Captures the underlying feelings | "You're very concerned about him." |

## Changes in Rogers's View of Therapy

Rogers's earlier writings on therapeutic techniques stressed the idea that the potential for better health lies in the client. The counselor's role was essentially that of making the kinds of reflective responses that would enable the client's potential to flower. Later, Rogers shifted from his emphasis on technique to therapist genuineness and use of self in therapy (Bozarth, 1990).

In later years, Rogers was less interested in individual counseling and more interested in group counseling, as well as broader social concerns. He was a leader in the field of encounter groups and sponsored some interracial and intercultural groups. Under the guidance of a facilitator, rather than a traditional leader, *encounter groups* seek to create an atmosphere in which members can express their feelings, focus on their experience, and acknowledge how they are perceived by others in the group. Although not as popular as they were in the 1960s and 1970s, encounter groups can be seen as a forerunner of the support and help groups that many people today find very useful.

Rogers challenged some of the concepts on which our society is based, such as that power is power over other people or that strength is the strength to control. Instead he suggested that influence is gained only when power is shared and that control is constructive when it is self-control. He wrote about education, particularly higher education, describing a plan for radical change in teacher education and researching the effects of teachers' attitudes on students' learning. He emphasized the importance of combining experiential with cognitive learning. He also explored various forms of partnership unions or alternatives to

---

**THINKING CRITICALLY**

## *Cultivating a More Reflective Response*

Rogers suggested this exercise as a way of cultivating a more reflective response to other people. The next time you become deeply engrossed in a conversation or an argument, agree to obey the following rule. Each person may speak only after reflecting the thoughts and feelings of the previous speaker accurately and to that person's satisfaction. What initially sounds simple proves difficult, but it leads to a much more constructive discussion as it focuses on understanding one another rather than simply presenting different points of view.

Understanding is particularly difficult when one is dealing with a group that involves people of different genders, backgrounds, races, native languages, and/or cultures. Try this activity with many diverse people and see how it helps to improve your communication.

Actually, there is no written exercise or book that can improve your ability to communicate reflectively. It requires continual practice, interaction, and feedback from others. Nevertheless, in everyday communications, you can try to attune yourself to the kinds of responses that are offered. You can ask yourself, "Do my responses reflect what the speaker really means?" You can also ask the speaker if you are reflecting accurately by prefacing or ending a comment with a phrase such as, "Do you mean . . ." or ". . . is that it?"

---

marriage as well as other interpersonal relationships in contemporary society. His later workshops have been depicted as entailing a spiritual dimension, perhaps reflecting Rogers's (1980) openness to mysticism and his belief that subjective experiences were compatible with science.

---

## Assessment and Research in Rogers's Theory

Rogers was exceptionally open to the empirical test of his theories. The private, confidential character of clinical treatment has made it very difficult to study in its natural setting. With the permission of his clients, however, Rogers introduced the tape recorder and film camera into the treatment room. He did not believe that they detract from the therapy. Within a short time, both client and counselor forget about the recording equipment and act naturally and spontaneously.

The recordings Rogers made have provided a group of actual transcriptions of therapeutic sessions that can be observed and studied. The sessions have been analyzed in various ways. A classification system permits us to note the kinds of statements made by both the client and the counselor. Rating scales monitor the progress and change that occur during therapy from the viewpoints of both the client and the counselor.

Thus in describing the case of Mrs. Oak, Rogers was able to illustrate in her therapeutic experience and in her performance on a variety of test and research instruments,

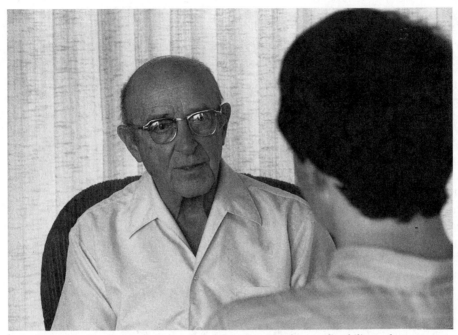

*From his work with clients, Rogers concluded that there is a clear predictability to the therapeutic process as the perceived self and the self ideal become more congruent.*

such as pre- and post-therapy Thematic Apperception Tests, the process of her psychotherapy and its results (Rogers & Dymond, 1954). In his analysis, changes in the perceived self and the self-ideal, as well as changes in their relationship, were readily apparent. In the beginning of therapy, the self-ideal bears little resemblance to the perceived self. However, during the process, congruence increases, so that at the conclusion and in the follow-up study, there is marked congruence.

One method that Rogers used for studying changes in a person's self-concept is the **Q-sort technique,** developed by William Stephenson. The Q-sort test uses a packet of one hundred cards containing descriptive statements or words that can be used to describe the self. The person is given the cards and asked to sort them according to his or her self-perception into a prearranged order, which resembles a normal curve of distribution. The Q-sort technique has been used to measure changes that occur throughout therapy. In short, Roger provided an impetus to developing means for ongoing empirical research on the processes of therapy and the self.

From his studies, Rogers concluded that there is a clear predictability to the therapeutic process. Given certain conditions, such as the three therapist attitudes outlined earlier, certain predictable outcomes may be expected. The client will express deep motivational attitudes and begin to explore and become more aware of attitudes and reactions. The client will begin to accept him- or herself more fully and will discover and choose more

## Assessment with the Q-Sort Test

You may explore the Q-sort technique by making and sorting a set of cards. Copy the following list of twenty-five different ways in which you might perceive yourself onto individual index cards:

I make strong demands on myself.
I often feel humiliated.
I often get down on myself for the things I do.
I doubt my sexual powers.
I have a warm emotional relationship with others.
It is difficult to control my aggression.
I am responsible for my troubles.
I tend to be on my guard with friendly people.
I am a responsible person.
I usually feel driven to work hard.
Self-control is no problem for me.
I am disorganized.
I express my emotions freely.

I feel apathetic.
I am optimistic.
I try not to think about my problems.
I am sexually attractive.
I am shy.
I am liked by most people who know me.
I am afraid of a full-fledged disagreement with a person.
I can usually make up my mind and stick to it.
I can't seem to make up my mind one way or another.
I am impulsive.
I am afraid of sex.
I am ambitious.

Sort the cards into seven different piles, ranging from "least like me" to "most like me." In order to have your piles follow a normal curve of distribution, you will need to place most of the cards in the middle piles, indicating that the characteristic is somewhat like you but not the most or least like you. Your final distribution should be like this:

|  | (least like me) | | | | (most like me) | | |
|---|---|---|---|---|---|---|---|
| pile # | 1 | 2 | 3 | 4 | 5 | 6 | 7 |
| no. of cards | 1 | 2 | 5 | 9 | 5 | 2 | 1 |

After you have sorted the cards to describe your self-concept as you perceive it, you may wish to re-sort the cards to describe your ideal self—the person that you would most like to be. A comparison of these two sortings will give you a rough idea of the discrepancy between your self-concept and your self-ideal. You might also wish to ask some friends to sort the cards as they perceive you, to gain an idea of the image you project to others in comparison with your own self-perception.

satisfying goals. Finally, the client will begin to behave in a manner that indicates greater psychological growth and maturity.

| PHILOSOPHY, | **Rogers's Theory** |
|---|---|
| SCIENCE, | |
| AND ART | |

Rogers did a great deal to bring the human being back as the primary focus of psychological study. In doing so, he clearly reasserted the philosophical character of personality theorizing. At the same time, he was very careful to distinguish between his philosophical assumptions and his scientific hypotheses. For instance, in Rogers's theory the self is not a philosophical concept but a name for a group of processes, which can be studied scientifically. The issue of the usefulness of the concepts of self and self-actualization continue to attract discussion and debate (see Geller, 1984; Ginsburg, 1984).

Still, Rogers's emphasis on subjectivity and the individual's internal frame of reference made scientific research difficult. Researchers have traditionally stressed the role of the external observer because, as we have seen, introspective reports are much more difficult to validate than extrospective reports. Rogers was criticized for using self-reports in his research, and many scientific psychologists have rejected Rogers's notion of the self because of his methods.

However, Roger encourages us to invite the person as a co-investigator in personality research. The concept of self, which he revitalized, is increasingly described as a complex psychological construct stemming from interpretations of cognitive, affective-motive, and attitudinal facets. Within individuals, there is one self with varied interrelated aspects as compared to a multiplicity of selves. The existence of a harmony between the pattern and typology of the personality and the self provides a framework for explaining both realities (Zlate, 1989).

Tendencies to suppress data or to supply socially acceptable data instead of the truth do exist in subjective reporting. However, if we are aware of these tendencies toward error, we can take steps to avoid them. In this sense, introspection is no different from any other scientific method. Extrospection is also open to a great deal of error: sense organs may be defective or deluded. Psychologists have known for a long time that there is hardly a perfect correspondence between the stimulus, or the evidence of the world that reaches our senses, and our perception of the world. Introspection does not involve the sense organs to the same extent as extrospection and so in some respects may be more trustworthy. Thus, Rogers's emphasis on introspection was a useful correction of the emphasis on extrospection that characterized American psychology. Introspective self-reports have gained wider acceptance with social and cognitive behavior theorists with the present emphasis on cognition.

Nevertheless, a major criticism of Rogers's position is that it is based on a simplistic concept of phenomenology and does not reflect a sophisticated understanding of the complexity of the processes underlying human awareness. It also does not take into account a child's immature cognitive structures and inability to make clear distinctions between feelings and actions. To say that the best vantage point for understanding an individual is that of the individual minimizes how frequently human beings deny or distort the truth about themselves to themselves. Many of us seem bent on self-deception rather than on self-understanding. Although Rogers acknowledged that there are experiences of which a person may be unaware through the processes of denial and distortion, he did not believe that repression is inevitable and held that an atmosphere of acceptance is sufficient to lift repression. Critics suggest that this belief is naive and that Rogers failed to recognize the power and intensity of unconscious forces.

Rogers's own example of the two men, one of whom saw a boulder and the other a tumbleweed, depicts the limitations of his approach. In spite of how an object is perceived, or even if it is not perceived, its reality has an impact. After all, "contact with a boulder will hurt no matter how it is perceived." "Reality is not wholly determined internally" (Lerman, 1992). Research in feminist psychology shows that individuals' personalities are intimately related to the world they live in and the conditions of worth that are imposed upon them. The reality of women's subjugation (and I might add that of other oppressed groups) influences what they can be, how they conceive of themselves, and their personality development (Miller, 1976). Thus, Lerman (1992) points out that Rogers does not seem to fully appreciate the impact of external influences. Patriarchy has, in fact, limited options for women. A woman's belief that she is entitled to leave an abusive situation does not necessarily imply that she will be able to leave safely. Changing women's self-perceptions will not, in itself, eliminate external barriers.

Moreover, Rogers's view of the development and actualization of self may be highly culture-bound. He has been accused of encouraging selfishness (Marin, 1975; Wallach & Wallach, 1983) and making interpersonal relations "instrumental" and "competitive" (Geller, 1982). His portrait of the healthy self as an actualizing being, differentiated from others and dependent on achievement, may not be relevant to non-Western cultures where the self is delineated in terms of relation to others, particularly within the family (Markus & Kitayama, 1991). This may be strange, because Rogers (1963) indicated that one of the outcomes of self-actualization is harmonious and deep social relations. Das (1989) argues that Rogers's view can be seen as complementary to the concept of self-realization in Vedandic Hinduism and the two major schools of Buddhism—Thervada and Mahayana. Hermsen (1996) has suggested that the concept of self, central to Rogers's psychotherapy, may be helpful in developing a synthesis of the psychology of religion, psychotherapy, and Taoism, while recognizing the cultural differences.

At the same time, a phenomenological view gives balance to psychology by providing a human voice in an expanding electronic world of computerization and reminds us that psychology is principally a human science (Mruk, 1989).

Rogers's careful empirical study of the therapeutic process has shed considerable light on the phenomenon and practice of therapy. Scientific research has helped to clarify the types of situations and relationships that are conducive to change. Rogers's discussion of the therapist's attitude of acceptance is a helpful correction of Freud's overemphasis on transference. It is the real, personal relationship between therapist and client that fosters personality change. Rogers's most lasting contribution may be the therapeutic impact of the art of listening (Cain, 1990): An attitude of openness and readiness to hear, that is generally taken for granted and sounds so easy, but in fact is exceedingly difficult to do. Rogers, in encouraging empirical validation of his theories, has facilitated the development of person-centered therapeutic techniques.

Rogers (1961) criticized the social and philosophical implications of a rigid behavioral science, like that proposed by B. F. Skinner, who advocated the development of a technology to control human behavior (see Chapter 8). Rogers believed that kind of society would destroy our personhood. He acknowledged that science brought us the power to manipulate; if we value the ability to control other people, our scientific technology can tell how to achieve this goal. On the other hand, if we value individual freedom and creativity, our scientific technology can facilitate these ends as well. In either case, the goal that directs the

## PHILOSOPHICAL ASSUMPTIONS

 *Examining Maslow and Rogers*

How would you rate Maslow and Rogers on each of the basic philosophical assumptions described in Chapter 1? Consult the chart on the inside front cover. Each basic issue is presented as a bipolar dimension along which a person's view can be placed according to the degree of agreement with one or the other extreme: *freedom/determinism, hereditary/environmental, uniqueness/universality, proactive/reactive, optimistic/pessimistic.* Rate Maslow and Rogers's views on these issues.

When you have determined where you think Maslow and Rogers stand, compare your responses with those of your classmates and your instructor. You should be willing to defend your ratings, but also be prepared to change them in light of others' compelling arguments. Afterward, compare your rating of Maslow and Rogers with your own position on each issue and with those of other theorists. Does this comparison help you understand why their theories do or do not appeal to you?

scientific enterprise lies outside of the scientific enterprise. The basic difference between a behavioristic approach and a humanistic approach is a philosophical choice (1980). Each choice leads to different topics of research and different methods of validation (see also DeCarvalho, 1989; Harari, 1989).

Rogers suggested that we need to be explicit about the goals we want our scientific endeavor to serve. Rogers, in his role as scientist, studied the predictability of the therapeutic process, not to control his client's behavior but to help his client be less predictable and more free, responsible, and spontaneous.

Psychologists have welcomed Rogers's reintroduction of the importance of subjectivity and perception in determining behavior, a theme consistent with the current cognitive emphasis. His therapeutic techniques have been widely applauded and adopted in education, industry, and social programs. Moreover, Rogers's theory prompted a great deal of further study and research, particularly concerning his concept of the self and the process of psychotherapy. His emphasis on human potentiality and freedom provides an attractive alternative to theories that emphasize the idea that we are largely controlled by external or unconscious forces. His theory has tremendous appeal for those who share his humanistic and optimistic philosophy of the human being.

Tena (1993) argues that Rogers's theory of an "emerging new person" can best be conceived in the framework of a "World evolutionary-revolutionary process not limited by any one specific culture." In Latin America, where people are actively involved in transpersonal psychology, these ideas are seen as relevant. In this connection, Smith (1990) reminds us that humanistic psychology originated as a social movement as well as a perspective on human nature. O'Hara (1995) suggests that Rogers's work is at the edge of nineteenth-century positivism and twentieth-century postpositive constructivism. He had a mystical commitment to truth and a scientific way of looking for it.

## *Summary*

1. Abraham Maslow has been called the spiritual father of humanistic psychology. He criticized psychoanalysis for being pessimistic and negative, and behavior and learning theories for being mechanistic.

2. Maslow distinguished between *motivation* and *metamotivation,* which entail *D-needs* and *B-needs* respectively. Motivation and the D-needs take precedence over metamotivation and the B-needs.

3. Maslow's *hierarchy of human needs* includes physiological, safety, belonging and love, self-esteem, and *self-actualization.*

4. *Self-actualized persons* fulfill themselves and do the best that they are capable of doing. Maslow's investigations of self-actualized people were not conducted along strict scientific lines, as he felt that those limitations would not be suitable for his research. He described several characteristics of self-actualizers.

5. A self-actualized person will often have a *peak experience,* which can be provoked by both religious and secular events.

6. Some critics suggest that Maslow's picture of self-actualized persons is simplistic and neglects the hard work that is involved in growth and development. Others suggest it is based on American values and a Western male paradigm of individual achievement.

7. Maslow's theory points in a direction away from pure science. His work underscores the fact that rigorous scientific procedures may not emcompass or permit research into important human questions.

8. Rogers's humanist theory is influenced by *phenomenology,* which emphasized that what is important is not an object or event in itself but how it is perceived. In psychology this means an emphasis on human awareness and the conviction that the best vantage point for understanding an individual is that of the individual him- or herself. The *phenomenal field* refers to the total sum of experiences an organism has, the organism is the individual as a process, and the *self* is a concept of who one is. Self-actualization is the dynamic within the organism leading it to actualize, fulfill, and enhance its potentials. Emotions accompany and facilitate the process of self-actualization. Fully experiencing emotions facilitates growth and repression is unnecessary.

9. A state of *congruence* exists when a person's symbolized experiences reflect actual experiences. When denial or distortion is present in the symbolization, there is a state of *incongruence.*

10. The young child has a strong need for *positive regard.* Ideally, positive regard is *unconditional.* If it is contingent upon specific behaviors it becomes *conditional positive regard* and posits *conditions of worth* that may lead the child to introject values of others and become incongruent.

11. Rogers is best known for his method of person-centered therapy. He believed that there are three necessary and sufficient therapeutic attitudes for change: *empathy, acceptance,* and *genuineness.*

12. Rogers distinguished among five different *responses* to emotional communications: *evaluative, interpretative, reassuring, probing,* and *reflective.* Each of them has different effects. Rogers encouraged the cultivation of the reflective response.

13. *Person-centered therapy* tends to be *supportive* rather than *reconstructive.* In his later writings, Rogers stressed the need for the therapist to be present as a person in the relationship and showed more interest in group therapy and social change. He has encouraged the empirical test of his theories and developed methods of assessing and predicting therapeutic change.

14. Rogers was very careful to distinguish between his philosophical assumptions and his scientific hypotheses. He criticized Skinner's view of science and his goal of controlling human nature rather than increasing human freedom, responsibility, and spontaneity. He pointed out that our technology may be used to foster many different goals. His own position has been criticized for its reliance on a simplistic phenomenology and for being highly culture-bound and praised for increasing our understanding of interpersonal relationships. Rogers's careful empirical study of the therapeutic process has shed considerable light on the phenomenon of therapy and counseling.

## Suggestions for Further Reading

Maslow's best-known work is *Motivation and Personality* (Harper & Row, 1970), which presents his theory of personality and describes in full his concepts of the hierarchy of needs and self-actualization. Originally published in 1954, it was completely revised shortly before his death. *Religions, Values, and Peak Experiences* (Viking, 1964) presents Maslow's argument that religion should be viewed as a normal, potentially healthy phenomenon and studied scientifically. In this work he outlined his concept of peak experiences, although he did not limit them to religious experiences. Nevertheless, Maslow pointed out the need of human beings for spiritual expression and he suggested that science can assist us in understanding this need and its expressions. *Toward a Psychology of Being* (Van Nostrand, 1968) is a collection of papers in which Maslow discussed his theory of B-values as well as peak experiences and self-actualization; the book also makes clear Maslow's humanistic stance as opposed to those who present a mechanistic or negative picture of human nature. Maslow's last work, *The Farther Reaches of Human Nature* (Viking, 1971), is a cumulative effort to integrate his theory with the latest developments in science. It covers topics such as biology, creativity, cognition, and synergy.

Two readable secondary sources on Maslow's thought are Frank Goble, *The Third Force: The Psychology of Abraham Maslow* (Grossman, 1970) and Colin Wilson, *New Pathways in Psychology: Maslow and the Post-Freudian Revolution* (Taplinger, 1972). A biography of Maslow, based on diaries, interviews with friends and associates, and his published works is Edward Hoffman, *The Right to Be Human* (Tarcher, 1988).

Carl Rogers was a lucid writer whose works are relatively easy for the lay person to understand. In *Counseling and Psychotherapy* (Houghton Mifflin, 1942), Rogers first introduced his therapy technique, gave examples, and compared it with other therapeutic methods. *Client-Centered Therapy* (Houghton Mifflin, 1951) reflects the change in name Rogers gave his technique in order to focus attention on the client as the center of the therapeutic process. This book discusses the practice and implications of client-centered therapy and also described his theory of personality and behavior. With Rosalind Dymond, Carl Rogers edited *Psychotherapy and Personality Change* (University of Chicago Press, 1954), which presents thirteen empirical studies investigating hypotheses that arose out of the client-centered approach. In a group of significant articles organized into the book *On Becoming a Person* (Houghton Mifflin, 1961), Rogers described his own experiences as a counselor, his view of the fully functioning person, the place of research in psychotherapy, and its implications for education, family life, and group functions. Also included is Rogers's critique of

B. F. Skinner. *Freedom to Learn* (Charles E. Merrill, 1969) discusses ways of making class-room learning more relevant and meaningful to students. Rogers explained how the atmosphere that makes learning effective is similar to those attitudes that are conducive to personality change in therapy. *A Way of Being* (Houghton Mifflin, 1980) describes the changes that occurred in Rogers's life and thought during the 1970s. Rogers felt that the best and most rigorous presentation of his theory is his article in Koch, *Psychology: A Study of a Science* (McGraw-Hill, 1959).

  Summaries of Rogers's own research may be found in a book edited by him, *The Therapeutic Relationship and Its Impact* (University of Wisconsin Press, 1967), and the Rogers and Dymond book mentioned above. For a discussion of the research generated by self-theory, the reader is referred to R. Wylie's chapter on "The Present Status of Self-Theory" in E. F. Borgotta and W. W. Lambert, *Handbook of Personality and Research* (Rand McNally, 1968) and his book *The Self-Concept* (University of Nebraska Press, 1974, 1978), as well as D. N. Aspy, *Toward a Technology for Humanizing Education* (Research Press, 1972), and R. Tausch's article "Facilitating dimensions in interpersonal relations: Verifying the theoretical assumptions of Carl Rogers," *College Student Journal*, 1978, 12 (1).

# Existential Psychoanalysis

## ROLLO MAY

## *Your Goals for This Chapter*

1. Identify two major traditions that Rollo May combines.
2. Describe the philosophy of *existentialism.*
3. Explain the existentialist approach to scientific methodology.
4. Describe the central problem May believed we face at the end of the twentieth century.
5. Explain how May conceived of *anxiety* and tell how it is intensified in contemporary culture.
6. Discuss the source of the human dilemma according to May.
7. Identify four ontological assumptions May made concerning human beings and explain how they can give us a structural basis for a science of personality.
8. Discuss what is involved in rediscovering selfhood.
9. Show how May confronted the *paradoxes* involved in each of the following goals of integration: love, *intentionality,* the *daimonic,* courage and creativity, power, freedom and destiny.
10. Explain how May defined *myth* and why he believed we need new myths.
11. Describe the existentialist approach to psychotherapy.
12. Describe May's methods of assessment and research.
13. Evaluate May's theory in terms of its function as philosophy, science, and art.

Existentialism and psychoanalysis grew out of the same cultural situation. Both seek to understand anxiety, despair, and the alienation that people feel from themselves and society. During the last half of the nineteenth century, there was a strong tendency to make the person over into a machine, thinking of people in terms of the industrial system for which they worked. This segmentation of culture had a psychological counterpart in extreme repression within the individual. It was Freud's genius to speak to, and help cure, the problem of repression (May, Angel, & Ellenberger, 1958). However, the problem went deeper than neurotic repression in the individual. Kierkegaard, Nietzsche, and other forerunners of the existentialist position foresaw that the forces of disintegration were gradually destroying the inner emotional and spiritual life of the person and leading to ultimate despair and alienation from self and society.

Rollo May's work brings together the psychoanalytic tradition in psychology and the existentialist movement in philosophy. As we have seen, Freud's writings, though transcending his own era, nevertheless clearly reflect tendencies of nineteenth-century philosophy that are considered inappropriate today. In combining the insights of psychoanalysis and existentialism, May not only clarified the continued relevance of many of Freud's contributions but also developed his own original stance. In doing so, he helped underscore the importance of philosophy and the understanding of values for the psychologist and the theory of personality. His work has earned him the title of father of American existential psychology (Bugental, 1996a).

## Biographical Background

Rollo May was born on April 21, 1909, in Ada, Ohio, and grew up in Marine City, Michigan, where a middle-American anti-intellectual attitude prevailed. His father commented several times that a psychotic breakdown experienced by Rollo's older sister was due to "too much education." May felt that the comment was "inhumane and destructive" and came to hate the disease of anti-intellectualism. However, he indicates that in other respects his father was a very sympathetic man (1983).

May graduated from Oberlin College in Ohio where he completed the A.B. in 1930. There, he marveled at the simple yet beautiful lines of an antique Greek vase displayed on a table in one of the classrooms and resolved to go to Greece, which he did immediately after his graduation. He worked in Greece for three years, teaching at Anatolia College in Salonika and traveling during the summer. He spent two summers with a group of modern artists, painting and studying peasant art. The impact of Greek philosophy and mythology is clear in his writings. He also went to Vienna and studied briefly with Alfred Adler, whose approach influenced him considerably.

Europe's tragic view of human nature prevented May from ever accepting a mechanistic concept of the person (see also Bugental, 1996b). Upon his return, American psychology seemed "naive and simplistic." So he enrolled at Union Theological Seminary in New York—not with the intent of becoming a preacher, but with the intent of asking ques-

*Rollo May's work brings together the psychoanalytic tradition in psychology and the existentialist movement in philosophy.*

tions. There he could raise penetrating inquiries into the meaning of despair, suicide, and anxiety, issues largely ignored by psychologists. He also hoped that in doing so he might learn about their counterparts: courage, joy, and the intensity of living (1983; see also Abzug, 1996). At Union, he began a lifetime friendship with the eminent Protestant theologian Paul Tillich, an association that enriched the lives, work, and writings of both of them.

May's parents were divorced while he was at Union, so he interrupted his studies and returned to East Lansing, Michigan, to take care of what remained of his family, his mother, a younger sister, and a brother. During that time, he served as an advisor to students at Michigan State College. He was able to return to New York and complete the B.D. in 1938. During his senior year at Union, his first book, *The Art of Counseling,* was written.

Thereafter, May served briefly as a parish minister in Montclair, New Jersey, before going back to New York to study psychoanalysis at the William Alanson White Institute for Psychiatry, Psychoanalysis, and Psychology. He enrolled at Columbia University and received its first Ph.D. in clinical psychology.

May's life was sharply interrupted when he came down with tuberculosis in his early thirties. At that time there was no medication for the disease. May spent three years at the Saranac TB Sanatorium in upstate New York, not knowing whether he would live or die. During his illness, he read, among other works, *The Problem of Anxiety* by Freud and *The Concept of Dread* by Sören Kierkegaard, the founder of the existential movement in philosophy. He appreciated Freud's careful formulations but felt that Kierkegaard "portrayed what is immediately experienced by human beings in crisis" (1969). May's illness helped him to appreciate the importance of an existential point of view. His own book *The Meaning of Anxiety* (1977) has been widely recognized as the first in America to encourage a genuine union between psychology and philosophy and to demonstrate the importance of values for psychology.

May's professional life was busy and productive. He served as a counselor to college students at City College of New York, developed a private practice in psychoanalysis, and became a member of the White Institute. He taught at The New School for Social Research, New York University, Harvard, Yale, and Princeton. He has numerous publications and was honored with several awards. May died in 1994.

## The Existential Attitude

**Existentialism** is a movement in contemporary philosophy and psychology that sprang up spontaneously in differently parts of Europe and among different schools of thought. It has its roots in the resistance movements during World War II and in the philosophies of Sören Kierkegaard (1813–1855), Martin Heidegger (1889–1976), and Jean-Paul Satre (1905–1980). The name existentialism comes from the Latin *exsistere*, which means "to stand out" or "to emerge," and the existential approach focuses upon the human being as he or she is emerging and becoming.

In the past, Western philosophy has traditionally looked for the **essence** of being, the unchangeable principles and laws that are believed to govern existence. Mathematics is the purest form of this approach. In psychology, the essentialist attitude expresses itself in the effort to understand human beings in terms of forces, drives, and conditioned reflexes. Existentialists point out that a law can be true and still not be real. "Two unicorns plus two unicorns equals four unicorns" is a logically true statement but it does not talk about anything that is real. Existentialism seeks to bridge the gap between what is abstractly true and what is existentially real (May et al., 1958).

The existential attitude can be a bewildering one that defies simple definition. We can illustrate it, however, by comparing two possible postures that a person might have at a football game. The first is that of the spectator up in the stands; the second is that of the player on the field. Both spectator and player are involved in the football game, but there is a considerable difference in their involvement. The spectator may get very agitated and excited as the game proceeds, urging and cheering on a favorite team. But this involvement is very different from that of the player. The outcome of the game does not depend on the activity of the spectator, who remains outside the game as an observer. The outcome does depend very much on how the player behaves and performs on the field. What the player does is not indifferent to the game. The player cannot stand back and observe the game while being involved in it.

The posture of existentialism is that of the player, and the game of existentialism is the game of life. In life, existentialists point out, we cannot play the role of a detached or uninvolved spectator because we are already participants in the game.

Existentialists suggest that there is no truth or reality for us as human beings except as we participate in it, are conscious of it, and have some relation to it. Knowledge is not an act of thinking but an act of doing. Existentialists do not necessarily rule out essences, but "existence precedes essence." May, for example, did not deny the validity of concepts such as conditioning or drives; he simply pointed out that we cannot adequately explain a person on that basis because when we try to, we end up talking about abstractions rather than the living person. It is all right to have concepts, but we must recognize that they are only tools and not substitutes for the living person. Thus, when we use concepts, we must make it clear that we are abstracting them from the living person and we are not talking about the real person.

Psychologists have generally tended to study those phenomena that lend themselves to control and analysis and permit one to formulate abstract laws. They are not particularly concerned with whether or not the phenomena are real or even close to everyday life. Indeed, in some laboratory experiments, the phenomenon under consideration is far removed from real life. Existentialists believe that psychologists' preoccupation with lawfulness and predictability stands in the way of understanding the real person. May pointed out that the behavior of a neurotic is quite predictable because it is compulsive, whereas the healthy person is "predictable" in that behavior is integrated and unified, but at the same time can be flexible and spontaneous. The existentialist approach has been criticized for rendering the individual unlawful and unpredictable. It is true that existentialists do not see the human being in terms of our traditional conceptual theories, looking instead at the structure of a particular person's existence and its own lawfulness.

The existentialist approach is not antiscientific. It arose out of a desire to be not *less* but *more* empirical, but it does urge a greater breadth to our scientific methodology. Contrary to the conventional approach of the scientist in which the more complex is explained by the simpler, existentialists believe that a reductionistic approach misleads and that the "simpler can be understood and explained only in terms of the more complex" (May, 1969). When a new level of complexity emerges, it becomes crucial for understanding the forms that have preceded it. What makes a horse a horse is not what it shares with the organisms it evolved from but what constitutes its distinctive "horseness" (1983). Science, therefore, must look for the distinguishing characteristic of what it is trying to understand, namely, the human being.

The existentialist view takes the inquiry to a deeper level to look at the structure in which those concepts are rooted. It seeks to develop an empirical science that deals with the whole of our knowledge of what it means to be human. As such, it looks at the unity of the person prior to any split into subject versus object, body versus mind, nature versus nurture, or any other conceptual "either-or" dimensions. It asks what it means to be and to exist under these particular psychological, cultural, and historical conditions.

In studying the structure of human existence, the very nature of the subject shapes the science that investigates it. Existentialists have made clear the limits of objectivity in our understanding and the need to broaden the scope of our methodology. Objectivity is a goal that many psychologists have prized and sought to achieve. They believe that unless we are objective, our emotions and prejudices will come between us and the facts, clouding our reasoning processes. Students of psychology are encouraged to take a detached, objective stance. At times, however, objectivity prevents understanding. Some truths, such as understanding what it means to be, are discovered not by objectivity but by intense personal involvement. The existentialist attitude strongly resists the tendency to treat a person as an object.

In their insistence that human knowledge is ultimately interpersonal, May and other existentialists are indebted to the thought of Martin Buber (1878–1965), whose book *I and Thou* made a classic distinction between knowing that is transpersonal (I-Thou) and knowing that is objective or subjective (I-it). In his book, Buber describes an entirely different way in which the world, particularly the world of persons, reveals itself to us. Knowledge is not simply objective (of an external object) or subjective (of the self) but also interpersonal, arising out of the encounter of human beings with one another. Understanding through encounter is just as real as understanding through objectification.

Existentialism begins with personal existence. It asks, "What does it mean to be a self?" It questions the purpose and nature of existence. It views individuals as agents with free choices who are responsible for their actions. Each one of us carves out his or her own destiny. We are literally what we do. The existentialist posture leads to an emphasis on choice and responsibility and to the view that a worthwhile life is one that is authentic, honest, and genuine.

## Our Predicament

May pointed out (1967) that in the second half of the twentieth century, the central problem that we face is a feeling of *powerlessness,* a "pervasive conviction that the individual cannot do anything effective in the face of enormous cultural, social, and economic problems." Our feelings of powerlessness are compounded by anxiety and the loss of traditional values.

### *Powerlessness*

The problem of powerlessness goes much deeper than the fact that this is an age of uncertainty and social upheavals. May believed that the unwanted war in Vietnam and the continued unrest in the Middle East illustrate how we can become caught in a historical situation in which no one person or group of persons feels capable of exercising significant power. With our increased technology, power has become impersonal, an autonomous force acting on its own behalf (1967).

In the early 1950s, May observed that many of the patients who came to see him were suffering from inner feelings of emptiness (1953). He noted that the neurotic frequently acts out what others are temporarily unaware of. May anticipated that the experience of emptiness and powerlessness he was seeing in his patients would in time become epidemic, and of course it did. The 1970s saw considerable talk about human potentialities, yet very little confidence on the part of individuals about their power to make a significant difference (1975). This feeling of paralysis accompanied us throughout the 1980s and even into the 1990s.

May believed that the most striking example of the individual's sense of insignificance and powerlessness is the impotence many of us feel concerning the threat of nuclear war or accident. The potentiality for such disaster rapidly increases along with a recognition that it could begin through a simple incident such as a computer malfunction. The threat of nuclear war and other unsettling social conditions are but symptoms of the deeper problem. Contemporary men and women feel helpless and insignificant. Our impotence leads to anxiety and repression, leading in turn to apathy, which is a form of protection. Impotence and apathy, however, also breed violence and hostility that further alienate us from one another and only serve to increase our isolation (1972).

## Anxiety

It has become commonplace to describe our age as an age of anxiety. However, prior to 1950, only two books had been written that concerned themselves specifically with presenting an objective picture of anxiety and suggesting constructive ways of dealing with it: Freud's *The Problem of Anxiety* and Kierkegaard's *The Concept of Dread*. After May wrote *The Meaning of Anxiety,* which was first published in 1950, hundreds of works followed on the same topic. May's efforts helped to spur research into this area. *The Meaning of Anxiety* was revised in 1977 and at that time May pointed out that the tremendous interest in anxiety that attended its initial publication had indicated the need for an integrated theory of anxiety. May's work is distinguished by its efforts to synthesize the insights of both psychology and philosophy. Since that time, he has applied his analytic synthesis to the dilemmas of love and will, power and innocence, creativity, and freedom and destiny.

Some psychologists prefer to use the term "stress" in place of anxiety. May believed that this tendency is unfortunate and inaccurate. The word *stress* has become popular because it comes from engineering and physics; it can be defined easily and measured accurately. The problem with the concept of stress is that it does not adequately describe the apprehension we ordinarily refer to as anxiety. Moreover, it puts the emphasis on what happens *to* a person, whereas anxiety is distinctly bound up with consciousness and subjectivity (1977).

May proposed the following definition of **anxiety:** "Anxiety is the apprehension cued off by a threat to some value that the individual holds essential to his or her existence as a person" (1977). Anxiety is an inevitable characteristic of being human (1983), a given. Anxiety is objectless, "because it strikes at that basis of the psychological structure on which the perception of one's self as distinct from the world of objects occurs" (1977). Thus, in anxiety, the distinction between self and object breaks down.

The potential for anxiety is innate, although the particular events that may become threatening are learned. Fear is the expression of anxiety in a specific objectified form. May suggested that anxiety is intensified in our contemporary competitive culture by the interpersonal isolation and alienation that have emerged out of a particular pattern in which one's self is viewed as an object and self-validation depends upon winning over others (1977). Anxiety, therefore, is another symptom of the deeper problem. Kagan (1994) reminds us that the primary source of anxiety in our time is not the major source of anxiety in all of time, reflecting a universal truth about human nature. A particular culture may elevate one facet of anxiety to a dominant position, but only temporarily. The situations that provoke anxiety in our time would be incomprehensible to a Tibetan villager.

Our current stepped-up efforts to dispel anxiety actually end up increasing it. May reminded us that we cannot live in an empty condition for a sustained period of time (1953). We need something to fill the gap, be it a destructive authority, drugs, or alcohol. Earlier in this century, the emotional vacuum in Europe permitted fascist dictators to seize power. Today, many young people "waste" themselves on alcohol and drugs. The problem is that human consciousness, responsibility, and intentions have not been able to keep up with all of the rapid changes in contemporary society. If we were able to recognize our historical situation and its psychological implications, we might be able to move from self-defeating activities to constructive ones.

## The Loss of Values

The source of our problem lies in the loss of the center of values in our society (1967). Ever since the Renaissance, the dominant value in Western society has been competitive prestige measured in terms of work and financial success. Such values are no longer effective in the postmodern world in which we have to learn to work with other people in order to survive. Individual competition no longer brings the greatest good to one's self or to the community. Instead, it creates problems where previously it did not.

Our ability to stand outside of ourselves and relate to ourselves permits us to create values that help to shape our lives (1967). For several centuries, we were able to validate ourselves by our power over nature. Then we began to supply the methods that had been so successful in understanding and controlling nature to ourselves. In so doing, we rendered ourselves impersonal objects that could be exploited. Along with the loss of the dominant value of individualism, we lost a sense of the worth and dignity of the human being. We became estranged from nature and from one another. Today, many people are more comfortable conversing with a computer than with another human being. The loneliness and isolation that were potential in Western society have become widely apparent in our time.

The answer to our dilemma is to discover and affirm a new set of values. There are those who would suggest that we need to reaffirm the traditional values, embodied in earlier philosophies and religion, that we have permitted to go by the wayside. Here, May's existential stance becomes apparent. Because we have no "essence," there are no given or pre-established values to which we can turn. Our values are established in the course of our existence and our destiny now includes the historical situation in which we have placed ourselves (1981). There can be no simple reaffirmation of our human "essence," because there is none; the human being is forever in the process of becoming. We have to choose our values in the process of living.

The choice is ours, and so is the responsibility. We can withdraw in anxiety, giving up our distinctive human capacity to influence our own development through our awareness; we can surrender to the power of the technology that we created; or we can muster the courage that we need to preserve our sensitivity and responsibility and consciously work together in developing a new society (1975).

**THINKING CRITICALLY**

## *The Viability of a Traditional Ethic*

Rollo May suggested that many of our traditional values are no longer effective and that we need to develop and affirm a new set of values. For example, a dominant value in Western society has been competitive prestige, measured in terms of work and the reward of financial success that attends it. Many of us have grown up hearing about the importance of the "work ethic." When queried about what life would be like if they were poor, most students indicate that they would work very hard, save money, and move out of poverty.

The following activity may help you appreciate some of the structural and resource constraints on people who live in poverty. Imagine that you are a welfare mother of two preschoolers who is being battered by her husband and deciding whether to leave him. You are to base your decision on a budget in which you will either continue to work full time at minimum wage or go on welfare. In order to do this, you need to contact the local welfare office and ask the following questions:

1. What is the grant for your size family?
2. How much will you get in food stamps?
3. Is public housing available? Immediately, or will you need to be on a waiting list?
4. If you work, how much of your income will you be permitted to keep?
5. What daycare is available, and how will you pay for it?

The information you receive will vary in its "generosity" depending on local welfare policies. In answering your dilemma, you can also assume the following facts: You do not have a credit card or good credit. Your family is unable to help you out. Any child-support money would also probably reduce the size of your grant.

Once you've gathered your information, do you see any options other than staying with your abusive husband, abandoning your children, or going on welfare and "cheating" by failure to report some of your income or other sources of money? What does this tell you about the effectiveness of the "work ethic" in contemporary society for self-validation for people living in poverty?

America is the land of opportunity. We are all familiar with stories of rags to riches. But are your parents multimillionaires? Why not? Were they unwilling to work? Are they lazy? Bill Gates was able to do it. Why not your parents? Why not you? What does this tell you about the effectiveness of the "work ethic" and competitive prestige for self-validation for middle-class people in today's society?

Do these activities help you to think differently about the viability of the work ethic in providing a value that helps shape our lives? What value or ethic do you suggest might be developed in its place?

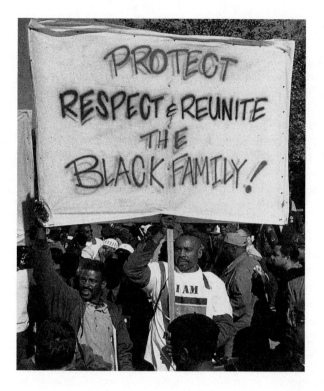

The purpose of the Million Man March was to discover and affirm a new set of values, particularly in reference to the role of men in African-American families.

## Rediscovering Selfhood

May (1953) believed that *consciousness of self* is the unique mark of the human person. Self-consciousness enables us to distinguish between ourselves and the world, to learn from the past and to plan for the future, to see ourselves as others do, and to have empathy with others. However, such self-consciousness comes at the risk of anxiety and inward crisis. It means that we must stand on our own and develop an identity apart from that of our parents and forebears. We can even stand against them, if necessary.

Unlike the acorn that grows automatically into an oak tree, the human being, in self-actualizing, must do so consciously through choice and affirmation. Selfhood is not automatic but is born in a social context and grows in interpersonal relations. However, May's emphasis is not on the extent to which we are created by others, but rather on our capacity to create and experience our own selves.

Some psychologists avoid the concept of self because it separates humans from animals and complicates scientific experimentation. May, along with Rogers and Maslow, believed that in doing so psychologists miss an important feature of the human experience. Our capacity for self-relatedness is prior to, not established by, our science. It is presupposed in the fact that one can be a scientist. May wanted to see us develop a science to illuminate the concept of self.

## Ontological Assumptions Concerning the Person

Many psychologists emphasize the study of behavior, but May believed that they need to ask questions on a deeper *ontological* level, the level of being. They need to ask what is the nature of the person as a person and how can we best describe human existence?

As a clinician, May frankly admitted that he made certain ontological and philosophical assumptions about what it means to be a human being (1967). First, he assumed that all living organisms are potentially centered in themselves and seek to preserve that center. In psychotherapy, a patient is engaged in the process of such preservation. Second, human beings have the need and the possibility of going out from their centeredness to participate with other people. This entails risk and is illustrated in psychotherapy in the encounter with the therapist. Third, May suggested that sickness is a method whereby an individual seeks to preserve his or her being, a strategy for survival, even though that method may be limiting and may block off potentials for knowledge and action. Finally, May asserted that human beings can participate in a level of self-consciousness that permits them to transcend the immediate situation and to consider and actualize a wider range of possibilities. These ontological assumptions can give us a structural basis for a science of personality. They precede analytic activity and make it possible. In turn, our analytic activity can help to illumine them.

Psychological concepts need to be oriented within an ontological framework. Thus, May suggested that the concept of *unconscious experience* can be understood in terms of self-deception and experiences that an individual cannot actualize. May interpreted the Oedipal myth and conflict as indicative of the problems involved in a person's relation to the world through the emergence and development of consciousness (1967). The main question in the drama does not concern murder and incest but is "Shall Oedipus recognize what he has done?" It is significant that Oedipus plucks out his eyes and thereby blinds himself, rather than, for example, attacking his genitals. What is at issue is seeing reality and the truth about oneself.

May believed that the theme of exile in the story is very important. Oedipus was exiled as a baby and at the end of the drama he exiles himself. Being aware that one is responsible for one's life, a person can confront life and death. This is why the symbol of suicide is centrally placed in the existentialist approach.

## Rediscovering Feelings

In rediscovering selfhood, most people have to start back at the beginning and rediscover their feelings (1953). Many of us have only a vague idea of what we are feeling at any given time. We react to our bodies as if they were separate and distinct. While denying our own emotions, we ascribe feelings to machines, describing them as "friendly," "affectionate," and so forth. We need to recognize that we play an active role in creating our bodies and feelings. Awareness of one's body and feelings lays the groundwork for knowing what one wants. Surprisingly few people are actually clear on what they want. Being aware of one's desires does not imply that one must act on them. But we cannot have any basis for judging what we will and will not do unless we first know what we want to do.

Becoming a person requires not only getting in touch with one's feelings and desires but also fighting against those things that prevent us from feeling and wanting (1953). The development of a human being is a process of differentiation from an original unity with the mother toward freedom as an individual. The physical umbilical cord is cut at birth, but the infant is still dependent on its mother. Unless the psychological cord is severed in due time, the individual's growth is stunted. In order to advance and be oneself, a person has to become free of domineering and authoritarian powers even if that requires taking a stand against one's parents or other authorities. It is our infantile ties of dependency that keep us from being clear as to our feelings and wants. The early struggle against authority is external; as we grow, the problem becomes internal. Thus, as adults many of us continue to act as if we still have to fight the original forces that enslaved us when in fact we are now enslaving ourselves.

## *Four States of Consciousness of Self*

May (1953) suggested that there are four stages of consciousness of self. The first is the *stage of innocence* before consciousness of self is born. This stage is characteristic of the infant. The second is the *stage of rebellion* in which the individual seeks to establish some inner strength. The toddler and the adolescent illustrate this stage, which may involve defiance and hostility. The third stage is *ordinary consciousness of self.* This is the stage most people refer to when they speak of a healthy personality. It involves being able to learn from one's mistakes and live responsibly. May referred to the last stage as *creative consciousness of self.* It involves the ability to see something outside one's usual limited viewpoint and gain a glimpse of ultimate truth as it exists in reality. This level cuts through the dichotomy between subjectivity and objectivity. Not everyone achieves each level of consciousness. The fourth stage, achieved only rarely, is somewhat analogous to Maslow's peak experience. Nevertheless it is the level that gives meaning to our actions and experiences on the lesser levels.

## The Goals of Integration

May conceived of the human being as conscious of self, capable of intentionality, and needing to make choices. In his existential analysis of personality, May sought to undercut the traditional dualism of subject and object that has haunted Western self-understanding ever since Descartes, who said that we are conscious of ourselves either as a subject or as an object. May considered the self as a unity. In his discussion of the goals of integration, May further revealed an intent to discuss key issues in personality in such a way as to avoid the tendency to abstract the real person and life itself into artificial dualisms and constructs. Instead of abstract conceptualizations, we need to recognize and confront the paradoxes of our own lives (1981). In **paradox** two opposing things are posited against and seem to negate each other yet they cannot exist without each other. Thus, good and evil, life and death, beauty and ugliness appear to be at odds with each other but the very confrontation with the one breathes life and meaning into the other. "Harmony," as Heraclitus reminded us, "consists of opposing tension, like that of the bow and the lyre" (May, 1981). The goals of integration include confronting one's potentialities for the daimonic, power, love, intentionality, freedom and destiny, and courage and creativity.

## The Daimonic

In a world that vaunts rationality, May (1969) reintroduced the concept of the daimonic and insists that we come to terms with it. The **daimonic** is "any natural function which has the power to take over the whole person." Sex, anger, a craving for power, all of these may become evil when they take over the self without regard for the integration of the self. We can repress the daimonic but we cannot avoid its consequences. In repressing it, we become its pawns.

The daimonic is potentially creative and destructive at the same time. By becoming aware of it, we can integrate it into ourselves. We can learn to cherish our internal demons and permit them to give us the salt of life. The daimonic begins as impersonal; by bringing it into consciousness, one makes the daimonic urges personal. With a more sensitive understanding of these forces in one's body and life, the daimonic pushes one toward the universal structure of reality. The movement is from impersonal to personal to a transpersonal dimension of consciousness (1969).

## Power

As we have seen, a basic factor in our contemporary crisis is the feeling of insignificance and powerlessness. Human life can be seen as a conflict between achieving a sense of the significance of one's self on the one hand and the feeling of powerlessness on the other. We tend to avoid both sides, the former because of evil connotations associated with being too powerful and the latter because our powerlessness is too painful to bear.

Violence has its breeding ground in impotence and apathy. As we make people powerless, we encourage their violence rather than control it. Violent deeds such as the taking of hostages are done by those who seek to enhance their self-esteem. Powerless people sometimes invite exploitation in order to feel significant or seek revenge in passive-aggressive ways, such as the ways of drugs and alcohol.

May pointed out that the argument against violence on television would be stronger if it were made against the passive character of television viewing rather than the emulation of aggressive models. Televised entertainment cultivates the spectator role rather than active participation; as such, its greatest danger may lie in the cultivation of feelings of impotence that contribute to violent behavior.

"The culture admittedly has powerful effects upon us. But it could not have these effects were these tendencies not already present in us, for, . . . we constitute the culture" (1983). Power is an ontological state of being. The potentiality to experience and to express

*According to May, televised entertainment cultivates the spectator role, which leads to feelings of impotence and contributes to violent behavior.*

power is present in all of us. No one can escape experiencing power in desire or in action. Our goal is to learn how to use our power in ways that are appropriate for the situation, to be assertive rather than aggressive. We must find social ways of sharing and distributing power so that every person can feel significant.

## Love and Sex

Love used to be seen as the answer to human problems. Now love itself has become the problem (1969). The real problem is being able to love. Our world is schizoid, out of touch, unable to feel or to enter into a close relationship. Affectlessness and apathy are predominant attitudes toward life, forms of protection against the tremendous overstimulation of modern society.

May believed that our highly vaunted sexual freedom has turned out to be a new form of puritanism in which emotion is separated from reason and the body is used as a machine. Pornography and commercialization have also turned sex into a vehicle for power. We have set sex against *eros,* the drive to relate to another person and create new forms of life. It is now socially sanctioned to repress eros, and we rush to the sensation of sex in order to avoid the passion and responsibility that eros commands. The sexual freedom established during the 1960s and 1970s has not led to the increase in happiness that many thought would follow a freeing of sexual mores. The premature awakening of sex so prevalent in our time can lead us to dodge awakening at other levels (1991). In the midst of wide availability of information and birth control, unwanted pregnancies and sexually transmitted diseases continue. Why? The real issue is not on the level of conscious rational intentions but in the deeper realm of intentionality, where a deep defiance mocks our withdrawal of feeling.

May (1969) suggested that only the experience and rediscovery of *care,* the opposite of apathy, will enable us to stand against the cynicism that characterizes our day. The mythos of care points to the need to develop a new morality of authenticity in human relations.

## Intentionality

May believed that we must put decision and will back into the center of our picture of personality. His intent is not to rule out deterministic influences but to place the problem of determinism and freedom on a deeper level. May does this by introducing the concept of **intentionality** (1969), which underlies will and decision.

By intentionality, May meant "the structure which gives meaning to experience." A distinctly human capacity, intentionality is an imaginative attention that underlies our intentions and informs our actions. It is the capacity to participate in knowing. How a piece of paper is perceived will differ depending on whether one intends to write on it or to make a paper airplane. It is the same piece of paper that provides the stimulus and the same person responding to it but the paper and experience will have a different meaning.

Intentionality bridges the gap between subject and object because it is the structure of meaning that permits a subject to understand the world as object. Perception is directed by intentionality. Contrary to the popular belief that truth is perceived through a detached objective stance, May held that we cannot know the truth until we have taken a stand on it. Both the detached type and the asocial personality avoid confronting their intentionality. When you face your intentionality, then you can decide whether or not to act it out in your behavior.

## Freedom and Destiny

The existentialist attitude is sometimes mistakenly criticized for portraying the individual as absolutely free with no restraints whatsoever. May, however, reminded us that freedom can be considered only together with destiny (1981). Freedom means "openness, readiness to grow, flexibility, and changing in pursuit of greater human values" (1953). It entails our capacity to take a hand in our own development. Freedom is basic to the existentialist understanding of human nature because it underlies our ability to choose and to value. However, freedom can be experienced only in juxtaposition with human destiny.

May (1981) defined *destiny* as the vital design of the universe expressed in each one of us. In its extreme form, our destiny is death, but it also expresses itself in our individual talents, our personal and collective histories, and the culture and society into which we were born. Destiny sets limits for us but it also equips us to perform certain tasks. Confronting these limits yields constructive values.

Freedom is in crisis today because we have viewed it without its necessary opposite. We have become irresponsible with our laissez-faire free enterprise system and culture of narcissism. We have lost sight of the fact that we can exist only as a community. The tendency to believe that nothing is fixed and that we can change everything we wish is not only a misperception of life but also a desecration of it. When people cannot or will not accept their destiny, it is repressed and often projected onto others, such as the perception of one's enemy as totally bad (1981).

May pointed out that "freedom and determinism give birth to each other. Every advance in freedom gives birth to a new determinism, and every advance in determinism gives birth to a new freedom" (1981). Freud's and Darwin's theories, deterministic as they were, opened the door to new possibilities. However, the word **determinism,** borrowed from physics, is not very adequate for the rich nuances of human experience. To the extent to which one is unaware of one's responses, the term *determinism* may be appropriate, yet May suggested that we reserve it for inanimate objects, such as billiard balls, and use the term *destiny* for human beings. Determinism is merely one aspect of destiny. The shift from determinism to destiny occurs when a person is self-conscious about what is happening to him or her (1981).

Are we responsible for our destiny? May reminded us that responsibility is inseparable from freedom. To acknowledge one's destiny is to accept personal responsibility. In the terms of our psychology, freedom is the capacity to pause between a stimulus and a response. The key word here is *pause.* The significance of the pause is that it breaks the rigid chain of cause and effect. In the debate between situational and dispositional factors, May reminded us that there is a third alternative. Human beings can choose when and whether they are to be acted upon or do the acting. In moving between being controlled and controlling, one moves on a deeper level of freedom, the freedom of being (1981).

The past and future live in the psychological present. On the deepest level, the question of which age we live in is irrelevant. Instead the question is how, in our awareness of self and the period we live in, we are able through our choices to attain inner freedom and live according to our own inner integrity (1953). One reason we are reluctant to confront our destiny is that we are afraid it will lead us to despair. But despair may be a prelude to better things. Indeed, authentic despair is the emotion that forces us to come to terms with our destiny and permits us to let go of false hopes (1981).

## Courage and Creativity

Courage is the capacity to move ahead in spite of despair. In human beings, courage is necessary in order to make being and becoming possible. Courage is not a virtue but a foundation that underlies and gives reality to all other values. The paradox of courage is that we must be fully committed but we must also be aware at the same time that we might be wrong. Creative courage is the discovery of new forms, symbols, and patterns on which a new society can be built. The creative person must fight the actual order so as to bring about what is new. Thus, creativity brings upon us the wrath of the gods, the anger of the authority of the past. Psychologists frequently ignore creativity because, as an act of encounter between two poles, it is very difficult to study. Yet our contemporary crisis requires creativity if we are to deal with it effectively (1975).

## A Cry for Myth

In his book *The Cry for Myth* (1991), May argued passionately that many of the problems we confront, such as increases in suicide, anxiety, depression, substance abuse, and the growth of cults, stem from the absence of myths that would help us make meaning in what has become a "senseless world." May defined **myths** as "narrative patterns that give significance to our existence" and deemed them essential for psychological health. Our current myths no longer play that role; rather, they increase our frustrations.

We do not generate the necessity for myths. That necessity comes from our destiny as humans, our language, and a mode of knowing one another. May described the pseudomyths that are filling the vacuum created by the lack of genuine myths for people living today in the West. Our denial of myth in the West reflects our overemphasis on left-brain activities, rationalistic speech, and "our refusal to confront our own reality and that of our society."

The myths that we create are both conscious and unconscious, personal and collective. Thus each of us develops our own unique narrative in which we play the primary role, and by which we model our lives. That myth may follow infinite patterns, but generally also reflects a primary motif of classical myths, such as that of Satan, who appears over and over again under many different names in our literature. This is because "myths are archetypal patterns in human consciousness": being born, dying, making choices, and so forth.

The need for myth is also the need to belong to a community and to have heroes who act as role models as compared to celebrities who are simply well known. Martin Luther King, Alex Haley, and Mother Teresa are heroes whom we can identify with, as compared to celebrities such as Donald Trump and Madonna.

"Myth leads to fact rather than the reverse" (May, 1991). The American myth of the frontier permitted many people to make a new, more constructive, beginning of their lives. But there was also the myth of the Lone Ranger, which eventually became the myth of lonely individualism that characterizes the narcissistic personality and expresses itself in our loneliness and violence.

The most influential myth in America during the twentieth century has been that of Horatio Alger, which couples individualism with success and leads people to be driven, competitive, tense, and predisposed to stress and depression. Meanwhile anxiety disorders and depression have soared, and we must rediscover myths that can help us combat them. If not, our gambling (which defrauds primarily the poor) and use of drugs will continue to skyrocket.

Dante's *The Divine Comedy* tells us we must go through hell before we can love and live "life as community." May reminded us that "a person's hell may consist of confronting the fact that his mother never loved him; or it may consist of fantasies of destroy-

**THINKING CRITICALLY**

## *The Myth That Surrounds Our Birth*

We have noted that "myths are archetypal patterns in human consciousness" surrounding the existential crises of life. Birth is the first of these crises. Even though we are not aware of it at the time, a lot of fuss (or lack of it) is made over our birth. You may recall that Freud was born in a caul, a sign that his mother took to mean he was destined for greatness. Our parents may or may not have told us stories about it. In any event, in time each of us gives our birth a special meaning accompanied by strong feelings. We may be proud of it, perplexed by it, or wish that it had never occurred. Such response constitutes our personal myth.

What is the myth that surrounds your birth? Do you recall any stories your parents told concerning your birth? What narrative can you tell? How do you believe your parents reacted to your particular gender? Were they happy or would they have preferred a child of the opposite sex? Even though you may never have thought about these questions before, taking the time to do so now and writing down your narrative can help you to become more aware of the myth that surrounds your birth.

---

ing those a person loves most, like Medea destroying her children; or undergoing the hideous cruelty released in wartime when it becomes patriotic to hate and to kill" (1991). What is important is not the particulars of one's own hell but the journey itself.

In the nineteenth century, Ibsen anticipated the twentieth and tolled the death of hyperindividualism. Counterposing humans and subhuman trolls, his *Peer Gynt* describes the conflicting life of a man who wished to be honored and taken care of by one woman. The struggle rendered him passive, dependent, and powerless.

Goethe's *Faust* is the myth of patriarchal society and power that has dominated the West. Much as we would like to believe that our tremendous technology is leading to progress, the tale of Faust reveals that, in a patriarchal society, men have a serious problem with the feminine dimension of life. Washington politics, some say, demands a Faustian pact from even its finest people. Vince Foster, Jr., President Clinton's boyhood chum and later his aide, is said to have commented before he committed suicide, "Before we came here, we thought of ourselves as good people" (Farmer, 1993). Faust steered Gretchen into condemnation. In the twentieth century, May suggested, Germany itself became Faust and tumbled to its death in Nazism, a guilt that is shared by all in the West. One does not have to commit the specific evil to be guilty. We are guilty because we are human and the only way we can save ourselves is to assume responsibility.

Myths motivate us because they imply new potentialities and interpretations. Our current distress with parental sexual abuse of children is a new form of the Oedipal myth. May was amazed that Sophocles' sequel to *Oedipus Rex, Oedipus in Colonus,* is neglected in American psychoanalytic circles because in that drama the blind Oedipus comes to terms with what he has done. Oedipus knows that he is not guilty because he was unaware that the man he murdered was his father, but he must assume responsibility for his action.

Finally, May asked if we can construct a new myth for our survival. The Peer Gynt and Faust myths teach us that we must develop a myth of equality between men and women to undermine the primarily male, left-brain concepts of reason and hyperindividualism that have misled us. We need myths that give meaning to a woman's life other than just in the context of her relationship to men. The Navaho have a myth in which women, by their power of creativity, save the world from chaos, much as Ma Joad in Steinbeck's *The Grapes of Wrath* holds a migrant family together.

May believed we can develop a new myth out of our explorations of the heavens. On Christmas Eve 1968, three astronauts circled the moon and read from the Bible, making that experience sacred. Those astronauts could become heroes in a myth in which they look back in space upon the earth and recognize that the borders over which people kill each other are not really there and were a terrible, demented mistake. Pictures of the earth from space tell us that we must develop a new myth that fosters world community and learn to live in one global family (see also Kaplan, 1994).

## Psychotherapy

The existential approach to psychotherapy maintains that the central goal of therapy is to help promote understanding of the self and one's mode of being in the world. Psychological constructs for understanding human beings are, therefore, placed on an ontological basis and take their meaning from the present situation. Drives, dynamisms, or behavior patterns are understood only in the context of the structure of the existence of the particular person.

May pointed out that *being* in the human sense is not given once and for all. As humans we have to be aware of ourselves, be responsible for ourselves, become ourselves. "To be *and* not to be" (May's rephrasing of Hamlet) is a choice we make at every moment. An "I am" experience is a precondition for solving specific problems (1983). Otherwise, we merely trade one set of defenses for another.

Becoming aware of one's own being is not to be explained in social terms. The acceptance of the therapist may facilitate the "I am" experience but it does not automatically lead to it. "The crucial question is what the individual himself, in his own awareness of and responsibility for his existence, does with the fact that he can be accepted" (1983). Nor is the emergence of an "I am" experience identical to the development of the ego. It occurs on a more basic level, an ontological one, and is a precondition for subsequent ego development.

In order to grasp what it means to exist, one also needs to grasp the option of nonbeing. Death is an obvious form of the threat of nonbeing, but conformity is an alternative mode that May found very prevalent in our day. People give up their own identity in order to be accepted by others and avoid being ostracized or lonely, but in doing so they lose their power and uniqueness. Whereas repression and inhibition were common neurotic patterns in Freud's day, today *conformism* is a more prevalent pattern. Such denial of one's potentialities leads to the experience of guilt. Ontological guilt does not come from cultural prohibition but arises from the fact of self-awareness and the recognition that one has not fulfilled one's potentialities. Facing such guilt in the process of therapy leads to constructive effects.

Thus, the central task of the therapist is to seek to understand the patient's mode of being and nonbeing in the world. It is the context that distinguishes the existential approach rather than any specific techniques. The human being is not an object to be managed or analyzed. Technique follows understanding. Various psychotherapeutic devices may be used, depending on which method will best reveal the existence of a particular patient at any given time.

May believed that free association is particularly useful in revealing intentionality. The relationship between the therapist and patient is seen as a real one. When transference occurs, May pointed out that it distorts the therapeutic encounter. The therapist seeks to help the patient experience existence as real. This does not imply simply adjusting to one's culture or relieving anxiety but rather experiencing one's existence or mode of being in the world.

May warned against the use of drugs in psychotherapy. For the most part, he believed they have a negative effect because, in removing the patient's anxiety, they may remove the motivation for change and thereby deny an opportunity for learning and destroy vital resources. Occasionally, May employed techniques developed by *gestalt* therapists such as Fritz Perls. An emphasis might be placed on nonverbal behaviors to show the inconsistency between a verbal and nonverbal statement. If a patient states that she is frightened but has a smile on her face, the therapist might point out that a frightened person does not smile and seek to explore the meaning of the smile. A patient might be asked to fantasize that a significant other was sitting in an opposite chair, to have a conversation with that person, and then to reverse roles. Such techniques are designed to help the patient confront and experience actual present feelings. Finally, May's approach emphasized commitment, believing that patients cannot receive any insight until they are ready to decide and take a decisive orientation to life.

## Assessment and Research in May's Theory

May believed that in their efforts to be "scientific" many psychologists have lost sight of the real person that they seek to understand. However, while May was critical of some of the so-called scientific forms of psychology, he was by no means antiscientific. His aim was to speak out against concepts of personality that dogmatically foreclose avenues of research.

In the 1950s, May criticized psychologists for having singled out for study those aspects of human behavior that overlap with animal behavior and can ultimately be described in physiological or stimulus-response terms. In doing so, May pointed out that psychologists neglected the problem of symbols, even though the use of symbols is part of the distinct human condition (May et al., 1958). Although cognitive psychology studies symbols and other events that occur in the mind, May did not look to cognitive psychology for answers because its conceptions are also too limited for the psychological problems of our time (1981).

May criticized contemporary psychological research for being impressed with data and numbers at the expense of theory. Psychologists tend to be contemptuous of imagination and speculation, yet the most important scientific discoveries (Copernicus's concept of the universe, Darwin's theory of evolution, Freud's construct of unconscious forces, Einstein's theory of relativity) were made not by accumulating facts but by perceiving the relationship among them (1983). Human nature can be understood only within a theoretical framework.

The existential approach suggests three basic changes in psychological methods of research on personality. First, "we must cut through the tendency in the West to believe we understand things only if we know their causes, and to find out and describe instead what the thing is as a phenomenon—the experience, as it is given to us, in its 'givenness.' First, that is, we must know what we are talking about. This is not to rule out causation and genetic development, but rather to say that the question of *why* one is what one is does not have meaning until we know *what* one is" (1967). This phenomenological approach is very similar to the view maintained by Rogers.

Second, psychologists must recognize that all ways of understanding what it means to be a human being are based on philosophical assumptions and myths. We need to examine these presuppositions continually, for it is one's philosophical concept of human being that guides one's empirical research. Here May also reminded us of Rogers's and Maslow's emphasis on science serving previously chosen goals.

Finally, we must ask the question of the nature of person as person, the ontological question of what it means to be. Understanding the being of another person occurs on a very different level from knowing specific things about the person. This is the classical distinction between *knowing* and *knowing about.* Our culture tends to believe that something is not real unless we can reduce it to a mathematical abstraction. But according to May, this denies the reality of our own experience. May suggested that it would be more scientific to first try to see clearly what we are talking about and then try to find symbols to describe what we see with a minimum of distortion (1983).

At this time, much of our research is governed by the myth of the technological man, which May described as "a set of assumptions of postulating that the human being is governed by what he can rationally understand, that his emotions will follow this understanding, and that his anxiety and dread will thus be cured" (1969). May tried to help us develop a new form, a new myth that will be more adequate for our day. After all, he reminded us, "Anyone can do the research. . . . The original contribution lies in seeing a new *form* for the problem" (1967). May believed that new forms of symbols and myths for understanding human nature are more likely to come from our art, literature, humanities, and religion than from our present psychology (1983; also see DeCarvalho, 1992).

Two particular areas that May researched are anxiety and dreams. May undertook a study of unmarried mothers in order to illuminate the meaning of anxiety (1969). Because he believed that there might be damaging effects in inducing anxiety experimentally, he took what was an anxiety-creating situation at that time in our society and studied it to reveal a pattern that would be characteristic of other anxiety-creating situations as well. May believed that the more intensely we study the individual, the more we arrive at data that lie below individual differences and are applicable to human beings in general.

His study led to some rich observations concerning the meaning of anxiety itself, the origin of neurotic anxiety in a particular parent-child relationship in which rejection is covered over with pretenses of love so that it cannot be appraised realistically, and the greater prevalence of neurotic anxiety among women of the middle class.

May believed that dreams reflect how we perceive, cope, and give meaning to our world. Our dream life reflects our intentionality and deepest concerns. It permits the person to experience rather than merely explain important symbols and myths. In analyzing dreams, May took them phenomenologically as self-revealing givens, patterns of data within themselves. He looked for consistency over a period of time and noticed that latent meanings in earlier dreams often become manifest in the later dreams. The latent meaning of dreams was thus reconceived by May as a dimension of communication that the patient is unwilling or unable as yet to actualize.

Each dream has a theme and a motif. The *theme* is the unity and inner consistency that is a part of the dreamer. It is characteristic of all dreams and reflects the unity of a person's character. The *motif* is the central thread running through the various dreams and the goal one is moving toward. The purpose of interpreting a dream is not to tell the individual what it means but to expand the individual's consciousness so that what is going on can be more fully and deeply experienced. In dreams we successfully resist the temptation to intellectualize and, instead, wrestle with our real problems.

After May had painted a portrait of one patient from her dreams, he compared his picture with that which had emerged in the course of her three-year analysis with Dr. Leopold Caligor by comparing his findings with the doctor's case notes. He found a remarkable consistency between the two accounts, confirming his hypothesis that one can get an accurate and meaningful picture of a person from the symbols and myths created in dreams.

| PHILOSOPHY, |
| SCIENCE, |
| AND ART |

## May's Theory

May clearly recognized that science derives from prior philosophical forms and is fundamentally dependent on them. He believed the reason we don't understand the truth about ourselves is not that we haven't amassed enough data, conducted the right experiments, or read enough books, but because we "do not have enough courage." Scientific facts and technical proofs rarely help us answer the questions that really matter. We have to "venture" (1953).

In psychotherapy May was "the implacable friend," insisting that his patients "grapple with the disabling forces inside of them and fight their way back into life" (Harris, 1969). He was not afraid to risk reintroducing concepts vehemently rejected by mainstream psychologists—intentionality, the will, the daimonic. He reintroduced these concepts because he believed that they are vital to an understanding of what it means to be human today. There is a prophetic note to his writing, reminiscent of Erich Fromm, and his thinking frequently has a theological quality. Indeed, there are those who suggest that May took up where Paul Tillich, the theological giant of our century, left off (Harris, 1969). May acknowledged that for him the great periods in history were not those when psychological concerns were dominant but those when philosophical and religious concerns were uppermost (1983).

May did not give us a series of hypotheses that may be tested by empirical procedures. Instead, he gave us a philosophical picture of what it means to be a person in today's world. Reasons are offered in support of his affirmations, but they do not serve as proof; they cooperate as pieces of evidence in favor of a certain picture of reality. To reduce our understanding of personality to scientific, causative, and abstract terms means that we will lose some significant content and fail to understand the full reality of a human being. May encouraged us to examine the philosophical assumptions of our scientific endeavor so that we can maintain a creative dialogue between our science and our philosophy.

May's philosophical picture of human nature is coherent, relevant, comprehensive, and compelling. He successfully avoided dualisms that have troubled us since the philosophy of Descartes. The existential framework that informs his theory is more compatible with our world than the philosophical assumptions of nineteenth-century science that informed Freud's work. An existential philosophy provides a helpful background for discussing what Freud meant to say about the nature of psychic functioning. Although Freud was not an existentialist, existentialism provides categories that clarify Freudian thought and intent. Thus, May fruitfully reconceived many Freudian concepts.

Whereas Freud's philosophy was an extension of the assumptions inherent in the scientific community of his time, May began as a philosopher. His image of human nature provides a welcome antidote to the technological view of the person that permeates radical behavior and learning theories as well as the naive optimism of the humanists. May differed from traditional learning and behavior theories in his open examination of his philosophical assumptions. He differed from the humanists in his insistence that we directly confront our own evil.

## PHILOSOPHICAL ASSUMPTIONS

### *Examining May*

How would you rate May on each of the basic philosophical assumptions described in Chapter 1? Consult the chart on the inside front cover. Each basic issue is presented as a bipolar dimension along which a person's view can be placed according to the degree of agreement with one or the other extreme: *freedom/determinism, hereditary/environmental, uniqueness/universality, proactive/reactive, optimistic/pessimistic.* Rate May's views on these issues. How does his concept of paradox influence your completion of this activity?

When you have determined where you think May stands, compare your responses with those of your classmates and your instructor. You should be willing to defend your ratings, but also be prepared to change them in light of others' compelling arguments. Afterward, compare your rating of May with your own position on each issue and with those of other theorists. Does this comparison help you understand why his theory does or does not appeal to you?

For the most part, psychologists have tended to ignore May's theory because they cannot treat it as a scientific hypothesis. Concepts like intentionality and the daimonic are virtually impossible to define operationally and test empirically, but the findings of an empirical test do not establish a philosophical assumption; they may not even significantly relate to it. Nevertheless, the very strength of May's theory, the fact that it has its roots in a new philosophical conception of human life, may also be its greatest liability. May runs a strong risk of being given short shrift by the psychological establishment and having little impact on personality theorizing. This is ironic because in many ways the humility and openness to change characteristic of May's theory are more in keeping with the nature of the scientific enterprise than the attitude of those who seek to limit and confine research. By ignoring May, psychologists deprive themselves of the challenge of reexamining their own philosophical assumptions and, perhaps, reconceiving the goals and methods of their science.

## Summary

1. Rollo May's work brings together the psychoanalytic tradition in psychology and the existentialist movement in philosophy.

2. *Existentialism* emphasizes *existence* rather than *essence*. It suggests that there is no truth or reality except as we participate in it. Knowledge is an act of doing.

3. Existentialists believe that the psychologist's preoccupation with lawfulness and predictability stands in the way of understanding the real person and they urge a greater breadth to our scientific methodology. They seek to study the structure of human existence and to look at the unity of the person prior to any split into subject and object.

4. The central problem we face in the second half of the twentieth century, according to May, is a feeling of *powerlessness* in the face of nuclear war.

5. May defined *anxiety* as the apprehension cued off by a threat to an essential value. It is intensified in contemporary culture by the interpersonal isolation and alienation that have come out of the way in which we view ourselves. Many of our present efforts to dispel anxiety actually end up increasing it.

6. The source of the human dilemma lies in the loss of the center of values in our society. A distinguishing mark of the human animal is that of creating values. The need today is to discover and affirm a new set of values.

7. May assumed that (a) all living organisms are centered on themselves and seek to preserve that center; (b) they can go out from their centeredness to participate with other people; (c) sickness is a means of preserving one's

being; (d) human beings can engage in a level of self-consciousness that permits them to transcend the present and consider alternatives. These *ontological assumptions* precede our scientific activity and make it possible, but our analytic activity may in turn illumine them.

8. *Rediscovering selfhood* involves rediscovering our own feelings and desires and fighting against those things that prevent us from feeling and wanting. There are *four stages of consciousness* of self: innocence, rebellion, ordinary consciousness of self, and creative consciousness of self.

9. May discussed key issues in personality in ways that avoided abstraction and facilitated the confronting of *paradoxes*. *Love,* which used to be seen as the answer to human problems, has now become the problem. We are unable to love. We need to experience and rediscover *care*. May introduced the concept of *intentionality* to bridge the gap between subject and object and to place the problem of determinism and freedom on a deeper level. He reintroduced the concept of the *daimonic* and insisted that we must come to terms with it. He emphasized our need to be *courageous* and *creative*. We also need to rediscover our *power* and express it in constructive ways. May pointed out how our *freedom* needs to be considered in light of our *destiny*.

10. May defined *myth* as "narrative patterns that give significance to our existence." He believed pseudomyths, such as that of Horatio Alger, are filling the vacuum created by the lack of genuine myths of people living today in the West. We need new myths to give our lives meaning, provide heroes, suggest new possibilities. Two possible new myths that we need are equality between women and men, and a global community with no boundaries.

11. In psychotherapy the existentialist seeks to understand the patient's mode of being in the world. It is the context that distinguishes the existential approach rather than any specific technique. Use has been made of the psychotherapeutic devices of both Freud and gestalt psychotherapists.

12. May criticized contemporary psychological research for being impressed with data and uninterested in theory. We need continually to reexamine our presuppositions and raise ontological questions. Two specific research activities that May engaged in were a study of unmarried mothers and the study of a dream sequence.

13. May's theory is not a scientific theory of personality giving us a series of hypotheses that may be tested by an empirical procedure. Instead he suggested a philosophical picture of human nature that is coherent, relevant, comprehensive, and compelling.

## Suggestions for Further Reading

Rollo May's books are extremely readable and enlightening for the lay person. His theory of personality was initially outlined in *Man's Search for Himself* (Norton, 1953) and *Psychology and the Human Dilemma* (Van Nostrand Reinhold, 1967). *The Meaning of Anxiety* (Norton,

1950; revised, 1977) is now considered a classic. In it May encouraged a genuine union between psychology and philosophy and demonstrated the importance of values for psychology. *Love and Will* (Norton, 1969) explores the experience of sex and love in contemporary society. It was hailed by the *New York Times* as the "most important book of the year." May's most important later works were *Freedom and Destiny* (Norton, 1981), which rethinks the problem of determinism and personal freedom, *The Discovery of Being* (Norton, 1983), which describes the human search for being and nonbeing in an age of anxiety, *My Quest for Beauty* (Saybrook, 1985), which describes the creative and therapeutic role of art, and *The Cry for Myth* (Norton, 1991), a passionate plea for a new myth to guide our lives. For a biography of Rollo May, see R. deCarvalho (1996), "Rollo R. May (1909–1994): A biographical sketch." *Journal of Humanistic Psychology, 36,* 8–16.

PART **VII**

# Cognitive Theories

Cognitive theories of personality, exemplified here by George Kelly and the cognitive behavioral theories of Albert Ellis, Aaron Beck, and Arnold Lazarus, emphasize the processes by which an individual becomes aware of the world and makes judgments about it. Cognitive theories stress that behavior is determined not simply by the environment but also, and primarily, by an individual's attitudes, expectations, and beliefs.

Other theories have recognized the importance of cognition, but they did not make it the mainstay of their theory. Freud emphasized emotional processes of the heart rather than intellectual processes of the mind. The behavior and learning tradition, until recently, was concerned with the analysis of environmental stimuli and the individual's final overt response to the environment rather than with the intermediate subjective processes that led to the behavior.

### CHAPTER 15

# Personal Constructs

## GEORGE KELLY

## Your Goals for This Chapter

1. Explain why Kelly suggested that we view ourselves as scientists.
2. Describe the philosophical position of *constructive alternativism*.
3. Discuss Kelly's fundamental postulate and identify eleven corollaries that support it.
4. Explain how Kelly reconceived traditional concepts in personality theorizing.
5. Describe the Rep Test.
6. Discuss Kelly's view of and contributions to psychotherapy.
7. Identify some of the criticisms of Kelly's theory.
8. Evaluate Kelly's theory in terms of its function as philosophy, science, and art.

R eading Kelly is like entering a new terrain, as he avoided many of the concepts traditionally present in personality theorizing. Kelly was forthright in describing the differences between his approach and that of others. "It is only fair," he wrote, "to warn the reader about what may be in store for him. In the first place, he is likely to find missing most of the familiar landmarks. . . . For example, the term *learning*, so honorably embedded in most psychological texts, scarcely appears at all. That is wholly intentional; we are for throwing it overboard all together. There is no *ego*, no *emotion*, no *reinforcement*, no *drive*, no *unconscious*, no *need*" (1955). It is not that these concepts are entirely omitted from Kelly's work; rather, they are given new meanings and incorporated into his philosophy of constructive alternativism.

## Biographical Background

George Kelly was born on a farm in Perth, Kansas, in 1905. His father was a Presbyterian minister, but ill health prevented him from actively leading a church congregation. Kelly's parents were devout fundamentalists who practiced their faith, prescribed hard work, and rigorously shunned the evils of dancing, drinking, and card playing. As an only child, Kelly received extensive attention and love. His mother, in particular, was devoted to him.

Kelly's early education was somewhat sporadic. He attended a one-room country school and was taught by his parents at home. He was sent to Wichita, Kansas, for high school, where he attended four different schools. He studied for three years at Friends University and received the B.A. degree one year later (1926) from Park College. Kelly had majored in physics and mathematics and planned a career in mechanical engineering. However, his interests were turning to social problems. While holding a number of different jobs related to engineering and education, he pursued the M.A. degree in educational sociology at the University of Kansas.

In 1929, Kelly was awarded a fellowship for study at the University of Edinburgh in Scotland. He earned the B.Ed. degree there based on his previous academic experience and his year of residency in Scotland. Kelly wrote his dissertation on the problem of predicting teaching success and discovered that his interests were turning to psychology. On his return to the United States, he enrolled as a doctoral student in psychology at the State University of Iowa. He received the Ph.D. in 1931 with a dissertation on speech and reading disabilities.

Kelly began his career as an academic psychologist in the middle of the Depression of the 1930s. Opportunities for work in physiological psychology, his specialty, were scarce, so he turned his attention to clinical psychology, a growing field. During the next twelve years, Kelly taught at Fort Hays Kansas State College and developed a program of traveling psychological clinics that sought to identify and treat emotional and behavioral problems in students in the state's public school system. His experience with the clinics was crucial to his later development and theorizing. Not committed to any one theoretical approach, Kelly experimented with several different methods in his work with students referred for counseling. His position gave him a unique opportunity to try out innovative as well as tradi-

*George Kelly's theory of personality is based on his philosophical position of constructive alternativism.*

tional clinical approaches. His work with the clinics sparked several ideas that later found application in his own theory of personality and therapy.

World War II briefly interrupted Kelly's academic career. He enrolled in the navy as an aviation psychologist, headed a training program of local civilian pilots, and worked for the bureau of medicine and surgery, gaining recognition for his clinical services. After the war, a significant demand for clinical psychologists appeared as returning servicemen required help with personal problems. Clinical psychology came to be seen as an essential part of health services. Kelly played a leading role in fostering the development and integration of clinical psychology into the mainstream of American psychology. After teaching one year at the University of Maryland, he joined the faculty of Ohio State University as professor and director of clinical psychology. During the next twenty years at Ohio State, Kelly built a distinguished program of clinical psychology and refined and published his theory of personality.

In 1965, Kelly received a prestigious appointment to the Riklis Chair of Behavioral Science at Brandeis University. This appointment would have given him great freedom to pursue his research, but he died in 1967.

Kelly did not publish a great deal but he lectured extensively in the United States and abroad and he exerted a significant influence on psychology through his personal impact on his students and friends. In his later years, he spent considerable time suggesting how personal construct theory could be applied to help resolve social and international problems. He held several important positions, such as president of both the Clinical and Counseling Divisions of the American Psychological Association. He assisted in developing and also served as president of the American Board of Examiners in Professional Psychology.

## The Person as Scientist

George Kelly invited us to look at ourselves and other people as scientists, an image that he noted psychologists are quick to ascribe to themselves but perhaps not as readily to other people. Kelly suggested that the posture we take as we attempt to predict and control the events in our world is similar to that of the scientist who develops and tests hypotheses. In our efforts to understand the world, we develop **personal constructs** that serve as hypotheses that make the world meaningful to us. This is the core of Kelly's **personal construct theory.** If these constructs appear to fit our subsequent experience, we find them useful and hold onto them. Thus, if we construe the world or certain events as hostile, we will act in certain ways to protect ourselves. If our protective behaviors appear to be useful ways to cope with the events, we will continue to hold onto the hostile interpretation. If the pattern or construct does not lead to behaviors that help us adjust to events in our world, we will seek to alter or change the construct in order to develop a better one. Just as the scientist employs hypotheses to make predictions about certain consequences, people employ their constructs to predict what is going to happen to them in the future. Subsequent events are then used to indicate whether the predictions and underlying constructs were correct or were misleading.

Because of the emphasis he placed on the ways in which people construe the world, Kelly is often perceived as a cognitive theorist who stressed the process of knowing as the primary factor in personality development (see also Warren, 1990). One could also easily defend labeling Kelly a humanist (Epting & Leitner, 1992) or a phenomenologist. Kelly repeatedly protested that his was not a cognitive theory: "I have been so puzzled over the early labeling of personal construct theory as 'cognitive' that several years ago I set out to write another short book to make it clear that I wanted no part of cognitive theory" (Mahler, 1969, p. 216). He felt that his theory belied any such classification and should be considered independently. However, interest in Kelly's approach has grown in recent years in that it has been seen as compatible with the growing interest in cognition that characterizes contemporary psychology.

The cognitive movement in contemporary psychology rejects the behaviorist view that people react passively to stimuli. It explores the various ways in which we respond to the environment by actively processing the information we receive into new forms, categories, and "mental representations of the world" (Klatzky, 1980) and thereby actively construe reality (Soffer, 1993). Kelly's theory is cognitive because he stressed that an individual's behavior is determined not simply by the environment or heredity but also, and primarily, by attitudes, expectations, and beliefs.

# Constructive Alternativism

Kelly's theory of personality is based on his philosophical position of **constructive alternativism:** the assumption that any one event is open to a variety of interpretations. The world, in and of itself, does not automatically make sense to us. We have to create our own ways of understanding the events that happen. In effect, there is no reality outside our interpretations of it. Take, for example, the situation of a boy who is late for school. His father may think that it is because the boy is lazy. His mother may suggest that her son is forgetful and daydreams on the way to school. His teacher may view the pupil's tardiness as an expression of his distaste and hostility toward academic work. His best friend might see it as an accident. The boy himself could construe his lateness as an indication of his inferiority. The event itself is merely a given datum but it gives rise to many different alternative constructions that may lead to different actions. For Kelly, the individual's complex constructions are the appropriate object of study. The objective truth of a person's interpretations are unimportant because they are unknowable. What is important is their implications for behavior and life.

In our efforts to understand the world, we develop constructs or patterns that make the world meaningful to us. We look at the world "through transparent patterns or templates" of our own creation (Kelly, 1955). It is as if each person can view the world only through sunglasses of his or her own choosing. No one construct or pattern is final and a perfect reflection of the world. There is always an alternative construct that might do a better job of accounting for the facts that we perceive. Thus, our position in the world is one of constructive alternativism, as we change or revise our constructs in order to understand it more accurately.

For example, at the beginning of a semester, students develop certain constructs or ideas about the subjects that they are studying. Usually, these constructs are based on a very limited sample of the actual course or the instructor's behavior. One student may conclude that a particular course will be a snap, requiring a minimum of time and preparation. Another student may conclude that the same course will be a challenge, requiring considerable effort. As the semester progresses, each student acts on and gradually tests the preliminary hypothesis for its accuracy. The lectures, reading assignments, written papers, and tests are all subsequent events that serve to confirm or disprove the initial assumptions. By the middle of the semester, a student has a much clearer idea of the accuracy of the original construct concerning the course.

A student's behavior in a college course is simply an example in miniature of what happens to us all throughout our lives. As was pointed out earlier, the world is not a fixed given that can be immediately comprehended and understood. In order to understand the world, we have to develop constructs or ways of perceiving it. During the course of our lives, we develop many different constructs. Further, we continually test, revise, and modify them. As none of our constructs is ultimate, alternative constructs that we could choose from are always available. Thus, a person is free to change constructs in an effort to make sense out of, predict, and control the world. This validation process is central to the psychology of personal constructs (Landfield, 1988).

**THINKING CRITICALLY**

## How We Behave as Scientists

Kelly (1955) suggested that each one of us behaves as a scientist in our efforts to understand the world. You can gain a deeper appreciation of your own attempts to understand other people by analyzing a recent situation and your effort to understand it in terms of the scientific method. Suppose one night, when you arrive home, you observe that there are tears in your roommate's eyes. You might conclude that your roommate was upset about something. However, when you inquire what the problem is your roommate says, "Nothing is the matter" and points to a pile of onions recently chopped for tonight's stew.

Analyze this situation, or another one, in terms of the scientific method. What was the problem? What hypothesis did you develop? What prediction did you make about possible experiences you could have if the hypothesis were useful? How did you test your hypothesis and what conclusions did you draw?

Anderson and Kirkland (1990) suggest that in his metaphor of the personal scientist, Kelly provides a constructive alternative to the mechanistic metaphor of the machine. What do you think?

## Fundamental Postulate and Corollaries

In order to present and explain his theory, Kelly (1955) set forth one basic assumption, or fundamental postulate, and then elaborated on it with eleven corollaries (see Table 15.1).

The *fundamental postulate* reads:

> A person's processes are psychologically channelized by the ways
> in which he anticipates events.

Probably the most important word in Kelly's primary assumption is *anticipates*. Essentially, Kelly suggested that the way in which an individual predicts future happenings is crucial to behavior. As scientists, people seek to forecast what is going to happen. They orient their behaviors and ideas about the world toward the goal of accurate, useful predictions. According to Kelly, the future, rather than the past, is the primary impetus of behavior.

Each of the eleven corollaries that Kelly presented to elaborate his fundamental postulate focuses on a primary word that sums up the essence of these supportive statements and his theory.

1. *Construction*   "A person anticipates events by construing their replications" (Kelly, 1955). The term *construe* means to place an interpretation on an event. As we have seen, the universe is not an automatically knowable given. We must create constructs or ways in which to understand it.

TABLE 15.1   **Kelly's Fundamental Postulate and Corollaries**

Kelly presents a *fundamental postulate* with eleven corollaries.

FUNDAMENTAL POSTULATE

A person's processes are psychologically channelized by the ways in which he anticipates events.

COROLLARIES

1. *Construction*   People anticipate events by interpreting them.
2. *Individuality*   Each person construes events differently.
3. *Organization*   People develop an organized system of constructs.
4. *Dichotomy*   Constructs are of a bipolar nature.
5. *Choice*   People choose from among alternatives the most useful construct.
6. *Range*   Each construct has a limited range or focus.
7. *Experience*   Constructs are changed in the light of experience.
8. *Modulation*   Constructs are open to change and alteration.
9. *Fragmentation*   People may use constructs that seem to be incompatible.
10. *Communality*   Communication is based on similar personal constructs.
11. *Sociability*   Social interaction entails understanding constructs.

2. *Individuality*   "Persons differ from each other in their construction of events" (Kelly, 1955). No two people interpret events in the same way. Each of us experiences an event from our own subjective point of view. This corollary underscores Kelly's belief that it is the subjective interpretation of an event, rather than the event itself, that is most important.

3. *Organization*   "Each person characteristically evolves, for his convenience in anticipating events, a construction system embracing ordinal relationships between constructs" (Kelly, 1955). Our interpretation of events in the world is neither haphazard nor arbitrary. Each one of us organizes constructs in a series of ordinal relationships in which some constructs are more important and others are less important. The fact that our constructs fall into an organized pattern means that we develop a system of constructs rather than simply a number of isolated ones.

4. *Dichotomy*   "A person's construction system is composed of a finite number of dichotomous constructs" (Kelly, 1955). In making an interpretation about an event, we not only make an assertion about it, but we also indicate that the opposite quality is not characteristic of it. A dichotomy is an opposition; Kelly suggested that all of our constructs are of a bipolar form. When we construe that a person is strong, we also imply that the person is not weak. The dichotomous form of our constructs provides the basis for constructive alternativism. Riemann (1990), however, suggests that bipolarity is an important but not necessary aspect of personal constructs.

5. *Choice*   "A person chooses for himself that alternative in a dichotomized construct through which he anticipates the greater possibility for extension and definition of his system" (Kelly, 1955). The choice corollary is a very important one. It underlines Kelly's belief that a person is free and able to choose from among the various alternatives the construct that will be most useful.

6. *Range*   "A construct is convenient for the anticipation of a finite range of events only" (Kelly, 1955). Each construct has a certain range or focus. The construct of *tall versus short* is useful for describing people, trees, or horses, but virtually useless for understanding the weather. Some people apply their constructs broadly and others limit their constructs to a narrow focus.

7. *Experience*   "A person's construction system varies as he successively construes the replication of events" (Kelly, 1955). People change their interpretation of events in the light of later experience. Such reconstruction forms the basis for learning.

8. *Modulation*   "The variation in a person's construction system is limited by the permeability of the constructs within whose range of convenience the variants lie" (Kelly, 1955). The extent to which a person's constructs may be adjusted or modulated depends on the existing framework and organization of the constructural system. Constructs are *permeable,* that is, they are open to change and alteration.

   Some constructs are more permeable than others. Concrete constructs are rather difficult to change because of their specificity in definition and range. The construct *good versus evil* might be narrowly conceived by one individual so as to contain relatively few experiences. In that case it would be very difficult for the individual to change the construct. For another individual, the same construct might be much more permeable and easily penetrated by new experiences.

9. *Fragmentation*   "A person may successfully employ a variety of construction subsystems which are inferentially incompatible with each other" (Kelly, 1955). There are times when people employ constructs that appear to be incompatible with each other. Because of this, we are often surprised by other people's behavior and we cannot always infer what people are going to do tomorrow from the way they behave today. Such fragmentation is particularly apt to occur either when a person's constructs are impermeable and concrete or when they are undergoing change.

10. *Communality*   "To the extent that one person employs a construction of experience which is similar to that employed by another, his psychological processes are similar to the other person" (Kelly, 1955). This does not mean that their experiences are identical, but our ability to share and communicate with other people is based on the fact that we share similar personal constructs with them.

11. *Sociability*    "To the extent that one person construes the construction processes of another, he may play a role in a social process involving the other person" (Kelly, 1955). Our ability to interact socially with other people entails understanding a broad range of their constructs and behaviors. Thus other people are also important for testing one's construing system (Walker, 1990).

## The Reconstruction of Old Concepts

Kelly avoided many of the concepts traditionally associated with personality theorizing. He gave familiar landmarks and terms new meanings and subordinated them to his theory of personal constructs.

Some of Kelly's constructs refer to self-identity or the identity of others. The **self-construct** is based primarily on what we perceive as consistencies in our own behavior. For example, we believe that we are honest, sincere, friendly, and so forth. The self-construct is developed out of our relationships with other people. When we construe other people, we also construe ourselves. When we think of another person as "hostile" or "aggressive," we are making those qualities and their opposites a dimension of our own experience. Our self-interpretation is linked to our role relationships with other people.

A **role** is a process or behavior that people engage in based on their understanding of the behavior and constructs of others. We do not have to be accurate in our constructions to enter into a role. A student may play a certain role with a professor believed to be unduly demanding and unfair when in fact the professor is not. Nor does a role have to be reciprocated by the other person. The professor may remain fair in spite of the student's misconstruction. What is needed in order to play a role is simply some construct of the other person's behavior.

Kelly's use of the term "role" should not be confused with its use in social psychology. In social psychology, "role" usually refers to a set of behavioral expectations such as mother, teacher, physician, ruler, and so on, set forth by a particular society and fulfilled by its members. In Kelly's theory, the role is defined by the individual in an effort to understand the behavior of other people and relate to them. One's self-construct may be seen as a core or basic role structure by which one conceives of oneself as an integral individual in relation to other people.

For Kelly, the person is a process, an organism in continual activity, whose behavior is governed by a system of personal constructs. *Development* is based on one's choice of constructs and viewed in psychological rather than biological terms (Vaughn & Pfenninger, 1994). *Learning* and *motivation* are built into the very structure of the system. Kelly believed that no special inner forces, such as drives, needs, instincts, or motives, are needed to account for human motivation. Human nature in and of itself implies motivation because it is alive and in process. Nor need behavior be accounted for in terms of external forces, such as stimuli and reinforcements. Learning is synonymous with all of the psychological processes themselves. It is simply inappropriate to conceive of an individual as motivated by other internal or external forces. Kelly (1958) declared that "there are pitchfork theories on the one hand and the carrot theories on the other. But our theory is neither of these.

Since we prefer to look at the nature of the animal itself, ours is probably best called a jack-ass theory."

Not all constructs are verbalized; therefore, conscious and unconscious processes may be accounted for by our capacity to form constructs that are not put into words. *Emotions* are also subsumed under the general framework of personal constructs. Although some critics (e.g., Bruner and Rogers, 1965) suggest that Kelly's theory is too intellectual and mentalistic, Kelly refused to divide the person into cognitive and emotional states. Feelings and emotions refer to inner states that need to be construed. They arise when constructs are in a state of change.

Traditional psychological concepts such as anxiety, guilt, and aggression were also reconceived by Kelly in accordance with his personal construct theory. *Anxiety* is "the recognition that the events with which one is confronted lie outside the range of one's construct system" (1955). In other words, we feel anxious when we can no longer understand ourselves and the events of our lives in terms of our past experiences. Such discrepancy can lead to construct change. If a change is merely incidental, the individual may experience some fear, but if the change is comprehensive, the individual will feel deeply threatened.

*Guilt* is a "perception of one's apparent dislodgement from his core role structure" (1955). In our relationships with significant others, we develop a *core role* in which we construe ourselves in certain ways, such as loving or responsible. If we behave, either intentionally or unintentionally, in a way that violates the core role structure, we will experience guilt.

*Aggression* entails "the active elaboration of one's perceptual field" (1955). Aggression involves action: the deliberate placement of oneself into situations that call for decisions. Such aggression is distinguished from hostility, in which an individual forces other people or events to fit into the current personal construct system. In Kelly's theory, *hostility*, the "conflicted effort to extort validational evidence in favor of a type of social prediction which has already proven itself a failure," (1955) is the opposite of aggression. Kelly uses the term aggression in the way most of us would use the term assertiveness.

## Assessment and Research in Kelly's Theory

Clinical experience with public school and college students provided the basis for Kelly's theory of personal constructs. Although these students may have had problems, they were essentially functioning normally in the academic setting. In assessing the students who came to him, therefore, Kelly primarily used the interview. "If you don't know what is going on in a person's mind," Kelly wrote, "ask him; he may tell you!" (1958). Kelly might have asked his client to respond to questions such as, "What kind of child were you?" "What kind of a person do you expect to become?" and "What do you expect from therapy?" Such questions, and their answers, were useful in elaborating the construct system.

At other times, Kelly would ask his clients to write a character sketch of themselves as if they were the primary character in a play. Written in the third person and beginning "The client's name is . . .", the character sketch was to be written as if by an intimate and sympathetic friend who knew the individual better than anyone else. Such character sketches were also helpful in determining the individual's constructs and relations with others.

In order to understand further how a person interprets the world, Kelly developed the Role Construct Repertory Test, known more simply as the **Rep Test** (see Figure 15.1). Essentially, the Rep Test permits a person to reveal constructs by comparing and contrasting a number of significant persons in her or his life. You will have an opportunity to learn about the Rep Test and to explore your own constructs in the "Thinking Critically" exercise that follows.

The philosophical aspect of Kelly's theory may help account for the fact that his work initially generated little research. Most of the empirical studies based on his work concern the Rep Test (Bannister & Mair, 1968). Other studies like Bannister and Fransella (1966) and Bannister and Salmon (1966) suggest that the Rep Test and Kelly's constructs can help us understand the disturbance of thought in schizophrenia. They conclude that the thought constructs of a schizophrenic are less interrelated and more inconsistent than other people's, particularly regarding interpersonal constructs.

The Rep Test has also been used to explore the complexity of an individual's construct system and changes in the construct system throughout the lifespan (Crockett, 1982).

**FIGURE 15.1  Rep Test Grid**  *(SOURCE: Reprinted from* The Psychology of Personal Constructs, *Volume One, by George A. Kelly, Ph.D., by permission of Mrs. Gladys Kelly. Copyright 1955 by George A. Kelly.)*

# *Assessing Personal Constructs: The Rep Test*

The following activity will help you become acquainted with the Rep Test and also tell you about some of your own personal constructs.

Make up a list of representative persons in your life by choosing from among people you know the individual who most suits each description below. Using the form provided (Figure 15.1 on page 410), write the name of the person in the grid space above the column with the number corresponding to the description.

#### LIST OF REPRESENTATIVE PERSONS

1. Write your own name in the first blank.
2. Write your mother's first name. If you grew up with a stepmother, write her name instead.
3. Write your father's first name. If you grew up with a stepfather, write his name instead.
4. Write the name of your brother who is nearest your own age. If you had no brother, write the name of a boy near your age who was most like a brother to you during your early teens.
5. Write the name of your sister who is nearest your own age. If you had no sister, write the name of a girl near your own age who was most like a sister to you during your early teens.

   *From this point on do not repeat any names. If a person has already been listed, simply make a second choice.*

6. Your wife (or husband) or, if you are not married, your closest present girl (boy) friend.
7. Your closest girl (boy) friend immediately preceding the person mentioned above.
8. Your closest present friend of the same sex as yourself.
9. A person of the same sex as yourself whom you once thought was a close friend but in whom you were badly disappointed later.
10. The minister, priest, or rabbi with whom you would be most willing to talk over your personal feelings about religion.
11. Your physician.
12. The present neighbor whom you know best.
13. A person with whom you have been associated who, for some unexplained reason, appeared to dislike you.
14. A person whom you would most like to help or for whom you feel sorry.
15. A person with whom you usually feel most uncomfortable.
16. A person whom you have recently met and would like to know better.
17. The teacher who influenced you most when you were in your teens.
18. The teacher whose point of view you found most objectionable.
19. An employer, supervisor, or officer under whom you served during a period of great stress.

*(Continued next page)*

20.    The most successful person whom you know personally.
21.    The happiest person whom you know personally.
22.    The person known to you personally who appears to meet the highest ethical standards.

After you have written the names in the space above the columns, look at the first row. There are circles under three persons' names (20, 21, 22). Decide how two of them are alike in an important way and how they differ from the third person. Put an X in each of the two circles under the names of the persons who are alike. Then write on the line under the column headed "Construct" a word or phrase that identifies the likeness. Write the opposite of this characteristic under the heading "Contrast." Now go back and consider all the other people you listed on your grid. If any of them also share the same characteristic, put a check mark under their name. Repeat this procedure until you have completed every row on the form.

When you have completed the form, take a close look at your results. First consider the nature of the constructs you listed. How many different constructs did you list? What kind of constructs were they? Did you tend to make comparisons on the basis of appearance (skinny versus fat) or personality characteristics (thoughtful versus unthoughtful; honest versus dishonest)? Do any of the constructs overlap? You can discover this by examining the pattern of checks and X's in the various rows. If the pattern for one construct (such as honest versus dishonest) is identical to that of another construct (such as sincere versus insincere), you can suspect that these two constructs may really be one and the same for you. To how many different people did you apply each of the constructs? A construct that is applied to a large number of people may be more permeable than one that is restricted to only one person. Are the constructs divided in terms of their application to persons of the same age or sex? This may give you some idea of the limits on the range of your constructs. Now take a look at your list of contrasting constructs. Are there any constructs that you list only as a difference and never as a similarity? If so, you may be reluctant to use that construct. If you list a contrasting pole for one person only, perhaps that construct is impermeable and limited to that person. Are any names associated only with contrasting poles? If so, your relationship to those persons may be rigid and unchanging even though you get along with them. Finally, compare your own column with those of the other people on the list. Which of the three people are you most like?

This analysis will not give you definitive answers; it will simply provide a starting point for further questions. Rather than consider the results on the grid as final, use your findings as the basis for additional study of yourself. For example, if you discover identical patterns for two constructs, such as honest versus dishonest and sincere versus insincere, you might ask yourself, "Do I believe that all honest people are sincere?" In other words, use your findings for further questions. Numerous possibilities for self-exploration are initiated by the Rep Test.

SOURCE: Reprinted from The Psychology of Personal Constructs, *Volume One*, by George A. Kelly, Ph.D., by permission of Mrs. Gladys Kelly. Copyright 1955 by George A. Kelly. Additional quotes reprinted by permission of W. W. Norton and Company, Inc.

Such research has focused on **cognitive complexity,** the ability to perceive differences in the way in which one construes other people. Individuals who are high in cognitive complexity are better able to predict what others will do and to relate with them.

As psychologists pay increased attention to the role of cognitive factors in personality, personal construct theory has generated more and more research (Chambers & Epting, 1985; Chambers & Graves, 1985; Chambers & Stonerock, 1985; Tobacyk & Downs, 1986). Recent research has used the Rep grid to asses values and beliefs (Horley, 1991) and to analyze content and structural form in personality description (Donahue, 1994); in addition, computer-based methods of analysis have been developed (Bringmann, 1992; see also Ford & Adams-Webber, 1991).

# Psychotherapy

According to Kelly (1955), psychological disorders arise when a person clings to and continues to use personal constructs in spite of the fact that subsequent experience fails to validate them. Such a person has difficulty anticipating and predicting events and is unable to learn from experiences. The neurotic flounders in an effort to develop new ways to interpret the world or rigidly holds onto constructs that are useless. Instead of developing more successful constructs and solving problems, the neurotic develops symptoms.

Kelly conceived of his therapeutic methods as "reconstruction" rather than psychotherapy. He sought to help his patient reconstrue the world in a manner that would foster better predictions and control. The first step in his therapy is usually that of "elaborating the complaint." In this step, the therapist seeks to identify the problem, discover when and under what conditions it first arose, indicate what changes have occurred in the problem, discover any corrective measures that the client may have already taken, and find out under what conditions the problem is most and least noticeable. Elaboration of the complaint usually reveals many aspects of the person's construct system, but Kelly conceived of a second step as that of elaborating the construct system itself. Such elaboration gives a fuller picture of the elements encompassed in the complaint, allows more alternatives to arise, broadens the base of the relationship between therapist and client, and reveals the conceptual framework that created and sustained the symptoms.

Many of the techniques that Kelly employed to effect psychotherapeutic change are similar to those used by other therapists. However, in part through exposure to the psychodrama of J. Moreno (Stewart & Barry, 1991), Kelly made a unique contribution to therapeutic methodology by developing and fostering the use of **role-playing.** In the course of therapy, if a client mentioned difficulty with a particular interpersonal relationship, such as an overly demanding boss or unsympathetic professor, Kelly would suggest that they pretend they were in the boss's or the professor's office and re-enact the troublesome scene. Afterward, alternative methods of handling the scene would be explored and the scene itself re-enacted and changed in the light of alternative ways in which the client might deal with it in the future. Kelly encouraged the use of role reversal, having the client play the role of the significant figures while he played the client. Role reversal allows the client to understand his or her own participation more fully and also to understand the framework of the other person.

Kelly also used fixed-role therapy, in which he had the client enact the role of

## Role-Playing

Kelly's method of role-playing can be fruitfully employed as a way of understanding one's own interpersonal relationships. Ask a close friend to help as you play the role of an important figure in your life. You might wish to play the role of your mother, father, instructor, boss, or boy or girl friend. Ask your friend to play yourself. Identify a problem situation or a potential problem. First consider how your parent, or whoever, would handle the situation. Then act it out, with your friend playing yourself. It is important that you try to look at the situation and behave as you believe your mother, or the other figure, would. Afterward, discuss with your friend what happened and consider alternative ways of handling the scene. Seeing yourself through your friend's eyes may help you to a closer understanding of how you come across to other people. Playing the role of other important people in your life can help you construe their interpretation of the way in which you behave.

It is also possible for the reader to obtain some of the benefits of fixed-role therapy by employing it in a limited scope. Choose one aspect of your personality that you would like to work on. It is important that you choose only one aspect at a time and one with which you feel you can deal relatively comfortably. If you believe that you are generally too passive, you might try to become more assertive. Ask yourself, "How does an assertive person think, respond, or behave in certain situations?" Then for a period of one day, try to pretend that you are an assertive person. You might even give yourself a new name. Of course, all of your friends will call you by the same old name and assume that you are your same old passive self. However, unknown to them, the passive you is taking a day off and the new you is going to respond to them and other events as an assertive person would. When the day is over, take time to consider how you performed in your new role. How did other people react to you? You may find yourself quite surprised by the impact that your new role has had on other people.

someone else for a more protracted period of time. Beginning with the client's own character sketch, developed during the phase of elaborating the construct system, the therapist creates a fictitious role for the client to play that is different from the normal role and is designed to help the client explore possible ways of reconstruing experiences. The client is introduced to the fictitious role and asked to try to think, talk, and behave like that other person for a period of a few days or weeks. Obviously, the role must be carefully contrived ahead of time. It must be realistic and not too threatening for the client. Eventually the client may discover that the construct system of the character played is more effective and adopt some of those constructs. More importantly, the client learns that change is a real possibility. Fixed-role therapy has proved to be a very creative way to reconstrue the self under professional guidance. Mair (1988) believes that Kelly was reaching toward a new conception of inquiry in which the narrative form becomes very important and psychology is seen as a story-telling discipline.

Kelly believed that his theory had wide implications for social and interpersonal relationships. By actively considering alternative constructions, Kelly suggested, it is possible for us individually and collectively to envision new, more creative ways of dealing with a problematic situation. Take the problem that arises when a teacher observes an inattentive student who does not listen, turns in work late, and appears to put forth very little effort. The teacher might conclude that the pupil is lazy. Kelly would ask us to pose the question: Is this the most fruitful interpretation that the teacher can make, or is it simply a cop-out? Perhaps a different construction would give the teacher more latitude in creatively dealing with the problem. At the same time, the student may have a construction of the classroom situation that is hindering rather than facilitating learning. The student may, for instance, perceive that teachers are out to prove the stupidity of their pupils and play an obliging role.

Kelly acknowledged the integral relation of values and theory. Indeed, his metaphor of the scientist may be seen as a proscription instead of a description of human nature (Walker, 1992). Kalekin-Fishman (1993) believes that Kelly's theory escapes the limitation of radical individualism and enriches our understanding of sociocultural processes by emphasizing shared social construction of reality. As such, it may help us to build a bridge to the social constructionists and deal with the problem of alienation.

Kelly also encouraged the use of group therapy to help solve individual and common problems. The technique of role-playing is particularly well adapted to groups, where several people may assist an individual in acting out a scene. By the end of his life, Kelly was suggesting ways in which his theory could be applied to help solve social and international problems. Much of our difficulty as Americans in international relations has been our problem as a nation in understanding how different events are construed or interpreted variously by people in other countries. An enrichment of Kelly's theory, termed *perspectivism*, conceives of other people as equal partners and promotes tolerance of multiple perspectives (Warren, 1992). In this way, personal construct theory can underlie a theory of social action because its central task is to help people reconstrue their lives (Butt, 1995).

## Kelly's Theory

PHILOSOPHY,<br>SCIENCE,<br>AND ART

Although Kelly encouraged us to think of the person as a scientist, his discussion of the way we validate personal constructs involved the compelling character of philosophical insights as well. Kelly's theory suggests that a construct is validated if the anticipations it gives rise to occur. *Validation* refers to the compatibility between one's predictions and one's observation of the outcome, both of which are subjectively construed. This form of everyday validation does not precisely parallel the controlled procedures of science. A scientist testing hypotheses does not look for events that will verify the hypotheses but rather sets up conditions that might falsify them. In a well-designed experiment one's anticipations are of little consequence to the outcome of the hypothesis (Rychlak, 1973, 1990). In Kelly's theory people are philosophers as well as scientists, or, at least, the scientific activities in which they engage are predicated on a philosophical stance. Kelly candidly acknowledged that his view of the person as a scientist was based on the philosophical position of constructive alternativism.

Kelly's theory is better known in England and Europe than in the United States (see also Feixas, 1989). There, industrial-organizational psychologists, management development specialists, and occupational counselors have computerized the Rep Test and grid and have seen enormous potential for the instrument as an assessment device in industry. In spite of the fact that Kelly's own writings were scholarly and academic in tone, replete with their own technical vocabulary, his personal construct theory lends itself well to industrial-organizational psychology, in which there is a need for the psychologist to speak the language of the employee rather than that of the psychologist (Jankowicz, 1987). Translated into lay terms and concretely applied to the everyday lives of individuals, Kelly's theory is particularly relevant in the workplace.

Kelly emphasized the rationality of the human being. He believed that as the scientific world becomes increasingly sophisticated, the constructs we form are increasingly more successful approximations of reality. Nevertheless, he did not believe that the world or the person is ultimately knowable through a scientific methodology. Science is simply a construct system that helps us explain events. It is one system of constructs among many alternatives. Since we cannot posit any objective reality apart from our understanding of it, we cannot assert that science can ever comprehend the real person. It can, however, provide useful constructions that assist us in making predictions. This point of view characterized Kelly's attitude toward his own philosophizing and theorizing as well, since he readily acknowledged and expected that his own theory would ultimately be succeeded by an alternative construction (1970). "At best," he wrote, "it is an ad interim theory" (1955).

## PHILOSOPHICAL ASSUMPTIONS

 *Examining Kelly*

How would you rate Kelly on each of the basic philosophical assumptions described in Chapter 1? Consult the chart on the inside front cover. Each basic issue is presented as a bipolar dimension along which a person's view can be placed according to the degree of agreement with one or the other extreme: *freedom/determinism, hereditary/environmental, uniqueness/universality, proactive/reactive, optimistic/pessimistic.* Rate Kelly's on these issues.

When you have determined where you think Kelly stands, compare your responses with those of your classmates and your instructor. You should be willing to defend your ratings, but also be prepared to change them in light of others' compelling arguments. Afterward, compare your rating of Kelly with your own position on each issue and with those of other theorists. Does this comparison help you understand why his theory does or does not appeal to you?

In spite of the "ad interim" character of Kelly's theory, it has attracted considerable attention and controversy. Kelly has been brought to task for his overly intellectual view of the individual and therapy, his neglect of developmental antecedents, his failure to deal adequately with human emotions, and his insistence on dichotomous concepts. The biggest criticism of Kelly's work has been that he ignored the full range of the human personality in his effort to do justice to the human intellect (Bruner & Rogers, 1965). He has been praised, however, for providing a model of uniqueness versus universality; "construct systems can have unique content elements but follow common principles of functioning" (Pervin, 1996).

Although Kelly insisted that his theory was not a cognitive one, his work foreshadowed the contemporary interest in cognitive factors in personality. As such, some critics suggest that Kelly's theory is a "classic that was ahead of its time" (Rorer & Widiger, 1983, p. 426). At the same time, psychologists who are influenced by information processing models often conceive of Kelly's constructs as schemas, scripts, or neural networks when in fact Kelly's personal constructs are structures of the phenomenal field. Mancuso (1996) suggests that Kelly's personal construct theory shares assumptions with social constructionism and narrative psychology and can help to illumine the emerging discussions on narrative as a highly suitable mode for personality expression.

By viewing personal constructions as the primary factor governing personality, Kelly developed a theory that encompasses cognitive, emotional, behavioral, perceptual, and motivational aspects of personality. Perhaps this is why Kelly was entertained by various efforts to classify his theory. After he gave a lecture at Harvard, Kelly noted that "Professor Gordon Allport explained to the students that my theory was not a 'cognitive' theory but an 'emotional' theory. Later the same afternoon, Dr. Henry Murray called me aside and said, 'You know, don't you, that you are really an existentialist'" (in Mahler, 1969, p. 216; see also Soffer, 1993).

However one wishes to classify Kelly's theory, his emphasis on construction is compatible with recent trends in cognitive psychology, and, thus, his theory is likely to continue to attract attention. Moreover, his techniques of assessment and role-playing have proved to be very useful tools in psychotherapy, education, and industry.

## *Summary*

1. Kelly suggested that we view ourselves as scientists because, in our efforts to understand the world, we develop *personal constructs* that act as hypotheses that make the world meaningful to us.

2. His theory is based on the philosophical position of *constructive alternativism,* the assumption that any one event is open to a number of interpretations.

3. Kelly's fundamental postulate is "A person's processes are psychologically channelized by the ways in which he anticipates events." He elaborates on his fundamental postulate with eleven corollaries: construction, individuality, organization, dichotomy, choice, range, experience, modulation, fragmentation, communality, and sociality.

4. Kelly gave new meanings to many traditional concepts in personality theorizing, such as the *self-construct,* role, learning, motivation, and emotion.

5. Kelly developed the Rep Test, which permits a person to reveal his or her constructs by comparing and contrasting a number of different persons in his or her life.

6. In his psychotherapy Kelly sought to help his patient reconstrue the world by first elaborating the complaint and then elaborating the construct system. His unique contribution was the technique of *role-playing.*

7. Kelly has been criticized for being too intellectual and for failing to deal with the whole of personality or the emotions.

8. The way in which we validate personal constructs involves philosophical insights as well as scientific methods.

## Suggestions for Further Reading

George Kelly was not a prolific writer. Two books and about a dozen articles constitute the sum of his publications. His basic theory was published in a two-volume work called *The Psychology of Personal Constructs* (Norton, 1955). The first three chapters of those volumes were published separately as *A Theory of Personality: A Psychology of Personal Constructs* (Norton, 1963). Kelly's writing is rather academic and difficult reading for the lay person, who might be better advised to begin with a good secondary source such as D. Bannister and F. Fransella, *Inquiring Man: The Theory of Personal Constructs* (Penguin, 1966) or D. Bannister, *New Perspectives in Personal Construct Theory* (Academic Press, 1985). Donald Bannister, an Englishman, is Kelly's most fervent disciple.

The *Journal of Constructivist Psychology* devoted a special issue (Jul–Sep 1994) to the elaboration of personal construct psychology.

# Cognitive-
# Behavioral Theories

## ALBERT ELLIS ❖ AARON BECK
## ❖ ARNOLD LAZARUS

### *Your Goals for This Chapter*

1. Discuss the philosophical origins of Ellis's *rational emotive behavior therapy.*
2. Explain the theory behind Ellis's rational emotive behavior therapy.
3. Discuss the *A-B-C theory of personality* and tell how people develop irrational and *mustabatory* belief systems.
4. Explain how people get their belief systems.
5. Explain the goal of rational emotive behavior therapy and tell how it is achieved.
6. Compare and contrast Ellis's theory with those of other theorists.
7. Discuss the philosophical origins of Beck's cognitive theory.
8. Discuss the theory of personality behind *cognitive therapy.*
9. Explain what is meant by *cognitions, schemas,* and *cognitive distortions.*
10. Discuss the dimensions of *sociotrophy* and *autonomy.*
11. Describe the *cognitive triad.*
12. Give an overview of Beck's cognitive therapy.
13. Describe some cognitive and behavioral techniques used in cognitive therapy.
14. Discuss assessment and research in Beck's theory and compare him with other theorists.
15. Discuss the development of Lazarus's theory and the *BASIC-ID.*
16. Describe the personality theory behind *multimodal therapy.*
17. Describe *multimodal therapy.*
18. Evaluate behavioral cognitive therapies and theories in terms of their function as philosophy, science, and art.

I n recent years, behavioral cognitive therapies have revolutionized the fields of psy-chotherapy and counseling. Albert Ellis, Aaron Beck, and Arnold Lazarus are primar-ily clinicians who have developed techniques and strategies for helping people cope better with their problems. These theorists were frustrated with the relatively long (and to them inefficient) process of psychoanalysis; they devised counseling methods that are often very brief, client-centered, and to the point. Rather than take a long time to bring out issues that are related to events in the distant past, they deal directly with elements of the client's im-mediate present and attempt to change existing thoughts or client values. In their writing, they primarily talk about the type of therapy that they do. Nevertheless, their counseling and therapy strategies are based on underlying theories (although they are not necessarily clearly articulated or a primary concern of these thinkers, who emphasize practical advan-tages over theoretical orientations). While these theories are a little difficult to extract from their writings, we can try to examine them as theories of personality. They emphasize and cultivate conscious forces, recognizing that a primary goal in life and analysis is to become more aware and conscious. The significance of these clinicians is apparent when we note that a survey of clinical and counseling psychologists on the "Ten Most Influential Psy-chotherapists" (D. Smith, 1982) placed Ellis second, Beck seventh, and Lazarus fifth.

## Albert Ellis: Biographical Background

Albert Ellis (1991) does not believe that his childhood experiences shaped his becoming a psychotherapist. Born September 27, 1913, in Pittsburgh and raised "on the streets of the Bronx," Ellis says that he was a "semiorphan" because his father (before his parents were di-vorced) did a great deal of traveling and spent little time with him and his younger brother and sister. He believes that his mother was totally unprepared to raise children. As a result, Ellis suggests, "I was almost as instrumental in raising my mother (and, to an even greater degree my younger brother and sister) as she was in raising me."

Neglected by his parents, he was also ill (with nephritis, chronic inflammation of the kidney, which led to severe headaches), frequently hospitalized, and not permitted to engage in active childhood play. Shy and introverted, he was readily exceeded by his brave extraverted brother. To top things off, during the Great Depression, the family just barely managed without having to go on welfare.

With an incompetent mother, a brother who "acted out" and a sister who "whined," you might think that the stage was set for a pretty miserable childhood. Nevertheless, Ellis "refused to be miserable." In his immediate family, only his sister suffered from depression and anxiety, leading him to speculate that emotional disorders are due to genetics rather than environmental factors. Fortunately, when they became adults, Ellis's rational emotive behavior therapy (REBT) was able to help her.

He went to the High School of Commerce in New York with the intent to quickly become a millionaire, but upon graduation the Great Depression shattered that dream. He enrolled in City College, where he ended up majoring in English. He did a great deal of

*Albert Ellis developed an A-B-C theory of personality that influences his rational emotive behavior therapy.*

writing, supporting himself with odd jobs. When he could not get any of his six novels published, he decided to focus on nonfiction.

It was sex that launched him into clinical psychology. Wanting to write about promiscuity, he did a great deal of reading in erotic fiction and nonfiction. Friends began to ask him to assist them in solving some of their problems. He found that he was good at helping and enjoyed doing it, and decided to begin graduate training. At Teachers College of Columbia University he received his M.A. degree and matriculated for the Ph.D. Ellis wanted to write his dissertation on love, but two members of the department censored the topic, leading him to deliberately choose and successfully defend a dull and harmless topic, *A Comparison of the Use of Direct and Indirect Phrasing with Personality Questionnaires.* He thereby became very knowledgeable about personality inventories.

Returning to his love of research on sex, Ellis wrote a great many articles and books that became very popular. He spent two years in analysis and was subsequently "unofficially" trained by his analyst, who was associated with the Horney Institute for Psychoanalysis, which at that time did not permit the training of psychologists. Ellis found he was an effective analyst but gave it up in 1953 because he was looking for a more "efficient" method. Ellis had rapidly risen to a position of high authority in the state of New Jersey, but "prudes" in the state system objected to his research on sex, so he left New Jersey in 1952, became a well-known practicing psychologist in New York, and continued to write. In 1955, Ellis introduced a new approach—*rational psychotherapy*—so called to emphasize its focus on rational rather than irrational thinking. When wrongly criticized for neglecting emotions, Ellis changed the name to rational emotive therapy (RET). In the late 1960s and early 1970s, Ellis began to remake RET, "making it both simpler and more complex" (1991). In 1991, he amended the name once again to **rational emotive behavior therapy** to acknowledge the behavioral aspect that was always emphasized. Because the term is rather cumbersome, we will primarily refer to it by its acronym, **REBT.**

REBT is the first primarily cognitive behavioral therapy, and Ellis is proud to have been its founder. His career soared in the 1960s due to the popularity of his books and therapy method and he founded the Institute for Rational Emotive Therapy in New York. The institute has grown enormously, and the therapy it proposes has been widely adopted throughout the world.

Partially disabled with diabetes, poor hearing, weak vision, and other physical handicaps during most of his life (1997), this incredible busy, productive, and controversial man, who is in his eighties, has used some of his own basic principles to help him continue to actively practice, train, write, and conduct workshops.

## Philosophical Origins

The philosophic origins of REBT go back to the Stoic philosophers, particularly Marcus Aurelius (121–180) and Epictetus (60–120), who wrote in the *Encheiridion* (or Handbook). "People are not disturbed by things, but by the view which they take of them," a position that is the cornerstone of REBT. He was also influenced by Immanuel Kant's writings on cognition and ideation, as well as by the philosophers of science, such as Bertrand Russell, who emphasized the importance of testing hypotheses. He allies himself with the philosophy of ethical humanism. REBT challenges self-defeating absolutistic beliefs, not religious beliefs (1994a; Nielsen & Ellis, 1994). Ellis concurs with the Christian stance of accepting the sinner but not the sin (1996).

In psychology, the modern precursor of REBT was Alfred Adler, whose emphasis on inferiority feelings, goals, education, and social interest is also apparent in Ellis's work. Adler's (1927) motto "Everything depends on opinion" is an essential tenet of REBT.

## The Theory of Rational Emotive Behavior Therapy (REBT)

Ellis (1978) points out that from the beginning REBT has denoted a theory of personality that arises from its theory of personality change.

Ellis (1958) suggests that human beings are "sign-, symbol-, and language-creating" animals who have four fundamental processes: *perception, movement, thinking,* and *emotion.* These are all necessarily interrelated. Thinking not only entails brain activity (such as remembering, learning, and problem solving); it also entails perception, emotion, and movement. Therefore it would be more accurate to say that a person "perceives-moves-feels-THINKS about" a problem than to simply say he or she "thinks" about it. Likewise emotion is not one thing but a combination of related phenomena. Thus cognitions, emotions, and behavior are consistently interactional and transactional. The theory behind REBT is a comprehensive cognitive-affective behavioral one (Ellis, 1962). Because thoughts and emotions frequently overlap, much of what we consider emotion is a type of evaluative thinking. Perhaps it is somewhat less dispassionate than that which we usually label thinking, but nevertheless it may be seen as a type of thought. Because humans are raised in a social culture in which thinking and emoting are highly interrelated, thinking and emotion tend to develop into a cause and effect relationship, "so that one's thinking *becomes* one's emotion and emoting *becomes* one's thought." These processes tend to assume a type of "self-talk" in which our "internalized sentences" determine our thoughts and emotions. Although it is conceivably possible to have a momentary outburst of emotion without thought, in order to sustain the emotion it has to be backed up by some form of thought (1958). Thus the basic personality theory of rational emotive behavior theory suggests that human beings largely create their own emotional consequences.

Ellis believes that people have strong innate inclinations to live and be happy, to seek pleasure and to avoid pain. They are goal-oriented active and changing creatures with a strong compulsion to fulfill their potential.

Nevertheless, people of all ages engage in numerous irrational thoughts, unsuitable feelings, and dysfunctional behaviors that are inclined to sabotage their potential. People are born with a distinct proneness to engage in self-destructive behavior and learn, through social conditioning, to exacerbate rather than to minimize that proneness.

Most of these human self-sabotaging tendencies may be summarized by stating that humans are born with an exceptionally strong tendency to want, to "need," and to condemn first themselves, others, and then the world when they do not immediately get what they supposedly "need." They consequently think "childishly" or "humanly" all their lives and are able only with enormous difficulty to achieve and maintain "mature" or realistic behavior (1976).

People grow up in social groups and spend much of their energy trying to impress, live up to the expectations of, and outdo the performances of other people. On the surface they are "ego-oriented," "identity seeking" or "self-centered." Even more importantly, however, they usually define themselves as "good" or "worthwhile" when they believe that others accept and approve of them. Ellis says that it is realistic and sane for people to find or fulfill "themselves" in their interpersonal relations and to have a considerable amount of what Adler called social interest.

However, what we call emotional disturbance is frequently associated with people's caring too much about what others think and stems from their believing they can accept themselves only if others think well of them. When disturbed, people escalate their desire for others' approval and the practical advantages that normally go with such approval into an absolute *dire need* to be liked, and they can hardly avoid becoming anxious and prone to depression (Bernard, 1986; Ellis, 1962, 1987, 1988; Ellis & Dryden, 1987; Ellis & Harper, 1975). It is our tendency to exaggerate the importance of others' acceptance that often causes our inappropriate emotions (Ellis, 1985a, 1985b; Ellis & Becker, 1982; Ellis & Dryden, 1987).

The **A-B-C theory of personality** behind rational emotive behavior therapy holds that when a highly charged *emotional consequence* (C) (such as being very frightened) follows a significant *activating event* (A) (such as being chased by a large dog as a child), A may seem to but actually does not cause C. Instead, in subsequent situations, emotional consequences are largely created by (B), the individual's *belief system* (Oh, dear, all dogs are dangerous and that is horrible). "If two people get labeled 'stupid,' and one laughs at the statement and the other feels depressed, we cannot explain these radically different Consequences by A (the Activating Event) but rather by B (the Belief System) *about A*" (1978). Although the sequence may appear to be linear, the theory is actually interactive and bidirectional (1996).

When an undesirable emotional consequence occurs, such as severe anxiety, it can usually be traced to the person's irrational beliefs. When these beliefs are effectively challenged (at point D) by *disputing* them rationally and behaviorally (Some, but not all, dogs are dangerous, thus while it pays to be prudent, you don't have to be afraid of and avoid all dogs), the disturbed consequences are minimized and greatly decreased (see Figure 16.1).

A Activating event

B Belief system

Oh dear, all dogs are dangerous and that is horrible.

C Emotional consequence

**A does *not* cause C; rather, B does.**

**FIGURE 16.1**    Ellis's A-B-C Theory

The A-B-C theory of personality holds that when a highly charged emotional consequent (C) follows a significant activating event (A), in subsequent similar situations A may seem to, but actually does not, cause C. Instead, subsequent emotional consequences are largely created by B—the individual's belief system.

Emotional disturbance results from the interdependence of cognition, emotion, and action. Thus it is too simplistic to say that irrational beliefs cause or determine unhealthy negative emotions. Rather, we are dealing with a complex of thoughts, feelings, and action tendencies that are more likely to become disturbed when they are grounded in dogmatic **musturbatory belief systems** that take the form of **absolute musts,** such as: "I *absolutley must* perform well and be lovable!" "Other people *absolutely must* treat me considerately and fairly!" and "My life conditions *absolutely must* be comfortable and not too frustrating" (1978, 1996).

Recently, Ellis acknowledges that his choice of the word *irrational* to describe beliefs that are not only unrealistic and illogical but also, and primarily, self-defeating was not the wisest choice and suggests that instead these beliefs be called *dysfunctional beliefs* (1996).

If people think and work hard at understanding and contradicting the "absolute musts" of their musturbatory belief systems, they can make amazing curative and preventive changes in their disturbance-creating tendencies. Instead of thinking "I must always have the approval of other people," they can think "I like to have the approval of other people, but I know I am not always going to get it." Thus the personality theory behind REBT "may at first sound grim and pessimistic" (1987; Ellis & Dryden, 1987), but it is actually very realistic. It is also highly optimistic and pragmatic. Ellis debunks as myths the notions that personality disorders mainly stem from parental rejection, that feelings of worthlessness usually arise from constant criticism, or that sexual-abuse victims invariably continue to suffer as adults (1995). Posttraumatic stress disorder victims may create their severe distress by having dysfunctional beliefs (1994b).

How do people get their belief systems? Ellis increasingly believes that heredity has a large influence in that as human beings we inherit a great many biological hedonistic predispositions and a high degree of "teachability." Ellis believes that "probably 80 percent of the variance of human behavior rests on biological bases and about 20 percent on environmental training" (1978). We inherit a tendency to raise cultural *preferences* into *musts* and social *norms* into absolute *shoulds.*

There are so many variables (both internal and external, conscious and unconscious) that lead to the origin and maintenance of personality that Ellis believes there are no simple answers concerning the existence of traits or explanations of certain behavior. While behavior is somewhat determined by internal and external forces, Ellis believes people do have *some,* albeit limited, free will and capability of changing their behavior patterns. While he recognizes that we can make some general statements about what people have in common, he also believes that each individual is unique and must assume responsibility for his or her behavior. In spite of his strong emphasis on heredity, Ellis would place himself firmly in the proactive camp.

## Rational Emotive Behavior Psychotherapy

Albert Ellis takes a very directive approach in his rational therapy and argues strongly for the view that people must judge their behavior not in terms of what others may believe but in terms of what they sense is right for them. The goal of therapy for Ellis is to enable clients to commit themselves to actions that correspond to their true value system. The goal of therapy should not be to understand the causes or to remove the symptoms of pathological behavior, but rather to free individuals to develop a constructive and confident image of their self-worth. Clients should be led to appreciate their "true identity" and encouraged to venture forth to test their personal tastes and values.

If clients are helped to focus on their irrational thinking and inappropriate emoting and behaving by a highly active, directive, didactic, philosophic, homework-assigning therapist, they are more likely to change their symptom-creating beliefs than if they mainly work with a dynamically oriented, client-centered, existentialist, or classical behavior-modification therapist (Ellis, 1978, 1985a, 1987a; Ellis & Dryden, 1987).

Three main therapeutic processes are used in rational emotive behavior therapy: (1) cognitive, (2) emotive evocative, and (3) behavioral.

Rational emotive **cognitive therapy** attempts to show clients how to recognize their *should* and *must* thoughts, how to separate rational from irrational beliefs, and how to accept reality. It assumes that clients can think, can think about their thinking, and can even think about thinking about their thinking. In one-to-one sessions, the therapist not only listens but also gives information and seeks to stimulate the client to explore his or her own philosophy of life. In group therapy or workshops, members are encouraged to discuss, explain, and reason with one another.

**Emotive evocative therapy** employs role-playing, psychodrama, humor, and other ideas such as unconditional acceptance to reduce disturbance-creating ideas to absurdity; to convince clients that others can accept them with their failings; and to get in touch with their "shameful" feelings so they can zero in on the exact things they are telling themselves to create these feelings.

**Behavior therapy** is employed in REBT not only to help clients change maladaptive patterns of behavior but also to help change their cognition. Thus, clients can be told to deliberately fail at a small task in order to survive a failure and thus learn that it is not dangerous. Clients may be persuaded to momentarily stay in a difficult situation, such as an uncomfortable job or marriage, in order to work on the problem. REBT therapists give specific active homework assignments and may suggest that clients develop penalties for failure to do their assignments.

Ellis's first paper on rational psychotherapy (1958) pointed out how cognitions, emotions, and behaviors are consistently interactional and transactional. Early papers advocated **in vitro desensitization,** a process whereby anxieties and fears are reduced by repeated imagined exposure to the noxious stimuli paired with relaxation, skill training, and other behavioral techniques. Thus individuals who were anxious about driving on major high-speed highways might first be taught how to deeply relax (a skill that can be learned, but takes practice) and then to imagine themselves driving on a highway as a safe, competent driver. If there was any question about their driving ability, they might be encouraged to take a driving class. Other goal-oriented steps might be encouraged as well to help them maintain a reasonable speed, and so forth. REBT favors **in vivo desensitization,** in which the client is actually exposed to gradually more threatening versions of the anxiety-provoking situation. Some REBT therapists prefer **implosive** (or sudden, instead of gradual) confrontation of phobic situations, depending on the circumstances. Later REBT embraced experiential-encounter techniques, and Ellis invented some of his own.

The rational emotive theory of psychotherapy asserts that there are many kinds of psychological treatment and that most of them work to some degree. An efficient system of therapy includes (a) economy of time and effort, (b) rapid symptom reduction, (c) effec-

**THINKING CRITICALLY**

## A Self-Help Form

The Institute for Rational-Emotive Therapy has developed a Self-Help Form that can be useful for individuals trying to identify irrational beliefs that lead to emotional disturbance or self-defeating behavior.

First you are asked to identify an activating event that precipitates a negative consequence or condition that you would like to change. For example, the prospect of having to drive on a high-speed highway makes me very anxious and leads me to avoid such trips.

Then you identify those irrational beliefs that lead to your self-defeating feelings and behavior. For example:

1. I *must* do things perfectly.
2. I am a *worthless person* if I become anxious.
3. I *must* be approved and accepted by other people.
4. People *must* live up to my expectations, and if they don't it is terrible.
5. It is *awful* or *horrible* when major things don't go my way.

Next you develop a dispute for each of your irrational beliefs. For example:

1. Why *must* I do things perfectly?
2. Where is it written that I am a worthless person if I become anxious?
3. Why do people *have to* approve or accept everything I do?
4. Many people do not live up to my expectations. It's disappointing, but not terrible.
5. Is it really *awful* or *horrible* when major things don't go my way? Or only a hassle or inconvenience?

Finally, work on coming up with an effective rational belief to replace your irrational beliefs. For example:

1. I'd *prefer* to do very well, but I don't always *have* to.
2. I can be a worthwhile person and still feel a little anxious.
3. While it is nice to be approved and accepted by everybody, it isn't absolutely necessary. I won't die of rejection.
4. It's disappointing when people don't live up to my expectations but it is not the end of the world.
5. It's pretty inconvenient when major things don't go my way; and I don't *like* it, but I can stand it.

After you have come up with some effective rational beliefs for some of the activating events that used to create problems for you, notice the different types of feelings and behaviors that you experience. By thinking rationally when negative events occur, you will be more likely to feel *appropriate* feelings, such as disappointment or frustration—rather than *disturbed* feelings such as rage, anxiety, or depression. Regularly practice and repeat these rational beliefs to yourself—out loud—in order to help yourself feel better and behave more rationally.

---

*SOURCE: This exercise is based on the RET Self-Help Form published by the Institute for Rational-Emotive Therapy, 45 E. 65th Street, New York, NY 10021.*

tiveness with a large cross-section of clients, (d) solution-oriented discussions, and (e) long-term results that last. Ellis (1987a) says that rational emotive theory is realistic and unindulgent. It gets to the core of and ruthlessly persists at undermining childish demand-ingness, the main element of serious emotional disturbance.

Unlike many other systems of psychotherapy, Ellis emphasizes the biological aspects of human personality. Although Ellis holds that people have vast untapped resources for growth and that they are in many important ways able to change their social and personal destinies, he also holds that they have exceptionally powerful innate tendencies to think irrationally and to harm themselves (Ellis, 1976).

The rational therapist assumes that people imbibe goals, standards, and values from their parents and culture and then add their own musts and demands to these ideals. Along the way, they also construct illogical ideas or irrational modes of thinking and that, without doing so, they could hardly be as disturbed as they are. It is the therapist's function not merely to show clients their irrational ideas or thinking processes but to persuade them to change and substitute for them more rational ideas and thought processes. Rational emotive behavior therapy employs many techniques such as role-playing, or free association and other expressive emotive techniques, but the therapist does not isolate her- or himself but rather acts "as his or her own person" (1987) so that these relationship-building techniques really get to the core of illogical thinking and induce clients to think in a more rational manner.

The rational emotive behavior therapist will keep pounding away, time and again, at the illogical ideas that underlie the client's fears. This means showing the client that it is not fear of father but fear of being blamed, of being disapproved, of being unloved, of being imperfect, of being a failure.

Ellis (Ellis & Dryden, 1987) points out that eclecticism is "hardly new to REBT." His willingness to draw creatively from many areas of effective psychotherapy is impressive.

Like most Western therapies. REBT tends to adopt a more universalist (and also more individualistic) position than would be appropriate to the cultures that many of the world's people are reared in. However, dysfunctional beliefs occur in all cultures, albeit in various forms. Since REBT specializes in uncovering such beliefs, it can make a significant contribution to the study of cultural diversity.

## Comparisons and Contrasts with Other Theorists

Ellis largely agrees with Freud that the pleasure principle tends to run most people's lives. He agrees with Karen Horney and Erich Fromm that cultural influences as well as early family influence tend to play a significant part in building up people's irrational thinking; with Alfred Adler that fictitious goals tend to order and run human lives; with Gordon Allport that once individuals begin to think and act in a certain manner, they find it very difficult to think or act differently, even when they really want to. He also agrees with Ivan Pavlov that humans' large cerebral cavities provide them with a secondary signaling system through which they often become cognitively conditioned; with Jerome Frank that people are especially prone to the influence of suggestion; and with Jean Piaget that active teaching is much more effective than passive learning. Moreover, he agrees with Sigmund and Anna Freud that people frequently refuse to acknowledge their mistakes and resort to defenses and rationalizations that cover up underlying feelings of shame and self-deprecation; and with Abraham Maslow and Carl Rogers that humans, however disturbed they may be, have great potential for continued growth and development.

On the other hand, Ellis has serious objections to certain aspects of many popular personality theories. He opposes the Freudian concept that people have clear-cut libidinous instincts, which if unduly satisfied or thwarted lead to emotional disturbance. Human senses become needs only when people define them as such. The Oedipus complex is a relatively minor subheading under people's major irrational belief that they absolutely have to receive the approval of their parents.

Ellis recognizes the importance of empirical research for supporting and maintaining the effectiveness of REBT (1996). The vivid informality of his descriptions could easily mislead us into thinking that his ideas are not scientific. Because they are interdependent, his concepts are more difficult to measure and study than single isolated concepts, but that is not to say that they are untestable. We can observe the different complexes entailed in absolute musts as compared to preferences and also the consequent thoughts, feelings, and actions and convert these into variables for empirical study, an activity that Ellis would strongly encourage.

## Aaron Beck: Biographical Background

Aaron T. Beck was born in Providence, Rhode Island, on July 18, 1921. He is the third surviving son and youngest child of Russian Jewish immigrants to the United States. His mother's depression following the death of her only daughter in an influenza epidemic lifted when her youngest child was born, and Beck would joke that his ability to cure his mother at an early age illustrated his need to control. Young Aaron developed a near fatal illness following an infection of a broken arm, which led him to be anxious and to believe that he was inept and stupid. At an early age, he began to work cognitively through some of his problems and fears. Later, his theory and therapy would help others overcome the types of negative beliefs that he himself experienced. His father encouraged his interest in science and nature, but his career interests did not coalesce until he had almost finished college. Beck graduated from Brown University magna cum laude in 1943 and was elected to Phi Beta Kappa. The Yale School of Medicine granted him the M.D. in 1946, and the American Board of Psychiatry and Neurology certified him in psychiatry in 1953. The following year, he joined the faculty of the Department of Psychiatry of the University of Pennsylvania Medical School where he has been ever since. In his early years at the university, he received training in psychoanalysis from the Philadelphia Psychoanalytic Institute, where he graduated in 1958.

Following his education, Beck, concerned with the lack of scientific basis for psychoanalysis, embarked on research intended to substantiate psychoanalytic concepts. In a study of depressed people's dreams, Beck hypothesized that their dreams "would contain more hostility than those of nondepressed people. . . . Instead their dreams reflected three common themes: defeat, deprivation, and loss" (1991). This failure led him eventually to develop cognitive therapy as a way of understanding and treating depression. He began to believe that "depressed people did not seek failure; rather they distorted reality to the point where they could not recognize success when it happened" (Greenberg, 1981).

*Aaron Beck views personality as shaped by schemas, cognitive structures or beliefs, and assumptions about how the world operates.*

In addition to his teaching duties at the University of Pennsylvania, Beck has administered research of issues such as depression, suicide, anxiety and panic disorders, substance abuse, marital problems, and personality disorders. He has received a number of honors for his contributions to the comprehension and therapy of depression, anxiety, and suicidal behaviors. His alma mater, Brown, gave him an honorary Doctor of Medical Science in 1982 and the Distinguished Alumnus Award in 1990. In 1987, he was elected a fellow of the Royal College of Psychiatrists. Beck has written or coauthored over 350 articles and 12 books. He has also developed a number of assessment instruments.

## Philosophical Origins

Cognitive therapy's theoretical foundation is derived from three main sources: the phenomenological approach to psychology, structural theory and depth psychology, and cognitive psychology. The phenomenological approach holds that an individual's view of self and the personal world are central to behavior. This approach is demonstrated in the writings of Adler (1936), Alexander (1950), Horney (1950), Sullivan (1953), and Rogers (1959).

The second major influence is the structural theory and depth psychology of Kant (1798) and Freud, particularly Freud's concept of the hierarchical structuring of cognition into primary and secondary processes.

Finally, more modern developments in cognitive psychology have had an impact on this theory. George Kelly (1955) is credited with being the first among contemporaries to derive the cognitive model through his use of "personal constructs" and his emphasis on the role of beliefs in behavior change, even though he did not like being called a cognitivist. Cognitive theories of emotion, such as those of Magda Arnold and Richard Lazarus, which stress the importance of cognition in emotional and behavioral change, have also contributed to cognitive theory. Cognitive theory was originally developed to facilitate treatment for depression, and it is still one of the best effective treatments for that disorder.

## The Theory Behind Cognitive Therapy

Cognitive therapy is based on a theory of personality that maintains that how one thinks largely determines how one feels and behaves. Similar in many ways to rational emotive behavior theory and therapy, which preceded but developed parallel to Beck's cognitive theory and therapy, Beck's system has acquired strong empirical support for its theoretical foundations. Both Ellis and Beck believe that people can consciously adapt reason, and both view the client's underlying assumptions as targets of intervention. While Ellis confounded and persuaded clients that the philosophies they lived by were irrational, Beck "turned the client into a colleague who researches verifiable reality" (Wessler, 1986, p. 5).

Beck views personality as reflecting the individual's cognitive organization and structure, which are both biologically and socially influenced. Within the constraints of one's neuroanatomy and biochemistry, personal learning experiences help determine how one develops and responds. Beck further views personality as shaped by central values, or superordinate schemas, and sees psychological distress as "caused" by a number of factors. People may have biochemical predispositions to illness. Childhood depression may foreshadow depression later in life (Goleman, 1994). However, people respond to specific stressors because of their learning. Thus Beck has said, "People are missing the boat if they say that because it can be treated by drugs, depression is primarily biological in nature. . . . People who receive psychotherapy learn something; people on drugs don't. . . . Biochemical changes probably do occur in the brain during depression, but those come back into balance once the person recovers through therapy" (Greenberg, 1981). Psychopathology is on a continuum with normal emotional reactions. Sometimes emotions are exaggerated. In depression, sadness and loss of interest are intensified and prolonged, in mania there is grandiosity, and in anxiety there is fear of fear.

The concepts involved in Beck's cognitive theory include cognitions, schemas, and cognitive distortions or errors in logic (Beck & Emory, 1979). **Cognitions** refer to a person's awareness. They can be viewed in terms of information processing (Beck & Hollon, 1993) and are rather changeable and brought about by stimuli.

## Cognitive Schemas

**Schemas** are cognitive structures that consist of an individual's fundamental core beliefs and assumptions about how the world operates. At birth we are preprogrammed with certain types of proto-schemas (referring to survival, bonding, autonomy, etc.), which vary in propensity from person to person (Beck & Hollon, 1993). The environment then facilitates or inhibits the emergence of the schema in a way that may or may not assist in adaptation. Schemas, therefore, develop early in life from personal experiences and identification with significant others. People form concepts about themselves, others, and the world. These schemas shape personality. Schemas may be adaptive or maladaptive. They may be general or specific in nature. The behavioral and emotional patterns that make up personality, therefore, are derived from individual rules about life and beliefs about the self. Examples of schemas are "Unless other people approve of me, I am worthless" or "Unless I can do something perfectly, I should not do it at all." Schemas are much more stable than cognitions but they are somewhat dependent on a person's moods.

## Cognitive Distortions

Systematic errors in reasoning called **cognitive distortions** are evident during psychological distress (Beck, 1967). Distortions in cognitions arise when stressful events trigger an unrealistic schemata. Each individual has a set of idiosyncratic vulnerabilities that predispose the person to psychological distress in a unique way. These vulnerabilities appear related to personality structure and cognitive schema. Examples are given in Table 16.1.

Frequently people express their cognitive distortions in terms of *conditional assumptions,* beliefs that are dependent on certain conditions. Such assumptions frequently begin with an *if.* A depression-prone patient may say: "If I don't succeed, nobody will respect me," or "If that one person doesn't like me I must be unlovable." Such persons may function rather well until they experience a series of failures or rejections. Such *errors in logic* frequently entail a systematic negative style of thinking.

## Dimensions of Sociotropy and Autonomy

Beck further describes personality in terms of two dimensions. The **sociotropic dimension** is characterized by dependence on interpersonal relationships and needs for closeness and nurturance. This dimension is organized around closeness, nurturance, and dependency. The **autonomous dimension** is characterized by independence and organized around goal setting, self-determination, and self-imposed obligations (Beck, Epstein, & Harrison, 1983).

While "pure" cases of sociotropy and autonomy do exist, most people display features of each, depending on the situation. Thus, sociotropy and autonomy are modes of behavior, not fixed personality structures. This position stands in marked contrast with psychodynamic theories of personality that hold to fixed personality dimensions.

Beck's research shows that dependent individuals become depressed when their

**TABLE 16.1   Cognitive Distortions**

Beck provides several definitions and examples of cognitive distortions.

| COGNITIVE DISTORTION | DEFINITION | EXAMPLE |
| --- | --- | --- |
| Arbitrary inference | Drawing a specific conclusion without supporting evidence or even in the face of contradictory evidence | After getting a C rather than an A on the first test, a student erroneously concludes that she would not be able to pass the course. |
| Selective abstraction | Conceptualizing a situation on the basis of a detail taken out of context and ignoring all other possible explanations | An individual who is nervous about getting into an accident while driving will zero in on all the reports about traffic accidents while listening to the morning news, reconfirming the belief that driving is a dangerous activity. |
| Overgeneralization | Abstracting a general rule from one or two isolated incidents and applying it too broadly | Hearing about a robbery in the city leads one to conclude that everyone is being robbed. |
| Magnification and minimization | Seeing an event as more significant or less significant than it actually is | A high school girl thinks that if she is not asked to go to the senior prom, her life is over. |
| Personalization | Attributing external events to oneself without evidence of connection | Parents assume that they are to blame every time their children misbehave. |
| Dichotomous thinking | Categorizing situations in extremes | A person sees his or her performance on a task as either a complete success or a total failure. |

relationships are disrupted. Autonomous people become depressed when they fail to achieve a certain goal.

## Cognitive Triad

According to Beck (1967), the depressed individual has a negative view of the self, the world, and the future. These three perceptions are known as the **cognitive triad.** The world seems devoid of pleasure or gratification. The depressed person's view of the future is pessimistic or nonexistent. The increased dependency often observed in depressed patients reflects the view of self as incompetent, an overestimation of the difficulty of normal life tasks, the expectation of failure, and the desire for someone more capable to take over. Indecisiveness similarly reflects the belief that one is incapable of making correct decisions. The physical

**THINKING CRITICALLY**

## *Cognitive Distortions*

Can you think of ways in which you make the errors in logic that Beck describes as cognitive distortions? Which ones can you identify in your own thinking? Rate yourself on a scale of 1–5 (1 = never; 5 = frequently) for each of the distortions listed in Table 16.1. This will help you see if you are more prone to make certain types as opposed to other ones. Do you believe that any of these types of errors could underlie your own depressive mood changes? Being aware of the tendency to make cognitive distortions can be helpful, because if we are aware of our tendencies we can take steps to control them.

symptoms of depression—low energy, fatigue, and inertia—are also related to negative expectations.

## Cognitive Psychotherapy

Borrowing some of its concepts from psychodynamic therapy and a number of techniques from behavior therapy and client-oriented psychotherapy, **cognitive therapy** consists of a broad theoretical structure of personality and psychopathology, a set of well-defined therapeutic techniques. The ultimate goal of cognitive therapy is to remove systematic biases in thinking by correcting faulty information processing, thus helping clients to modify assumptions that maintain maladaptive behaviors and emotions. Cognitive and behavioral methods are used to challenge dysfunctional beliefs and to promote more realistic thinking.

Cognitive therapy fosters change in clients' beliefs by conceiving of beliefs as testable hypotheses to be examined through behavioral experiments jointly agreed upon by client and counselor. The cognitive therapist does not tell the client that the beliefs are irrational or wrong. Instead, the therapist asks questions that elicit the meaning, function, usefulness, and consequences of the client's beliefs. It is up to the individual client to decide which beliefs to keep and which ones to eliminate.

Cognitive therapy is not as simple as replacing negative thoughts with positive self-statements. Change can occur only if the client experiences **affective arousal.** In the language of cognitive therapy, **hot cognitions** happen when a person experiences arousing emotions and reality testing at the same time. For example, a hot cognition is the actual phrase, fear, or critical self-blaming thought, such as "Oh, what a klutz I am." An examination of personal experience and logic at the same time allows the client to change the inner attitude or belief.

Cognitive therapy is present-centered, directive, active, problem-oriented, and best suited for cases in which problems can be delineated and cognitive distortions are apparent. It is not designed for personal growth or developmental work. Cognitive therapy is widely recognized as an effective treatment for unipolar depression. Sometimes cognitive therapy is used in combination with medication (Beck, Rush, Shaw, & Emery, 1979).

Cognitive therapy consists of highly specific learning experiences designed to teach clients to do five things: (1) to monitor their negative, automatic thoughts or cognitions; (2) to recognize the connections between cognition, affect, and behavior; (3) to examine the evidence for and against distorted automatic thoughts; (4) to substitute more reality-oriented interpretations for these biased cognitions; and (5) to learn to identify and alter the beliefs that predispose them to distort their experiences (Beck, Rush et al., 1979).

## Cognitive Techniques

*Decatastrophizing,* also known as the "what if" technique (Beck & Emory, 1979), helps clients prepare for anticipated consequences. Anxious clients commonly "catastrophize" and anticipate the worst possible outcome of a situation. Specifically asking a client, "What if the worst possible thing did happen?" can be helpful in decreasing phobic avoidance, particularly when combined with exposure plans (Beck & Emory, 1985). *Retribution* techniques test automatic thought and assumptions by using reality testing in the present situation of therapy. *Redefining* a problem is used to mobilize clients who believe themselves to be out of control. *Decentering* is used for clients who focus on their own discomfort to the extreme. *Imagery* encourages clients to use their imagination. Some clients report images more easily than thoughts and thus provide useful data before and during episodes of anxiety.

## Behavioral Techniques

Clients are given *homework* assignments focusing on self-observation and self-monitoring. In *hypothesis testing,* specific criteria are listed for monitoring so that the client sets up a framework for feedback during actual life experience. During *exposure therapy,* self-reported levels of tension are examined during specific practice sessions according to the individual client's needs. Clients are asked to **role-play** or rehearse situations that will later happen in real life. Their performance is jointly evaluated by the client and the therapist. In *diversion,* self-rating of tension levels provides structure while fluctuation of moods are tracked during normal everyday activities. Giving *graduated task assignments* that gradually become more difficult enables the client to begin assignments at a low level of tension.

These various cognitive and behavioral techniques enable the client and therapist or counselor to work together to effect genuine changes.

# Assessment, Research, and Comparison with Other Theorists

Aaron Beck developed an instrument to measure depression called the **Beck Depression Inventory,** which is widely seen as the finest psychometric instrument for this objective. Equally important have been his longitudinal studies on suicide and its deterrence. Other assessment devices that Beck has published include Beck Anxiety Scale, Beck Hopelessness Scale, Beck Scale for Suicide Ideation, and Beck Self-concept Test.

Ninety percent of the two hundred studies testing the cognitive model have supported it. More than thirty outcome studies have corroborated the power of the cognitive theory of depression. Other studies show cognitive therapy is helpful in panic disorders, obsessive-compulsive disorder, substance abuse, personality disorders, marital problems, and sex offenses (Beck, 1991). Effectiveness is usually determined on the basis of percentage of improvement and maintenance of gains at follow-up and in terms of comparison with other types of therapy (including pharmacotherapy) or other controls (Beck & Hollon, 1993).

Beck acknowledges that more decisive tests of the kinds of cognitive change or causal structures entailed in his theory would have to consider that some cognitive schema may be latent and therefore difficult to assess unless primed or activated; that the model is a *diathesis-stress* one, which sees disorders as joint functions of a diathesis, or predisposition, and environmental stress, so that simply assessing cognitions in the absence of live events would not be sufficient; and that attention must be given to idiographic methodologies that would be sensitive to individual vulnerabilities (Beck & Hollon, 1993).

Beck's cognitive therapy disagrees with Ellis's rational emotive behavior therapy in several ways: (1) it does not dispute the client's cognitive distortions as actively and directly; (2) it never uses the word "irrational" and would never, never interrupt a client in midsentence; (3) it does not hold that major cognitive distortions stem from "shoulds" and "musts"; (4) it does not believe that appropriate negative feelings are responsible for depression; (5) it does not generally think of self-talk as provoking emotions, albeit in some situations self-talk may. However, it does favor and employ in vivo (in actual life) desensitization.

At present, more than fifty books have been published on cognitive therapy, and two scholarly journals focus on the topic. Most big cities in North America and numerous cities in other nations have centers for instruction in cognitive therapy.

Donald Meichenbaum has taken Beck's cognitive restructuring and behavioral methods and developed techniques such as Stress Inoculation Training (Meichenbaum & Deffenbacher, 1988). He is a leader in the application of operant conditioning principles in settings ranging from classrooms to institutions for exceptional individuals.

Because of his work in controversial domains, Aaron Beck is often seen as a "maverick." His "approach is so straightforward in shunning traditional complexities that Dr. Beck says it befuddles many psychiatrists. 'Analysts view me as a behaviorist and behaviorists view me as an analyst.' . . . He says simply, 'I am a researcher'" (Greenberg, 1981).

## Arnold Lazarus: Biographical Background

Johannesburg, South Africa, was the birthplace of Arnold A. Lazarus on January 17, 1932. When he was born, his older sisters were seventeen and fourteen and his brother was almost nine. "'A skinny kid, who was bullied a lot,'" Lazarus took to lifting weights, and at seventeen he left school thinking he would open a health and training center. Two years later, he was convinced it would be smarter to return and finish his education (Dryden, 1991).

All of his degrees are from the University of Witwatersrand in Johannesburg: a B.A. in psychology and sociology in 1955, a B.A. with honors in psychology in 1956, an M.A. in experimental psychology in 1957, and a Ph.D. in clinical psychology in 1960. At first he thought he would major in English, but he was fascinated by psychology.

In the 1950s, while Lazarus was a student at the University of Witwatersrand, the psychotherapeutic climate was predominantly Freudian and Rogerian. Visiting lectures by

*Arnold Lazarus's multimodal behavior therapy is informed by his theory of the BASIC-ID.*

Joseph Wolpe, a general medical practitioner who was applying "conditioning methods" with his patients, led to the formation of a small group of "neobehaviorists." The members of this group knew that performance-based methods were usually better in clinical practice than purely verbal and cognitive approaches. Whereas the psychotherapeutic establishment viewed behavior as the outward manifestation of more fundamental psychic processes, the neobehaviorists stressed that behavior per se is often clinically significant. People can acquire insight and change significant beliefs and still use maladaptive coping behavior and self-destructive behavior.

To legitimize behavioral intervention as an essential part of clinical practice, Lazarus in 1958 introduced the terms "behavior therapy" and "behavior therapist" (Lazarus, 1958).

"New Group Techniques in the Treatment of Phobic Conditions" was the first study to explore the use of systematic desensitization in groups and included the development of objective scales for assessing phobic avoidance (Dryden, 1991).

In 1959, Lazarus began private practice. He began to use hypnosis and was elected to the presidency of the South African Society for Clinical and Experimental Hypnosis.

Growing distress with apartheid led the Lazaruses to the United States, and in 1967 he began working with Joseph Wolpe as a professor in the Department of Behavioral Science at Temple University Medical School in Philadelphia. However, it quickly became apparent that Wolpe's and Lazarus's interests and thinking were headed in different directions. After teaching briefly at Yale University in 1970 and publishing *Behavior Therapy and Beyond* (1971), Lazarus assumed the rank of Distinguished Professor at Rutgers University in 1972.

Lazarus has received several honors and been president of many professional organizations. He has written sixteen books and over 200 journal articles. He has lectured widely and is often cited as "one of the most influential psychotherapists of the twentieth century" (Dryden, 1991). In 1992 he received the Distinguished Psychologist Award, Division of Psychotherapy, from the American Psychological Association. In 1996 he was awarded the highly prestigious Cummings PSYCHE Award, and in 1997 he received an award from the Division of Clinical Psychology for Distinguished Professional Contributions. He retired from Rutgers in 1998 and is now the President of the Center for Multimodal Psychological Services in Princeton, New Jersey.

## The Development of His Theory and the BASIC-ID

In 1966 Lazarus published an article that challenged narrow stimulus-response formulations of the early 1960s and focused on dyadic transactions, or significant interpersonal relationships, as a significant part of the maintenance of maladaptive behavior. This was the first step in a significant movement in contemporary behavior theory and therapy, away from the radical behaviorism of an earlier period. Contemporary behavior theory and therapy has moved from the individual to the group and to society at large.

No one exemplifies these developments more than Lazarus (Franks, 1976). Spurning psychoanalytic methods in favor of the apparently more favorable pattern of early stimulus-response conditioning therapy, Lazarus soon became disillusioned with the then current behavioral strategies. Slowly and carefully, he developed a new set of clinical strategies that has come to be known as **multimodal behavior therapy.**

The importance of feeling, behavior, and thought (*Affect-Behavior-Cognition*) is well documented in the writings and practices of behavior theorists and therapists, but Lazarus felt that they gloss over other significant modalities such as our senses, our tendency to form pictures of events, and crucial interpersonal factors. A comprehensive appraisal based on the observation that clients are usually troubled by a multitude of specific problems called for an examination of behavior, affect, sensation, imagery, cognition, and interpersonal relationships. The first letter of each word forms the acronym BASIC-I.

*Behavior* entails overt behaviors. *Affect* refers to the emotions. *Sensation* entails the wide realm of sensory stimuli. *Imagery* may entail a memory or the deliberate imaging of a relaxing image or scene. *Cognition* includes the intuition, ideology, concepts, and judgments that make up our basic attitudes, values, and beliefs. *Interpersonal relations* entails one's social life and issues of intimacy with others (1976). *D* was added to the acronym to stand for *drugs* (neurological and biochemical factors that influence behavior). Lazarus is aware that some clients may require medication, but *D* has also come to stand for all aspects of physical well-being. With the addition of drugs, the acronym became **BASIC-ID** (see Figure 16.2).

| 1 | **B**ehavior | What the individual does |
| 2 | **A**ffect | The predominant emotions |
| 3 | **S**ensation | Specific sensory stimuli |
| 4 | **I**magery | Predominant fantasies and images |
| 5 | **C**ognition | Primary attitudes, values, beliefs, and opinions |
| 6 | **I**nterpersonal | Relationships with other people |
| 7 | **D**rugs/Biology | Physical well-being |

FIGURE 16.2    The BASIC-ID

In Lazarus's theory, seven modalities, known as the BASIC-ID,
make up personality. The first letters of each modality
make up the acronym BASIC-ID.

## Theory of Personality

Lazarus believes that the seven modalities—behavior, affect, sensation, imagery, cognition, interpersonal processes, and drugs/biology—may be said to make up human personality. The BASIC-ID is presumed to comprise human temperament and personality, and it is assumed that everything from anger, disappointment, greed, fear, grief, awe, contempt, and boredom to love, hope, faith, and joy can be accounted for by examining components and interactions within a person's BASIC-ID.

Lazarus holds that each person is a product of genetic history, environment, and learning. He gives great importance to the concept of individual physical **thresholds.** People have different thresholds, or tolerance levels, for pain, frustration, or stress. These thresholds are unique and individual. Psychological interventions can bolster physical thresholds but genetics, which also influences thresholds, cannot be overcome.

People tend to favor some BASIC-ID modality; thus, we may speak of a "sensory reactor" or an "imagery reactor" or a "cognitive reactor." This does not imply that a person will always react in a certain way, but over time, a tendency to value certain response patterns can be noted. As Bandler and Grinder (1976) say, visualizers tend to "make pictures" out of what they hear. In terms of split-brain research (Galin, 1974; Kimura, 1979), imagery reactors are probably right-hemispheric dominant, whereas cognitive reactors are frequently left-hemispheric dominant (see Ornstein, 1997).

The totality of habits that make up a personality are acquired through genetics, but also through association and conditioning. A good bit of human thoughts, feelings, and behaviors are due to the simple conditioning of family life. Many aversions appear to result from an association of one stimulus with another. Bandura (1969, 1977) speaks of imitation, observational learning, modeling, and vicarious processes as means of acquiring life-styles and habits that make up our personalities. As Bandaura's (1978) principle of reciprocal determination underscores, people do not react automatically to external stimuli. Their thoughts about those stimuli will determine which stimuli are noticed, how much they are valued, and how long they are remembered. Lazarus's view of the role for the unconscious is related to the recognition that different people have different levels of self-awareness and also that nonawareness (subliminal) or nonrecognition of thoughts and feelings does not prevent these nonconscious processes from influencing a person's attitudes and behaviors. Lazarus simply does not deal with traditional psychoanalytic notions and concepts in his writing.

In the multimodal orientation, it is acknowledged that people are capable of denial, displacement, and projection of thoughts and feelings. Impulses and aggressions are recognized and displaced. When accounting for these important human reactions, multimodal theory adds the concept of **metacommunication,** which is to say that people not only communicate, they also can think and communicate about their communications. The use of **paradox,** or contradictions, in therapy, in which the therapist or counselor exaggerates the client's irrationality, so popular nowadays, draws its energy from the process of metacommunication (e.g., Fay, 1978; Foa, 1990; Frankl, 1960, 1978; Zeig, 1982).

Fay (1976) gives the following example of the effectiveness of paradox:

> A twelve-year-old boy, whose over-protective mother constantly peppered him with solicitous questions about his health, vociferously protested but to no avail. However, he virtually extinguished the undesired behavior when on several occasions, in response to her frantic "Are you alright?" he clutched his abdomen and said, "No, I'm not all right. I'm dreadfully ill and I don't think I can last much longer!"

Mental and emotional disorders arise due to the genetic inheritance of certain vulnerabilities combined with the learning of faulty cognition, exposure to inadequate or abusive role models, and the collection of a variety of inhibitions and needless defenses. Emotional problems and disorders also arise from inadequate attention to learning. People with inadequate social learning cannot cope with the demands of everyday life and society's demands. "Adaptive living among the Hottentots or the Nilotes of Africa calls for different behavioral repertoires than those demanded by Western society" (Lazarus, 1976).

## Multimodal Therapy

Multimodal therapy rests primarily on the theoretical base of social learning theory (Bandura, 1969, 1977, 1986) while also drawing from general systems theory (Bertalanffy, 1974; Buckley, 1967) and group communications theory (Watzlawick, Weakland, & Fisch, 1974).

Lazarus's search for systematic therapies led him to the awareness that changing a client's cognitive modality often called for more than the correction of misconceptions. Lazarus needed to help clients change the messages conjured up by their imaginations. He added *goal rehearsal,* imagining yourself fulfilling your goal, *time projection,* imagining yourself projected into the future, and other coping imageries to his repertoire (see Lazarus, 1978, 1982).

Lazarus takes a holistic approach to his clients. Initially (Lazarus, 1973, 1976) the term "multimodal behavior therapy" was used to describe BASIC-ID assessment and treatment, but because emphasis is on comprehensive coverage of all the modalities, it is misleading to single out any one dimension over another. In a critical review of multimodal therapy, Kwee (1981) underscores its historical development from a narrow band of stimulus-response conditioning therapy by way of broad-spectrum behavior therapy to its present multimodal therapy and concludes that "whether or not multimodal therapy can be classified as behavior therapy is less important than the method itself" (p. 65).

Detailed accounts of multimodal assessment and therapy have been presented in several textbooks (for example Dryden & Golden, 1986; Jacobson, 1987; Norcross, 1986; Norcross & Goldfried, 1992). Books, articles, and chapters on multimodal therapy have been written or translated into German, Italian, Portuguese, Spanish, and Dutch. Multimodal therapy has been proven effective beyond the traditional therapeutic settings and can be found in day hospitals, nursing homes, and self-help support programs (Brunell & Young, 1982; O'Keefe & Castaldo, 1981; Roberts, Jackson, & Phelps, 1980). Training in multimodal therapy has been a formal aspect of the clinical doctoral program at Rutgers University since 1972.

Another fundamental multimodal therapy assumption is that without new experiences there can be no change. The multimodal therapy methods, therefore, are *performance based.* Woody puts it very clearly when he says that an effective therapist "must be more than a 'nice guy' who can exude prescribed interpersonal conditions—he must have an armamentarium of scientifically derived skills and techniques to supplement this effective interpersonal relations" (1971).

Multimodal therapy is predicated on the assumption that the more disturbed the client is, the greater the specific excesses and deficits there will be throughout the BASIC-ID. Lazarus bases his model on actualization and self-determination rather than on pathology. His theory places primary emphasis on the uniqueness of each person. Maximum flexibility rather than fixed rules is demanded of the therapist in selecting and matching therapeutic interventions to each client (1994, 1996a, 1996b). The fundamental question is always "what is best for this particular client?"

While multimodal therapy draws heavily from several systems (both rational emotive and cognitive), there are distinctive features that set multimodal therapy apart: (1) its holistic approach of giving attention to the full BASIC-ID; (2) the use of **modality profiles,** or a specific list of problems and proposed treatments across the client's BASIC-ID; (3) the use of a **structural profile,** or a quantitative assessment of the relative involvement of each of the elements of the BASIC-ID; (4) the use of **bridging,** a multimodal technique used by counselors to deliberately begin work in terms of their client's preferred modality. With a feeling-sensory client it can be detrimental to insist on cognitive restructuring right at the onset of treatment. Multimodal therapy starts where the client is and bridges into more challenging areas as the therapeutic relationship develops; (5) the use of **tracking,** paying careful attention to the "firing order" of the different modalities. The "firing order" refers to "how the modalities interact to cause the client's problems" (Lazarus, 1985) or the order in which the modalities appear. Most people report a reasonably stable range of firing order much of the time. Recognition of these patterns permits intervention at any point in the firing sequence. Tracking also enables one to select the most appropriate intervention techniques.

---

**THINKING CRITICALLY**

## *Using the BASIC-ID*

The following are sample questions that are used to rate BASIC-ID. Use a scale from six to zero. High scores characterize you. A zero means that the tendency does not describe you at all. How would you rate yourself on the following questions?

1. *Behavior:* Are you active, a doer, always busy?
2. *Affect:* How emotional are you?
3. *Sensation:* How intently do you monitor your bodily sensations?
4. *Imagery:* Do you think in pictures, fantasy?
5. *Cognition:* Do you like to make plans, anticipate?
6. *Interpersonal:* Are you gregarious, intimate?
7. *Drugs/Biology:* Are you healthy? Do you abuse drugs or alcohol?

In reference to a specific problem, asking the following can also help to access the BASIC-ID:

1. *Behavior:* When you have the problem, what are you usually doing at the time?
2. *Affect:* How are you feeling? Fearful, depressed, discouraged . . . ?
3. *Sensation:* Do any parts of your body feel tense or uncomfortable?
4. *Imagery:* What pictures come to mind when you dwell on your problem?
5. *Cognition:* What thoughts, irrational and rational, do you have about the problem?
6. *Interpersonal:* Who are the other people involved in your problem?
7. *Drugs/Biology:* Do you ever resort to alcohol or sleeping pills while experiencing the problem?

It takes a considerable amount of skill for a therapist or a counselor to diagnose a client's BASIC-ID, but these questions may give you an idea of the type of questions that would be asked.

---

Multimodal therapy offers a precise and disciplined behavioral retraining process. Behaviorists are sometimes insensitive to the individual's interpersonal needs and affective reactions. Multimodal therapy helps them to meet this challenge (Lazarus, 1989, 1997).

---

## Technical Eclecticism

Lazarus is also very well known for advocating **technical eclecticism** (1995, 1996c). He maintains that good treatment methods may be derived from many sources without necessarily agreeing with the theories that generated them. He further believes that if therapists or counselors use only the methods included in their favored theoretical view, they will invariably neglect effective techniques that are used by therapists or counselors of other persuasions. Thus Lazarus may borrow techniques that were generated at Gestalt therapy, Transactional Analysis, or existential therapy without embracing the theory held by their founders and disciples. Lazarus says he prefers to operate out of social and cognitive learning theory as "its tenets are grounded in research and are open to verification and disproof. . . . [moreover] I have yet to find any effective procedure that cannot be readily explained in terms of social and cognitive learning theory" (Dryden, 1991).

Lazarus further maintains that the greater number of coping skills clients develop, the less likely they will backslide. Thus Lazarus's method is performance based. He starts by observing behavior and develops a re-education plan custom-made for each client.

Lazarus's eclectic multimodal theory and therapy, performance-based and tailor-made for each client, is demonstrably effective; however, the inherent limitations of controlled evaluations make it difficult to attend to the idiographies of individual cases (Davison & Lazarus, 1994).

|  |
|---|
| PHILOSOPHY, |
| SCIENCE, |
| AND ART |

# Cognitive Behavioral Therapies and Theories

Although cognitive behavioral therapies and theories clearly emphasize the art of psychotherapy and counseling, one can find some key underlying philosophical assumptions. Ellis's roots in Stoic philosophy and his realistic attitude of both pessimism and optimism concerning human nature (that human beings have a strong tendency to sabotage themselves but at the same time have enormous potential for change and self-actualization) are important philosophical assumptions. Beck's strong roots in phenomenology, the structural theory and depth psychology of Kant and Freud, and more modern developments in cognitive psychology lead him also to concur that people have great potential to change. Lazarus further agrees with the crucial significance of emotional freedom and rational thinking. These theorists recognize that behavior is both determined and free, that both hereditary and environmental factors influence behavior, and that while there are similarities among people, each one of us develops a unique way of coping with life's problems. Although learning is important in shaping our behaviors, people can also act primarily on their own initiative.

In neurotic clients, dysfunctional beliefs (Ellis) and cognitive schemas (Beck) function as philosophical assumptions. The client is compelled by them and tenaciously clings to them out of that compulsion. The therapist helps the patient to treat the dysfunctional beliefs and cognitive schema as working hypotheses and to test them. In the process, they may be successfully falsified and changed, leading the client to new epiphanies and alternative beliefs and schemas.

The emphasis on behavior, "rational" thinking, and science in behavioral and cognitive theories of personality clearly fits and perpetuates the preferred philosophical models and functions of white male Euro-Americans. It may not be suitable for the diverse ways of knowing and being of other populations. For example, the emphasis on thinking

## PHILOSOPHICAL ASSUMPTIONS

### Examining Cognitive Behavioral Therapists

How would you rate the cognitive behavioral therapists on each of the basic philosophical assumptions described in Chapter 1? Consult the chart on the inside front cover. Each basic issue is presented as a bipolar dimension along which a person's view can be placed according to the degree of agreement with one or the other extreme: *freedom/determinism, hereditary/environmental, uniqueness/universality, proactive/reactive, optimistic/pessimistic.* Rate Ellis's, Beck's, and Lazarus's views on these issues.

When you have determined where you think Ellis, Beck, and Lazarus stand, compare your responses with those of your classmates and your instructor. You should be willing to defend your ratings, but also be prepared to change them in light of others' compelling arguments. Afterward, compare your rating of these theorists with your own position on each issue and with those of other theorists. Does this comparison help you to understand why their theories do or do not appeal to you?

as primary and the need to challenge beliefs may be inappropriate for Asians, who emphasize emotional harmony with cultural norms (Kantrowitz & Ballou, 1992).

These methods of therapy and counseling have received considerable empirical and scientific support. In particular, Ellis's research at the Institute for Rational-Emotive Therapy confirm his approach to counseling; Beck's research studies into many areas of maladaptive behaviors and his development of assessment inventories demonstrate the effectiveness of his cognitive therapy; and Lazarus's development of objective scales for assessing phobic avoidance, pre- and posttreatment assessments, and research on the BASIC-ID demonstrates the effectiveness of multimodal therapy.

The current emphasis on managed care has led to an increase in short-term psychotherapy that is directed toward the active resolution of specific problems and is frequently limited to a specific number of sessions. "Not unreasonably managed care demands demonstrably effective interventions that are valid, short-term, of minimal cost, and consumer-friendly" (Franks, 1997). Some critics are concerned that managed-care companies are making decisions on the basis of cost effectiveness rather than medical desirability and that these decisions may be jeopardizing the quality of mental health care (Goleman, 1996). At the same time, the demands of managed care have led to the development of innovative models for meeting the challenges of providing adequate psychotherapy and keeping costs reasonable (MacKenzie, 1996). Lazarus reminds us that short-term therapy can be practiced without shortchanging the patient (1997).

*Much of the therapeutic work that Ellis, Beck, and Lazarus do can be done in groups,
a cost-saving factor that is very attractive in a climate of managed care.*

It is in the application and art of psychotherapy and counseling
that these behavioral cognitive therapies and theories really shine. Extremely practical, down to earth, directive, and eclectic, these theorists
are determined to help people change and to improve their life-style.
And they are effective! Moreover, much of the work that they do can be
done in groups—a cost-saving factor that is important in this climate of
economic concerns. Twelve-step programs frequently employ cognitive
tools to foster behavioral change. While Ellis, Beck, and Lazarus are criticized for being simple, incomplete, and one-sided as philosophers of
human nature, there is little reason to doubt that they will continue to
have an enormous impact in the areas of therapy and counseling.

## Summary

1. The philosophical origins of Ellis's *rational emotive behavior therapy* go back
   to the Stoics. The most important modern precursor was Alfred Adler.

2. Ellis suggests that human beings are "sign-, symbol-, and language-creating"
   animals who have four fundamental processes: perception, movement,
   thinking, and emotion. These are all necessarily interrelated and tend to

assume a type of "self-talk" in which our "internalized sentences" determine our thoughts and emotions. Ellis believes that people have a strong tendency to engage in dysfunctional behaviors but that they also have potential to change and self-actualize. Emotional disturbance usually arises when people care too much about what others think of them.

3. The *A-B-C theory of personality* suggests that people develop irrational and *musturbatory* belief systems when a highly charged emotional consequence (C) follows a significant *activating event* (A). A may seem to but does not actually cause C. Instead, emotional consequences are largely created by inappropriate *irrational beliefs* (B's).

4. As human beings we inherit a tendency to raise cultural *preferences* into *musts* and social *norms* into absolute *shoulds*.

5. The goal of rational emotive behavior therapy is for people to commit themselves to actions that correspond to their true value system. The three main therapeutic processes are *cognitive, emotive evocative,* and *behavioral.*

6. Ellis's theory has many points of comparison with other theorists. For example, in comparison to Freud's theory, Ellis believes that virtually all so-called sexual problems result from people's irrational beliefs that they need approval.

7. The philosophical origins of Beck's cognitive theory are the phenomenological approach to psychology, structural theory and depth psychology, and cognitive psychology.

8. *Cognitive therapy* is based on a theory of personality that maintains that how one thinks largely determines how one feels and behaves. Personality reflects the individual's cognitive organization and structure, which are both biologically and socially influenced.

9. *Cognitions* refer to a person's awareness. *Schemas* are cognitive structures that consist of an individual's fundamental core beliefs and assumptions about how the world operates. *Cognitive distortions* are systematic errors in reasoning. Examples of cognitive distortions are: *arbitrary inference, selective abstraction, overgeneralization, magnification and minimization, personalization, dichotomous thinking,* and *conditional assumptions.*

10. The *sociotropic dimension* is characterized by dependence on interpersonal relationships and needs for closeness and nurturance. The *autonomous dimension* is characterized by independence.

11. The *cognitive triad* refers to the fact that depressed individuals have a negative view of the self, the world, and the future.

12. Beck's *cognitive therapy* consists of a broad theoretical structure of personality and psychopathology and a set of well-defined therapeutic techniques designed to help the client experience *affective arousal.*

13. Some cognitive and behavioral techniques are *decatastrophizing, retribution, redefining, decentering, imagery, homework, hypothesis testing, exposure therapy, role-playing, diversion,* and *graduated task assignments.*

14. Beck developed several assessment instruments, among them the *Beck Depression Inventory,* widely seen as the finest psychometric instrument for this objective. Unlike other behaviorists, Beck believes it is essential that people understand that their unrealistic view of the world and life is responsible for their depression.

15. Lazarus's theory developed out of an emphasis on *dyadic transactions.* He developed a comprehensive appraisal of personality called the *BASIC-ID.* These letters stand for the following words: *behavior, affect, sensation, imagery, cognition, interpersonal relations,* and *drugs.*

16. Lazarus says people have different physical *thresholds* and tend to favor some BASIC-ID. The habits that make up a personality are acquired through genetics, association, and conditioning. Multimodal theory also talks about *metacommunication* and the use of *paradox.*

17. *Multimodal therapy* methods are *performance based.* Lazarus added *goal rehearsal* and *time projection* as therapeutic methods. Some other features that set it apart from other therapies are the use of *modality profiles, structural profiles, bridging, tracking,* and Lazarus's emphasis on *technical eclecticism.*

18. While behavioral cognitive therapies and theories function as philosophy, science, and art, it is the application and art of psychotherapy and counseling that they really shine.

## Suggestions for Further Reading

Albert Ellis is witty, humorous, pragmatic, and highly readable. Most recommended are *The Handbook of Rational-Emotive Therapy* (Springer, 1986); *How to Live with a Neurotic* (Crown, 1957); *The Art and Science of Love* (Lyle Stuart, 1966); *How to Stubbornly Refuse to Make Yourself Miserable about Anything—Yes Anything* (Lyle Stuart, 1988); *How to Live With—and—Without Anger* (Reader's Digest Press, 1977); with R. Harper, *A New Guide to Rational Living* (Wilshire Books, 1975); and with W. Dryden, *The Practice of Rational Emotive Therapy* (Springer, 1987). The titles are all self-explanatory.

Good secondary sources include W. Dryden's *Rational Emotive Therapy: Fundamentals and Innovations,* published in Beckenham, England, by Croom-Helm, 1984; and M. E. Bernard's *Staying Alive in an Irrational World: The Psychology of Albert Ellis,* published in South Melbourne, Australia, by Carlton and Macmillan in 1986.

A little bit more technical but still very readable are Aaron T. Beck's works. Most recommended are *Depression: Causes and Treatment* (University of Pennsylvania Press, 1967); *Cognitive Therapy and the Emotional Disorders* (International Universities Press, 1976); *Cognitive Therapy of Depression* (Guildford, 1987); and with G. Emory, *Cognitive*

*Therapy of Anxiety and Phobic Disorders* (Center for Cognitive Therapy, 1979). A biography about Aaron Beck written by Marge Weishaar is *Dr. Beck Biography* (Sage, 1993).

Again, a wee bit more technical yet still readable by the lay person are Arnold Lazarus's works. Most recommended are *Behavior Therapy and Beyond* (McGraw-Hill, 1971); *Multimodal Behavior Therapy* (Springer, 1976); *In the Mind's Eye: The Power of Imagery for Personal Enrichment* (Rawson, 1978); and *The Practice of Multimodal Therapy* (McGraw-Hill, 1981).

PART

# VIII

# *A Non-Western Approach*

As Westerners, we are frequently unaware of or tend to depreciate other psychologies, such as those that come from the Eastern traditions. We have made enormous progress in gathering together a significant amount of information about human nature and personality. However, although we have learned a great deal about ourselves, we are still far from an adequate understanding of what it means to be a human being. There has been a growing feeling that the dominant concerns of Western science and psychology have ignored the inner nature of the person. Our modern technology and culture have given rise to practices that may relieve many forms of human illness and suffering, but they have yet to provide satisfactory answers to the most fundamental questions of human existence.

Many movements of Eastern thought raise questions about the ultimate meaning and purpose of human life and have developed theories of personality insofar as they have investigated what it means to be a human being. In many respects these thought systems do not resemble philosophy or religion as much as they resemble the art of psychology and psychotherapy (Watts, 1961). Their basic concern is with the human situation: the suffering and frustrations of people. They emphasize the importance of techniques to accomplish change. Eastern thought aims at transformations in consciousness, feelings, emotions, and one's relation to other people and the world.

There are many varieties of Eastern thought: Hinduism, Buddhism, Confucianism, Taoism, and Sufism, among others. Chapter 17 will focus on one of them, Zen Buddhism, in order to help us recognize that the assumptions that constitute the consensus about reality in the modern-day Western world are not necessarily universal and shared by other cultures. From the viewpoint of many of these movements, several of our contemporary Western ideas about personality are very alien. No wonder we often have difficulty communicating, as long as we tacitly assume that our comprehension of human behavior is universally shared.

# Zen Buddhism

## Your Goals for This Chapter

1. Discuss the origins of *Zen* by describing the story of the *Buddha,* the teachings of Buddhism, and the main branches of thought that stemmed from early Buddhism.
2. Discuss the principle of *dependent origination.*
3. Discuss the three characteristics of existence: *anicca, dukkha,* and *anatta.*
4. Explain what is meant by *satori.*
5. Discuss the five *skandhas* and explain what is meant by the statement that they are empty.
6. Describe the eight consciousnesses and explain what is meant by "seeding the *alaya-vijnana.*"
7. Describe *zazen,* and contrast *shikantaza* with the *koan* method.
8. Learn to actually practice Zen meditation.
9. Compare the modes of liberation or psychotherapeutic change developed by the East and the West.
10. Evaluate Eastern theories of personality in terms of their function as philosophy, science, and art.

P onder this story before reading this chapter. A professor once asked a Zen master to teach him about Zen. The master agreed, and offered him a cup of tea. He accepted. The master prepared the tea and filled his guest's cup, continuing to pour tea until it was overflowing. The professor exclaimed, "What are you doing? Can't you see that the cup is already full?" "Ah," replied the master, "it is just like your mind, which is full with your ideas and misconceptions. How can I teach you something about Zen? Before you can receive more fresh tea, you must first empty your cup." Only if you empty your cup and approach the material in this chapter with an open mind will you be able to appreciate and understand it.

## The Introduction of Zen to the West

Daisetz Teitaro Suzuki (1870–1966) is often credited with singlehandedly introducing Zen Buddhism to the West. A follower of the Rinzai school of Zen, Suzuki seldom mentioned the Soto school, although it was and is the main form of Zen in Japan. Alan Watts (1915–1973) later popularized the ideas of Suzuki in America. As a result, Rinzai Zen became well known in the West and Soto Zen remained virtually unknown. Paradoxically, the Zen of D. T. Suzuki, although stressing **satori,** or enlightenment, as the goal to Zen, never provided a practice method or any practical guidance to experience it.

In the 1960s and 1970s, due to the efforts of several masters such as Shunryu Suzuki and Dainin Katagiri in America and Taisen Deshimaru in Europe, Zen spread. These masters, among others, deserve credit for being the true introducers of Zen in the West.

## The Origins of Zen

Zen is a school of Buddhism that claims to represent the purest essence of Buddhist teachings. The origins of Zen trace back to the story of Siddhartha Gautama, born about 563 B.C. in northern India, the son of a king. Upon his birth, the story goes, a local sage prophesied that the child would become either a great sage or a conquering monarch. His father, preferring the latter, decided to accustom the child to a life of luxury and comfort, as befitted a future king. Siddhartha grew up a virtual prisoner in the palaces his father built for him, married a princess from a neighboring kingdom, and had a son.

Wanting to know the kingdom he was to rule one day, he finally got his father's permission to leave the palaces and see the country, but he was greatly disturbed by seeing on successive occasions a very old man, a severely ill person, and a funeral procession. These were his first encounters with old age, sickness, and death, since information about such aspects of the human condition had been withheld from him. Recognizing impermanence and suffering, he was so moved that he vowed to forsake his kingdom and to dedicate his life to finding a solution to the problem of suffering. He left in the middle of the night, leav-

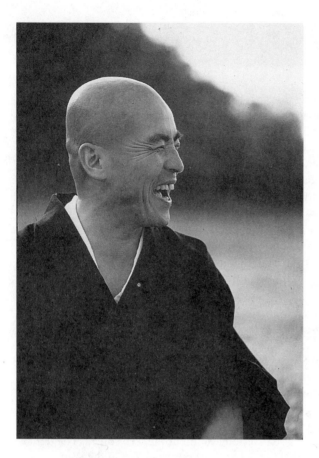

*The joy and radiance of an enlightened master are evident in this photograph of Dainin Katagiri-roshi (1928–1990), who brought Zen to the American Midwest.*

ing behind his wealth as well as his family, knowing that they would be cared for. He was twenty-nine years old.

For six years, Siddhartha sought out and trained under the greatest Yoga teachers of northern India. He learned and practiced their meditation techniques and achieved the most advanced states of altered consciousness his teachers had accomplished. But he was dissatisfied, for he realized that regardless of the nature of the mental trance he experienced, it provided only a temporary escape—not a permanent cure for human suffering. He tried all the methods and studied under all available teachers, even engaging in intense ascetic practices and self-mortification designed to liberate the mind from the demands of the body, but to no avail.

In desperation, leaving the ascetic practices that brought him near to death from starvation, he accepted food, regaining his strength, and sat down under a great peepul tree (an Indian fig tree, which would become known as the *bodhi tree* of enlightenment). He determined not to rise again until he found the answer to the problem of suffering. After seven days of intense concentration, he reached a profound flash of awakening, and the nature of reality as well as the solution to the problem that had tormented him were clear. From that moment on, he was known as **Buddha,** the Awakened One. He was then thirty-five years old, and spent the following forty-five years of his life traveling, teaching others, and sharing his great discovery. He made no claims of divine origin or of having received a divine revelation. When asked whether he was a god, or a supernatural being, he always replied no. When asked what he was, he said "I am Awake" ("I am Buddha"). Radiant, peaceful, compassionate, and charismatic, he continued his work until he died at the age of eighty, in about 483 B.C.

The Buddha's teachings, preserved initially through an oral tradition, were eventually written down in the form of three collections or "baskets," known as the **Tripitaka.** The oldest version of these is believed to have been written in Pali, an ancient Indic language; it constitutes the scriptures of one of the two main branches of Buddhism, sometimes called the **Hinayana,** or "small vehicle," and represented today by the **Theravada** school. Theravada Buddhism is dominant today in parts of Southeast Asia. The second major branch, the **Mahayana,** uses primarily the Sanskrit version of the *Tripitaka,* in addition to which it recognizes a large number of additional scriptures not in the Pali Canon, some attributed to the historical Buddha and others to diverse authors. The total number of scriptures in Buddhism surpasses 85,000, a massive body of literature. The Mahayana (or "great vehicle") branch of Buddhism is dominant in East Asia. Zen belongs to the Mahayana tradition, developing from roots in India through the filter of Taoism in China, passing from there to Korea and to Japan, and to the rest of the world. A primary difference between Theravada and Mahayana Buddhism lies in their ideals of personal development. The former stresses renunciation of worldly life and a monastic life-style, seeking to develop the practitioner into an *arhat,* a sage who through practice and discipline is liberated from suffering. The latter accepts that enlightenment is possible also for lay practitioners. Its ideal is the **bodhisattva,** a person who vows to dedicate life to the salvation of all sentient beings, not accepting full liberation until all others are free from suffering. Of the two key virtues in Buddhism, wisdom and compassion, Theravada stresses the former, while Mahayana emphasizes the latter. As we will see below, this does not necessarily represent a contradiction.

## The Teachings of the Buddha

What the Buddha discovered at the time of his awakening is very profound, complicated, and difficult to understand, and yet amazingly simple, direct, and self-evident. To appreciate his great insight, it is helpful first to reflect on the philosophical background in India two and a half millennia ago.

There were then more philosophical schools and positions in India than ever developed in ancient Greece. These ranged from a form of Vedic mysticism that postulated a universal creator, or *Brahma,* and individual souls (**atman**) who transmigrated through many lives in order to become purified and rejoin the universal *Brahma,* to those who believed that all that existed was the material substance evident to the senses, and that at death the individual was totally extinguished. One extreme was the externalist position, where a person's soul or atman continues eternally, and the other annihilationist position, postulating that a human being is completely destroyed at death. The Buddha discovered a position between these extremes. He called this position **dependent origination.** He also advocated a life-style that avoided the extremes of self-indulgence and self-mortification. His position became known as "the Middle Way."

The teaching of dependent origination is at the core of the Buddha's **Dharma** (meaning "Doctrine," "Truth," or "Law"). Simply stated, dependent origination is a law of causality that says "this is, because that is; this is not, because that is not; when this arises, that arises; when this ceases, that ceases." Despite the apparent simplicity of this law, it is a far-reaching truth that leaves nothing untouched and causally connects everything in the universe, for it implies that all phenomena, whether they be external or internal events, come into existence depending on causes and conditions without which they could not be. These causes and conditions can themselves be either internal or external.

As Hanh (1988) suggests, consider the page of the book you are reading. This piece of paper can be, because a tree was, since the tree had to be in order to be cut down to make the paper. This same piece of paper is also because there was rain and sunshine; without them the tree could not have grown. The same is true for the seed and the fertile soil, and the logger who cut the tree down. Without them, the tree would not have been there for the paper to be. But for the logger to be, his parents had to be, and the food they consumed, and all the conditions that made their lives possible, and those lives upon which theirs depended, and on, and on. There is no end to this causal interconnectedness. Everything in the universe is connected to this piece of paper. If the component conditions are seen as elements, we can say that this piece of paper is composed of non-paper elements: conditions other than the paper itself are necessary for the paper to exist. The paper cannot exist by itself. Neither can you or anything else in the universe. The same is true of cognitive or mental states. For every emotion, every perception, every thought, there are necessary causal conditions without which they would not have come into being. Everything is dependently arisen, everything exists only if the necessary conditions are there. This means nothing is ever truly independent or separate from everything else. Dependent origination is not simply A causing B, but simultaneously A being a necessary condition for B to occur, and B being necessary for A to arise. Thus the best label is that used by Katagiri (1988), "interdependent co-origination," or Hanh's (1988) "interbeing," where things and mental states "inter-are." Modern general systems theory, derived from our relatively recent awareness of the interconnectedness of ecological factors, approximates this, although the theory lacks the generality and universality of the Buddha's position (Macy, 1991).

The concept of dependent origination results in an understanding of existence as a process of change, the result of an infinite web of causal conditions, with birth and death marking neither the start nor the end. The conditions that result in our present existence represent a beginningless chain; the consequences of our actions become causal conditions whose effects will continue after we die. While there is no separate, immutable self or soul that can continue forever, the process of which we are a part continues forever (Katagiri, 1988). The Buddha talked about "rebirth." By this expression he did not mean reincarnation in the Vedic sense, where a soul (atman) inhabits a succession of bodies, but continuation in the sense in which a wave is "reborn" in the ocean after apparently "dying" on the seashore. All the water is still there, and the process continues endlessly, but no "soul" travels from one wave to the other. There are no transmigrating souls, only a continuing karmic process. Who we are lives on in the effects we have on others and on our world.

## The Three Characteristics of Existence

The Buddha realized that there are three characteristics of existence: anicca, dukkha, and anatta. **Anicca** or impermanence means that everything is always changing. Nothing is immutable or permanent. Children grow, people age, things break down, spring follows winter, rivers flow, subatomic particles fluctuate, galaxies spin, everything is in a state of flux. Impermanence is not good or bad, it's just the way things are. Understanding and accepting impermanence leads to the avoidance of unrealistic expectations. Ultimately there is nothing we can hold onto or keep forever. Attachment and aversion will not change this.

**Dukkha,** usually translated as suffering, refers to the dissatisfaction and distress that results from attachment and aversion. The Buddha's solution to the problem of suffering, which has been called "the most important psychological discovery of all time" (Mosig, 1989), represents an application of the far-reaching principle of dependent origination. If suffering is, it must have come into being as the result of causal conditions, and if suffering is to cease, those conditions must cease. His solution was expressed in the form of the **Four Noble Truths.**

The *first noble truth* describes the problem of suffering, the universal dissatisfaction that characterizes human existence: our perception of pain, illness, old age, and death; not getting what we want and being exposed to what we don't want; not being able to keep forever what we love and not being able to eliminate what we hate.

The *second noble truth* begins the application of dependent origination to the problem, identifying the causal conditions on which suffering depends. Suffering and dissatisfaction, the "dis-ease" of human existence, cannot be by themselves, but arise due to our craving, our "thirsting" and desiring for things to be other than what they are. Old age is not suffering, it is just old age. Suffering arises because we do not want to be old. This thirsting for things not to be as they are comes in two "flavors," attachment (which includes greed and possessive love) and aversion (including anger, resentment, and hate).

The *third noble truth* derives a solution through the application of the same principle. Since human suffering arose out of craving, to bring our "dis-ease" to an end we must cease the self-defeating liking and disliking that causes it, we must stop the "picking and choosing" that is "the sickness of the mind" (Seng T'san in Sheng-Yen, 1987). While we cannot get rid of illness, physical pain, aging, and death, we can eliminate the anxiety we cause ourselves with our cognitive processing. In doing so, we can achieve freedom from unnecessary psychological pain (Kalupahana & Kalupahana, 1982). To eliminate suffering, we must get rid of craving.

The answer to how we can do this is contained in the Buddha's *fourth noble truth,* known as the **Eightfold Path.** It consists of *Right Understanding* (understanding the interconnectedness and impermanence of everything, and specifically the Four Noble Truths); *Right Thinking* (cultivating thoughts of selfless detachment, compassion, and non-harming, and extending these to all sentient beings); *Right Speech* (abstaining from lying, slander, gossip, and injurious speech, speaking only that which is positive and constructive, otherwise maintaining a "noble silence"); *Right Action* (acting in ways that will benefit and not cause suffering to others or oneself); *Right Livelihood* (avoiding ways of making a living that are based on the exploitation of the suffering of animals or people); *Right Effort* (cutting off unwholesome thoughts before they can be transformed into actions and nurturing wholesome ones); *Right Mindfulness* (maintaining full awareness of our actions and experiences in the present moment, and their likely consequences); *Right Concentration* (the disciplining, concentration, and one-pointedness of mind resulting from the practice of meditation) (Piyadassi, 1974; Rahula, 1974).

The first two components of the Eightfold Path are related to wisdom; the following three, to moral conduct; and the last three, to mental discipline. The different aspects of the Path are themselves interdependent. Without wisdom one would not see the necessity of undertaking the Path, without moral development one would not be ready to undertake it, and without mental discipline one would not be able to do it! The moral conduct aspects of the Path relate also to the concept of karma. **Karma** means volitional action, whether of word, deed, or thought. Every action has effects or consequences, which "rebound." One could hardly expect to free oneself from suffering while inflicting it on others.

The third characteristic of existence, **anatta** or non-self, is the one that sets Buddhism apart from practically all other religious, philosophical, and psychological theories and positions.

> Buddhism stands unique . . . in denying the existence of a soul, self, or *atman*. According to the teaching of the Buddha, the idea of a [personal] self is an imaginary, false belief which has no corresponding reality, and it produces harmful thoughts of "me" and "mine," selfish desire, craving, attachment, hatred, ill-will, conceit, pride, egoism, and other defilements, impurities and problems. It is the source of all the troubles in the world, from personal conflicts to wars between nations . . . to this false view can be traced all the evil in the world. (Rahula, 1974)

Craving is one of the links in the chain of dependent origination, and suffering the end product. The doctrine of *anatta* links craving to the false idea of a separate ego or self. It is important to realize what is meant by the "self" that the Buddha rejected as illusory. Not only are human beings said to lack a soul or self, so is everything else: rivers, mountains, this book, and your pencil. This means they cannot have any reality except in terms of the interconnected net of causal conditions that made their existence possible. All things (including human beings) are composites; they are composed of parts and have no real existence other than as temporary collections of parts. There is no separate essence, self, or soul, that could exist by itself, apart from the component parts and conditions.

What we call a "person" is the composite of five groups of elements or **skandhas.** The skandhas are *form, feelings, perceptions, impulses,* and *consciousness.* Just as an automobile is a temporary collection of car parts, a person is a temporary arrangement of these five skandhas. There is no separate, independent self or soul that would be left if we removed form (which includes the body), feelings, perceptions, impulses, and consciousness. While these aggregates are together, the functioning gestalt we call a person exists; if they are removed, the gestalt ceases to be. For this reason, the self can be said to be "empty": a view of the self radically different from Western perspectives (Page & Berkow, 1991).

Close your hand into a fist and look at it. What do you see? A fist. Is it real? It certainly seems to be. Now open your fingers. What happened to the "real" thing called "fist" that was there a moment ago? Where did it go? Consider your self, your ego. Is it real? Certainly. Or is it? What would remain of it if you removed form, feelings, perceptions, impulses, and consciousness? Just as the term "fist" is a convenient label to designate a transient arrangement of the fingers, the term "self" or "I" is nothing but a label for an impermanent arrangement of the skandhas. There is no little person inside the head, no inner ego or self, other than the temporary gestalt formed by the skandhas. This is the Buddha's concept of anatta, and why the self is an illusion.

The concept of anatta does not negate the person, nor does it diminish it. Rather, it empowers the individual by erasing the boundaries of separateness that limit the personal ego or self. The person becomes transformed from an isolated and powerless individual struggling against the rest of the world, into an interconnected integral part of the universe. The person's boundaries dissolve, and the person *becomes* the universe. This is the realization known as enlightenment, the emergence of the big self, the Self with capital *S*, which is boundless.

Consider a wave in the ocean. It has no reality apart from the water. Although its form seems to last as it continues to move on the surface of the ocean, it is composed each moment of different water particles. It seems so real, and yet we can see that there is no thing called "wave" there at all; there is only the movement of the water. The wave has no separate "self," no reality apart from the water. The separation is just an illusion created by our perceptions and by the words we use to describe them. Now assume that the collection of elements forming the wave had resulted in the phenomenon of consciousness. As long as the wave was unaware of the nature of the ocean, believing itself to be separate and independent of it, it might develop attachments and aversions, fears, jealousies, and worries about its size, its purpose, its importance, or its destination. Any such concerns would vanish instantly upon realizing the water-nature of the ocean, and its oneness with it. In the same way, all human problems disappear when the illusion of a separate self is eliminated.

The transcendent wisdom of realizing the universal oneness generates compassion and caring for everyone as oneself. To hurt or help another is to hurt or help oneself. True wisdom is automatically manifested as universal compassion, and true compassion manifests itself as wisdom. Wisdom and compassion "inter-are." In the final analysis, wisdom is compassion, and compassion is wisdom (Mosig, 1989).

The ultimate state of mind in Buddhism is **nirvana,** not a place like heaven, but a mental state, where all cravings, desires, and dualistic ideas have been completely extinguished, through the complete realization of *anicca* and *anatta*. The Buddha taught that liberation is within the grasp of everyone. Just as he said that there had been many fully enlightened beings or buddhas before him, he indicated that there would be countless buddhas after him.

## Vasubandhu and the Eight Consciousnesses

The psychological insights of the Buddha have been explicated by a number of commentators. One of the most important ones was **Vasubandhu,** an outstanding Buddhist scholar living in the fourth century. He was a founder of the school known as the *Vijnanavada* ("path of knowledge") or *Yogacara* ("application of yoga"), and the author of one of the most important books of Buddhist psychology, the *Abhidharmakosa* (de La Valle Poussin, 1990).

According to Vasubandhu, all that can be experienced to exist is "mind only," or the mental processes of knowing. There is experience, but there is no subject (no *atman*) having the experience. **Vijnana,** or "consciousness," the last of the five skandhas, is a multi-layered concept, including both conscious and unconscious aspects.

There are eight consciousnesses, not just one. (See Figure 17.1.) The first five correspond to the five basic sense fields and share the same level of depth. They are the consciousnesses of seeing, hearing, smelling, tasting, and touching. Below is the **manovijana,** the integrating basis of the five sense consciousnesses, which has functions such as knowing, evaluating, imagining, conceiving, and judging. It is essentially a perceptual and cognitive processing center. Next comes **manas** ("mind"), which is where the illusion of a subjective "I" or "ego" arises. This sense of self or ego-individuality defiles the first six consciounesses and is the source of all sorts of psychological problems and delusions. Finally comes the vast **alayavijnana,** or "storehouse consciousness," which is the passive or potential ground out of which emerge the other seven consciousnesses. It is the repository of all potential activities of the other consciousnesses. These potentials exist in the form of "seeds" (*bija*) (Epstein, 1985; Hanh, 1974). These "seeds," upon development, produce all sorts of mental phenomena. Furthermore, in the *alayavijnana,* the "seeds" affect each other in various ways. These "seeds" are "watered" by conscious activities, so that, for example, engaging in kind or compassionate thoughts makes the seeds of compassion ripen and grow (i.e., become more powerful), so that it will be easier to think compassionately next time. Allowing oneself to indulge in anger or hatred waters the corresponding seeds, so that it becomes easier to grow angry and to experience hate. This is why mindfulness of thoughts is so important, and why the "right effort" aspect of the Eightfold Path deals with cutting off negative or destructive thoughts as soon as they appear, while nurturing positive ones. This develops positive mental habits rooted in the seeds of the *alayavijnana* and has far-reaching effects on the life and well-being of the individual.

The *alayavijnana* is a vast unconscious realm, which is often compared to a stream, constantly flowing and renewing itself. If the individual is likened to a wave in the ocean, then the *alayavijnana* is the unconsciousness (or subconsciousness) of the ocean, providing the continuity of the karmic process. Jung's collective unconscious is the closest concept in Western psychology, with the archetypes being somewhat analogous to "seeds," but the Buddhist concept is more vast and more dynamic, allowing as it does for the "seeding" of the unconscious (Hanh, 1991).

The eight consciousnesses should not be conceived as separate but rather as eight manifestations or functions of an ongoing process. Think of a room illuminated by several lightbulbs. The illumination is one ongoing phenomenon, integrating the contributions of the individual bulbs. In this example, the electricity that activates them is the equivalent of the *alayavijnana*. There are eight consciousnesses, and yet these are ultimately one (Epstein, 1985).

## Bodhidharma and the Transmission of Zen to China

Zen Buddhism was introduced to China around 520 A.D. by the Buddhist monk Bodhidharma. Upon his arrival in China, Bodhidharma met with the emperor, a devout but superficial Buddhist who asked, "I have built temples, support the monks, and have had the

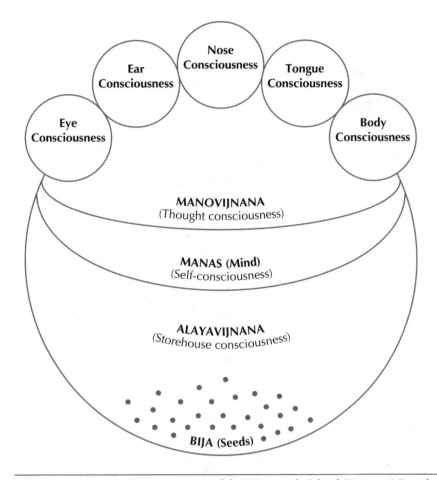

**FIGURE 17.1** The Eight Consciousnesses of the Vijnanavada School (Yogacara) Founded by Vasubandhu and Asanga in the Fourth Century C.E.

The eight consciousnesses are not conceived as separate but rather as eight manifestations of an ongoing process, such as the illumination of a room to which individual bulbs contribute. *(SOURCE: Courtesy Yōzan Dirk Mosig, adapted from a lecture by Thich Nhat Hanh at the Retreat for Psychotherapists held in Boulder, Colorado, in 1989.)*

scriptures translated, tell me, what will all of this bring me?" "It will bring you nothing," replied Bodhidharma. "Then tell me, what are the sacred things in Buddhism?" "There are no sacred things—only vast emptiness." Irritated, the emperor asked, "And who are you to stand in front of me and talk to me like this?" "I do not know," said Bodhidharma, and he left. The emperor was functioning at the relative plane, while Bodhidharma made repeated references to the absolute one, where there are no "things," nothing can be sacred or profane, and there is no "I" or "self" to know.

Bodhidharma is said to have practiced sitting meditation for nine years at the Shaolin Temple, teaching the monks with his example. He is also said to have summarized his teaching as "a special transmission outside of the scriptures; no reliance upon words and letters; direct pointing to the heart of man, and the realization of enlightenment" (Hoover, 1980). This statement emphasizes that the scriptures must be practiced and not just read, for words by themselves are as useless as a picture of a cake is to satisfy hunger. Only an enlightened teacher can verify the awakening of a disciple, which is thus transmitted "from mind to mind" (or "from heart to heart").

As Zen Buddhism passed into China, it adopted expressions from **Taoism,** which helped to convey Buddhist ideas. The philosophy of Taoism, attributed to the Chinese philosopher Lao-tse (approximately fourth century B.C.), the author of the *Tao Te Ching* ("The Way and Its Power"), is essentially compatible with that of Buddhism. Lao-tse referred to the absolute as the **Tao,** or the "Way" of Nature, which is inexpressible in words, and stressed the desirability of harmonizing with nature. Many references to the "Way" (Tao) appear in Chinese Zen literature, usually to express the Buddha-nature.

In China, the Tao was thought to manifest itself in the form of two forces: **yin** and **yang**. Yin stands for the feminine, receptive, internal, negative aspect of nature, while yang represents the masculine, active, external, positive aspect. The yin and yang are not merely opposites, but exist in a state of dynamic complementation, expressing the unity of the Tao. In Buddhist terms, we can say that yin and yang are dependently arisen, so that yin is yin because of yang, and yang is yang because of yin. The yin and yang symbol thus becomes a convenient expression of the principle of dependent origination, its dynamic quality corresponding to the impermanence and constant change the Buddha saw in the universe. The white dot in the black yin signifies that there is yang in the yin, while the black dot on white field reflects the yin in the yang.

## The Practice of Zen

We need to distinguish between Zen as a school of the Mahayana division of Buddhism, and Zen as an experience. To speak of the latter is immediately to distort and misrepresent it. Zen masters have often said that those who say what Zen is do not know what it is, while those who know what it is, do not talk about it, but teach the practice of Zen, so that others will be able to experience it.

The practice of Zen entails a systematic training of the mind designed to create in the disciple a state of mind that will permit the realization of enlightenment. The indispensable form of Zen practice is **zazen,** which is traditionally practiced sitting cross-legged on a firm, round cushion or *zafu,* maintaining a precise physical posture for a period of time. Eastern psychologies, and especially Zen, do not regard the mind and the body as separate, but as intimately interconnected, to the point that one could more properly refer to a "body-mind" than to a body *and* a mind. The posture of the body in zazen is extremely important, and is expressed in the mental state that accompanies it.

The main position recommended for zazen is the full lotus, with the right foot placed on the left thigh, and the left foot on the right thigh. This position expresses the oneness of duality. Even though we have two legs, in this posture they have become one. The head, neck, and spine are kept in a straight vertical line, which is the hallmark of all proper zazen postures. When one sits correctly, the body is held in perfect balance. Everything exists in the right place and in the right way. In such a position, a person can maintain physi-

*Zazen can be practiced by young and old.
The preferred body position is the full lotus,
which requires a measure of flexibility.*

cal and mental balance and can breathe naturally and deeply. The state of consciousness
that exists when one sits in the correct posture is, itself, enlightenment.

The harmonization of the mind with the posture of zazen is usually accomplished
through awareness of one's breathing. The mind tends to act like a monkey or a misbehav-
ing child, constantly engaging in discursive thought. As the practitioner notices that the
mind is climbing the treetops, he or she returns awareness to the breath, and continues to
repeat this process.

Any thoughts, ideas, visions, or unusual experiences that may occur while one is
practicing zazen are to be dismissed as *makyo*, delusions or hallucinations. The student is to
attach no significance to them. Zazen is not the pursuit of mystical experiences. Zazen done
properly is just sitting, body and mind together, right here and now—*just sitting*. While
some recommend that beginners count their breaths, follow a mental sound or mantra, use
some sort of visualizations, or ponder a paradoxical riddle during zazen, these are "unnecessary training wheels" (Kosko, 1993)

Zazen is not a means to reach enlightenment, thus it is not a tool to be discarded once the mind has become awakened. At that point, zazen becomes a manifestation of this realization. "The reason why you have to practice zazen is that if you do not practice zazen, things stick to you, and you cannot let go of them" (Katagiri, 1988). In the same way that showering allows us to wash away dust and dirt, practicing zazen allows us to let go of past regrets and future worries. Just as it would not occur to us to discontinue showering because the body is now clean, we should not regard any mental state as an indication that zazen is no longer necessary.

In the **Rinzai** school of Zen, **koans** are often used as themes for Zen meditation. The term "koan" literally means a "public document." It consists of an apparently paradoxical anecdote, statement, or question that has no logical, rational, or intellectual solution, as long as the student continues functioning at the level of the *relative,* the realm of duality. The koan statement is perfectly clear to an enlightened individual able to experience the *absolute* realm of nonduality. Since language is a tool developed to express dualistic concepts, it is totally inadequate to convey a nondualistic experience or understanding. For this reason, any attempt to provide an answer based on language or discursive Aristotelian-style logic is futile.

The koan usually describes actions or words by an enlightened teacher attempting to jolt a student out of discursive thinking into an intuitive realization. The use of such incidents as meditation aids is relatively recent in the long history of Zen Buddhism. Examples of koans are "What was your face before your parents were born?" and "What is the sound of one hand clapping?"

Students using a koan typically have individual daily interviews (called *sanzen*) with the master, to express their current understanding of the koan. Students' answers are almost invariably rejected, and they are sent back to meditate on the koan until they become one with it and arrive at a breakthrough, transcending dualistic thinking. Once they have broken through the koan, they are assigned another one, and the process is repeated. It may take weeks, months, or years for a student to work through a particular koan.

Teachers of the **Soto** school of Zen also use koans, but not as meditation themes. Zazen in Soto Zen is essentially **shikantaza,** themeless, just sitting. Shikantaza is not based on trying to realize anything. It is a pure practice that allows any effects to take place without being sought after. A Soto Zen teacher may use a koan as a focal point for a *teisho,* a "dharma talk" offered by a master to his students to enhance their understanding. A koan can be seen as a miniature exaggeration of the problem of life. Just as the koan seems to defy logical comprehension and resolution, so life itself cannot be held or contained within the categories constructed by dualistic thinking.

A number of studies have examined the physiological responses that occur during the practice of Zen meditation (Murphy & Donovan, 1988). In experienced meditators, the respiratory rate has been found to typically slow down during zazen, from the normal of 18–20 breaths per minute to 4–6 per minute or less, with a marked increase in the tidal volume of air displaced. The electroencephalographic record shows a predominance of alpha along with theta waves, although zazen is normally practiced with the eyes partially open. Oxygen consumption shows a marked decrease, and metabolic rates slow down (Hirai, 1989). Although some of these changes can be brought about through simple relaxation, they are not critical to the experience of zazen. Simple relaxation cannot produce the transpersonal awareness and present-centering that result from a proper meditative practice. There is a considerable body of literature supporting the notion that zazen, as well as other Eastern meditative disciplines, can lead to better health and an increased ability to deal with stress and tension (e.g., Brazier, 1995; Epstein, 1995; Hirai, 1989; Kabat-Zinn, 1990; Miller, Fletcher, & Kabat-Zinn, 1995; Urbanowski & Miller, 1996). Such practices emphasize internal rather than external control, as well as the unity of mind and body, and they are gaining recognition from contemporary Western medicine for their efficacy.

Zen practice has many other forms, which serve to extend the mindfulness of zazen to daily life. **Kinhin** is a slow walk performed between consecutive periods of zazen, while maintaining concentration and mindfulness. The kinhin walk allows for rest and normalization of circulation in the legs when one is doing several sittings. As during zazen one just sits, when walking in kinhin one just walks. In a more informal form of walking meditation, a person, alone or in a group, just walks (in the park, around the block, or wherever), maintaining awareness of the breath and of everything experienced during the walk, but without labeling or discussing what is being experienced. In order to maintain mindfulness when walking in this manner, it is recommended that the person notice the number of steps taken while inhaling, and also the number while exhaling (Hanh, 1985). Counting the steps and maintaining awareness of the breathing keeps the individual focused on the present, and this mindfulness is extended to everything encountered. If you try this exercise, you may be amazed at how many things you notice during your walk that you had never noticed before.

*Gathas,* short verses to help focus attention on the task at hand, by mentally dedicating the activity to the benefit of all sentient beings, may also be used. This practice makes every activity into something sacred and clarifies that no activity is more or less valuable than any other activity—as we engage in it, it is our life at that moment.

Another form of Zen practice is the **gassho,** the putting together of the hands, palm to palm. The gassho position is a symbol of nonduality. It reminds us that the mind and body are one. One hand stands for you, the other for the person you are greeting, or for the entire universe, and you become aware that you and the other are one. When you put the hands together in gassho, just do gassho. Zen teaches to do each action completely and for its own sake.

Chanting sutras is Zen, too; here the important thing is to just chant, expecting nothing out of it, as an **autotelic** activity, in other words, an activity that contains its own goal. Chanting is not a form of prayer. It is not aimed at a superior power, nor does it petition anything. When chanting, just experience the sound.

A practice that many Westerners find difficult at first because of their cultural upbringing is bowing. In Zen, bowing is not an act of worship but an action expressing respect and gratitude. You may put your hands in gassho and bow to give thanks or to show appreciation for another, or merely as a greeting. Bowing in front of an altar, whether it be a standing bow or a full prostration, is an exercise that helps to subdue the ego and expresses gratitude. All the statues found in a Zen temple are symbolic of mental states and abilities, and do not represent external deities. In Zen you can bow to anything, people, statues, animals, your meditation cushion, a cup of tea. The important thing when bowing is to just bow, expecting nothing out of it.

Eating can also be a form of Zen practice, whether it be with the traditional *oryoki* bowls often used in Zen centers and monasteries, or in the everyday setting of the Western dining room. The key element in this is the maintenance of mindfulness. When you eat, just eat. Give your food your undivided attention—you can take care of other matters when their turn arrives.

# Meditation

Unlike Western personality theories, Zen cannot be grasped by thinking, critically or otherwise—it must be experienced. Here are instructions on how to practice zazen.

Wear loose-fitting clothes. Find a quiet, temperate, and neat place where you are not likely to be disturbed. Put a mat or folded blanket on the floor close to a wall, and place a thick cushion above it. Facing the wall, you should sit on the edge of the cushion, which should support the base of your spine, elevating it 6–8 inches from the floor. The cushion should allow you to sit straight and be stable, with your spine and your two knees forming three points of a tripod. The knees must be on the mat, not elevated from it.

Place your legs in one of the following positions (in descending order of stability and desirability): *full lotus* (right foot on left thigh and left foot on right thigh), *half lotus* (one foot on the opposite thigh, the other tucked underneath), *quarter lotus* (one foot on the opposite calf, the other tucked underneath), *burmese* (both legs flat on the mat), or *seiza* (kneeling, with the cushion on edge between your legs). If none of these are possible for you, sit on a cushion at the edge of a chair (keep your back straight, do not lean on the backrest). Put your hands on your knees, palms up. Breathing deeply, slowly arch your body back and then forward, and then sway from side to side in *decreasing* arcs, until you are perfectly centered. Then put your right hand on your lap (resting on your left foot, if you are in a lotus position), palm up, and the left hand on top of it, with the thumbs slightly touching over your middle fingers. Your hands should now be forming an oval, with the blades touching the stomach a few inches below the navel. The arms are relaxed and extend slightly forward, without touching the sides of your body.

Push your lower back slightly forward, then straighten your back, pushing upward with the top of your head. Keep your neck straight and tuck your chin slightly in. There should be a straight line now from the bottom of your spine to the top of your head. Your nose and navel should be in a vertical line, and your ears and shoulders on a horizontal line. Your eyes should remain slightly open, with your gaze cast downward at a 45-degree angle. Don't look at a specific spot—just let your eyes rest; don't try to see or visualize anything. Your mouth should be closed, with lips and teeth touching. Rest the tongue against the roof of the palate. Swallow any saliva, creating a vacuum inside your mouth. Breathe in and out through your nose and let the air go down to your lower abdomen so that you are breathing with the diaphragm. Breathe naturally, don't force the breath.

Keep your mind with your breath. When you inhale, be aware of your lower abdomen going out. When you exhale, notice your lower abdomen going in. Maintain this awareness. If you become distracted, don't get upset. If thoughts arise, notice them and let them go, gently returning to your breath. Keep repeating this. Just sit there, doing nothing, just being present in the reality of your life, beyond likes and dislikes. Sit firmly and immovable, like a mountain. At the end of your sitting period, release the posture of your hands, and put them on your knees, palms up. Gently sway from side to side in *increasing* arcs, exhaling each time as you sway to one side and then the other; then undo the position of your legs and stretch them out. Stand up slowly and carefully.

Sit every day, expecting nothing, for at least five minutes, working up to 40 as time allows. Early morning and end of day are the best times to practice..

Many aspects of Japanese culture show the imprint of Zen. This is true of the tea ceremony, the Noh theatre, the art of calligraphy, ink brush painting, haiku poetry, flower arranging, the *shakuhachi* flute, as well as the martial arts, such as karate, aikido swordsmanship, and archery. These are meditative arts based on the discipline of zazen. These and other forms of Zen practice are no substitutes for zazen, but serve to extend the mindfulness of zazen to everyday life (Mosig, 1988, 1990, 1991). The martial arts in particular necessitate the development of two mental states associated with Zen: "no-mindedness," the ability to react without conscious thought, and the "immovable mind," the ability to remain calm and undisturbed regardless of the circumstances (Mosig, 1988).

But you do not need to bow, chant, play the shakuhachi, write haikus, recite gathas, learn calligraphy, or engage in a martial art in order to practice Zen. All those manners of Zen expression, however helpful they may be, are ultimately superfluous and can be dispensed with. The only Zen practice that is completely indispensable is zazen.

It is important to find a master or a teacher to learn the correct way to practice Zen. The most important thing to look for in a teacher is not the depth of his or her enlightenment—that is secondary. The most important point is how much the truth the teacher has experienced has been "digested" and manifests itself in the teacher's life (Katagiri, 1988). Only a teacher who has received "Dharma transmission," in other words, whose experience has been verified and authenticated by an enlightened master, is in a position to verify and authenticate the awakening of others.

## The Five Approaches to Zen Practice

There are five basic approaches to Zen practice. **Bompu Zen** is Zen practiced for a profit, such as mental health, stress management, improved sports performance, inner peace, or effective salesmanship. Today most Westerners who take up the practice of zazen do so with some benefit in mind. They are also likely to quit if the expected results are not experienced in a short time. **Gedo Zen** is practice unconnected with the Buddha's teachings. It is exemplified by New Age practitioners who engage in zazen in order to reach higher levels of consciousness, visions, or mystical experiences. People of diverse religious backgrounds may also attempt to use Zen to deepen their religious experiences. **Shojo Zen**, or "small vehicle" Zen, is zazen practiced for the sake of one's own liberation from suffering or for one's personal enlightenment. It is similar to the approach to meditation in the Theravada tradition. **Daijo Zen** is Zen practiced for the sake of liberating all sentient beings, seeking enlightenment to help others. This approach is the one found in most Mahayana schools, including Rinzai Zen. **Saijojo Zen,** meaning "great and perfect practice," is zazen practiced for the sake of practicing zazen, with no idea of gain and no expectations. This is the *shikantaza,* or "just sitting," emphasized in Soto Zen. It is called great and perfect because it is not based on trying to realize anything. It is a pure practice that allows any effects to take place without being sought after.

An analogy to learning to swim may make this clearer. You could learn swimming in order to improve your health (*bompu*), in order to have a mystical experience of oneness with the ocean (*gedo*), in order to save yourself from drowning (*shojo*), in order to save others from drowning (*daijo*), or just in order to swim (*saijojo*). Notice that the latter approach does not preclude improved health, oceanic experiences, or salvation from drowning for oneself or others. Instead, it pursues swimming for its own sake and allows any benefits to come of themselves. Thus it is the pure and perfect practice of just swimming.

## Enlightenment

The reflective illumination or awakening of Zen is known as **satori.** Satori, or enlightenment, cannot be communicated with words, any more than words could communicate the experience of color to someone who is blind. In the Rinzai school, satori is regarded as the goal of Zen practice, and zazen as a method to achieve it. Practitioners sit in meditation, attempting to circumvent linear, rational thought through the use of a koan.

The Soto school, in comparison, stresses that satori is not a goal to be attained but is identical with the practice of zazen, which must be engaged in with no gaining idea in mind. Dogen Zenji (1200–1253), the founder of the Soto school in Japan, interpreted the Buddha's statement that everyone has the Buddha-nature as *everyone is the Buddha nature.* This is because the Buddha-nature is not something outside or inside of the individual, but the absolute universal reality. Each and every one of us is the universe, whether we realize it or not. Satori means to wake up to this fact, to the way things are and have always been, a transformative experience that entails the realization of the universal Self.

To clarify satori, Loori (1988) tells the story of the ugly duckling who felt terrible because he was so different from the other ducks who made fun of him. One day, as he was looking at his reflection in the water, he noticed the reflection of another ugly duckling just like him. As he looked up, he discovered a group of swans, and *in that moment* he realized that he himself was a swan. He instantly became a perfect and complete swan. Suddenly everything was right and he was free from all his psychological suffering. He was enlightened, and yet, nothing had changed, for he had always been a perfect swan. The difference, though, was transformative, for he was liberated from the delusion of his imperfection.

Okumura (1985) wrote, "satori is nothing but being aware of, or being alert in whatever activity you are doing right now, right here. Any activity is not a step, means, or preparation for other things, but rather should be done for its own sake, being accomplished in each moment." This description is a far cry from the mystical misconceptions often connected with the subject of enlightenment.

It is just as important to let go of the good as of the bad features of the past. As Okumura (1997) points out:

> If we did something good yesterday, we should forget it and face what is in front of our eyes today. What we did yesterday is not reality anymore. We cannot be proud of what we did in the past and think we are great people because we did such and such. Even if we make mistakes, we shouldn't be caught up in them. Let go of them and start again. Start right from this posture in silence, right from the ever fresh life force that is free from any defilement. Moment by moment, we start again and again.

This is the enlightened state, where human evaluations are no longer important.

The activities of an enlightened individual are autotelic. Such enlightened functioning is similar to Csikszentmihalyi's "flow" (1975, 1990). When we become totally immersed in an activity, we can "flow" with it to the point that we lose awareness of ourselves as separate from the activity.

When an enlightened person eats, that person just eats, when resting, just rests, in the same manner that one just sits when practicing zazen. The awakened one does not discriminate between activities, knowing that no task is intrinsically better or worse than any other. Whatever is being done, painting a landscape or cleaning the toilet bowl, is one's life at that moment. Giving the activity full attention is to be able to flow with it, without attempting to get it out of the way to do something else that may be more enjoyable. One is thus fully living one's life. Zen is the art of losing the self (the ego) in the everyday flow of autotelic activities.

The awakening of Zen can be precipitated by any stimulus or event occurring at the right time in the life of a person who is ready to experience it. Recorded instances provide the subject matter for numerous Zen stories. The manner in which a given incident manages to trigger the awakening of a specific individual cannot be understood intellectually, and any attempt to imitate another's realization experience is futile.

Satori must be personally experienced. A master can point the way but cannot experience it for the student. If we are hungry or thirsty, another person's eating or drinking will not fill our stomach or moisten our throat. This is why Zen masters insist that they have

*The performance of work, when done with mindfulness,*
*is a meditative experience in the Zen tradition.*

nothing to teach or impart. All they can do is show how Zen is practiced and exemplify it in their lives.

*Enlightenment is not the end of Zen practice.* If it were, it would represent the outcome of a selfish interest in one's own happiness and fulfillment. Practitioners seek enlightenment not for themselves but for the benefit of all sentient beings. Zen teaches that in the enlightenment of one person, all sentient beings are enlightened, for all boundaries are illusions. It has been said that Zen training is like climbing a mountain. Satori is being on top of the mountain. But after reaching the top, coming down the other side of the mountain and returning to the "marketplace" to help everyone else is the bodhisattva spirit, exemplified in the enlightened master.

## Eastern Thought and Psychotherapy

Alan Watts (1961) has compared the modes of liberation or psychotherapeutic change developed by the East and the West. Both Western psychotherapy and Eastern ways of life aim at change. However, whereas Western psychotherapy has emphasized change for neurotic or disturbed individuals, Eastern disciplines are concerned with change in the consciousness of normal or healthy people. Eastern psychotherapies recognized long ago that the culture in which one lives not only defines what is normal and abnormal in that particular society but also provides the context for and fosters a more pervasive form of neurosis that is endured by all of its members.

In the West, Sigmund Freud drew our attention to the offenses that are committed against the human being by social repression. In large measure, the task of the psychoanalyst is to liberate the patient from stressful social conditioning to facilitate more effective functioning. Recent studies have shown that Eastern perspectives on mental health and Buddhist meditative disciplines can facilitate the psychotherapeutic process in psychoanalysis and other forms of psychotherapy (Epstein, 1995; Metzger, 1996) and that Zen meditation can be conceptualized in psychoanalytic terms (Leone, 1995). Eastern psychotherapy, however, goes further than do classical Freudian psychoanalysis and other Western psychotherapies. It seeks not just to restore the disturbed individual to normal, healthy social functioning but to point out that the distress of the normal, as well as the abnormal, person is caused by **maya** or illusion. The neurosis of all humanity lies in the fact that we take the world picture of our culture too literally and identify ourselves with our social roles.

The construct of the self as an "individual" is a social process created in the history of our relations with others that gives us our categories of subjective identity but cannot be identified with anything ultimate or real. We need to recognize the relative and impermanent nature of the self, while being aware of the absolute interconnected reality. When crossing the street, it is not enough to contemplate an approaching car and to realize that we are one with it. True, the car, the road, our body, and everything else are nothing more than temporary collections of energy and particles and have no more reality than the transient shape of a wave on the surface of the ocean. Nevertheless, unless we act in the relative plane, and get out of the way of the car, the collection of skandhas that allows this awareness to occur will be promptly dissolved. What is needed is appropriate action in the relative world, while maintaining awareness of the big picture.

The Eastern disciplines provide a path of liberation from unnecessary psychological suffering and its aggravation into mental illness. Western psychotherapy, as Watts points out, falls short of being a way of liberation because it fails to deal with the bigger problem of rectifying the breach between the individual and the world. It is content to limit itself to the individual's adjustment to society. Frequently its aim is to fortify the ego rather than to dissolve it. Such an approach cannot heal the alienation experienced by the ego as the result of the delusion of separation.

There may be another way in which Western psychotherapy has failed, and that is in terms of the development of a method to enhance and protect the mental health of the practicing clinician. Western psychotherapists have rightly stated that it is not possible to bring someone to a higher level of mental health than one has accomplished oneself, but Western psychotherapy has failed to develop the equivalent of zazen as a method to dissolve the delusion of the ego in therapists and patients alike. Therapists need to heal themselves before they are in a position to help others. They need to develop inner peace, and the capacity for compassionate action, to be able to be islands of refuge for those immersed in psychological pain. This is the mental characteristic known as the "immovable mind" of Zen, the natural outcome of the practice of zazen. Echoing Zen master Katagiri's words: if we don't practice zazen, painful events stick to our consciousness and we cannot let go of them.

With the current meeting of East and West, more Western psychotherapists are discovering the value of adopting a meditative discipline as part of their training and, in general, of regarding meditation as a powerful therapeutic tool (e.g., Brazier, 1995; Epstein, 1995; Fickling, 1991; Fuld, 1991; Hirai, 1989; Kabat-Zinn, 1990; Miller, 1991; Urbanowski & Miller, 1996).

Perhaps one of the most significant developments in the field of psychotherapy over the past couple of decades has been the introduction in the West of several Eastern systems of treatment. Reynolds (1980) identified several Japanese forms of psychotherapy, which he called the "quiet therapies" because their main therapeutic tool is some form of silent meditation, in contrast with the "talking cures" so prevalent in the West. **Morita therapy** was developed by Japanese psychiatrist Shoma Morita in the early 1900s and is founded on the theoretical concepts and practice of Zen, as shown by Rhymer (1988). The method consists of isolated bedrest (to force patients to come in touch with themselves), followed by periods of light and then heavier manual work, and a period of retraining to help patients rejoin normal life. During part of the treatment patients keep a diary that is annotated by the therapist. Standard hospitalization lasts usually from 40 to 60 days (Reynolds, 1976).

The Moritist method requires that patients acknowledge their feelings and take full responsibility for their actions, being trained to behave appropriately despite any feelings that might arise. In other words, they learn to gradually develop a degree of "immovable mind," realizing that if they do not react to their feelings, these feelings have no power over them. This is similar to a person sitting in zazen learning that whatever thoughts, stimuli, or feelings pop up in consciousness and are noticed but not reacted to will pass away, demonstrating their impermanent character. Instead of attempting to remove symptoms, Morita therapy regards patients as students and teaches them to live constructively despite any symptoms or feelings that may be present.

██ **THINKING CRITICALLY** ██

## *Mindfulness and the Search for a Higher Synthesis*

At this point you would normally be asked to rate Zen Buddhism on each of the philosophical assumptions described in Chapter 1. However, such an activity would be contrary
to the spirit of Zen, which aims at a higher synthesis and asks that we experience rather than
analyze. Can you see how the experience of Zen undercuts traditional dualisms such as freedom versus determination, uniqueness versus universality, proactive versus reactive? Can
you suggest ways in which thinking in terms of these dualisms may stand in the way of our
experiencing ourselves? Can you further suggest ways in which people in the West can benefit from the teachings of the East?

As an additional experiential exercise to appreciate the power of mindfulness, try
the following. Select a task you normally dislike or avoid. For example, let's say that you hate
to wash dishes. The next time the opportunity presents itself, approach this task as something to be done as a meditative experience. Do the job with full concentration, without
rushing through it to get it out of the way to do something else that you regard as more interesting or enjoyable. While you are washing dishes, this is your life at the moment. No activity is intrinsically better or worse than any other activity; it is merely the content of your
life at the moment. Pick up each dish, each cup, each glass, each utensil, and carefully wash
it, one by one, as if you were polishing a precious jewel. Look at each item in your hands and
actually see it. Don't allow your attention to wander. Don't think of anything else. Be there,
in the present moment. Maintain awareness of your breath, of your inhalations and exhala-
tions while you do the washing—it will help you to stay in the present moment. Don't look
at the clock. Don't talk with someone else while doing this. Just wash the dishes, one at a
time, carefully, mindfully, with your whole being. Afterward you may wish to reflect on this
experience. Was the task distasteful? Was it enjoyable? What would your life be like, if you
did everything with mindfulness? What is keeping you from it? You will find other mindfulness exercises in Hanh (1975, 1993) and Kabat-Zinn (1990).

---

Morita therapy seems to be most effective with neuroses grouped under the name
**shinkeishitsu,** which overlap primarily with anxiety disorders in the standard DSM-IV
classification. The rates of success of Morita therapy, as reported by Rhymer (1988), are very
high, over 90 percent when significant improvement and cures are combined.

**Naikan** introspective therapy emphasizes the development of a sense of responsibility and obligation in the patient, consonant with the principle of interconnectedness or
dependent origination stressed in all Buddhist schools, as well as with the sense of societal
and familial responsibility associated with Confucian ethics. For instance, the patient may
be instructed to sit in introspective meditation, recording all the things her mother has
done for her, and on a following day, all the things she has done for her mother, and similarly with respect to her father, her siblings, her teachers, and others in her life. What
emerges is a deep insight into the imbalance of the relationships and a desire to repay others for their care and support (Reynolds, 1980).

Morita and Naikan therapies have demonstrated their effectiveness in the West and are regarded with growing respect in psychotherapeutic literature (Bankart, 1997; Walsh, 1995). The two approaches have been successfully combined into the "constructive living" system championed by Reynolds in the United States; the system is rapidly growing in popularity here and abroad (Reynolds, 1995).

The value of Zen meditation as therapy and as an adjunct to other forms of psychotherapy has been documented by Hirai (1989) and others. A more general application of mindfulness therapy is advocated by Hanh (1991, 1992), where awareness of emotions (such as anger) is used to transform the energy of the emotion into constructive channels. Kabat-Zinn (1990) has also developed a program based on mindfulness meditation for stress reduction and is currently helping develop similar programs across the country. We are likely to continue to see the increasing impact of Zen and other Eastern disciplines on Western psychotherapy in the future.

| PHILOSOPHY, |
| :---: |
| SCIENCE, |
| AND ART |

# Eastern Theories

An extensive literature on Buddhist psychology exists, including diagnosis and psychotherapy. In the East, the emphasis is relational rather than individual; the person is not considered in isolation but in relation to the self, to others, and to the larger cosmos.

Most certainly, Eastern concepts of personality do not qualify, nor do they aspire to qualify, as science. The very need to evaluate and demonstrate a personality theory's usefulness constitute a bias that is foreign to Eastern thought. Although Eastern theories are sometimes considered a philosophy or a religion, they do not entail the same logic or speculation that characterizes Western religion and philosophy. Zen and Eastern personality theories in general are in many ways closer to science than to philosophy or religion, but since they do not utilize the scientific method of investigation, it is perhaps most accurate to describe them as art.

Eastern theories are highly practical. They offer a variety of techniques for cultivating a deeper understanding of the self. These practices move the individual away from intellectual, rational consciousness and cultivate a deeper awareness that transcends everyday consciousness. Systematically training the body and the mind, Eastern disciplines aim at enabling the individual to perceive the truth that lies within the inner being.

There has been a steady growth of interest in the ideas and practices of the East. The influence of Eastern concepts is apparent in the work of several personality theorists included in this book: Jung explicitly incorporated Eastern concepts into his theory; Fromm and Horney turned to the East to enrich their theories and practices, and the same is true to some extent of Rogers, Maslow, and many others, particularly in the emerging field of transpersonal psychology. By looking for the commonalities between Buddhism and Western thought, especially existentialism, we may be taken to even greater insights. Exciting new holistic metatheories of personality integrate Western psychology's obsession with early development and self-esteem with Eastern traditions concerned with self-transcendence and enlightenment. Today, with increasing opportunities for cooperation, it is vitally important that East and West appreciate each other's attempts to understand the self. To do so can only enrich both.

# *Summary*

1. Siddhartha Gautama, the *Buddha,* renounced everything he had and left home in search of a solution to the problem of human suffering. After six years he attained enlightenment. Theravada and Mahayana Buddhism grew out of his teachings. *Zen Buddhism,* a branch of the Mahayana, adopted *Taoist* language in China and spread from there to Japan and the rest of the world.

2. The principle of *dependent origination* says "this is because that is; this is not, because that is not; when this arises, that arises; when this ceases, that ceases."

3. The three characteristics of existence are **anicca** (impermanence), *dukkha* (suffering), and *anatta* (non-self). The Buddha's solution to the problem of suffering was expressed in the form of the *Four Noble Truths.*

4. The experience of enlightenment, or *satori,* is an awakening to the reality of the universe that cannot be grasped through intellectual analysis, but must be experienced personally.

5. The five *skandhas* are form, feelings, perceptions, impulses, and consciousness. A person is a temporary arrangement of these aggregates or skandhas and has no reality separated from them.

6. Of the eight consciousnesses, the first five correspond to the basic sense fields: seeing, hearing, smelling, tasting, and touching. Below that are the *manovijnana,* the integrating basis of the five sensory consciousnesses; *manas* ("mind"), where the illusion of a separate "I" or "ego" arises; and the *alayavijnana* ("storehouse consciousness"), the ground of knowledge and impressions that exist in the form of "seeds" affecting each other in various ways.

7. The practice of Zen entails a systematic training of the mind through the practice of *zazen,* sitting meditation, and the extension of the mindfulness and concentration of zazen to daily life. The two main schools of Zen are *Soto,* which stresses the practice of zazen as "just sitting," or *shikantaza,* and *Rinzai,* which employs the *koan* (an apparently paradoxical statement, question, or anecdote) as a focus of concentration during zazen.

Furthermore, the Rinazi school sees zazen as a method to reach enlightenment, while the Soto school stresses that practice and enlightenment are one and the same.

8. It is necessary to actually practice zazen in order to understand it. Detailed instructions are given on page 464.

9. Whereas Western psychotherapy has emphasized change for neurotic or disturbed individuals, Eastern disciplines are concerned with change in the consciousness of normal or healthy people, pointing out that the distress of both is caused by *maya,* or illusion.

10. Eastern theories do not entail the speculation or the kind of logic characteristic of Western theories. For our purposes, it is most accurate to characterize them as art.

## Suggestions for Further Reading

It is often said that the best Zen books are those that make you put them down and head for the meditation cushion. Suzuki's *Zen Mind, Beginner's Mind* (Weatherhill, 1970) and Katagiri's *Returning to Silence* (Shambhala, 1988) do an excellent job of explaining and encouraging the practice and application of Zen in daily life. The best manual of Zen meditation, clearly illustrated and including a number of classic and modern texts, is Okumura's *Shikantaza* (Kyoto, 1985). A lot of common questions about Zen are answered in Deshimaru's *Questions to a Zen Master* (Dutton, 1985).

For a good introduction to the basic teachings of Buddhism, the two best works are Piyadassi's *The Buddha's Ancient Path* (B.P.S., 1974) and Rahula's *What the Buddha Taught* (Grove, 1974). An excellent approach from a Zen perspective can be found in Hagen's *Buddhism Plain and Simple* (Tuttle, 1997). Three worthwhile biographies of the Buddha from different perspectives are Kalupahana's novelized *The Way of Siddhartha* (Shambhala, 1982), Nanamoli's *The Life of Buddha,* based on the Pali Canon, and the historical Carrither's *The Buddha* (Oxford, 1983).

A fair historical outline of the development of Zen can be found in Hoover's *The Zen Experience* (New American Library, 1980) and the history of the coming of Buddhism to America is extensively treated in Fields's *How the Swans Came to the Lake* (Shambhala, 1992). A delightful account by a writer of her relationship with her Zen teacher is to be found in Goldberg's *Long Quiet Highway* (Bantam, 1993).

To begin an exploration of the works of that deepest of Zen masters, Eihei Dogen, the student is referred to Cleary's *Rational Zen* (Shambhala, 1992), the Dogen and Uchiyama volume *Refining Your Life* (Weatherhill, 1983), and Abe's challenging *A Study of Dogen* (State University of New York, 1992).

For the practice of mindfulness and an understanding of "dependent origination" in everyday life, the various books by Thich Nhat Hahn are without peer. Especially recommended are *Being Peace* (Parallax, 1987), *Touching Peace* (Parallax, 1992), *Peace Is Every Step* (Bantam, 1991), and *The Heart of Understanding* (Parallax, 1988).

Those interested in feminist issues will find of value several volumes on the contributions of women teaching Zen Buddhism in America, such as Boucher's *Turning the*

*Wheel* (Harper & Row, 1988) and Friedman's *Meetings With Remarkable Women* (Shambhala, 1987). Also worthwhile are several excellent books on Zen practice by Western women, such as Beck's *Everyday Zen*, Mountain's *The Zen Environment* (Morrow, 1982), and Packer's *The Work of This Moment* (Shambhala, 1990), as well as the collections of essays by the Japanese Zen nun Shundo Aoyama, *Zen Seeds* (Kosei, 1990).

A good history of psychotherapy East and West is Bankart's *Talking Cures: A History of Western and Eastern Psychotherapies* (Brooks/Cole, 1997). For applications of Zen in the field of psychotherapy, you may wish to start with Reynold's *The Quiet Therapies* (Hawaii, 1980), Wellwood's *Awakening the Heart* (Shambhala, 1983), Claxton's *Beyond Therapy* (Wisdom, 1986), and Brazier's *Zen Therapy* (Wiley, 1995). Further reading on the Zen-based Morita therapy can be found in the many excellent books on the subject by David K. Reynolds, especially *Morita Psychotherapy* (University of California, 1976), *Playing Ball on Running Water* (Morrow, 1984), and *Plunging Through the Clouds* (State University of New York, 1993). A more general application of Buddhist meditation in the area of stress management is Kabat-Zinn's *Full Catastrophe Living* (Delacorte, 1990), and for the stresses of college life Gibbs's *Dancing With Your Books* (Penguin, 1990) is highly recommended.

Finally, Kosko's *Fuzzy Thinking* (Hyperion, 1993) and Darling's *Zen Physics* (HarperCollins, 1996) explore the impact of Zen ideas at the cutting edge of modern science, and Hagen's *How the World Can Be the Way It Is* (Theosophical House, 1995) makes clear the interaction between Buddhist thought and the view of reality emerging from quantum mechanics—a tremendously stimulating and enjoyable volume.

Beyond reading, you may wish to practice zazen. A traditional meditation cushion (*zafu*) and mat (*zabuton*) will make this easier. You might also want to locate a Zen center and try practicing Zen under the guidance of a qualified teacher. If you cannot find one in your area, a handy reference is Morreale's *Buddhist America* (John Muir, 1988), which in addition to giving addresses and descriptions of numerous centers contains many interesting articles.

# *Personality Theory in Perspective*

## *Your Goals for This Chapter*

1. Compare different personality theories in terms of their emphasis on philosophy, science, and art.

2. Compare different personality theories in terms of their stand on some basic philosophical issues.

3. Discuss the history of the terms *psyche* and *psychology* from their origins in Greek thought to their present-day use.

4. Indicate how Western psychology has narrowed the definition of *empirical*. Explain how the scientific method may separate us from experience rather than illuminate it.

5. Describe some signs of change on the horizon.

6. Explain why it is important to conceive of personality theories as philosophy and art as well as science.

T his final chapter seeks to place the personality theories we have studied into perspective by making some comparisons and contrasts among them and by pointing to a problem in contemporary personality theorizing, suggesting a view toward the future.

# Personality Theories

Although personality theories are a branch of academic scientific psychology, they also entail philosophy and art. As scientists, personality theorists seek to develop workable hypotheses that enable us to understand human behavior. As philosophers, personality theorists seek to give us insight into what it means to be a person. As artists, personality theorists seek to apply what is known about people and behavior to foster a better life. Some critics evaluate theories simply in terms of their efficacy as science. Yet, as we have seen, few of the theories described in this text demonstrate purely scientific concerns. This text has described a variety of theories ranging from Freud's emphasis on the ego to Eastern psychology's denial of it. Most theories reflect a great variety of concerns and need to be evaluated in terms of the criteria that suit their goals.

Some of the theories we have considered clearly reflect philosophical concerns. The psychoanalytic tradition, for instance, tends to be philosophical, rather than scientific, in its approach. Psychoanalytic theorists, by and large, are clinicians who develop their theoretical structures within the context of therapy. Although their methods and results are frequently empirical, that is, based on observation, they could not be described as rigorous or precise scientific techniques. Psychoanalytic theorists tend to consider proof as arising from the internal consistency of a theory and the ability of the theory to illumine the human condition. Their work is ultimately evaluated in terms of its coherence, relevance, comprehensiveness, and compellingness. The theories of Sigmund Freud, Carl Jung, Alfred Adler, Erich Fromm, and Rollo May represent a deep commitment to an underlying philosophy of life. More recent psychoanalytic theorists appreciate the need to validate their constructs and are thus open to scientific test. But psychoanalytic theory remains largely philosophical. This is best seen in the work of Erik Erikson who did not insist on a scientific pretense for his work but tried to make his philosophical assumptions explicit.

Other theories make a greater effort to be successful scientific theories. Behavior and learning theories are expressly scientific in their approach. Committed to a rigorous methodology, behavior and learning theories shun theoretical speculation in favor of careful observation and experimentation. Thus, John Dollard and Neal Miller emphasized empirical research in their efforts to combine psychoanalytic theory with the behaviorist tradition. B. F. Skinner's view also evolved from experimental laboratory investigations. This emphasis has continued in the work of cognitive and social learning theorists, like Albert Bandura and Julian Rotter, whose theories are superb examples of a rigorous scientific approach to personality. Their methodologies have produced precise and economical theories and have given strong empirical support to their constructs. Psychometric trait theories also demonstrate a deep commitment to scientific methodologies and validating evidence; Raymond Cattell, Hans Eysenck, and the Big Five theorists are also excellent examples of theorists who try to comprehend personality through a scientific model.

Some theorists deliberately seek an interdisciplinary approach. Henry A. Murray was one of the first to recognize the value of an interdisciplinary methodology; the diagnostic council that he established at Harvard was unprecedented in its vision and scope. Jung, Fromm, Gordon Allport, and Abraham Maslow all drew upon several areas of research—art, literature, history, philosophy, and science—in their efforts to understand human nature. Carl Rogers very carefully distinguished between his philosophical assumptions and his scientific hypotheses, emphasizing the need for a balanced view.

Other theories are primarily concerned with the art of personality theory, or the practical applications. We saw how Eastern thinkers do not seek to demonstrate the validity of their constructs or engage in philosophical speculation; rather, they are concerned with offering a variety of practices for cultivating a deeper understanding of the self. Likewise, Ellis, Beck, and Lazarus are best known for their contributions in the area of counseling. Freud, Horney, Adler, Rogers, and Kelly also made substantial contributions to the understanding and practice of psychotherapy.

None of the personality theories that we have studied can be appropriately labeled as simply philosophy, science, or art. For instance, although behavior and learning theories largely seek to present a scientific conception of personality, they also reflect basic philosophical assumptions that influence their scientific hypotheses and their practical applications.

Initially, behavior and learning theorists were unable to recognize the philosophical roots of their approach. In recent years, however, they have acknowledged the philosophical assumptions that undergird their work. It is now widely recognized that even the most scientific approach to understanding personality addresses philosophical questions and suggests philosophical answers. Indeed, the basic difference among personality theories appears to be one of philosophical stance.

## Philosophical Issues

Personality theories, then, can be compared in terms of where they stand on each of the basic philosophical issues outlined in Chapter 1.

For example, theorists differ as to whether they believe people are basically free to control their own behavior or whether they believe that behavior is essentially determined by forces over which people have little, if any, control. Both Freud and Skinner saw the individual as determined but for very different reasons. For Freud, the individual is motivated by internal unconscious forces. For Skinner, the individual is shaped by forces within the environment. Theorists also differ in the extent to which they would like their theories to be used to cultivate freedom in human nature or to exercise greater control over it. Skinner sought to develop a technology to control human behavior, whereas Rogers tried to increase a client's sense of freedom and responsibility.

As we have seen, another of the most puzzling questions in personality theorizing has been the dichotomy between hereditary and environmental determinants of behavior. Theorists differ over whether they believe that inborn characteristics or factors in the environment have the more important influence on a person's behavior. Dispositional theorists stress the importance of long-term personality traits in understanding behavior; behaviorists emphasize stiuational factors. These philosophical differences also lead to different recommendations for action. An emphasis on inborn factors sometimes leads to the support of selective breeding; an emphasis on situational factors may lead to efforts to change the environment. Thus, Cattell urged consideration of *eugenics,* the study of improving hereditary qualities by genetic control, and Bandura encouraged *euthenics,* the study of advancing human life by improving living conditions. The most recent theories stress an interactionist and biosocial view.

A third major issue is that of uniqueness versus universality. Allport clearly grappled with this issue. On one hand he recognized that common traits permit us to make generalizations and comparisons among individuals, but in the final analysis he held that each individual is particular and unique. Eastern theories point out that we need to see through the illusion of individual existence, called maya. Jung described a twofold process of individuation and transcendence.

Proaction versus reaction is a fourth dimension that influences personality theories. Allport discovered in a study of psychological terms with the prefixes *re-* and *pro-* that most theories tend to be reactive. Concepts such as "repression" and "regression" in psychoanalysis and "reflex" and "reinforcement" in stimulus-response theory suggest an emphasis on the past and a preoccupation with homeostasis. Humanist theories, on the other hand, suggest that the human being is motivated toward heterostasis, that is, growth and self-actualization. Cognitive theories also emphasize the present and the future rather than the past, viewing the individual as purposeful and active rather than passive.

Finally, personality theories can be compared according to whether they are optimistic or pessimistic about the possibility of change. Freud is generally seen as a pessimist because he believed that adult behavior is deeply structured by early childhood. Dispositional theorists believe that some constitutional factors place firm limits on personality change. Behavior and learning, cognitive, and humanist theorists, on the other hand, are usually very optimistic concerning the possibility of change.

These basic issues are typically presented as bipolar dimensions. However, Rollo May reminded us that they are actually paradoxes of human existence that seek resolution in a creative synthesis. An either/or position is generally misleading. Personality theorists must avoid being impaled on either horn of the dilemma as they try to reflect the truth of human existence.

In any event, a response to a theorist can take one of three forms. We can agree with the theorist and adopt his or her philosophical categories as part of our scientific activity. We can object to a theorist's own philosophical grounds and maintain that another view is more compelling. Or, we can maintain that none of these views is adequate. If we adopt the third position, we are then faced with the responsibility of suggesting an alternative philosophical framework that provides a more convincing model for understanding personality.

## The Challenge of Contemporary Personality Theorizing

Although psychology is a young science, it represents the oldest of human concerns. Our Western tradition initially fostered a mystical view of the self, emphasizing the spiritual side of the person. The effort to comprehend the human personality within the framework of a scientific methodology is largely the recent product of the twentieth century.

The term *psychology* comes from the ancient Greek word *psyche,* first introduced by the poet Homer to express the essence of a human being, or "the self." During the early Christian era, as philosophy and rhetoric replaced poetry and mythology, the term *psyche* came to be identified with *pneuma,* or "spirit." It later became identified with the more rationalistic and intellectual concept of *nous,* or "mind." By the time of the Enlightenment, "psyche" had become synonymous with consciousness or mental processes. As we have seen, John Watson, the founder of behaviorism, subsequently pointed out that states of consciousness are not objectively verifiable. He deemed them unfit as data for science and encouraged psychologists simply to study behavior. Under Watson's leadership, psychology was transformed from the largely introspective study of consciousness into the study of overt or observable behaviors. Thus, in the typical American university a strange situation prevailed throughout most of the twentieth century. Students of psychology discovered that, for the most part, they were not engaged in the study of the psyche; they were engaged in the study of behavior.

Behaviorism came to be the dominant position of psychology in American universities. Psychologists sought to pursue psychology as an experimental science that emulated the natural science of physics. The mainstream of American psychology still tends to emphasize extrospective observation and a rigorous scientific methodology. This emphasis is found in the cognitive approach, which has superseded behaviorism as the dominant trend.

Not all of the personality theorists that we have considered agree that a rigorous scientific method is the best way to understand personality. Indeed, some (Allport, Maslow, Rogers, and May, for example) have been very critical of the narrow view of psychology as an experimental science. Their critiques have fostered trends toward a more humanistic approach and an interest in alternative means of studying the person.

Unfortunately, however, humanistic psychology became a "divisive force." Psychologists tend to be divided as to whether they belong to a "humanistic" or a "scientific" camp. Thus, "the early promise of this approach, as emphasized by Abraham Maslow and Carl Rogers, was never realized in the mainstream of psychology" (Ornstein, 1977; see also Boneau, 1992). Humanistic psychology and mainstream psychology share the same problem: How do we overcome the tension between the demands of good science and the demands of the subject matter (Giorgi, 1987)?

The behaviorist and cognitive positions, with their emphasis on extrospective observation and experimental research, continue to represent the strongest and most predominant modes of psychological study in the American academy today. Those theorists who choose not to imitate the mainstream run the risk of being considered less respectable because of their lack of allegiance to a purely scientific approach and methodology. They are tolerated, particularly when they are willing to subject their findings to scientific scrutiny, but their theories are not fully recognized as sound.

We have seen that the keynote of science is observation. Scientific theories rest on empirical data, that which is based on experience. In Western psychology, however, the term *empirical* has been rendered practically synonymous with "relying on or derived from extrospective observation." Empirical data have been largely limited to objective findings. Other data of experience or observation, such as subjective introspection, have been discouraged or depreciated, largely because it is so difficult to test these findings experimentally.

Historical, philosophical, and mythological data, because they invariably entail subjective as well as objective elements, are often viewed as incompatible with science. According to this conception, a competent scientist generally does not permit subjective assumptions to interfere with his or her work. The scientist remains detached, objective, and value free, which Maslow and Fromm said is an error. As a result, Western psychology has tended to isolate itself. It has divorced itself from other possible modes of investigation on the grounds that their findings, because they are difficult to test experimentally, are not objective and are therefore incompatible with science.

David Bakan has pointed out that the rigorous scientific methodology of the Western experimental psychologist may, at times, actually stand in the way of the empirical and divorce us from experience rather than illuminate it (1969). In a well-developed experiment the experimenter does not deal with the everyday world; instead, she or he creates a **paraworld** of quantified, logico-mathematical imaginary constructs. In this paraworld, events are carefully chosen and precisely controlled in order to avoid the haphazard occurrences of the everyday world that might jeopardize the results. Further, in a well-designed experiment all the possible alternatives and outcomes are anticipated in advance. The experimenter can predict within limits what is going to happen as a result of the manipulation of the variables in the experiment. And so the more carefully designed an experiment is, the more separate it becomes from the world of experience that it seeks to clarify. The Western psychologist's reliance on a rigid experimental method may, therefore, interfere with the possibility of learning from experience.

The emphasis on extrospection and rigorous scientific methodology also limits the findings of psychology to those that can be demonstrated within the experimental laboratory. It circumscribes the study of personality to merely those aspects about the person that can be comprehended in specifically scientific terms. Because of this, many questions about the ultimate meaning, purpose, and goal of human living, questions that traditionally have been and could be included in the study of personality, and are addressed by some theorists, are ruled out of inquiry.

Few theories of personality resemble an ideal scientific theory. Their assumptions lack explicitness, making it difficult for us to derive empirical statements that would permit us to move from abstract theory to empirical observation. Many personality theories, although provocative, have failed to generate a significant amount of research, thus depriving us of some of the "most important evaluative comparison" that can be made among theories (Hall & Lindzey, 1978; see also Hall, Lindzey, & Campbell, 1998). And yet, those personality theories that successfully emulate a scientific model can be criticized as gaining their precision, accuracy, and predictive power at the price of evoking little depth of insight or new understanding.

In part, the problem results from the fact that theories of personality explore phenomena that by their very nature elude a narrow definition of science. At the heart of the experimental method is the search for cause and effect. Theories that emphasize motivation or free will make it difficult to look for underlying causes and limit the possibility of prediction and control. Moreover, they call into question the value of experimentation as a primary means of gaining insight into the human condition.

We need to recall that American psychology struggled valiantly to become a respectable science. This struggle entailed severing its early ties with philosophy and modeling itself along the lines of the natural sciences. Sound training in experimental design and statistical methods characterize the curriculum of academic psychology. Because of the earlier struggle to gain recognition as a science, many psychologists, particularly those with a behaviorist orientation, are suspicious of recent efforts by personality theorists to defy strict scientific methodology and reassert the philosophical character of psychology.

As a result, much of the current research in personality is fragmented (cf. Magnusson & Törestad, 1993; Sarason, 1989) and isolated (Ehrenreich, 1997), limited to a special domain that can be precisely defined, articulated, measured, and tested. Feshbach (1984) suggested that "the study of personality has not moved in the direction of actualization; rather it appears to have become constricted, dissociated, and overly defensive." A particular variable, such as locus of control, need to achieve, or cognitive style, is isolated for study, leading to a multiplicity of interesting and reliable empirical findings.

Many current texts in personality, after providing a brief introduction to theories, concentrate on major research issues such as intelligence, anxiety and stress, perceived control, aggression, altruism, sex roles, and gender differences. But as May reminded us, contemporary psychological research is preoccupied with data and numbers at the expense of theory. The most important scientific discoveries were not made by accumulating facts but by perceiving relationships among the facts (1983). Retief (1986) points out that "data and methods, no matter how profuse and sophisticated they may be, can lead nowhere on their own: it is obvious that good theories are needed to guide them. . . . Psychology has made a firm commitment to method: the time for an equal commitment to theory is overdue." Human nature can be understood only within a theoretical framework. The real contribution lies in seeing a new *form* that avoids the misconceptions of an existing mythology (see also Noble, 1993).

A new framework is needed within which the study of personality can develop into a more cumulative science (Shoda & Mischel, 1996). Recently, McAdams (1996a; see also 1995, 1996b), whose work was described in Chapter 6, has suggested an integrative framework of three levels for studying personality: personality traits, goals and motives, and personal life stories. He believes that his framework will enable us to place recent advances in the study of personality within the cultural context of modernity. As time goes on, it will be interesting to see the response to this effort to provide a comprehensive new theory.

The reluctance to reassert the philosophical character of psychology to some extent reflects a realistic fear that our present disillusionment with science may foster a tendency to disregard the substantial contributions that it has made to our understanding. We developed the experimental method as a tool because we discovered that we could increase our understanding and act more efficiently if our activities were guided by information about the determined aspects of our everyday world. Although it may be true that the experimental method cannot establish truth, it has provided a very pragmatic means of testing some of our assumptions.

Still, we should recognize that a purely experimental approach is not the only option available to the personality theorist and we should be aware of the effects of a narrow scientific conception of psychology. Moreover, we must not allow the popularity of the experimental approach in the American academy to close our eyes to the importance of other methods or to the reality of the phenomena that other methods draw to our attention. We should seek a higher perspective in which science and philosophy are no longer in opposition to one another but complement each other.

Many contemporary personality theorists urge us to be *more*, not less, empirical— that is, *more* empirical in the original sense of the term, "based on experience." They point out that our traditional scientific methods may not only fail to do justice to the experiential data but may also camouflage it. They suggest that when we limit our analysis to those phenomena that can be comprehended in terms of current experimental methodology, we prejudice our results. By becoming "less scientistic," psychology could become "more scientific" (Bakan, 1969).

Although psychology represents the oldest of human concerns, the science of psychology and the effort to comprehend the human personality within the framework of a scientific methodology is largely a product of the twentieth century. We have seen (in Chapter 1) that Wilhelm Wundt conceived of psychology as an experimental science that ought to emulate the natural science of physics. Psychology may have failed as a scientific enterprise because it did not develop its own methodology but borrowed it from the physical sciences (Kruger, 1986). Many psychologists have been moving away from the social sciences toward the biological sciences and clinical practice. This has led to an increased isolation of scientific psychology from the insights and problems of other social sciences (Harzem, 1987). In contemporary sciences from biology to physics, the concept of *pattern* has replaced earlier concepts, such as cause and effect, as the key principle of explanation. Psychology has yet to incorporate that view (Rychlak, 1986).

There are signs of change on the horizon. Rychlak (1981) and Valentine (1988) argue for a teleological (goal-oriented) perspective. Motivation has reemerged as a central player in personality theory (Pervin, 1996). The renewed interest in idiographic methods of research is heartening. In 1988, the *Journal of Personality* devoted an entire issue to psychobiography and life narratives. These are contemporary forms of case histories and studies of the unique life stories of individuals such as those explored by Freud, Erikson, Murray, and Allport. MacIntyre (1984) has suggested that narrative history may be "the basic and essential genre for the characterization of human actions." Davidson (1987) suggests that if psychology reconceives itself as based on an analysis of motivational/intentional relations, it will place itself in a closer and more appropriate relationship to the sociocultural sciences than to the physical sciences. McClelland (1996) points out that when the study of personality is expanded to include topics such as values, motives, and life stories, it becomes a much more exciting area to explore.

The narrative form is increasingly being seen as the most appropriate form for understanding the construction of self in a postmodern era (Atkinson, 1990; Freeman, 1992; McAdams, 1995, 1996a, 1996b; Miller, Potts, Fung, & Hoogstra, 1990). "Instances of cultural diversity take on a different hue when viewed from a narrative perspective" (Howard, 1991). A study of Japanese children's personal narratives may help us to understand how those children are trained in empathy (Minami & McCabe, 1991). Gardner (1992) suggests that psychology turn toward literature and other artistic studies in an effort to help understand issues such as self, will, consciousness, and personality. His suggestion has stirred considerable discussion (see Markova, 1992; Oatley, 1992; Potter & Wetherell, 1992; Sternberg, 1992; and Woodward, 1992). Students of personality would do well to emulate van Krogten's interpretive-theoretical research method modeled in his *Proustian Love* (1992), in which he presents a complex theory on the psychology of love built on principles originating from a study of Proust's *Remembrance of Things Past*. "The stories we live by" (McAdams, 1993) and the scientific method itself (Suchecki, 1989) are being seen as mythical texts.

Mahers (1991) has argued that the meager real increase in our understanding of the psychology of personality in recent years may be due to methodological procedures and our underlying notion of human behavior. These notions and procedures induced us to "invent artificial problems to solve" instead of focusing on real ones, "namely the identification of the processes that govern" human behavior "in the natural habitat" (1991). As psychologists increasingly argue that psychology needs to be relevant, to "adequately explain the immediate causes influencing people's lives" (Retief, 1989), and to take a proactive role in helping us to understand our values and moral development in a postmodern society (Neufeldt, 1989; Packer, 1992), narrative thought is being seen as a major form of cognition and an important part of moral education (Vitz, 1990).

No more can we assume that science considers facts and ethics considers values living in different domains. Ethics are the result of social life and need to be studied "in their own right." "When we do this, the outlines of a different kind of ethical justification becomes apparent, one that legitimatizes multiple objective moralities rather than a universal moral system" (Packer, 1992).

As we focus on cultural diversity, we also must recognize that ideas such as actualization, individuation, and autonomy and the psychotherapies rooted in them are not apt to be immediately germane to other portions of U.S. society or to people who relate to diverse other societies that do not cultivate or prize these notions. Many theories of personality "imply that their stance is apolitical, while in actuality, they serve a highly political function—in service of the continued acceptance of the specifically patriarchal status quo of present society in the United States" (Lerman, 1992). Sexism and racism as ideologies that try to justify white male supremacy need to be challenged (Anderson, 1991). We need to specifically ask of personality theories whether they embrace the diversity and complexity of women and other minorities and insist that they begin to address those issues (Espin & Gawelek, 1992). As technologies are increasing our communication with people of diverse cultures and values, we need to recognize that "there is no distinct American identity. America exists as it does because of the relationships of which it is a part" (Gergen, 1992).

Burkitt (1991) suggests that we try to understand people as social selves rather than self-contained individuals. It may be desirable to develop indigenous psychologies more appropriate to various cultures (Naidu, 1991; Puhan & Sahoo, 1991) or at least a pluralistic psychology aiming to transform dehumanizing social contexts (O'Hara, 1992).

Concentration on the biological basis of personality will also increase. As we turn to genetics and neurobiology we will be looking at temperament or traits that are innate and explore how these are changed by social and developmental events (Woodall & Matthews, 1993). An evolutionary perspective will also be apparent, looking at how personality traits adapt and have helped to ensure the survival of the human race (Buss, 1991). Personality theory cannot afford to ignore principles derived from genetics, biology, and evolution (Epstein, 1996). Indeed, contemporary personality theories are more "threatened" by developments in neuropsychology, biochemistry, and computer technology than by rival personality theories (Loevinger, 1996).

The spirit of the new physics combats the estrangement and segmentation of life in the twentieth century and supplants it with a view of reality in which the human consciousness is just one form of consciousness within a wider cosmic consciousness. Such a quantum worldview goes beyond the two poles of individual and relationship by demonstrating that human beings can only be the persons they are within a framework. "The quantum self thus mediates between the extreme isolation of Western individualism and the extreme collectivism of Marxism or Western mysticism" (Zohar, 1991). A therapeutic universal narrative is now coming into consciousness from many diverse fields of science and telling us that it is futile to be disconnected. The cosmos is "one system of which we're one part integrated into the totality. . . . The fate of the earth is our fate as we're part of the same totality" (Coelho, 1993).

Boneau (1992) predicts students and faculty will be leaving psychology "to become interdisciplinary cognitive scientists and neuroscientists." However, he adds, these subjects are only concerned with parts of a larger picture. We "need to have a science of humanity, a discipline concerned with understanding and explaining the human individual coping in a social-cultural-environmental context? . . . That is not what psychology is now, but perhaps it should be."

It is not wise for a field of investigation that claims to explore the human condition to refuse to deal with a wide variety of concepts and data simply because they are difficult to state in narrow, preconceived scientific terms. The crises in living that we face today mandate that we marshal whatever means are available to assist us in self-understanding. A true portrait of personality must come to terms with all the experiences that are central to being a person, even though they may be difficult to conceptualize, test, or express. Lopsided theories err not simply because they present us incomplete portraits that are often biased or stereotyped but because they fail to develop concepts that adequately represent human potential. In doing so, lopsided theories deprive us of important aspects of our own consciousness.

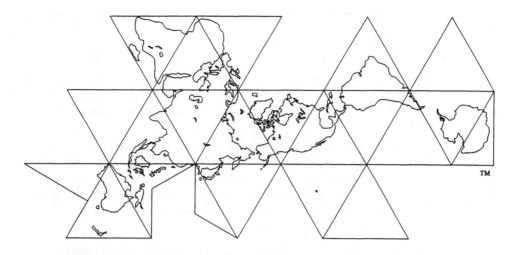

**FIGURE C.1    Dymaxion Map**

Here is a map that seeks to portray more accurately the world that we all share.
*(SOURCE: The Buckminster Fuller Institute owns all rights in and to the Dymaxion™
Map design. The word Dymaxion and the Dymaxion Map design are trademarks of The
Buckminster Fuller Institute. The Map is also copyrighted by The Buckminster Fuller
Institute, 1983, 1967 & 1982. All rights reserved. The Dymaxion World Map, invented by
Buckminster Fuller, shows our planet without any visible distortion of the relative shapes
and sizes of the land and sea areas, and without any breaks in the continental contours.
The Dymaxion Map is used here by permission. Additional information and maps
available through the Buckminster Fuller Institute, 1743 South La Cienega Blvd.,
Los Angeles, CA 90035 (213) 837-7710.)*

This book has suggested that personality theorizing invariably entails more than
science; it also involves philosophy and art. Every activity that we engage in rests on certain
philosophical assumptions. Contemporary personality theorizing is tied to and limited by
certain assumptions that characterize our view of the world. Frequently, these assumptions
are implicit rather than explicit; that is, they are not clearly recognized. Nevertheless, they
profoundly influence our concept of the world and its inhabitants. Only by making our assumptions explicit and continually re-examining them can we place ourselves in a better
position to understand ourselves. Herein lies the value of the scientific method: it has provided us with a means of testing and consensually validating our theoretical speculations.
What we need to do is twofold. We need to evaluate our philosophical assumptions in the
light of contemporary scientific information and to judge our scientific findings in the light
of their adequacy as philosophy. In the final analysis, however, neither the speculations of
science nor the speculations of philosophy can express the ultimate meaning of personality.
The ultimate expression of personality does not lie in the constructs of science or psychology. It lies in the art of living.

# Summary

1. Personality theories can be compared in terms of their emphasis on philosophy, science, and art. For example, psychoanalytic theories tend to emphasize philosophy, whereas behavior and learning theories emphasize science.

2. They can also be compared in terms of where they stand on basic philosophical issues, like freedom versus determinism, heredity versus environment, uniqueness versus universality, proactive versus reactive emphases, and optimism versus pessimism. For instance, humanist theories stress an individual's responsibility and free will; psychoanalytic and behaviorist theories see the individual as determined.

3. Although psychology is a young science, it represents one of the oldest human concerns. The term *psyche* is an ancient Greek term that originally referred to "the self." Later it came to mean "spirit" and, finally, "mind." Through the influence of the behaviorist movement, *psychology* came to be the study of behavior, emphasizing a rigorous scientific method based on extrospective observation.

4. In Western psychology the term *empirical* has been rendered synonymous with "relying on or derived from extrospective observation." The rigorous scientific methodology of the Western experimental psychologist may at times tend to divorce us from experience, rather than illumine it, by separating us from the everyday world.

5. Some signs of change are the emphasis on the narrative form, the introduction of values, an emphasis on cultural diversity, and a possible reconceptualization of psychology.

6. Personality theories need to be seen as philosophy, science, and art in order to do justice to the full range of human existence and potentiality.

## Suggestions for Further Reading

For additional information on problems in current psychological research, see David Bakan, *On Method: Toward a Reconstruction of Psychological Investigation* (Jossey-Bass, 1969). Bakan points out that our enormous expenditures on psychological research are not yielding much new information. He suggests ways in which psychology might become "more scientific" and "less scientistic."

The following three books were previously recommended in conjunction with the Introduction; they are again suggested as invaluable for the student who is interested in pursuing personality theory in greater depth: Joseph Rychlak, *A Philosophy of Science for Personality Theory* (Houghton Mifflin, 1968); T. S. Kuhn, *The Structure of Scientific Revolu-*

*tions,* 2nd ed. (University of Chicago Press, 1970); and I. Chein, *The Science of Behavior and the Image of Man* (Basic Books, 1972).

More recent books include Danah Zohar in collaboration with I. N. Marshall, *The Quantum Self: Human Nature and Consciousness Defined by the New Physics* (Morrow, 1990) and Ian Burkitt, *Social Selves: Theories of the Social Formation of Personality* (Sage, 1991). Igor van Krogten's interpretive-theoretical research method is described in *Proustian Love* (Swets & Zeitlinger, B. V. Amsterdam/Lisse, 1992).

# Glossary

**A-B-C theory of personality** In Ellis's rational emotive behavior therapy, the theory that a highly charged *emotional consequence* (C) is caused not by a significant *activation event* (A), but by the individual's *belief system* (B).

**acceptance** A nonjudgmental recognition of oneself, others, and the world.

**active imagination** In Jung's psychotherapy, a method for getting in touch with the archetypes.

**affective arousal** The arousal of emotions in conjunction with cognitions.

**alayavijnana** Sanskrit for the storehouse consciousness, the last of the eight consciousnesses.

**alienation** In Horney's theory, a state in which the real self and the idealized self are disjunct.

**amplification** In Jungian therapy, an analytical method whereby one focuses repeatedly on an element and gives multiple associations to it.

**anal stage** One of Freud's psychosexual stages, in which the major source of pleasure and conflict is the anus.

**analytical psychology** The school of psychology founded by Carl Jung.

**anatta** Pali for non-selfness, the lack of a permanent separate self, one of the three characteristics of existence in Buddhism.

**androgyny** The presence of both masculine and feminine qualities in an individual and the ability to realize both potentials.

**anicca** Pali for impermanence and transiency, one of the three characteristics of existence according to the Buddha.

**anima** In Jung's theory, an archetype representing the feminine side of the male personality.

**animus** In Jung's theory, an archetype representing the masculine side of the female personality.

**anxiety** An emotional state characterized by a vague fear or premonition that something undesirable may happen. In May's theory, the apprehension cued off by a threat to some value that the individual holds as essential to his or her existence as a person.

**archetype** In Jung's theory, a universal thought form or predisposition to perceive the world in certain ways.

**assessment** Evaluation or measurement.

**atman** Sanskrit for soul, self, or ego.

**attitude** A positive or negative feeling toward an object. a) In Jung's theory, a basic psychotype. b) In Cattell's theory, a surface dynamic trait.

**authoritarian ethics** In Fromm's theory, a value system whose source lies outside the individual.

**authoritariansim** In Fromm's theory, a way of escaping from freedom by adhering to a new form of submission or domination.

**autoeroticism** Self-love. In Freud's theory, the child's sexual activity.

**automaton conformity** In Fromm's theory, a way of escaping from freedom by adopting the personality proffered by one's culture.

**autonomous dimension** In Beck's theory, a personality dimension characterized by independence.

**autonomous self** In Kohut's theory, an ideal self with qualities of self-esteem and self-confidence.

**autonomy versus shame and doubt** Erikson's psychosocial stage, corresponding to Freud's anal stage, in which the child faces the task of developing control over his or her body and bodily activities.

**autotelic** Containing its own goal, an activity done for its own sake.

**avoiding type** In Adler's theory, people who try to escape life's problems and who engage in little socially constructive activity.

**basic anxiety** In Horney's theory, feelings of insecurity in which the environment as a whole is dreaded because it is seen as unrealistic, dangerous, unappreciative, and unfair.

**basic evil** In Horney's theory, all of the negative factors in the environment that can provoke insecurity in a child.

**BASIC-ID** In Lazarus's theory, an examination of the seven modalities, behavior, affect, sensation, imagery, cognition, interpersonal relationships, and drugs, that make up human personality.

**basic needs therapy** Therapeutic procedures that seek to meet the primary needs of people.

**basic orientations** In Horney's theory, fundamental modes of interaction with the world.

489

**Beck Depression Inventory** An instrument developed by Beck to measure depression.

**behavior** The activity of an organism. a) In learning theory, a response to stimuli. b) In Rogers's theory, the goal-directed attempt of the organism to meet its needs as it perceives them.

**behavior modification** A form of therapy that applies the principles of learning to achieve changes in behavior.

**behavior potential** In Rotter's theory, a variable that refers to the likelihood that a particular behavior will occur.

**behavior therapy** a) A form of therapy that aims to eliminate symptoms of illness through learning new responses. b) In Ellis's theory, helping clients change maladaptive patterns of behavior and their cognition.

**behaviorism** A movement in psychology founded by John Watson, who suggested that psychologists should focus their attention on the study of overt behavior.

**being mode** In Fromm's theory, a way of life that depends solely on the fact of existence.

**Big Five** Five primary factors that typically surface from personality questionnaires and inventories: openness, conscientiousness, extraversion, agreeableness, and neuroticism.

**biophilia hypothesis** In Wilson's theory, an intense need to belong to the rest of the living world.

**biophilous character** In Fromm's theory, a character orientation that is synonymous with the productive orientation.

**B-needs** A term used by Maslow to refer to being needs that arise from the organism's drive to self-actualize and fulfill its potential.

**bodhisattva** Sanskrit for "enlightenment being," a person who has vowed not to accept final liberation from suffering until all sentient beings are liberated; the ideal of the Mahayana tradition.

**bodily self** In Allport's theory, a propriate function that entails coming to know one's body limits.

**Bompu Zen** Zen practiced for a profit, such as stress management or increased mental health.

**borderline patients** In Kernberg's theory, patients with oral tendencies but also powerful aggressive tendencies.

**bridging** A multimodal technique used by counselors to deliberately begin work in terms of their client's preferred modality.

**Buddha** "Awake" or "enlightened one." One who has fully awakened to the Turth.

**cardinal disposition** In Allport's theory, a personal disposition so pervasive that almost every behavior of an individual appears to be influenced by it.

**castration anxiety** In Freud's theory, the child's fear of losing the penis.

**catharsis** An emotional release that occurs when an idea is brought to consciousness and allowed expression.

**central disposition** In Allport's theory, a highly characteristic tendency of an individual.

**central relational paradox** The phenomenon by which people who have experienced trouble in relationships continue to try to make new connections but are hindered in doing so.

**cerebrotonia** In Sheldon's theory, a component of temperament characterized by a predominance of restraint, inhibition, and the desire for concealment.

**choleric** One of Hippocrates' temperaments, referring to an individual who tends to be irascible and violent.

**classical conditioning** A form of learning in which a response becomes associated with a previously neutral stimulus.

**client-centered psychotherapy** A therapeutic technique developed by Rogers that focuses attention on the person seeking help.

**closed system** A concept of personality that admits little or nothing new from outside the organism to influence or change it in any significant way.

**cognition** The process of knowing.

**cognitions** In Beck's theory, a person's awareness.

**cognitive complexity** The ability to perceive differences in the way in which one construes other people.

**cognitive distortions** In Beck's theory, systematic errors in reasoning.

**cognitive neuroscience** A field that concentrates on how mental activities occur in the brain.

**cognitive theories** Theories of personality that emphasize cognitive processes such as thinking and judging.

**cognitive therapy** In Ellis's theory, showing clients how to recognize their "should" and "must" thoughts, how to separate rational from irrational beliefs, and how to accept reality.

**cognitive triad** In Beck's theory, the depressed individual has a negative view of the self, the world, and the future.

**coherence** One of the criteria for judging philosophical statements: the quality or state of logical consistency.

**collective unconscious** In Jung's theory, a shared, transpersonal unconscious consisting of potential ways of being human.

**common traits**  In Allport's theory, hypothetical traits that permit us to compare individuals according to certain shared dimensions.

**compatibility**  A criterion for evaluating rival hypotheses: the agreement of the hypothesis with other previously well-established information.

**compellingness**  One of the criteria for evaluating philosophical statements: the quality of appealing to someone with a driving force.

**compensation**  Making up for or overcoming a weakness.

**compensatory function**  In Jung's theory, an effort to complement one's conscious side and speak for the unconscious.

**compensatory mechanisms**  In Adler's theory, safeguarding tendencies that ward off feelings of inferiority.

**complex**  In Jung's theory, an organized group of thoughts, feelings, and memories about a particular concept.

**comprehensiveness**  One of the criteria for evaluating philosophical statements: the quality of having a broad scope or range and depth of coverage.

**conditional positive regard**  In Rogers's theory, positive regard that is given only under certain circumstances.

**conditioned response**  A response that becomes associated with a stimulus through learning.

**conditioned stimulus**  A previously neutral stimulus that becomes associated with a response.

**conditions of worth**  In Rogers's theory, stipulations imposed by other people indicating when an individual will be given positive regard.

**conflict**  a) In Freud's theory, the basic incompatibility that exists among the id, ego, superego, and the external world. b) In Dollard and Miller's theory, frustration that arises from a situation in which incompatible responses occur at the same time.

**congruence**  In Rogers's theory, the state of harmony that exists when a person's symbolized experiences reflect the actual experiences of his or her organism.

**connections**  In relational/cultural theory, the basic origins of growth and development.

**conscience**  In Freud's theory, a subsystem of the superego that refers to the capacity for self-evaluation, criticism, and reproach.

**conscious**  In Freud's theory, the thoughts, feelings, and wishes that a person is aware of at any given moment.

**consensual validation**  Agreement among observers about phenomena.

**constellating power**  In Jung's theory, the power of a complex to admit new ideas into itself.

**constellatory construct**  In Kelly's theory, a construct that sets clear limits to the range of its elements but also permits them to belong to other realms.

**constitutional traits**  In Cattell's theory, traits that have their origin in heredity or the physiological condition of the organism.

**constructive alternativism**  In Kelly's theory, the assumption that any one event is open to a variety of interpretations.

**continuity theory**  A theory that suggests that the development of personality is essentially an accumulation of skills, habits, and discriminations without anything really new appearing in the make-up of the person.

**continuous reinforcement**  A schedule of reinforcement in which the desired behavior is reinforced every time it occurs.

**control group**  In an experiment, a group equally matched to the experimental group and used for comparison.

**conversion disorder**  A reaction to anxiety or stress expressed through physical symptoms; the modern term for hysteria.

**correlation**  A statistical tool for making comparisons by expressing the extent to which two events covary.

**covert behavior**  A behavior that can be observed directly only by the individual actually experiencing it.

**creative self**  In Adler's theory, that aspect of the person that interprets and makes meaningful the experiences of the organism and establishes the life-style.

**criterion analysis**  A method of analysis employed by Eysenck that begins with a hypothesis about possible variables and conducts statistical analyses in order to test the hypothesis.

**critical periods**  Periods during which an organism is highly responsive to certain influences that may enhance or disrupt its development.

**cue**  In Dollard and Miller's theory, a specific stimulus that tells the organism when, where, and how to respond.

**Daijo Zen**  Zen practiced for the sake of liberating others.

**daimonic**  In May's theory, any natural function that has the power to take over a person.

**defense mechanism**  In Freud's theory, a procedure that wards off anxiety and prevents its conscious perception.

**definition**  A statement that is true because of the way in which we have agreed to use words.

**delayed reinforcement**  Reinforcement that is delayed after a response.

**denial**  In Freud's theory, a defense mechanism that entails refusing to believe a reality or a fact of life.

**dependent origination**  The Buddhist concept of interconnected causality.

**dependent variable**  In an experiment, the behavior under study.

**destructiveness**  In Fromm's theory, a way of escaping from freedom by eliminating others and/or the outside world.

**determinism**  The philosophical view that behavior is controlled by external or internal forces and pressures.

**developmental line**  In A. Freud's theory, a series of id-ego interactions in which children increase ego mastery of themselves and their world.

**Dharma**  Sanskrit for the truth or law of the universe discovered by the Buddha; the Buddha's teaching.

**diagnostic profile**  A formal assessment procedure developed by Anna Freud that reflects developmental issues.

**directive**  A term used to describe therapies whose course is primarily structured by the therapist.

**disconnection**  The break that is experienced when a person cannot engage in mutually empathetic and empowering relationships.

**discontinuity theory**  A theory of personality that suggests that in the course of development an organism experiences genuine transformations or changes so that it reaches successively higher levels of organization.

**discrimination**  The learned ability to distinguish among different stimuli.

**displacement**  In Freud's theory, a defense mechanism in which one object of an impulse is substituted for another.

**D-needs**  A term used by Maslow to refer to deficiency needs that arise out of a lack.

**dream analysis**  A technique used by Freud and other analysts to uncover unconscious processes.

**dream work**  In Freud's theory, the process that disguises unconscious wishes and converts them into a manifest dream.

**drive**  The psychological correlate of a need or stimulus that impels an organism into action. a) In Freud's theory, a psychological representation of an inner bodily source of excitement characterized by its source, impetus, aim, and object. b) In Dollard and Miller's theory, the primary motivation for behavior.

**drive reduction**  A concept forumated by Hull that suggests that learning occurs only if an organism's response is followed by the reduction of some need or drive.

**dukkha**  Pali for suffering, dissatisfaction, imperfection, incompleteness; one of the three characteristics of existence according to the Buddha.

**dynamic traits**  In Cattell's theory, traits that motivate an individual toward some goal.

**eclectic**  Selecting the best from a variety of different theories or concepts.

**ego**  The self. a) In Freud's theory, a function of the personality that follows the reality principles and operates according to secondary processes and reality testing. b) In Jung's theory, one's conscious perception of self.

**ego-ideal**  In Freud's theory, a subsystem of the superego consisting of an ideal self-image.

**ego identity versus role confusion**  Erikson's psychosocial stage of adolescence in which one faces the task of developing a self-image.

**ego integrity versus despair**  Erikson's psychosocial stage of maturity that entails the task of being able to reflect on one's life with satisfaction.

**ego-psychoanalytic theory**  Psychoanalytic theory that emphasizes the role of the ego in personality development.

**Eightfold Path**  The Buddha's prescription for living constituting the fourth Noble Truth; the "Middle Way" leading to nirvana.

**Electra complex**  A term that some critics have used to express the feminine counterpart to the male Oedipus complex.

**emotionality versus stability**  One of Eysenck's personality dimensions, involving an individual's adjustment to the environment and the stability of his or her behavior over time.

**emotive-evocative therapy**  In Ellis's theory, helping clients to get in touch with their feelings.

**empathy**  The ability to recognize and understand another's feelings.

**empirical**  Based on experience and observation.

**empiricism**  The philosophical view that human knowledge arises slowly in the course of experience through observation and experiment.

**environmental-mold traits**  In Cattell's theory, traits that originate from the influences of physical and social surroundings.

**epiphany**  A usually sudden manifestation of the essential nature of something.

**equilibrium** Balance or harmony.

**Eros** In Freud's theory, life impulses or drives—forces that maintain life processes and ensure reproduction of the species.

**erg** In Cattell's theory, a constitutional dynamic trait.

**erogenous zones** Areas of the body that provide pleasure.

**essence** In philosophy, the unchangeable principles and laws that govern being.

**evaluative response** In Rogers's theory, a response that places a value judgment on thoughts, feelings, wishes, or behavior.

**evolutionary psychology** The branch of psychology that considers the impact of evolution on psychological mechanisms.

**expressive psychoanalytically oriented psychotherapy** Kernberg's method of treatment.

**existential dichotomy** In Fromm's theory, a dilemma or problem that arises simply from the fact of existence.

**existentialism** A philosophical movement that studies the meaning of existence.

**expectancy** In Rotter's theory, the individual's subjective expectation about the outcome of his or her behavior.

**experimental method** A scientific method involving a careful study of cause and effect by manipulating variables and observing their effects.

**exploitative orientation** In Fromm's theory, a character type in which a person exploits others and the world.

**expressive behavior** In Allport's theory, an individual's manner of performing.

**extinction** The tendency of a response to disappear when it is not reinforced.

**extrinsic** A quest that serves other purposes outside the original goal.

**extraversion** An attitude of expansion in which the psyche is oriented toward the external world.

**extraversion versus introversion** One of Eysenck's personality dimensions, involving the degree to which a person is outgoing and participative in relating to other people.

**factor analysis** Employed by Cattell, a procedure that interrelates many correlations at one time.

**falsification** The act of disproving.

**family atmosphere** In Adler's theory, the quality of emotional relationships among members of a family.

**family constellation** In Adler's theory, one's position within the family in terms of birth order among siblings and the presence or absence of parents and other caregivers.

**feeling** One of Jung's functions, involving valuing and judging the world.

**fictional finalism** In Adler's theory, a basic concept or philosophical assumption that cannot be tested against reality.

**finalism** In Adler's theory, a principle that reflects the concept of goal orientation.

**fixation** In Freud's theory, a concept in which there is an arrest of growth, and excessive needs characteristic of an earlier stage are created by overindulgence or undue frustration.

**fixed schedule of reinforcement** A schedule of reinforcement in which the time period or number of responses before reinforcement is identical.

**Four Noble Truths** The essence of the practical teaching of the Buddha, specifying the nature of suffering, its cause, its cessation, and the path to accomplish liberation from suffering.

**frame of orientation and object of devotion** In Fromm's thought, the need for a stable thought system by which to organize perceptions and make sense out of the environment.

**free association** In Freud's psychoanalysis, a technique in which a person verbalizes whatever comes to mind.

**freedom of movement** In Rotter's theory, the degree of expectation a person has that a particular set of responses will lead to a desired reinforcement.

**frustration** In Dollard and Miller's theory, an emotion that occurs when one is unable to satisfy a drive because the response that would satisfy it has been blocked.

**fully functioning program** A term used by Rogers to indicate an individual who is functioning at an optimum level.

**functional autonomy** In Allport's theory, a concept that present motives are not necessarily tied to the past but may be free of earlier motivations.

**functions** In Jung's theory, ways of perceiving the environment and orienting experiences.

**gassho** Japanese for "palms of the hands pressed together," expressing the unity of the person and the universe, a gesture commonly used for greeting in many cultures in the East.

**Gedo Zen** Zen practiced without connection to the Buddha's teachings, generally in order to attain mystical experiences.

**generalization** A statement that may be made, when a number of different instances coincide, that something is true about many or all of the members of a certain class.

**generalized conditioned reinforcers** In Skinner's theory, learned reinforcers that have the power to reinforce a great number of different behaviors.

**generativity versus stagnation** Erikson's psychosocial stage of the middle years, in which one faces the dilemma of being productive and creative in life.

**genital stage** Freud's final psychosexual stage, in which an individual reaches sexual maturity.

**genotype** The genetic makeup of an individual.

**genuineness** A therapist's attitude characterized by congruence and awareness in the therapeutic relationship.

**gestalt** Configuration or pattern that forms a whole.

**gestalt principle** The notion that the whole is more than the sum of its parts.

**gestalt psychology** A branch of psychology that studies how organisms perceive objects and events.

**getting type** In Adler's theory, dependent people who take rather than give.

**goal of superiority** In Adler's theory, the ultimate fictional finalism, entailing the desire to be competent and effective in whatever one strives to do and to actualize one's potential.

**gradient** The changing strength of a force, which may be plotted on a graph.

**habit** In Dollard and Miller's theory, the basic structure of personality: a learned association between a stimulus and response.

**habitual responses** In Eysenck's theory, clusters of specific behaviors that characteristically recur in similar circumstances, such as buying groceries or giving parties.

**having mode** In Fromm's theory, a way of existence that relies on possessions.

**heterostasis** The desire not to reduce tension, but to seek new stimuli and challenges that will further growth.

**heuristic value** The ability of a construct to predict future events.

**hierarchy of needs** Maslow's theory of five basic needs ranked in order of strength: physiological, safety, belonging and love, self-esteem, and self-actualization.

**hierarchy of response** In Dollard and Miller's theory, a tendency for certain responses to occur before other responses.

**Hinayana** Sanskrit for "small vehicle," a designation for the southern schools of Buddhism concerned with personal liberation. One of the two major divisions of Buddhism.

**historical dichotomy** In Fromm's theory, a dilemma or problem that arises out of human history because of various societies and cultures.

**hoarding orientation** In Fromm's theory, a character type in which the person seeks to save or hoard and protects him- or herself from the world by a wall.

**homeostasis** Balance or harmony.

**homosexuality** Primary attraction to the same sex.

**hormones** Chemicals released into the blood stream by the endocrine glands.

**hot cognitions** In Beck's therapy, experiencing arousing emotions and reality testing at the same time.

**humanist theories** Theories of personality that emphasize human potential.

**Humanistic Communitarian Socialism** The name of Fromm's ideal society.

**humanistic ethics** In Fromm's theory, a value system that has its source in the individual acting in accord with the law of his or her human nature and assuming full responsibility for his or her existence.

**humors** In earlier psychology, bodily fluids thought to enter into the constitution of a body and determine, by their proportion, a person's constitution and temperament.

**hypercompetitiveness** In Horney's theory, American society's sweeping desire to compete and win.

**hypothesis** A preliminary assumption that guides further inquiry.

**hysteria** An earlier term for an illness in which there are physical symptoms, such as paralysis, but no organic or physiological basis for the problem.

**id** In Freud's theory, the oldest and original function of the personality, which includes genetic inheritance, reflex capacities, instincts, and drives.

**idealization** In Kohut's theory, the tendency children have to idealize their parents.

**idealized self** In Horney's theory, that which a person thinks he or she should be.

**identification** In Freud's theory, (a) a defense mechanism in which a person reduces anxiety by modeling his or her behavior after that of someone else, and (b) the process whereby the child resolves the Oedipus complex by incorporating the parents into the self.

**identity crisis** In Erikson's theory, transitory failure to develop a self-image or identity.

**idiographic** In Allport's theory, an approach to studying personality that centers on understanding the uniqueness of the individual.

**I-E Scale** A questionnaire developed by Rotter to measure internal versus external locus of control.

**imagoes** In McAdams's theory, main characters that represent our primary social roles and cravings for power and love.

**immediate reinforcement** Reinforcement that immediately follows a response.

**implosive** A sudden, instead of gradual, confrontation of a phobic situation.

**imprinting** A bond of attraction that develops among members of a species shortly after birth.

**incongruence** In Rogers's theory, the lack of harmony that results when a person's symbolized experiences do not represent the actual experiences.

**independent variable** In an experiment, the factor that is manipulated by the experimenter.

**individual psychology** The school of psychology developed by Adler.

**individuation** In Jung's theory of self-realization, a process whereby the systems of the individual psyche achieve their fullest degree of differentiation, expression, and development.

**industry versus inferiority** Erikson's psychosocial stage, corresponding to Freud's latency period, in which children face the task of learning and mastering the technology of their culture.

**inferiority complex** In Adler's theory, a neurotic pattern in which an individual feels highly inadequate.

**inferiority feelings** In Adler's theory, feelings of being inadequate that arise out of childhood experiences.

**infrahuman species** Species lower than human organisms.

**inhibition** The prevention of a response from occurring because it is in conflict with other strong unconscious responses.

**initiative versus guilt** Erikson's psychosexual stage, corresponding to Freud's phallic stage, in which children face the task of directing their curiosity and activity toward specific goals and achievements.

**inner space** In Erikson's theory, tendency on the part of girls to emphasize qualities of openness versus closedness in space.

**insight** A form of therapeutic knowing that combines intellectual and emotional elements and culminates in profound personality change.

**insight therapy** Therapeutic procedures that seek to increase self-understanding and lead to deep motivational changes.

**intentionality** In May's theory, a dimension that undercuts conscious and unconscious, and underlies will and decision.

**interpretative response** In Rogers's theory, a response that seeks to interpret a speaker's problem or tell how the speaker feels about it.

**interpsychic** Between psyches or persons.

**interval reinforcement** A schedule of reinforcement in which the organism is reinforced after a certain time period has elapsed.

**intimacy versus isolation** Erikson's psychosocial stage of young adulthood in which one faces the task of establishing a close, deep, and meaningful genital relationship with another person.

**intrapsychic** Within the psyche or individual self.

**introversion** An attitude of withdrawal in which personality is oriented inward toward the subjective world.

**intuition** One of Jung's functions, entailing perception via the unconscious.

**in vitro desensitization** A process whereby anxieties and fears are reduced by repeated imagined exposures to the noxious stimuli paired with relaxation, skill training, and other behavioral techniques.

**in vivo desensitization** A process in which a client experiencing anxiety is exposed to gradually more threatening versions of the anxiety-provoking situation.

**IQ** Intelligence quotient: a number used to express the relative intelligence of a person.

**karma** Sanskrit for volitional action.

**kinhin** Japanese for the meditational walking performed between periods of zazen.

**koan** Japanese for "public document," an apparently paradoxical story, anecdote, or statement expressing the realization of a Zen master.

**latency period** A period in Freud's psychosexual stages of development in which the sexual drive was thought to go underground.

**latent dream** In Freud's theory, the real meaning or motive that underlies the dream that we remember.

**law of effect** A law formulated by Thorndike that states that when a behavior or a performance is accompanied by satisfaction it tends to increase; if accompanied by frustration, it tends to decrease.

**L-data** In Cattell's theory, observations made of a person's behavior in society or everyday life.

**learning dilemma** In Dollard and Miller's theory, the situation an individual is placed in if present responses are not reinforced.

**libido** a) In Freud's theory, an emotional and psychic energy derived from the biological drive of sexuality. b) In Jung's theory, an undifferentiated life and psychic energy.

**life crisis** In Erikson's theory, a crucial period in which the individual cannot avoid a decisive turn one way or the other.

**locus of control** In Rotter's theory, the belief that reinforcements are controlled either by one's own behavior (internal) or by outside forces (external).

**logotherapy** Frankl's theory that suggests people have realized freedom but we have not necessarily taken responsibility for our freedom.

**love** In Fromm's theory, the productive relationship to others and the self, entailing care, responsibility, respect, and knowledge.

**Mahayana** Sanskrit for "great vehicle," one of the two major divisions of Buddhism, concerned with the liberation of all sentient beings.

**manas** Sanskrit for "mind," the seventh of the eight consciousnesses, where the illusion of the ego arises.

**mandala** A concentrically arranged figure often found as a symbol in the East that denotes wholeness and unity. In Jung's theory, a symbol for the emerging self.

**manifest dream** In Freud's theory, the dream as it is remembered the next morning.

**manovijnana** Sanskrit for "mental consciousness," the sixth of the eight consciousnesses and the basis for the five sensory consciousnesses.

**marketing orientation** In Fromm's theory, a character type in which the person experiences him- or herself as a commodity in the marketplace.

**masculine protest** In Adler's early theory, the compensation for one's inferiorities.

**masochism** A disorder in which a person obtains pleasure by receiving pain.

**maya** Sanskrit for deception, delusion, or illusion.

**melancholic** One of Hippocrates' temperaments, referring to an individual characterized by depression.

**mergers** In Orlofsky's theory, individuals who commit themselves to a relationship at the price of their own independence.

**metacommunication** In Lazarus's theory, the fact that people not only communicate but also think and communicate about their communications.

**metamotivation** A term used by Maslow to refer to growth tendencies within the organism.

**metapsychological** A term used by Freud to indicate the fullest possible description of psychic processes.

**minimum goal level** In Rotter's theory, the lowest level of potential reinforcement that is perceived as satisfactory in a particular situation.

**mirrored** In Kohut's theory, the need for children to have their talk and their accomplishments acknowledged, accepted, and praised.

**mistaken style of life** In Adler's theory, a style of life that belies one's actual capabilities and strengths.

**modality profiles** In Lazarus's therapy, a specific list of problems and proposed treatments across the client's BASIC-ID.

**moral anxiety** In Freud's theory, fear of the retribution of one's own conscience.

**Morita therapy** A system of psychotherapy developed in Japan early in the twentieth century by Shoma Morita, combining elements of Zen Buddhism and psychoanalysis.

**motivation** Maslow's term for the reduction of tension by satisfying deficit states or lacks.

**moving against** One of Horney's three primary modes of relating to other people, in which one seeks to protect him- or herself by revenge or controlling others.

**moving away** One of Horney's three primary ways of relating to other people, in which one isolates him- or herself and keeps apart.

**moving toward** One of Horney's three primary modes of relating to other people, in which one accepts his or her own helplessness and becomes compliant in order to depend on others.

**multimodal behavior therapy** Lazarus's method of therapy.

**musturbatory belief systems** In Ellis's theory, escalating probalistic statements into absolutes.

**myths** In May's theory, narrative patterns that give significance to our existence.

**Naikan therapy** In Japanese culture, a form of introspective therapy emphasizing the development of responsibility and obligation.

**narcissim** A form of self-encapsulation in which an individual experiences as real only that which exists within him- or herself.

**necrophilous character** In Fromm's theory, a character orientation in which an individual is attracted to that which is dead and decaying and seeks to destroy living things.

**need** a) In Murray's theory, a force in the brain that organizes perception, understanding, and behavior in such a way as to change an unsatisfying situation and increase satisfaction. b) In Rotter's theory, a behavior that leads to a reinforcement.

**need potential** In Rotter's theory, the likelihood that a set of behaviors directed toward the same goal will be used in a given situation.

**need value** In Rotter's theory, the importance placed on a goal.

**negative identity** In Erikson's theory, an identity opposed to the dominant values of one's culture.

**negative reinforcement** Unpleasant or aversive stimuli that can be changed or avoided by certain behavior.

**NEO-PI** The Neuroticism Extraversion Openness Personality Inventory developed by Costa and McCrae.

**NEO-PI-R** The Neuroticism Extraversion Openness Personality Inventory, Revised, developed by McCrae and Costa.

**neopsychoanalytic theories** Psychoanalytic theories that revise or modify Freud's original theories.

**neurotic anxiety** In Freud's theory, the fear that one's inner impulses cannot be controlled.

**neurotic needs or trends** In Horney's theory, exaggerated defense strategies that permit an individual to cope with the world.

**nirvana** Sanskrit for a mental state where craving and suffering have been completely extinguished.

**nomothetic** In Allport's theory, an approach to studying personality that considers large groups of individuals in order to infer general variables or universal principles.

**nondirective** A term used by Rogers to describe therapies whose course is primarily determined by the patient.

**normal curve of distribution** A bell-shaped curve representing many events in nature in which most events cluster around the mean.

**nuclear self** In Kohut's theory, a well-developed self that ideally emerges in the second year.

**object relations** The intrapsychic experience of early relationships with others.

**objective data** Data acquired through extrospection, the act of looking outward on the world as object.

**objectivism** The philosophical view that valid knowledge arises gradually in the course of experience through observation and experimentation.

**objectivity** The quality of recognizing or expressing reality without distortion by personal feeling. In test construction, construction of a test in such a way that it can be given and scored in a way that avoids the scorer's subjective bias.

**observational learning** In Bandura's theory, learning that occurs through observation without any direct reinforcement.

**Oedipus complex** In Freud's theory, an unconscious psychological conflict in which the child loves the parent of the opposite sex.

**open system** A concept of personality that conceives of it as having a dynamic potential for growth, reconstitution, and change through extensive transactions within itself and the environment.

**operant behavior** In Skinner's theory, a response that acts on the environment and is emitted without a stimulus necessarily being present.

**operant conditioning** In Skinner's theory, the process by which an operant response becomes associated with a reinforcement through learning.

**operational definition** A definition that specifies those behaviors that are included in the concept.

**oral stage** One of Freud's psychosexual stages, in which the major source of pleasure and potential conflict is the mouth.

**organismic valuing process** In Rogers's theory, a subconscious natural phenomenon that guides an individual towards productive growth experiences.

**outer space** In Erikson's theory, tendency on the part of boys to emphasize qualities of highness or lowness in space.

**overcompensation** In Adler's theory, an exaggerated effort to cover up a weakness that entails a denial rather than an acceptance of the real situation.

**overt behavior** Behavior that can be observed by an external observer.

**paradigm** A pattern or model.

**paradox** In Lazarus's therapy, the use of contradictions. Two opposites that seem to negate each other but cannot exist without each other.

**paraworld** A world of quantified, logical, and mathematical imaginary constructs used by the scientist to draw conclusions about the everyday world.

**peak experience** In Maslow's theory, an intensified experience in which there is a loss of self or transcendence of self.

**penis envy** In Freud's theory, the concept that women view themselves as castrated males and envy the penis.

**performance phase** In Dollard and Miller's therapy, a phase in which the patient acquires new, more adaptive responses and habits.

**perseverative functional autonomy** In Allport's theory, acts or behaviors that are repeated even though they may have lost their original function.

**persona** In Jung's theory, an archetype referring to one's social role and understanding of it.

**personal construct** In Kelly's theory, a hypothesis an individual forms in order to predict and control events, which makes the world meaningful and which is tested by later experience.

**personal dispositions** In Allport's theory, traits that are unique to an individual.

**personal unconscious** In Jung's theory, experiences of an individual's life that have been repressed or temporarily forgotten.

**personality** a) In social speech, one's public image. b) In Fromm's theory, the totality of an individual's psychic qualities. c) In Cattell's theory, that which permits prediction of what a person will do in a given situation.

**personology** Murray's term for his study of individual persons.

**phallic stage** One of Freud's psychosexual stages, in which pleasurable and conflicting feelings are associated with the genital organs.

**phenomenal field** In Rogers's theory, the total sum of experiences an organism has.

**phenomenology** The study of phenomena or appearances.

**phenotype** An individual's observable appearance and behavior.

**philosophical assumption** An underlying view of the world that influences a person's thinking.

**philosophy** The systematic love and pursuit of wisdom.

**phlegmatic** One of Hippocrates temperaments, referring to an individual who is slow, solid, and apathetic.

**pleasure principle** In Freud's theory, the seeking of tension reduction followed by the id.

**polymorphous perverse** A phrase used by Freud to emphasize the point that children deviate in many ways from what is thought to be normal reproductive sexual activity.

**positive regard** In Rogers's theory, being loved and accepted for who one is.

**positive reinforcement** Anything that serves to increase the frequency of a response.

**positive self-regard** In Rogers's theory, viewing the self favorably and with acceptance.

**predictive power** A criterion for evaluating rival hypotheses: the range or scope of the hypothesis.

**pre-emptive construct** In Kelly's theory, a construct that limits its elements to one range only.

**press** In Murray's theory, a force coming from the environment that helps or hinders an individual in reaching goals.

**primary drive** A drive associated with a physiological process that is necessary for the organism's survival.

**primary process** In Freud's theory, a psychological activity of the id characterized by immediate wish fulfillment and the disregard of realistic concerns.

**primary reinforcer** A reinforcer that is inherently rewarding as it satisfies a primary drive.

**proactive** Referring to theories of personality that view the human being as acting on his or her own initiative rather than simply reacting.

**probing response** In Rogers's theory, a response that seeks further information.

**proceeding** In Murray's theory, a short, significant behavior pattern that has a clear beginning and ending.

**productive orientation** In Fromm's theory, the character type that represents the ideal of humanistic development.

**projection** In Freud's theory, a defense mechanism that refers to the unconscious attribution of an impulse, attitude, or behavior to someone else or some element in the environment.

**projective techniques** Personality tests in which an ambiguous stimulus is presented to the subject who is expected to project aspects of his or her personality into the response.

**propositional construct** In Kelly's theory, a construct that leaves its elements open to other constructions.

**propriate functional autonomy** In Allport's theory, acquired interests, values, attitudes, intentions, and life-style that are directed from the proprium and are genuinely free of earlier motivations.

**propriate functions** In Allport's theory, the functions of the proprium.

**propriate striving** In Allport's theory, a propriate function that entails projection of long-term purposes and goals and development of a plan to attain them.

**proprium** In Allport's theory, a term that refers to the central experiences of self-awareness that a person has as he or she grows and moves forward.

**psyche** From the Greek term meaning "breath" or "principle of life," often translated as "soul" or "self." a) In Freud's theory, the id, ego, and superego. b) In Jung's theory, the total personality encompassing all psychological processes: thoughts, feelings, sensations, wishes, and so on.

**psychoanalysis** A method of therapy developed by Freud that concentrates on cultivating a transference relationship and analyzing resistances to the therapeutic process.

**psychohistory** The combined use of psychoanalysis and history to study individuals and groups.

**psychological situation** The psychological context within which an organism responds.

**psychometrics** The quantitative measurement of psychological characteristics through statistical techniques.

**psychophysical** Entailing components of both the mind and the body.

**psychosexual stages** In Freud's theory, a series of developmental stages through which all people pass as they move from infancy to adulthood.

**psychosis** An abnormal personality disturbance characterized by loss or distortion of reality testing and the inability to distinguish between reality and fantasy.

**psychosocial stages** A series of developmental stages proposed by Erikson to emphasize the social dimension of personality.

**psychotherapy** Treatment of emotional disorders by psychological means.

**psychoticism** One of Eysenck's personality dimensions, involving the loss or distortion of reality and the inability to distinguish between reality and fantasy.

**punishment** An undesirable consequence that follows a behavior and is designed to stop or change it.

**Q-sort technique** A card-sorting technique employed by Rogers for studying the self-concept.

**radical behaviorism** A label that has been given to B. F. Skinner's point of view.

**random assignment** In an experiment, insuring that every subject has an equal chance of being assigned to any of the treatment groups.

**ratio reinforcement** A schedule of reinforcement in which the organism is reinforced after a number of appropriate responses.

**rational emotive behavior therapy** Ellis's method of psychotherapy.

**rationalism** The philosophical view that the mind can, in and of its own accord, formulate ideas and determine their truth.

**rationalization** In Freud's theory, a defense mechanism that entails dealing with an emotion or impulse analytically and intellectually, thereby not involving the emotions.

**reaction formation** In Freud's theory, a defense mechanism in which an impulse is expressed by its opposite.

**reactive** Referring to theories of personality that view the human beings as primarily responding to external stimuli.

**real self** In Horney's theory, that which a person actually is.

**reality anxiety** In Freud's theory, the fear of a real danger in the external world.

**reality principle** In Freud's theory, the way in which the ego satisfies the impulses of the id in an appropriate manner in the external world.

**reassuring response** In Rogers's theory, a response that attempts to soothe feelings.

**receptive orientation** In Fromm's theory, a character type in which the individual reacts to the world passively.

**reciprocal determinism** In Bandura's theory, the regulation of behavior by an interplay of behavioral, cognitive, and environmental factors.

**reconstructive (or intensive) psychotherapy** Therapeutic methods that seek to remove defenses and reorganize the basic personality structure.

**reflective response** In Rogers's theory, a response that seeks to capture the underlying feeling expressed.

**reflexes** Inborn automatic responses.

**regression** In Freud's theory, a defense mechanism that entails reverting to earlier forms of behavior.

**reinforcement** The process of increasing or decreasing the likelihood of a particular response.

**reinforcement value** In Rotter's theory, a variable that indicates the importance or preference of a particular reinforcement for an individual.

**reinforcer**  Any event that increases or decreases the likelihood of a particular response.

**relatedness**  In Fromm's theory, the basic need to relate to and love other people.

**relational/cultural theory**  A perspective for understanding personality developed by scholars working out of the Stone Center at Wellesley College.

**relevance**  One of the criteria for evaluating philosophical statements, the quality of having some bearing or being pertinent to one's view of reality.

**reliability**  The quality of consistently yielding the same results over time.

**reproduction of mothering**  Chodorow's belief that women's mothering reproduces itself cyclically.

**Rep Test**  Role Construct Repertory Test: a device developed by Kelly to reveal personal constructs.

**repression**  a) In Freud's theory, the key defense mechanism, which entails blocking a wish or desire from expression so that it cannot be experienced consciously or directly expressed in behavior. b) In Dollard and Miller's theory, a learned process of avoiding certain thoughts and thereby losing verbal control.

**resignation solution**  One of Horney's three basic orientations, representing the desire to be free of others.

**respondent behavior**  In Skinner's theory, reflexes or automatic responses elicited by a stimulus.

**response**  A behavior that results from a stimulus. In Dollard and Miller's theory, one's reaction to a cue or stimulus.

**Rinzai**  One of the two major schools of Zen Buddhism in Japan, stressing the use of koans and zazen to reach enlightenment.

**role**  a) In social psychology, a set of behavioral expectations set forth by a particular society and fulfilled by its members. b) In Kelly's theory, a process or behavior that a person plays based on his or her understanding of the behavior and constructs of other people.

**role confusion**  In Erikson's theory, an inability to conceive of oneself as a productive member in one's society.

**role-playing**  A therapeutic technique in Kelly and Beck's therapy, in which clients are asked to rehearse situations that will later happen in real life.

**rootedness**  In Fromm's theory, the basic need to feel that one belongs in the world.

**ruling type**  In Adler's theory, aggressive, dominating people who have little social interest or cultural perception.

**sadism**  A disorder in which a person obtains pleasure by inflicting pain.

**safeguarding tendencies**  In Adler's theory, compensatory mechanisms that ward off feelings of insecurity.

**Saijojo Zen**  Zen practiced for its own sake, with no expectations and no thought of gain.

**sanguine**  One of Hippocrates' temperaments, referring to a personality marked by sturdiness, high color, and cheerfulness.

**sanzen**  Individual consultations between a Zen Buddhist monk and his master.

**satiation**  Engaging in a behavior until one tires of it.

**satori**  Japanese for "enlightenment," the goal of Zen practice.

**schedule of reinforcement**  A program for increasing or decreasing the likelihood of a particular response.

**schemas**  In Beck's theory, cognitive structures that consist of an individual's fundamental core beliefs and assumptions about how the world operates.

**science**  A system or method of acquiring knowledge based on specific principles of observation and reasoning.

**scientific construct**  An imaginary or hypothetical construct used to explain what is observed in science.

**scientific (or empirical) generalization**  An inductive conclusion based on a number of different instances of observation.

**scientific method**  A method of inquiry that consists of five steps: recognizing a problem, developing a hypothesis, making a prediction, testing the hypothesis, and drawing a conclusion.

**scientific statement**  A statement about the world based on observations arising from a currently held paradigm.

**scientism**  Exclusive reliance on a narrow conception of science.

**secondary dispositions**  In Allport's theory, more specific, focused tendencies of an individual that tend to be situational in character.

**secondary drive**  A drive that is learned or acquired on the basis of a primary drive.

**secondary processes**  In Freud's theory, higher intellectual functions that enable the ego to establish suitable courses of action and test them for their effectiveness.

**secondary reinforcer** A reinforcer that is originally neutral but that acquires reward value on the basis of association with a primary reinforcer.

**self** a) In Jung's theory, a central archetype representing the striving for unity of all parts of the personality. b) In Rogers's theory, the psychological processes that govern a person's behavior.

**self-actualization** In the theories of Rogers and Maslow, a dynamic within the organism leading it to actualize, fulfill, and enhance its inherent potentialities.

**self-analysis** In Horney's theory, a systematic effort at self-understanding conducted without the aid of a professional.

**self-as-rational coper** In Allport's theory, a propriate function that entails the perception of oneself as an active problem-solving agent.

**self-concept** In Rogers's theory, a portion of the phenomenal field that has become differentiated and is composed of perceptions and values of "I" or "me."

**self-construct** In Kelly's theory, perception of similarities in one's behavior based on role relationships with other people.

**self-effacing solution** One of Horney's three basic orientations toward life, which represents an appeal to be loved by others.

**self-efficacy** In Bandura's theory, a person's perception of his or her effectiveness.

**self-esteem** In Allport's theory, a propriate function that entails feelings of pride as one develops the ability to do things.

**self-expansive solution** One of Horney's three basic orientations toward life, which represents a striving for mastery.

**self-extension** In Allport's theory, a propriate function that entails a sense of possession.

**self-identity** In Allport's theory, a propriate function that entails an awareness of inner sameness and continuity.

**self-image** In Allport's theory, a propriate function that entails a sense of the expectations of others and its comparison with one's own behavior.

**self-love** In Fromm's theory, love of self that is a prerequisite for love of others.

**self-orientation** A new character type, informed by Fromm's theory, that is highly narcissistic.

**self-realization** In Jung's theory, a drive within the self to realize, fulfill, and enhance one's maximum human potentialities.

**self-sentiment** In Cattell's theory, an environmental-mold dynamic source trait composing a person's self-image.

**self-system** In Bandura's theory, cognitive structures that underlie the perception, evaluation, and regulation of behavior.

**sensation** One of Jung's functions, referring to sense perception of the world.

**sense of identity** In Fromm's theory, the need to be aware of oneself as an individual.

**sentiment** In Cattell's theory, an environmental-mold dynamic source trait.

**separation-individuation process** A sequence of stages posited by Mahler through which the ego passes in the process of becoming an individual.

**shadow** In Jung's theory, an archetype that encompasses one's animalistic and unsocial side.

**shaping** In Skinner's theory, a process by which an organism's behavior is gradually molded until it approximates the desired behavior.

**shikantaza** Japanese for "just sitting," the form of zazen practice stressed particularly in the Soto Zen tradition.

**shinkeishitsu** A Japanese label for a group of neuroses overlapping with the anxiety disorders in the DSM-IV classification.

**Shojo Zen** Zen practiced for personal enlightenment or for relief from suffering.

**simplicity** A criterion for evaluating rival hypotheses: the quality of being simple and avoiding complicated explanations.

**skandha** Sanskrit for "aggregate" or "heap." The five *skandhas* are form, feelings, perceptions, impulses, and consciousness.

**slips** In Freud's theory, bungled acts, such as a slip of the tongue, a slip of the pen, or a memory lapse.

**social interest** In Adler's theory, an urge in human nature to adapt oneself to the conditions of one's environment and society.

**social learning theories** Theories that attempt to explain personality in terms of learned behavior within a social context.

**social psychoanalytic theories** Psychoanalytic theories that emphasize the role of social forces in shaping personality.

**socially useful type** In Adler's theory, people who have a great deal of social interest and activity.

**sociotropic dimension** In Beck's theory, a personality dimension characterized by dependence on interpersonal relationships and needs for closeness and nurturance.

**somatotonia**  In Sheldon's theory, a component of temperament characterized by a predominance of muscular activity and vigorous bodily assertiveness.

**somatotype**  Sheldon's term for the expression of body type through three numbers that indicate the degree of each physical component.

**Soto**  One of the two major schools of Zen Buddhism in Japan, stressing the practice of zazen as shikantaza and the identity of practice and enlightenment.

**source traits**  In Cattell's theory, underlying variables that determine surface manifestations.

**species-specific behavior**  Complex automatic behaviors that occur in all members of a species.

**specific responses**  In Eysenck's theory, behaviors that we can actually observe, such as someone answering a phone.

**specification equation**  An equation by which Cattell suggests we may eventually be able to predict human behavior.

**splitting**  In Kernberg's theory, failing to consolidate positive and negative experiences between oneself and other people.

**spontaneous recovery**  Following extinction, the return of a learned behavior.

**standardization**  Pre-testing of a large and representative sample in order to determine test norms.

**statement**  An utterance that makes an assertion or a denial.

**statistics**  The application of mathematical principles to the description and analysis of measurements.

**stereotype**  Prejudgment that we make about people on the basis of their membership in certain groups.

**stimulus**  An agent that rouses or excites a response.

**structural profile**  In Lazarus's therapy, a quantitative assessment of the relative involvement of each of the elements of the BASIC-ID in a client.

**structuralism**  Early school of psychology that suggested that psychology study conscious experience.

**stupidity-misery syndrome**  Dollard and Miller's term for a neurosis.

**style of life**  In Adler's theory, the specific ways in which an individual seeks to attain the goal of superiority.

**subception**  In Rogers's theory, a discriminative evaluative response of the organism that precedes conscious perception.

**subjective data**  Data acquired through introspection, the act of looking inward on the self as subject.

**subjectivism**  A philosophical view that constructs of knowledge are creations of the self.

**sublimation**  In Freud's theory, a defense mechanism that refers to translating a wish, the direct expression of which is socially unacceptable, into socially acceptable behavior.

**subsidiation**  In Cattell's theory, the principle that certain traits are secondary to other traits.

**successive approximations**  In Dollard and Miller's therapy, the interpretations of the therapist that provide increasingly more accurate labels for the patient's responses.

**superego**  In Freud's theory, a function of the personality that represents introjected and internalized values, ideals, and moral standards.

**superiority complex**  In Adler's theory, a neurotic pattern in which an individual exaggerates his or her importance.

**supportive psychotherapy**  Therapeutic measures that seek to strengthen adaptive instincts and defenses.

**surface traits**  In Cattell's theory, clusters of overt behavior responses that appear to go together.

**sutra**  Sanskrit for a sermon or discourse, usually of the Buddha.

**symbiotic relationship**  In Fromm's theory, a relationship in which one or the other of two persons loses or never attains his or her independence.

**symbol**  An element in a dream that stands for something else.

**synchronicity**  A phenomenon in which events are related to one another through simultaneity and meaning.

**syntality**  In Cattell's theory, the behavior of a group as a whole or its "group personality."

**talking phase**  In Dollard and Miller's therapy, a phase in which neurotic habits are studied, examined, and identified so that the patient may unlearn them.

**Tao**  A Chinese term for "Way" or "Path"; the absolute and ineffable nature of ultimate reality.

**Taoism**  A Chinese philosophy and way of life based on the teachings of Lao-tse (ca. 4th century B.C.), stressing harmony with the Tao.

**T-data**  In Cattell's theory, objective tests.

**technical eclecticism**  In Lazarus's therapy, deriving treatment methods from many sources without necessarily agreeing with the theories that generated them.

**telos**  A purpose or goal.

**temperament traits**  In Cattell's theory, traits that determine how a person behaves in order to obtain his or her goal.

**Thanatos**  In Freud's theory, the death impulse or drive, the source of aggression, the ultimate resolution of all of life's tension in death. A projective test consisting of ambiguous pictures to which a subject is asked to respond.

**Thematic Apperception Test (TAT)**  A projective test consisting of ambiguous pictures to which a subject is asked to respond.

**theory**  A set of abstract concepts made about a group of facts or events to explain them.

**therapy**  The practical application of psychology in ways that will assist individuals.

**Theravada**  Pali for "the teaching of the Elders," the form of Buddhism dominant in Sri Lanka, Burma, Thailand, Laos, and Cambodia. Sometimes referred to as the Hinayana.

**thinking**  One of Jung's functions, referring to giving meaning and understanding to the world.

**thresholds**  In Lazarus's theory, tolerance levels for pain, frustration, or stress.

**token economy**  A community based on Skinnerian principles in which individuals are rewarded for appropriate behavior with tokens that can be exchanged for various privileges.

**tracking**  In Lazarus's therapy, paying careful attention to the "firing order" of the different modalities.

**trait**  Continuous dimension that an individual can be seen to possess to a certain degree. a) In Allport's theory, a determining tendency to respond that represents the ultimate reality of psychological organization. b) In Cattell's theory, an imaginary construct or inference from overt behavior that helps to explain it.

**trait theories**  Theories that conceive of personality as being composed primarily of traits.

**transcendence**  a) In Jung's theory of self-realization, a process of integrating the diverse systems of the self toward the goal of wholeness and identification with all humanity. b) In Fromm's theory, the basic human need to rise above the accidental and passive creatureliness of animal existence and become an active creator.

**transference**  In Freudian psychoanalysis, a process in which the patient projects onto the analyst emotional attitudes felt as a child toward important persons.

**Tripitaka**  Sanskrit for the "three baskets" or collections of Buddhist scriptures.

**trust versus mistrust**  Erikson's psychosocial stage, corresponding to Freud's oral stage, in which infants face the task of trusting the world.

**typology**  Division of human beings into distinct, separate categories.

**tyranny of the should**  In Horney's theory, creating false needs instead of meeting genuine ones.

**unconditional positive regard**  In Rogers's theory, positive regard that is not contingent on any specific behaviors.

**unconditioned response**  A reflex or automatic response to a stimulus.

**unconditioned stimulus**  A stimulus that normally elicits a particular reflex or automatic response.

**unconscious process**  a) In Freud's theory, processes of which a person is unaware because they have been repressed or never permitted to become conscious. b) In Dollard and Miller's theory, drives or cues of which we are unaware because they are unlabeled or repressed.

**usefulness**  a) In scientific theorizing, the ability of a hypothesis to generate predictions about experiences that we might observe. b) In Adler's theory, the ability of a goal to foster productive living and enhance one's life.

**validating evidence**  Observable consequences that follow an experiment designed to test a hypothesis and are used to support a construct or theory.

**validity**  The quality of measuring what a construct is supposed to measure.

**variable**  A characteristic that can be measured or controlled.

**variable schedule of reinforcement**  A schedule of reinforcement in which the time period or number of responses prior to reinforcement varies.

**vijnana**  Sanskrit for "consciousness."

**virtues**  In Erikson's theory, ego strengths that develop out of each psychosocial stage.

**Walden II**  Skinner's name for his utopian comunity.

**wish fulfillment**  In Freud's theory, a primary-process activity that seeks to reduce tension by forming an image of the object that would satisfy needs.

**wishes**  In Freud's theory, desires that may be rendered unconscious if they go against a person's ego-ideal.

**withdrawal-destructiveness relationship**  In Fromm's theory, a relationship characterized by distance, apathy, or aggression.

**womb envy**  In Horney's theory, the concept that men and boys experience jealousy over women's ability to bear and nurse children.

**yang**  Chinese Taoist term for the positive, masculine, active, external aspect of the complementary yin and yang polarity.

**yin**  Chinese Taoist term for the negative, feminine, passive, internal aspect of the complementary yin and yang polarity.

**zazen**  Japanese for "sitting meditation," the most important and indispensable aspect of Zen practice. The typical length of a period of *zazen* in Japan is 40 minutes.

**Zen**  Japanese rendering of the Chinese *ch'an,* meaning absorption or meditation. It can refer to a school of Buddhism or to the ineffable experience of oneness with reality.

# References

Abzug, R. H. (1996). Rollo May as friend to man. *Journal of Humanistic Psychology, 36,* 17–22.

Adler, A. (1917). *Study of organ inferiority and its psychical compensation.* New York: Nervous and Mental Diseases Publishing Co.

Adler, A. (1927). *The practice and theory of individual psychology.* New York: Harcourt, Brace, & World.

Adler, A. (1929a). *The science of living.* New York: Greenberg.

Adler, A. (1929b). *Problems of neurosis.* London: Kegan Paul.

Adler, A. (1930). Individual psychology. In C. Murchison (Ed.), *Psychologies of 1930.* Worcester, MA: Clark University Press.

Adler, A. (1931). *What life should mean to you.* Boston: Little, Brown.

Adler, A. (1936). The neurotic's picture of the world. *International Journal of Individual Psychology, 2,* 3–10.

Adler, A. (1939). *Social interest.* New York: Putnam.

Adler, A. (1954). *Understanding human nature.* New York: Fawcett.

Adler, A. (1964). *Superiority and social interest: A collection of later writings.* H. L. & R. R. Ansbacher (Eds.). Evanston: IL: Northwestern University Press.

Agarwal, R., & Misra, G. (1986, January). Locus of control and attribution for achievement outcomes, *Psychological Studies, 31*(1), 15–20.

Akhtar, S. (1994). Object constancy and adult psychopathology. *International Journal of Psycho-Analysis, 75,* 441–455.

Alexander, F. (1950). *Psychosomatic medicine: Its principles and applications.* New York: Norton.

Allport, G. W. (1937). *Personality: A psychological interpretation.* New York: Holt.

Allport, G. W. (1954). *The nature of prejudice.* Boston: Beacon Press.

Allport, G. W. (1955). *Becoming: Basic considerations for a psychology of personality.* New Haven: Yale University Press.

Allport, G. W. (1960). The open system in personality theory. *Journal of Abnormal and Social Psychology, 60,* 301–310.

Allport, G. W. (1961). *Pattern and growth in personality.* New York: Holt, Rinehart, and Winston.

Allport, G. W. (1965). *Letters from Jenny.* New York: Harcourt Brace and World.

Allport, G. W. (1968). *The person in psychology: Selected essays.* Boston: Beacon.

Allport, G. W., & Odbert, H. S. (1936). Trait-names: A psycholexical study. *Psychological Monographs, 47,* 1–211.

Anderson, M. (1991). *Thinking about women: Sociological perspectives on sex and gender* (3rd ed.). New York: Macmillan.

Anderson, R., & Kirkland, J. (1990). Constructs in context. *International Journal of Personal Construct Psychology, 3*(1), 21–29.

Ansbacher, H. L. (1990). Alfred Adler's influence on the three leading co-founders of humanistic psychology. *Journal of Humanistic Psychology, 30*(4), 45–53.

Ansbacher, H. L., & Ansbacher, R. R. (1956). *The individual psychology of Alfred Adler.* New York: Basic Books.

Archer, S. L. (1989). Gender differences in identity development: Issues of process, domain, and timing. *Journal of Adolescence, 12,* 117–138.

Aries, E., & Moorehead, K. (1989). The importance of ethnicity in the development of identity of Black adolescents. *Psychological Reports, 65*(1), 75–82.

Aron, L. (1996). From hypnotic suggestion to free association: Freud as a psychotherapist, circa 1892–1893. *Contemporary Psychoanalysis, 32,* 99–114.

Atkinson, R. (1990). Life stories and personal myth-making. *Humanistic Psychologist, 18*(2), 199–207.

Bacciagaluppi, M. (1996). Guilt according to Erich Fromm. *Contemporary Psychoanalysis, 32,* 455–462.

Badcock, C. (1992). *Essential Freud* (2nd ed.). Oxford, England: Blackwell Publishers.

Bagby, L. J. (1995). The question of Jung and racism reconsidered. *Psychohistory Review, 23,* 283–298.

Bakan, D. (1966). *The duality of human existence: Isolation and communion in Western man.* Boston: Beacon Press.

Bakan, D. (1969). *On method: Toward a reconstruction of psychological investigation.* San Francisco: Jossey-Bass.

Balter, L., & Spencer, J. H. (1991). Observation and theory in psychoanalysis: The self psychology of Heinz Kohut. *Psychoanalytic Quarterly, 60*(3), 361–395.

Bandler, R., & Grinder, J. (1976). *The structure of magic: A book about communication and change* (Vol. 2). Palo Alto, CA: Science and Behavior Books.

Bandura, A. (1969). *Principles of behavior modification.* New York: Holt, Rinehart & Winston.

Bandura, A. (1973). *Aggression: A social learning analysis.* Englewood Cliffs, NJ: Prentice-Hall.

Bandura, A. (1974). A behavior theory and the models of man. *American Psychologist, 29,* 859–869.

Bandura, A. (1977). *Social learning theory.* Englewood Cliffs, NJ: Prentice-Hall.

Bandura, A. (1978). The self system in reciprocal determinism. *American Psychologist, 33,* 344–358.

Bandura, A. (1986). *Social foundations of thought and action: A social cognitive theory.* Englewood Cliffs, NJ: Prentice-Hall.

Bandura, A. (1986). The explanatory and predictive scope of self-efficacy theory. *Journal of Social and Clinical Psychology, 4*(3), 359-373.

Bandura, A. (1989). Human agency in social cognitive theory. *American Psychologist, 44*(9), 1175-1184.

Bandura, A. (1990). Some reflections on reflections. *Psychological Inquiry, 1*, 101-105.

Bandura, A. (1991a). The changing icons in personality psychology. In J. Cantor (Ed.), *Psychology at Iowa: Centennial Essays.* Hillsdale, NJ: Lawrence Erlbaum.

Bandura, A. (1991b). Self-efficacy. In R. Schwarzer & R. Wicklund (Eds.), *Anxiety and self-focused attention.* New York: Harwood Academic.

Bandura, A. (1991c). Social cognitive theory of moral thought and action. In W. Kurtines & J. Gewirtz (Eds.), *Handbook of Moral Behavior and Development* (pp. 45-103). Hillsdale, NJ: Lawrence Erlbaum.

Bandura, A. (1991d). Social cognitive theory of self-regulation. *Organizational Behavior & Human Decision Processes, 50*(2), 248-287.

Bandura, A. (1992). Social cognitive theory. In R. Vasta (Ed.), *Six theories of child development: Revised formulations and current issues* (pp. 1-60). England: Jessica Kingsley.

Bandura, A. (Ed.). (1995). *Self-efficacy in changing societies.* New York: Cambridge University Press.

Bandura, A. (1996). Ontological and epistemological terrains revisited. *Journal of Behavior Therapy and Experimental Psychiatry, 27*, 323-345.

Bandura, A. (1997a). Health promotion from the perspective of social cognitive theory. *Psychology and Health*, 1-27.

Bandura, A. (1997b). *Self-efficacy: The exercise of control.* New York: Freeman.

Bandura, A., Adams, N. E., Hardy, A. B., & Howells, G. N. (1980). Tests of the generality of self-efficacy theory. *Cognitive Therapy and Research. 4*, 39-66.

Bandura, A., Barbaranelli, C., Caprara, G. V., & Pastorelli, C. (1996). Mechanisms of moral disengagement in the exercise of moral agency. *Journal of Personality and Social Psychology, 71*, 364-374.

Bandura, A., & Mischel, W. (1965). Modifications of self-imposed delay of reward through exposure to live and symbolic models. *Journal of Personality and Social Psychology, 2*, 698-705.

Bandura, A., & Walters, R. (1963). *Social learning and personality development.* New York: Holt, Rinehart, & Winston.

Bankart, C. (1997). *Talking cures: A history of Western and Eastern psychotherapies.* Pacific Grove, CA: Brooks/Cole.

Banks, W., Ward, W., McQuater, G., & DeBritto, A. (1991). Are blacks external: On the status of locus of control in black populations. In J. Reginald (Ed.), *Black psychology* (pp. 181-192). Berkeley, CA: Cobb & Henry.

Bannister, D., & Fransella, F. (1966). A grid test of schizophrenic thought disorder. *British Journal of Social and Clinical Psychology, 5*, 95-102.

Bannister, D., & Mair, J. M. M. (1968). *The evaluation of personal constructs.* New York: Academic Press.

Bannister, D., & Salmon, P. (1966). Schizophrenic thought disorder: Specific or diffuse? *British Journal of Medical Psychology, 39*, 215-219.

Barrett, P., & Eysenck, S. (1994). The assessment of personality factors across 25 countries. *Personality and Individual Differences, 5*, 615-632.

Barrick, M. R., & Mount, M. K. (1991). The Big Five personality dimensions and job performance: A meta-analysis. *Personnel Psychology, 44*, 1-26.

Basch, M. F. (1995). Kohut's contribution. *Psychoanalytic Dialogues, 5*, 367-373.

Baumrind, D. (1972). Socialization and instrumental competence in young children. In W. W. Hartup (Ed.), *The young child: Reviews of research* (Vol. 2, 202-224. Washington, DC: National Association for the Education of Young Children.

Beck, A. (1991). *Biological sketch.* Unpublished manuscript.

Beck, A., & Freeman, A. (1990). *Cognitive therapy of personality disorders.* New York: Guilford Press.

Beck, A. T. (1967). *Depression: Clinical, experimental, and theoretical aspects.* New York: Hoeber. (Republished as *Depression: Causes and treatment.* Philadelphia: University of Pennsylvania Press, 1972.)

Beck, A. T. (1972). *Depression: Causes and treatments.* Philadelphia: University of Pennsylvania Press.

Beck, A. T., & Emory, G. (1979). *Cognitive therapy of anxiety and phobic disorders.* Philadelphia: Center for Cognitive Therapy.

Beck, A. T., & Emory, G. (1985). *Anxiety disorders and phobias: A cognitive perspective.* New York: Basic Books.

Beck, A. T., Epstein, N., & Harrison, R. (1983). Cognitions, attitudes, and personality dimensions in depression. *British Journal of Cognitive Psychotherapy, 1*(1), 1-16.

Beck, A. T., & Hollon, S. (1993). Controversies in cognitive therapy: A dialogue with Aaron T. Beck and Steve Hollon. *Journal of Cognitive Psychotherapy, 7*, 79-93.

Beck, A. T., Rush, A. J., Shaw, B. F., & Emery, G. (1979). *Cognitive therapy of depression.* New York: Guilford.

Benjamin, J. (1988). *The bands of love.* New York: Pantheon Books.

Berkowitz, L., & Powers, P. (1979). Effects of timing and justification of witnessed aggression on observers' punitiveness. *Journal of Research in Personality, 13*, 71-80.

Bernadez, T. (1988). Women and anger—Cultural prohibitions and the feminist ideal. *Work in Progress.* The Stone Center. Wellesley College, Wellesley, Massachusetts.

Bernal, M. E., Knight, G. P., Garza, C. A., Ocampo, K. A. et al. (1990). The development of ethnic identity in Mexican-American children. *Hispanic Journal of Behavioral Sciences, 12*(1), 3-24.

Bernard, M. E. (1986). *Staying alive in an irrational world: The psychology of Albert Ellis.* Melbourne, Australia: Carlton & Macmillan.

Bernstein, D. (1991). The female oedipal complex. In P. Hartocollis & I. D. Graham (Eds.), *The personal myth in psychoanalytic theory.* Madison, CT: International Universities Press.

Bertalanffy, L. von. (1974). General systems theory and psychiatry. In S. Arieti (Ed.), *American handbook of psychiatry* (Vol. 1), 1095-1117. New York: Basic Books.

Bettelheim, B. (1977). *The uses of enchantment.* New York: Knopf.

Bettelheim, B. (1982). *Freud and man's soul.* New York: Knopf.

Bezjak, J., & Lee, W. (1990). Relationship of self-efficacy and locus of control constructs in predicting college students' physical fitness behaviors. *Perceptual & Motor Skills, 71*(2), 499–508.

Bitter, J. R. (1991). Conscious motivations: An enhancement to Dreikurs' goals of children's misbehavior. *Individual Psychology: Journal of Adlerian Theory, Research & Practice, 47*(2), 210–221.

Blackman, D. (1991). B. F. Skinner and G. H. Mead: On biological science and social science. *Journal of the Experimental Analysis of Behavior, 55*(2), 251–265.

Boneau, C. A. (1992). Observations on psychology's past and future. *American Psychologist, 47*(12), 1586–1596.

Bouchard, T. J., Jr. (1994). Genes, environment, and personality. *Science, 264,* 1700–1701.

Bouchard, T. J., Lykken, D. T., McGue, M., Segal, N., & Tellegen, A. (1990). Sources of human psychological differences: The Minnesota study of twins reared apart. *Science, 250,* 223–228.

Bouchard, T. J., Jr., & Propping, P. (Eds.). (1993). *Twins as a tool of behavioral genetics.* New York: Wiley.

Bozarth, J. D. (1990). The evolution of Carl Rogers as a therapist. Special Issue: Fiftieth anniversary of the person-centered approach. *Person-Centered Reievw, 5*(4), 387–393.

Brazier, D. (1995). *Zen therapy: Transcending the sorrows of the human mind.* New York: Wiley.

Breger, L., Hunter, I., & Lane, R. W. (1971). The effect of stress on dreams. *Psychological Issues, 7* (3, Monograph 27), 1–213).

Bringmann, M. W. (1992). Computer-based methods for the analysis and interpretation of personal construct systems. In R. A. Neimeyer & G. J. Neimeyer (Eds.), *Advances in personal construct psychology, 2,* 57–90. Greenwich, CT: JAI Press.

Brooke, R. W. (1991). Psychic complexity and human existence: A phenomenological approach. *Journal of Analytical Psychology, 36,* 505–518.

Brumann, H. (1996). Metapsychology and professional politics. The Freud-Klein controversy. *Luzifer-Amor: Zeitschrift zur Geschichte der Psychoanalyse, 9,* 49–112.

Brunell, L. J., & Young, W. T. (Eds.). (1982). *Multimodal handbook for a mental hospital.* New York: Springer.

Brunner, J. (1991). The (ir)relevance of Freud's Jewish identity to the origins of psychoanalysis. *Psychoanalysis & Contemporary Thought, 14*(4), 655–684.

Brunner, J. (1994). Looking into the hearts of the workers: Or how Erich Fromm turned critical theory into empirical research. *Political Psychology, 15,* 631–654.

Bryant, B. L. (1987, March). Birth order as a factor in the development of vocational preferences. *Individual Psychology: Journal of Adlerian Theory, Research and Practice, 43*(1), 36–41.

Buckley, W. (1967). *Modern systems research for the behavioral scientist.* Chicago: Aldine.

Bugental, J. F. T. (1996a). Rollo May (1909–1994): Obituary. *American Psychologist, 51,* 418–419.

Bugental, J. F. T. (1996b). Aristophanes, William James, Rollo May, and our dog Dickens. *Humanistic Psychologist, 24,* 221–230.

Bullock, W. A., & Gilliland, K. (1993). Eysenck's arousal theory of introverstion-extraversion: A converging measures investigation. *Journal of Personality and Social Psychology, 64,* 113–123.

Burkitt, I. (1991). *Social selves: Theories of the social formation of personality.* Newbury Park, CA: Sage.

Burlingham, M. J. (1990). The relationship of Anna Freud and Dorothy Burlingham. *Journal of the American Academy of Psychoanalysis, 19*(4), 612–619.

Buss, A. (1991). The EAS theory of temperament. In J. Stelau & A. Angleitner (Eds.), *Exploration in temperament: International perspectives on theory and measurement* (p. 43). New York: Plenum Press.

Buss, A. H., & Plomin, R. A. (1984). *Temperament: Early developing personality traits.* Hillsdale, NJ: Erlbaum.

Buss, D. (1990). Biological foundations of personality. *Journal of Personality, 58,* 1–345.

Buss, D. (1991a). Evolutionary personality psychology. *Annual Review of Psychology, 42,* 459–491.

Buss, D. (1991b). Evolutionary personality psychology. *Annual Review of Psychology, 42,* 161–190.

Buss, D. M. (1984). Evolutionary biology and personality psychology: Toward a conception of human nature and individual differences. *American Psychologist, 39,* 1135–1147.

Butt, T. (1995). Ordinal relationships between constructs. *Journal of Constructivist Psychology, 8,* 227–236.

Cain, D. J. (1990). Celebration, reflection, and renewal: 50 years of client-centered therapy and beyond. Special Issue: Fiftieth anniversary of the person-centered approach. *Person-Centered Review, 5*(4), 357–363.

Campbell, J. (1949). *The hero with a thousand faces.* New York: Pantheon.

Campbell, J. B., & Hawley, C. W. (1982). Study habits and Eysenck's theory of extraversion-introversion. *Journal of Research in Personality, 16,* 139–146.

Cantor, N. (1990). From thought to behavior: "Having" and "doing" in the study of personality and cognition. *American Psychologist, 45*(6), 735–750.

Capps, W. H. (1996). Erikson's contribution toward understanding religion. *Psychoanalysis and Contemporary Thought, 19,* 225–236.

Cartwright, D. S. (1979). *Theories and models of personality.* Dubuque, IA: W. C. Brown Co.

Carver, C. S. (1996). Emergent integration in contemporary personality psychology. *Journal of Research in Personality, 30,* 319–334.

Cattell, R. B. (1943). The description of personality: Basic traits resolved into clusters. *Journal of Abnormal and Social Psychology, 38,* 476–506.

Cattell, R. B. (1948). Concepts and methods in the measurement of group syntality. *Psychological Review, 55,* 48–63.

Cattell, R. B. (1950). *Personality: A systematic, theoretical and factual study.* New York: McGraw-Hill.

Cattell, R. B. (1960). The multiple abstract variance analysis equations and solutions for nature-nurture research on continuous variables. *Psychological Review, 67,* 353–372.

Cattell, R. B. (1965). *The scientific analysis of personality.* Chicago: Aldine.

Cattell, R. B. (Ed.). (1966). *Handbook of multivariate experimental psychology.* Chicago: Rand McNally.

Cattell, R. B. (1972). *A new morality from science: Beyondism.* New York: Pergamon.

Cattell, R. B. (1990). Advances in Cattellian personality theory. In L. A. Pervin (Ed.), *Handbook of personality: Theory and research* (pp. 101–110). New York: Guilford Press.

Cavell, M. (1991). The subject of mind. *International Journal of Psycho-Analysis, 72*(1), 141–154.

Chambers, W. V., & Epting, F. R. (1985, Dec.). Personality and personal construct: Logical consistency. *Psychological Reports, 57*(3), 1120.

Chambers, W. V., & Graves, P. (1985, Dec.). A technique for eliciting personal construct change. *Psychological Reports, 57*(3), 1041–1042.

Chambers, W. V., & Stonerock, B. (1985, Dec.). Truth and logical consistency of personal constructs. *Psychological Reports, 57*(3), 1178.

Chandler, C. K. (1995). Guest editorial: Contemporary Adlerian reflections on homosexuality and bisexuality. *Individual Psychology: Journal of Adlerian Theory, Research and Practice, 51*, 82–89.

Chang, R., & Page, R. C. (1991). Characteristics of the self-actualized person: Visions from the East and West. *Counseling & Values, 36*(1), 2–10.

Chernin, J., & Holdren, J. M. (1995). Toward an understanding of homosexuality: Origins, status, and relationship to individual psychology. *Individual Psychology: Journal of Adlerian Theory, Research and Practice, 51*, 90–101.

Cheshire, N., & Thoma, H. (1991). Metaphor, neologism, and "open texture": Implications for translating Freud's scientific thought. *International Review of Psycho-Analysis, 18*(3), 429–455.

Chodorow, N. (1985). Gender, relation, and difference in psychoanalytic perspective. In H. Eisenstein & A. Jardine (Eds.), *The future of difference.* New Brunswick, NJ: Rutgers State University.

Chodorow, N. J. (1978). *The reproduction of mothering.* Berkeley: University of California Press.

Chodorow, N. J. (1989). *Feminism and psychoanalytic theory.* New Haven, CT: Yale University Press.

Chodorow, N. J. (1991). "Freud on women" in J. Neu (Ed.), *The Cambridge companion to Freud.* New York: Cambridge University Press.

Chodorow, N. J. (1994). *Femininities, masculinities, sexualities: Freud and beyond.* Lexington, KY: University of Kentucky Press.

Chodorow, N. J. (1995). Gender as a personal and cultural construction. *Signs, 20*, 516–544.

Chodorow, N. J. (1996a). Nancy J. Chodorow talks to Anthony Elliot. *Free Associations, 6*, 161–173.

Chodorow, N. J. (1996b). Reflections on the authority of the past in psychoanalytic thinking. *Psychoanalytic Quarterly, 65*, 32–51.

Chomsky, N. (1959). Review of Skinner's *Verbal behavior. Language, 35*, 26–58; 234; 246–249.

Clarke, J. J. (1992). *In search of Jung: Historical & philosophical enquiries.* London, England: Routledge.

Coan, R. W. (1991). Self-actualization and the quest for the ideal human. Special Issue: Handbook of self-actualization. *Journal of Social Behavior & Personality, 6*(5), 127–136.

Coelho, M. C. (1993). *The universe story.* Unpublished manuscript.

Coles, R. (1970). *Erik H. Erikson: The growth of his work.* Boston: Little, Brown.

Coles, R. (1974). Karen Horney's flight from orthodoxy. In J. Strouse (Ed.), *Women and analysis.* New York: Grossman.

Comstock, G., & Strasburger, V. (1990). Deceptive appearances: Television violence and aggressive behavior. *Journal of Adolescent Health Care, 11*(1), 31–44.

Cooper, J., & Mackie, D. (1986). Video games and aggression in children. *Journal of Applied Social Psychology, 16*(8), 726–744.

Cooper, S. H. (1989). Recent contributions to the theory of defense mechanisms: A comparative view. *Journal of the American Psychoanalytic Association, 37*, 865–891.

Corcoran, D. W. J. (1964). The relation between introversion and salivation. *American Journal of Psychology, 77*, 298–300.

Corcoran, K. (1991). Efficacy, "skills," reinforcement, and choice behavior. *American Psychologist, 46*(2), 155–157.

Costa, P., & McCrae, R. (1992). Revised NEO Personality Inventory: NEO PI and NEO Five-Factor Inventory (NEO FFI) professional manual. Odessa, FL: Psychological Assessment Resources.

Costa, P. T., Jr., & McCrae, R. R. (1985). *The NEO Personality Inventory manual.* Odessa, FL: Psychology Assessment Resources.

Costa, P. T. Jr., & McCrae, R. R. (1997). Stability and change in personality assessment: The revised NEO Personality Inventory in the year 2000. *Journal of Personality Assessment, 68*, 86–94.

Crews, F. (1996). The verdict on Freud. *Psychological Science, 7*, 63–68.

Crockett, W. H. (1982). The organization of construct systems: The organization corollary. In J. C. Mancuso & R. Adams-Webber (Eds.), *The construing person.* New York: Praeger.

Darling, D. (1996). *Zen physics.* New York: HarperCollins.

Das, A. K. (1989). Beyond self-actualization. *International Journal for the Advancement of Counseling, 12*, 13–27.

Davidson, L. (1987, Fall). What is the appropriate source for psychological explanation? *Humanistic Psychologist, 15*(3), 150–166.

Davis, P. J. (1987, September). Repression and the inaccessibility of affective memories. *Journal of Personality and Social Psychology, 53*(3), 585–593.

Davison, G. C., & Lazarus, A. A. (1994). Clinical innovation and evaluation: Integrating practice with inquiry. *Clinical Psychology: Science and Practice, 1*, 157–168.

de Brabander, B., & Boone, C. (1990). Sex differences in perceived locus of control. *Journal of Social Psychology, 130*(2), 271–272.

de Courcy-Hinds, M. (1993, October 19). Not like the movie: A dare leads to death. *The New York Times,* p. C-1.

de Mann, A., Leduc, C., & Labreche-Gauthier, L. (1992). Parental control in child rearing and multidimensional locus of control. *Psychological Reports, 70*(1), 320–322.

DeCarvalho, R. J. (1989). Contributions to the history of psychology: LXII. Carl Rogers' naturalistic system of ethics. *Psychological Reports, 65*(3, Pt. 2), 1155–1162.

DeCarvalho, R. J. (1990). Contributions to the history of psychology: LXIX. Gordon Allport on the problem of method in psychology. *Psychological Reports, 67*(1), 267–275.

DeCarvalho, R. J. (1991). *The founders of humanistic psychology.* New York: Praeger.

DeCarvalho, R. J. (1992). The humanistic ethics of Rollo May. *Journal of Humanistic Psychology, 32,* 7–18.

DeCarvalho, R. J. (1996). Rollo R. May (1909–1994): A biographical sketch. *Journal of Humanistic Psychology, 36,* 8–16.

DeMartino, R. J. (1991). Karen Horney, Daisetz T. Suzuki, and Zen Buddhism. *American Journal of Psychoanalysis, 51*(3), 267–283.

Demont, W. C., & Wolper, E. A. (1958). The relationship of eye movements, body motility, and external stimuli to dream content. *Journal of Experimental Psychology, 55,* 543–553.

Digman, J. M. (1990). Personality structure: Emergence of the five-factor model. *Annual Review of Psychology, 41.* 417–440.

Digman, J. M., & Inouye, J. (1986). Further specification of the five robust factors of personality. *Journal of Personality and Social Psychology, 50,* 116–123.

Diller, J. V. (1991). *Freud's Jewish identity: A case study in the impact of ethnicity.* Rutherford, England: Fairleigh Dickinson University Press/Associated University Press.

Dinkmeyer, D. (1989). Adlerian psychology. *A Journal of Human Behavior, 26*(1).

Dinkmeyer, D., & McKay, G. (1976). *Systematic training for effective parenting.* Circle Pines, MN: American Guidance Service.

Dixon, P. N., & Strano, D. A. (1989). The measurement of inferiority: A review and directions for scale development. *Individual Psychology, 45,* Austin: University of Texas Press.

Doherty, W. J., & Baldwin, C. (1985, April). Shifts and stability in locus of control during the 1970s: Divergence of the sexes. *Journal of Personality and Social Psychology, 48*(4), 1048–1053.

Dollard, J. (1937). *Caste and class in a southern town.* New Haven, CT: Yale University Press.

Dollard, J., Doob, L. W., Miller, N. E., Mowrer, O. H., & Sears, R. R. (1939). *Frustration and aggression.* New Haven, CT: Yale University Press.

Dollard, J., & Miller, N. (1941). *Social learning and imitation.* New Haven, CT: Yale University Press.

Dollard, J., & Miller, N. (1950). *Personality and psychotherapy: An analysis in terms of learning, thinking, and culture.* New York: McGraw-Hill.

Dolliver, R. H. (1994). Classifying the personality theories and personalities of Adler, Freud, and Jung with introversion/extraversion. *Individual Psychology: Journal of Adlerian Theory, Research, and Practice, 50,* 192–202.

Dolliver, R. H. (1995). Carl Rogers's personality theory and psychotherapy as a reflection of his life and personality. *Journal of Humanistic Psychology, 35,* 111–128.

Donahue, E. M. (1994). Do children use the Big Five, too? Content and structural form in personality description. *Journal of Personality, 62,* 45–66.

Donaldson, G. (1996). Between practice and theory: Melanie Klein, Anna Freud and the development of child analysis. *Journal of the History of the Behavioral Sciences, 32,* 160–176.

Dornbusch, S., Gross, R., Duncan, P., & Ritter, P. (1987). Stanford studies of adolescence using the national health examination survey. In R. Lerner & T. Fuch (Eds.), *Biological-psychosocial interactions in early adolescence* (pp. 189–206). Hillsdale, NJ: Erlbaum.

Douglas, C. (1993). *Translate this darkness: The life of Christiana Morgan.* New York: Simon & Schuster.

Dreikurs, R., & Soltz, V. (1964). *Children: The challenge.* New York: Hawthorne.

Drwal, R. L., & Wiechnik, R. (1984). The effect of locus of control and self-esteem on attributions and expectancies after success and failure. *Polish Psychological Bulletin, 15*(4), 257–266.

Dryden, W. (1991). *A dialogue with Arnold Lazarus: "It depends."* Philadelphia: Open University Press.

Dryden, W., & Golden, W. (Eds.). (1986). *Cognitive behavioral approaches to psychotherapy.* London: Harper & Row.

Ducat, S. (1985). Science and psychoanalysis: The implications of recent findings in psychopathology research and neurophysiology for the Freudian theory of the mind. *International Journal of Biosocial Research, 7*(2), 94–107.

Duhs, L., & Gunton, R. (1988). TV violence and childhood aggression: A curmudgeon's guide. *Australian Psychologist, 23*(2), 183–195.

Duke, M. P. (1986, February). Personality science: A proposal. *Journal of Personality and Social Psychology, 50*(2), 382–385.

Dyer, R. (1983). *Her father's daughter: The work of Anna Freud.* New York: Jason Aronson.

Eagle, M. N. (1984). *Recent developments in psychoanalysis: A critical evaluation.* New York: McGraw-Hill.

Eckhardt, M. H. (1991). Feminine psychology revisited: A historical perspective. *American Journal of Psychoanalysis, 51*(3), 235–243.

Edelson, M. (1986, October). The convergence of psychoanalysis and neuroscience: Illusion and reality. *Contemporary Psychoanalysis, 22*(4), 479–519.

Ehrenreich, J. H. (1997). Personality theory: A case of intellectual and social isolation. *Journal of Personality, 131,* 33–44.

Eisenman, R. (1992). Birth order, development, and personality. Acta Paedopsychiatrica: *International Journal of Child & Adolescent Psychiatry, 55,* 25–27.

Ellenberger, H. F. (1970). *The discovery of the unconscious.* New York: Basic Books.

Elliot, B. A. (1992). Birth order and health: Major issues. *Social Science & Medicine, 35*(4), 443–452.

Ellis, A. (1955). New approaches to psychotherapy techniques. *Journal of Clinical Psychology Monograph Supplement,* Brandon, VT.

Ellis, A. (1958). Rational psychotherapy. *Journal of General Psychology, 59,* 35–49.

Ellis, A. (1962). *Reason and emotion in psychotherapy.* New York: Lyle & Stuart.

Ellis, A. (1969). A weekend of rational encounter. *Rational Living, 4*(2), 1–8.

Ellis, A. (1973). *Humanistic psychotherapy.* New York: Julian Press.

Ellis, A. (1976). The biological basis of human irrationality. *Journal of Individual Psychology, 32,* 145–168.

Ellis, A. (1978). Toward a theory of personality. In R. J. Corsini (Ed.), *Readings in current personality theories.* Itasca, IL: Reacock.

Ellis, A. (1985a). *Overcoming resistance: Rational-emotive therapy with difficult clients.* New York: Springer.

Ellis, A. (1985b). Expanding the ABC's of rational emotive therapy. In M. Mahoney & A. Freemany (Eds.), *Cognition and psychotherapy* (pp. 313–323). New York: Plenum.

Ellis, A. (1985c). Two forms of humanistic psychology: Rational-emotive therapy vs. transpersonal psychology. *Free Inquiry, 15*(4), 14–21.

Ellis, A. (1987a). How rational-emotive therapy (RET) helps to actualize the human potential. *New Jersey Journal of Professional Counseling, 50,* 2.

Ellis, A. (1987b). A sadly neglected cognitive element in depression. *Cognitive Therapy and Research, 11,* 121–146.

Ellis, A. (1988). *How to stubbornly refuse to make yourself miserable about anything—yes anything.* Secaucus, NJ: Lyle & Stuart.

Ellis, A. (1991). My life in clinical psychology. In C. E. Walker (Ed.), *The history of clinical psychology in autobiography* (Vol. 1, pp. 1–37). Pacific Grove, CA: Brooks/Cole.

Ellis, A. (1994a). My response to "Don't throw the therapeutic baby out with the holy water": Helpful and hurtful elements of religion. *Journal of Psychology & Christianity, 13,* 323–326.

Ellis A. (1994b). Post-traumatic stress disorder (PTSD): A rational emotive behavior theory. *Journal of Rational-Emotive and Cognitive Behavior Therapy, 12,* 3–25.

Ellis, A. (1995). Psychotherapy is alarmingly encumbered with disposable myths. *Psychotherapy, 32,* 495–499.

Ellis, A. (1996). Responses to criticsms of Rational Emotive Behavior Therapy. *Journal of Rational-Emotive and Cognitive Behavior Therapy, 14,* 97–121.

Ellis, A. (1997). Using Rational Emotive Behavior Therapy techniques to cope with disability. *Professional Psychology: Research and Practice, 28,* 17–22.

Ellis, A., & Becker, I. (1982). *A guide to personal happiness.* North Hollywood, CA: Wilshire.

Ellis, A., & Bernard, M. E. (Eds.). (1983). *Rational-emotive approaches to the problems of childhood.* New York: Plenum.

Ellis, A., & Bernard, M. E. (Eds.). (1985). *Clinical applications of rational-emotive therapy.* New York: Plenum.

Ellis, A., & Dryden, W. (1987). *The practice of rational emotive therapy.* New York: Springer.

Ellis, A., & Harper, R. A. (1975). *A new guide to rational living.* North Hollywood, CA: Wilshire.

Epstein, M. (1995). *Thoughts without a thinker: Psychotherapy from a Buddhist perspective.* New York: Basic Books.

Epstein, R. (1985). The transformation of consciousness into wisdom: The path of the bodhisattva according to the Ch'eng Wei-shih Lun. *Vajra Bodhi Sea, 15,* (176) 22–23; (177) 15–17; (178) 14–15.

Epstein, S. (1994). Integration of the cognitive and the psychodynamic unconscious. *American Psychologist, 49,* 709–724.

Epstein, S. (1996). Recommendations for the future development of personality psychology. *Journal of Research in Personality, 30,* 435–446.

Epting, F. R., & Leitner, L. M. (1992). Humanistic psychology and personal construct theory. Special Issue: The humanistic movement in psychology: History, celebration, and prospectus. *Humanistic Psychologist, 20*(2–3), 243–259.

Erikson, E. H. (1958). *Young man Luther.* New York: Norton.

Erikson, E. H. (1963). *Childhood and society* (2nd ed.). New York: Norton.

Erikson, E. H. (1964). *Insight and responsibility.* New York: Norton.

Erikson, E. H. (1968). *Identity, youth and crisis.* New York: Norton.

Erikson, E. H. (1969). *Gandhi's Truth,* New York: Norton.

Erikson, E. H. (1974). *Dimensions of a new identity.* New York: Norton.

Erikson, E. H. (1975). *Life history and the historical moment.* New York: Norton.

Erlenmeyer-Kimling, L., & Jarvik, L. F. (1963). Genetics and intelligence: A review. *Science, 142,* 1477–1479.

Espin, O., & Gawelek, M. (1992). Women's diversity: Ethnicity, race, class, and gender in theories of feminist psychology. In L. Brown & M. Ballou (Eds.), *Personality and psychopathology: Feminist reappraisals.* New York: Guilford Press.

Esterson, A. (1998). Jeffrey Masson and Freud's seduction theory: A new fable based on old myths. In *History of the Human Sciences,* vol. 11, No. 1, pp. 1–21. London.

Evans, R. I. (1967). *Dialogue with Erik Erikson.* New York: Harper & Row.

Evans, R. J. (1976). *The making of psychology: Discussions with creative contributors.* New York: Knopf.

Evans, T. D., & Meredith, D. W. (1991). How far can you go and still be Adlerian? Special Issue: "On beyond Adler." *Individual Psychology: Journal of Adlerian Theory, Research & Practice, 47*(4), 541–547.

Eysenck, H. (1990). Biological dimensions of personality. In L. A. Pervin (Ed.), *Handbook of personality: Theory and research.* New York: Guilford Press.

Eysenck, H. (1990). Genetic and environmental contributions to individual differences: The 3 major dimensions of personality. *Journal of Personality, 58,* 245–261.

Eysenck, H. (1991). Dimensions of personality: The biosocial approach to personality. In J. Strelau & A. Angleitner (Eds.), *Exploration in temperament: International perspectives on theory and measurement* (p. 365). New York: Plenum Press.

Eysenck, H. J. (1947). *Dimensions of personality.* London: Routledge & Kegan Paul.

Eysenck, H. J. (1952). The effects of psychotherapy: An evaluation. *Journal of Consulting Psychology, 16,* 319–324.

Eysenck, H. J. (1956). The inheritance of extraversion-introversion. *Acta Psychologica, 12,* 95–110.

Eysenck, H. J. (1957). *The dynamics of anxiety and hysteria.* London: Routledge & Kegan Paul.

Eysenck, H. J. (Ed.). (1961). *Handbook of abnormal psychology: An experimental approach.* New York: Basic Books.

Eysenck, H. J. (1964). Involuntary rest pauses in tapping as a function of drive and personality. *Perceptual and Motor Skills, 18,* 172–174.

Eysenck, H. J. (1965). *Fact and fiction in psychology.* Baltimore: Penguin.

Eysenck, H. J. (1967). *The biological basis of personality.* Springfield, IL: Charles C. Thomas.

Eysenck, H. J. (1970). *The structure of human personality* (3rd ed.). New York: Methuen.

Eysenck, H. J. (1972). *Psychology is about people.* New York: The Library Press.

Eysenck, H. J. (1975). *The inequality of man.* San Diego: EdITS.

Eysenck, H. J. (1976). The learning theory model of neurosis—a new approach. *Behavior Research and Therapy, 14,* 251–267.

Eysenck, H. J. (Ed.). (1981). *A model for personality.* New York: Springer-Verlag.

Eysenck, H. J. (1982). *Personality, genetics, and behavior: Selected papers.* New York: Praeger.

Eysenck, H. J. (1985). Revolution in the theory and measurement of intelligence. *Evaluación Psicológica, 1*(1–2), 99–158.

Eysenck, H. J. (1989, December). Health's character. *Psychology Today,* 28–32, 34–35.

Eysenck, H. J. (1993). The relationship between IQ and personality. In G. L. Van Heck, (Ed.), *Personality psychology in Europe* (Vol. 4, pp. 159–181). Tilbur, Netherlands: Tilbourg University Press.

Eysenck, H. J. (1994). The outcome problem in psychotherapy: What have we learned? *Behavior Research and Therapy, 32,* 477–495.

Eysenck, H. J. (1994a). Personality and intelligence: Psychometric and experimental approaches. In R. J. Sternberg (Ed.), *Personality and intelligence* (pp. 3–31). New York: Cambridge University Press.

Eysenck, H. J. (1994b). Personality and temperament. In D. Tantam & M. Birchwood (Eds.), *Psychology and the social science* (pp. 187–202). Gaskell, United Kingdom: Royal College of Psychiatrists.

Eysenck, H. J. (1995b). Mental health and physical disease: A new paradigm. *Journal of Mental Health, 4,* 221–225.

Eysenck, H. J. (1996). Personality and the experimental study of education. *European Journal of Personality, 10,* 427–439.

Eysenck, H. J., & Eysenck, M. W. (1985). *Personality and individual differences.* London: Plenum.

Eysenck, H. J., & Eysenck, S. B. G. (1976). *Psychoticism as a dimension of personality.* New York: Crane, Russak.

Eysenck, H. J., & Rachman, S. (1965). *The causes and cures of neurosis.* San Diego, CA: Knapp.

Eysenck, S. B. J., Eysenck, H. J., & Barrett, P. (1985). A revised version of the psychoticism scale. *Personality and Individual Differences, 6,* 21–29.

Farmer, J. J. (1993, July 29). Vince Foster's reasons may never be known. *Newark Star Ledger.*

Farran, D., Haskins, R., & Galligher, J. (1980). Poverty and mental retardation: A search for explanations. *New Directions for Exceptional Children, 1,* 47–66.

Fay, A. (1976). Clinical notes on paradoxical therapy. In A. A. Lazarus, *Multimodal behavior therapy.* New York: Springer.

Fay, A. (1978). *Making things better by making them worse.* New York: Hawthorne.

Feixas, G. (1989). Personal construct psychology in Spain: A promising perspective. *International Journal of Personal Construct Psychology, 2*(4), 433–442.

Feldmann, T. B., & Johnson, P. W. (1995). Cult membership as a source of self-cohesion: Forensic implications. *Bulletin of the American Academy of Psychiatry and the Law. 23,* 239–248.

Feshbach, S. (1984, September). The "personality" of personality theory and research. *Personality and Social Psychology Bulletin, 10*(3), 446–456.

Fickling, W. (1991), Fall/Winter). Zen as therapy, *The Ten Directions,* pp. 38–40.

Fiebert, M. S. (1997). In and out of Freud's shadow: A chronology of Adler's relationship with Freud. *Individual Psychology: Journal of Adlerian Theory, Research and Practice, 53,* 241–269.

Fingarette, H. (1963). *The self in transformation: Psychoanalysis, philosophy, and the life of the spirit.* New York: Basic Books.

Fisher, S., & Greenberg, R. P. (1977). *Scientific credibility of Freud's theory and therapy.* New York: Basic Books.

Flax, J. (1994). Final analysis? Psychoanalysis in the postmodern West. *Annual of Psychoanalysis, 22,* 1–20.

Foa, E. B. (1990). Continuous exposure and complete response prevention of obsessive compulsive neuroses. *Behavior Therapy, 32,* 821–829.

Ford, J. G. (1991). Inherent potentialities of actualization: An initial exploration. *Journal of Humanistic Psychology, 31*(3), 65–88.

Ford, K. M., & Adams-Webber, J. R. (1991). The structure of personal construct systems and the logic of confirmation, *International Journal of Personal Construct Psychology, 4*(1), 15–41.

Fordham, F. (1953). *An introduction to Jung's psychology.* Baltimore: Penguin.

Forisha-Kovach, B. (1983). *The experience of adolescence: Development in context.* New York: Scott, Foresman & Co.

Frank, C. M. (1956). Conditioning and personality: A study of normal and neurotic subjects. *Journal of Abnormal and Social Psychology, 52,* 143–150.

Frankl, V. E. (1960). Paradoxical intention: A logo-therapeutic technique. *American Journal of Psychotherapy, 14,* 520–535.

Frankl, V. E. (1978). *The unheard cry for meaning.* New York: Simon & Schuster.

Franks, C. M. (1976). Foreword. In A. A. Lazarus, *Multimodal behavior therapy.* New York: Springer.

Franks, C. M. (1997). Foreword. In A. A. Lazarus, *Brief but comprehensive Psychotherapy: The multimodal way.* New York: Springer.

Freeman, M. (1992). Self as narrative: The place of life history in studying the life span. In T. Brinthaupt & R. Lipka (Eds.), *The self: Definitional and methodological issues.* New York: State University of New York.

Freud, A. (1946). *The ego and the mechanisms of defense.* New York: International Universities Press.

Freud, A. (1958). Adolescence. In *The Writings of Anna Freud.* New York: International Universities Press.

Freud, A. (1965–  ). *The Writings of Anna Freud.* New York: International Universities Press.

Freud, S. (1953–  ). *The complete psychological works: Standard edition* (24 vols.). J. Strachey (Ed.). London: Hogarth Press. (Hereafter referred to as *SE* with year of original publication.)

Freud, S. (1895). Studies in hysteria. *SE* (Vol. 2).

Freud, S. (1900). The interpretation of dreams. *SE* (Vols. 4 & 5).

Freud, S. (1901). The psychopathology of everyday life. *SE* (Vol. 6).

Freud, S. (1905). Three essays on sexuality. *SE* (Vol. 7).

Freud, S. (1910). Five lectures on psychoanalysis. *SE* (Vol. 11).

Freud, S. (1917). Introductory lectures on psychoanalysis. *SE* (Vols. 15 & 16).

Freud, S. (1923). The ego and the id. *SE* (Vol. 19).

Freud, S. (1926b). The question of lay analysis. *SE* (Vol. 20).

Freud, S. (1933). New introductory lectures on psychoanalysis. *SE* (Vol. 22).

Freud, S. (1940). An outline of psychoanalysis. *SE* (Vol. 23).

Fromm, E. (1941). *Escape from freedom.* New York: Rinehart.

Fromm, E. (1947). *Man for himself.* New York: Rinehart.

Fromm, E. (1955). *The sane society.* New York: Rinehart.

Fromm, E. (1956). *The art of loving.* New York: Harper & Row.

Fromm, E. (1964). *The heart of man.* New York: Harper & Row.

Fromm, E. (1973). *The anatomy of human destructiveness.* New York: Rinehart.

Fromm, E. (1976). *To have or to be.* New York: Harper & Row.

Fromm, E., & Maccoby, M. (1970). *Social character in a Mexican village.* Englewood Cliffs, NJ: Prentice-Hall.

Fuld, P. J. (1991, Fall/Winter). Zen and the work of a psychotherapist. *The Ten Directions,* pp. 40–41.

Fullerton, C. S., Ursano, R. J., Harry, P., & Slusarcick, A. (1989). Birth order, psychological well-being, and social supports in young adults. *Journal of Nervous & Mental Disease, 177*(9), 556–559.

Funder, D., & Sneed, C. (1993). Behavioral manifestations of personality: An ecological approach to judgmental accuracy. *Journal of Personality and Social Psychology, 64.* 479–490.

Furnham, A. (1990). Can people accurately estimate their own personality test scores? *European Journal of Personality, 4*(4), 319–327.

Gaillard, C. (1995). The presbyopic vision of C. G. Jung. *Cahiers Jungiens de Psychanalyse, 82,* 105–118.

Galin, D. (1974). Implications for psychiatry of left and right cerebral specialization. *Archives of General Psychiatry, 31,* 572–583.

Gallard, M. (1995). Jung and Nazi Germany: The facts, the context. *Cahiers Jungiens de Psychanalyse, 82,* 69–76.

Gardner, H. (1992). Scientific psychology: Should we bury it or praise it? *New Ideas in Psychology, 10*(2), 179–190.

Gardner, W. L., & Martinko, M. J. (1996). Using the Myers-Briggs Type Indicator to study managers: A literature review and research agenda. *Journal of Management, 22,* 45–83.

Garfield: S. (1992). Response. In W. Dryden & C. Feltham (Eds.), *Psychotherapy and its discontents* (pp. 124–137). Buckingham, England: Open University Press.

Garofalo, D. (1996). The clinical application of Karen Horney's theory to group psychoanalysis. *American Journal of Psychoanalysis, 56,* 193–202.

Garrison, D. (1981). Karen Horney and feminism. *Signs: Journal of Women in Culture and Society, 6,* 4.

Geisler, C. (1985). Repression: A psychoanalytic perspective revisited. *Psychoanalysis and Contemporary Thought, 8*(2), 253–298.

Geller, L. (1982). The failure of self-actualization theory. *Journal of Humanistic Psychology, 22,* 56–73.

Geller, L. (1984, Spring). Another look at self-actualization. *Journal of Humanistic Psychology, 24*(2), 93–106.

Gergen, K. (1992, November/December). The decline and fall of personality. *Psychology Today,* pp. 59–60.

Gilligan, C. (1977). In a different voice: Women's conception of self and morality, *Harvard Educational Review, 47,* 481–517.

Gilligan, C. (1982). *In a different voice.* Cambridge, MA: Harvard University Press.

Gilligan, C. (1990). Joining the resistance: Psychology, politics, girls and women, *Michigan Quarterly Review, 29,* 501–536.

Ginsberg, C. (1984, Spring). Toward a somatic understanding of self: A reply to Leonard Geller. *Journal of Humanistic Psychology, 24*(2), 66–92.

Giora, Z. (1991). *The unconscious and its narratives.* Budapest, Hungary: Twins Publishing House.

Giorgi, A. (1987, Spring). The crisis of humanistic psychology. *Humanistic Psychologist, 15*(1), 5–20.

Glucksberg, S., & King, I. (1967, October 27). Motivated forgetting mediated by implicit verbal chaining: A laboratory analog of repression. *Science,* 517–519.

Glymour, C. (1991). Freud's androids. *The Cambridge companion to Freud. Cambridge companions to philosophy.* New York: Cambridge University Press.

Goldberg, L. R. (1981). Language and individual differences: The search for universals in personality lexicons. In L. Wheeler (Ed.), *Review of personality and social psychology* (Vol. 2, pp. 141–165). Beverly Hills, CA: Sage.

Goldberg, L. R. (1990). An alternative "description of personality": The big-five factor structure. *Journal of Personality and Social Psychology 59,* 1216–1229.

Goldberg, L. R. (1993). The structure of phenotypic personality traits. *American Psychologist, 48,* 26–34.

Goldstein, J., Freud, A., & Solnit, A. J. (1973). *Beyond the best interests of the child.* New York: The Free Press.

Goldstein, J., Freud, A., & Solnit, A. J. (1979). *Before the best interests of the child.* New York: The Free Press.

Goleman, D. (1985*). Vital lies, simple truths.* New York: Simon & Schuster.

Goleman, D. (1987, February 6). Carl R. Rogers, 85, leader in psychotherapy, dies. *The New York Times,* pp. D16.

Goleman, D. (1992). New light on how stress erodes health. *New York Times,* p. C-1.

Goleman, D. (1993a, May 4). Some patients arouse hatred, therapists find. *New York Times,* p. C-1.

Goleman, D. (1993b, April 6). Studying the secrets of childhood memory. *The New York Times,* p. C-1.

Goleman, D. (1994, January 11). Childhood depression may herald adult ills. *The New York Times,* p. C-1.

Goleman, D. (1994, March 22). The "wrong" sex: A new definition of childhood pain. *The New York Times.*

Goleman, D. (1996, January 24). Critics say managed-care savings are eroding mental care. *The New York Times,* p. C9.

Green, C. D. (1992). Of immortal mythological beasts: Optionism in psychology. *Theory & Psychology, 2*(3), 291–320.

Greenberg, G. (1995). If a self is a narrative: Social construction in the clinic. *Journal of Narrative and Life History, 5,* 269–283.

Greenberg, J. 1981, August 11). A psychiatrist who wouldn't take no for an answer. *The New York Times*, pp. C1–C2.

Greisers, C., Greenberg, R., & Harrison, R. H. (1972). The adaptive function of sleep: The differential effects of sleep and dreaming on recall. *Journal of Abnormal Psychology, 80*, 280–286.

Grotstein, J. S. (1991). An American view of the British psychoanalytic experience: Psychoanalysis in counterpoint: The contributions of the British Object Relations School. *Melanie Klein & Object Relations, 9*(2), 34–62.

Grotstein, J. S. (1997). "Internal objects" or "chimerical monsters"?: The demonic "third forms" of the internal world. *Journal of Analytical Psychology, 42*, 47–80.

Grünbaum, A. (1984). *The foundations of psychoanalysis: A philosophical critique.* Berkeley, CA: University of California Press.

Grünbaum, A. (1993). *Validation in the clinical theory of psychoanalysis.* New York: International Universities Press.

Guilford, J. P. (1967). *The nature of human intelligence.* New York: McGraw-Hill.

Gupta, M. D. (1987, January). Role of age and birth order in Machiavellianism. *Psychological Studies, 32*(1), 47–50.

Guy-Gillet, G. (1996). Oedipus confronting the Sphinx. *Cahiers Jungiens de Psychanalyse, 87*, 31–40.

Hagen, S. (1995). *How the world can be the way it is: An inquiry for the new millennium into science, philosophy, and perception.* Wheaton, IL: Theosophical Publishing House.

Hagen, S. (1997). *Buddhism plain and simple.* Rutland, VT: Tuttle.

Haitch, R. H. (1995). How Tillich and Kohut both find courage in faith. *Pastoral Psychology, 44*, 83–97.

Hall, C. S., & Lindzey, G. (1978). *Theories of personality* (3rd ed.). New York: Wiley.

Hall, C. S., Lindzey, G., & Campbell, J. B. (1998). *Theories of personality,* 4th ed. New York: John Wiley and Sons.

Hall, C. S., & Van de Castle, R. (1965). An empirical investigation of the castration complex in dreams. *Journal of Personality, 33*, 20–29.

Hall, M. (1968, July). A conversation with Abraham H. Maslow, *Psychology Today,* 34–37; 54–57.

Hall, M. (1983, June). A conversation with Erik Erikson. *Psychology Today, 17*(6).

Hamacheck, D. (1990). Evaluating self-concept and ego status in Erickson's last three psychosocial stages. *Journal of Counseling & Development, 68*(6), 677–683.

Hammer, J. (1970). Preference for gender of child as a function of sex of adult respondents. *Journal of Individual Psychology, 33*, 20–29.

Hamon, S. A. (1987, Summer). Some contributions of Horneyan theory of enhancement of the Type A behavior construct. *American Journal of Psychoanalysis, 47*(2), 105–115.

Hanh, T. N. (1974). *Zen keys.* Garden City, NY: Anchor/Doubleday.

Hanh, T. N. (1975). *The miracle of mindfulness! A manual on meditation.* Boston: Beacon.

Hanh, T. N. (1985). *A guide to walking meditation.* Nyack, NY: Fellowship.

Hanh, T. N. (1988). *The heart of understanding.* Berkeley, CA: Parallax.

Hanh, T. N. (1991). *Peace is every step: The path of mindfulness in everyday life.* New York: Bantam.

Hanh, T. N. (1992). *Touching peace.* Berkeley, CA: Parallax.

Hanh, T. N. (1993). *The blooming of a lotus: Guided meditation exercises for healing and transformation.* Boston: Beacon.

Harari, C. (1989). Humanistic and transpersonal psychology: Values in psychotherapy. *Psychotherapy in Private Practice, 7*(4), 49–56.

Harrington, D. M., Block, J. H., & Block, J. (1987, April). Testing aspects of Carl Rogers's theory of creative environments: Child-rearing antecedents of creative potential in young adolescents. *Journal of Personality and Social Psychology, 52*(4), 851–856.

Harris, K. A., & Morrow, J. B. (1992). Differential effects of birth order and gender on perceptions of responsibility and dominance. *Individual Psychology: Journal of Adlerian Theory, Research & Practice, 48*(1), 109–118.

Harris, T. (1969). *I'm OK—You're OK.* New York: Harper & Row.

Harrison, W., Lewis, G., & Straka, T. (1984, September). Locus of control, choice, and satisfaction with an assigned task. *Journal of Research in Personality, 18*(3), 342–351.

Hartmann, H. (1958). *Ego psychology and the problem of adaption.* New York: International Universities Press.

Hartmann, H. (1964). *Essays in ego psychology: Selected problems on psychanalytic theory.* New York: International Universities Press.

Harzem, P. (1987, Fall). On the virtues of being a psychologist. *Behavior Analyst, 10*(2), 175–181.

Hayes, S., & Hayes, L. (1988). Inadequacies not just obstacles. *Counseling Psychology Quarterly, 1*(2–3), 291–294.

Hayes, T. L. (1996). Personality correlates of performance: Does disability make a difference? *Human Performance, 9*, 121–140.

Henwood, K. L., & Pidgeon, N. F. (1992). Qualitative research and psychological theorizing. *British Journal of Psychology, 83*(1), 97–111.

Hermans, J. J., Kempen, H. J., & Van Loon, R. J. (1992). The dialogical self: Beyond individualism and rationalism. *American Psychologist, 47*(1), 23–33.

Hermsen, E. (1996). Person-centered psychology and Taoism: The reception of Lao-tzu by Carl R. Rogers. *International Journal for the Psychology of Religion, 6,* 107–125.

Heston, L. L. (1966). Psychiatric disorders in foster home reared children of schizophrenic mothers. *British Journal of Psychiatry, 112*, 819–825.

Hibbard, S. (1993). Behavior, adaption, and intentionality. *Journal of Mind and Behavior, 14,* 373–384.

Hinds, M. (1993, October 19). Not like the movie: A dare leads to death. *The New York Times,* p. C-1.

Hirai, T. (1989). *Zen meditation and psychotherapy.* Tokyo: Japan Publications.

Hjelle, L. A. (1991). Relationship of social interest to internal-external control and self-actualization in young women. Special Issue: Social interest.

*Individual Psychology: Journal of Adlerian Theory, Research & Practice, 47*(1), 101–105.

Hoffman, E. (1988). *The right to be human: A biography of Abraham Maslow.* Los Angeles: Tarcher.

Hoffman, E. (1994a). *The drive for self: Alfred Adler and the founding of individual psychology.* Reading, MA: Addison-Wesley.

Hoffman, E. (1994b, November 20). Karen Horney, *New York Times Book Review,* p. 20.

Hogan, R. (1982). A socioanalytic theory of personality. In M. Page (Ed.), *Nebraska symposium on motivation.* Lincoln: University of Nebraska Press.

Hogan, R., & Hogan, J. (1995). *Hogan Personality Inventory manual* (2nd ed.). Tulsa, OK: Hogan Assessment Systems.

Hogan, R., Hogan, J., & Roberts, B. W. (1996). Persaonlity measurement and employment decisions: Questions and answers. *American Psychologist, 5,* 469–477.

Hogan, R. J. (1976). *Personality theory: The personological tradition.* Englewood Cliffs, NJ: Prentice-Hall.

Holland, J. L. (1996). Exploring careers with a typology: What we have learned and some new directions. *American Psychologist, 51,* 397–406.

Honey, P., & Mumford, A. (1992). *The manual of learning styles,* Peter Honey and Alan Mumford (Publishers), Maidenhead, U.K.

Hoover, I. (1980). *The Zen experience,* New York: New American Library.

Horley, J. (1991). Values and beliefs as personal constructs. *International Journal of Personal Construct Psychology, 4*(1), 1–14.

Horney, K. (1937). *The neurotic personality of our time.* New York: Norton.

Horney, K. (1939). *New ways in psychoanalysis.* New York: Norton.

Horney, K. (1942). *Self-Analysis.* New York: Norton.

Horney, K. (1945). *Our inner conflicts.* New York: Norton.

Horney, K. (1950). *Neurosis and human growth.* New York: Norton.

Horney, K. (1967). *Feminine psychology.* New York: Norton.

Howard, R., & McKillen, M. (1990). Extraversion and performance in the perceptual maze test. *Personality and Individual Differences, 11,* 391–396.

Iaccino, J. F. (1994). *Psychological reflections on cinematic terror: Jungian archetypes in horror films.* London: Praeger.

Ingram, D. H., & Lerner, J. A. (1992). Horney theory: An object relations theory. *American Journal of Psychoanalysis, 52*(1), 37–44.

Ishiyama, F. I., Munson, P. A., & Chabassol, D. J. (1990). Birth order and fear of success among midadolescents. *Psychological Reports, 66*(1), 17–18.

Jackson, C., & Lawty-Jones, M. (1996). Explaining the overlap between personality and learning style. *Personality and Individual Differences, 20,* 293–300.

Jackson, D. J. (1991). Contributions to the history of psychology: LXXXI. The friendship of Anna Freud and Dorothy Burlingham. *Psychological Reports, 68*(3, Pt. 2), 1176–1178.

Jacobson, L. (1996). The Grünbaum debate: Introduction. *Psychoanalytic Dialogues, 6,* 497–502.

Jacobson, N. S. (1987). *Psychotherapists in clinical practice: Cognitive and behavioral perspectives.* New York: Guilford Press.

Jager, B. (1989). Language and human science: The vocabularies of academic psychology and psycholanalysis. *Humanistic Psychologist, 17*(2), 112–130.

Jankowicz, A. D. (1987, May). Whatever became of George Kelly? Applications and implications. *American Psychologist, 42*(5), 481–487.

Jensen, A. R. (1969). How much can we boost IQ and scholastic achievement? *Harvard Educational Review, 39,* 1–123.

John, O. P. (1990). The "Big Five" factor taxonomy: Dimensions of personality in the natural language and in questionnaires. In L. A. Pervin (Ed.), *Handbook of personality: Theory and research* (pp. 66–100). New York: Guilford Press.

John, O. P., & Robins, R. W. (1993). Gordon Allport: Father and critic of the Five-Factor Model. In K. H. Craik, R. Hogan, & R. N. Wolfe (Eds.). *Fifty years of personality psychology* (pp. 215–236). New York: Plenum Press.

Johnson, R. A. (1991). *Understanding the dark side of the psyche.* San Francisco, CA: Harper San Francisco.

Jones, E. (1953–1957). *The life and work of Sigmund Freud* (3 vols.). New York: Basic Books.

Jones, E. E., & Pulos, S. M. (1993). Comparing the process in psychodynamic and cognitive behavioural therapy. *Journal of Consulting and Clinical Psychology, 61,* 306–316.

Jordan, J. V. (1990). Courage in connection: Conflict, compassion, creativity. *Work in Progress.* The Stone Center, Wellesley College, Wellesley, Massachusetts.

Jordan, J. V. (1991). Women and empathy: Implications for psychological development and psychotherapy. In J. V. Jordan et al. (Eds.), *Women's growth in connection: Writings from the Stone Center,* 27–50. New York: Guilford Press.

Jordan, J. V. (1994). A relational perspective on self esteem. *Work in Progress.* Stone Center, Wellesley College.

Jordan, J. V. (Ed.). (1997a). *Women's growth in diversity.* New York: Guilford Press.

Jordan, J. V. (1997b). Clarity in connection: Empathic knowing, desire, and sexuality. In J. V. Jordan (Ed.), *Women's growth in diversity,* 50–73. New York: Guilford Press.

Jordan, J. V. (1997c). Relational development: Therapeutic implications of empathy and shame. In J. V. Jordan (Ed.), *Women's growth in diversity.* New York: Guilford Press.

Jordan, J. V., Kaplan, A. G., Miller, J. B., Stiver, I. P., & Surrey, J. L. (Eds.). (1991). *Women's growth in connection: Writings from the Stone Center.* New York: Guilford Press.

Josephs, R., Markus, R., & Tafarodi, R. (1992). Gender and self-esteem. *Journal of Personality and Social Psychology, 63,* 391.

Juda, D. P. (1991). Freud versus Freud: Healing the divided field of victimization. *Psychoanalysis & Psychotherapy, 9*(1), 3–17.

Jung, C. G. (1953– ). *Collected works.* H. Read, M. Fordham, & G. Adler, (Eds.). Princeton: Princeton

University Press. (Hereafter referred to as *CW* with year of original publication.)

Jung, C. G. (1916). Symbols of transformation. *CW* (Vol. 5).

Jung, C. G. (1933). *Psychological types.* New York: Harcourt, Brace.

Jung, C. G. (1934). A review of complex theory. *CW* (Vol. 8).

Jung, C. G. (1936). The archetypes and the collective unconscious. *CW* (Vol. 9).

Jung, C. G. (1938). Psychology and religion. *CW* (Vol. 11).

Jung, C. G. (1939). The integration of the personality. *CW* (Vol. 17).

Jung, C. G. (1948). On psychic energy. *CW* (Vol. 8).

Jung, C. G. (1951). Two Essays on Analytical Psychology. *CW* (Vol. 7).

Jung, C. G. (1954). Psychological aspects of the mother archetype. *CW* (Vol. 9).

Jung, C. G. (1955). Mandalas. *CW* (Vol. 9).

Jung, C. G. (1960). Synchronicity: An acausal connecting principle. *CW* (Vol. 8).

Jung, C. G. (1961). *Memories, dreams, and reflections.* New York: Random House.

Jung, C. G. (1964). *Man and his symbols.* New York: Doubleday.

Kabat-Zinn, J. (1990). *Full catastrophe living: Using the wisdom of your body and mind to face stress, pain, and illness.* New York: Delacorte.

Kaczor, L. M., Ryckman, R. M., Thornton, B., & Kuelnel, R. H. (1991). Observer hyper-competitiveness and victim precipitation of rape. *Journal of Social Psychology, 131,* 131–134.

Kagan, J. (1972). Motives and development. *Journal of Personality and Social Psychology, 22,* 51–56.

Kagan, J. (1991). The theoretical utility of constructs for self. Special Issue: The development of self: The first three years. *Developmental Review, 11*(3), 244–250.

Kagan, J. (1994). *Galen's prophecy: Temperament in human nature.* New York: Basic Books.

Kalekin-Fishman, D. (1993). The two faces of hostility: The implications of personal construct theory for understanding alienation. *International Journal of Personal Construct Psychology, 6*(1), 27–40.

Kalupahana, D. J., & Kalupahana, I. (1982). *The way of Siddhartha: A life of the Buddha.* Boulder, CO: Shambhala.

Kant, I. (1798). *Anthropology from a pragmatic point of view.* ts. by V. L. Dowdel. Carbondale and Edwardsville: Southern Illinois University Press. A new translation published in 1978.

Kantrowitz, R. E., & Ballou, M. A. (1992). A feminist critique of cognitive-behavioral therapy. In L. S. Brown & M. Ballou (Eds.), *Personality and psychopathology: Feminist reappraisals* (pp. 70–87). New York: Guilford Press.

Kaplan, L. J. (1996). The stepchild of psychoanalysis, adolescence. *American Imago, 53,* 257–268.

Kaplan, R. D. (1994, February 20). There is no "Middle East." *The New York Times Magazine,* p. 14.

Katagiri, D. (1988). *Returning to silence: Zen practice in daily life.* Boston: Shambhala.

Keirsey, D., & Bates, M. (1984). *Please understand me: Character and temperament types.* Del Mar, CA: Prometheus Nemesis.

Kelly, G. A. (1955). *The psychology of personal constructs* (2 vols.). New York: Norton.

Kelly, G. A. (1958). Man's construction of his alternatives. In G. Lindzey (Ed.), *Assessment of human motives.* New York: Rinehart & Winston.

Kelly, G. A. (1970). A brief introduction to personal construct theory. In D. Bannister (Ed.), *Perspectives in personality construct theory.* New York: Academic Press.

Kelly, W. L. (1991). *Psychology of the unconscious.* Buffalo, NY: Prometheus Books.

Kernberg, O. F. (1975). *Borderline conditions and pathological narcissism.* New York: Jason Aronson.

Kernberg, O. F. (1990). Sexual excitement and rage: Building blocks of the drives. *Sigmund Freud House Bulletin, 15*(1), 3–38.

Kernberg, O. F. (1992). *Aggression in personality disorders and perversions.* New Haven and London: Yale University Press.

Kernberg, O. F. (1994). The present state of psychoanalysis. *Psyche: Zeitschrift für Psychoanalyse und ihre Anwendungen, 48,* 483–508.

Kernberg, O. F. (1995a). Omnipotence in the transference and in the countertransference. *Scandinavian Psychoanalytic Review, 18,* 2–21.

Kernberg, O. F. (1995b). Technical approach to eating disorders in patients with borderline personality organization. *Annual of Psychoanalysis, 23,* 33–48.

Kernberg, O. F. (1996a). Hatred as the core affect of aggression. *Zeitschrift für Psychosomatische Medizin und Psychoanalyse, 42,* 281–305.

Kernberg, O. F. (1996b). The analyst's authority in the psychoanalytic situation. *Psychoanalytic Quarterly, 65,* 137–157.

Kernberg, O. F. (1996c). Thirty methods to destroy the creativity of psychoanalytic candidates. *International Journal of Psycho-Analysis, 77,* 1031–1040.

Kernberg, O. F., Selzer, M. A., Koenigsberg, H. W., Carr, A. C., & Appelbaum, A. H. (1989). *Psychodynamic psychotherapy of borderline patients.* New York: Basic Books.

Kidwell, J. (1982). The neglected birthorder: Middleborns. *Journal of Marriage and the Family, 44,* 225–235.

Kihlstrom, J. F., Barnhardt, T. M., & Tataryn, D. J. (1992). The psychological unconscious: Found, lost, and regained. *American Psychologist, 47,* 788–791.

Kimura, D. (1979). The asymmetry of the human brain. *Scientific American, 2128,* 70–78.

Kinkead, G. (1994, April 10). Spock, Brazelton, and now Penelope Leach. *The New York Times Magazine,* p. 32.

Kiracofe, N. M., & Kiracofe, H. N. (1990). Child-perceived parental favoritism and birth order. *Individual Psychology: Journal of Adlerian Theory, Research & Practice, 46*(1), 74–81.

Kitayama, S., & Markus, H. R. (1992, May). *Construal of self as cultural frame: Implications for internationalizing psychology.* Paper presented to symposium on Internationalization and Higher Education, Ann Arbor, MI.

Klatzky, R. L. (1980). *Human memory: Structures and processes* (2nd ed.). San Francisco: Freeman.

Klein, M. (1932). *The psychoanalysis of children.* London: Hogarth.

Klein, M. (1975). The writings of Melanie Klein, vol. 3. London: Hogarth.

Klein, S. (1984, March). Birth order and introversion-extraversion. *Journal of Research in Personality*, 18,(1), 110–113.

Kline, P. (1972). *Fact and fantasy in Freudian theory*. London: Methuen.

Kline, P. (1987, September). The experiential study of the psychoanalytic unconscious. *Personality and Social Psychology Bulletin*, 13(3), 363–378.

Koch, E. (1991). Nature-nurture issues in Freud's writings: The complemental series. *International Review of Psycho-Analysis, 18*, 473–487.

Kohut, H. (1971). *The analysis of the self*. New York: International Universities Press.

Kohut, H. (1977a). *The restoration of the self*. New York: International Universities Press.

Kohut, H. (1977b). Preface. In *Psychodynamics of drug dependence* (NIDA Research Monograph No. 12, pp. vii–ix). Washington, DC: U.S. Government Printing Office.

Kohut, H. (1978). The psychoanalyst in the community of scholars. In P. Ornstein (Ed.), *The search for the self: Selected writings of Heinz Kohut* (Vol. 2, pp. 685–724). New York: International Universities Press.

Kohut, H. (1984). *How does analysis cure?* In A. Goldberg and P. Stepansky (Eds.), *Contributions to the psychology of the self*. Chicago, IL: University of Chicago Press.

Kolata, G. (1994, March 8). In ancient times, flowers and fennel for family planning. *The New York Times*, p. C-1.

Kolb, D. (1984). *Experiential learning*, Englewood Cliffs, NJ: Prentice-Hall.

Kosko, B. (1993). *Fuzzy thinking: The new science of fuzzy logic*. New York: Hyperion.

Kruger, D. (1986, December). Phenomenology and the fundamentals of psychology. *South African Journal of Psychology, 16*(4), 109–116.

Krystal, H. (1990). An information processing view of object-relations. *Psychoanalytic Inquiry, 10*(2), 221–251.

Kuhn, T. S. (1970). *The structure of scientific revolutions*. Chicago: University of Chicago Press.

Kwee, M. G. T. (1981). Towards the clinical art and science of multimodal psychotherapy. *Current Psychological Reviews, 1*, 55–68.

Lachmann, F. M., & Beebe, B. (1995). Self psychology: Later, the same day. *Psychoanalytic Dialogues, 5*, 415–419.

Lambert, M. (1988). Beyond psychology as the science of behavior. *Counselling Psychology Quarterly, 1*(2–3), 313–315.

Lamielle, J. T. (1981). Toward an idothetic psychology of personality. *American Psychologist, 36*, 276–289.

Lamielle, J. T., & Trierweiler, S. J. (1986, June). Interactive measurement, idiothetic inquiry, and the challenge to conventional nomotheticism. *Journal of Personality, 54*(2), 460–469.

Landfield, A. W. (1988). Personal science and the concept of validation. *International Journal of Personal Construct Psychology, 1*(3), 237–249.

Landman, J. T., & Dawes, R. M. (1982). Psychotherapy outcomes. *American Psychologist, 37*(5), 504–516.

Landrine, H., & Klonoff, E. (1992). Culture and health-related schemas: A review and proposal for interdisciplinary integration. *Health Psychology, 11*, 267–276.

Lang, K. L., & Livesley, W. J. (1996). Heritability of the big five personality dimensions and their facets: A twin study. *Journal of Personality, 64*, 577–597.

Lawton, H. W. (1990). The field of psychohistory. *Journal of Psychohistory, 17*(4), 353–364.

Lazarsfeld, S. (1991). The courage for imperfection. Special Issue: Social interest. *Individual Psychology: Journal of Adlerian Theory, Research & Practice, 47*(1), 93–96.

Lazarus, A. A. (1956). A psychological approach to alcoholism. *South African Medical Journal, 30*, 707–710.

Lazarus, A. A. (1958). New methods in psychotherapy: A case study. *South African Medical Journal, 32*, 660–664.

Lazarus, A. A. (1966). Broad spectrum behavior therapy and the treatment of agoraphobia. *Behavior Research and Therapy, 4*, 95–97.

Lazarus, A. A. (1971). *Behavior therapy and beyond*. New York: McGraw-Hill.

Lazarus, A. A. (1973). Multimodal behavior therapy: Treating the BASIC-ID. *Journal of Nervous and Mental Disorders, 156*, 404–411.

Lazarus, A. A. (1976). *Multimodal behavior therapy*. New York: Springer.

Lazarus, A. A. (1978). *In the mind's eye: The power of imagery for personal enrichment*. New York: Rawson.

Lazarus, A. A. (1982). Personal enrichment through imagery. New York: BMA Audio Cassettes.

Lazarus, A. A. (1985). *Casebook of multimodal therapy*. New York: Guilford Press.

Lazarus, A. A. (1989). *The practice of multimodal therapy*. Baltimore: Johns Hopkins University Press.

Lazarus, A. A. (1993). Theory, subjectivity and bias: Can there be a future? *Psychotherapy, 30*, 674–677.

Lazarus, A. A. (1994). How certain boundaries and ethics diminish therapeutic effectiveness. *Ethics and Behavior, 4*, 255–261.

Lazarus, A. A. (1995). Different types of eclecticism and integration: Let's be aware of the dangers. *Journal of Psychotherapy Integration, 5*, 27–39.

Lazarus, A. A. (1996a). Fixed rules versus idiosyncratic needs. *Ethics and Behavior, 6*, 80–81.

Lazarus, A. A. (1996b). Some reflections after 40 years of trying to be an effective psythotherapist. *Psychotherapy, 33*, 142–145.

Lazarus, A. A. (1996c). The utility and futility of combining treatments in psychotherapy. *Clinical Psychology: Science and Practice, 3*, 59–68.

Lazarus, A. A. (1997). *Brief but comprehensive psychotherapy: The multimodal way*. New York: Springer.

Leak, G. K., Gardner, L. E., & Pounds, B. (1992). A comparison of Eastern religion, Christianity, and social interest. *Individual Psychology: Journal of Adlerian Theory, Research & Practice, 48*, 53–64.

Lefcourt, H. (1976). *Locus of control: Current trends in theory and research*. Hillsdale, NJ: Erlbaum.

Lefcourt, H. (1992). Durability and impact of the locus of control construct. *Psychological Bulletin, 112*(3), 411–414.

Lefcourt, H. M., Martin, R. A., & Saleh, W. E. (1984, August). Locus of control and social support: Interactive moderators of stress. *Journal of Personality and Social Psychology, 47*(2), 378–389.

Leith, G. (1974). Individual differences in learning: Interaction of personality and teaching methods. In *Personality and Academic Process* (pp. 14–25). London: Association of Educational Psychologists.

Leone, G. (1995). Zen meditation: A psychoanalytic conceptualization. *Journal of Transpersonal Psychology, 27,* 87–94.

Lerman, H. (1992). The limits of phenomenology: A feminist critique of the humanistic personality theories. In L. S. Brown & M. Ballou (Eds.), *Personality and psychopathology.* New York and London: Guilford Press.

Lester, D. (1992). Cooperative/competitive strategies and locus of control. *Psychological Reports, 71*(2), 594.

Lester, D., Eleftheriou, L., & Peterson, C. A. (1992). Birth order and psychological health: A sex difference. *Personality & Individual Differences, 13,* 379–380.

Levitz-Jones, E. M., & Orlofsky, J. L. (1985). Separation-individualization and intimacy capacity in college women. *Journal of Personality and Social Psychology, 49,* 156–169.

Lewis, A. (1991). Developing social feeling in the young child through his play life. *Individual Psychology: Journal of Adlerian Theory, Research & Practice, 47*(1), 72–75.

Lewis, H. B. (1988, Winter). Freudian theory and new information in modern psychology. *Psychoanalytic Psychology, 5*(1), 7–22.

Lewis, J. L. (1995). Two paradigmatic approaches to borderline patients with a history of trauma. *Journal of Psychotherapy Practice and Research, 5,* 1–19.

Lieberman, L., Shaffer, T. G., & Reynolds, L. T. (1985, September). Scientific revolutions and birth order. *Individual Psychology: Journal of Adlerian Theory, Research and Practice, 41*(3), 328–335.

Likierman, M. (1990). "Translation in transition": Some issues surrounding the Strachey translation of Freud's works. *International Review of Psycho-Analysis, 17,* 115–120.

Likierman, M. (1995). The debate between Anna Freud and Melanie Klein: An historical survey. *Journal of Child Psychotherapy, 21,* 313–325.

Lindorff, D. (1995). Psyche, matter and synchronicity: a collaboration between C. G. Jung and Wolfgang Pauli. *Journal of Analytical Psychology, 40,* 571–586.

Loehlin, J. C. (1992). *Genes and environment in personality development.* Newbury Park, CA: Sage.

Loevinger, J. (1996). In defense of the individuality of personality theories. *Psychological Inquiry, 7,* 344–346.

Lombardi, D. N., & Elcock, L. E. (1997). Freud versus Adler on dreams. *American Psychologist, 52,* 572–573.

Loomis, M. E. (1991). *Dancing the wheel of psychological types.* Wilmette, IL: Chiron Publications.

Loori, J. D. (1988). *Mountain record of Zen talks.* Boston: Shambhala.

Lovaas, O. T., et al. (1966). Acquisition of imitative speech in schizophrenic children. *Science, 151,* 705–707.

Maccoby, E. E., & Martin, J. A. (1983). Socialization in the context of the family: Parent-child interaction. In E. M. Hetherington (Ed.), *Handbook of child psychology: Socialization, personality, and social development* (Vol. 4), 1–102. New York: Wiley.

Maccoby, M. (1976). *The gamesman.* New York: Simon & Schuster.

Maccoby, M. (1981). *The leader.* New York: Simon & Schuster.

MacIntyre, A. (1958). *The unconscious: A conceptual analysis.* London: Routledge & Kegan Paul.

MacIntyre, A. (1984). *After virtue* (2nd ed.). Notre Dame, IN: University of Notre Dame Press.

MacKenzie, K. R. (1996). Group psychotherapy: Managed care's reluctant bride. *Behavioral Health Management, 16,* 18–24.

Macmillan, M. (1991). *Freud evaluated: The completed arc.* Advances in Psychology 75. Amsterdam: North-Holland.

Macy, J. (1991). *Mutual causality in Buddhism and general systems theory.* Albany: State University of New York.

Magid, B. (Ed.). (1993). *Freud's case studies.* Hillsdale, NJ: Analytic Press.

Magnusson, D., & Torestad, B. (1993). A holistic view of personality: A model revisited. *Annual Review of Psychology, 44,* 427–452.

Mahers, B. A. (1991). Deception rational man and other rocks on the road to a personality psychology of real people. In P. E. Meehl (Ed.), *Matters of public interest:* Vol. 2. *Personality and psychopathology.* Minneapolis: University of Minnesota Press.

Mahler, B. (Ed.). (1969). *Clinical psychology and personality: The selected papers of George Kelly.* New York: John Wiley.

Mahler, M. (1975). *The psychological birth of the human infant.* New York: Basic Books.

Maiello, S. (1996). Epistemological contribution of the Horney theory to group psychoanalysis. *American Journal of Psychoanalysis, 56,* 187–192.

Mair, M. (1988). Psychology as storytelling. *International Journal of Personal Construct Psychology, 1*(2), 125–137.

Mancuso, J. C. (1996). Constructionism, personal construct psychology and narrative psychology. *Theory and Psychology, 6,* 47–70.

Mansfield, V., & Spiegelman, J. M. (1991). The opposites in quantum physics and Jungian psychology: I. Theoretical foundations. *Journal of Analytical Psychology, 36*(3), 267–287.

Marcia, J. E. (1966). Development and validation of ego-identity status. *Journal of Personality and Social Psychology, 49,* 156–169.

Marcia, J. E. (1980). Identity in adolescence. In J. Adelson (Ed.), *Handbook of adolescent psychology.* New York: Wiley.

Margolis, D. P. (1989). Freud and his mother. *Modern Psychoanalysis, 14,* 37–56.

Marin, P. (1975). The new narcissism. *Harper's,* 45–56.

Markova, I. (1992). On solos, duets, quartets, and quintets: A response to Gardner. *New Ideas in Psychology, 10*(2), 215–221.

Markstrom-Adams, C. (1992). A consideration of intervening factors in adolescent identity formation. In G. R. Adams, T. P. Gullotta, & R. Montemayor (Eds.), *Adolescent identity formation. Advances in adolescent development, 4,* 173–192. Newbury Park, CA: Sage.

Markus, H. R., & Kitayama, S. (1991). Culture and the self: Implications for cognition, emotion, and motivation. *Psychological Review, 98,* 224–253.

Masling, J. M., Rabie, L., & Blondheim, S. H. (1967). Obesity, level of aspiration, and Rorschach and TAT measures of oral dependence. *Journal of Consulting Psychology, 31,* 233–239.

Maslow, A. (1970). *Motivation and personality* (2nd ed.). New York: Harper & Row.

Masse, G. (1994). From complex to spirit: Jung and the spiritual dimension. *Cahiers Jungiens de Psychoanalyse, 80,* 81–94.

Masson, J. M. (1983). *The assault on the truth: Freud's suppression of the seduction theory.* New York: Farrar, Straus, & Giroux.

May, R. (1953). *Man's search for himself.* New York: Norton.

May, R. (1967). *Psychology and the human dilemma.* New York: Van Nostrand Reinhold.

May, R. (1969). *Love and will.* New York: Norton.

May, R. (1972). *Power and innocence.* New York: Norton.

May, R. (1975). *The courage to create.* New York: Norton.

May, R. (1977). *The meaning of anxiety.* New York: Norton.

May, R. (1981). *Freedom and destiny.* New York: Norton.

May, R. (1983). *The discovery of being.* New York: Norton.

May, R. (1991). *The cry for myth.* New York: Norton.

May, R., Angel, E., & Ellenberger, H. F. (Eds.). (1958). *Existence: A new dimension in psychiatry and psychology.* New York: Basic Books.

Mayer, E. L. (1996). Erik H. Erikson on bodies, gender, and development. *Psychoanalysis and Contemporary Thought, 19,* 237–257.

McAdams, D. P. (1992). Unity and purpose in human lives: The emergence of identity as a life story. In R. A. Zucker, A. I. Rabin, J. Aronoff, & S. J. Frank (Eds.), *Personality structure in the life course: Essays on personology in the Murray tradition,* 323–375. New York: Springer.

McAdams, D. P. (1993). *The stories we live by: Personal myths and the making of the self.* New York: William Morrow.

McAdams, D. P. (1994). A psychology of the stranger. *Psychological Inquiry, 5,* 145–148.

McAdams, D. P. (1995). What do we know when we know a person? *Journal of Personality, 63,* 366–396.

McAdams, D. P. (1996a). Personality, modernity, and the storied self: A contemporary framework for studying persons. *Psychological Inquiry, 4,* 295–321.

McAdams, D. P. (1996b). Alternative futures for the study of human individuality. *Journal of Research in Personality, 30,* 374–388.

McAdams, D. P. (1997). Three voices of Erik Erikson. *Contemporary Psychology, 42,* 575–578.

McAdams, D. P., & de St. Aubin, E. (1992). A theory of generativity and its assessment through self-report, behavioral acts, and narrative themes in autobiography. *Journal of Personality and Social Psychology, 62,* 1003–1015.

McAdams, D. P., Diamond, A., de St. Aubin, E., & Mansfield, E. (1997). Stories of commitment: The psychosocial construction of generative lives. *Journal of Personality and Social Psychology, 72,* 678–694.

McAdams, D. P., & Ochberg, R. C. (Eds.). (1988, March). Special Issue: Psychobiography and Life Narratives. *Journal of Personality, 56*(1).

McCartney, K. (Rapporteur). (1993). Group report: What can twin studies contribute to the understanding of personality? In T. J. Bouchard, Jr., & P. Propping (Eds.), *Twins as a tool of behavioral genetics.* New York: Wiley.

McClelland, D. C. (1961). *The achieving society.* New York: Free Press.

McClelland, D. C. (1996). Does the field of psychology have a future? *Journal of Research in Personality, 30,* 429–434.

McClelland, D. C., Atkinson, J. W., Clark, R. A., & Lowell, E. L. (1953). *The achievement motive.* New York: Appleton-Century-Crofts.

McCrae, R. R. (1996). Integrating the levels of personality. *Psychological Inquiry, 7,* 353–356.

McCrae, R. R., & Costa, P. T. (1989). Validation of the five-factor model of personality across instruments and observers. *Journal of Personality and Social Psychology, 52,* 81–90.

McCrae, R. R., & Costa, P. T. (1990). *Personality in adulthood.* New York: Guilford Press.

McCrae, R. R., & Costa, P. T., Jr. (1985). Updating Norman's adequate taxonomy: Intelligence and personality dimensions in natural language and in questionnaires. *Journal of Personality and Social Psychology, 49,* 710–721.

McCrae, R. R., & Costa, P. T., Jr. (1987). Validation of the five-factor model of personality across instruments and observers. *Journal of Personality and Social Psychology, 52,* 81–90.

McCrae, R. R., & Costa, P. T. Jr. (1997). Personality trait structure as a human universal. *American Psychologist, 52,* 509–516.

McKay, J., Pyke, S. W., & Goranson, R. (1984, November–December). Whatever happened to "inner-space": A failure to replicate. *International Journal of Women's Studies, 7*(5), 387–396.

McLaughlin, R. J., & Eysenck, J. J. (1967). Extraversion, neuroticism, and paired-associate learning. *Journal of Experimental Research in Personality, 2,* 128–132.

Meares, R. (1996). The psychology of self: An update. *Australian & New Zealand Journal of Psychiatry, 30,* 312–316.

Meichenbaum, D., & Deffenbacher, J. L. (1988). Stress inoculation training. *The Counseling Psychologist, 16,* 69–90.

Mencher, J. (1997). Intimacy in lesbian relationships: A critical reexamination of fusion. In J. V. Jordan (Ed.), *Women's growth in diversity,* 311–330. New York: Guilford Press.

Metzger, R. (1996). The Buddhist six-worlds model of consciousness and reality. *Journal of Transpersonal Psychology, 28,* 155–166.

Miccolis, G. (1996). Sociocultural influences in the theory of Karen Horney. *American Journal of psychoanalysis, 56,* 141–147.

Miller, C. (1991). Self-actualization and the consciousness revolution. Special Issue: Handbook of self-actualization. *Journal of Social Behavior & Personality, 6*(5), 109–126.

Miller, J. (1976). *Toward a new psychology of women.* Boston, MA: Beacon Press.

Miller, J., Fletcher, K., & Kabat-Zinn, J. (1995). Three-year follow-up and clinical implications of a mindfulness meditation-based stress reduction intervention in the treatment of anxiety disorders. *General Hospital Psychiatry, 17,* 192–200.

Miller, J. B. (1984). *The development of women's sense of self.* Work in Progress Series. The Stone Center for Development Studies, Wellesley College, MA.

Miller, J. B. (1986). What do we mean by relationships? *Work in Progress.* No. 22. Stone Center, Wellesley College.

Miller, J. B. (1991). The development of women's sense of self. In J. V. Jordan, A. G. Kaplan, J. B. Miller, I. P. Stiver, & J. L. Surrey (Eds.), *Women's growth in connection: Writings from the Stone Center*, 11–26. New York: Guilford Press.

Miller, J. B., & Stiver, I. P. (1997). *The healing connection: How women form relationships in therapy and in life*. Boston: Beacon Press.

Miller, J. B., & Surrey, J. L. (1997). Revisioning women's anger: The personal and the global. In J. V. Jordan (Ed.), *Women's growth in diversity*, 199–216. New York: Guilford Press.

Miller, N. E. (1944). Experimental studies of conflict. In J. McV. Hunt (Ed.), *Personality and the behavior disorders* (Vol. 1). New York: Ronald Press.

Miller, N. E. (1951). Comments on theoretical models: Illustrated by the development of a theory of conflict behavior. *Journal of Personality, 20*, 82–100.

Miller, N. E. (1959). Liberalization of basic S-R concepts: Extensions to conflict behavior, motivation, and social learning. In S. Koch (Ed.), *Psychology: A study of a science* (Vol. 2). New York: McGraw-Hill.

Miller, N. J. (1991, Fall/Winter). To study the self. *The Ten Directions*, pp. 35–37.

Miller, N. S., Katz, J. L. (1989). The neurological legacy of psychology: Freud as a neurologist. *Comprehensive Psychiatry, 30*, 128–134.

Miller, P., Potts, R., Fung, H., & Hoogstra, L. (1990). Narrative practices and the social construction of self in childhood. *American Psychologist, 17*(2) 292–311.

Miranda, A. O., Goodman, E. D., & Kern, R. M. (1996). Similarities between social interest and contemporary definitions of corporate leadership. *Individual Psychology: Journal of Adlerian theory, Research & Practice*, 261–269.

Mischel, W. (1968). *Personality and assessment*. New York: Wiley.

Mischel, W. (1973). Toward a cognitive social learning reconception of personality. *Psychological Review, 80*, 252–283.

Mischel, W. (1983). Alternatives in the pursuit of the predictability and consistency of persons: Stable data that yield unstable interpretations. *Journal of Personality, 51*, 578–604.

Mischel, W., & Shoda, Y. (1995). A cognitive-affective system theory of personality: Reconceptualizing situations, dispositions, dynamics, and invariance in personality structure. *Psychological Review, 102*, 246–268.

Mitchell, J. (1974). *Psychoanalysis and feminism: Freud, Reich, Laing and women*. New York: Vintage.

Mitchell, J. (1991). "Deconstructing difference: Gender, splitting and transitional space": Commentary. *Psychoanalytic Dialogues, 1*(3), 353–357.

Mogenson, G. (1990). The resurrection of the dead: A Jungian approach to the mourning process. *Journal of Analytical Psychology, 35*(3), 317–333.

Moore, J. (1992). On private events and theoretical terms. *Journal of Mind and Behavior, 13*(4), 329–345.

Moraglia, G. (1994). C. G. Jung and the psychology of adult development. *Journal of Analytical Psychology, 39*, 55–75.

Mosig, Y. D. (1988). Karate-do and the actualization of enlightenment. *Udumbara: Journal of Zen Practice, 4*(2)/5(1), 45–50.

Mosig, Y. D. (1989). Wisdom and compassion: What the Buddha taught. *Theoretical and Philosophical Psychology, 9*(2), 27–36.

Mosig, Y. D. (1990). Zen meditation and the art of kobudo. *U.S.K.A. Forum, 1*(1), 2–3.

Mosig, Y. D. (1991). A guide to Zen practice. *U.S.K.A. Forum, 2*(1), 2–3.

Mruk, C. J. (1989). Phenomenological psychology and the computer revolution: Friend, foe, or opportunity? *Journal of Phenomenological Psychology, 20*(1), 20–39.

Mueller, E., & Tingley, E. (1990). The Bears' Picnic: Children's representations of themselves and their families. *New Directions for Child Development, 48*, 47–65.

Murk, D., & Addleman, J. (1992). Relations among moral reasoning, locus of control, and demographic variables among college students. *Psychological Reports, 70*(2), 467–476.

Murphy, M., & Donovan, S. (1988). *The physical and psychological effects of meditation*. San Rafael, CA: Esalen Institute.

Murray, H. A. (1938). *Explorations in personality*. New York: Oxford University Press.

Myers, I. B., & McCaulley, M. H. (1985). *A guide to the development and use of the Myers-Briggs Type Indicator*. Palo Alto, CA: Consulting Psychologists Press.

Myyra, J. (1992). The great mother. In K. Bjorkqvist & P. Niemela (Eds.), *Of mice and women: Aspects of female aggression* (pp. 263–271). San Diego, CA: Academic Press.

Naidu, R. (1991). Etic principles in psychology: An evaluation of the myth in support of indigenous psychologies. *Indian Journal of Current Psychological Research, 5*(2), 93–100.

Narayan, C. (1990). Birth order and narcissism. *Psychological Reports, 67*(3, Pt. 2), 1184–1186.

Neubauer, P., & Neubauer, A. (1990). *Nature's thumbprint: The new genetics of personality*. Reading, MA: Addison-Wesley.

Neufeldt, A. (1989). Applying psychology: Some real world possibilities for scientists and practitioners. *Canadian Psychology, 30*(4), 681–691.

Nielsen, S. L., & Ellis, A. (1994). A discussion with Albert Ellis: Reason, emotion and religion. *Journal of Psychology and Christianity, 13*, 327–341.

Noble, B. P. (1993, February 21). Infant bonding and guilty mothers. *The New York Times*, p. 25.

Noel, D. C. (1991). Traveling with Jung toward an archetypal ecology. *Quadrant, 24*(1), 83–91.

Norcross, J. C. (1986). *Handbook of eclectic psychotherapy*. New York: Brunner/Mazel.

Norcross, J. C., & Goldfried, M. R. (Eds.). (1992). *Handbook of psychotherapy integration*, New York: Basic Books.

Norman, W. T. (1963). Toward an adequate taxonomy of personality attributes. *Journal of Abnormal and Social Psychology, 66*, 574–583.

Oatley, K. (1992). Not psychologists but psychology: A response to Gardner. *New Ideas in Psychology, 10*(2), 207–214.

O'Hara, M. (1992). Relational humanism: A psychology for a pluralistic world. *Humanistic Psychologist, 20*(2–3), 439–446.

O'Hara, M. (1995). Carl Rogers: Scientist and mystic: *Journal of Humanistic Psychology, 35,* 40–53.

O'Keefe, E. J., & Castaldo, C. (1981). Multimodal management: A systematic and holistic approach for the 80's. *Proceedings of the Marist College Symposium on Local Government Productivity,* Poughkeepsie, NY.

Okumura, S. (Ed.). (1985). *Shikantaza.* Kyoto, Japan: Kyoto Soto-Zen Center.

Okumura, S. (1997, May 1). Untitled. *Sanshin Zen Community Newsletter, 2,* 1.

Orlofsky, J. L. (1976). Intimacy status: Relationship of interpersonal perception. *Journal of Youth and Adolescence, 5,* 73–88.

Ornstein, A. (1993). Little Hans. In B. Magid (Ed.), *Freud's case studies.* Hillsdale, NJ: Analytic Press.

Ornstein, R. (1997). *The right mind: Making sense of hemispheres.* New York: Harcourt, Brace.

Ornstein, R. E. (1977). *The psychology of consciousness.* New York: Harcourt Brace Jovanovich.

Packer, M. (1992). Toward a postmodern psychology of moral action and moral development. In W. Kurtines, M. Azmitia, & J. Gewirtz (Eds.), *The role of values in psychology and human development* (pp. 30–59). New York: John Wiley.

Packer, M. J. (1991). Interpreting stories, interpreting lives: Narrative and action in moral development research. In M. B. Tappan & M. J. Packer (Eds.), *Narrative and storytelling: Implications for understanding moral development. New directions for child development.* San Francisco, CA: Jossey-Bass.

Page, R. C. & Berkow, D. N. (1991). Concepts of the self: Western and Eastern perspectives. *Journal of Multicultural Counseling and Development, 19,* 83–93.

Papini, D. R., Micka, J. C., & Barnett, J. K. (1989). Perceptions of intrapsychic and extrapsychic functioning as basis of adolescent ego identity statuses. *Journal of Adolescent Research, 4*(4), 462–482.

Paris, B. J. (1994). *Karen Horney: A psychoanalyst's search for self-understanding.* New Haven, CT: Yale University Press.

Paris, B. J. (1996). Introduction to Karen Horney. *American Journal of Psychoanalysis, 56,* 135–140.

Patterson, S. J., Sochting, I., & Marcia, J. E. (1992). The inner space and beyond: Women and identity. In G. R. Adams, T. P. Gullotta, & R. Montemayor (Eds.), *Adolescent identity formation: Advances in adolescent development, 4,* 9–24. Newbury Park, CA: Sage.

Paul, R. A. (1985, Summer). Freud and the seduction theory: A critical examination of Masson's *The Assault on Truth. Journal of Psychoanalytic Anthropology, 8*(3), 161–187.

Paul, R. A. (1989). Psychoanalytic anthropology. *Annual Review of Anthropology, 18,* 177–202.

Paul, R. A. (1992). Bettelheim's contribution to anthropology. *Educating the emotions: Bruno Bettelheim and psychoanalytic development.* New York: Plenum.

Pelham, B. W. (1993). The idiographic nature of human personality: Examples of the idiographic self-concept. *Journal of Personality & Social Psychology, 64*(4), 665–677.

Perrez, M. (1991). The difference between everyday knowledge, ideology, and scientific knowledge. *New Ideas in Psychology, 9,* 227–231.

Pervin, L. A. (1994). A critical analysis of current trait theory. *Psychological Inquiry, 5,* 103–113.

Pervin, L. A. (1996). Personality: A view of the future based on a look at the past. *Journal of Research in Personality, 30,* 309–318.

Pine, F. (1994). The era of separation-individuation. *Psychoanalytic Inquiry, 14,* 4–24.

Piyadassi, T. (1974). *The Buddha's ancient path.* Kandy, Sri Lanka: Buddhist Publication Society.

Place, U. (1988). What went wrong? *Counselling Psychology Quarterly, 1*(2–3), 307–309.

Plomin, R., Chipuer, H. M., & Loehlin, J. C. (1990). Behavioral genetics and personality. In L. A. Pervin (Ed.), *Handbook of personality: Theory and research* (pp. 225–243). New York: Guilford Press.

Potter, J., & Wetherell, M. (1992). On the literary solution: A response to Gardner. *New Ideas in Psychology, 10*(2), 223–227.

Powell, L. (1992). The cognitive underpinnings of coronary-prone behaviors. *Cognitive Therapy & Research, 16*(2), 123–142.

Power, M. (1988). Seven sins of behaviourism. *Counselling Psychology Quarterly, 1*(2–3), 279–286.

Power, T., & Chapleski, M. (1986). Childrearing and impulse control in toddlers: A naturalistic investigation. *Developmental Psychology, 22,* 271–275.

Privette, G. (1986, April). From peak performance and peak experience to failure and misery. *Journal of Social Behavior and Personality, 1*(2), 233–243.

Puhan, B. N., & Sahoo, F. M. (1991, October). Indigenization of psychological studies: Research agenda. *Indian Journal of Current Psychological Research, 6*(2), 101–107.

Quinn, S. (1994). Awakened to life: Sources of independence in the girlhood of Karen Horney. In M. Berger (Ed.), *New concepts of feminine psychology,* New York: Brunner/Mazel.

Rahula, W. (1974). *What the Buddha taught.* New York: Grove.

Rapaport, D. (1953). A critique of Dollard and Miller's *Personality and psychotherapy. American Journal of Orthopsychiatry, 23,* 204–208.

Rattner, J. (1983). *Alfred Adler.* New York: Ungar.

Reichlin, R. E., & Niederehe, G. (1980). Early memories: A comprehensive bibliography. *Journal of Individual Psychology, 36*(2), 209–218.

Retief, A. (1986, September). The need for theory development in psychology: Some care studies. *South African Journal of Psychology, 16*(3), 71–78.

Retief, A. (1989). The debate about the relevance of South African psychology: A metatheoretical imperative. *South African Journal of Psychology, 19*(2), 75–83.

Reynolds, D. (1995). *A handbook for constructive living.* New York: William Morrow.

Reynolds, D. K. (1976). *Morita psychotherapy.* Berkeley: University of California.

Reynolds, D. K. (1980). *The quiet therapies: Japanese pathways to personal growth.* Honolulu: University of Hawaii.

Rhymer, B. (1988). *Morita-Psychotherapie und Zen-Buddhismus.* Zurich, Switzerland: Volkerkundemuseum der Universitat Zurich.

Richards, A. D. (1990). The future of psychoanalysis: The past, present, and future of psychoanalytic theory. *Psychoanalytic Quarterly, 59,* 347–369.

Rieken, B. (1996). "Fiction" in the works of Vaihinger and Adler, *Zeitschrift für Individualpsychologie, 21,* 280–291.

Roberts, T. K., Jackson, L. J., & Phelps, R. (1980). Lazarus' multimodal therapy model applied to an institutional setting. *Professional Psychology, 11,* 150–156.

Robinson, F. G. (1992). *Love's story told: A life of Henry A. Murray.* Cambridge, MA: Harvard University Press.

Robinson, P. (1993). *Freud and his critics.* Berkeley: University of California Press.

Rogers, C. R. (1951). *Client-centered therapy: Its current practice, implications, and theory.* Boston: Houghton Mifflin.

Rogers, C. R. (1959). A theory of therapy, personality, and interpersonal relationships as developed in the client-centered framework. In S. Koch (Ed.), *Psychology: A study of a science* (Vol. 3). New York: McGraw-Hill.

Rogers, C. R. (1961). *On becoming a person.* Boston: Houghton Mifflin.

Rogers, C. R. (1963). The concept of a fully functioning person. *Psychotherapy: Theory, Research, and Practice, 1*(1), 17–26.

Rogers, C. R. (1964). Toward a modern approach to values: The valuing process in the mature person. *Journal of Abnormal and Social Psychology, 68,* 160–167.

Rogers, C. R. (1980). *A way of being.* Boston: Houghton Mifflin.

Rogers, C. R., & Dymond, R. S. (Eds.). (1954). *Psychotherapy and personality change.* Chicago, IL: University of Chicago Press.

Rogers, C. R., & Roethlisberger, F. J. (1952, July–August). Barriers and gateways to communication. *Harvard Business Review,* 28–35.

Romaniello, J. (1992). Beyond archetypes: A feminist perspective on Jungian theory. In L. S. Brown & Mary Ballou (Eds.), *Personality and psychopathology: Feminist reappraisals.* New York: Guilford Press.

Rorer, L. F., & Widiger, T. A. (1983). Personality structure and assessment. *Annual Review of Psychology, 34,* 401–430.

Rosolack, T., & Hampson, S. (1991). A new typology of health behaviours for personality–health predictions: The case of locus of control. *European Journal of Personality, 5*(2), 151–168.

Rotter, J. B. (1954). *Social learning and clinical psychology.* Englewood Cliffs, NJ: Prentice-Hall.

Rotter, J. B. (1966). Generalized expectancies for internal versus external control of reinforcement. *Psychological Monographs, 80* (whole no. 609).

Rotter, J. B. (1982). *The development and application of social learning theory: Selected papers.* New York: Praeger.

Rotter, J. B., Chance, J. E., & Phares, E. J. (1972). *Applications of a social learning theory of personality.* New York: Holt, Rinehart & Winston.

Rotter, J. B., & Hochreich, D. J. (1975). *Personality,* Glenview, IL: Scott, Foresman.

Rottschaefer, W. (1991). Some philosophical implications of Bandura's social cognitive theory of human agency. *American Psychologist, 46*(2), 153–155.

Rousselle, R. (1990). On the nature of psychohistorical evidence. *Journal of Psychohistory, 17*(4), 425–434.

Runco, M. A., & Bahleda, M. D. (1987, March). Birth-order and divergent thinking. *Journal of Genetic Psychology, 148*(1), 119–125.

Russell, G. (1992). Response of the macho male to viewing a combatant sport. *Journal of Social Behavior & Personality, 7*(4), 631–638.

Rychlak, J. (1968). *A philosophy of science for personality theory.* Boston: Houghton Mifflin.

Rychlak, J. F. (1973). *Introduction to personality and psychotherapy.* Boston: Houghton Mifflin.

Rychlak, J. F. (1981). Logical learning theory: Propositions, corollaries, and research evidence. *Journal of Personality and Social Psychology, 40*(4), 731–749.

Rychlak, J. F. (1986, December). Logical learning theory: A teleological alternative in the field of personality. *Journal of Personality, 54*(4), 734–762.

Rychlak, J. F. (1990). George Kelly and the concept of construction. *International Journal of Personal Construct Psychology, 3*(1), 7–19.

Ryckman, R. M., et al. (1985, September). Physical self-efficacy and actualization. *Journal of Research in Personality, 19*(3), 288–298.

Ryckman, R. M., & Malikiosi, M. X. (1975). Relationship between locus of control and chronological age. *Psychological Reports, 36,* 655–658.

Ryckman, R. M., Hammer, M., Kaczor, L. M., & Gold, A. (1990). Construction of a hypercompetitive attitude scale. *Journal of Personality Assessment, 55,* 630–639.

Saeeduzzafar, R., & Sharma, R. (1991). A study of independence-proneness among Hindu and Muslim youths in relation to locus of control. *Journal of Personality & Clinical Studies, 7*(2), 199–202.

Sampson, E. E. (1991). The democraticization of psychology. *Theory & Psychology, 1*(3), 275–298.

Samuels, A. (1992). National psychology, national socialism, and analytical psychology: Reflections on Jung and anti-Semitism: II. *Journal of Analytical Psychology, 37*(2), 127–147.

Sarason, S. (1989). The lack of an overarching conception in psychology. *Journal of Mind and Behavior, 10*(3), 263–279.

Sarbin, T. (Ed.). (1986). *Narrative psychology: The storied nature of human conduct.* New York: Praeger.

Sass, L. (1982, August 22). The borderline personality. *New York Times Magazine.*

Saudino, K. J., & Plomin, R. (1996). Personality and behavioral genetics: Where have we been and where are we going? *Journal of Research in Personality, 30,* 335–347.

Sayers, J. (1987). Freud revisited: On gender, moral development, and androgyny. *New Ideas in Psychology, 5*(2), 197–206.

Schafer, R. (1995). In the wake of Heinz Hartmann. *International Journal of Psycho-Analysis, 72,* 223–235.

Schimek, J. G. (1987). Fact and fantasy in the seduction theory: A historical review. *Journal of the American Psychoanalytic Association, 35*(4), 937–965.

Schultz, D. (1990). *Theories of personality* (4th ed.). Pacific Grove, CA: Brooks/Cole.

Schwartz, J. (1996). Physics, philosophy, psychoanalysis, and ideology: On engaging with Adolf Grünbaum. *Psychoanalytic Dialogues, 6,* 503–513.

Sears, R. R. (1943). Survey of objective studies of psychoanalytic concepts. *Social Science Research Council Bulletin, 51.*

Shea, C. (1997, April 4). No less violence on TV, study says. *Chronicle of Higher Education.*

Shell, W. E., Hargrove, L., & Falbo, T. (1986, September). Birth order and achievement motivation configurations in women and men. *Individual Psychology: Journal of Adlerian Theory, Research and Practice, 42*(3), 428–438.

Sheng-Yen (1987). *The advantages one may derive from Zen meditation.* Elmhurst, NY: Dharma Drum.

Sherman, N. (1995). The moral perspective and the psychoanalytic quest. *Journal of the American Academy of Psychoanalysis, 23,* 223–241.

Shevrin, H. (1995a). Is psychoanalysis one science, two sciences, or no science at all? A discourse among friendly antagonists. *Journal of the American Psychoanalytic Association, 43,* 963–986.

Shevrin, H. (1995c). Is psychoanalysis one science, two sciences, or no science at all? Commentary reply. *Journal of the American Psychoanalytic Association, 43,* 1035–1049.

Shoda, Y., & Mischel, W. (1996). Toward a unified, intra-individual dynamic conception of personality. *Journal of Research in Personality, 30,* 414–428.

Shur, M. (1972). *Freud: Living and dying.* New York: International Universities Press.

Shurcliff, J. (1968). Judged humor, arousal, and the relief theory. *Journal of Personality and Social Psychology, 8,* 360–363.

Shweder, R. A., & Bourne, E. J. (1984). Does the concept of person vary cross-culturally? In R. A. Shweder & R. Levin (Eds.), *Culture theory: Essays on mind, self, and emotion* (pp. 158–199). New York: Cambridge University Press.

Silverman, L. H. (1976). Psychoanalytic theory: The reports of my death are greatly exaggerated. *American Psychologist, 31,* 621–637.

Silvern, S. B., & Williamson, P. A. (1987, October–December). The effects of video game play on young children's aggression, fantasy, and prosocial behavior. *Journal of Applied Developmental Psychology, 8*(4), 453–462.

Singer, J. (1991). Closeness and androgyny. In H. A. Wilmer (Ed.), *Closeness in personal and professional relationships.* Boston, MA: Shambhala Publications.

Singh, K. (1990). Tough-mindedness in relation to birth order, family size, and sex. *Individual Psychology: Journal of Adlerian Theory, Research & Practice, 46*(1), 82–87.

Singh, R. P. (1984, January). Experimental verification of locus of control as related to conformity behavior. *Psychological Studies, 29*(1), 64–67.

Skhiri, T., & Gaha, L. (1994). Evolution of ideas on the psychogenesis of depression. *Psychologie Medicale, 26,* 511–514.

Skinner, B. F. (1938). *The behavior of organisms.* New York: Appleton-Century-Crofts.

Skinner, B. F. (1948). *Walden II.* New York: Macmillan.

Skinner, B. F. (1953). *Science and human behavior.* New York: Macmillan.

Skinner, B. F. (1969). *Contingencies of reinforcement: A theoretical analysis.* New York: Appleton-Century-Crofts.

Skinner, B. F. (1971). *Beyond freedom and dignity.* New York: Knopf.

Skinner, B. F. (1972, November). Will success spoil B. F. Skinner? (Interview). *Psychology Today, 6,* 66–72, 130.

Skinner, B. F. (1983a, Spring). Can the experimental analysis of behavior rescue psychology? *Behavior Analyst, 6*(1), 9–17.

Skinner, B. F. (1983b, September). Origins of a behaviorist. *Psychology Today, 17*(7).

Skinner, B. F. (1984, December). Selection by consequences. *Behavior and Brain Sciences, 7*(4), 477–510.

Skinner, B. F. (1985). *The shaping of a behaviorist.* New York: New York University Press.

Skinner, B. F. (1986, January). The evolution of verbal behavior. *Journal of the Experimental Analysis of Behavior, 45*(1), 115–122.

Skinner, B. F. (1987, August). Whatever happened to psychology as the science of behavior? *American Psychologist, 42*(8), 780–786.

Sliker, G. (1992). *Multiple mind: Healing the split in psyche and world.* Boston, MA: Shambhala Publications.

Small, F. E. (1989). The psychology of women: A psychoanalytic review. *Canadian Journal of Psychiatry, 34*(9), 872–878.

Smelser, N. J. (1996). Erik Erikson as social scientist. *Psychoanalysis and Contemporary Thought, 19,* 207–224.

Smith, D. (1982). Trends in counseling and psychotherapy. *American Psychologist, 37*(7), 802–809.

Smith, M. B. (1990). Humanistic psychology. *Journal of Humanistic Psychology, 30*(4), 6–21.

Smith, M., & Glass, J. (1977, September). Metaanalysis of psychotherapy outcome studies. *American Psychologist,* 752–760.

Soffer, J. (1993). Jean Piaget & George Kelly: Toward a stronger constructivism. *International Journal of Personal Construct Psychology, 6*(1), 59–77.

Solnit, A. J. (1994). Heinz-Hartmann—Psychoanalysis and health values unfolding. *Psychoanalytic Study of the Child, 49,* 36–45.

Spiegel, R. (1994). Reflections on our heritage from Erich Fromm. *Contemporary Psychoanalysis, 30,* 419–424.

Spranger, E. (1928). *Types of men.* New York: Stechert.

Steelman, L. C. (1985). A tale of two variables: A review of the intellectual consequences of sibship size and birth order. *Review of Educational Research, 55,* 353–386.

Steelman, L. C. (1986). The tale retold: A response to Zajonc. *Review of Educational Research, 56,* 373–377.

Stein, D. J. (1997). *Cognitive science and the unconscious.* Washington, DC: American Psychiatric Press.

Stelmack, R. M. (1990). Biological basis of extraversion: Psychophysiological evidence. *Journal of Personality, 58,* 291–311.

Stern, D. (1985). *The interpersonal world of the infant: A view from psychoanalysis and development psychology.* New York: Basic Books.

Sternberg, R. (1992). Too young to die—Let's not bury psychology alive: A response to Gardner. *New Ideas in Psychology, 10*(2), 195–205.

Stevens, A. (1994). *Jung. Past masters.* Oxford, England: Oxford University Press.

Stewart, A. E., & Barry, J. R. (1991). Origins of George Kelly's consctuctivism in the work of Korzybski and Moreno. *International Journal of Personal Construct Psychology, 4*(2), 121–136.

Stiver, I. P. (1991a). Beyond the Oedipus complex: Mothers and daughters. In J. V. Jordan et al. (Eds.), *Women's growth in connection: Writings from the Stone Center.* New York: Guilford Press.

Stiver, I. P. (1991b). The meanings of "dependency" in female-male relationships. In J. V. Jordan et al. (Eds.), *Women's growth in connection: Writings from the Stone Center.* New York: Guilford Press.

Stolorow, R. D. (1995). An intersubjective view of self psychology. *Psychoanalytic Dialogues, 5,* 393–399.

Straussner, S. L., & Spiegel, B. R. (1996). An analysis of 12-step programs for substance abusers from a developmental perspective. *Clinical Social Work Journal, 24,* 299–309.

Strickland, B. R. (1978). I-E expectations and health-related behaviors. *Journal of Consulting and Clinical Psychology, 46,* 1192–1211.

Strickland, B. R. (1979). I-E expectations and cardiovascular functioning. In L. C. Perlmuller & R. A. Monty (Eds.), *Choice and perceived control.* Hillsdale, NJ: Erlbaum.

Suchecki, J. (1989). Can scientific method be perceived as mythical text? *Polish Psychological Bulletin, 20*(2), 83–93.

Sullivan, H. S. (1953). *The interpersonal theory of psychiatry.* New York: Norton.

Sullivan, H. S. (1954). *The psychiatric interview.* New York: Norton.

Sulloway, F. J. (1996). *Born to rebel: Birth order, family dynamics, and creative lives.* New York: Pantheon.

Sumerlin, J. R., & Bundrick, C. M. (1996). Brief Index of Self-Actualization: A measure of Maslow's model. *Journal of Social Behavior & Personality, 11,* 153–172.

Surrey, J. L. (1990). Empathy revisisted. *Works in Progress* No. 40. The Stone Center, Wellesley College, Wellesley, Massachusetts.

Surrey, J. L. (1991). The self-in-relation: A theory of Women's development. In J. V. Jordan et al. (Eds.), *Women's growth in connection: Writings from the Stone Center.* New York: Guilford Press.

Swann, W. B., Stein-Seroussi, A., & Giesler, R. B. (1992). Why people self-verify. *Journal of Personality and Social Psychology.* Austin: University of Texas.

Swenson, C. R. (1994). Freud's "Anna O.": Social work's Bertha Pappenheim. *Clinical Social Work Journal, 22,* 149–163.

Symonds, A. (1991). Gender issues and Horney theory. *The American Journal of Psychoanalysis, 51*(3).

Tacey, D. (1997). Jung in the academy: Devotions and resistance. *Journal of Analytical Psychology, 42,* 269–283.

Tappan, M. B. (1991). Narrative, authorship and the development of moral authority. In M. B. Tappan & M. J. Packer (Eds.), *Narrative and storytelling: Implications for understanding moral development. New directions for child development.* San Francisco, CA: Jossey-Bass.

Tart, C. T. (Ed.). (1975). *Transpersonal psychologies.* New York: Harper & Row.

Tatum, B. D. (1997). Racial identity development and relational theory: The case of black women in white communities. In J. V. Jordan (Ed.), *Women's growth in diversity.* New York: Guilford Press.

Tena, C. (1993). Impact of the theories of Carl Rogers and Teihard De Chardin in Mexico. In G. M. Gonzalez, I. Alvarado, & A. S. Segrera (Eds.), *Challenges of cultural and racial diversity to counseling, 2,* (p. 105).

Tett, R. P., Jackson, D. N., & Rothstein, M. (1991). Personality measures as predictors of job performance: A meta-analytic review. *Personnel Psychology, 44, 703–742.*

Thompson, M. G. (1996). The rule of neutrality. *Psychoanalysis and Contemporary Thought, 19, 57–84.*

Thompson, S., & Spacapan, S. (1991). Perceptions of control in vulnerable populations. *Journal of Social Issues, 47*(4).

Thorne, B. (1990). Carl Rogers and the doctrine of original sin. Special Issue: Fiftieth anniversary of the person-centered approach. *Person-Centered Review, 5*(4), 394–405.

Thrasher, P. (1991). A Jungian view of postmodernism: A response to "Psychology and postmodernity." *Humanistic Psychologist, 19*(2), 242–245.

Thurstone, L. L. (1948). Psychological implications of factor analysis. *American Psychologist, 3,* 402–408.

Tobacyk, J. J., & Downs, A. (1986, Oct.). Personal construct threat and irrational beliefs as cognitive predictors of increases in musical performance anxiety. *Journal of Personality and Social Psychology, 51*(4), 779–782.

Tokar, D. M., & Subich, L. M. (1997). Relative contributions of congruence and personality dimensions to job satisfaction. *Journal of Vocational Behavior, 50,* 482–491.

Tolpin, M. (1993). The unmirrored self, compensatory structure, and cure. In B. Magid (Ed.), *Self-Psychological Perspectives.* Hillsdale, NJ: Analytic Press.

Tompkins, S. S. (1992). Script theory. In R. A. Zucker, A. I. Rabin, J. Aronoff, & S. J. Frank (Eds.), *Personality structure in the life course: Essays on personology in the Murray tradition.* New York: Springer.

Toronto, E. L. (1991). The feminine unconscious and psychoanalytic theory. *Psychoanalytic Psychology, 8*(4), 415–438.

Torrey, E. F. (1992). *Freudian fraud: The malignant effect of Freud's theory on American thought and culture.* New York: HarperCollins.

Tribich, D., & Messer, S. (1974). Psychoanalytic character type and states of authority as determiners of suggestibility. *Journal of Consulting and Clinical Psychology, 42,* 842–848.

Ugwu-Oju, D. (1993, November 14). Hers: Pursuit of happiness. *The New York Times Magazine.*

Urbanowski, F., & Miller, J. (1996). Trauma, psychotherapy, and meditation. *Journal of Transpersonal Psychology, 28,* 31–48.

Vaillant, G. E. (1992a). *Ego mechanisms of defense: A guide for clinicians and researchers.* Washington, DC: American Psychiatric Press.

Vaillant, G. E. (1992b). The historical origins and future potential of Sigmund Freud's concept of the mechanisms of defense. *International Review of Psycho-Analysis, 19*(1), 35–50.

Valentine, E. (1988). Teleological explanations and their relation to causal explanations in psychology. *Philosophical Psychology, 1*(1), 61–68.

Vande Kempe, H. (1995). Religion in college textbooks: Allport's historic 1948 report. *International Journal for the Psychology of Religion, 5,* 199–211.

Van den Daele, L. (1987, Summer). Research in Horney's psychoanalytic theory. *American Journal of Psychoanalysis, 47*(2), 99–104.

Van Eenwyk, J. R. (1991). Archetypes: The strange attractors of the psyche. *Journal of Analytical Psychology, 36,* 1–25.

Van Kalmthout, M. A. (1995). The religious dimension of Rogers's work. *Journal of Humanistic Psychology, 35,* 23–39.

van Krogten, I. (1992). *Proustian love.* B. V. Amsterdam. Lisse: Swets & Zeitlinger.

Vaughn, C. M., & Pfenninger, D. T. (1994). Kelly and the concept of developmental stages. *Journal of Constructivist Psychology, 7,* 177–190.

Viner, R. (1996). Melanie Klein and Anna Freud: The discourse of the early dispute. *Journal of the History of the Behavioral Sciences, 32,* 4–15.

Visher, S. (1986, May). The relationship of locus of control and contraception use in the adolescent population. *Journal of Adolescent Health Care, 7*(3), 183–186.

Vitz, P. (1990). The use of stories in moral development: New psychological reasons for an old education method. *American Psychologist, 45*(6), 709–720.

W., Bill (1988). *The language of the heart: Bill W's Grapevine writings.* New York: The AA Grapevine, Inc.

Walker, A. & Parmar, P. (1993). *Warrior marks: Female genital mutilation and the sexual blinding of women.* New York: Harcourt Brace.

Walker, B. M. (1990). Construing George Kelly's construing of the person-in-relation. *International Journal of Personal Construct Psychology, 3*(1), 41–50.

Walker, B. M. (1992). Values and Kelly's theory: Becoming a good scientist. Special Issue: Papers from the Eighth International Congress on Personal Construct Psychology. *International Journal of Personal Construct Psychology, 5*(3), 259–269.

Wallach, M. A., & Wallach, L. (1983). *Psychology: Sanction for selfishness.* San Francisco, CA: Freeman.

Wallwork, E. (1991). *Psychoanalysis and ethics.* New Haven, CT: Yale University Press.

Walsh, R. (1995). Asian psychotherapies. In J. Corsini & D. Wedding (Eds.), *Current psychotherapies* (pp. 387–398). Itasca, IL: Peacock.

Warner, S. L. (1991). Freud and the mighty warrior. *Journal of the American Academy of Psychoanalysis, 19*(2), 282–293.

Warren, W. G. (1990). Is personal construct psychology a cognitive psychology? *International Journal of Personal Construct Psychology, 3*(4), 393–414.

Warren, W. G. (1992). Personal construct theory and mental health. Special Issue: Papers from the Eighth International Congress of Personal Construct Psychology. *International Journal of Personal Construct Psychology, 5*(3), 223–237.

Wastell, C. A. (1996). Feminist developmental theory: Implications for counseling. *Journal of Counseling and Development, 74,* 575–581.

Waterman, A. S. (1982). Identity development from adolescence to adulthood: An extension of theory and a review of research. *Developmental Psychology, 18,* 341–358.

Watson, P. J., Little, T., & Biderman, M. D. (1992). Narcissism and parenting styles. *Psychoanalytic Psychology, 9*(2), 231–244.

Watts, A. W. (1961). *Psychotherapy east and west.* New York: Ballantine.

Watzlawick, P., Weakland, J., & Fisch, R. (1974). *Change: Principles of problem formation and problem resolution.* New York: Norton.

Weingberg, L. (1991). Infant development and the sense of self: Stern vs. Mahler. *Clinical Social Work Journal, 19*(1), 9–22.

Weinraub, W. (1993, December 28). Despite Clinton, Hollywood is still trading in violence. *The New York Times,* A1.

Weiss-Rosmarin, T. (1990). Adler's psychology and the Jewish tradition. *Individual Psychology: Journal of Adlerian Theory, Research & Practice, 46,* 108–118.

Wengler, B. (1995). Reflections on Alfred Adler's treatment technique. *Zeitschrift für Individualpsychologie, 20,* 273–287.

Wertsch, J. V. (1990). A meeting of paradigms: Vygotsky and psychoanalysis. *Contemporary Psychoanalysis, 26*(1), 53–73.

Wessler, R. L. (1986). Conceptualizing cognitions in the cognitive-behavioral therapies. In W. Dryden & W. Golden (Eds.), *Cognitive-behavioral approaches to psychotherapy* (pp. 1–30). London: Harper & Row.

Whitbourne, S. K., Zuschlag, M. K., Elliot, L. B., & Waterman, A. S. (1992). Psychosocial development in adulthood: A 22-year sequential study. *Journal of Personality & Social Psychology, 63*(2), 260–271.

White, R. W. (1992). Exploring personality the long way: The study of lives. In R. A. Zucker, A. I. Rabin, J. Aronoff, & S. J. Frank (Eds.), *Personality structure in the life course: Essays on personology in the Murray tradition* (pp. 3–21). New York: Springer.

Widiger, T. A. (1993). The DSM-III-R categorical personality disorder diagnoses: A critique and an alternative. *Psychological Inquiry,* in press.

Widiger, T. A., & Trull, T. J. (1997). Assessment of the five-factor model of personality. *Journal of Personality Assessment, 68,* 228–250.

Wiggins, J. S. (1984, April–July). Cattell's system from the perspective of mainstream personality theory. *Multivariate Behavioral Research, 19*(2–3), 176–190.

Wilson, A. (1996). The irrelevance of infant observations for psychoanalysis: Commentary. *Journal of the American Psychoanalytic Association, 44,* 452–464.

Winnicott, D. W. (1993). C. G. Jung's memories, dreams, reflections. *Cahiers Jungiens de Psychoanalyse, 78,* 83–92.

Winter, D. G. (1993). Gordon Allport and "Letters from Jenny." In K. H. Craik, R. Hogan, & R. N. Wolfe (Eds.), *Fifty years of personality psychology* (pp. 147–163). New York: Plenum Press.

Wolberg, A. (1989). Pilgrim's progress through the psychoanalytic maze. *Psychoanalysis & Psychotherapy, 7*(1), 18–26

Wood, R. E., & Bandura, A. (1989). Impact of conceptions of ability on self-regulatory mechanisms and complex decision making. *Journal of Personality and Social Psychology, 56,* 407–415.

Woodall, K., & Matthews, K. (1993). Changes in and stability of hostile characteristics: Results from a 4-year longitudinal study of children. *Journal of Personality and Social Psychology, 64,* 491–499.

Woodward, W. (1992). On opening the psychology of personality to philosophy and literature in our time: A response to Gardner. *New Ideas in Psychology, 10*(2), 191–194.

Woody, R. H. (1971). *Psychobehavioral counseling and therapy: Integrating behavioral and insight techniques.* New York: Appleton-Century Crofts.

Wright, J. C., & Mischel, W. (1988). Conditional hedges and the intuitive psychology of traits. *Journal of Personality and Social Psychology, 55,* 454–469.

Wrightsman, L. S. (1993). Allport's personal documents: Then and now. In K. H. Craik, R. Hogan, & R. N. Wolfe (Eds.), *Fifty years of personality psychology* (pp. 165–175). New York: Plenum Press.

Yang, K., & Bond, M. H. (1990). Exploring implicit personality theories with indigenous or imported constructs: The Chinese case. *Journal of Personality and Social Psychology, 58,* 1087–1095.

Young, T. W., & Shorr, D. N. (1986, November). Factors affecting locus of control in school children. *Genetic, Social and General Psychology Monographs, 112*(4), 405–417.

Zajonc, R. B. (1986). Family factors and intellectual test performance: A reply to Steelman. *Review of Educational Research, 56,* 365–371.

Zajonc, R. B., & Markus, G. B. (1975). Birth order and intellectual development. *Psychological Review, 82,* 74–88.

Zeig, J. K. (Ed.). (1982). *Eriksonian approaches to hypnosis and psychotherapy.* New York: Brunner/Mazel.

Zlate, M. (1989). The place and role of the self in the pattern of personality: Controversial questions. *Revue Roumainē des Sciences Sociales—Serie de Psychologie, 33*(1), 3–15.

Zohar, D., & Marshall, I. (1990). *The quantum self: Human nature and consciousness defined by the new physics.* New York: William Morrow.

Zuckerman, M. (1991). *Psychobiology of personality.* Cambridge, England: Cambridge University Press.

# Index

A-B-C theory of personality, Ellis on, 423–424
Abraham, Karl, 31, 114
Absolute musts, 425
Abzug, R. H., 374
Academic psychology, 5, 6
Acceptance, 358
Achievement, need for, 276–277
Acquisition, 232
Activity, 308
Actualization, 17, 117, 352–353, 366
    self-, 344–350
Adams-Webber, J. R., 411
Adaptation, Hartmann on, 143
Addiction, 172
Addleman, J., 246
Adler, Alfred, 93–111, 431
    assessment and research in theory of, 106–108
    biographical background of, 94–95
    on birth order, 100–102, 106–107
    on creative self, 103–104, 109
    on dreams, 107
    Ellis and, 109, 428
    evaluation of, 108–110
    on family atmosphere, 102–103
    on female development, 99, 121
    finalism of, 96–97
    Freud and, 95, 103
    on inferiority feelings, 98–99
    Kelly and, 422
    mentioned, 31, 69, 139, 242, 243, 293, 342, 476,
        477
    on parenting, 102–103, 105, 106
    psychotherapy of, 104–105, 108, 109
    Rotter and, 109
    on social interest, 96, 105, 108, 110
    on style of life, 99–103, 104, 107
    on superiority striving, 97–99
    writings of, 111
Adlerian Individual Psychology, 109
Adolescence
    Allport on, 262
    Erikson on, 149–151, 153, 158
    Freud (Anna) on, 142
    Surrey on, 182
Adoption studies, 295, 297, 331
Aesthetics, 7
Affective arousal, 434
Agarwal, R., 244
Agency, 159
Aggression
    depression and, 56
    Fromm on, 131
    Kelly on, 409
    Kernberg on, 175
    television and, 234–236
Aggressor, identification with, 142
Agoraphobia, 238

Agreeableness, as Big Five factor, 289, 290–291, 292, 293,
    296, 297
Akhtar, S., 170
Al-Anon, 105
Alayavijnana, 458
Alcoholics Anonymous, 90, 170, 189
Alexander, F., 431
Alienation, 118
Allport, Gordon, 255, 257–269
    assessment and research in theory of, 266–268
    biographical background of, 257–258
    Ellis and, 428
    evaluation of, 268–270, 279
    Freud and, 257–258, 259
    on functional autonomy, 263–264, 268–269
    Kelly and, 417
    language and, 290
    Maslow and, 266, 268
    maturity definition and, 264–266
    mentioned, 15, 271, 275, 285, 477, 478, 479, 483
    personality definition and, 2, 258–259, 266, 269
    proprium and, 261–263
    traits and dispositions concept and, 259–261
    writings of, 267, 281
Alpha press, 273, 275
American hypercompetitiveness, 123
American Institute of Psychoanalysis, 115
American Psychological Association, 248, 302
Amplification, 86
Anal stage, 42–43, 57, 129, 206
Analytical psychology, 70–92. *See also* Jung, Carl
Analytic process of psychoanalysis, 54–56
Anatta, 456
Anderson, M., 179, 483
Anderson, R., 405
Androgyny, 78, 90
Angel, E., 373
Anger, 189
Anicca, 455, 457
Anima, Jung on, 77–78, 79
Anna O., 32–34, 35, 53
Ansbacher, H. L., 99, 109
Ansbacher, R. R., 99
Anticipates, Kelly and, 405
Anxiety, 349
    Freud on, 50–53, 58
    Horney on, 115–116
    Kelly on, 409
    May on, 378–379, 392
Appelbaum, A. H., 175
Approach-approach conflict, 204, 205
Approach-avoidance conflict, 203, 204, 205
Aquinas, Thomas, 40
Arbitrary inference, Beck and, 433
Archer, S. L., 158
Archetypes, 73, 76–81, 90
Aries, E., 158

Aristotle, 4, 62, 83
Arnold, Magda, 431
Aron, L., 34
Art
     Jungian therapy and, 89
     personality theories and, 6, 23–24, 476, 477
     productive love as, 131
     *see also* Eastern thought
Artistic studies, psychology and, 483
Asanga, 459
Assertiveness training, 248
Assessment of personality, 16–18, 107–108. *See also under*
     *individual psychologists*
Association for the Advancement of Psychoanalysis,
     115
Atkinson, J. W., 276
Atkinson, R., 483
Atman, 453
AT&T, 275
Attentional processes, 231, 251
Attitudes, Jung on, 81, 82
Aurelius, Marcus, 422
Authoritarian ethics, 130
Authoritarianism, 126
Autism, normal, 169
Autoeroticism, 41
Automatic response, 201
Automation conformity, 126–127
Autonomous dimension, 432–433
Autonomous self, 172
Autonomy
     functional, 263–264, 268–269
     versus shame and doubt, 147, 153
Autotelic activity, 463, 467
Aversive conditioning, 248
Avoidance-avoidance conflict, 204, 205
Avoiding type, of style of life, 100

Bacciagaluppi, Marco, 134
Badcock, C., 40
Bagby, L. J., 90
Bahleda, M. D., 107
Bakan, David, 159, 480, 482
Baldwin, C., 244
Ballou, M. A., 444
Balter, L., 172
Bandler, R., 439
Bandura, Albert, 226–240, 439, 440
     biographical background of, 226–227
     evaluation of, 240–241, 252
     mentioned, 15, 208, 249, 477, 478
     modeling and, 230–231, 238
     observational learning theory of, 229–234
     on psychotherapy and behavior modification,
          238–240
     reciprocal determinism theory of, 227–229, 239
     on self-efficacy, 226, 236–237, 243
     on television and aggression, 234–236
     writings of, 254
Bankart, C., 470
Banks, W., 246
Bannister, D., 410
Barbaranelli, C., 240
Barnett, J. K., 158
Barnhardt, T. M., 59
Barrett, P., 315, 318
Barrick, M. R., 292
Barry, J. R., 411

Basic anxiety, 115–116
Basic evil, 115
Basic human conditions and needs, Fromm on, 126–129
BASIC-ID, 438–439, 441, 442
Basic orientations toward life, 116, 117
Basic relational paradox, 188
Bates, M., 87
Baumrind, D., 123, 172
Beck, Aaron, 429–436
     Beck Depression Inventory and, 435
     biographical background of, 429–430
     on cognitive distortions, 432, 433, 434
     cognitive therapy theory of, 430–434
     on cognitive triad, 433–434
     on depression, 432–434
     Ellis and, 431, 436
     evaluation of, 435–436, 443, 444, 445
     mentioned, 208, 399, 420, 477
     philosophical origins and, 430–431
     psychotherapy of, 434–435, 436, 445
     on schemas, 432
     on sociotropy and autonomy dimensions, 432–433
     writings of, 447–448
Beck Anxiety Scale, 435
Beck Depression Inventory, 435
Becker, I., 423
Beck Hopelessness Scale, 435
Beck Scale for Suicide Ideation, 435
Beck Self-concept Test, 435
Becoming, Allport on, 265
Behavior
     biological basis of, 322–324, 333, 484
     causal agents of, 292, 318–326, 334
     covert versus overt, 4, 13
     experimental analysis of, 200–201
     expressive, 267
     operant, 213
     respondent, 212–213
     Rogers on, 2, 353
     superstitious, 215
Behavioral genetics, 294–299, 302
Behavioral specificity, 250
Behavioral training, 248
Behaviorism, 4, 201, 330, 479
Behaviorist theories, 197–224, 477. *See also* Cognitive-
     behavioral theories; Dollard, John; Miller, Neal;
     Skinner, B. F.
Behavior modification, 216–218, 238–240, 331–333
Behavior potential, 246, 247
Behavior therapies, 22–23
     cognitive behavioral, 443–445
     Eysenck and, 331–333
     Lazarus and, 437
     multimodal, 438–439, 440–442, 444
     rational emotive behavior, 422–428
Being mode, 131
Belief systems, Ellis on, 424–425. *See also* Eastern
     thought
Belonging needs, 343, 344
Benedict, Ruth, 342
Benjamin, Jessica, 170
Bergman, S. J., 191
Berkow, D. N., 456
Berkowitz, L., 234
Bernadez, T., 189
Bernal, M. E., 158
Bernard, M. E., 423
Bernstein, Doris, 45

Bertalanffy, L. von., 440
Beta press, 275
Bettelheim, B., 37, 39, 47, 61
Beyondism, 301
Bezjak, J., 244
Biderman, M. D., 172–173
Big Five personality traits, 268, 289–294, 309, 477
    applications of, 292–294
    evaluation of, 301–303
    evolution and, 300
    Eysenck and, 315–316, 334
    Five Factor Model and, 289, 290, 291–294, 301–302
    genetic influence on, 296, 297
    language analysis and, 290, 293–294
    personality questionnaires and ratings and, 290–291
Biological determinism, 46, 57, 133
Biological intelligence, 325
Biological therapies, 333
Biology, personality and, 322–324, 333, 484
Biophilous character, 131
Biosocial approach, 305–338. *See also* Eysenck, Hans
Birth order, 100–102, 106–107
Bitter, J. R., 105
Blackman, D., 221
Bleuler, Eugen, 72
Block, J., 357
Block, J. H., 357
Blondheim, S. H., 57
Blos, Peter, 145
B-needs, 343
Bobo doll, 230–231, 234
Bodhidharma, 458–460
Bodhisattva, 453, 468
Bodhi tree, 452
Bodily self, 262
Body measurements, Kretschmer and, 309
Bompu Zen, 465
Bond, M. H., 293
Boneau, C. A., 480, 484
Boone, C., 244
Borderline personality disorders, 173–175
Bouchard, Thomas J., 296, 299
Bourne, E. J., 293
Bozarth, J. D., 361
Brahma, 453
Brain, causal agents of behavior and, 318–326, 334
Bray, Douglas, 275
Brazier, D., 463, 469
Breeding, selective, 295, 298
Breger, L., 56
Breuer, Joseph, 31, 32, 33, 86
Bridgeman, Percy, 14
Bridging, 441
Briggs, Katherine, 87
Brill, A. A., 31
Bringmann, M. W., 411
Brooke, R. W., 75
Brumann, H., 167
Bruner, 409, 417
Brunnell, L. J., 441
Brunner, José, 29, 132
Bryant, B. L., 107
Buber, Martin, 377
Buckley, W., 440
Buckminster Fuller Institute, 485
Buddha, 452–457, 466. *See also* Buddhism; Zen Buddhism

Buddhism, 110
    mandalas and, 78, 80
    Rogers and, 366–367
    *see also* Zen Buddhism
Bugental, J. F. T., 373
Bullock, W. A., 321
Bundrick, C. M., 343
Burkitt, I., 484
Burlingham, Dorothy, 139
Buss, A. H., 297, 484
Buss, David, 300, 302
Butt, T., 415

Cain, D. J., 367
Campbell, J. B., 328, 481
Campbell, Joseph, 78–79
Cantor, N., 261
Capps, W. H., 151
Caprara, G. V., 240
CAPS (cognitive-affective personality system), 250–252
Cardinal disposition, 260
Care, as ego strength or virtue, 151–152, 153
Carr, A. C., 175
Cartwright, D. S., 250
Carver, C. S., 62
Case history, 18
Castaldo, C., 441
Castration anxiety, 44, 56
CAT (Children's Apperception Test), 276
Catharsis, 33
Cattell, Raymond, 268, 283–289, 301
    assessment and research in theory of, 286–289
    beyondism and, 301
    Big Five model and, 290, 292, 301
    biographical background of, 283–284
    evaluation of, 300–301, 302–303
    Eysenck and, 315–316, 334
    heredity versus environment and, 294
    mentioned, 15, 19, 259, 290, 309, 311, 313, 477, 478
    personality definition and, 284–285
    selective breeding and, 295
    on surface versus source traits, 285–286
    writings of, 304
Causal agents of behavior, 292, 318–326, 334
Cause, 36, 83, 88
Cavell, M., 40
Central disposition, 260, 261
Central relational paradox, 186
Chabassol, D. J., 107
Chambers, W. V., 410–411, 411
Chandler, C. K., 109
Chang, R., 349
Change
    possibility of, 478–479
    therapeutic, 358
Changeability, Wundt and, 308, 309
Chapleski, M., 235
Character orientations, 129–132
Charcot, Jean, 31
Chernin, J., 109
Cheshire, N., 47
Child development
    Allport on, 261–263
    Dollard and Miller on, 206
    Erikson on, 146–154, 155–157
    Kohut on, 172–173
    McAdams on, 159

Child development (*cont.*)
   Rogers on, 355–357
   *see also* Psychosexual stages of development;
      Psychosocial stages of development
Children
   birth order and, 100–102, 106–107
   family atmosphere of, 102–103
   Freud (Anna) on, 138–142
   Freud (Sigmund) on, 41
   Horney on, 115–116
   Klein on, 167–168
   Mahler on, 169–170
   19th-century views of, 40
   sexual abuse of, 43, 389, 425
   television violence and, 234–236
   *see also* Child development; Parenting
Children's Apperception Test (CAT), 276
China, transmission of Zen to, 458–460
Chipner, H. M., 302
Chodorow, Nancy, 176–179, 181, 191, 192, 195
Choice, Kelly and, 406, 408
Choleric personality, 308, 309, 313, 314
Chomsky, N., 221
Circumcision, 180
Clark, R. A., 276
Clarke, J. J., 90
Classical conditioning, 201, 212–213, 214
Client-centered therapy, 357–362
Clinical practice, 5, 6
Clinical psychology, Kelly and, 402, 409
Clinical research, 18–19
Clinton, Bill, 298
Clitoridectomy, 180
Closed systems, 259
Coan, R. W., 349
Codependence, 105
Coelho, M. C., 484
Cognitions, Beck and, 431
Cognitive-affective personality system (CAPS), 250–252
Cognitive behavioral psychotherapy, 443–445
Cognitive-behavioral theories, 399, 419–448
   evaluation of, 443–444
   *see also* Beck, Aaron; Ellis, Albert; Lazarus, Arnold
Cognitive complexity, 413
Cognitive distortions, 432, 433, 434
Cognitive psychology, 5, 58–59
Cognitive psychotherapy, Beck on, 434–435, 436
Cognitive schemas, 432
Cognitive social learning theory, 109
Cognitive style, intelligence and, 326
Cognitive techniques, in cognitive therapy, 435
Cognitive theories, 104, 109, 399–418, 478, 479, 480. *See also* Bandura, Albert; Cognitive-behavorial theories; Kelly, George; Rotter, Julian
Cognitive therapies
   Beck and, 430–434
   behavioral, 443–445
   personality concept and, 431–434
   philosophical origins, 430–431
   psychotherapy, 434–435, 436
   rational emotive behavior, 422–428
Cognitive triad, 433–434
Coherence, as criterion, 10
Coles, R., 121, 153
Collective efficacy, 236–237
Collective unconscious, 73, 75–81, 89
Common traits, 260, 261
Communality, Kelly on, 407, 408

Communion, 159
Compatibility of hypotheses, 16
Compellingness, criterion, 9, 10, 12
Compensation, 98, 99, 104, 105
Compensatory function, of dreams, 86
Competence
   as ego strength or virtue, 148–149, 153
   industry versus inferiority and, 149, 153
Complex, Jung on, 75
Complex themas, 276
Comprehensiveness, as criterion, 10
Computer-assisted instruction, 217
Comstock, G., 234, 235
Conditional assumptions, Beck and, 432
Conditional-positive regard, 356
Conditioned response, 201
Conditioned stimulus, 201
Conditioning
   aversive, 248
   classical, 201, 212–213, 214
   operant, 212–213, 214, 218
Conditions of worth, 356
Confession, 86
Conflict, learning and, 203–205
Conformity
   automation, 126–127
   May on, 390
Confucius, 470
Congruence, Rogers and, 354–355
Connectedness, Stone Center group and, 181, 182–183
Connections, 182, 188, 189
Conscience, 48
   Allport on, 265
Conscientiousness, as Big Five factor, 289, 290–291, 292, 296, 297
Consciousness, 382
   Adler on, 103
   id, ego, and superego and, 49–50
   of self, 380, 382–383
   Wundt on, 4
   Zen Buddhism and, 457–458, 459
Consensual validation, 13
Consolidation, in separation-individuation process, 170
Constellating power, 75
Construction, Kelly and, 405, 408
Constructive alternativism, 401, 404–407
Constructs
   Kelly on, 401, 404–411, 412–413, 415, 416–417
   scientific, 14–15
Contemporary personality theories, 479–485
   writing on, 486–487
Content analysis, 266–267, 269
Continuity theory, of personality, 259
Continuous reinforcement, 215
Control, *see* Locus of control
Conversion disorders, 33
Cooper, J., 234
Cooper, S. H., 53
Copernicus, 62, 391
Coping aspect, of behavior, 267
Corcoran, D. W. J., 321, 322
Corcoran, K., 238
Core role, Kelly on, 409
Corollaries, Kelly on, 405–407, 408
Corporal punishment, 235–236
Correlational study, 19, 20
Costa, Paul T., 289, 290, 291, 292, 293
Countertransference, 56, 189

Courage, 189
  May and, 387–388
Covert behaviors, 4
Covert sensitization, 248
Creative achievement, Eysenck and, 329
Creative consciousness of self, 383
Creative self, 103–104, 109, 265
Creativity
  Eysenck on, 329
  May on, 387–388
  Rogers on, 357
Crews, F., 58
Criminal behavior, genetic factor in, 331
Criterion analysis, 317
Crockett, W. H., 410
Csikszentmihalyi, M., 467
Cues
  in learning process, 202, 203, 204
  unlabeled, 205
Cult membership, 172
Culture
  Adler on, 99
  basic needs and, 128, 129
  character orientations and, 129, 132
  see also Multiculturalism

Daijo Zen, 465
Daimonic, May and, 384
Dante, 388
Darwin, Charles, 62, 63, 107, 218, 387, 391
Das, A. K., 366
Data
  empirical, 480, 482
  objective versus subjective, 13
Davidson, Larry, 483
Davis, P. J., 58
Davison, G. C., 443
Dawes, R. M., 22
Death, Fromm on, 126
Death impulses, Freud on, 40
Death wish, 58
De Brabander, B., 244
De Britto, A., 246
De Carvalho, R. J., 257, 269, 341, 368, 392
Decatastrophizing, in cognitive therapy, 435
Decentering, in cognitive therapy, 435
Defense mechanisms
  Freud on, 50–53
  learning and, 206
Deffenbacher, J. L., 436
Definitions
  operational, 14
  scientific, 14
Delay of gratification, 239–240
De Mann, A., 244
DeMartino, R. J., 123
Demont, W. C., 56
Demosthenes, 98
Denial, 51
Dependence, 189
Dependent origination, 454, 460
Dependent variable, 19
Depression, 349
  aggression and, 56
  Beck and, 431, 432–434, 435–436
  behavior therapy for, 332
  cognitive therapy for, 434
Descartes, René, 39–40, 62, 200, 383, 394

Desensitization, in vitro, 426
Deshimaru, Taisen, 451
Despair, ego integrity versus, 152–153
De St. Aubin, E., 160
Destiny, May on, 386–387
Destructiveness, 126
Determinism, 46, 57, 206, 387, 478
  biological, 46, 57, 133
  freedom versus, 8
  reciprocal, 227–229, 239
Development
  Kelly and, 408
  psychosexual stages of, 41–46
  see also Child development
Developmental line, 141–142
Devil's pact, see Alienation
Devotion, object of, 127, 128, 129
Dharma, 454
Diagnostic profile, Freud (Anna) and, 141
Diamond, A., 160
Diathesis-stress model, 436
Dichotomous thinking, Beck and, 433
Dichotomy, Kelly and, 406, 408
Differentiation, in separation-individuation process, 170
Digman, J. M., 290
Diller, J. V., 29
Dinkmeyer, D., 105, 109
Disconnections, 182, 185–188, 189
Discontinuity theory, of personality, 259, 269
Discovery learning, 327–328
Displacement, 51, 52, 53, 206
Dispositional theories, 255, 478–479. *See also* Factor
  analytic theories; Traits and personality
Dispositions
  cardinal, 260
  central, 260, 261
  personal, 260–261
  secondary, 260–261
Diversion, in cognitive therapy, 435
Dixon, P. N., 108
Dizygotic (DZ), 294
DNA markers, 296, 297
D-needs, 343
Doherty, W. J., 244
Dollard, John, 119, 200–208, 221
  biographical background of, 200
  evaluation of, 207–208, 221
  on experimental analysis of behavior, 200–201
  Freudian psychoanalysis and, 205–206
  on frustration and conflict, 203–205
  on learning, 201–203, 204
  mentioned, 217, 477
  psychotherapy of, 206–207
  writings of, 208, 223
Dolliver, R. H., 81, 350
Donahue, E. M., 411
Donaldson, G., 167
Donovan, S., 462
Doob, L. W., 208
Dornbusch, S., 236
Double approach-avoidance conflict, 204, 205
Doubt, autonomy versus, 147, 153
Douglas, C., 271
Downs, A., 411
Dread/Anger Impasse, 191
Dreams
  Adler on, 107
  Freud on, 37–38, 57

Dreams (*cont.*)
    Horney on, 121
    Jung on, 86
    May on, 392–393
Dream work, 37
Dreikurs, R., 105
Drive reduction, 201–202, 206
Drives, 201
    Dollard and Miller on, 201–203
    Freud on, 39–40
    in learning process, 201–202, 203, 204
    primary, 202
    reduction of, 201–202
    secondary, 202
    unlabeled, 205
Drugs, in psychotherapy, 391
Drwal, R. L., 244
Dryden, W., 423, 425, 426, 428, 436, 441, 443
Ducat, S., 57
Duhs, L., 234–235
Duke, M. P., 18
Dukkha, 455
Duncan, P., 236
Dyadic transactions, 438
Dyer, R., 167, 168
Dymaxion Map, 485
Dymond, R. S., 357, 363
Dysfunctional beliefs, 425

Eagle, M. N., 173
Eastern thought, 449–474, 478
    evaluation of, 470–472
    Jung and, 78, 80, 84, 90
    Rogers and, 366–367
    self-actualization and, 349
    Taoism, 460
    *see also* Zen Buddhism
Eating disorders, 175
Eckhardt, M. H., 120
Edelson, M., 58
Education, Eysenck and, 327–328
Edwards Personal Preference Schedule, 276
Effect, law of, 201, 211
Ego, 46
    Erikson on, 145–146, 148–149
    Freud (Anna) on, 139, 141, 142
    Freud (Sigmund) on, 47, 48, 49, 50, 58, 63–64, 74,
        139
    Hartmann on, 142–143
    Jung on, 73, 74
    Murray on, 272
Ego defenses, 50–53, 142
Ego-ideal, 34, 44, 48, 119, 124
Ego identity versus role confusion, 149–151, 153
Ego integrity versus despair, 152–153
Ego psychology, 138–165. *See also* Erikson, Erik;
    Freud, Anna; Freud, Sigmund; Hartmann, Heinz
Ego strengths/virtues, 146
    care, 147, 151–152, 153, 156, 162
    competence, 148–149, 153
    fidelity, 149–151, 153
    love, 151, 153
    purpose, 148, 153
    will, 147, 153
    wisdom, 152–153
Ehrenreich, J. H., 481
Eight consciousnesses, in Buddhism, 457–458, 459
Eightfold Path, 455–456, 458

Einstein, Albert, 62, 391
Eisenman, R., 107
Elaborating the complaint, Kelly and, 411
Elcock, L. E., 107
Electra complex, 44
Eleftheriou, L., 107
Ellenberger, H. F., 62, 87, 373
Elliot, B. A., 107
Elliot, L. B., 158
Ellis, Albert, 420–429, 422, 423, 425, 426, 428
    A-B-C theory of personality and, 423–424
    Adler and, 109
    Beck and, 431, 436
    biographical background of, 420–422
    evaluation of, 443, 444, 445
    mentioned, 208, 399, 477
    other theorists and, 422, 428–429
    psychotherapy of, 425–428, 445
    rational emotive behavior therapy and, 109, 422–428
    writings of, 447
Emory, G., 431, 434, 435
Emotional consequence, 423–424
Emotionality versus stability, 312, 313, 314
Emotions
    Eysenck on, 312, 313, 314
    Kelly on, 409, 417
    in rational emotive behavior therapy, 422–423
    Rogers on, 358–360, 361, 362
    Wundt on, 308, 309
    *see also* Feelings
Emotive evocative therapy, 426
Empathy, 134, 172, 182, 184–185, 189, 191, 358
Empirical data, 480, 482
Empirical generalization, 13–14
Empirical statements, 8, 9, 13
Empiricism, 200
Encounter groups, 361
Enlightenment, 479
Enlightenment (Zen), 451, 460–462, 466–468
Environment
    heredity versus, *see* Heredity versus environment
    style of life and, 99
Epictetus, 422
Epigenetic stages, 146
Epiphany, 8, 61
Epstein, N., 432
Epstein, Raissa, 99
Epstein, S., 58, 458, 463, 468, 469, 484
Epting, F. R., 403, 410–411
Erikson, Erik H., 19, 144–164
    assessment and research in theory of, 153–158
    biographical background of, 144–145
    on child development, 146–154, 155–157
    ego and, 145–146
    empirical research in theory of, 158–159
    evaluation of, 162–164
    Freud (Anna) and, 145
    Freud (Sigmund) and, 145, 146, 157
    Fromm and, 162
    McAdams and, 159–162
    mentioned, 182, 262, 293, 483
    psychohistories and, 154–155, 157–158
    on psychosocial stages of development, 146–153
    womb envy and, 119, 120
    writings of, 155, 165
Erlenmeyer-Kimling, L., 295
Erogenous zones, 41
Eros, 40

Escape mechanisms, 126–127
Espin, O., 484
Essence of being, 375
Esterson, A., 43
Ethics, 7, 23
    authoritarian versus humanistic, 130
    of behavior therapy and modification, 333
    Cattell and, 301
    in contemporary theories, 483
    Fromm and, 134
Eugenics, 478
Euthenics, 478
Evaluative response, 359, 361
Evans, R. D., 110
Evans, R. I., 147, 148, 149
Evans, Richard J., 240, 312, 335
Evoked potential, intelligence and, 326
Evolutionary psychology, 299–300, 302
Excitation, 127, 128, 129, 319
Existentialism, 375–377. *See also* May, Rollo
Existential psychoanalysis, 339, 372–398, 442. *See also*
        May, Rollo
Existential therapy, 442
Expectancy, 246
Experience, Kelly and, 406, 408
Experimental analysis, of behavior, 200–201
Experimental method
    limitations of, 480, 482
    Wundt and, 4
Experimental psychology, 480
Experimental research, 19, 21
Exploitative orientation, 129, 130
Exposure therapy, in cognitive therapy, 435
Expressive behavior, 267
Expressive psychoanalytically oriented psychotherapy,
        175
External locus of control, 244, 245
Extinction, of response, 203
Extraversion, 81, 82, 87, 308
    as Big Five factor, 289, 290–291, 293, 296, 297
    education and, 328
    introversion versus, 15, 312, 313, 314, 318–
        321, 322–326, 334
Extrinsic reinforcement, 233
Extrospection, 4–5, 13, 60, 201, 365, 479
    limitations of, 480–481
Eysenck, Hans J., 268, 305–377, 314, 315, 321, 325, 326, 327,
        328
    application of theories of, 327
    Big Five and, 301, 315–316, 334
    biographical background of, 306–308
    on biological basis of behavior and neurosis,
        322–324, 331, 333
    Cattell and, 315–316, 334
    on causal agents for behavior, 292, 318–326
    on creativity, 329
    educational implications of, 327–328
    evaluation of, 333–336
    historical predecessors of, 308–310
    on intelligence, 325–326
    mentioned, 15, 19, 22, 290, 303, 477
    on personality and genetics, 314–315, 327, 329,
        330–331, 335
    personality model of, 310–311, 312–315
    psychotherapy of, 331–333
    on superfactors, 306, 311–318
    on trait measurement, 317, 318
    writings of, 307, 332, 337

Eysenck, J. J., 320–321
Eysenck, M. W., 315, 326
Eysenck, S. B. G., 313, 315, 318
Eysenck Personality Inventory, 317
Eysenck Personality Questionnaire, 317
Eysenck Personality Questionnaire-Revised, 318

Factor analysis, 19, 267, 283, 286–289, 290, 301, 311–312,
        315–316, 325, 330
Factor analytic theories, 282–304
    behavioral genetics and, 294–299, 302
    evolutionary psychology and, 299–300, 302
    *See also* Big Five personality traits; Cattell,
        Raymond
Falbo, T., 107
Family, dysfunctional, 193
Family atmosphere, 102–103
Family constellation, 100, 102, 109
Fantasy, 43
Farmer, J. J., 389
Farran, D., 236
Fay, A., 440
Feelings
    Jung and, 82
    Kant and, 308
    May and, 382–383
    *see also* Emotions
Feixas, G., 416
Feldmann, T. B., 172
Feminist psychology, 121
    Chodorow and, 176–179, 191, 192, 195
    Freud and, 57
    Horney and, 114, 119–121, 123, 124
    Morgan and, 271
    Rogers and, 366
    *See also* Gender; Stone Center group; Women
Ferenczi, Sandor, 31
Feshbach, S., 481
FFM (Five Factor Model), 269, 289, 290, 291–294,
        301–302
Fickling, W., 469
Fictional finalisms, 97, 99
Fidelity, as ego strength or virtue, 149–151, 153
Fiebert, M. S., 95
Finalisms, 96–97
    fictional, 97, 99
Fingarette, H., 58
Fisch, R., 440
Fisher, S., 56
Five Factor Model (FFM), 269, 289, 290, 291–294,
        301–302
Fixation, 45–46
Fixed interval reinforcement, 215
Fixed ratio reinforcement, 215
Fixed-role therapy, Kelly and, 411, 414
Flax, J., 61
Fletcher, K., 463
Flooding, 332
"Flow," 467
Foa, E. B., 440
Ford, J. G., 352
Ford, K. M., 411
Fordham, F., 74
Forisha-Kovach, B., 157
Foster, Vince, Jr., 389
Four Noble Truths, 455
Fragmentation, Kelly and, 407, 408
Frank, C. M., 319

Frank, Jerome, 428
Frankfurt Institute of Social Research, 132
Frankl, V. E., 440
Franks, C. M., 438, 444
Fransella, F., 410
Free association, 31, 35–36, 39, 54, 86, 87, 121, 172, 391
Freedom
    determinism versus, 8
    Fromm on, 126–127
    May on, 386–387
Freedom of movement, 247
Freeman, M., 483
Freud, Anna (daughter), 57, 139–142, 167, 428–429
    biographical background of, 139
    child analysis and, 139–142
    developmental line theory and, 141–142
    Erikson and, 145
    Freud (Sigmund) and, 139, 142
    on object relationships, 167
    writings of, 165
Freud, Anna (sister), 29
Freud, Jacob, 29
Freud, Sigmund, 28–67, 126
    Adler and, 95
    Allport and, 257–258, 259
    anxiety and, 115
    Beck and, 431, 443
    biographical background of, 29–31
    Chodorow and, 179
    clinical practice and, 6
    on defense mechanisms, 50–53
    Ellis and, 428–429
    Erikson and, 145, 146, 157
    evaluation of, 59–64
    existentialism and, 394
    Freud (Anna) and, 139, 142
    Fromm and, 125, 126, 133, 134
    Horney and, 115, 119, 121, 122, 123, 124
    impact of, 62–64
    introspection and, 5, 60
    Jung and, 72–73, 74, 75–76, 77, 79–80, 81, 83, 85, 86
    Klein and, 167
    on memory, 107
    mentioned, 5, 6, 19, 21, 96, 98, 100, 106, 108, 113, 114,
        116, 129, 130, 139, 173, 184, 208, 221, 242, 259, 262,
        276, 367, 373, 374, 378, 387, 390, 391, 399, 476, 477,
        478, 483
    Murray and, 272, 277
    personality definition and, 2
    on personality development, 38–46, 139
    personality structure concept of, 46–50
    philosophy and, 9
    psychoanalysis concept, 23, see also Freudian
        psychoanalysis
    on psychosexual stages, 41–46
    sexuality theory of, 38–41, 179
    Skinner and, 217
    writings of, 31, 32, 36, 38, 46, 47, 49, 68
    see also Freudian psychoanalysis
Freudian psychoanalysis, 2, 5, 21, 31–38, 53–64, 85, 103,
        104, 105, 193, 207, 285
    analytic process in, 54–56
    countertransference in, 189
    Eastern psychotherapy and, 468
    Erikson and, 163–164
    learning theory integrated with, 205–206
    methodology of, 35–38
    origins of, 31–38

training for, 125
transference in, 53–54, 55, 105
unconscious in, 32–35, 58, 73–74, 75
validation of concepts in, 56–59
Freudian slips, 36–37
Fromm, Erich, 113, 124–136, 393
    assessment and research in theory of, 132
    on basic human conditions and needs, 126–129
    biographical background of, 124–125
    on character orientations, 129–132
    Eastern thought and, 471
    Ellis and, 428
    Erikson and, 162
    on escape mechanisms, 126–127
    evaluation of, 133–134
    on female development, 121
    Freud and, 125, 126, 133, 134
    Horney and, 115, 127
    mentioned, 69, 109, 139, 342, 476, 477, 480
    writings of, 132, 136
Frost, Robert, 210
Frustration, learning and, 203
Fuld, 469
Fuller, F. Buckminster, 485
Fullerton, C. S., 107
Fully functioning person, 357
Functional autonomy, 263–264, 268–269
Functions, Jung on, 81, 82
Fundamental postulates (Kelly), 405–407, 408
Funder, D., 293
Fung, H., 483
Furnham, A., 87
Fusion, 190

Gaha, L., 170
Gaillard, C., 73
Galen, 308
Galin, D., 439
Gallard, M., 73
Galligher, J., 236
Galton, Francis, Sir, 290, 325
Gandhi, Mahatma, 19, 155
Gardner, H., 483
Gardner, L. E., 110
Gardner, W. L., 87
Garfield, S., 22
Garofalo, D., 124
Garrison, D., 124
Gassho, 463
Gates, Bill, 381
Gautama, Siddhartha, 451–452. See also Buddha
Gawelek, M., 484
Gedo Zen, 465
Geisler, C., 56
Geller, L., 365, 366
Gender
    Adler on, 99
    androgyny and, 78, 90
    anima-animus archetypes (Jung) and, 77–78
    Chodorow on, 176–179
    dialogue and, 191
    Erickson on children's play construction and,
        155–157
    genetic factors in sexual behaviors and, 331
    myths and, 390
    personality and, 107
    personality theories and, 484
    psychological health and, 107

psychoticism and, 321–322
self-actualization and, 349
*see also* Feminist psychology; Women
Generalization, scientific (or empirical), 13–14
Generalized conditioned reinforcers, 215
Generativity
    McAdams and, 159–160, 161
    versus stagnation, 151–152, 153
Genetics
    behavioral, 294–299, 302
    personality and, 314–315, 327, 329, 330–331, 335
Genital stage, 45, 130
Genotype, personality and, 323–324
Genuineness, 358
Gergen, K., 484
Gestalt therapists, 391, 442
Getting type, of style of life, 99–100
*g* factor (general factor), 325
Giesler, R. B., 357
Gilligan, Carol, 181
Gilliland, K., 321
Ginsburg, C., 365
Giora, Z., 37
Giorgi, A., 480
Giovacchini, 171
Glass, J., 22
Glucksberg, S., 58
Glymour, C., 30
Goal rehearsal, Lazarus and, 440
Goals
    Adler on, 96–97, 99, 104
    of integration (May), 383–390
Goethe, 389, 390
Gold, A., 123
Goldberg, L. R., 289, 290, 293, 316
Golden, W., 441
Goldfried, M. R., 441
Goldstein, J., 139
Goleman, D., 47, 56, 107, 343, 352, 431, 444
Goodman, E. D., 109
Goranson, R., 156
Graduated task assignments, in cognitive therapy, 435
Gratification, delay of, 240
Graves, P., 411
Green, C. D., 14
Greenberg, G., 21
Greenberg, J., 429, 431, 436
Greenberg, R., 107
Greenberg, R. P., 56
Greisers, C., 107
Grinder, J., 439
Gross, R., 236
Grotstein, J. S., 168
Group therapy, 361, 415, 437
Grünbaum, A., 58
Guilford, J. P., 325
Guilt
    Fromm on, 134
    initiative versus, 147–148, 153
    Kelly on, 409
    May on, 390
Gunton, R., 234–235
Gupta, M. D., 107
Guy-Gillet, G., 85

Habits, learning and, 201–203, 204
Habitual responses, Eysenck and, 312–313
Hall, C. S., 56, 290, 481

Hall, G. Stanley, 31
Hall, M., 163, 342
Hamacheck, D., 157–158
Hammer, J., 58
Hammer, M., 123
Hamon, S. A., 123
Hampson, S., 244
Hanh, T. N., 454, 458, 463, 470, 471
Harari, C., 368
Hargrove, L., 107
Harper, R. A., 423
Harrington, D. M., 357
Harris, K. A., 107
Harris, T., 393
Harrison, R. H., 107, 432
Harrison, W., 244
Harry, P., 107
Hartmann, Heinz, 142–143
Harvard Psychological Clinic, 271, 278
Harzem, P., 482
Haskins, R., 236
Having mode, 131
Hawley, C. W., 328
Hayes, L., 221
Hayes, S., 221
Hayes, T. L., 293
Health problems, personality traits and, 333
Heidegger, Martin, 375
Help groups, 361
Henwood, K. L., 21
Heraclitus, 384
Heredity versus environment, 8, 283, 294, 478
    behavioral genetics and, 294–299, 302
    *see also* Traits and personality
Heritability, 296
Hermans, J. J., 12
Hermsen, E., 367
Heston, L. L., 295
Heterostasis, 478
Hibbard, S., 218
Hierarchical model of personality, 312–315
Hierarchy of needs, 272, 343–345
Hierarchy of response, 202
Hinayana, 453
Hinds, M., 234
Hinduism
    mandalas and, 78, 80
    Rogers and, 366
Hippocrates, 308, 313, 314
Hirai, T., 462, 463, 469, 470
Hjelle, L. A., 108
Hoarding orientation, 129, 130
Hochreich, D. J., 246, 247
Hoffman, E., 115, 341
Hogan, J., 292, 293
Hogan, R., 292, 293
Hogan, Robert, 155
Holdren, J. M., 109
Holland, J. L., 293
Hollon, S., 431, 432, 436
Homer, 479
Homework, in cognitive therapy, 435
Homosexuality
    Freud on, 46
    lesbian relationships and, 190
    19th-century views of, 40
Honey, P., 328
Hoogstra, L., 483

Hoover, I., 460
Hope, as ego strength or virtue, 147, 153
Horley, J., 411
Hormones, psychoticism and, 321–322
Horney, Karen, 113–124, 431
    on anxiety, 115–116
    assessment and research in theory of, 121–123
    biographical background of, 113–115
    Eastern thought and, 471
    Ellis and, 428
    evaluation of, 123–124, 133
    feminine psychology of, 114, 119–121, 123, 124
    Freud and, 115, 119, 121, 122, 123, 124
    Fromm and, 115, 127
    on idealized self, 117–119, 123
    mentioned, 69, 109, 139, 293, 342, 354, 477
    on neurotic needs on trends, 116–119, 124, 127
    psychotherapy and, 124
    on self-analysis, 121
    writings of, 135–136
Hostility, Kelly and, 409
Hot cognitions, 434
Howard, R., 326
Hull, Clark, 201–202, 243, 319
Human Genome Project, 297
Humanistic ethics, 130
Humanistic theories, 103, 109, 134, 178, 248, 339, 340–371, 478, 480
    Allport and, 257, 268, 269
    see also Maslow, Abraham; Rogers, Carl R.
Human needs, Murray on, 272–275, 278–279
Human relations theories, 166–196
    evaluation of, 191–193
    see also Object relations theorists; Relational/cultural theory
Human society, Adler on, 96
Humor, Allport on, 265
Hunter, I., 56
Hypercompetitive Attitude Scale, 123
Hypercompetitiveness, 123
Hypnosis, 33, 34
Hypothesis testing, in cognitive therapy, 435
Hysteria, 33

Iaccino, James, 79
Ibsen, Henrik, 389, 390
I Ching, 84
Id, 46, 47–48, 49, 50, 58, 139, 142, 143, 272
Idealization, of parents, 172
Idealized self, 117–119, 123
Identification, 51, 52–53, 206
    with the aggressor, 142
Identity, sense of, 127, 128, 129
Identity crisis, 150–151, 158
Idiographic approach, 266, 269, 482
Idiothetic approach, 269
I-E Scale, 243–244, 245, 250
Imagery, in cognitive therapy, 435
Imaginal symbols, in observational learning, 232
Imagoes, 159
Imitation, 208, 232
Implosive confrontation, 426
Incest, 43
Incongruence, Rogers and, 354–355
Independent variable, 19
Individuality, Kelly and, 406, 408
Individualized instruction, 217
Individual psychology, 93–111. See also Adler, Alfred

Individuation, 84–85
    separation-individuation process and, 169–170, 182, 183
Industry versus inferiority, 148–149, 153
Infant, Allport on, 261–262
Inferiority
    feelings of, 98–99
    industry versus, 148–149, 153
Inferiority complex, 104
Information processing, 59
    Kelly and, 417
Infrahuman species, 204, 220
Ingram, D. H., 116, 124
Inhibition, Eysenck and, 319
Initiative versus guilt, 147–148, 153
Innocence, stage of, 383
Insight, 217
Institute for Rational-Emotive Therapy, 427, 444
Integration, goals of (May), 383–390
Integrative life story, 21
Intelligence
    biological, 325
    evoked potential and, 326
    g factor and, 325
    heritability of, 330, 331
    IQ and, 14, 295, 325, 326
    personality and, 325–326
    practical, 325
    psychometric, 325
Intentionality, 218, 386
Internal locus of control, 243–246
International Psychoanalytic Association, 94
International Psychoanalytic Society, 73
Interpersonal school of psychoanalysis, 123, 124
Interpretative response, 359, 361
Interpsychic phenomena, 94, 95
Interval reinforcement, 215
Intimacy versus isolation, 151, 153
Intrapsychic phenomena, 94, 95
Intrinsic reinforcement, 233
Introspection, 4–5, 13, 60, 172, 250, 365–366
Introversion, 14–15, 81, 82, 87, 308
    education and, 328
    extraversion versus, 15, 312, 313, 314, 318–321, 322–326, 334
Intuition, Jung and, 82
Inventories, personality, 317–318
In vivo desensitization, 426
IQ (intelligence quotient), 14, 295, 325, 326. See also Intelligence
Ishiyama, F. I., 107
Isolation, intimacy versus, 151, 153
I-Thou, Buber on, 377

Jackson, C., 328
Jackson, D. J., 140
Jackson, D. N., 292
Jackson, L. J., 441
Jackson Personality Research Form, 276
Jacobson, L., 58
Jacobson, N. S., 441
Jager, B., 192
James, William, 108
Jankowicz, A. D., 416
Jarvik, L. F., 295
Jensen, A. R., 295

Job performance, personality questionnaire predicting, 292–293
Job satisfaction, personality measures predicting, 293
John, O. P., 269, 289, 290, 293
Johnson, P. W., 172
Johnson, R. A., 77
Jones, Ernest E., 22, 31, 33
Jordan, Judith V., 179, 184, 190
Joseph, R., 349
*Journal of Personality,* 482–483
Juda, D. P., 43
Jung, Carl, 70–92
    assessment and research in theory of, 86–88
    biographical background of, 71–73
    on collective unconscious, 73, 75–81, 89
    Eastern thought and, 471
    evaluation of, 88–90
    Freud and, 72–73, 74, 75–76, 77, 79–80, 81, 83, 85, 86
    mentioned, 18, 31, 69, 96–97, 98, 116, 123, 139, 264, 265, 308, 476, 477, 478
    Murray and, 271
    on personal unconscious, 73, 74–75
    psychotherapy of, 85–86
    on self-realization, 83–85
    structure of personality (types) and, 73–83
    writings of, 84, 91

Kabat-Zinn, J., 463, 469, 470, 471
Kaczor, L. M., 123
Kagan, J., 262, 378
Kalekin-Fishman, D., 415
Kalupahana, D. J., 455
Kalupahana, I., 455
Kant, Immanuel, 308, 422, 431, 443
Kantrowitz, R. E., 444
Kaplan, L. J., 142
Kaplan, R. D., 390
Karma, 456
Katagiri-roshi, Dainin, 451, 452, 454, 462, 465, 469
Katz, J. L., 30
Keirsey, D., 87
Kelly, George, 250, 400–418
    Allport and, 417
    assessment and research in theory of, 409–411, 412
    Beck and, 431
    biographical background of, 401–403
    on constructive alternativism, 401, 404–407
    evaluation of, 415–417
    fundamental postulate and corollaries and, 405–407, 408
    mentioned, 399, 477
    personal constructs theory and, 403, 404–411, 412–413 415, 416–417
    on person as scientist, 403, 405, 415, 416
    psychotherapy of, 411, 414–415
    reconstruction of old concepts by, 407–409
    Rep Test and, 409–410, 411, 412–413, 415–416
    role-playing and, 411, 414, 415
    writings of, 418
Kelly, W. L., 193
Kelly's Role Construct Repertory test, 293
Kempen, H. J., 12
Kern, R. M., 109
Kernberg, Otto F., 171, 173–176, 191, 192
Kidwell, J., 107

Kierkegaard, Sören, 373, 374–375, 378
Kihlstrom, J. F., 59
Kimura, D., 439
King, I., 58
Kinhin, 463
Kinkead, G., 178
Kiracofe, H. N., 107
Kiracofe, N. M., 107
Kirkland, J., 405
Kitayama, S., 64, 349, 366
Klatzky, R. L., 403
Klein, Melanie, 167–168
Klein, S., 107
Kline, P., 56, 57, 58
Klonoff, E., 64
Knowledge, need for, 344, 345
Koans, 462
Koch, E., 62
Koenigsberg, H. W., 175
Kohut, Heinz, 116, 124, 170–173, 175, 184
Kolata, G., 298
Kolb, David, 328
Kosko, B., 461
Krafft-Ebing, Richard, 72
Kretschmer, Ernest, 308–309
Kruger, D., 482
Krystal, H., 193
Kuelnel, R. H., 123
Kuhn, Thomas, 12
Kwee, M. G. T., 441

Labeling, 205
Labrèche-Gauthier, L., 244
Lambert, M., 220
Lamielle, J. T., 269
Landfield, A. W., 404
Landman, J. T., 22
Landrine, H., 64
Lane, R. W., 56
Lang, K. L., 296, 297
Language
    Big Five and, 290, 293–294
    Skinner and, 220–221
Lao-tse, 460
Lao Tzu, 349
Latency period, 45
Latent dream, 37
Law of effect, 201, 211
Lawton, H. W., 155
Lawty-Jones, M., 328
Lay analysts, 124–125
Lazarsfeld, S., 110
Lazarus, Arnold A., 436–445, 443
    BASIC-ID and, 438–439, 441, 442
    biographical background of, 436–438
    evaluation of, 443, 444, 445
    mentioned, 208, 399, 420, 477
    multimodal behavior therapy of, 438–439, 440–442, 443, 444
    personality theory of, 439–440
    technical eclecticism of, 442–443
    writings of, 438, 448
Lazarus, Richard, 431
Leak, G. K., 110
Learned helplessness, behavior therapy for, 332
Learning
    Eysenck and, 327–328
    Kelly and, 408

Learning dilemma, 203
Learning Style Questionnaire (LSQ), 328
Learning theories, 197, 200–201, 477
    history of, 200–201
    observational, 229–234
    psychoanalytic, 199, *see also* Dollard, John; Miller, Neal
    radical behaviorism, 199, *see also* Skinner, B. F.
    social, *see* Bandura, Albert; Rotter, Julian
    *see also* Behaviorist theories; Cognitive theories
Leduc, C., 244
Lee, W., 244
Lefcourt, H. M., 244, 246
Leith, G., 328
Leitner, L. M., 403
Lemon test, 322
Leonardo da Vinci, 19
Leone, G., 468
Lerman, H., 366, 483
Lerner, J. A., 116, 124
Lesbian relationships, 190
Lester, D., 107, 244
Levitz-Jones, E. M., 158
Lewin, Kurt, 203, 242–243
Lewis, A., 96
Lewis, G., 244
Lewis, H. B., 59
Lewis, J. L., 175
LGS (Loyola Generativity Scale), 160
Libido, 38, 40, 41, 45, 46, 47, 58, 74, 119, 129, 171
Lieberman, L., 102, 107
Life crisis, 146
Life cycle, Erickson and, 153
Life histories, *see* Life narratives
Life impulses, Freud on, 40
Life lie, *see* Mistaken style of life
Life narratives, 21
    in contemporary theories, 482–483
    Five Factor Model and, 293
Life style, *see* Style of life
Likierman, M., 47, 167
Lindorff, D., 84
Lindzey, Gardner, 267, 290, 481
Literature, psychology and, 483
Little, T., 172–173
Livesley, W. J., 296, 297
Locke, John, 200
Locus of control, 236
    internal-external, 243–246
    multiculturalism and, 246
Loehlin, J. C., 289, 296, 302
Loevinger, J., 484
Logic, 7
Lombardi, D. N., 107
Loneliness, Fromm on, 126, 131
Longitudinal studies, 192
Loomis, Mary, 84
Loori, J. D., 466
Lovaas, O. I., 217
Love
    Erikson on, 151, 153
    Fromm on, 126, 131
    May and, 385–386
Love needs, 343, 344
Lowell, E. L., 276
Loyola Generativity Scale (LGS), 160, 161

LSQ (Learning Style Questionnaire), 328
Luther, Martin, 19, 155

McAdams, Dan P., 159–162, 160, 163, 278, 301, 482, 483
McCabe, A., 483
McCaulley, M. H., 87
McClelland, David C., 276–277, 483
Maccoby, E. E., 123
Maccoby, Michael, 132
McCrae, Robert R., 21, 289, 290, 291, 292, 293
MacIntyre, Alasdair, 58, 61, 483
McKay, G., 105
McKay, J., 156
MacKenzie, K. R., 444
Mackie, D., 234
McKillen, M., 326
McLaughlin, R. J., 320–321
Macmillan, M., 58
McQuater, G., 246
Macy, J., 454
Magid, B., 56, 62
Magnification and minimization, Beck and, 433
Magnusson, D., 481
Mahayana Buddhism, 453, 460, 464
Mahers, B. A., 483
Mahler, B., 403, 417
Mahler, Margaret, 169–170
Maiello, S., 124
Mair, J. M. M., 410
Mair, M., 414
Malcolm X, 155
Male dominance, Adler on, 99
Malikiosi, M. X., 244
Managed care, short-term psychotherapy and, 444
Manas, 458
Mancuso, J. C., 417
Mandalas, 78, 80
Manifest dream, 37
Manovijana, 458
Mansfield, E., 160
Mansfield, V., 85
Marcia, J. E., 158
Marcus, H. R., 349
Margolis, D. P., 29
Marin, P., 366
Marketing orientation, 129, 130
Markova, I., 483
Markstrom-Adams, C., 158
Markus, G. B., 106
Markus, H. R., 64, 349, 366
Markus, R., 349
Martial arts, Zen and, 464
Martin, J. A., 123
Martin, R. A., 244
Martinko, M. J., 87
Marx, Karl, 126
Masculine protest, 99
Masling, J. M., 56
Maslow, Abraham, 339, 341–350
    Allport and, 266, 268
    biographical background of, 341–343
    Eastern thought and, 471
    Ellis and, 429
    evaluation of, 348–350
    hierarchical theory of motivation of, 272, 343–345
    May and, 380, 392
    mentioned, 265, 272, 477, 479, 480
    on self-actualization, 344–350

Watson and, 342
writings of, 370
Masochism, 42–43, 46
Masse, G., 72
Masson, J. M., 43
Masterson, Jenny, 266–267
Masturbation
Freud on, 43
19th-century views of, 40, 41
Matthews, K., 302, 484
Maturity
Allport on, 264–266
Freud on, 45, 46
Jung on, 71
Maudsley Personality Inventory, 317
MAVA (multiple abstract variance analysis), 294
May, Rollo, 43, 105, 110, 339, 372–398, 373
on anxiety, 378–379, 392
assessment and research in theory of, 391–393
biographical background of, 373–375
on courage, 387–388
on creativity, 387–388
on daimonic, 384
on dreams, 392
evaluation of, 393–395
existentialism of, 375–377
on feelings, 382–383
on freedom and destiny, 386–387
Freud and, 394
on integration goals, 383–390
on intentionality, 386
on love, 385–386
Maslow and, 380, 392
mentioned, 476, 479, 481
on myth, 388–390, 392
on ontological assumptions concerning the person, 382
on power, 384–385
on powerlessness, 377–378, 384
psychotherapy of, 390–391, 393
on rediscovering selfhood, 380, 382–383
Rogers and, 380, 392
on sex, 385–386
on values, 379, 381
writings of, 374, 375, 388, 396–397
Maya, 468, 478
Mayer, E. L., 155–156
MBTI (Myers-Briggs Type Indicator), 87, 88
Mead, Margaret, 221
Meditation, Zen, 460–466, 469, 470
Meichenbaum, David, 436
Melancholic personality, 308, 309, 313, 314
Memory
Adler on, 107
Freud on, 107
Mencher, J., 190
Meredith, D. W., 110
Messer, S., 57
Meta-analyses, of psychotherapy outcome studies, 22
Metacommunication, 440
Metamotivation, 343
Metaphysics, 7
Metzger, R., 468
Miccolis, G., 121
Michelangelo, 19
Micka, J. C., 158
Miller, Jean Baker, 179, 181, 182, 184, 185, 187, 188, 189, 195–196, 349, 366, 463, 469

Miller, N. J., 469
Miller, N. S., 30
Miller, Neal, 199, 200–208, 221
biographical background of, 200
evaluation of, 207–208, 221
on experimental analysis of behavior, 200–201
Freudian psychoanalysis and, 205–206
on frustration and conflict, 203–205
on learning, 201–203, 204
mentioned, 217, 477
psychotherapy of, 206–207
writings of, 208, 223
Miller, P., 483
Minami, M., 483
Mindfulness therapy, 470, 471
Minnesota Center for Twin and Adoption Research, 296
Minnesota Multiphasic Personality Inventory (MMPI), 17–18
Minorities, personality theories and, 483–484. *See also* Multiculturalism
Miranda, A. O., 109
Mirroring, 172
Mischel, Walter, 240, 250–252, 251, 254, 268, 482
Misra, G., 244
Mistaken style of life, 104, 105
Mistrust, trust versus, 147, 153
Mitchell, Juliet, 57
MMPI (Minnesota Multiphasic Personality Inventory), 17–18
Modality profiles, in multimodal therapy, 441
Modeling, 230–231, 238
Modulation, Kelly and, 406, 408
Monozygotic (MZ), 294, 295
Montessori philosophy, 145
Moore, J., 211
Moorehead, K., 158
Moraglia, G., 90
Moral anxiety, 50
Moreno, J., 411
Morgan, Christiana, 271, 277
Morgenson, G., 90
Morita, Shoma, 469
Morita therapy, 469–470
Morrow, J. B., 107
Mosig, Y. D., 455, 457, 465
Mothering, *see* Parenting
Motivation
in cognitive-affective personality system, 251
in contemporary theories, 482
hierarchical theory of, 343–345
Kelly and, 408
metamotivation versus, 343
in observational learning, 232
Rotter on, 246–247
Yerkes-Dodson law of, 320–321
Motives, 36
Motor production processes, in cognitive-affective personality system, 251
Motor reproduction processes, in observational learning, 232
Mount, M. K., 292
Movement, Ellis and, 422–423
Moving against, away, or toward, Horney on, 116, 117
Mowrer, O. H., 208
MPDQ (Mutual Psychological Development Questionnaire), 192–193
Mruk, C. J., 367
Mueller, E., 21

Multiculturalism
  Big Five and personality structure and, 290, 293–294
  Cattell and, 289
  child development and, 153–154
  child's will and, 147
  circumcision and, 180
  cognitive-behavioral theories and, 443–444
  generativity and, 152
  genetic basis for personality dimensions and, 314–315
  Jung and, 90
  Kelly and, 415
  labeling and, 205
  learning process and, 204
  locus of control and, 246
  May and, 390
  Mutual Psychological Development Questionnaire and, 192–193
  narrative perspective and, 483
  personality theories and, 2, 16, 63–64, 483–484
  postmodernism and, 12
  prejudice and, 267–268
  psychosocial stages and, 158
  reinforcement and, 203
  in relationships, 191
  Rogers and, 366–367, 368
  self-actualization and, 349–350
  sexual excitement and, 175–176
  similarities and differences among all people and, 335–336
  Stone Center group and, 190–191
  *see also* Culture; Eastern thought
Multimodal behavior therapy, 438–439, 440–442, 443, 444
Multiple abstract variance analysis (MAVA), 294
Mumford, A., 328
Munson, P. A., 107
Murk, D., 246
Murphy, M., 462
Murray, Henry A., 87, 250, 257, 270–279, 417
  assessment and research in theory of, 275–277
  biographical background of, 270–271
  evaluation of, 277–279
  Freud and, 272, 277
  on human needs, 272–275, 278–279
  Jung and, 271
  mentioned, 18, 477, 483
  personology theory and, 271–272, 278
  psychoanalysis and, 271
  writing of, 281
Musturbatory belief systems, 425
Mutilation, culturally sanctioned, 179
Mutual empathy, 185
Mutuality, 184
Mutual Psychological Development Questionnaire (MPDQ), 192–193
Myers, Isabel Briggs, 87
Myers-Briggs Type Indicator (MBTI), 87, 88
Myths
  McAdams on, 159, 160, 162
  May on, 388–390, 392
Myyra, J., 79

Naidu, R., 484
Naikan introspective therapy, 470
Napoleon, 75
Narayan, C., 107
Narcissism, 170–173

Narrative histories, *see* Life narratives
Native Americans, Erikson's study of, 153–154
Nature versus nurture, *see* Heredity versus environment
Necrophilous character, 131
Needs
  achievement, 276–277
  basic (Fromm), 126–129
  hierarchy of (Maslow), 272, 343–345
  Murray on, 272–275, 276, 278–279
  neurotic (Horney), 116–119
Need value, 247
Negative identity, 150, 155
Negative reinforcement, 215
Negative transference, 54, 55
Neobehaviorists, 437
NEO-PI (Neuroticism Extraversion Openness Personality Inventory), 290
NEO-PI-R (Neuroticism Extraversion Openness Personality Inventory, Revised), 290–291, 293
Neopsychoanalytic approach, *see* Adler, Alfred; Fromm, Erich; Horney, Karen; Jung, Carl
Neubauer, A., 46, 57
Neubauer, P., 46, 57
Neufeldt, A., 483
Neuroses, 31, 43, 53
  Adler on, 104
  Allport on, 263, 264–265
  Dollard and Miller on, 206–207
  Eastern psychotherapy and, 468
  Eysenck on, 314, 322–324, 331
  Freud on, 31, 46, 85
  Horney on, 116–119, 124, 127
  Jung on, 85, 308
  Kelly on, 411
  Skinner on, 216–217
Neurotic anxiety, 50
Neuroticism, as Big Five factor, 289, 290–291, 293, 296, 297
Neuroticism Extraversion Openness Personality Inventory (NEO-PI), 290
Neuroticism Extraversion Openness Personality Inventory, Revised (NEO-PI-R), 290–291, 293
Neurotic needs/trends, 116–119, 124, 127
Neutral stimulus, 201
New Age practitioners, 464
Niederehe, G., 107
Nielsen, S. L., 422
Nietzsche, 373
Nirvana, 457
Noble, B. P., 481
Noel, D. C., 90
Nomothetic approach, 266, 269
Nonbeing, May and, 390–391
Nondirective therapy, 357–362
Nonverbal behaviors, in psychotherapy, 391
Norcross, J. C., 441
Normal autism, 169
Normalcy, 266
Normal symbiosis, 169
Norman, W. T., 290
Nuclear episodes, 159
Nuclear self, 172
Nurture versus nature, *see* Heredity versus environment

Oatley, K., 483
Objective data, 13

Objectivity, 201
  assessment and, 17
Object of devotion, 127, 128, 129
Object relations, 167, 184
  object relationships versus, 167
Object relationships, 167
Object relations theorists, 116, 124, 167–179
  Chodorow, 176–179, 191, 192, 195
  Kernberg, 173–176, 192, 195
  Klein, 167–168
  Kohut, 170–173
  Mahler, 169–170
Observation, 13
Observational learning theory, 229–234
Obsessive-compulsive disorder, 332
Occasional self-analysis, 122
*OCEAN* personality factors, 289
Oedipus complex
  Ellis on, 429
  Erikson on, 148, 149
  Freud on, 29, 38, 43–44, 46, 48, 56–57
  Horney on, 116, 119
  Kohut on, 116, 172
  Mahler on, 169
  May on, 382, 389
  Stiver on, 184
Ogwu-Oju, D., 180
O'Hara, M., 368, 484
O'Keefe, E. J., 441
Okey, Jeffrey, 57
Okumura, S., 466–467
Ontological assumptions, May and, 382
Openness, as Big Five factor, 289, 290–291, 296,
  297
Operant behavior, 213
Operant conditioning, 212–213, 214, 218
Operational definition, 14
Opposite-sex archetype, 77
Optimistic theories, pessimistic theories versus, 9,
  478–479
Oral stage, 41–42, 57, 129, 206
Ordinary consciousness of self, 383
Ordination, Murray and, 272
Organ inferiority, 98
Organismic valuing process, 353
Organization, Kelly and, 406, 408
Orientation, frame of, 127, 128, 129
Orientations, basic (Horney), 116, 117
Originality, Eysenck and, 329
Orlofsky, J. L., 158
Ornstein, A., 56, 172
Ornstein, R. E., 439, 480
Overcompensation, 104
Overdetermination, 36
Overgeneralization, Beck and, 433
Overinclusive cognitive style, Eysenck and, 329
Overt behaviors, 4, 13

Packer, M. J., 21, 483
Page, R. C., 349, 456
Papini, D. R., 158
Pappenheim, Bertha (Anna O.), 32–34, 35, 53
Paradigm, 12, 24
Paradox, 383–384, 440
Parapsychology, 84
Paraworld, experiments and, 480
Parental inaccessibility, disconnection and, 187
Parentification, disconnection and, 187

Parenting
  Adler on, 102–103, 105, 106
  Chodorow on, 176–178
  family atmosphere established by, 102–103
  Horney on, 123
  Kohut on, 172–173
  shared, 178
  *see also* Children
Paris, B. J., 123, 124
Parmar, P., 180
Parsimony, as criterion, 16
Participant observation, 105, 157
Pastorelli, C., 240
Patterson, S. J., 158
Paul, R. A., 43, 119, 193
Pauli, Wolfgang, 84
Pavlov, Ivan, 200–201, 210, 212, 428
Peak experiences, 346–347, 350
Pelham, B. W., 269
Penis envy, 44, 56, 119
Perception, Ellis and, 422–423
Performance, 232
  Yerkes-Dodson law of, 320–321
Performance phase, of therapy, 207
Perls, Fritz, 391
Permeability, Kelly and, 406–407
Perrez, M., 24
Perseverative functional autonomy, 264
Persona, Jung on, 76–77, 78, 79
Personal construct theory, Kelly on, 403, 404–411,
  412–413, 415, 416–417
Personal dispositions, 260–261
Personality
  academic psychology and, 5, 6
  Allport on, 258–259, 266
  assessment of, 16–18, 107–108, *see also under*
    *individual psychologists*
  biological factors in, 322–324, 333, 484
  birth order and, 100–102, 107
  changes in, 358
  clinical practice and, 5, 6
  cultural differences in, 290, 293–294
  definitions of, 2–3, 15, 258–259, 266, 269, 284–285,
    312–315
  Five Factor Model of, 269, 289, 290, 291–294,
    301–302
  Freud on development of, 38–46
  genetics and, 314–315, 327, 329, 330–331
  as habits, 201–203
  hierarchical model of, 312–315
  intelligence and, 325–326
  Jung on nature of, 73–83
  psychosexual stages of, 41–46
  sexuality and, 38–41
  structure of, 46–50, 73–83
  *see also* Big Five personality traits; Traits and
    personality
Personality disorders, NEO-PI-R for, 293
Personality inventory questionnaires, 317–318
Personality phenotype, 323–324
Personality questionnaires and ratings
  Big Five model and, 290–293
  job performance and, 292–293
  job satisfaction and, 293
Personality theories
  application of, 16–23
  contemporary, 479–487
  culture and, *see* Culture; Multiculturalism

Personality theories (*cont.*)
  evaluation of, 5–6, 23–24, 476–478, *see also* Art;
      Philosophy; Science
  overview of, 4–24
  in perspective, 475–487
  psychotherapy and, 21–22
  racism and, 483–484
  role of in psychology, 4–5
Personality traits, *see* Traits
Personalization, Beck and, 433
Personal unconscious, 73, 74–75
Person-centered therapy, 357–362
Personnel selection, Cattell and, 289
Personology, 271–272, 278
Perspectivism, 415
Pervin, L. A., 301, 417, 482
Pessimistic theories, optimistic theories versus, 9,
      478–479
Peterson, C. A., 107
Pfenninger, D. T., 408
Phallic stage, 43–45, 206
Phelps, R., 441
Phenomenal field, 352
Phenomenology, 352, 366, 367, 392
  Beck and, 430–431
Phenotype, 294
  personality and, 323–324
Phenylketonuria (PKU), 299
Philosophical assumptions, 7–12
  basic, 8–9
  evaluation of, 9–12
  recognition of, 7–8
  scientific statements versus, 8
Philosophy, 4, 482, 485
  Adler and, 108–109
  Allport and, 265, 268, 478
  Bandura and, 241, 478
  Beck and, 443
  Cattell and, 301, 478
  comparison of personality theories based on, 478–479
  definition of, 7
  Ellis and, 422, 443
  Erikson and, 162
  Eysenck and, 335–336
  Freud and, 60–61, 478
  Fromm and, 133
  Horney and, 123
  Jung and, 89, 478
  Kelly and, 401, 404–407, 410, 415, 416
  May and, 392, 393–394, 395, 479
  Murray and, 278
  personality theories and, 5–9, 23–24, 476, 477–479
  psychoanalysis and, 476
  Rogers and, 368, 478
  science and, 12–13
  Skinner and, 219, 241, 478
Phlegmatic personality, 308, 309, 313, 314
Physics, 484
Physiological needs, 343
Physique, temperament and, 309
Piaget, Jean, 428
Pidgeon, N. F., 21
Pine, F., 170
Piyadassi, T., 456
Place, U., 220
Plato, 4, 49
Play, gender and, 155–157
Pleasure principle, 47

Plomin, R. A., 297, 302
Politics, 7
Polygraph (lie detector), 87
Polymorphous perversity, 41
Porter, E. H., Jr., 362
Positive regard, 355–356
Positive reinforcement, 215
Positive self-regard, 356
Positive transference, 54
Postmodernism
  Jung and, 90
  philosophical assumptions of, 12
Posttraumatic stress disorder, 425
Postulates, fundamental, 405–407, 408
Potter, J., 483
Potts, R., 483
Pounds, B., 110
Powell, L., 244
Power
  May and, 384–385
  predictive, 16
Power, M., 220
Power, R., 235
Powerlessness, anxiety and, 377–378, 384
Powers, P., 234
Practical intelligence, 325
Practicing, in separation-individuation process, 170
Predictive power, 16
Prejudice, Allport on, 267
Prepotent needs, 272–273
Presley, Sidney, 217
Press, Murray on, 272, 273, 275, 276
Primary drives, 202
Primary processes, 47–48
Primary reinforcers, 202
Privette, G., 347
Proactive theories, reactive theories versus, 9, 478
Probing response, 359–360, 361
Proceeding, Murray and, 271–272
Productive love, 131
Productive orientation, 129, 130, 131
Product/Process Impasse, 191
Programmed instruction, 217
Projection, 51, 86, 206
Projective techniques, 87
Projective tests, 18
Propriate functional autonomy, 264
Propriate functions, 261–262, 269
Propriate striving, 262
Proprium, 261–263
Prosocial constructionism, 160
Prospective function, of dreams, 86
Psyche, 73, 479
Psychic energy, 74
Psychoanalysis, 2, 19, 22, 139, 192
  Allport and, 269
  analytic process in, 54–56
  current work in, 193
  evaluation of, 476, 477
  existential, 339, 372–398, 442, *see also* May, Rollo
  feminist, 176–179
  interpersonal school of, 123, 124
  learning theory integrated with, 205–206
  medical background for, 125
  Morgan and, 271
  neo-, *see* Adler, Alfred; Fromm, Erich; Horney,
      Karen; Jung, Carl
  transference and, 53–54, 55, 86, 105, 188

*see also* Freudian psychoanalysis; Object relations theorists; Relational/cultural theory
Psychoanalytic learning theory, 199. *See also* Dollard, John; Miller, Neal
Psychoanalytic social psychology, 112–136. *See also* Fromm, Erich; Horney, Karen
Psychobiography, 482–483
Psychodrama, 411
Psychohistory, 154–155, 157–158
Psychological situation, 246
Psychological types, Jung on, 81–83
Psychology
    academic, 5, 6
    analytical, 70–92, *see also* Jung, Carl
    contemporary, 479–487
    ego, 138–165, *see also* Erikson, Erik; Freud, Anna; Freud, Sigmund; Hartmann, Heinz
    evolutionary, 299–300, 302
    individual, 93–111, *see also* Adler, Alfred
    origin of term, 479
    psychoanalytic social, 112–136, *see also* Fromm, Erich; Horney, Karen
    role of personality theories in, 4–5
    of women, *see also* Feminist psychology
Psychometric intelligence, 325
Psychometric tests, 17–18
Psychometric trait theory, 309
Psychophysiological monitoring, 87
Psychosexuality, Freud and, 40
Psychosexual stages of development, 41–46
    anal, 42–43, 57, 129, 206
    effects of, 45–46
    genital, 45, 130
    latency, 45
    oral, 41–42, 57, 129, 206
    phallic, 43–45, 206
    psychosocial stages and, 146, 147, 148, 149, 151, 152, 153
Psychosocial stages of development, 146–153
    autonomy versus shame and doubt, 147, 153
    ego identity versus role confusion, 149–151, 153
    ego integrity versus despair, 152–153
    generativity versus stagnation, 151–152, 153
    industry versus inferiority, 148–149, 153
    initiative versus guilt, 148, 153
    intimacy versus isolation, 151, 153
    McAdams and, 159–162
    psychosexual stages and, 146, 147, 148, 149, 151, 152, 153
    trust versus mistrust, 147, 153
Psychotherapy, 21–23, 188
    Adler and, 104–105, 108, 109
    art of, 21
    Bandura and, 238–240
    behavior modification and, 216–218
    client-centered, 357–362
    cognitive (Beck), 434–435, 436
    cognitive behavioral, 443–445
    Dollard and Miller and, 206–207
    drugs in, 391
    Eastern thought and, 468–470
    evaluation of, 22–23
    Eysenck and, 331–333
    Fromm and, 134
    goals of, 21–22
    group, 361, 437, 445
    Horney and, 124, 129–130
    Jung and, 85

Kelly and, 411, 414–415
Kernberg and, 174–175
May and, 390–391, 393
nondirective, 357–362
personality theory and, 21–22
person-centered, 357–362
rational emotive behavior, 422–428
reconstructive, 360
Rogers and, 85, 357–362, 367
Rotter and, 247–249
short-term, 444
Stone Center group and, 188–189
supportive versus reconstructive, 360
*see also* Psychoanalysis; Therapy
Psychoticism, Eysenck and, 313, 314, 315, 321–322, 329, 331
Puhan, B. N., 484
Pulos, S. M., 22
Punishment, Skinner on, 215
Purpose, as ego strength or virtue, 148, 153
Pyke, S. W., 156

Q-sort technique, 363, 364
Quantitative trait loci (QTL), 297
Quantum theory, 484
Questionnaires, *see* Personality inventory questionnaires; Personality questionnaires and ratings
Quiet therapies, 469
Quinn, S., 116

Rabie, L., 56
Rachman, S., 313, 321
Racism, personality theories and, 483–484
Radical behaviorism, 199. *See also* Skinner, B. F.
Rahula, W., 456
Range, Kelly and, 406, 408
Rapaport, D., 208
Rapprochement, in separation-individuation process, 170
RAS, *see* Reticular activating system
Rational emotive behavior therapy (REBT), 422–428
Rational-emotive therapy (RET), 109, 422. *See also* Rational emotive behavior therapy
Rationalization, 51, 52, 206
Ratio reinforcement, 215
Rattner, J., 107
Reaction formation, 51, 52, 206
Reactive theories, proactive theories versus, 9, 478
Reality anxiety, 50
Reality principle, 48
Real self, 117–118
Reasoning, 203
Reassuring response, 359, 361
Rebellion, stage of, 383
REBT (rational emotive behavior therapy), 422–428
Reception learning, 327–328
Receptive orientation, 129, 130
Reciprocal determinism, 227–229, 239
Reconstruction, Kelly and, 411
Reconstructive psychotherapy, 360
Redefining, in cognitive therapy, 435
Rediscovery of self, 380, 382–383
Reflective response, 360, 361, 362
Reflexes, 202
Regard, Rogers and, 356
Regression, 51, 52, 143
Reichlin, R. E., 107
Reid, Theodore, 39

Reinforcement
    continuous, 215
    Dollard and Miller on, 201–203
    extrinsic, 233
    interval, 215
    intrinsic, 233
    locus of control and, 243–246
    multiculturalism and, 203
    negative, 215
    in observational learning, 233–234
    positive, 215
    primary, 202
    punishment as, 215
    ratio, 215
    schedules of, 215–216
    secondary, 202
    self-, 234
    Skinner on, 212, 213, 214–216
    vicarious, 233
Reinforcement value, 246
Reinforcers, 202
    generalized conditioned, 215
    primary, 202
    secondary, 202
Relatedness, 127, 128, 129
Relational/cultural theory, 167, 179–191, 193. See also
        Stone Center group
Relationship-differentiation process, 182
Relevance, as criterion, 10–11
Reliability, assessment and, 17
Religion
    Allport on, 267
    Maslow and, 350
    see also Eastern thought; Zen Buddhism
REM (rapid eye movement) sleep, 59
Repression, 34–35, 51, 52, 58, 116, 205
Reproduction, sex for, 40
Rep Test (Role Construct Repertory Test), 410, 411,
        412–413, 415–416
Research, differing methods of, 18–21. See also under
        individual psychologists
Resignation solution, 116, 117
Resistance, 34, 36, 56
Respondent behavior, 212–213
Responses, 203
    conditioned and unconditioned, 201
    extinction of, 203
    habitual and specific, 312–313
    hierarchy of, 202
    in learning process, 202, 203, 204
    Rogers and, 358–360, 361, 362
RET (rational-emotive therapy), 109
Retentional processes
    in cognitive-affective personality system, 251
    in observational learning, 231–232
Reticular activating system (RAS), introversion-
        extraversion and, 319, 320–321, 322, 323, 334
Retief, A., 481, 483
Retribution, in cognitive therapy, 435
Reynolds, D. K., 469, 470
Reynolds, L. T., 102, 107
Rhymer, B., 469, 470
Richards, A. D., 46
Ricoeur, 61
Rieken, B., 97
Rinzai Zen, 462, 464, 466
Ritter, P., 236
Roberts, B. W., 293

Roberts, T. K., 441
Robins, R. W., 269, 289, 293
Robinson, F. G., 271
Robinson, P., 43, 58
Roethlisberger, F. J., 359
Rogers, 409, 417
Rogers, Carl R., 350–368, 357, 431
    actualization theory of, 352–353, 366
    Allport and, 268
    assessment and research in theory of, 362–365
    biographical background of, 350–352
    on child development, 355–357
    on congruence and incongruence, 354–355
    Eastern thought and, 471
    Ellis and, 429
    on emotions, 358–360, 361, 362
    evaluation of, 365–368
    feminist critique of, 366
    May and, 380, 392
    mentioned, 15, 22, 85, 265, 339, 341, 349, 392, 477, 478,
        479, 480
    personality theory of, 2, 352–357
    philosophy and, 9
    psychotherapy of, 357–362, 367
    on self-concept, 341, 353–358, 365, 366–367
    writings of, 370–371
Rogers, David, 352
Role, 289
    Kelly and, 407–408
    in social psychology, 408
Role confusion, ego identity versus, 149–151, 153
Role Construct Repertory Test, see Rep Test
Role-playing
    in cognitive therapy, 435
    Kelly and, 413, 414, 415
Role reversal, Kelly and, 411
Romaniello, J., 78
Rootedness, 127, 128, 129
Rorer, L. F., 417
Rorschach, Hermann, 87
Rorschach Inkblot Test, 18, 87, 132, 276
Rosolack, T., 244
Rothstein, M., 292
Rotter, Julian, 226, 241, 242–252
    Adler and, 109
    basic concepts and, 246–247
    biographical background of, 242–243
    evaluation of, 249–250, 252
    on internal-external locus of control, 243–246
    mentioned, 208, 477
    psychotherapy of, 247–249
    writings of, 243, 254
Rottschaefer, W., 241
Rousselle, R., 155
Ruling type, of style of life, 99
Runco, M. A., 107
Rush, A. J., 434, 435
Russell, F., 234
Rychlak, Joseph F., 21–22, 133, 162, 221, 415, 482
Ryckman, R. M., 123, 244

Sachs, Hans, 114
Sadism, 42–43, 46
Saeeduzzafar, R., 246
Safeguarding tendencies, 104
Safety needs, 343–344
Sahoo, F. M., 484
Saijojo Zen, 465

Saleh, W. E., 244
Salmon, P., 410
Sampson, E. E., 143
Samuels, A., 73
Sanguine personality, 308, 309, 313, 314
Sarason, S., 481
Sarbin, T., 21
Sass, L., 174
Satiation, 215
Satori (enlightenment), 451, 460–462, 466–468
Satre, Jean-Paul, 375
Saudino, K. J., 297
Sayers, J., 57
Scapegoats, 52
Scattergram, 19, 20
Schafer, R., 143
Schedules
    Murray and, 272
    of reinforcement, 215–216
Schemas, 432
Schimek, J. G., 43
Schizophrenia, 410
Schorr, D. N., 244
Schultz, D., 56, 88, 123
Science, 485
    Allport and, 268
    Bandura and, 241
    behavior theories and, 477
    Cattell and, 300–301
    definition of, 12
    Dollard and Miller and, 207–208
    Eastern thought and, 470
    Ellis and, 444
    Erikson and, 146, 162–163
    existentialism and, 376
    Eysenck and, 335
    Freud and, 59–60
    Fromm and, 133
    Horney and, 123
    human relations theorists and, 191–192
    Jung and, 88–89
    Kelly and, 403, 405, 415, 416
    learning theories and, 477
    limitations of, 479–481, 482
    Maslow and, 248
    May and, 391, 393, 394–395
    Murray and, 277
    personality theories and, 4, 5–6, 23–24, 476, 477
    philosophy and, 5–6, 12–13
    Rogers and, 365, 368
    Rotter and, 249–250
    Skinner and, 211, 219
Scientific constructs, 14–15
Scientific generalization, 13–14
Scientific method, 5
Scientific statements, 12–16
    basic constructs, 14–15
    definition of, 12–13
    evaluation of, 15–16
    philosophical assumptions versus, 8
    recognition of, 13–14
Scientific validation, 13
Scientism, 133
Scientist, person as (Kelly), 403, 405, 415, 416
Sears, R. R., 56, 208
Secondary dispositions, 260–261
Secondary drives, 202
Secondary processes, 48
Secondary reinforcers, 202
Secrecy, disconnection and, 187
Seduction theory, Freud on, 43
Selective abstraction, Beck and, 433
Selective breeding, 295, 298
Self
    -as-rational-coper, 262
    autonomous, 172
    bodily, 262
    consciousness of, 380, 382–383
    construct of, 15
    creative, 103–104, 109, 265
    Eastern psychotherapy and, 468
    Greeks and, 479
    idealized, 117–119, 123
    Jung on, 78–80, 90
    Maslow on, 344–350
    normal versus neurotic, 118
    nuclear, 172
    real, 117–118
    rediscovery of (May), 380, 382–383
    Rogers on, 352–353, 366
    stages in consciousness of, 380, 382–383
Self-acceptance, 265
Self-actualization, 17, 117, 344–350
Self-analysis, 60, 121–122
Self-as-rational coper, 262
Self-concept, 37, 108
    Rogers and, 341, 353–358, 365, 366–367
Self-confidence, 172
Self-consciousness, May and, 380, 382–383
Self-construct, 407–408
Self-control, 239–240
Self-effacing solution, 116, 117
Self-efficacy, 226, 236–237, 243
Self-esteem, 172, 189, 262, 349
Self-esteem needs, 344
Self-expansive solution, 116, 117
Self-extension, 262
Self-Help Form, of Institute for Rational-Emotive
    Therapy, 427
Self-identity, 262, 407
Self-image, 262
Self-insight, 265
Self-objectification, 265
Self-orientation, 132
Self-psychology, 175–176
Self-realization, 83–85, 98, 117, 123, 265
Self-regard, 355–356
Self-reinforcement, 234
Self-report inventory, Mutual Psychological
    Development Questionnaire and, 192–193
Self-system, 228
Self-theory, 170–173
Selzer, M. A., 175
Sensation, Jung and, 82
Sensitization, covert, 248
Sentence completion, 87
Separation-individuation process, 169–170, 182, 183
Serial, Murray and, 271–272
Serial program, Murray and, 272
Sex differences, see Gender
Sex hormones, psychoticism and, 321–322
Sexual abuse, of children, 43, 389, 425
Sexual desire, 190
Sexuality
    circumcision and, 180
    clitoridectomy and, 180

Sexuality (*cont.*)
    culture and, 175–176
    Ellis on, 421–422
    Freud on, 38–41, 179
    Jung versus Freud on, 74
    May and, 385–386
Shadow, Jung on, 77, 78, 79
Shaffer, T. G., 102, 107
Shakuhachi, 464
Shame, 189–190
    autonomy versus, 147, 153
Shaping, 213–215
Sharma, R., 246
Shaw, B. F., 434
Shea, C., 235
Sheldon, William, 309
Shell, W. E., 107
Sheng-Yen, 455
Sherman, N., 62
Shevrin, H., 58, 59
Shikantaza, 462
Shinkeishitsu, 470
Shoda, Yuichi, 250–252, 251, 254, 482
Shojo Zen, 465
Short-term psychotherapy, 444
Shur, M., 31
Shurcliff, J., 58
Shweder, R. A., 293
Sibling rivalry, 102
SII (Social Interest Index), 107–108
Silverman, Lloyd H., 56, 58
Silvern, S. B., 234
Simple themas, 276
Simplicity, as criterion, 16
Singer, J., 78
Singh, K., 107
Singh, R. P., 244
Sioux tribe, Erikson's study of, 153–154
SIS (Social Interest Scale), 108
Sixteen Personality Factor Questionnaire (16PF),
    286
Skandhas, 456–457
Skhiri, T., 170
Skinner, B. F., 199–200, 209–221, 477
    behavior change and psychotherapy of, 216–218
    on behavior development and learning, 211–216
    behaviorism of, 4–5
    biographical background of, 209–211
    evaluation of, 219–221, 241
    Freud and, 217
    mentioned, 9, 207, 249, 332, 367, 478
    operant conditioning and, 212–213
    personality theory and, 2, 211
    on schedules and types of reinforcement, 215–216
    on shaping, 213–215
    on social utopias, 210, 218–220
    Watson and, 211
    writings of, 210, 218, 224
Skinner box, 213
Sliker, G., 90
Slips, Freud on, 36–37
Slusarcick, A., 107
Small, F. E., 56, 57
Smelser, N. J., 153
Smith, D., 420
Smith, L., 218
Smith, M., 22
Smith, M. B., 368

Sneed, C., 293
Sochting, I., 158
Sociability, Kelly and, 407, 408
Social character, Fromm on, 129–131
Social interest, 96, 105, 108, 110
Social Interest Index (SII), 107–108
Social Interest Scale (SIS), 108
Social learning theories, 225–254
    Mischel and Shoda and, 250–251
    *see also* Bandura, Albert; Rotter, Julian
Socially useful type, of style of life, 100
Social utopias, Skinner on, 210, 218–220
Sociobiology, 300
Sociotropic dimension, 432–433
Socrates, 54
Soffer, J., 403, 417
Solnit, A. J., 139, 143
Soltz, V., 105
Sophocles, 43, 389
Soto Zen, 462, 464, 466
Source traits, 285–286
Spacapan, S., 246
Spearman's *g* factor, 325
Species-specific behavior, 208
Specification equations, 287–289
Specific responses, Eysenck and, 312
Speech, *see* Language
Spencer, J. H., 172
Spiegel, B. R., 170
Spiegel, R., 132
Spiegelman, J. M., 85
Splitting, 174, 192
Spotnitz, 171
Spranger, E., 267
Stability, emotionality versus, 312, 313, 314
Stages of development, *see* Child development
Stagnation, generativity versus, 151–152, 153
Standardization, assessment and, 17
State, 289
Stein, D. J., 59
Steinbeck, John, 390
Stein-Seroussi, A., 357
Stellman, L. C., 106–107
Stelmack, R. M., 321
STEP (Systematic Training for Effective Parenting),
    106
Stephenson, William, 363
Stern, D., 170
Sternberg, R., 483
Stevens, A., 90
Stewart, A. E., 411
Stimulation, 127, 128, 129
Stimulus
    conditioned and unconditioned, 201
    neutral, 201
Stiver, Irene P., 179, 181, 182, 184, 185, 187, 188, 190
Stoicism, 422, 443
Stolorow, R. D., 173
Stone Center group, 167, 179–191
    connectedness and, 181, 182–183
    connections and, 182, 184–185, 187, 188, 189
    disconnections and, 182, 185–188, 189
    evaluation of, 193
    Mutual Psychological Development Questionnaire
        and, 192–193
    psychotherapy and, 188–189
    writings of, 195–196
Stonerock, B., 411

Straka, T., 244
Strano, D. A., 108
Strasburger, V., 234, 235
Straussner, S. L., 170
Stress, 378. *See also* Anxiety
Stress Inoculation Training, 436
Strickland, B. R., 244
Striving for superiority, 97–99
Structural profile, in multimodal therapy, 441
Study of Values Scale, 267
Study places, personality and, 328
Stupidity-misery syndrome, 206–207
Style of life, 99–103, 107
    mistaken, 104, 105
Subien, L. M., 293
Subjective data, 13
Sublimation, 41, 51, 52, 53
Suchecki, J., 483
Sullivan, Harry Stack, 105, 157, 431
Sulloway, F. J., 107
Sumerlin, J. R., 343
Superego, 46, 47, 48–49, 50, 53, 58, 119, 139, 142, 272
Superfactors, 306, 311–318
Superiority, striving for, 97–99
Superiority complex, 104
Superstitious behaviors, 215
Support groups, 361
Supportive psychotherapy, 360
Suppression, 207
Surface traits, 285
Surrey, Janet L., 179, 182, 189, 191
Suzuki, Daisetz Teitaro, 451
Suzuki, Shunryu, 451
Swann, W. B., 357
Swenson, C. R., 34
Symbiosis, 126, 131
    normal, 169
Symbols
    in dream work, 37
    May and, 391
Symonds, A., 120, 268
Symonds, Percival, 276
Synchronicity, 83–84
Syntality, 289
Systematic desensitization, 248
Systematic self-analysis, 122

Tacey, D., 89
Tafarodi, R., 349
Talking phase, of therapy, 207
Tao, 460
Taoism, 460
    Rogers and, 367
Tappan, M. B., 21
Tart, C. T., 13
TAT (Thematic Apperception Test), 18, 87, 271, 275–277, 279, 363
Tataryn, D. J., 58
Tatum, B. D., 191
Teaching machine, 217
Technical eclecticism, 442–443
Teleology, 83, 88, 96–97
Television
    aggression and, 234–236, 384
    modeling and, 231
Telos, 83
Temperaments, Sheldon and, 309. *See also* Traits and personality

Tena, C., 368
Teresa, Mother, 260
Tests
    projective, 18
    psychometric, 17–18
    word-association, 86–87
Tett, R. P., 292
Thanatos, 40
Themas, Murray on, 276
Thematic Apperception Test (TAT), 18, 87, 271, 275–277, 279, 363
Thematic lines, 159
Theory, definition of, 3–4
Therapeutic change, 358
Therapy
    behavioral cognitive, 443–445
    conditions for change, 358
    Eastern thought and, 468–470
    group, 361, 415, 437
    multimodal behavior, 438–439, 440–442, 444
    reconstructive, 360
    *see also* Behavior therapies; Cognitive therapies; Psychotherapy
Theravada Buddhism, 453, 464
Thinking
    Ellis and, 422–423
    Jung and, 82
Thomas, H., 47
Thompson, M. G., 55
Thompson, S., 246
Thorndike, Edwin L., 201, 211–212, 243
Thorne, B., 350
Thornton, B., 123
Thrasher, P., 90
Thresholds, Lazarus and, 439
Thurstone, Lewis L., 290, 325
Tillich, Paul, 374, 393
Time projection, Lazarus and, 440
Tingley, E., 21
Tobacyk, J. J., 411
Tokar, D. M., 293
Token economy, 217–218
Tolpin, M., 33
Tompkins, S. S., 278
Törestad, B., 481
Toronto, E. L., 57
Torrey, E. F., 63
Tracking, in multimodal therapy, 441
Traits
    Allport on, 259–261
    common, 260, 261
    construct of, 14–15
    measurement of, 316–318
    source, 285–286
    surface, 285
    *see also* Factor analysis; Traits and personality
Traits and personality, 256–281, 308, 477
    background of, 308–310
    Cattell and, 285–286
    *see also* Allport, Gordon; Eysenck, Hans; Murray, Henry A.
Transactional Analysis, 442
Transcendence, 84–85, 127, 128, 129
Transference, 53–54, 55, 86, 105, 188, 391
Tribich, D., 57
Trierweiler, S. J., 269
Tripitaka, 453
Trull, T. J., 293

Trust, mistrust versus, 147, 153
Turner, 190
12–step programs, 170, 189
Twin studies, 294–296, 297, 298, 331
Type A behavior, 123
Typologies, 308
Tyranny of the should, 118, 119

Unconditional positive regard, 356
Unconditioned response, 201
Unconditioned stimulus, 201
Unconscious
    collective, 73, 75–81, 89
    Freud on, 32–35, 49, 50, 58, 103
    Freud versus Jung on, 73–74, 75–76, 79–80
    personal, 73, 74–75
Unconscious experience, 382
Unconscious processes, 34, 205
Understanding, need for, 344, 345
Uniqueness versus universality, 9, 478
Urbanowski, F., 463, 469
Ursano, R. J., 107
Usefulness
    Adler on, 108
    of fictional finalisms, 97
Utopias, Skinner on, 210, 218–220

Vaihinger, Hans, 97
Vaillant, G. E., 53
Valentine, E., 482
Validation, Kelly and, 415
Validity, assessment and, 17
Values
    in contemporary theories, 483
    May and, 379, 381
Van de Castle, R., 56
Vande Kempe, H., 267
Van den Daele, L., 123
Van Eenwyk, J. R., 85
Van Kalmthout, M. A., 352
Van Krogten, I., 483
Van Loon, R. J., 12
Variable interval reinforcement, 215
Variable ratio reinforcement, 215
Variables, independent and dependent, 19, 20
Vasubandhu, 457–458, 459
Vaughn, C. M., 408
Vedandic Hinduism, Rogers and, 366
Verbal symbols, in observational learning, 232
Vernon, Philip, 267
Vicarious reinforcement, 233
Vienna Psychoanalytic Society, 94
Vijnana, 458
Viner, R., 167
Violence
    May and, 384
    punishment and, 215
    television and, 234–236, 384
Visceral brain activity, emotional stability versus
    neuroticism and, 319–320, 322, 323
Visher, S., 244
Vitz, P., 483
Voyeurism, 46
Vygotsky, L., 193, 221

Walden II, Skinner and, 218
Walker, A., 180

Walker, B. M., 407, 415
Wallach, L., 366
Wallach, M. A., 366
Walsh, R., 470
Walters, A., 230
Ward, W., 246
Warner, S. L., 30
Warren, W. G., 403, 415
Wastell, C. A., 157
Waterman, A. S., 158
Watson, John, 4, 5, 13, 201, 210, 211, 342, 479
Watson, P. J., 172–173
Watts, Alan W., 449, 451, 468, 469
Watzlawick, P., 440
Weakland, J., 440
Weingberg, L., 170
Weinraub, W., 235
Weiss-Rosmarin, T., 110
Wengler, B., 104
Wertsch, J. V., 193
Wessler, R. L., 431
Wetherell, M., 483
"What if" technique, 435
Whitbourne, S. K., 158
White, R. W., 278
Widiger, T. A., 293, 417
Wiechnik, R., 244
Wiggins, J. S., 300
Wilkinson, 57
Will, as ego strength or virtue, 147, 153
William Alanson White Institute for Psychiatry,
    Psychoanalysis, and Psychology, 125
Williamson, P. A., 234
Wilson, A., 46, 59
Winnicott, D. W., 71
Winter, D. G., 266
Wisdom, as ego strength or virtue, 152–153
Wishes, Freud on, 34, 35
Wish fulfillment, 47–48
Within-subjects techniques, 269
Wolberg, A., 56
Wolpe, Joseph, 437–438
Wolper, E. A., 56
Womb envy, 119, 120
Women
    Adler on, 99, 121
    Allport on, 267
    Chodorow on, 180–183
    clitoridectomy, 180
    Erikson on, 156–157
    Freud on, 44–45, 56, 57, 179
    Fromm on, 121
    Horney on, 124
    identity development in, 158
    Jung on, 77–78
    lesbian relationships and, 190
    May and, 390
    Miller on, 181
    19th-century views of, 40
    personality theories and, 483–484
    sexism and personality theories and, 483–484
    see also Feminist psychology; Gender; Stone Center
      group
Wood, R. E., 237
Woodall, K., 302, 484
Woodward, W., 483
Woody, R. H., 441